Euston
Knettishall
Hopton
Coney Weston
Market Weston
Barningham
Thelnetham
Hinderclay
Redgrave
Wortham
Palgrave
Stuston
Oakley
Brome
Fakenham Magna
Sapiston
Honington
Hepworth
Thrandeston
Troston
Ixworth Thorpe
Bardwell
Stanton 2
Wattisfield
Rickinghall Inferior
Rickinghall Superior
Botesdale
Burgate
Mellis
Yaxley
Eye
Thornham Parva
Great Livermere
Ixworth
Walsham le Willows
Gislingham
Braiseworth
Thornham Magna
Occold
Redlingfield
Langham
Finningham
Westhorpe
Stoke Ash
Pakenham
Stowlangtoft
Hunston
Badwell Ash
Wyverstone
Wickham Skeith
Thwaite
Thorndon
Rishangles
Great Ashfield
Cotton
reat Barton
Thurston
Norton
Bacton
Wetheringsett cum Brockford
Aspall
Mendlesham
Rougham
Tostock
Elmswell
Wetherden
Haughley
Old Newton
Gipping
Beyton
Bushbrooke
Hessett
Woolpit
Drinkstone
Harleston
Stowupland
Little Whelnetham
Bradfield St George
Shelland
reat etham
Bradfield St Clare
Gedding
Rattlesden
Onehouse
Stowmarket
Creeting St Peter
Felsham
Buxhall
Combs
Great Finborough
Creeting All Saints
Bradfield Combust
ngfield
Cockfield
Thorpe Morieux
Brettenham
Little Finborough
g
pheton
Hitcham
Wattisham
Lavenham
Preston
Kettlebaston
Bildeston
Chelsworth
Nedging
Naughton
Brent Eleigh
Monks Eleigh 1
Semer
Whatfield
Elmsett
Acton
Little Waldingfield
Milden
Lindsey
Aldham
Great Waldingfield
Chilton
Edwardstone
Groton
Kersey
Hadleigh 1
Great Cornard
Newton
Layham
Little Cornard
Assington
Boxford
Polstead
Stoke by Nayland
Bures St Mary
Nayland with Wissington

THE WILLS
OF THE ARCHDEACONRY
OF SUDBURY

1630–1635

Edited by Nesta Evans

The Boydell Press

Suffolk Records Society
VOLUME XXIX

Editorial matter © Nesta Evans 1987

Published by
The Boydell Press

Suffolk Records Society

Boydell & Brewer Ltd
PO Box 9, Woodbridge, Suffolk IP12 3DF
and Wolfeboro, New Hampshire 03894-2069, USA

First published 1987

ISBN 0 85115 492 1

Issued to subscribing members for
the years 1985/6 and 1986/7

British Library Cataloguing in Publication Data

The Wills of the Archdeaconry of Sudbury
    1630–1635. – (Suffolk Records Society;
    V.29)
    1. Church of England – Archdeaconry of
    Sudbury. *Court*   2. Probate records –
    England – Suffolk   2. Suffolk –
    Genealogy
    I. Evans, Nesta   II. Suffolk Records
    Society   III. Series
    929'.342644   CS435.S7
    ISBN 0-85115-492-1

Library of Congress Cataloging-in-Publication Data applied for

Printed and bound in Great Britain by
Short Run Press Ltd, Exeter

Contents

General Editor's Introduction:
The Society's First Thirty Years

In 1987, the Suffolk Records Society is completing its thirtieth year in excellent health, with the production of Volume 29 – a substantial double volume of edited abstracts of seventeenth-century Suffolk wills – and with lively ambitions for the next thirty years.

Ever since Samuel Tymms edited the volume known as *Bury Wills and Inventories* (Camden Society, 1850), it has been clear that early wills make surprisingly compulsive reading; and that, *fully indexed*, they supply invaluable information for social and economic historians, for local historians, and – perhaps above all – for genealogists.

This new double volume of Suffolk wills presents very full abstracts of no fewer than 894 wills. The indexes refer to several thousands of Suffolk people of the first half of the seventeenth century, and inevitably give insights into their family lives, their relationships, their occupations and trades. The editor has based the introduction to her volume on its particular contents, and thereby reflected shades of difference perhaps implicit in date, and in fashion, and in the nature and social structure of the western part of the county. The period they cover – 1630–1635 – is certainly one of great interest not only to Old Englanders but also to New Englanders interested in English forebears. This brings me to the principal begetter of the volumes.

For some years now, Mr John Brooks Threlfall, of Madison, Wisconsin, a keen and accomplished genealogist in his own right, has generously financed the work of scholarly abstraction and edition of wills, most notably those in the record offices of Essex and Suffolk. Two Suffolk volumes, both from the Archdeaconry of Suffolk (broadly speaking, of 'East' Suffolk), covering the years 1629–1636 and 1637–1640, and abstracted by Marion Allen, Richard Allnutt and Nesta Evans, were published in 1986 in Boston, Massachusetts, by the New England Historic Genealogical Society. In the course of two visits I paid to their splendid library and headquarters in Boston, it became clear that the NEHGS would be happy for the Suffolk Records Society to take over publication of future Suffolk volumes. We would retail their existing two volumes, and they would reciprocate with ours as they appeared. We are indebted to Mr John Sears, their Interim Director, and to Mr Donald Nielsen, their Associate Editor, for their friendly offices in these transactions. We are especially pleased to be able to play our part in bringing the results of Mr Jack Threlfall's very generous sponsorship to our members and to the general public. The chronology of years covered by these first seventeenth-century volumes is hard to explain: they had been planned without our involvement. We can only state our determination to cover completely all surviving Suffolk will-records from the end of the Middle Ages to the end of the seventeenth century, and then perhaps beyond.

1988 will bring this Society's thirtieth anniversary. In our first thirty years, our most notable achievements were perhaps the eight classic volumes of *John Constable's Correspondence*, acknowledged by students of his work all over the world, and most warmly in Graham Reynolds' great catalogue, *The Later Paintings and Drawings of John Constable, 1817–1837*, superbly published in 1984 by Yale University Press. But, apart from notable volumes in our main series, we are very proud indeed to have celebrated our twenty-first anniversary by launching, with our publishers, the Boydell Press, and with the aid of generous benefactors, Professor Allen Brown's admirably ambitious additional series of annual volumes of Suffolk Charters – a *Monasticon Suffolkianum*, its own ninth volume already in the press.

To celebrate our thirtieth year, we intend to make strenuous efforts to double our membership, which has remained, loyally, at about 320. Our plan for increased membership goes with a rise in subscription, but our intention is to step up our production and make full use of increasing revenue from subscriptions and subventions; we dare to hope that double volumes, like these seventeenth-century Suffolk will-abstracts, will appear with encouraging frequency. Our other long-term plans include a major series of medieval manorial records, set in train under the editorship of Dr John Ridgard, with amateur as well as specialist students of Suffolk history in mind.

There is one more landmark to chart in our first thirty years. The first 18 volumes were printed, and bound, by our original printers, Messrs W. S. Cowell of Ipswich. Their managing director, Mr R. Geoffrey Smith, was one of the very kind sponsors who helped, most practically, with the inauguration of the Society's work: what a pleasure it always was to work with his firm. When W. S. Cowell was taken over, we looked naturally to Richard Barber, whose local firm, the Boydell Press, was already making a name for itself with its scholarly publications. Our next two volumes appeared with the coy acknowledgement 'Distributed by the Boydell Press'. With Volume 21, Boydell became our publisher, and Richard Barber's remarkable expertise has shaped the costing, production and marketing of our last ten regular volumes, as well as the eight volumes of Suffolk Charters. This is a proper moment for the Hon Editors and officers of the Society to express their appreciation to him.

Norman Scarfe
April 1987

Editor's Introduction

This volume, published by the Suffolk Records Society in 1987, inaugurates what is planned to be a long-term series of printed Suffolk wills. The introduction is intended to give a guide to the contents of the volume, and to explain points that may be obscure to some readers. There are five indexes, which should guide users to the varied material in the wills. These are indexes of testators, of other persons mentioned in the text, of places, of the occupations of testators and of subjects.

Contained in this volume are the 894 surviving wills proved in the Court of the Archdeacon of Sudbury during the old style calendar years 1630 to 1635 inclusive, thus covering 25 March 1630 to 24 March 1636. An unusually low number of wills, only eighty, were proved in 1633 and none earlier than July. These wills are preserved in two registers, Corner and Colman. The former contains those for 1630 and the latter the wills registered in 1631 to 1635. Register Corner measures 14 by 9½ by 1¼ inches, is 186 folios long and is bound in vellum. Colman is the largest register in the records of the Archdeaconry and measures 16½ by 11½ by 5½ inches. It contains 554 folios and is bound in vellum on boards. Both volumes have been recently repaired, but unfortunately nothing could be done to make good the damage caused by the acid ink, which in places has literally eaten away the paper. The registers had to be de-acidified before they were laminated. Some folios are difficult to read, others are illegible, while the remainder are in good condition. Fortunately, virtually all the original wills for 1630 to 1635 have survived and were used for the abstracts whenever the registers were difficult or impossible to read.

The area covered by the Archdeaconry of Suffolk is roughly the same as that of the old county of West Suffolk, but it also includes a handful of Cambridgeshire parishes which lay within the deanery of Fordham. The map shows the boundaries of the Archdeacon's jurisdiction, and also marks the names and boundaries of all the parishes included within it.

Practically no probate inventories survive for this period, but occasionally the total value of an inventory appears at the end of the probate clause in the original will. Where this occurs, the figure has been included in the text. The only will with an inventory is 310, which has the brief nuncupative will and the inventory on one sheet of paper. The inventory is printed with will 310.

Until 1858 virtually all wills were proved in the ecclesiastical courts, of which there were four kinds as far as probate is concerned. In theory probate was granted by the archdeaconry court covering the area in which the testator's property lay, but if it came under the jurisdiction of more than one archdeaconry, then the Consistory or Bishop's Court was used; the Diocese of St Edmundsbury and Ipswich was not established until 1914, so this would have been the Norwich Consistory Court. In the case of persons with property in more than one diocese probate was granted by the Prerogative Court of Canterbury; this was the court of the Archbishop of Canterbury, which covered the whole of the southern half of England. In practice these rules were not always followed, and many wills were proved in a higher court than was strictly necessary. Social aspirations were probably a factor which encouraged the proving of wills in PCC rather than in the court of the local archdeaconry. This and geographical convenience could account for the use of the Norwich Consistory Court when this was not legally required. It seems to have been commoner in East than in West Suffolk to resort to this court, and this lends weight to the view that geography was a factor in chosing a probate court. There are a handful of wills in the two registers used in this volume which were proved in PCC. It is not clear why the unusual procedure of including these in the Archdeaconry registers was followed. One will was proved in the Court of the Bishop of Durham, and seems to have been included here because the testator owned property in Norfolk. Logic would suggest it should rather have appeared in the Norwich Consistory Court register. The fourth type of court, those of Peculiars, need not concern us here.

The just under 900 wills included in this volume can only represent a fraction of the adults who died during the six years it covers. Estimates of the proportion of the population that made wills range from five to 20 percent, but this writer prefers a low figure. No precise figure can be given for the size of the population of the archdeaconry in the 1630s, but a very rough estimate can be made of the population at the beginning of the seventeenth century. In 1603 a return was made to the Bishop of Norwich of all communicants in his diocese.[1] A total of 37,012 communicants are listed for the Archdeaconry of Sudbury, including the Fordham Deanery parishes in Cambridgeshire. On the assumption that there were 2.8 communicants per household, and that 40 percent of the population was too young to communicate, it can be suggested that there may have been 61,686 persons living in 13,218 households in the Archdeaconry in 1603. By 1630 the population was almost certainly larger. An interesting subject for research would be to relate the number of surviving wills to recorded burials for the same period.

To what extent are these wills representative of the society of their time as a whole? The answer must be a negative one. The richest and most influential persons, many of the gentry and some wealthy yeomen had their wills proved in the Prerogative Court of Canterbury. This explains why the Bury testators in this volume seem rather unrepresentative of the

[1] 'The Condition of the Archdeaconries of Suffolk and Sudbury in the year 1603', *Proceedings of the Suffolk Institute of Archaeology*, XI (1903), pp. 2–46.

wealth of one of the principal towns in East Anglia. For the majority of the population poverty must have made the making of a will superfluous. Even amongst those who had something to leave, many did not bother to make wills because they had already disposed of their property, or relied on manorial custom to deal with real estate. In other cases the heir may have been obvious and so the making of a will could have been considered superfluous.

There are three groups of persons who predominate amongst will makers: widows, men with at least some under-age children and those with no obvious heir; this last group consists of the unmarried of both sexes, and of apparently childless married men. Widows form 16 percent of the will makers in this volume; men with children who are minors 18.5 percent and childless testators 22 percent. Together the three groups make up well over half the total number of testators. As far as occupations are concerned it is agriculturalists, craftsmen and tradesmen who predominate.

It is often thought that wills are principally of interest to genealogists, but this is to undervalue them. They are a rich source of information for the social and economic historian as will be shown in the following pages. The subject index should help researchers to find topics of interest.

Virtually every will, except the nuncupative ones, begins with a preamble setting out the testator's religious beliefs. On the whole it is likely that the words used are not those of the testator, but were selected from one of the formulary books available or were those the writer of the will was accustomed to use. It is not uncommon to find that certain people, not necessarily clergymen, are regular writers of wills. In this volume Henry Spurgen appears frequently as a scribe, but most will writers do not indicate that it is they who have done the actual writing of a will. Some preambles do appear to express personal beliefs and feelings and the wording of these has been included in the abstracts. Most of the religious preambles can be described as either mainstream Anglican or Puritan in tone. The principal distinction being that the latter use the words saved or elect. Only one will in this volume has a preamble which could be described as expressing recusant beliefs; this is will 841. When more volumes in the wills series have appeared, it may be possible to see whether there was an increase over time in the number of testators expressing Calvinist beliefs about salvation. In the following paragraph examples are given of the standard form, and of the specifically Puritan spirit, in these preambles, which are given in abbreviated form in the text of this volume.

Will 184: 'First I Comitt my sowle into the hands of allmightie god, my maker and of Jesus Christ my Redemer and saviour.' Will 89: 'First and principally I doe com[m]end and bequeath my soule to Almightye god the giver thereof, trustinge hopinge and assuredly beleevinge to be saved and to enioye eternall life in the kingdome of heaven, onely by the mediation, merrittes, death, passion and resurrection of my lord and Saviour Jesus Christ the sonne of the eternall God.'

The majority of testators do not say precisely where they wish to be buried, but merely in the parish where they die or where the executor thinks best. When testators ask to be buried in a named churchyard or church, this has been included in the religious preamble. Only a few request interment inside a church; in will 333 John Robson asks to be buried in the sanctuary of Soham church [Cambridgeshire].

In contrast to pre-Reformation wills, bequests for the repair of church fabric are few, but a Preston yeoman gave 20s towards the leading and repairing of the parish church (will 395). The widow of a cleric left 20s towards enlarging the communion cup of Risby (will 440) and Thomas Downham of Assington (will 335) gave the parson 10s towards his enlarging of the vicarage house.

Bequests to the poor of the testator's parishes are very common, but a few leave money to more than one parish; presumably because they have connections in several places. An example is will 566. Most of these bequests consist of a sum of money to be distributed soon after the donor's death, often on the day of burial; frequently the distribution is to be at the discretion of the churchwardens and overseers of the poor of the parish. A few testators make more enduring bequests in the form of money to be invested, or land or livestock to be used as a stock to provide an income for the parish poor. John Jolly of Langham (will 68) asked his executors to lay out £100 in purchasing land to be held in trust in perpetuity for the benefit of the poor. Other gifts take the form of permanent doles. John Bentlie (will 113) of Newmarket instructed his wife to see that the poor of this town received 2 loads of wood on 29 December and a cade of red herrings on the second Sunday of Lent each year. Edward Darbey of Bury (will 296) left £300 to the aldermen and burgesses of the town on condition that they paid £17 6s 8d yearly towards catechising and instructing the poor people in St James's parish every fortnight. A handful of testators named poor persons whom they wished to receive their charity. Thomas Wymarke of Denham (will 315) left 5s each to 6 poor houses in Denham and named their occupants. In addition to giving £5 to the poor at his burial, Ambrose Harvy of Honington (will 713) instructed his executors to expend £10 on a dinner for the entertainment of his friends on the day of his burial.

Unlike many others, Edward Darbey's bequest has survived. It is now administered by the Guildhall Trustees, and forms part of the sum of money paid annually by them to the cathedral in Bury St Edmunds.

A number of testators requested a funeral sermon and left a small sum, usually 10s, to pay the preacher. Jeffery Tanner of Bures (will 225) gave the parish curate such a sum. Others made bequests to several named preachers; the Edward Darbey already mentioned was one, and a Mendlesham testator (will 627) left 10s each to 15 named preachers when they came to preach in the parish.

Only one will (310) is accompanied by an inventory, but many others contain such long lists of furnishings and items of domestic equipment that they make up for this lack. The list of possessions of a governor of the hospital at Long Melford is virtually an inventory (will 506). To have included in the subject index every will that mentions any item of furniture would have made it impossibly long; only those with significant quantities of furniture or particularly interesting items have been included. The same applies to clothing; it is mainly widows who detail articles of attire.

It is not unusual to find bequests of tools of trade, amongst which looms are probably the most common. Thomas Pretty, a woollen weaver of Eye (will 147) left looms to two of his sons. Not all testators state their occupation, and it is sometimes possible to deduce what this was from possessions itemised in the will. A Lavenham clothier (will 893) mentioned the cocks, cisterns and lead pipes belonging to his messuage in Water Street. It is rare to find such unusual light being thrown on industrial processes. Several millers, including one from Hundon (will 241), bequeathed mills.

Bibles are the book most commonly mentioned in wills, but a handful bequeath others. These are listed in an appendix, together with notes on their authors. Will 355, for instance, mentions Foxe's Book of Martyrs and will 871 includes a bequest of divinity books and a Tremelius bible.

Not many wills make provision for the education of children in the modern meaning of the word. In the 1630s that word was still frequently used in the sense of bringing up. One of the few testators to make specific arrangments for the education of a son was Ralph Waller of Drinkstone (will 9), who asked that his namesake son should learn Latin. Another yeoman testator, this time of Thurston (will 272), refers to his son's education at the University of Cambridge.

The wording of a few wills suggests that a child may have suffered from mental or physical incapacity. A Boxted clothier provided an income for his wife to keep one of their sons with meat, drink and apparel even though he was adult. A Lakenheath man willed his wife to keep his son Robert in a decent and orderly manner so that he did not become chargeable to the parish (will 834). A charitably inclined clergyman (will 258) gave his 'poor blind cousin £20 towards maintaining her.

Some children seem to be long-term absent, judging from such phrases as 'if he comes again'. William Sampson of Newmarket (will 528) apparently had a son who was abroad, as did Giles Franck of Pakenham (will 777). Bequests to adult children of 12 pence are not uncommon. These should not be seen as the traditional being 'cut off with a shilling', but more probably as token gifts to children who had already received their portions. One widow (will 734) makes this clear in saying 'I give my son Joseph, to whom I have freely been beneficial, 12 pence.'

Many men made careful provision for the future wellbeing and comfort of their wives. Some were left the use of part of the family house (will 141), and annual deliveries of wood are common; will 264 is an example. Roger Manning of Cockfield (will 710) arranged for his wife to live with their daughter, who was to see she was 'carefully tended and looked unto during her life'. Another testator, worried that his wife might fall on hard times in old age, said she could sell his goods if she fell into want (will 284). Lawrence Stone is of the opinion that true affection between

xiii

spouses and towards children was uncommon in the early modern period, but sufficient testators express fondness for their wives to give the lie to this view.[2] William Frend (will 234) said 'God has bestowed on me a loving and comfortable wife'; Thomas Whithead (will 300) describes his as 'loving and wellbeloved'; Edward Kempe (will 329) had always found his 'a kind and loving help to me'; William Peirson, in his nuncupative will (374), called his wife 'sweetheart'; and Robert Glover and his wife (will 829) had lived together 52 years and 'lovingly and jointly' made their last will. Many other men described their wives as wellbeloved. Similarly, affection and concern is often expressed for children.

Terms to describe relationships were not always used in the seventeenth century in the same way as they are today. Cousin occasionally means nephew or niece, and they in their turn sometimes replace grandchild. Son or daughter-in-law can have the meaning stepchild, and the same applies to mother and father-in-law. The intended meaning is usually clear from the context.

In the 17th century the legal position of women was poor, and married women had no rights to property. Many husbands bequeathed to their wives their personal clothing or goods which had been theirs before marriage; an example of the latter can be found in will 742. To modern eyes the necessity to do this seems strange, but it is possible that by positively leaving a wife what in effect were her own possessions her husband was making sure that she was not deprived of them. However, wives had the right to one-third of their late husbands real estate during their widowhood. Many testators bequeathed their wives land and buildings on condition that they renounced their right to 'thirds'; alternative names were dowry and jointure. A handful of wills made by married women appear in this volume. They are all made in especial circumstances and with the consent of the husband. Usually a married woman made a will because she was acting as executrix of the will of a parent or of a previous husband. Will 350 is an example of the former and 437 of the latter. The widowed Alice Tillott's will (825) includes interesting details of her executorship of her late husband's will. The fact that a large proportion of men made their wives sole executrices of their wills indicates that women were not regarded as incapable of running a farm or business on their own.

There is a certain amount of information in these wills about the layout of houses, the building of new and repairs to existing ones. Thomas Barton (will 341) enjoined his wife to keep his house in repair with 'thatching and claying'. A Newmarket glover's will (528) includes a detailed description of at least part of a house he owned in Mustow Street in Bury. Houses were often divided between legatees, and examples can be found in wills 626 and 816.

Farming is a subject about which wills are very informative. Bequests of livestock are common, and crops are also mentioned. Will 471 refers to land 'new broken up' and sown with oats. Descriptions of land and

[2] Lawrence Stone, *Family, Sex and Marriage in England 1500–1800*, 1977

abuttals make it clear that open field farming was still widespread in certain parts of west Suffolk. This is particularly noticeable in Mildenhall. The Cambridgeshire parishes in Fordham deanery too retained their open fields, and wills from them also contain references to the exploitation of the fens in various ways. Several wills contain bequests that indicate that hops were being grown; will 354, for instance, mentions hop poles. Many field and other topographical names appear in these wills and should be of interest to local historians.

In the absence of banks and other financial institutions, money lending played an important part in the economic life of seventeenth-century society. An intricate network existed of lenders and borrowers; many of the former were widows or retired farmers with surplus capital in hand. Instructions to put out to the best profit the cash portions of children are common in wills, and this money too entered into the debt system. Many testators instructed their executors to pay the debts they owed and to collect in those owed to them. Most loans were made to people known to the lender and usually within his immediate neighbourhood. Very rarely debts are listed in wills. Francis Pattell (will 337) named six people to whom he owed sums of money ranging from 6s to 40s, and John Rogers (will 560) mentions four men indebted to him. A Bury blacksmith (will 475) left his son all the debts and money due to him from his customers, 'which are standing or marked up on marks or chalked scores in my shop.' Some debts were secured by bonds, often called specialty or obligations, but others were of the kind described in inventories as desperate debts. Mortgages are another kind of lending which occurs in several wills.

There are frequent references in these wills to obligations to enter into a bond to ensure the payment of legacies or the true performing of testators' wishes. It is usually wives who are obliged to take out these bonds, probably because their husbands were concerned about the effect on their children of a second marriage. Remarriage for widows was much commoner in the early modern period than it was to be in later centuries. It has been suggested that in the sixteenth century as many as 25 to 30 percent of marriages were second or subsequent marriages.[3]

Finally, there are some legal terms found in the wills which will be unfamiliar to many readers. A nuncupative will is an oral one recording the testator's wishes as expressed in the presence of witnesses. Although brief, these are often particularly interesting as they give us the actual words uttered by the dying man or woman. William Brooke (will 887) gave his daughter all his goods and as a token of this 'he took a sheet in his hand and gave it to his daughter' saying 'I do freely give to thee this sheet and with it all such moveable goods as I have'. Another man (will 243) pulled his handkerchief out of his pocket and gave it to his wife to put her in possession of his goods.

Copyhold land is frequently mentioned. This was land held at the will of the lord of the manor and according to custom. The tenant's title to his

[3] *Local Population Studies*, 23 (1979), p. 8

land was not a deed, but a copy of the entry in the court roll which recorded his acquisition of it by purchase or inheritance. Copyhold tenants paid rent, and in addition a fine (usually equivalent to two years' rent) each time such land or houses changed hands. On the majority of Suffolk manors the tenants had the right to leave their copyhold property by will, but, to ensure that land passed to the designated heir, it was usual to make a formal surrender to the use of the tenant's will. These surrenders are quite often recorded at the end of wills.

A very few wills refer to wardship of the heir. On the death of a person holding land by knight service or directly of the Crown, and whose heir was not of age (21 for boys and 14 for girls), the Crown was entitled to hold the land and draw its revenues until the heir came of age. Charles I ensured the strict application of this rule as he found it a useful source of income. Wardship was much disliked, because the custody of the heir and his or her lands was often farmed out to the highest bidder and this not infrequently led to the mismanagement of estates. In will 420 there is an example of a testator trying to avoid this eventuality by willing the wardship of his son to two kinsmen of his wife, and expressing the hope that the Master of the Court of Wards and Liveries would accede to his wishes. A very curious phrase occurs in will 793: the acknowledgement of 'a fine sur cognisance de droit come ceo' by the testator and his wife to four persons. The meaning of this is obscure.

Editorial Method

In order to keep this volume within a reasonable length, the abstracts are briefer than the originals which are full of double verbs and phrases such as 'I give and bequeath'. This was common form in the early seventeenth century and can also be found in the Book of Common Prayer e.g. 'We have erred and strayed'. However, nothing of substance has been omitted and the bequests appear in the order in which they are set down in the wills. All personal, place and topographical names, and all details of legacies are included.

When making the abstracts the original wills and the register copies have been collated, and where variations between the two have been found the form in the original will has been used. As far as possible the abstracts have been made from the registers, but as explained in the Introduction they are in poor condition and it was often necessary to use the original wills as the main source. How 'original' in fact are the original wills? Some of them are quite obviously copies and bear no signatures or marks of witnesses or testator. Presumably the executors needed to retain a copy of the will, but there is no means of telling whether that was the one originally drawn up; possibly it was usual to make two copies initially.

In abstracting the wills published in this volume certain conventions have been followed, and these are set out here. In order to save space, and to avoid tedious repetition, some frequently recurring and lengthy clauses have been abbreviated as follows. When authority is given to legatees to enter property or to distrain on property or goods to secure payment of a legacy, the phrase 'power to distrain' has been used, and the words 'benefit of survivorship' indicate that provision has been made for the eventuality of one or more legatees dying before inheriting.

Spelling of Christian and place names has been modernised as far as possible, but the spelling of topographical names has been left as it appears in the MSS. Surnames have also been left in their original form, and where there is a discrepancy between the spelling in the register copy and the original will the latter has been preferred. In indexing surnames, variant spellings have been brought together. Places are in Suffolk unless otherwise indicated. Archaic words are explained in the glossary.

Until 1751 the year began not on 1 January but on 25 March, so wills made or proved between 1 January and 24 March bear the date of the preceding year e.g. a will written on 26 February 1632 was in modern terms made on 26 February 1633. To avoid confusion all dates between 1 January and 24 March have been given in the form 26 February 1632/33.

Finally the following abbreviations have been used.

exor(s)	executor(s)
ex'trix/ex'trices	executrix/executrices
Let. ad.	Administration granted
(N)	Nuncupative will
PCC	Prerogative Court of Canterbury
Pr.	Proved
R	Register copy only of will available
R(W)	Abstract made from registered will and original also available
W	Original will only available
W(R)	Abstract made from original will and register copy also available
Wit.	Witness(es)
(X)	The person to whose name this is suffixed made his or her mark

1. R(W) WILLIAM CORNER (X) of Downham, shepherd. 2 March 1629/30

Commends soul to God and trusts to be inheritor of kingdom of heaven. Body to be buried in Downham churchyard.
To my wife Elizabeth for life my copyhold tenement and land in Downham. After her death to her exors for 3 months and then to my son Samuel. All my moveables to my wife towards bringing up of my children, the paying of my debts and my burial charges. Wife sole ex'trix. Wit. Thomas Maltyward Senior, William Maltyward. Pr. at Bury 30 March 1630

2. R(W) JOHN PRENTICE of Wissington yeoman. 17 November 1629.

Soul bequeathed to 3 persons of Trinity. To be buried in Wiston churchyard.
To my wife Mary for life the copyhold tenement wherein I now dwell called Keenes with its land, my copyhold land in Wiston called Foxfeilds, Calves pasture, Shardfeild, Harwardes and Slades. After her death I bequeath all my tenement and land called Keenes, except a little grove called Rushie grove and lying next to Broadfeild lane, to my eldest son John, who must pay £20 each within 3 years to my youngest sons Thomas and William. Foxfeild, Calves pasture and Rushie grove to be equally divided between my second and third sons Phillip and Peter, who must within 3 years pay £10 each to my daughters Mary and Sarah. They all have power to distrain. Gift of money to poor of Wiston, but sum erased. Residue of goods to wife, who must pay my debts and whom I make sole ex'trix. Wit. Charles Smith (X), Richard Robinson. Pr. at Sudbury 1 April 1630.

3. R(W) WILLIAM SMITH (X) of Stanstead, blacksmith. 10 January 1629/30

Soul bequeathed to God.
I give and bequeath to my son Thomas a piece of land in Stanstead called Long pasture. He must pay 30s p.a. to my daughter Bridget Guterson for life at 4 usual terms. She has power to distrain. If her husband, Matthew Gutterson, sells this legacy it will be void. To my wife Ann for life the house I now dwell in, a tenement let to Isaack Penall, my shop and chamber in tenure of my son Thomas and my orchard. After her death I give to my son Andrew the tenement let to Isaack Penall and the chamber adjoining it and now in occupation of my son Thomas, together with liberty of access to my well for water. To my son Thomas my other house and land. He must pay £10 each to my son John and to my daughter Elizabeth over 6 years. If these legacies are unpaid, legatees to inherit property left to Thomas. All my shop stuff to be equally divided between my sons Thomas and John. To my wife Ann all my household stuff for life, and after her death to be equally divided between my five children: Thomas, Andrew, John, Elizabeth and Ann. Wife sole ex'trix. Wit. Henry Walford, William Daye. Pr. at Bury 1 April 1630.

4. R(W) BRIDGET GARDNER of Finningham (N). March 1629/30.

She gave all her goods and household stuff to her brother John Steggall of Newton. He is to pay her debts, bury her and look to her girl Rachel Balls. John Steggall sole exor. Wit. Theophilus Lane, Margaret Sweteman. Pr. No date.

5. R(W) ADAM FORDHAM (X) of Hargrave, husbandman. 18 September 1629

Bequeaths soul to God and trusts to be saved.
To my wife Joan for life my close called Spring close and after her death to my son Thomas, and after his death to his son Thomas and his heirs. To Anne Bridges who hath long continued with us as a servant £5 in regard of her careful service and in satisfaction of a legacy left to her by Thomas Fletcher of Hargrave. I give to my grandchildren, Thomas and Elizabeth Fordham £10 each at age of 21. I bequeath the residue of my goods to my wife, whom I make sole ex'trix. Wit. Adam Halls, Simon Pitts (X). Pr. at Bury 5 April 1630.

6. R(W) FRANCIS BEVILL of Little Saxham, esquire. 12 April 1625

Trusts to be saved.
I bequeath to Elizabeth my wife for ever my close of pasture in Barrow called Lavenkins, which I and my wife lately purchased from Thomas Bilham. I give to Henry, son of my son-in-law Henry Leichfeild, £6 13s 4d, and to Francis his brother and my godson £13 6s 8d, and to Edward their brother £6 13s 4d. All these legacies to be paid at age of 21 with benefit of survivorship. I will that £20 be paid within 1 year to Alice Morrice, my wife's sister. I give to my friend Simon Pitts 20s. I bequeath to the poor of the parish where I am buried 40s. I give the residue of my goods to my wife whom I have always found a kind and loving wife to me and whom I make sole ex'trix. Wit. John Wymarke, Simon Pitts, Henry Holden. Pr. at Bury 9 April 1630.

7. R(W) SARAH NUTTEN of Edwardstone, widow woman. 4 April 1630

I give £10 to my son Samuel and the rest of my goods, money, cattle and corn to my son Abraham. I bequeath 20s to the poor of Edwardstone, and 20s to Mr Leigh, minister in the parish of Groton. Exors my sons Samuel and Abraham. Wit. Thomas Motte, John Brond, Richard Alstone (X). Pr. at Bury 12 April 1630.

8. R(W) JAMES HINSEBYE (X) of Cavenham. 21 November 1628

Bequeaths soul to God and trusts to be saved. To be buried in Cavenham churchyard.

I give and bequeath to Barbary my wife for her life my house and tenement in Cavenham and after her death it is to be equally divided between my son James and my daughter Mary. James must pay £10 to my daughter Esther over 4 years; she has power to distrain. If my wife fails to keep my house in repair or takes in any inmate or undersitter, male or female, then James and Mary are to have my house and land immediately. I give to my daughter Mary a flockbed, a pair sheets and the coffer that was mine before I married. If my wife has any sows or bullocks when she dies, I bequeath a bullock each to my daughters Mary and Esther. The residue of my goods, after my debts and legacies have been paid, I give to my wife whom I make sole ex'trix. Wit. Jeremy Baldod, Peter Cater. Pr. at Bury 5 April 1630.

9. R(W) RALPH WALLER of Drinkstone, yeoman. 15 January 1629/30

Gives his soul to God and trusts to be saved.

I give to the poor of Drinkstone half the debt of £35 that Mr John Wrenn owes me; the other half to be paid to my exors. This debt was given to me by the Lord Chancellor for arrearages of money I laid out at the suit of the poor of Drinkstone. I give to the poor of Brettenham 40s and to the poor of Rattlesden 40s. I bequeath to my wife Ann, until my youngest son Ralph is 21, a messuage and land called Forsters and Munfeilds lying in Rattlesden and Brettenham and now let to Thomas Sharp. My son Ralph and my daughter Anne are to be brought up to learning out of the income of this property. Ralph is to learn Latin. If Ralph dies before he is 21, my wife is to keep the property for 10 years and it is then to go to my son Thomas and my youngest daughter Anne. They must pay their mother £40 within 1 year if she is still alive. I give to my wife Anne 4 of my milk cows to be chosen out of my dairy, my nag called Bragg that I use to ride on, and the use of all my linen, except 1 pair sheets of the middle sort, until my youngest daughter Anne is 21. Then the linen is to be equally divided between my wife, my daughter Anne and my son Ralph. I bequeath to my son William a mazer cup of silver and gilt, and to my son Thomas 4 silver spoons. The rest of my plate to be equally divided between my wife, Ralph and daughter Anne. I give to my wife my down bed I sleep on and 2 other featherbeds. I give a featherbed each to my sons Thomas and Ralph and to my daughter Anne. I bequeath to my daughter Anne my messuage and land called Ridnalls in Brettenham and now let to John Heyward. Until Anne is 21 my wife is to take the income of this property to increase my daughter's portion. If Anne dies remainder to sons Thomas and Ralph. I give to my wife all my best tables, my cupboard in the parlour, my desk, my carpet on the parlour table, two of the best stools, all my chests, my livery cupboard in the parlour, all my pewter and brass, except one brass pot of the middle sort

3

which I give to my son Thomas. I also bequeath to my wife all my cobirons, tongs and firepans. She is to have all these goods until Ralph and Anne are 21 when they are to be divided equally between the three of them. If my wife remarries she is to enter into a bond to perform my will. I give to my son Thomas my messuages and land in Woolpit which I purchased of William Hawys and his son Thomas. I give to my son Thomas my tenement and smith's shop in Woolpit now let to William Curtys and young Daniel Baker. Remainder to Anne and Ralph. I give to my grandson, son of my deceased son Robert, my messuage and land called Stonhams in Rattlesden, Gedding and Brettenham and now occupied by Jeremy Wood. Until John is 21 my exors are to have the profits of this property to pay my debts. I give to my son William my messuage in Hitcham called Harrys with its land. I give to Susan my maid 20s, and to my man Thomas Woodward 20s. I bequeath 40s each to the children of my son William. I give 20s to Martha, wife of William Sylvester, and to my son John the £10 that I borrowed for him and that he owes me. I give to the daughter of my son John 20s to buy her a ring. I give to Anne my wife 5 combs of rye, 1 firkin of butter and 1 way of cheese. I bequeath to my son Thomas all my household and moveable goods in the hands of Scott [forename missing], tanner of Lavenham. Any goods, etc, left after my debts, legacies and funeral expenses have been paid are to be divided between my wife, my sons Thomas and Ralph and my daughter Anne. If my wife claims any dower, then all bequests to her shall be void. Exor. Peter Devereux, clerk of Rattlesden, to whom I give £5 for his pains. Supervisor: John Watson, clerk of Woolpit, who is given 20s. Wit. Richard Cobbold (X), William Tebbold (X), Thomas Walker, who wrote this will and William Carleton. Pr. at Bury 12 April 1630.

10. R(W) THOMAS CLAYDON of St Pernells in Bury St Edmunds. 22 October 1624.

Commends his soul to God.
I give to the poor living in the Southward in Bury 40s. I stand indebted to various persons, and my brother Robert and other good friends are bound with me for the payment of these debts. The debts are those of my father-in-law Smyth deceased, as may appear by bonds taken out by me since his death and to be found hanging on a file in my study. The debts are a life annuity of £20 to my mother-in-law and £100 to her daughter Adbury's children. None of my sureties are to be charged with the payment of my debts, and I desire my wife to sell the following property to pay them: Gipps close and Cleres close at Nowton, 8 acres of land and meadow in Bury which my father-in-law bought from Henry Apten, my messuage in Southgate Street in Bury now let to Robert Gault, the lands in Great and Little Whelnetham bought from George Kirbye and his wife Amy, and a messuage in Southgate Street now occupied by Richard Syllett and his wife. All this property, except the closes in Nowton, were bequeathed to me by my father-in-law Smyth to pay his debts and legacies. If these sales do not raise enough money to pay my debts, my

wife is to sell also my 12 acres of arable land in the Vinefield in Bury which I bought of Thomas Baker. If my wife does not sell this property and pay my debts within one year of my death, then my good friend Mr George Skarpe and my brother Robert shall do so. Any money left over from the sales is to be given to my wife if she is alive, and if not to my son Thomas with remainder to my nephew Robert, son of my brother Robert. I make my wife sole ex'trix. Wit. Anthony Scarpe, Thomas Corenbre. Pr. at Bury 17 April 1630.

Codicil dated 23 April 1629. If my wife will sell the houses in Southgate Street, late her father's, and the house and ground at Sicklesmere which are her inheritance within a year and a day of my decease, then the land I bought of Thomas Baker and Henry Apten and the land in the Vinefield is to go to my son Thomas.

Note: Thomas Claydon's house called St Pernells stood on the site of the former monastic hospital of St Petronilla, which was outside the Southgate. It was founded in the 12th century for female lepers, but was refounded in the 15th century to serve the poor. It was dissolved in 1539 at the same time as Bury Abbey.

11. ALICE ROBERTS (N) of Downham, singlewoman. 4 March 1629/30

She bequeathed to her brother John Roberts a bill of £4 owing to her by widow Trapper of Attleborough, and to her brother Thomas Roberts a bill of £10 owed to her by Robert Redder of Larling. She gave her sister Elizabeth, wife of Leonard James two bonds: £6 owed to her by Edward Lovette of Hockham [Norfolk] and £5 owed to her by Edward Balder of Hockham. She gave to her sister Mary, wife of John Carpenter, a bill of 40s owed to her by Thomas Fenne of Hockham. All these bills are in the custody of Ann Coward, widow, whom testator willed to give bills to persons to whom they are bequeathed. She gave £10 owed to her by her brother-in-law John Carpenter to him. She gave a featherbed and all that belongs to it and all her apparel to her sister James. To Ann Coward, widow, she gave a bond of £5 due to her from Robert Beales of Hockham on condition she paid 35s to George Hunt of Hockham for a debt which testator's brother Thomas owed to George Hunt; 8s to the widow Ward and 6s 8d each to Isaac, Robert, Elizabeth and Thomas Coward, and to Ann Welton her maid servant 5s. She gave to her brother Thomas two kettles and to her brother-in-law James a kettle and a posnet. She gave to Ann Coward an old chest and to Alice Largent a brass pot. And to the person that should see her decently buried a chest standing at the house of Francis Bens of Hockham with all in it. Wit. Ann Coward, Alice Largent. Let. ad. granted at Bury 12 April 1630 to Leonard James.

5

12. R(W) ROBERT DALE of Botesdale, joiner. 15 February 1629/30

Commends his soul to God.

I give to my wife Margery my best posted bedstead with the best featherbed, coverlet and all belonging to it now standing in my shop chamber, my livery table in the same room, my framed table, 4 buffet stools, my best cupboard back wicker chair, all the household goods she brought with her to me, a cheese press and all my other dairy vessels, my third kettle in greatness, a little skillet and a cloth press. I bequeath to her for life the use of my new barn with free access through the yard where it stands, and all my land leased from Sir Edmund Bacon baronet; also my 2 black cows. I give to my son Thomas my messuage and tenement where I now live, except the chamber where I now lie with my little chamber being my cheese chamber, which two rooms I bequeath to my wife for her life. I give £20 each to my daughters Anne and Estafidelis to be paid over 4 years out of the tenement bequeathed to my son Thomas; they have power to distrain. I give to my grand-daughter Joan Goodwyne £10 when she is 21, with remainder to my son Robert. My son Thomas is to pay this sum and Joan has power to distrain. I bequeath to my daughters Thama and Martha all my messuage and tenement wherein John Mills now dwells, together with the barn left to my wife after her death. They must pay annuity of 10s to Avis Willon until she is 18, and £10 to her a year after my wife's death; she has power to distrain. I give to my son Jonathan a pasture close in Botesdale bought of Robert Offwood, and he is to pay an annuity of 30s to my son Robert and another of 20s to Avis Wyllon; both have power to distrain. Jonathan can buy out these annuities by paying £20 to Robert and £15 to Avis. I bequeath to my daughter Estafidelis my second best featherbed, second best coverlet and second best bolster. I give to Avis Wyllon my second best kettle, second best brass pot, my brinded cow and 40s; and to her brother Robert Wyllon 20s. I give my god-daughter Elizabeth Greeneward 5s. I bequeath to my son Thomas all my shopstuff, benches, tools and implements belonging to my trade, together with all cutwork stuff and inlaid wainscot and all other old timber, as well broken as otherwise. Excepted from this gift are my green timber newly come into my yard, my stryces as ropes, barrell, my best hagsaw, my best handsaw, best hatchet, best throwyer, my chicksell and one holdfast, all which I give to my son Robert. I give my growing corn and all my swine to my wife; the residue of my goods are to be equally divided among my children. I ask my son Jonathan freely to give my wife 2 loads of smallwood and 1 of great wood, in consideration of which he shall have my best cloak and band. I give a pair of gloves worth 12 pence to each of 8 men who take the pains to carry me to church. Exors son Thomas and William Greenewood, who is given 20s for his pains. Wit. John Garrett, John Harvey. Pr. at Bury 9 April 1630.

13. R(W) AGNES MORLEY of Mildenhall, widow. 28 February 1629/30

I give to Margaret, daughter of John Burges my best gown, and to Agnes, wife of Thomas Young, my best red petticoat and my best waistcoat. I give to Joan, daughter of Thomas Young, one pewter platter, and to John Morley my son 12d. I give Grace Tompson, my daughter, my best cloak, and to my daughter, Mary Morley a bed that is in my son Henry's hands; also a flockbed, a bolster, a green coverlet, a blanket and the least of the 2 kettles. Exor: son Henry. Wit. Thomas Young, Nicholas Myne, Henry Younge. Pr. at Bury 19 April 1630.

14. R(W) ROSE DOWSING (N) of Hardwick, singlewoman. 17 March 1629/30. One of the poor people living in the almshouse in Hardwick.

She gave her nephew, Thomas Dowsing, a cupboard, a flockbed, a blanket, 2 pillows and a coverlet. To William Jony she left a flockbed and a blanket, and to John Dowsing a wheel, a chair and a gown. The rest of her goods and ready money, after debts and funeral expenses paid, to be equally divided between Thomas and John Dowsing and William Jony. Wit. Gilbert Spalding, Thomas Lilly. Let. ad granted in John Jewell's house at Bury 10 April 1630 to Thomas and John Dowsing and William Jony as exors.

15. R(W) JOHN DAVEY (X) of Hundon, tailor. 1 October 1627

Trusts to be saved. To be buried in Hundon churchyard.
I give and bequeath to Alice my wife for life my tenements and close of ground in Hundon and the use of all my moveables. I give her my warming pan to give and bestow as she pleases. After her death these gifts are to be divided among my 3 children as follows: to my daughter Frances my hall house which I now dwell in and all the rooms in the north end of the said hall house from the entry with the yards on both sides of the hall house. If she dies without heirs this property is to be equally divided between my son John and my daughter Alice. I also give to Frances my cloak, the middle kettle, the posted bed and all the bedding which I did lie upon being in the chamber over the buttery. I give to John and Alice, to be equally divided between them, the tenement adjoining to my hall house and the chamber over the hall and my close. I give to John my great hutch and the great kettle which I had of John Harvey. I give to Alice my brass pot and the little hutch. The residue of my goods to be divided between Alice and John. Ex'trix my daughter Alice. Wit. John Coggshall (X), William Pigg, who wrote will.

16. R(W) ELIZABETH GOODAY (X) of Chevington, singlewoman. 13 March 1629/30.

Bequeaths soul to God.
I bequeath money due to me by last will and testament of my father John

7

Gooday as follows: to my sister Susan Gooday £8 to be paid at Michaelmas after my decease in South porch of Chevington church; and to my sister Anne Gooday £8 to be paid on Whitsunday after my death. If one sister dies before her legacy is paid it is to be divided between survivor and my exors. I give 5s to be distributed to poor people of Chevington on day of my burial, and 5s to those that shall be ringers at my burial. The residue of my money and goods I bequeath to my good and loving mother Elizabeth Gooday and to my loving brother Christopher Gooday and I make them my exors. Wit. Robert Paman, John Gooday. Pr. at Bury 5 April 1630.

17. R(W) JEFFERY ERIE of Cavendish, husbandman. 15 March 1629/30

Bequeaths sinful soul to God and trusts to have sins washed away by precious blood of Jesus Christ.
I will that my wife Joan shall after my death have her dwelling in the house where I now inhabit and that my exor shall provide her with sufficient meat, drink, firing and lodging and all things needful in sickness and in health, using her during her natural life kindly, dutifully and lovingly. If she does not want to live with my exor, I will that she shall have for her life the house that Agnes Smyth now dwells in, and that is part of the farm I hold of Sir Henry Colt. This house was lately occupied by the widow Thetford. As long as my wife lives in this house my exor is to pay her £4 p.a. and to provide her with 2 loads of firewood. I give to my wife for life, and then to my exor, the best bedstead and bed furnished, 2 pairs of sheets, a warming pan, 3 pillows, the best kettle except one, a posnet, 2 of the lesser barrels, a tub, a keeler, a pair little cobirons, 1 little table with 4 feet, a long form, 2 little stools, 2 pewter dishes, 2 saucers, a salt cellar, a bowl to wash in, 2 hutches and 1 pail. If my wife does not reside with my exor he is to give her a shoate at All Saints each year. I give to my son George £11 to be paid within 3 years of my decease and 20s more if my wife dies within 4 years of my death. I owe George 40s which my exor is to pay him within 6 months. I give to my daughter Margaret £8 to be paid within 4 years, and 20s more if my wife dies within that time. To my daughter Ursula, wife of George Neale, 40s to be paid within 6 years of my death, and to their daughter Juda 20s when she is 20. I give to my son George a skep of bees. Exor my son Jeffery, who is to have the residue of my goods, cattle, corn in field and house, carts, plough and utensils of husbandry towards paying my debts, legacies and burial charges. Wit. Reginald Bell, Anthony Cooke (X). Pr. at Bury 5 April 1630.

18. R(W) GEORGE CAMPE (X) of Thwaite. 14 February 1629/30

Commends soul to God and trusts to be saved.
I give and bequeath to my daughter Esther 40s to be paid within one year of my death, and to my daughter Joan a cow left to her by her

grandmother. Also to Joan £3 10s 0d to be paid at once and another 10s to be paid within one year. The residue of my goods I bequeath to my wife Ursula for the bringing up of my children. I make her sole ex'trix. Wit. James Hatton, William Selfe. Pr. at Stowmarket 3 April 1630.

19. R(W) EDWARD ANDREWES of Long Melford, baymaker. 30 July 1628.

Bequeaths soul to God and hopes to attain everlasting kingdom.

I give and bequeath to my son Edward my copyhold tenement in Hall Street, Long Melford, with yard, garden and orchards, on condition he pays my daughter Anne, Henry Horne's wife, 40s within 2 years, and pays my daughter Margery £15 at £3 p.a. If all or part of this £15 is unpaid, then Margery is to have the house wherein Simon Clytter now dwells and the house next to it with the solar over it in which John Crysall now lives, with access to the well for water. I give to my son Edward two pairs of narrow combs, a posted bed, a great kettle, a great spit, a pair cobirons, a pewter platter, the great new chest, a pair malt querns, a pair of great combs and all my wedges with a kneading trough. I give to my daughter Horne's wife and to her husband for life the free tenement that I bought of John Crowch, and after their deaths to their son Henry. I give to my son-in-law Henry Horne a bed and bedstead wherein my daughter lieth, a middle kettle, a skillet, a pewter platter and my great old hutch. I give to my daughter Margery the bedstead and bed wherein I now lie with sheets, coverlet and blanket as it now standeth, a brass pot, a little kettle, the rest of my pewter, a little table, a little cupboard, a stool, 2 chairs, a trammell and a little spit. All other things unbequeathed my exors are to divide between them. Exors. son Edward and son-in-law Henry Horne. Wit. Francis Hamond, William King, Miles Haxall (X). Pr. at Long Melford 1 April 1630.

20. R(W) THOMAS VISE the elder of Burwell [Cambs], yeoman. 8 January 1628/29.

Gives soul to God trusting that he will place it in company of heavenly angels and blessed saints.

I give and bequeath to my son Thomas my messuage in Parsonage Lane, Burwell on condition he pays £20 to William Folkes yeoman of Exning and £20 to Simon Hering gentleman of Stetchworth plus the interest on both sums. If Thomas refuses to pay these sums, my exors are to sell the messuage and pay the £40. I give Thomas 2 copyhold meadows with the north end abutting on Parsonage Lane, and 11 acres copyhold arable land after the decease of Alice, my wife and his mother. I give my son John, after my wife's decease, the messuage wherein I now dwell in the High Street near the parish churchyard called St Mary's, all my freehold arable land, my meadows lying next to the messuage and meadow belonging to Benjamin Paine, and my meadow at High Town End next to William Rogers's pasture. I give my daughter Anne £40 within 2 years, and a bride chamber or £10 at her choice on her marriage day. I give my wife Alice for life all my messuages and land except the messuage in Parsonage Lane left to my son Thomas. I give 6s 8d to the churchwardens of Burwell towards the repair of St Mary's parish church, and 10s to be given to the poor at my burial. I give all my moveable goods to my wife and son John and make them exors. After my debts and legacies are paid, the residue is to be divided between my exors. I have surrendered all my copyhold land held of the manor of Ramsies to the use of my will by the hands of Edward Vaisey and in the presence of Barnaby Garner, and my copyhold land held of manor of Mrs Barrowe by hands of John Baron and in the presence of Barnaby Garner, and my copyhold land held of the parsonage by the hands of Richard Dixe and in the presence of Jeffery Vaisey. Wit. William Hopwood, John Baron, Barnaby Garner, Richard Dixe, Jeffery Vaisey, Edward Vaisey. Pr. at Newmarket 7 April 1630.

21. R(W) BENNITT HUNTE (X) of Lawshall, yeoman. 20 January 1629/30.

Commends soul to God and hopes to be partaker of life everlasting. I give and bequeath to my wife Katharine all my money absolutely, and to her for life all my household goods and implements of husbandry. After her death I leave them to my daughter Katharine, who must pay my son Richard 40s within 1 month of my wife's decease. Ex'trix to pay Richard 40s within 1 year of my death. I give 2s each to my son Bennitt and to my daughter Prudence Payne to be paid by my ex'trix within 1 year. Ex'trix my wife. Wit. Francis Smith (X), John Smith. Pr. at Bury 5 April 1630.

22. R(W) WILLIAM SHEPHEARD (X) of Wetheringsett, husbandman. 25 April 1629.

Commends soul to God in certain hope of everlasting life.
I give to Sarah my wife all my moveable goods on condition she pays, if she can spare it, 20s each when they are 21 to my 5 children: William, John, Joshua, Benjamin and Sarah. She must also give William the cupboard in the hall and Sarah a silver spoon. Ex'trix my wife Sarah. Wit. William Withers, Nicholas Daldye, George Brome. Pr. at Stowmarket 3 April 1630.

23. R(W) RICHARD HAIWARD the elder of Burwell [Cambs], husbandman. 13 November 1629.

Commends soul to God trusting to rest with Jesus Christ in his everlasting kingdom.
I give £4 each to my sons Thomas, Stephen, John and Richard to be paid within a year of the decease of my daughter Rose; and £4 to be paid at the same time to each of my daughters Mary, wife of Robert Baron, Margaret and Deborah. I give my son William 20s if he come again, and

if he come not I give this 20s and 20s more to his daughter Mary. I give another 20s to be divided equally amongst my above-named children after the decease of my daughter Rose. I give my daughter Deborah my brass pot and 15s; my daughter Margaret the great coffer and 15s; and my daughter Mary 10s. This sum of £2 is in the hands of Robert Caseburne. I give all the rest of my goods to my son-in-law Robert Baron and make him my exor on condition he sees my daughter Rose provided for and kept with all things necessary during her life, and after her decease performs my will. Wit. John Milkyns, Christopher Oliver senior, John Barone, William Hoppwoode. Pr. at Newmarket 7 April 1630.

24. R(W) ROBERT BEDDALL of Brockford, husbandman. 1 March 1629/30

Bequeaths soul to God and hopes to rise again to eternal life.
I bequeath to the 2 children of my kinsman James Beddall, otherwise called James Ostiler, now dwelling in Foulde [– perhaps Foulden, Norfolk]. All my goods, chattels, money and debts I give to my maid Constance Jessopp and make her sole ex'trix. Within one month she must enter into a bond for £10 with my landlord Samuel Colbey for payment of my legacies, or bequest to her becomes void and goes to Samuel Colbey, who in this case also becomes exor. The legacies to the two children are to be paid to their mother within 3 months of my death. Wit. William Smith, Samuel Colby. Pr. at Stowmarket 3 April 1630.

25. R(W) REGINALD REEVE (X) of Hepworth, yeoman. 20 May 1629

Bequeaths soul to God with hope of pardon and remission of sins.
To be buried in Hepworth churchyard.
I give to my son Francis my tenement wherein I now dwell. My wife Parnall is to have the use for life of my bedchamber wherein I usually lodge with the bedding and furniture. She is to have free access to one end of the chimney in the hall house. This gift is in lieu of dower. Francis is to pay my wife 40s a year for life at the 4 quarter days, and she has power to distrain. My daughter Margaret is to live for life in the house where she now dwells if she remains single. My son Francis is to pay her £10 at 20s p.a. after my wife's death; she has power to distrain. Wife and daughter have right to fetch water from any of my ponds at any time. Exor. son Francis. Wit. Francis Hawes, John Whithand, Richard Barker. Pr. at Bury 4 May 1630.

26. R(W) AGNES ROLFE (X) of Mildenhall, widow. 11 December 1629

Commends soul to God and hopes to attain kingdom of heaven.
I give to Richard my son the 7 rods copyhold land in Mondsfield, in Mildenhall, which I inherited from my husband Simon Rolfe, for his life and then to his daughter Jane Rolfe. Richard is to pay my daughter Agnes £10 within 18 months of my death, or Agnes will inherit land left to

Richard. Also to my daughter Agnes my great chest in the parlour with its contents, 6 pewter dishes, 2 pewter candlesticks, a chair in the parlour, a copper kettle, a brass skillet, my frying pan, and half of my dairy and brewing vessels. Also 2 combs good barley, 2 milch bullocks, one coloured red and the other brended. I give to my kinsman William Suckerman one comb barley. I give to Elizabeth, daughter of my brother-in-law Andrew Rolfe, 30s when she is 18. The residue of my goods, after debts, legacies and funeral expenses have been paid, I give to my son Richard whom I make sole exor. Wit. Andrew Rolfe (X), Mark Turner (X), William Dalleson.
Memorandum that I have surrendered my copyhold land into the hands of lord of manor by hands of Andrew Rolfe and Mark Turner, copyhold tenants of manor. Pr. at Bury 9 April 1630.

27. R(W) EDWARD HASELLWOOD (X) the elder of Wood Ditton [Cambs]. 20 October 1625.

Bequeaths soul to God. To be buried in Wood Ditton churchyard.
I give my son Edward the house Hector Vye now dwells in with the adjoining orchard and closes for one year after my decease, except for the herbage of the closes which I have let to John Powlter yeoman, late of Wood Ditton, and his assignees. I give my son Edward £14, being part of £20 due to me from Henry Visboroughe or John Powlter; the remaining £6 is to be used to pay my debts and funeral charges. Anything left over is to be divided between the rest of my children: William, John, Joan, Elizabeth and Agnes. Exor: son Edward. Wit. John Thomas, Thomas Chinnery (X), Pr. at Bury 10 May 1630.

28. R(W) MARTHA BARTON (X) of Combs, widow. 7 May 1630

Gives soul into hands of God and hopes to obtain eternal salvation.
I give to my daughters Margaret Beast and Martha Pattle my chest of linen to be equally divided between them. To Margaret Beast the bedstead in the chamber next to the hall with its bedding, but with a flockbed instead of the featherbed now on it as that belongs to my son Pattle. Also to her the lesser of my 2 brass pots and 2 brass candlesticks. I give to Martha Felgate, my husband's grandchild, the trundle bed in the parlour with a flockbed, bolster, 2 blankets, a coverlet and a pair of sheets. To my daughter, Margaret Beast, 6 pieces of my best pewter. I give to my grandchild Martha Pattle the bed in the parlour as it now stands, also the cupboard and table in the parlour. I give to Margaret Beast the biggest brass kettle but one and the joined chest in the parlour chamber. I give to the poor of Combs 40s. Exor. son-in-law Thomas Pattle. Wit. Thomas Sothebye, Robert Wellam. Pr. at Bury 13 May 1630.

29. R(W) GEORGE BOYTON (X) of Bury St Edmunds, plumber. 26 April 1630.

Commends soul to God.
I give and bequeath to Susan my wife all my goods and chattels on condition she pays my debts and performs my will. After her death my goods are to be equally divided between my sons John and George and my daughter Susan. My wife must allow my son George the peaceable occupation of the messuage in Whiting Street where he now lives; he must pay her £4 p.a. Ex'trix wife. If she does not prove my will within 14 days of my decease, then bequests to her are void and go to my brother Edward Boyton who also becomes exor. Wit. William Neale, Richard Howard (X), Oliver Johnson. Pr. at Bury 11 May 1630.

30. R(W) WILLIAM PEACH [no place given]. 18 April 1630

I give to my son William my house with adjoining acre of land when he is 26; until then my wife Agnes is to keep house in repair if she is able. I give to my wife one and a half acres copyhold land lying in Hallwellfield between meres, the north end on Styway and the south on Oldway. She is to sell this land to redeem one and half acres freehold land mortgaged to Francis Hunt. I give the freehold land to my daughters Agnes and Mary when they are 21. This land lies by Aspell way with north end abutting on Sir Roger North's land and the south on Styway. I give 10s each to Thomas and John sons of my brother Robert Peach. Exrx. wife. I have surrendered my copyhold land into hands of Thomas Barton and John Eagle. Wit. Thomas Barton, Henry Johnson, John Eagle, John Pay. Pr. at Bury 16 May 1630.

31. R(W) GRACE NORFOLKE (X) of Clare, widow. 26 January 1629/30.

Bequeaths soul to God. To be buried in churchyard at Clare.
I will that all my debts be paid. I bequeath the messuage I dwell in with its garden to my grandson Nicholas Fyler and to my sons Peter and Roger Norfolke. They are to sell it within a year and equally divide the proceeds. I bequeath all my goods to my 3 children: Peter, Roger and Sarah to be equally divided among them. Exor. George Finne of Clare, clothier. Wit. Richard Long, John Howe. Pr. at [no place given] 18 May 1630.

32. R(W) THOMAS GOODCHILD of Bury St Edmunds, physician. 10 April 1630.

Commends soul to God and hopes to be saved.
I give to Lucy my wife for life my freehold house in the ?Raingate Street which I bought from Thomas Church, and after her death to my daughter Elizabeth. If she dies without heirs, my son Thomas is to inherit house. I

give to Thomas a featherbed furnished, all my horses and carts with the harness belonging to them, and all my tools of husbandry. Half of my books are to be divided between my 2 children. The residue of my goods I give to my wife and daughter, who are joint ex'trices. Wit. Henry Pettiward, Thomas Rouland. Pr. at Bury 20 May 1630.

33. R(W) MARY SMITH (X) of Stradishall, widow of Bartholomew Smith of Great Bradley. 28 September 1619.

Commends soul to God and hopes to have a place of rest in his kingdom. To be buried in Stradishall churchyard.
I give to my eldest son John 5s in lieu of his portion. I give to my daughter Mary £5 and my best bedstead and a hutch; and to my daughter Avys £5, the bedstead that stands in the chamber over the parlour and the biggest chest in the chamber below. I give to my daughter Margaret Yackesley 5s for her portion. I give to my daughter Martha Chapman £5, and 2 forms with the long table that stands in the parlour. To my daughter Alice I give £5, the bedstead that stands in the upper chamber next the street and 2 of the smallest hutches. I give to my daughter Anne £5, the cupboard that stands in the parlour, the best unbequeathed hutch and a little brass pot. I give to my son Christopher £5, a trundle bed and the great chest that was his grandfather's. I give to my son Robert the table and form that stand in the parlour and 12d for his portion as his brother Bartholomew has already given him his portion. To my son Bartholomew I give my quern and a great chair that his father made. Also to him my house in Stradishall where I now dwell with a pightle on condition he pays my other children their portions within 1 year of my decease. If he fails to do this, my house is to go to my children whose portions are unpaid; they are to sell it to pay themselves their shares and must give £10 to Bartholomew. All my linen to be divided among my 6 daughters, except for my best sheet which is to be my winding sheet. Exor. son Bartholomew. Wit. William Veale, Thomas Gippes. Pr. at Bury 4 May 1630.

34. R(W) THOMAS DOBBES (X) of Soham [Cambs], blacksmith. 15 March 1629/30.

Commends soul to God and trusts to have a joyous resurrection.
I give Alice my wellbeloved wife for her life my copyhold messuage wherein I dwell, and after her decease to Thomas Dobbes, my godchild and son of William Dobbes of Soham. I give my wife 3 of my best milk bullocks, the best that she can choose, one hog and all the household stuff in the house and yard except my apparel and my working tools. I give Richard Dowe my working tools in the shop, my shop stuff, my irons and coals in the shop and all the debts due to the shop. He must take Bartholomew Wright as his apprentice to finish his time with him, or pay him 33s 4d on St John the Baptist day next. I give my kinsman William Dobbes my old garled cow, and my kinswoman Agnes Dobbes my black

howed cow; she must pay 10s to Robert Bentley within 1 month of my decease. If she refuses to pay this money, Richard Bentley is to have the cow. I give Richard Dowe my brinded cow and he must pay 10s to Robert Dawling, and 5s to the eldest child of [blank in MS] Syfers within a month of my decease. All the rest of my moveables I give to Alice my loving wife, whom I make ex'trix. Wit. John Norffolke, John Harvey (X), Henry Frost. On same day the testator surrendered his messuage to the use of his will by the hands of Robert Banyer. Pr. at Bury 20 April 1630.

35. R(W) MARTHA BREWSTER of Brandon, widow. 28 October 1629

Commits soul to God.

My exors are to pay all the as yet unpaid legacies bequeathed by my late husband William Brewster. I give my exors all the land in Hartest mortgaged to me and all monies due to me to enable them to pay my husband's legacies and my own. I give to my son William all those wainscots, benches and hangings in that part of the messuage where I now dwell and also in those houses and rooms how occupied by Nathaniel Howlett. Also to him a bedstead, a featherbed, a bolster, 2 pillows, a green rug coverlet, and the blankets, curtains and rods belonging to the bed which stands in my chamber called Roses chamber. I also give him a pair of my best sheets, a pair of the best pillowbeeres, my copper as it hangs and my horse mill as it goes. I give and bequeath to my son Thomas all the land in Foulden [Norfolk] left to me by my husband and which used to belong to Edmund Eastgates. Also to him a bedstead in my hall chamber, my new featherbed, a bolster, 2 pillows, a large darnacle coverlet of red and blue colour, 2 blankets and the curtains and rods belonging to the bed. Also to him a pair of my best sheets and a pair of my best pillowbeeres. Exors to pay him £20 when he is 21. I give and bequeath to my son John a bedstead with a featherbed, a bolster, 2 pillows, a rug coverlet, 2 blankets and the curtains and curtain rods for this bed which is in the chamber between the hall and parlour. Also to him a pair of the best sheets and a pair of the best pillowbeeres. Also to John £30 when he is 21. I give to my son Ambrose a bedstead standing in my servants' chamber, a featherbed, a bolster, 2 pillows, a coverlet with the blankets as they lie on the trundle bed in my parlour chamber. Also to him a pair of my best sheets and a pair of my best pillowbeeres. I give him £30 when he is 21. I bequeath to my daughter Martha a bedstead, a featherbed, a bolster, 2 pillows, a yellow rug coverlet, 2 blankets and the curtains and curtain rods belonging to the bed which stands in my parlour chamber. Also to her a pair of the best sheets, a pair of the best pillowbeeres, all my wearing linen and woollen, and the livery cupboard in the parlour chamber. I give her £20 when she is 21. I will my exors to hold my 2 leasehold closes of land and pasture in Brandon until my son William is 21 when he is to inherit this land. I give 20s each to my 3 daughters-in-law: Elizabeth Levick, Amy Howlett and Alice Beerewaye. I give £3 to the poor of Brandon to be distributed on day of my burial. The rest of my goods are to be sold by my exors and the money to be put out

15

and used for the maintenance and good education of my daughter and 3 youngest sons. When the youngest is 21 the principal sum is to be divided among these 4 children. They have benefit of survivorship. Exors. my 2 brothers Richard and Robert Cronshay, who are given £5 each. They are to be guardians of my son William until he is of age. Wit. Nathaniel Howlett, Silvester Spinke. Pr. at Bury 1 July 1630.

36. R(W) WILLIAM ONGE (X) OF BARNINGHAM, yeoman.
20 January 1625/26

Commends soul to mercy of God in hope of a joyful resurrection.
I give to Anne my well-beloved wife until the Michaelmas after my son William is 21 all my messuages, lands, sheep walks and fold courses in Barningham, which lately belonged to my uncle William Ong. Also all the rest of my land in Barningham which I have lately purchased. After my son William inherits this land my wife is to have for life the third part of my house and yards and of all the fruit trees together with the use of the ovens and brewing house. William must pay her an annuity of £20, and £100 to my younger son John when he is 24. Wife has power to distrain, and if John's legacy is not paid he is to inherit a close called Fishmeares and all my land in Stonyfield, Breach hearne or the Dales in Barningham, except 1 acre called Fould acre. If William dies before age of 21, John inherits his land and must pay annuity to my wife Anne. I give and bequeath to my wife for life one hundred and a half of wood yearly to be indifferently sized according to the custom of the country and taken from my land. If both sons die, heir is to be my brother Richard Ong. Ex'trix wife. Supervisor: Sir William Spring of Pakenham. Wit. John Craske, John Parkin (X), William Meaddowe. Pr. at Bury 24 April 1630.

37. R(W) BRIDGET SHERD alias SEYRD (N) of Great Livermere, singlewoman. No date, but buried 13 June 1628.

About 2 or 3 weeks before her death John Francis of Great Livermere asked how she would bestow her goods and she replied that all should go to her sister Elizabeth Harris because she is most worthy of them for she hath taken great pains about me. Wit. on 23 May 1630 by John Cater (X), John Francis (X). Pr. at Bury 25 May 1630.

38. R(W) ROBERT CARLTON the elder of Soham [Cambs], tailor.
15 February 1629/30.

Commends soul to God and trusts to be saved through Jesus Christ. To be buried in Soham churchyard.
I give my son Robert £6 13s 4d to be paid within 2 years of my decease and the same sum to my son Edward within 3 years. I give £3 6s 8d to each of the following of my children to be paid at the rate of 2 each year starting 4 years after my decease: my daughter Diana, wife of William Knocke; my daughter Edniah; my sons Thomas, John and Richard; my

16

daughter Elizabeth; and my sons Henry, William, Erasmus and Philip. All these legacies are to be paid in the common hall of the house wherein I now dwell in Soham and called by the sign of the George. I give my now wife Elizabeth for ever my messuage I now live in standing in Churchgate Street in Soham, with Carltons Lane on its south side and Paddock Street on the east side, with its outhouses, dovehouse, barn, stable, yards and orchards. She must pay my legacies and the sums of money for which I stand justly indebted to Mr Bentlye of Newmarket, Mr Drurie of Reach, [blank in MS] Stephenson of [blank in MS] and some others. I give my wife all my goods and chattels. If she sells my messuage, she is to pay all my legacies within 2 years of the sale. I make my wife sole ex'trix. Supervisors: Mr Roger Murden of Soham and my cousin John Hinson of Fordham. I have surrendered my copyhold land to the use of my will by the hands of William Goldsboroughe and in the presence of Roger Murden [both copyholders]. Wit. Roger Murden, Andrew Banyer, William Gouldsborough, John Bugge and me William Howe. Pr. at Soham 27 May 1630.

39. R(W) JOHN SOMER (N) of Rougham. Made about Easter 1629.

When asked if he would make a will his answer was no, and when asked how he would dispose of his estate and what his daughter should have to live with, replied that his son John knew his mind, which was that John should pay pay 20 marks to his daughter Margaret, 20s to grandson Robert Hunt and keep the rest of the estate for himself. When asked he said that this should be his will. Wit. John Drury, Thomas Borley (X). Let. ad. granted at Bury 10 May 1630 to son John.

40. R(W) ELIZABETH PAYNE (X) of Worlington, widow. 21 March 1629/30.

Commends soul to three persons of Trinity and trusts to be saved. To be buried in parish church of Worlington.
I give to my son Henry Payne my freehold messuage wherein I now dwell. I bequeath to my daughter Dister £20 within 6 months, and to my daughter Anne Guest £10 within 18 months. I also give her 2 wrought stools, a long table with 2 trestles belonging to it, 1 form, a great chest, the featherbed I lie on, 4 brass kettles, a pair malt querns and a barley screen. I give to my daughter Mary Biggs £10 within one year and also £5 that I lent to her husband Thomas Biggs. I also give her the featherbed in the parlour, a hutch with boules on the bottom, a little black chair and a little table in the buttery. I give 12d to every house or family of poor people in Worlington. The residue of my goods I give to my son Henry whom I make exor. Wit. Martin Warren, Elizabeth Dister (X). Pr. at Worlington 29 May 1630.

41. R(W) HELEN NEAVE (X) of Downham, widow. 11 May 1630

Bequeaths soul to God and trusts to have sins pardoned. To be buried in Downham churchyard.
I give all my goods and chattels to Olle Button, my youngest daughter, whom I make sole ex'trix. She is to pay my debts and pay 2s 6d each to my sons-in-law and daughters-in-law as well as 2s 6d to my son Richard and his wife. This last payment to be made at the church porch of Downham within a year of my decease. Wit. George Largent (X), Widow Cowherd (X). Pr. at Bury 24 May 1630.

42. R(W) FRANCES DENNANT of Stowmarket, wife of Walter Dennant. 27 January 1629/30.

Bequeaths soul to God and steadfastly believes to have eternal salvation. To be buried in Stowmarket churchyard.
I give and bequeath to my husband all my rights and title to a tenement in Lavenham wherein my father, William Haylock, and his wife Bridget now dwell. My husband must pay £10 to the children of my sister Ponder. Exor. Husband, Walter Dennant. Wit. John Glover, Philip Barne. Pr. at Stowmarket 17 June 1630.

43. R(W) JOHN BOROUGH of Haughley, yeoman. 25 June 1630.

Bequeaths soul to God and believes he will attain everlasting life. To be buried in Haughley churchyard.
I give to my son Thomas Borow the freehold tenement I live in with its land; also 33 acres copyhold land called Plashwood and Denner and another 3 acre piece called Grasselesse, all in Haughley. He is to pay my wife Rebecca an annuity of £7. I give my wife 2 cartloads of wood a year to be given to her by my son Thomas, and all the household goods within my house for life. She is to live in my house for her lifetime. If Thomas puts her out of the house, he must give her 40s p.a., and if he fails to provide her with wood the land left to him goes to her absolutely. I give to my son John Borough 13 acres copyhold land in 2 pieces called Oakes and lying in Haughley; also a copyhold tenement in Haughley called Newmans with its yard. Thomas must pay my daughter Rose £20 within 2 years and my daughter Rebecca £20 within 3 years of my death. If Thomas refuses to pay these legacies or my wife's annuity, then land left to him goes to son John. I give all unbequeathed moveable goods to my son Thomas whom I make exor. Supervisor: William Thorowgood of Haughley. Wit. John Raynold, William Thorowgood, who wrote this will. Pr. at Bury 26 July 1630.

44. R(W) AUDREY YOUNG (N) of Mildenhall, widow. No date.

She gave to her daughter Agnes her brass pot, a frying pan, a cradle, a hutch, a sieve, a tub, an overbody, 3 sheets, a table cloth, a coverlet, a pair of bedsteads and a linen apron. She gave to her son Henry a hutch, a pair of bedsteads, a pair sheets, a pillow and a pillow beere, a plank, a sholve and a crome. She gave to her daughter Mary a framed table, a hutch, 4 sheets, a moulding trough, a kettle, a posnet, a sieve, a bowl, a linen apron and a reel. She gave to her daughter Stephen Lilly [sic] a table, a form, a hat, a cloak, a sheet and a ring. All her clothes, both woollen and linen, she gave to be equally parted between her daughters Mary and Agnes. Wit. Edmund Petchey, John Winge. Let. ad. granted 5 July 1630 to son Henry, No place given.

45. R(W) JOHN GILLYE (X) of Troston, yeoman. 19 June 1630

Bequeaths soul to God.
I give to my wife Amy for life all my freehold and copyhold land in Pakenham. I bequeath to my son Clement £160 to be paid by my wife within 18 months into the hands of my landlord William Castleton, esquire, and of Richard Cooke, gent of Pakenham. I give to my son Robert £140 to be paid as above within two and a half years, and to my daughter Susan £100 to be paid as above within three and a half years of my decease. I give to my son John £100 to be paid by my wife within 4 years into the hands of John Cooke gent of Great Livermere and of my brother-in-law Simon Boxe, whom I entreat to be supervisor of my will. I give £5 to the town of Pakenham for the use of the poor for ever and similarly £2 to the town of Troston. I give 20s to the poor of Ixworth. I bequeath 40s to John Eagle, 20s to Robert Eagle and 5s each to all the rest of my present servants. I give my son John one featherbed. I bequeath the rest of my goods and chattels to my wife Amy to enable her to pay my debts and legacies, and I make her sole ex'trix. Wit. Thomas Nunne, Mary Pettit (X). Pr. at Bury 19 July 1630.

46. R(W) EDMUND RUMBELOWE of Dalham, yeoman. 2 April 1630.

Bequeaths soul to God and trusts to be saved.
I bequeath to my brother John my land and meadow ground at Great Bradley, and to my brother Martin my freehold messuage in Tuddenham with all its land, and £20 to be paid to him within 4 years of my decease. I give my brother Robert all my customary land and tenement in Dalham, my customary land held of the manor of Ousden and my freehold tenement at Dunston Green [in Dalham] if John Pratt does not redeem the mortgage on it. I also give my brother Robert all debts and monies owing to me, all my household stuff, all the corn in the chambers of the house where I live and my 10 sheep in a flock at Ashley [Cambs]. Also to him all the corn and grass growing on the land I have bequeathed to him.

19

I bequeath 20s to Bridget wife of Thomas Cobb and 20s to Jonas Cobb. I give £5 each to the sons and daughters of my uncle John Pettit: John, Ambrose, Mary, Bridget and Esther. I give £5 to Anne Rumbelowe, daughter of my uncle Thomas Rumbelowe; 20s to my servant Anne Cutting; and 6s 8d to each of my godchildren at age of 21. I bequeath 20s to increase the town stock of Dalham to the use and benefit of the poor, and 10s to be distributed at my funeral to the poor of Dalham. I give the residue of my goods to my brothers John and Robert, whom I make exors. Wit. Richard Palmer (X), Thomas Wakefeild. Pr. at Bury 12 July 1630.

47. R ROBERT FLOWER of Mildenhall. No date.

I give to Barbara my wife 4 milk bullocks, the best she can take, and all my household goods in the house. I bequeath to my sons Henry and Francis £4 each, and to my daughters Elizabeth, Barbara and Margaret £3 each. I give all this money to my wife so long as she lives and after her death to my children. Ex'trix wife. No witnesses. Pr. at Bury 12 July 1630.

48. R(W) STEPHEN HARDY (X) of the parish of St Mary, Bury St Edmunds, carpenter. 5 October 1629.

Bequeaths soul to God. To be buried in St Mary's churchyard.
I give all my goods and moveables to my loving wife Bridget, and appoint her sole ex'trix. I give my son Thomas 12d to be paid within a year of my decease. Wit. Da. Jones, Henry Plumbe, Henry Bathorne (X). Pr. at Bury 5 July 1630.

49. R(W) JOHN STEWARD (X) of Bury St Edmunds, carpenter. 19 June 1630.

Bequeaths soul to God.
I give and bequeath all my goods and chattels to my wife Elizabeth on condition she pays my debts. Exors wife and Bennitt Clerke of Nowton. Wit. John Hunt. Pr. at Bury 26 July 1630.

50. R(W) JOHN HEYWARD of Thorndon, husbandman. 28 April 1630.

I give to my beloved wife Thomazine all my moveable goods for ever, that is the clothes, household goods and ready money in my house at Thorndon. She is to pay my debts, and I trust that at her decease she will bestow my goods on my son John and his heirs. Wit. Katherine Clerke. Pr. at Thorndon 10 July 1630.

51. R(W) JAMES MOULTON (X) of Wortham, labourer. 17 October 1628.

Commits soul to God and hopes for salvation. To be buried in Wortham churchyard.
I give and bequeath to Mawnlinge my wife for life all my houses and hemplands towards the education of my younger children and the repairing of my houses. After her death they are to be sold for the best price by Thomas Nunne the younger and Nicholas Browne the elder, both of Wortham, and the money is to be equally divided among my children which I had of both my wives. If my children John and Elizabeth die before my wife, their portions are to go to their children. After my decease I give to my daughter Elizabeth one of my coffers, and another to my daughter Sibilla. After the death of my wife I give my bedstead to Elizabeth and the livery cupboard to Sibilla. If I die immediately I will that the year's profit of the little house wherein Thomas Langham lives shall be paid to my son John in consideration of 20s I owe him. The rest of my goods I give to my wife Mawnlinge, whom I make sole ex'trix. Wit. Thomas Leverington clerk, Nicholas Browne, Thomas Nun. Pr. at Wortham 7 July 1630.

52. R(W) HENRY ASTIN (N) of Braiseworth, husbandman. May 1630

Being required to settle his estate and make his will, he said my will is quickly made. All that I have my wife brought me and my meaning is that she shall have all that I leave. Wit. Francis Wood, Frances wife of Samuel Hunt. Let. ad. granted at Braiseworth 8 July 1630 to widow.

53. R(W) JOAN CANCELER of Wyverstone, widow. 13 May 1630.

Commits soul to God and hopes to be saved.
I give and bequeath to my god-daughter Rebecca Sweatman alias Bennet a flockbed, a feather bolster, 2 feather pillows, my best covering, 2 blankets and a livery bedstead. I give to my god-daughter Anne Beaton a feather bed and bedstead, which I now do lie upon, standing in the little chamber with all its bedding as it is now furnished with a bolster, 2 pillows, a covering and a pair blankets. All the rest of my goods, bonds and money I leave to be equally parted between my two god-daughters on condition they pay 5s each within a year to all their brothers and sisters, the children of Thomas Sweatman and Richard Beaton, who are to employ these legacies to the best profit until the children are 21. Six months after my decease the £10 of mine now in the hands of my son-in-law Richard Beaton is to be paid by him to Rebecca Sweatman and Anne Beaton, whom I make ex'trices. Wit. Richard Beaton, Elizabeth Blogget widow, John Watchame, who wrote will. Pr. at Bury 5 July 1630.

54. R(W) JOHN GRIMWADE of Aldham, yeoman. 1 March 1629/30

Commends soul to God and believes himself to be saved.
I give to my son William £20 when he is 24. I give 20 marks each to my daughters Dorcas, Sarah and Alice when 24 and 20 marks to my daughter Elizabeth at age of 21. All have benefit of survivorship. To my eldest daughter Mary I give 40s to be paid 3 months after my decease. All the rest of my goods, chattels, corn and implements of husbandry I bequeath to Frances my loving wife, whom I make sole ex'trix, to enable her to pay my debts and legacies and bring up my children. She is to enter into a bond of £180 for the performance of my will with my loving brother William Grimwade. If she refuses to do this, William Grimwade is to be exor, and if she remarries she must pay my children's legacies before she does so into the hands of William Grimwade and Richard Wixe, who must give her security for their payment and pay her interest at 8% until the legacies are paid. Supervisor: my loving brother Jacob Manning of Washbrook. Wit. George Carter, Richard Wyeller. Pr. at Elmsett 14 July 1630.

55. R(W) ROBERT BROOKE of Stanton, clerk. 10 March 1629/30

Commends soul into hands of God.
I give to my son William £60 to be paid by my exors within 6 months of my death. My will and mind is that my son William and son-in-law Robert Jenepie shall receive the first £100 due to be paid out of my debts and mortgages, and use the money to buy a house and land for my son John. After his decease this house and land are to go to his sons John, George and William. The residue of my goods, chattels, mortgages and debts I give to my wife Mary, whom I make ex'trix on condition she proves my will within 6 weeks of my death. If she fails to do this, I bequeath all my goods etc to my sons William and John and make them exors. Wit. Augustine Parker, Francis Hawys, Richard Browne the elder (X). Pr. at Bury 10 August 1630.

56. R(W) MARGARET COKEY of Groton, widow. 16 July 1626

Bequeaths soul to God trusting to have remission of her sins.
I give unto Mr Nickolson, our minister and teacher of God's word, 40s. I give to the poor of our parish 40s. I give to Nicholas Cokey of Milden 40s, to my kinswoman Dorothy Pooley 40s and to my kinsman Thomas Younge 20s. I give to my godchild Timothy of Monks Eleigh 20s, and to Seriant's wife the carpenter 20s. I give to my kinsman Samuel Wainfleet, citizen of London £5. I give 20s each to John Rawlin's wife and to Grove's wife, both of Edwardstone. I give to Rideldale's wife, the tailor of Groton, 10s. All these legacies are to be paid within 2 months of my decease. I give for life to my kinsman John Wainfleet, grocer of Boxford, my messuage in Groton with backhouses, outhouses, yards, orchard and garden with the millhouse and malt mill, and after his death to his son

Thomas. John Wainfleet must pay his daughter Margaret £20 on her marriage day. I give to John Wainfleet the lease of my watermill in Boxford and the leases of all my houses belonging to King's College, Cambridge, and after his death to his son John if the leases have not expired. I give to Margaret, daughter of John Wainfleet, my best bedstead with my best bed and bedding and all other things belonging to it, my virginals and my scarf, my gilt goblet, my silver beaker and all my riding furniture, that is saddle, bridle and saddle cloth. I give to Mary and Susan Wainfleet a dozen silver spoons to be divided between them, and to each a small jug tipped with silver. To my kinswoman Anne Grimstone I give the bedstead, bed and bedding wherein I lie with all things belonging to it. I give to my kinswoman Widow Swanton of Lavenham 40s to be paid within 2 months of my death. I give to Bridget, wife of John White of Edwardstone, my glass with the silver foot. To Anne Wainfleet I give my field bed with bed and bedding. The rest of my goods, my debts and funeral charges being paid and a dinner or supper of 40s bestowed upon my neighbours, I give to John Wainfleet, whom I make exor. Wit. John Coo, Thomas Grimwade, William Church. Pr. at Bury 2 August 1630.

57. R(W) GEORGE HAMMOND of Shipcoate in the parish of Denston, yeoman. 3 May 1630.

Commends soul to Jesus Christ in sure and certain hope of resurrection and eternal life.
I will that all my debts are discharged before any gifts or legacies are paid. I give to my wife Anne all the linen she brought when she first came to me, the bed and bedding standing in the parlour chamber. I give to my eldest son George the bed in the hall chamber with a pair blankets, a covering, a bed, a bolster and 2 pillows. The remainder of my estate is to be divided into 2 equal portions, one to be divided between my wife and my eldest son George and the other for my 4 children, Rebecca, Anne, Ambrose and Lydia when they are 21. They have benefit of survivorship. Ex'trix wife. Supervisor: Charles Owers of Giffordes, who is to have full power to dispose of my children and their portions if my wife remarries. Wit. Henry Whitehead, Charles Owers. Pr. at Bury 2 August 1630.

58. R(W) LAWRENCE HATFEILD alias MAIOR of Elmswell, yeoman. 12 February 1629/30.

Commends soul to God and Jesus Christ and trusts to be saved.
I give my wife Joan for life my parlour at my now dwelling house and the chamber next to the south side of it, with the use of waters belonging to my house and with a place in my yards to set her firewood. I also give her for life the posted bed in the parlour where I do now lie complete, a long framed table, a framed form and 2 buffet stools. I give and bequeath to my son John my 3 acre 3 rod copyhold close of arable and pasture abutting on south side of a common way leading from Elmswell to

Woolpit. John must pay £30 out of this land as follows: £10 each to my son William and to my daughters Anne and Elizabeth. Payments to be made within 6 months of my decease in south porch of Elmswell church. These legatees have benefit of survivorship and power of distraint. I give £10 to my son Robert to be paid within 6 months. I give my son William a 3 rods enclosed piece of copyhold pasture next to a way leading from Cockstreet to Wetherden. All the rest of my messuages and land in Elmswell I give to my son Thomas on condition he pays £20 each to my 3 sons, John, William and Robert and to my 2 daughters Anne and Elizabeth at £10 p.a. All five have power to distrain. I give my wife Joan an annuity of 40s. I bequeath to my son Thomas my framed table in the hall and my cupboard standing there, a chest in the chamber, a brazen cauldron, a pewter dish and a counter table in the parlour. Also to him I give my 3 mares, 2 bullocks, 4 milk cows, all my sheep, my hay, all my carts, plough and harness. The residue of my goods I give to my wife. Exor: son Thomas. Wit. Thomas Kettleborough, Robert Buckle (X), Thomas Walker, who probably wrote will. Pr. at Bury 2 August 1630.

59. R(W) LYDIA BOUGINGE of Tostock, singlewoman. 15 July 1630.

Commits soul into hands of God.
I give and bequeath to Francis Bouginge my brother £20, being part of £80 bequeathed to me by my late brother Thomas Bouginge. If Francis in any way molests my brother-in-law John Granger about any money or goods given by his late brother Thomas, then £20 left to Francis is to be paid instead in equal portions to his children Giles, Frances and Thomas when 21. I give to Elizabeth, wife of John Granger, £60 bequeathed to me by my brother Thomas. I give Elizabeth Bouginge, my sister, all my linen and woollen, and to my mother, Margaret Bouginge, £10. I leave £5 to Elizabeth daughter of John Granger when 21. All the residue of my goods I give to my brother-in-law John Granger, whom I make my exor. Wit. Thomas Carter, Miles Ralphe. Pr. at Bury 2 August 1630.

60. R(W) NICHOLAS BAXTER (X) of Barton, yeoman. 15 July 1630.

Commends soul to God. To be buried in Great Barton churchyard.
I give and bequeath to Richard my eldest son when he is 21 the messuage wherein I now dwell with its croft and orchard, and all my free and copyhold land in Westall field and Cancaster field. I also give to him all my land in Buryfield in Great Barton, and all my land in the parish of Fornham All Saints. When my second son James reaches age of 21, Richard must pay him £50. He must also pay £50 each at age of 21 to my sons Edmund and Isaac and to my daughter Margaret. All 3 have benefit of survivorship and power to distrain. I give to my wife Susan for life the house called Wrongeditche and all my free and copyhold land in Fitchmer field, Long Woodour field, Castle field and Enter Common field. After her death my fourth son Nicholas is to have the house called Wrongditch with an orchard and 2 pightles which I lately purchased of John Francke,

and another 1½ acre pightle called Berrie acre. I also give him 2 acres in Long Woodour field lying between the lands of William Rushbrook on either side and abutting on the red house. I also give him half an acre in Fitchmore field abutting on Peddars path and 2 acres abutting on Bouster way together with a 2 acre piece abutting on Fitchmore close and the vicarage lands to the north west. After my wife's death, I bequeath the residue of my land to my son Richard with a piece of pasture called the Grove when he is 21. Until he is 21 my wife is to enjoy the Grove, the tenement wherein I now dwell and all the land bequeathed to Richard. I give all my moveables to my wife provided that if she remarries she pays my children £10 each when they are 21. She is to bring up my children, pay my debts and pay 15s to the poor of the town of Barton. Ex'trix: wife. Supervisor: my brother Edward Baxter, whom I give 20s. Wit. John Knappe, George Crakenthorpe, Samuel Francke.
Memorandum that on 15 July 1630 Nicholas Baxter surrendered his copyhold land to the use of his will into hands of Mr John Knapp gent and Edmund Tuffeild, both customary tenants. Pr. at Bury 2 August 1630.

61. R(W) THOMAS EGGETT (X) of Soham [Cambs]. 23 May 1630.

Bequeaths soul to God. To be buried in Soham churchyard.
I bequeath to my son John 6d and to my son Thomas 6d. I give my son Robert my bay widgell that came of my bay mare, the chest which stands at my son John's house, 1 pair sheets and 2 pewter platters. I give my daughter Elizabeth £6 when she is 18 and when she is 14 a spreading sheet, a great kettle and [blank in MS] pewter platters. All the rest of my goods I bequeath to Elizabeth my now wife, whom I make ex'trix. Wit. Robert Banyer and me Robert Carlton. Pr. at Bury 28 June 1630.

62. R(W) ELIZABETH HAYWARD of Bury St Edmunds, widow. 22 May 1630.

Commends soul to God and trusts to be saved.
I give all my goods, plate, jewels, ready money, bonds and bills to my son-in-law Thomas Sandwith, whom I make exor. Wit. Katherine More, Dorothy Petchie (X), Isaac Francke. Pr. at Bury 25 July 1630.

63. R(W) WILLIAM STEGGELL (X) of Elmswell, yeoman. 10 August 1630.

Commends soul to God. To be buried in Elmswell churchyard.
I give to George my son the house wherein I now dwell with its adjoining land and a piece of land called Bulbrooke lying in 2 pieces for his life and then to his son Nicholas. I give to my son Simon a piece of pasture in Elmswell called Wrangelhedge. I give to Rose Banham my servant a milk cow, a bed complete and £5 to be paid within a year of my decease at my now dwelling house. I give to my sons George, Henry and Lawrence a

milk cow each. I give £6 to Anne Steggell, daughter of my son George, within 1 year. I give my son Lawrence £5 to be paid within a year out of the land called Wrangelhedge and £10 out of the land called Bulbrooke within 2 years of my decease. He has power to distrain. All my unbequeathed moveables I give to my son George, whom I make sole exor. Wit. Thomas Rose, Edward Raphe (X), Miles Raphe. Pr. at Bury 19 August 1630.

64. R(W) MARY DAYNES (X) of Mildenhall, widow. 24 July 1630.

Commends soul into merciful hands of God and Jesus Christ.

I give to my son Richard Ward my cottage in Mildenhall market place left to me my by late husband Robert Daynes, as well as my acre of copyhold arable land in Beckfeild. I give and bequeath to John Shelly my nephew [sic], son of my deceased daughter Marion, £5 when he is 21. I give my grand-daughter Marion Shelly £8 when she is 21. If John or Marion Shelly make any claim on the copyhold cottage where I now dwell, which belonged to Thomas Ward, my first husband and their natural father deceased [sic] they will lose their legacies. I give my kinswoman Mary Daynes 40s when she is 21, and a pewter platter and a little brass posnet immediately after my decease. I give 10s each when they are 21 to Alice and Mary, children of late James Turner. I give to my grand-daughter Marion Shelly my best gown, which is to be sold immediately after my death and the money put out by my exor to best profit for the benefit of Marion until she is 21. I also give her at once the little chest standing by my bedhead in the chamber. The residue of my goods I give to my son Richard Ward, whom I make exor. Wit. John Hargrave, Robert Watson, Edmund Hornigold (X), William Dallison.

Memorandum that I have surrendered my copyhold land to the use of my will into the hands of Edmund Hornigold and Robert Watson, customary tenants of the manor. Pr. at Bury 23 August 1630.

65. R(W) THOMAS STEWARD of Brockley, yeoman. 27 July 1630.

Commends soul to God.

I give and bequeath to my son Thomas all my houses and land in Brockley, Hartest and Lawshall. I also give him a featherbed furnished as it stands, half my brass and pewter, the long table and bench as they are in the hall and the cupboard in the hall. I give £150 to my daughter Lydia when she is 21. I give to my brother John Copping 20s. All the rest of my goods I give to my wife Lydia, whom I make ex'trix, desiring her to be a good guardian to my children. Wit. None. Pr. at Bury 23 August 1630.

66. R(W) FRANCES WICKES (X) of Fornham St Genevieve, widow.
10 August 1630.

Bequeaths soul to God.
I give £10 to be equally divided between the children of my brother John
Pryor, and similarly £10 for children of my sister Anne Boxe, £10 for
children of my late sister Elizabeth Ballye and £10 for children of my
brother William Prior. I bequeath £10 to my sister's son Thomas Frost as
soon as he shall come out of his apprenticeship. I give £5 to Mary,
daughter of Mr John Everard clerk, to be put out to her use. I give to my
sister Rose Frost for her life all my household stuff, and after her decease
I will it shall be equally parted among her children: Elizabeth, Anne,
John and Thomas. All the rest of my goods I give to my brother-in-law
John Frost clerk, whom I make exor. Wit. Thomas Sippes (X), John
Wells (X). Pr. at Bury 30 August 1630.

67. R(W) KATHERINE GOSLEN of Tostock, widow. 30 January
1621/22.

Commends soul to God and trusts to have remission of sins.
I give to my son James Goslyn a posted bedstead standing in the chamber
complete with all the bedding belonging to it, a long table in the hall, my
great keeler and my biggest kettle but one. I give to Elizabeth my
daughter 40s within 1 year of my death. I give my grandsons John and
Thomas Clarke 5s apiece to be paid within 1 year. I give and bequeath to
my daughter Anne, wife of George Creame, my great cupboard in my
bed chamber, my great coffer, all the bedding now lying on my livery bed
and 2 pewter dishes. I give my son William Goslinge my little cupboard
standing in the hall, my malt querns, 2 pewter dishes and a boarded
bedstead with the bed and all things belonging. I bequeath to my son
George 40s to be paid within a year and a dripping pan, a tub, a bowl, a
keeler, 2 pewter dishes, a little tub and a little coffer standing in the
chamber. I give Rose Greene my grandchild 20s when she is 21 or on her
marriage day. I give my daughter Anne my best gown and my best
petticoat, and to my daughter Elizabeth my watchet petticoat and my
grey waistcoat. I give my son James's wife my green petticoat and my
russet waistcoat. I give 6s 8d to my grandson Robert Goslen. To my sister
Isabel Lovenis I give my petticoat with the black fringe and green
binding, and to my son George's wife my mirrell gown. I give my
grandchild Priscilla Goslyn 10s when she is 21 or married, and to
grandchild Elizabeth Goslyn 10s when 21 or married and a great chair. I
give my grandson Robert Goslen a mortar and a pewter dish. To my son
William's wife I give a petticoat of a deroy colour. All my unbequeathed
linen is to be equally divided by my exor between my sons and daughters.
I give my daughter Anne 20s to be paid within 1 year. The residue of my
moveable goods I leave to my son Thomas, who is to bring my body to
the ground in decent and timely manner and is to be my exor. Wit.
Bennett Clarke (X), Robert Fiske, Katherine Goslin (X). Pr. at Bury 31
August 1630.

27

68. R(W) JOHN JOLLY (X) of Langham, yeoman. 12 August 1630.

Commits soul to God in full assurance of joyful resurrection.
I give and bequeath to my beloved wife Anne for life the messuage in Langham wherein I dwell with its yards, garden, orchard and land. I also give her all my free and copyhold land in Langham and Hunston for life, except the land let to Ezechias Rose and Millers tenement in Langham which lies between the land sometime Christopher Cope's to east and George Sparrowe's tenement to west with one end abutting on the king's highway leading from Badwell Ash to Ixworth. After my wife's death, the property left to her is to go to my sister Joan Jolly for ever. I give to Thomas Markes, labourer of Langham, my tenement called Millers. Several persons have mortgaged land to me; if any of them make default of payment I give the land so forfeited to my wife Anne for ever. All the rest of my land and tenements I give to my sister Joan for ever. I will that my exors, by the advice of the minister of the town of Langham and 6 other substantial men of the parish, lay out £100 in purchasing land in the name of the 6 men to hold it in trust for ever. The revenues and profits are to be used for the benefit of the poor of Langham and distributed yearly by the minister and churchwardens at Christmas and Midsummer. I give to my sister Joan Jolly £100 to be paid within a year of my decease. My bequests to my wife are in full satisfaction of her claims for dower. I give and bequeath to my kinsman George Chamberlyn and to each of his children £5 to be paid within a year. I give £5 to John Frost of Langham clerk, and £5 to Richard Chamberlyn of Hunston clerk, both to be paid within a year. I give 20s to the poor of each of the following parishes: Badwell, Walsham, Stanton, Ixworth and Hunston to be distributed at the discretion of their ministers and churchwardens. All the residue of my goods, debts owing to me and ready money I give to my wife Anne towards the performance of my will, my funeral expenses and her maintenance and livelihood, and I make her sole ex'trix. I give £5 to William Doe of Ixworth to be paid within a year and £5 to each of his children at age of 21. Wit. Humphrey Howlett, John Lurkyn. Pr. at Bury 4 September 1630.

69. R(W) MARGARET MULLYNER (X) of Stowupland, widow. 20 August 1630.

Bequeaths soul to God.
I give to Thomas Cuttinge my son 40s, and 20s each to his sons Thomas, Richard, John and James, all to be paid within 1 month. I give to Mary, daughter of Martha Cuttinge, £10 to be paid within 10 years, a dornix covering and my best kettle. I give to my son Francis Mullyner £20 to be paid at once, and all my rights in the tenement where I now dwell. All the rest of my goods and chattels I give to my son Francis Mullyner and my daughter Martha Cuttinge, whom I name my exors. Wit. John Sowgate, Thomas Cuttinge, Thomas Keable. Pr. at Bury 6 September 1630.

70. R(W) THOMAS AGNIS alias SMITH of Ketton hamlet [a hamlet of Kedington adjoining Sturmer] in Essex, yeoman. 6 August 1630.

Commends soul to God and trusts to be raised up to life everlasting at the general resurrection of all mankind.
I make my loving mother Joan Waltham alias Tanner my ex'trix. I give my mother all my messuages and land in Ketton and Sturmer in Essex until such time as their rents have paid my debts and funeral charges. After this is done, I give my sister Dorothy a 5 acre arable close called Hartscroft and 2 pieces arable in Sturmer field containing 5 rods. I bequeath my brothers Henry and John my messuage in which [blank in MS] Bickner now inhabits with 8 acres adjoining meadow or pasture and the yard and orchard. I also give them 2 closes called the Drugges containing 4 acres. I give my sister Elizabeth the 1½ acre Hopground meadow and 2 acres arable lying in 2 pieces in the common field called Wolves down, and another 2 acres in 2 pieces in Windmill field. I give my sister-in-law Anne Prewer 20s to be paid within 2 years, and to my god-daughter Anne Prewer the younger a silver spoon. I give my brother Robert Smith the reversion and all my rights in the messuage where my mother now dwells and all the land belonging to it. I give 20s to the poor of Ketton to be distributed with the assistance of the churchwardens, and 5s to the ringers to be paid by my ex'trix on the day of my burial. All my other goods I give to my ex'trix to pay my debts and legacies. Wit. Thomas Edwards senior, William Edwards and Thomas Donnell, who wrote this will. Pr. at Bury 14 September 1630.

71. R(W) ROBERT MALT (N) of Downham. 27 August 1630.

He gave £3 to his son Robert Malt to be paid to him at age of 7 by his wife Anne. He also gave him a cupboard and a brass pot to be delivered to him immediately after his mother's decease. The rest of his goods he gave to Anne his wife. Wit. John Malt, Anne Malt. Let. ad. granted to widow 9 September 1630. No place given.

72. R(W) JOHN FORD alias WORD of Nowton, yeoman. 1 June 1630.

Bequeaths soul to God.
I give to Barbara my wife for life all my free and copyhold land and tenements in Nowton. She must keep the buildings in repair. After her death I give the tenement wherein I now dwell with all its land to my son Thomas, except for some pieces of arable and pasture land otherwise bequeathed. Thomas must pay 50s a year to my daughter Barbara in 2 equal portions in Nowton parish church. She has power to distrain. Thomas must also pay my son John £10 within 3 years of my wife's decease. I bequeath to John 6 acres copyhold land in Millfield in Nowton and abutting on Pine Lane. I give to my son William my other copyhold tenement in Nowton and 16½ acres of land and pasture formerly belonging to the same tenement. William must pay my daughter Barbara

30s a year as above, and £5 to my son Anthony within 4 years of my wife's decease. I give and bequeath to my daughter Rose a 7 acre freehold close called Hencott close and a 2½ acre piece free land called Coes land and lying in Hencocke field. I give to my daughter Lucretia £80 to be paid over 3 years by my wife. I give to my wife 2 pieces of arable land containing 3 and a half acres lying in Backfield and abutting on Great Croft close. All my moveable goods I give to my wife, whom I make ex'trix. Wit. Thomas Hammond, Robert Fuller. Pr. at Bury 14 September 1630.

73. R(W) WILLIAM BURTON the elder of Hanchett End in the parish of Haverhill, yeoman. 3 February 1629/30.

Bequeaths soul to 3 persons of Trinity and hopes to receive everlasting life.
I give to my son William a piece of arable land called Hopley Well in Sandesfield. I give and bequeath to my youngest daughter Anne the tenement with yard and garden in Haverhill now in the occupation of [blank in MS] Daye, widow. I give to my sons Francis and Samuel the tenement and garden in Haverhill now occupied by John Wade, and also the running house, barn, stable and straw house now in the occupation of Richard Evans, butcher. I give to my son Thomas 40s. All the rest of my goods, unbequeathed land and tenements, and debts due to me I leave to be equally divided among my 3 sons: William, Francis and Samuel, and my five daughters: Susan, Margaret, Martha, Mary and Anna. Exor son William. Wit. John Hurst, Giles Bridge. Pr. at Bury 14 September 1630.

74. R(W) THOMAS BOUGING of Tostock, clothier. 11 July 1630.

Bequeaths soul to God.
I give to my brother Francis 40s to be paid 6 weeks after my decease, and to his daughter Frances and son Giles £5 to be put out to the best advantage until they are 22. I give to Thomas son of Francis Bouging £20 to be put out to his use until he is 22. His mother is to receive the income on condition he is sent to school until he can write and read, and is then bound apprentice to some trade by which he may earn his living. I give to my brother-in-law, John Granger, £10 on condition that he pays £5 8s 0d to Thomas Kittleburrough of Elmswell in performance of an obligation. I give to Elizabeth, wife of John Granger, all my household stuff, and to their children 10s apiece when 21. I give to my sister Lidia Bouging £80 to be paid within 9 months of my decease. I give 10s to him that preaches at my burial and buries me. I give to Thomas Carter, clothier of Ipswich, 40s. My will is that if any of my goods are lost by sea or land, my exors shall proportionately receive less of my goods. Exors John Granger, Thomas Carter. Wit. Anne Syer (X), Miles Raphe. Pr. at Bury 13 September 1630. Thomas Carter refused to act as exor.

75. R(W) JOHN DAYE (X) of Badwell Ash, husbandman. 24 February 1624/25.

Bequeaths soul to Jesus Christ and through faith is sure of salvation.
I give my son John £3, my son Roger 30s, my son William £3, my son George £3, my daughter Anne Kettle £3 and my daughter Lucy £3; all to be paid within 6 months of my decease. I give to my daughter Lucy a bond of £4 in the hands of Edward Harrison, clothier of Badwell Ash. I give to my daughters Priscilla Kettle, Margaret, Mary and Joan £3 each to be paid within 6 months of my death. I give to my daughter Elizabeth £5 lent to Thomas Syer yeoman of Langham. I give all my tools of husbandry, saws and the rest (except one hatchet and one hook) to be equally divided amongst my sons. I make my wife Mary my ex'trix and bequeath to her all the rest of my bonds, bills and sums of money lent out on condition she pays my children's legacies, and proves my will. The legacies are to be paid in my dwelling house in Badwell Ash. I have £35 in the hands of Thomas Syer the elder of Badwell Ash, £5 of which I have bequeathed to my daughter Elizabeth. The remaining £30 I give to my wife for life, and then to be equally divided among my surviving children. If my wife refuses to act as ex'trix, she loses all her bequests except £30 and my household goods, and I make Robert Daye, yeoman of Badwell Ash, my exor. Whereas I have given a bond of £4 to my daughter Lucy, my will is that this gift shall be void and I now give this sum to be divided between my sons John, William and George, whose legacies of £3 each are reduced to 40s each. Wit. Thomas Syer senior, Thomas Syer junior. Pr. at Bury 20 September 1630.

76. R(W) DOROTHY PRICKE (X) of Barrow, widow. 8 August 1630.

Commends soul to God and hopes assuredly to be saved.
I give to Susan, wife of John Clowe of Bury, a coverlet, my best gown, a brass pot, a pair sheets and a lockeram sheet. I bequeath the rest of my goods to be equally divided between my children, and I wish my daughter Susan Clowe to have an equal share. My children are to share costs of my funeral and the probate of my will. Exors sons Robert and Charles. Wit. Francis Heigham. Pr. at Bury 20 September 1630.

77. R(W) WILLIAM ELEY (X) of Lawshall, yeoman. 18 September 1628.

Commits soul to God and hopes to be saved by merits of Jesus Christ.
My son Robert is to have the profits and benefit of my messuage and lands until the Michaelmas after my decease. I give to my son-in-law, Giles Appleton a 1 acre close of pasture called Nether Copseys and lying between the messuage where I now dwell and his own tenement. But if my son John pays Giles Appleton £10 in the porch of Lawshall church within 2 years of my decease, then this close shall be his. I give to my daughter Alice Appleton my best kettle but two, my bedstead with a

tester of stained cloth, with a flockbed, a flock transon, a pillow, a pair of sheets, a pair of blankets and a covering as it stands in the chamber where I usually lie, and my 3-year old bullock. I give my sons-in-law, Francis Reighnoldes and Thomas Gills, 10s apiece. The residue of my moveable goods, cattle and corn I will to be equally divided between my son Robert and my son-in-law Richard Browne. Exor son Robert. Wit. Joseph Hammond, John Smith, who probably wrote this will. Pr. at Bury 30 September 1630.

78. R(W) PETER BACON (X) of Soham [Cambs], husbandman. 23 April 1629.

Bequeaths soul to God steadfastly hoping to be saved.
I give to my son John, shoemaker of Soham, my freehold messuage in Isleham wherein I lately dwelt and now occupied by Robert Hills and Richard Hyndes, my sons-in-law, with its land held of the manor of Beckhold at a yearly rent of threepence. John must pay the following legacies: £20 at £5 p.a. to my son George of Bury St Edmunds; £10 to my daughter Ellen, wife of Robert Hills of Isleham, 3 years after my decease; £10 to my daughter Jane, wife of Richard Hyndes, in 2 portions 2 and 4 years after my death. These legacies are to be paid in the north porch of Soham church. I give Elizabeth Bacon, daughter of my deceased son Thomas, £5 when she is 21. If my son John refuses to prove my will, I give the gifts made to him to my son George and make him exor. Exor: son John. Supervisors: my friends Christopher Ogrem and Thomas Brett, both of Soham. Wit. Christopher Ogrem, George Disborough (X) and me William Howe. Pr. at Bury 22 September 1630.

79. R(W) THOMAS PLUMMER of Dalham, yeoman. 11 August 1630.

Bequeaths soul to God and hopes to be saved by merits of Jesus Christ. To be buried in Dalham churchyard.
I give my house and all its lands to my wife Joan during her life, and after her decease they are to be sold and the money to be equally divided between my son Thomas and my daughters Elizabeth, Margaret and Susan. I give 20s each to Edward and Thomas, sons of my brother Robert Plummer, to be paid within 1 year. I make Joan my wife my ex'trix and give her the rest of my goods. Wit. Bartholomew Stutvile, Thomas Spencer (X), John Barrett (X). Pr. at Bury 30 September 1630.

80. R(W) EDMUND TUFFEILD (X) of Barton, tailor. 19 September 1630.

Bequeaths soul to God.
I will and bequeath to Edmund my son my now dwelling house with the home sitting and the ground about it amounting to 18 acres. I give my daughter Margaret a copyhold close lying by Shirmans bridge and 2 acres in Shrubfeild. I give my daughter Susan a freehold tenement in

Naughton. I give my daughters Margaret and Susan £40 each to be paid to them when 21. I give Mary Wickes my servant £3 to be paid within a month of my departure. I give to the poor of Barton 20s. I appoint Thomas Bryan, miller of Thurston, to be guardian to my children and to see them brought up, and I make him exor. I give to George Crakenkthorpe, clerk, 20s and I make him and Martin Cocksadge supervisors of my will. All my other goods shall be equally divided among my children. Wit. Thomas Salisbury senior, Thomas Salisbury junior. Pr. at Bury 27 September 1630.

81. R(W) JOHN COPSEY of Bury St Edmunds. 24 July 1630.

Bequeaths soul to God and trusts to have salvation.
I will that Agnes my wife shall pay £104, due on 10 December 1632, to Nicholas Baker tailor of Bury. This is a mortgage on my messuages, sometime 2 tenements with malthouses, millhouses, barns, stables, orchards and gardens in Whiting Street. I give and bequeath this property to my wife to sell for the best price within 1 year of my decease to enable her to pay £30 each to my sons James and Thomas when 24, and £30 each to my daughters Martha and Sarah when 22. I give to my wife for ever all my messuages and lands in Worlington. I give to my eldest son John my orchard, barn, stable and grounds in the backside in St Andrews Street [i.e. outside wall]. John must pay £10 each to my 4 children named above within 1 year of my wife's decease. Until my wife's death, she is to have the property left to John. All the residue of my goods, cattle, horses, carts, plate, debts, ready money, corn and wood I give to my wife Agnes, whom I make ex'trix. Wit. John Jewell, Henry Coe, Richard Wilkinson (X). Pr. at Bury 1 October 1630.

82. R(W) ROBERT RYMILL (X) of Glemsford, shoemaker. 3 August 1630.

Bequeaths soul to God.
I give to Alice my wife for life the messuage wherein I now dwell, and after her death to my daughter-in-law Thomazine Ellis for life. The messuage is to be let by the minister and churchwardens of Glemsford and the rent used to maintain her. If the rent is insufficient to support her, then the minister and churchwardens are to sell the messuage and put out the money to maintain her. If she dies before her mother, who is my wife, and my wife falls into sickness or need, then the messuage is to be sold as above for her benefit. If this is done and my wife can spare any money, I entreat her to give it to my brother Edward Rymill or his children if he has died. All the rest of my goods I give to Alice my wife towards the payment of my debts, proving my will and my burial charges and I make her ex'trix. Wit. Ambrose Bigges, Thomas Gardner, Richard Gardner. Pr. at Sudbury 2 October 1630.

83. R(W) WILLIAM ROWNINGE (X) of Badlingham in the parish of Chippenham [Cambs], yeoman. 3 May 1629.

Bequeaths soul to God and hopes to be saved. To be buried in Chippenham churchyard.
I give my son William my house and all my free and copyhold land in Badlingham. I give my son James £40 to be paid within 3 years. I give my daughter Phyllis £40 to be paid within 4 years of my decease. I give my son John £40 to be paid within 5 years, and my daughter Hodgkin £10 to be paid within 1 year. I give my daughter Phyllis a coffer. I will that my son William gives my wife her diet during her life, and that she shall have the chamber with a bed; he is to pay her 30s a quarter. I give to the poor of Chippenham 20s, the interest of which is to be distributed yearly by the churchwardens. I give Francis Porter 20s when he is 21, and Katherine Hearne 20s when she is 24. All the rest of my goods I give to my son William and my wife Phyllis, whom I make exors. Wit. Thomas Tolwardes, Nicholas Allen. Pr. at Bury 4 October 1630.

84. R(W) ISAAC MILLS of Cockfield, yeoman. 10 June 1630.

Commends soul to God and rests assured to be saved.
I have already surrendered the principal part of my estate to my wife Frances for her jointure and I do now, for the tender love and affection I bear her and for the care which I hope she will have in bringing up my children in the fear of God, bequeath to her for life all the residue of my land in Cockfield. After her death I give all my messuages and lands to my son Isaac. If my wife dies before my 2 younger children, Elizabeth and Simon, are 21, then half the profits of my land is to be employed in their education and upbringing until they reach 21. My father-in-law Simon Pitts and my brother Thomas Mills to be their guardians. I give £25 to my daughter Elizabeth when 18 and £25 to my son Simon when 21. Benefit of survivorship. I had intended to bestow larger legacies on my children, but I found my estate much abated and like to be more so by the tedious and grievous affliction it has pleased God to lay on me. Because of this and of the extraordinary care and pains my wife takes continually night and day for me, I intend to leave the more to her in recompense. If she marries again I entreat my father-in-law and brother to see my legacies are paid to Elizabeth and Simon. I give my son Isaac £5, the gift of his grandfather French, to be given to him when he has most need of it before he is 18 towards his bringing up to learning, which course of life I most desire for him. If my wife lives until Isaac is 21, I give him 20 marks. I give 20s to be distributed to the poor of Cockfield at my burial. I give the residue of my goods to my wife, whom I make ex'trix. Supervisor Simon Pitts. Wit. Simon Pitts, Thomas Mills, Thomas Browne, Isaac Miller. Pr. at Bury 4 October 1630.

85. R(W) JOHN DOBBS of Aspal, gentleman. 5 September 1608.

Commends soul to God and hopes to be partaker of the glorious resurrection.

I will that my exor pay my just debts. I give 20s to the poor of Aspal and 40s to the poor of Debenham to be paid immediately after my decease. I will that my well-beloved wife Margaret makes no claim on any land not bequeathed to her and that within a month of my death she surrenders to my son John all her rights to my lands and tenements. In consideration of this John is to pay her an annuity of £24 to be paid in my house at Lady Day and Michaelmas. I give to my son John several parcels of land amounting to 48 acres in Richmans field, Stonyland and Daniells lying in Aspal and Debenham. If he fails to pay my wife's annuity, I give to her for life the above land with remainder to John and his heirs. I give to my son Robert £20 and to my daughters Frances and Margaret £15 each to be paid my by brother-in-law John Grove, who owes me this sum. I give the messuage wherein I now dwell with all my unbequeathed land to my son John. I bequeath to him all my brewing vessels, my lead cistern, all my household [sic] in the parlour as it is ready furnished, a silver-gilt bowl, a silver salt, a dozen of the best silver spoons, a silver tunn, a silver bowl, 12 pairs of the best sheets and 4 pillows with beeres to them. I give to my son John £180, and to my daughter Anne £140 to be paid by my exors. I also give to Anne a dozen of silver spoons usually called maidenhead spoons, a silver tunn, a silver bowl, a great copper, 2 great kettles, 6 platters, 6 pewter dishes, 10 pairs of sheets, 2 feather beds with 2 feather bolsters, a bedstead in the parlour chamber, 1 pair blankets, a coverlet of tapestry work, a pot tipped with silver, and 4 pillows with beeres to them. I give to my daughter Thamar £140 to be paid by my exors when she is 21 or on her marriage day, until which time this sum is to remain in hands of my brother-in-law, John Fayerwether, towards Thamar's education and upbringing. I also give her a dozen silver spoons, a silver tunn, a silver bowl, a pot tipped with silver, a copper vessel, 2 other great kettles, 6 platters, 6 pewter dishes, 10 pairs sheets, 2 featherbeds with 2 feather bolsters, a bedstead in the buttery chamber, a pair blankets, a bird coverlet and 4 pillows with beeres to them. The rest of my moveable goods, corn and cattle are to be appraised by 3 or 4 honest men and sold by my exors, and the money equally distributed between my son and 2 daughters. Benefit of survivorship. I give my sister Emma Palmer £5, my sister Fayerwether £3 and my cousin Katharine, wife of William Blomefeild of Henley, 40s. I make my son John exor, and appoint Mr Serjeant Barker supervisor of my will and give him £10 for his pains. Wit. William Blomefeild, John Fairewether. My will further is that when a bond, dated 13 June 1607, for 200 marks for payment of £100 to my son Robert and daughters Frances and Margaret by John Gravett, citizen and goldsmith of London, falls due for payment, my son John should use his best endeavours to see that it is paid. Wit. same as above.

Memorandum that on 10 September 1608 John Dobbs surrendered his customary tenement called Fookes to use of his will by the hands of George Tovell senior and George Phillipps, both customary tenants. Pr. at Bury 5 October 1630.

86. R(W) STEPHEN DOE (X) of Hopton, yeoman. 30 August 1630.

Bequeaths soul to God and to Jesus Christ who will save me. To be buried in Hopton churchyard.
I give to my son Stephen the messuage I live in with all its outbuildings and land. I give my daughter Amy, wife of Edmund Acton, £20 half to be paid 2 years and half 4 years after my decease. If my son Stephen mortgages property left to him, he must pay £5 each when 21 to Anne and Mary, the children of Amy and Edmund Acton. The rest of my goods and chattels I give to Stephen who is to pay my debts and bring my body decently to the ground. He is exor. Wit. John Maryell, Thomas Windout. Pr. at Bury 5 October 1630.

87. R(W) JOHN ADSON of Glemsford, yeoman. 23 July 1630.

Bequeaths soul to God.
I give and bequeath to Alice my wife for life my messuage in Ixworth now occupied by Thomas Hye. After her death, I give it to Barbara Copsey, youngest daughter of John Copsey, my father-in-law. I give my wife an acre of land in Ixworth, sometime Felix Marshall's, and after her death to Barbara Copsey. The rest of my goods I give to my wife towards the payment of my debts and other charges, and I make her my ex'trix. Wit. John Lorkin, Thomas Grigges, Richard Gardner. Pr. at Bury 6 October 1630.

88. R(W) FRANCES BROWNINGE alias STEADMAN (N) of Thurston, wife of Thomas Browning yeoman. 4 August 1630.

Being sick in body and with a mind to settle the estate she had among her children and others, she sent for Mr William Onsloe to take a surrender of the lands she held of the manor of Norton Hall. She and her husband surrendered her land to the use of her husband on condition he paid £50 each to her daughters Sarah and Mary, in satisfaction of £30 each given to them by their father William Stedman in his will, of which she Frances was ex'trix. She also willed that her husband should take on the execution of William Stedman's will, and gave him all her interest in it towards the bringing up of her children and the education and upbringing of certain grandchildren of William Stedman as set out in his will. She gave Edmund Calye £20 in full satisfaction of a promise made to him in her widowhood. She gave an annuity of 10s to Mary Stedman widow towards her house rent. Wit. William Daniell esquire, Robert Jaques gent. Let. ad. granted at Bury 7 October 1630 in Richard Pead's house to Thomas Browninge.

89. R(W) WILLIAM STEDMAN of Tostock, yeoman. 26 January 1626/27.

Commends soul to God and trusts to be saved and to enjoy eternal life.
I give to my wife Frances for life my tenement in Tostock where I now dwell with its 8 acres of land, but excepting a 3 rods piece with a barn standing on it; and after her decease to my son William. If he dies without heirs before he is 21, this property is to go to William son of my late son Giles Stedman. I give to my son William all the household stuff found in my tenement when I die; to be given to him by my ex'trix when he is 22. I give my grandson Giles Stedman my unbequeathed free and copyhold land and tenements in Tostock when he is 24 and in Beyton when he is 28. Remainder to son William. I give £20 to my son Edmund and £30 to my daughter Margaret; both sums to be paid a year after my decease in the south porch of Tostock church if demanded. I give £30 each to Elizabeth and Anne, daughters of my son Giles, to be paid when they are 21 or on marriage day. Remainder to my daughters Sarah and Mary when 21 or married. I give Sarah and Mary £30 each when 21 or married with benefit of survivorship. I give £40 to John, son of my late son John Stedman, within a year of my decease if he demands it. I give £5 to my daughter Anne Hedge and 40s to my son-in-law Robert Brett to be paid within a year. I give 10s to the poor of Tostock to be distributed on my burial day. I give to my grandson William, when he is 24, all the household stuff that was in the house his father dwelt in at the time of his decease. Until then my ex'trix is to pay him £4 p.a. from such time as he shall depart from my wife Frances and take himself to some good and honest calling for his better education with the advice and consent of my supervisor. Until my grandson William reaches the age when he inherits my property in Tostock and Beyton, my wife is to hold it, keeping the buildings in good repair with claying and thatching, to the end that she may pay my debts and legacies and bring up my son Giles's 3 children and my own 3 in good education. The unbequeathed residue of my goods I give my wife Frances, whom I make ex'trix. I appoint my loving kinsman, Mr William Fiske of Hardinges, to be supervisor of my will. Wit. John Snellinge, John Bulbrooke, who wrote will and Mary Ballye. This will was originally proved at Norwich on 1 July 1629, but because of the change of exor from the testator's widow to her second husband let. ad. were granted to him at Bury on 7 October 1630.

90. R(W) ELIZABETH GOODINGE of Finningham, widow.
20 January 1629/30.

Commends soul to God and hopes to have remission of sins. To be buried in Mellis churchyard.
I give to my son Edmund my great chest now at my son-in-law Robert Rushe's house, 6 table napkins, the featherbed which I now lie in with the bolster belonging to it, a pair blankets, 2 pillows, a pair sheets, a coverlet which I lately bought and my great kettle. I give to my grandchild

Elizabeth, daughter of my son Edmund, a truckle bedstead with the feather bed belonging to it, a coverlet, a blanket, a pair sheets, a pillow and an old brass kettle. I give to my daughter Margery Rushe a trunk chest at her house, a posted bedstead with curtains and rods belonging to it, and a wicker chair. I give to Elizabeth Kersey, my daughter, my casting sheet, my bearing sheet, 3 pillowbeeres belonging to these sheets, a pair sheets and 6 napkins. To each of my grand-daughters Rachel and Judith Portte I give 3 pairs sheets, 4 pillowbeeres and a dozen table napkins. Also a long board cloth, 2 white aprons, 2 yard kerchers and 2 long towels equally to be divided between them. My son Edmund is to pay 20s each to my grandchildren John, Thomas and Robert Dowsen and Robert, Jasper and Edward Rush. These legacies are to be paid out of the bond of £20 he owes me, and I give the remainder of the bond to him. I give Avis Turner, my grandchild, my two-eared brazen pan. All my unbequeathed brass, pewter and linen are to be equally divided by my exor between my son Edmund and my daughters Margery Rush and Elizabeth Kersey. Exor my well-beloved son Jasper Gooding. Wit. Robert Rush (X), Thomas Preston, William Freman. Pr. at Bury 14 October 1630.

91. R(W) WILLIAM RUSHBROOKE of Thurston, yeoman.
24 September 1630.

Bequeaths soul to God and believes his sins forgiven through Jesus Christ. Body to be buried in Thurston churchyard believing that at the last day body and soul shall knit together and live with the blessed Trinity and Saints for evermore.
I bequeath 10s to the repair of Thurston church and 10s to the poor of the parish. I give to my son John my houses and tenements called Goodwyns in Blamorestreet with the home closes belonging, and my close called Denbies on condition he pays my daughter Mary £35 one year after my decease. If he defaults Denbies goes to Mary. I give to my son William my houses and lands at Stowe Green, which I bought from John Herd. I give to my sons Zachary and George my tenements and houses with yards and cellars in Mustow Street in Bury St Edmunds, standing near the well with two pumps. Henry Parker lives there, and my sister Smith in one little room, which I will she shall dwell in during her natural life. My son John is to have the benefit of this property until Zachary and George are 21, and he is to pay them 30s each p.a. I give my son John my freehold close called Kinges in Netherhall field on condition he pays £16 each to Zachary and George when they are 22. If John defaults they are to have this close for ever. I give my son William a freehold pightle next to the Wheatefield, half an acre at the church, 1½ rods I purchased from William Cobbold and all my copyhold land in Wheatefield on condition he pays my daughter Elizabeth £30 within a year of my decease; otherwise I give all this land to Elizabeth for ever. I bequeath my son William my piece of freehold land lying next to Bennett Hynard's house on condition he pays my daughter Sarah £10; if he defaults she has this

land. I give my son John all the rest of my land in the fields with a close by the church called the Sallow Row and an arable pightle between Goodwins way on the north and George Blackborne's close on the south. He must pay my daughter Sarah £20 within 3 years of my decease. If she defaults she is to have Sallow Row close and the piece at the Steeple's end for ever. To my son John I give Chelsale pightle, which I lately bought of my brother George, on condition he pays £5 each to my daughters Anne and Sarah within a year; if he defaults they have this property. I give to my son John my biggest bible and my musket. I will that he pays my daughter Elizabeth £5 within 2 years. I give my son William my least bible. I give John a horse, a cow and a bullock, the table and form in the hall, a pair of posted bedsteads in the parlour and a wetting fatt to wet barley in. I give to my son William all the lands left to him with all the profits immediately after my decease. I give to Anne my best-beloved wife all the rest of my moveable goods. I will that my sons Zachary and George shall pay my sister Smith's 3 children 6s 8d each 12 years after my death. I make my son John sole exor, and if he refuses to prove my will I make my son William exor and give him all the bequests made to John on the same conditions. Supervisors: my brothers Howe and George. Wit. James Margery, Robert Silvester, George Rushbrooke, Thomas Clarcke. Pr. at Bury 14 October 1630.

92. R(W) ANNE GROOME (X) of Brandon Ferry, widow. 20 September 1630.

Bequeaths soul to God. To be buried in Brandon churchyard.
I give and bequeath to my son Robert Groome that part of the house which my husband bought of Thomas Coward and which stands next to the common lane leading from Ferry street to Cowlsham. I give to my youngest son William the bedstead and beds as they stand furnished in the parlour where my son Francis and his wife now dwell, on condition that he allows my son Robert peaceably to take away all the corn, moveables and implements in the chambers over the parlour. I give my son Francis a milk cow at once and 40s within a year. I give my son Simon a milk cow within 2 years of my decease and 5s to his son Robert within a year. I give 40s within 2 years to my daughter Katharine, wife of George Crosse, and 10s each within 8 years to the 4 children she had by John Willett. I bequeath to the poor widows and aged people within the town of Brandon 13s 4d. The rest of my goods I give to my son Robert to discharge my debts and pay my legacies, and I make him sole exor. Wit. Thomas Jenninges, Thomas Rawling (X). Pr. at Bury 22 October 1630.

93. R(W) JOHN WETHERS of Stanton. 1 August 1630.

Bequeaths soul to God and trusts to be saved.
I will my wife Anne sells the tenement occupied by Mihill Knocke within 6 months of my decease and uses the money to pay my debts: £10 to Robert Carter of Honington, and the remainder to my other creditors. I

give to my wife the rest of my tenements and land in Stanton for life on condition she brings up my children until they are 21, keeps the houses and fences in repair and makes no strip or waste of land. I give my son Robert within a year of my wife's decease my tenements with adjoining crofts amounting to 5 acres on condition he pays my daughters Mary and Bridget £10 over 4 years, and £5 to my son James in 2 parts 5 and 6 years after my wife's death. If he defaults, this property is to go to James on the same conditions. I give to my wife's son Wether alias called John a 6 acre close in Stanton called Avina a year after my wife's decease, on condition he pays my daughter Elizabeth £10 over 2 years. I also will that he pays my daughter Frances £10 3 and 4 years after and my son Edmund £5 5 and 6 years after he enters his land. If Wether alias John defaults, my son James is to have Avina close and pay the above legacies. All cash legatees have benefit of survivorship. I give to my sons Edmund and James a 7 acre close in Stanton called Slytes. I bequeath to my wife Anne all my moveable goods and cattle on condition she pays £5 to Ann, daughter of Nicholas Bray, when she is 21. I make my wife sole ex'trix. Wit. John Dawson, Nicholas Warren (X), William Clarcke. Pr. at Ixworth 30 September 1630.

94. R(W) SAMUEL BARKER of Old Newton, yeoman. 3 June 1630.

Commends soul to God and hopes to receive pardon of sins.
I give to my wife Anne for life a close in Newton called Purles with reversion to my son Joseph. I also give her a close in Newton called ten acres and held copyhold of the manor of Dagworth Hall until Joseph is 21, and then to him. I give my messuage in Wimbish, Essex with its land in Wimbish and Thaxted to be equally divided between my daughters Susan and Margaret on condition they pay £25 to my daughter Sarah 2 years after they enter into possession and another £25 4 years after. If they default, Sarah is to have this property. In consideration of her renouncing all claim to my property in Essex, left to Susan and Margaret, my wife is to hold it for 3 years after my decease. I give to each of my 3 daughters a bed and bedstead furnished. All my other goods, corn and cattle I give to Anne my wife towards paying my debts and bringing up my children in their minority. I make her sole ex'trix. Wit. John Osbourne (X), Simon Wade, Edmund Heyward, Thomas Eley. Pr. at Stowmarket 28 September 1630.

95. R(W) WILLIAM BROOKE (X) of Weston Market, yeoman.
2 August 1630.

Bequeaths soul to God.
I give to my daughter Rebecca £5, a cow, the bed in the hall complete with a new covering in the chamber, a brass pot with a pair of pothooks to it and the best kettle. I give my daughter Alice £5 and 2 neats. I give my son Thomas of Hopton 20s, and 3s 4d each to all my grandchildren. I make my son Robert of Weston my exor. Wit. John Greene, Robert Peirson (X). Pr. at Bury 30 September 1630.

96. R(W) ROBERT SARGANT (N) of no place. No date.

He gave Agnes his wife his 2 milk cows. He gave his son Francis all his implements of husbandry, and 2 pewter platters. He gave 20s to his grand-daughter Annabel. He gave to Rose Smith one of the best of his 3 sheets after his wife's death. He gave Grace his sister 5s after the death of her sister Agnes. He gave Rose Smith and Annabel an ewe hogg each. All his other goods he left to his wife for her life, and after her decease to his son Francis. Wit. Robert Suckerman, Margaret Weetin. Let. ad. granted 25 September 1630 to widow. No place given.

97. R(W) MARGARET KEBLE (X) of Stowupland, singlewoman. 3 August 1630.

There are debts due to me of £10 from Samuel Smyth late of Haughley, of £3 from George Pratt and of £3 from Stephen Browne. After my burial charges have been paid, I leave the above sums to be equally divided between the 2 sons of John Sowgate senior and the 2 daughters of Christopher Bobye. I give John Sowgate a trundle bedstead with a flockbed, a coverlet, a sheet, a flock bolster and 2 old petticoats, one red and one blue. I give to Anne Boby 2 petticoats, a red and a black. I give 2 boxes to Christopher Boby's 2 daughters and 2 coffers to William and Helen Sowgate. My brother John Sowgate must see to the performance of my gifts as my trust is in him. Wit. John Goddard senior, William Keble. Pr. at Stowmarket 28 September 1630.

98. R(W) ROBERT TIFFIN of Hundon, yeoman. 25 July 1630.

Commends soul to God. To be buried in Hundon churchyard.
I give my eldest son Thomas 12d to be paid with a year. I give my second son John £30, £10 to be paid within 1 year and £20 within 3 years of my decease. I give my third son Robert £20 to be paid when he is 21, and £20 to my youngest son Peter when he is 21. I give my eldest daughter Mary 12d within a year, and my second daughter Anne £12 to be paid within 2 years. I give £20 each to my third daughter Jane and the youngest Grace when they are 21. All have benefit of survivorship. The residue of my goods, my debts, legacies and funeral charges paid, I give to Anne my wife, whom I make sole ex'trix. Supervisor: Mark Balls the elder, butcher of Hunsdon, to whom I give 20s for his pains. Wit. Mark Balls, William Pigg. Pr. at Clare 1 October 1630.

99. R(W) RICHARD CAMPIN (X) of Great Cornard, husbandman. 8 September 1630.

Commends soul to God and trusts to be saved. To be buried in Great Cornard churchyard.
I give to Elizabeth Campion my well-beloved wife £10 to be paid within a year. I bequeath to my eldest son John 40s to be paid within 2 years. I

give my son Richard £10 to be paid within a month and one great brass kettle. I leave my son Nicholas £10 to be paid within 2 years and my middle brass pot, and to my son Edmund £10 to be paid within 3 years and a little brass pot, the bedstead wherein I now lie and a great chest. I give my daughters Elizabeth and Joan 40s each within 3 years. I bequeath to my grandchildren John and Abigail, children of John Paine, 5s each within 1 year of my decease. I give to my servant Mary Upsonne 1 sheep. Finally I give to my son Richard all my unbequeathed goods, cattle and corn, he paying my debts, legacies and funeral charges. I make him sole exor. Wit. Henry Tanner, Joseph Harper (X). Pr. at Sudbury 2 October 1630.

100. R(W) RICHARD ARGENT (X) of Stoke by Clare, husbandman. 14 September 1630.

Bequeaths soul to God to dispose of it as it shall please him.
I give and bequeath to William my son my house and 2 tenements with yards, orchards and backside in Mill Lane in Stoke by Clare, now in the tenure of Richard Kent and one Pilgrime. William is to pay the money due to George Mills to whom this property is mortgaged. I give to William all my working tools, and all moneys due to me from sundry persons. I give 12d each to my sons Richard and Matthew. I give to my daughter Mary the half-headed bed standing in the chamber, after the decease of Margaret my wife. I give my daughter Anne the cupboard in the hall, and the bed which is called her bed, with a blanket and sheet to be set out by my wife. I give my wife all my crop of corn, hay and straw to pay my debts, and all my cattle and unbequeathed goods to her for life. After her death they are to be divided between my sons William and Ambrose, and my daughters Mary and Anne. Ex'trix: wife. Wit. Mark Reynolds, George Grimstone (X). Pr. at Clare 1 October 1630.

101. R(W) MARY TURNOR (X) of Haverhill, widow. 13 September 1630

Bequeaths soul to God and hopes to be saved. To be buried in Haverhill churchyard.
All my moveable goods and credits, except some money in my cousin Cole's hands, I give to be divided among my 5 youngest children now alive: Samuel, Daniel, Mary, Susan and Anne, and all the children of my deceased daughter Sarah King. Her children are to have a sixth part of my goods. There is £19 due to me from my son Samuel, who with my consent has lent this sum to my son-in-law James Fowler. For 6 years my above 5 children and those of Sarah King are to be paid interest on this money by my son Samuel, and at the end of that time the £19 is to be divided amongst them in the same way as my goods. I give the money now in my cousin Cole's hands to my daughter Anne, the wife of John Whiting, whom I make sole exor. Wit. Thomas Cole, John Crowe (X). Pr. at Clare 1 October 1630.

102. R(W) JOHN SMYTH of Lidgate, yeoman, made 4 August 1630.

Commends soul to God trusting to be saved.
I give and bequeath to Joan my wife 40s to be paid within 1 week of my burial. Also the bed and all the bedding wherein we usually lie, a hutch, a kettle, a skillet and 3 stools, the best that she can choose. I also give her an annuity of £8 to be paid quarterly. I give to my brother Clement Smyth £20 to be paid on 1 December 4 years after my decease, or to his children if he has died. I give to Marable Mayhew £7 besides the £3 I gave her, and to William Saunder £5; both legacies to be paid at Hallowmas 4 years after my decease. I give £40 to my servant William Jackson, £5 to my godson Robert Clement and £10 to Priscilla Hibbe. I bequeath £4 each to Thomas, Henry, Mary, Elizabeth and Margery, the children of my cousin Thomas Smyth. I give 20s each to the children my brother John Pollye had by his first wife Anne. I give £5 to the poor of Lidgate to be paid at £1 p.a. All the residue of my goods and chattels I give to my cousin Thomas Smyth, whom I make sole exor. Wit. Arthur Rogers, Thomas Wakefeild. Pr. at Bury 4 October 1630.

103. THOMAS WILLIS of Bury St Edmunds, singleman alias batchelor and son of Samuel Willis of Bury St Edmunds, yeoman. 17 June 1630.

Commends soul to God hoping for remission of sins.
I give to my sister Anne Willis my half share of the messuages and tenements in or near Garland Street, the messuage in Northgate Street and a close of pasture called Walnut Tree Close in Northgate Street, all of which were late in the possession of my grandfather Thomas Willis and the reversion of which was left to me in his will dated 17 July 1622. If my sister Anne has no heirs this property is to descend after her death to Thomas son of my uncle Thomas Baker, tailor of Bury St Edmunds, or to his brother Henry. I give the said Thomas Baker the younger £20 to be paid 1 year after the decease of my father Samuel Wyllis, and to his brother Henry £20 to be paid 1 year later. Benefit of survivorship. I give £5 each to John and Alice, children of my kinsman John Smyth, to be paid 3 years after my father's death. These legacies are to paid in the market cross at Bury by my sister Anne or by the owner of the property left to her. Legatees have power to distrain. I give my uncle Thomas Baker all my goods towards my funeral expenses and probate of my will, and I make him exor. Wit. John Gooderich, Samuel Mallowes, John Hart (X). Pr. at Bury 4 October 1630.

104. R(W) THOMAS NETHERCOTE (X) the elder of Soham [Cambs], thatcher. 17 August 1630.

Commits soul to God and trusts to be saved through Jesus Christ. To be buried in Soham churchyard.
I bequeath my goods and tenements not formerly conveyed as follows. I give my wife Margaret all my household stuff as long as she lives in the

house I have already assured to her and remains a widow. I also give her my 2 milk bullocks, one red and the other brown, and all the white meat (that is butter and cheese) and a great white hog with a black spot on his rump. I give her the linen and bedding already appointed to be hers to dispose of. I give my eldest son Thomas my copyhold tenement in Churchgate Street in Soham, and my freehold acre lying in the Croftes on the south side of the town and between the land of John Tiler gentleman and Thomas Wilken on the east and west sides. I also give him my half acre of demesne land, part of the demesnes granted to Thomas Hinson gentleman, lying in Bancroft in Soham and next to the land late Barber Seaman's and Mathew Pechey's to the east and west. Thomas must pay my son Richard £40 as follows: £25 within a year of my decease and £15 a month after my wife's death. If Thomas does not pay this legacy, the bequests made to him are to go to Richard. I give £5 to my daughter Bridget Egott within 1 year. All my other goods and stock I give to my son Thomas. I give 20s each to my daughters Marion Wrench and Elizabeth Kidd, and another 6s 8d to my daughter Bridget. Exor: my son Thomas. Supervisors: my loving brother John Nethercote and Roger Voyce. Lastly I give my son-in-law William Kidd my 2 best suits of apparel and to his wife my best hat. I give my sister Anne Nethercote 6s 8d. I have surrendered my copyhold land to the use of my will by the hands of Edward Wake and in the presence of Thomas Nethercote. I give my son Edward the 40s he owes me. I give my 5 grandchildren 6s 8d each. After my wife's death my 3 sons shall equally divide my household stuff. I give Henry Langham a heifer that is a 3-year old milk beast in calf when he has served out his apprenticeship with my exors. With the consent of my wife, she will not claim any thirds in my acre of freehold land in return for being provided with fodder from the commons for her 2 bullocks. Wit. Thomas Browne (X), Robert Maske (X) and me William Howe. Pr. at Bury 18 October 1630.

105. R(W) ROBERT BUCKLE (N) of Fornham All Saints, husbandman. No date.

He gave and bequeathed all his goods and chattels to his wife Anne for life, and then to be divided amongst his children. Wit. Thomas Prick, Anne Smyth, widow. Let. ad. granted to widow at Bury 11 October 1630.

106. R(W) MARK GEESON (X) of Mildenhall, yeoman. 1 May 1629.

Commends soul to God hoping assuredly to be associated and accompanied in the kingdom of heaven amongst the elect and chosen people of God.
I give 3s 4d to the repair of Mildenhall church, and 3s 4d to the poor man's box of the same town. The rest of my goods, after my funeral expenses have been paid, I give to be disposed of at the discretion of my kinsman Thomas Geeson the elder, whom I make exor. He is to receive and pay my debts. Wit. Nicholas Coates junior, Thomas Peacocke (X). Pr. at Bury 11 October 1630.

107. R(W) WILLIAM SPINKE of Thorpe Morieux, yeoman.
13 September 1630.

Bequeaths soul to God from whom it came. To be buried in churchyard of Thorpe Morieux.
My will is that Margaret my wife is to be sole ex'trix and pay my debts and funeral expenses. She is to have all my cattle, corn, hay, grass, implements of husbandry and household goods, and is to pay out of them, within 2 years of my decease, £100 to my son William. If he dies, the money is to go to the child my wife is believed to be carrying. If William and the unborn child both live, my wife is to pay £50 to the latter at age of 15. I give my wife for ever my 2 freehold closes in Brettenham containing 8 acres. I make my trusty and faithful friends William Crysall, yeoman of Pentlowe in Essex, and Thomas Purkis, yeoman of Cockfield, supervisors of my will. The £100 left to William is to be paid to them, and until he is 21 they are to use the benefit of this sum to bring him up in learning and what else may be most beneficial to him. When William reaches age of 21 the supervisors are to give him the £100. Within 3 months of my decease my ex'trix is to pay 5s to Bridget Thornton. Wit. William Crysall, Thomas Purkis, James Longe, Thomas Tayler. Pr. at Bury 18 October 1630.

Note: that in May 1648 William Spinke, son of the testator, presented an acquittance for receipt of £100 from goods in his mother's hands.

108. R(W) ROBERT SPINKE (X) of Great Saxham, yeoman. 17 April 1630.

Bequeaths soul to God, trusting to be saved eternally by merits of Jesus Christ.
The worldly goods, with which it hath pleased God to bless my labours, I give wholly to my wife Mary for whom I have a special care to provide she being a careful and loving wife. I trust her to bestow something on my kindred and her own where most need shall be. I wish her to take the advice of my neighbour Pitts. I make my wife ex'trix. Wit. Simon Pittes. Pr. at Bury 1 November 1630.

109. R(W) JOHN GREENEGRASSE (X) of Troston, yeoman.
20 October 1630.

Bequeaths soul to God.
I give to my kinsman Roger Greenegrasse, merchant tailor in London, my house wherein I now dwell with the barns, stables and land belonging to it, and part of a sheepwalk to enable him to pay my legacies. I give £5 each to Elizabeth and Bridget, daughters of my brother Francis Greenegrasse, when they are 21, and £6 13s 4d apiece when 21 to Thomas, John and a daughter, the children of my deceased brother Thomas. I give £6 13s 4d each when 21 to my sister Elizabeth Townsend's children. I give

20s to Richard Peak, who was my servant and 30s to my servant Margaret Greenegresse. I give for the benefit of the poor of Troston £10 to be laid out in land so that they may have the rent for ever. I give £10 to my kinswoman Mirablc Ezard, 10s to my servant Francis Knock, 20s to John Greenegresse of Pakenham and 5s apiece to the rest of my godchildren at their ages of 21. All the rest of my goods I give to Roger Greengrasse to pay my legacies and burial charges, and I make him sole exor. Wit. James Hodson, Francis Knocke (X). Pr. at Bury 1 November 1630.

110. R(W) PHILIP ADAMES (X) of Mildenhall, husbandman. 24 September 1630.

Commends soul to God. To be buried in parish church or churchyard of Mildenhall.

I give and bequeath to my brother Robert Adames, after the death of Katherine my wife, the house wherein I live and 1½ acres of adjoining arable land. Within 1 year of entering this property he must pay £4 to my brother Stephen Adames and £15 to the children of my sister Rose, wife of Nicholas Shellie. I give and bequeath to my brother Robert, after the death of my father James Adames, 4½ acres of land out of which he is to pay within 1 year £20 to Katherine and Joanna, my sister Shellie's 2 children, and £10 to Rose, daughter of my brother Stephen. I give to Katherine my wife for life the close I lately purchased from John Childerston and after her death to my brother Robert, who within a year must pay £20 to the son of my sister Rose Shellie if it shall please God that she have one. If she has no son, the money is to be divided between her daughters. I give to my wife, after my father's death, 5 rods land lying in 1 piece for ever, and for her life 1 acre of land my father lately bought of Andrew Rolfe. She must keep the buildings in good repair or forfeit this land to my brother Robert, who inherits it after her decease. I give all my goods to my wife and make her ex'trix. Wit. Simon Jerrold, Theodore Adame (X). Pr. at Bury 1 November 1630.

111. R(W) FRANCES RAYE of Barrow. 28 September 1630.

I give to Jeremy and Elizabeth, children of Robert Callowe and my godchildren, 5s each. I give to John and Joseph, sons of my brother Robert Callowe, 3s 4d each and to Frances, daughter of my brother Thomas Callowe 5s and to her brother Thomas 3s 4d. I give to Thomas, son of Anne Hamant my kinswoman, 5s, to Mary daughter of my brother Thomas Callowe 3s 4d and to Andrew, son of my kinsman Andrew Haward 5s. All these legacies are to be paid within a month of my decease. I give to the poor of Barrow 10s to be paid within 1 month. I give to William my godson and son of my brother Clement Callowe 5s, and to Dorothy my sister 40s. I also give her my black coat and a hempen smock. I give my sister Callowe, wife of my brother Robert, a stuff gown without lining or sleeves. I give to Clemence, daughter of my brother Clement Callowe, my old stuff gown. I give a great hutch with a spring lock to Thomas son of my brother Clement and to his sister Judith all the rest of my goods. I make Judith Callowe my ex'trix. Wit. Thomas Gault, Alice Callowe. Pr. at Bury 1 November 1630.

112. R(W) JOHN REEDE (X) of Stowmarket, yeoman. 26 April 1630.

Commends soul to God hoping to be made partaker of life everlasting.
I give to my son John when 21 my messuage with yard, garden and orchard in Stowmarket, which I purchased of William Blomefeild gent and [gap in MS] Baldery; and also part of a yard or orchard which I bought of [gap in MS] Damesden and his wife Margery; and also the adjoining part of this yard as it now divided and which I purchased from Miles and Frances Codd. I also give John that part of the above messuage in which widow Miller lately dwelt. If John dies without heirs, I give this property to be shared equally by Jane my wife and all my other children. I give my son John when he 21 a long table in the hall with the form belonging to it, a long joined bench standing in the parlour chamber of the house wherein I dwell and my greatest brass pot. I give to my son-in-law William Scrutton the messuage and yards as they are now divided in Stowmarket, which I bought from Miles and Frances Codd, on 22 October next on condition he pays my wife Jane £40 in my mansion house on or before 16 October next. If he defaults, the messuage is to go to my wife. I give my daughter Prudence a part of the messuage and yard in Stowmarket which I purchased of Francis Holmes and now occupied by Henry Bowier. I give my daughter Mary, after my wife's death, the chamber over the part of the parlour where Agnes Miller lately dwelt. I also give Mary the bedstead and bedding with its curtains, and a table standing in the parlour of the house wherein I now dwell. I also give her 2 forms, a new 4-gallon kettle and a spit. I give Mary also part of the messuage with yard in Stowmarket in which Nicholas Parish lives, and which I bought of Francis Holmes. Until Mary is 14, my wife is to use the rent of this property to bring her up and keep the house in repair. I will that my daughters Prudence and Mary shall have liberty to make gates out of the yards left to them into that left to my son John with access to draw water from the well there. I give to my daughter Anne and to my sons William, Thomas and Edward £5 each. I will that Jane my loving wife have the use of the messuage and yards given to my son John until he is 21. When my wife leaves the property, she must leave the yard or orchard as well stocked with hop plants and poles as it now is. I give my wife for her life the parlour wherein Thomas Blome now dwells and the chamber over part of the parlour in which Agnes Myller lately lived, and free access to the well in the yard to draw water and to the backhouse to brew and bake. She is also to have a place in the inner yard to lay her firewood. After my son John reaches age of 21 he is yearly to deliver to my wife at her parlour 16 bushels of apples growing in the orchards left to him. My unbequeathed goods and chattels I give to Jane my wife towards the bringing up of my children, and the payment of £86 8s 0d for which some of my tenements, yards and orchards are mortgaged to Thomas

Tastard of Combs, and the paying of my legacies and proving my will. I make her my ex'trix hoping she will be very careful to provide that my children are brought up in the fear of God, my mortgage redeemed and my debts paid. If my wife remarries and challenges my will, all gifts to her become void. Wit. William Heyward (X), John Goddard. Pr. at Bury 1 November 1630.

113. R(W) JOHN BENTLIE of Newmarket, yeoman. 23 September 1630.

Bequeaths soul to God and trusts to be make a partaker of his glorious kingdom and saved. To be buried in church or churchyard of Newmarket. I give and bequeath to Elizabeth my wife for life all my capital messuage or mansion house in Newmarket wherein I now dwell and which is commonly known by the sign of the Chequer, together with the brewhouse, millhouse, barns, stables, other outbuildings, yards, orchards and garden and adjoining croft of pasture. After her decease I give all the premises to my kinswomen Elizabeth White, widow of Newmarket, and Anne, wife of John Huske yeoman of Mildenhall. I give to my wife for life an inn or messuage in Newmarket, commonly called the Maidenhead and in which Richard Blowein now lives, with its outhouses, barns, stables, yard and garden. My wife must yearly pay out ot this property to Mary Stubbinge, widow of Thurlow, the dowry due to her from it. My wife must also on 29 December each year, if it is not a Sunday (and if it is on the following Monday) provide for the use of the poor of Newmarket 2 loads of great wood or half a hundred of 2-bond faggots. She must also provide yearly for the poor of Newmarket a cade of red herrings on the second Sunday in Lent or thereabouts. After my wife's death, I give the Maidenhead to my kinsman Stephen Bently, yeoman of Brinckley in Cambridgeshire. He must continue to pay the above gifts to the poor, and also pay £50 to Agatha, wife of William Bryant draper of Newmarket at the times hereinafter mentioned. I give to the said Agatha 3 copyhold shops in Newmarket near the back gate of the inn called the Maidenhead and now occupied by Henry Cobbyn, John Poulter and Robert Bennet. This bequest is on condition that within a year of my decease William Bryant discharges and releases my ex'trix from a bond for payment of £100 to Oliver Moorden gent of Exning deceased. I am bound to pay this sum together with William Bryant and John Nelson. If William Bryant fails to do this, I give the 3 shops to my wife for ever. I give £100 to Agatha Bryant: £50 to be paid by Stephen Bentley, and £50 by my ex'trix on condition that William Bryant discharges the above-mentioned bond. If he fails to do this, then the £100 is not to be paid to Agatha until 1 year after my wife's death. After my wife's decease I bequeath to Elizabeth White and Anne Huske, my kinswomen, my copper in the brewhouse with the iron grate belonging to it, a mash vat with the under back belonging to it, a yealde vat and a float, 3 coolers and a horse mill. I give to my kinswoman Mary, daughter of Thomas Coleman woollen draper of

Diss in Norfolk, 40s or a ring to that value. I bequeath the residue of my moveable and immoveable goods and chattels to my wife Elizabeth, whom I make sole ex'trix. Supervisor: my cousin Stephen Bentley of Brinckley. Wit. John Mathew (X), Richard Blowen, Richard Kidman. Pr. at Bury 1 November 1630.

114. R(W) THOMAS HINDLE of the hamlet of Ballingdon near Sudbury in Essex. 7 May 1630.

Bequeaths soul to God and hopes to inherit everlasting life.
I give and bequeath to Alice my wife for her life the messuage wherein I dwell and which I lately purchased of John Smythe. She is to sell my other 5 tenements in Ballingdon to pay my debts. They are occupied by William Inchbalde, Robert Cocke, William Fuller, William Bellowbie and George Hockett. I give 10s to my eldest son Peter to be paid 6 weeks after my decease, and £10 at 5s a quarter. If he finds fault and grudges at this gift, my wife is to pay him 5s only. I give to my second son Thomas all my tools which are to be given to him 4 days after my decease, and also the best flockbed with feather bolster and pillow, a pair blankets and a pair sheets, a good coverlet and a bedstead, a brass pot and the round trunk. My wife is to deliver these to him within a year of my decease. After my wife's death I give to my son Thomas the parlour and all those other rooms as they are ranged in the house where I now dwell and the sawing pits; also the timber yard. He must keep up the fence between the timber yard and the orchard with 5-foot pales. He must pay 40s to Matthew Bryant, and £5 each to my daughters Faith and Alice when they are 21. The occupants of the other tenements are to have free access with horse and cart and workmen to the timber yard left to Thomas, provided that timber is not left there for more than 3 days. I give all the rooms in my house not already bequeathed to Thomas to my sons James and John, together with the stone yard, after my wife's death. I give all my unbequeathed goods and all moneys due to me to my wife Alice, and I make her ex'trix. Wit. William Frost clerk, Robert Paine. Pr. at Bury 1 November 1630.

115. R(W) ROBERT FROST late of Whepstead and now of Great Barton, yeoman. 28 September 1630.

Bequeaths soul to God and hopes to have eternal life. To be buried in Whepstead churchyard.
I give 40s to the poor of Whepstead to be distributed on my burial day. I give to my son Abraham and his wife Mary and to their heirs 20 acres freehold land called Gatefield and Geddings in Brockley and Whepstead. Also to him my horse mill and all my brewing vessels with which he brews, my cupboard standing in the the kitchen chamber, and my great brass pot. I give my daughter Judith and her husband Samuel Allen my messuage in Whepstead near Dunston Street in which Thomas Hynes now lives with the land belonging to it. They are to pay my daughter

Grace Brooke an annuity of £6; she has right to distrain if this is not paid quarterly. I give to my daughter Mary 3 pieces freehold pasture: 2 pieces, which I lately had of my father Vincent Frost, lying in Ashfield and the other in Badwell [Ash] between the lands of Thomas Chenerie and Abraham Frost and which I bought from Mr Robert Bland. If my son Abraham pays Mary 40s p.a. for life he may have the above land. I give to my daughter Mary 40s to be paid within 1 year, my russet cloak and a silver spoon. I give to Mary, my son Abraham's wife, my posted bedstead, my trundle bed, my cupboard and joined table as they stand in the parlour. I give £40 to be distributed equally amongst my grand-children. Those who are 18 or more are to receive their legacies at once, and those of the younger ones are to be paid to their mothers: Mary wife of my son Abraham and my daughters Elizabeth, Grace, Sarah, Mary, Judith, Margaret and Lydia. I bequeath to my daughter Grace a pair of coarse sheets, a pot brass stealed, a posnet, my wife's gown and her kirtle, a cloak, a silver spoon and a pillow. I give my sister Bridget 10s and my sister Whitacre a yard of cloth worth 5s. I give Grace Mayhew a silver spoon. Jeffery Halles owes me £10 of a bond for £20. If he pays his 4 daughters 40s each on their marriage days, I give him this bond. I have certain writings in the keeping of Thomas Croplie which are to be delivered to my exor. Thomas Gault owes me £10 by bond, which I give to his wife Mary. All the rest of my goods and money, my legacies and funeral expenses paid, I give to be equally divided between my 4 daughters Elizabeth, Sarah, Judith and Margaret, and I ask them to preserve these gifts for their children. I make my son-in-law Samuel Allen sole exor. Wit. William Bronwyne, Thomas Atkynson, Robert Walker. Pr. at Bury 5 November 1630.

116. R(W) WILLIAM HELDER senior of Hargrave, yeoman.
16 September 1630.

Bequeaths soul to God.
I bequeath all my moveable goods, bonds, corn and cattle to my son Richard and make him my exor. Wit. Thomas Nunne, James Heyward (X). pr. at Bury 8 November 1630.

117. R(W) JOHN MARTYN of Barnham, cook. 28 December 1629.

Bequeaths soul to God.
I give and bequeath to my son Thomas for life the little house next the gate with its ground and yard, which I bought of Robert Davie, and after his death to my son John. I give my son John all that part of my house which I purchased of Elizabeth Andrews on condition he pays £16 to the rest of his brothers and sisters, and £4 to Judy daughter of my son-in-law Henry Write. These payments are to be £4 each at the rate of 1 p.a. and in the following order: my daughter Anne wife of Robert Buller, my son Thomas, my daughter Magdalen Martyn and my son William, and lastly to my belchild Judy Wryte when she is 14. If my son John refuses to enter

into a bond to pay these sums, my house is to be sold and the money divided amongst my children. I give my son Thomas a trundle bed and a flockbed with the furniture belonging to it. All my other moveable goods are to be divided among my children. I make my son John exor. Wit. John Largent (X), Hugh Hart (X), John Man (X). Pr. at Bury 8 November 1630.

118. W(R) THOMAS GOSHAWKE (X) of Little Waldingfield, yeoman. 1 October 1630.

Commends soul to God.
I give to William my eldest brother £5 to be paid to him by John Middleton of Little Waldingfield as due to me by bond. I give to Anne Goshauke my loving sister £5 and to my loving sister Susan Englishe 5s. I give my loving sister Elizabeth Aleward the 30s she owes me, and 20s to Mary English my sister's daughter. I give 20s each when 21 to my brothers Robert, Samuel, Isaac and Abraham. All the rest of my goods and chattels I give to my loving mother Mary Goshawke whom I make ex'trix. I make John Hamond, yeoman of Edwardstone, overseer of my will. Wit. Thomas Langton, John Garrad (X), Robert Man (X), Thomas Fordum (X). Pr. at Bury 11 October 1630.

119. W(R) THOMAS GOSHAUKE (X) of Little Waldingfield, yeoman. 8 September 1630.

Commends soul to God.
I give to my son William £5, my doublet, my jerkin, and 2 shirts. I give £5 each to sons Robert, Samuel, Isaac and Abraham to be paid by my exor when they are 21. I give 6s 8d to my daughter Elizabeth Allewarde, and 5s to my daughter Susan wife of Robert Englishe of Newton. I give £5 to my daughter Anne Goshauke, and 40s to my eldest son Thomas. I give the rest of my goods to my wife Mary. Exors: wife and son Thomas. Wit. John Wincoll, George Wincoll, Thomas Langton. Pr. at Bury 11 October 1630.

120. W(R) JOHN ALDERS (X) of Great Waldingfield, blacksmith. 20 August 1630.

Commends soul to God and expects to have life eternal with the elect in God's kingdom of glory.
I give my brother William 20s, my brother Samuel 5s, and my brother Isaac 10s. I give Mr Richard Peachie 10s, and to the poor of Great Waldingfield 6s 8d. I give to my kinsman Edmund Revill 10s. The residue of my goods I give to Winifred my wife, whom I make ex'trix. Wit. John Hubbard senior, Joshua Isaacke, John Hammond. Pr. at Sudbury 2 October 1630.

121. W(R) THOMAS BREWERTON (X) of Gazeley, blacksmith.
17 October 1630.

Bequeaths soul to God in sure hope of the resurrection.
My debts and funeral expenses being paid, I give to my sons Thomas and
Clement 6d each in full discharge of their portions. I give all my
moveable goods, except as after bequeathed, to be divided between my 3
daughters Elizabeth, Ursula and Alice. I give to my son John my long
table in the hall with its forms and stools and the great brass kettle. I give
the posted bedstead in the parlour with the bed and bedding to my
daughter Alice, and 2 lambs to my grandson John Burges. I give 10s to
my wife Anne and all the goods she brought at our marriage. I give to my
son John my house and grounds, and he must pay my daughter Alice £5
within 1 year of my decease. Exor: my son John. Wit. Edmund Moodye,
John Botthamley. Pr. at Bury 8 November 1630.

122. W(R) WILLIAM LOCK (X) of Hopton, husbandman.
20 September 1630.

Bequeaths soul to God.
I give and bequeath to Elizabeth my wellbeloved wife for life my
messuage in Hopton wherein I now dwell, and after her death to Marion
Turrill my sister's daughter on condition she pays her mother Marion an
annuity of 30s, and 40s to her sister Mary within 2 years of my wife's
decease. I give all my goods absolutely to my wife except for a cupboard
in the hall, my best table and my best ladder, which are to descend to my
kinswoman Marion after my wife's decease. Ex'trix: wife. Wit. Thomas
Goddard clerk, George Harvey (X). Pr. at Bury 22 November 1630.

123. W(R) THOMAS CLARKE of Norton, yeoman. 1 July 1630.

Bequeaths soul to God. To be buried in Thurston churchyard.
I give to Joan my beloved wife for life the house and land wherein I now
dwell, and after her decease to my sons Edmund and Thomas the
younger to be equally divided between them. My wife is to have all my
moveable goods for life, and then they are to go to my son Thomas.
Edmund is to have £10. I give my daughter Bridget Smith a featherbed
and a feather bolster. I give 10s each to my daughters Dorothy Gippes
and Mary Verby to buy a silver spoon. I give 40s to the poor of Thurston
to be distributed half at my death and half at the Christmas following at
the discretion of my sons Thomas and Edmund, who are living in
Thurston. I give 20s to the poor of Norton. My eldest son Thomas of
Thurston is to receive the moveable goods that belonged to my
son-in-law, John Verbie, and to see that they are conveyed to my
daughter Mary Verbie and her children. The rest of my goods I give to
my exors, who are my wife Joan and my youngest son Thomas.
Supervisor: my eldest son, Thomas of Thurston, to whom I give my best
rug for his pains. Wit. None. Pr. at Bury 2 December 1630.

124. W(R) JOHN REVELL of Cavendish, yeoman. 13 January 1623/24

Commends soul to God.
I freely remit to my son Prentise the money for which he is indebted to me. I give 10s to my reverend friend and ancient pastor William Fearmers, preacher of this parish. I bequeath to Mr Willmott, preacher of Clare, 6s 8d, and to Mr Stephenson of Hevingham preacher 5s and 30s to the poor of his parish. The rest of my goods I give to my son Thomas and make him sole exor. Wit. Mathew Crathoode, Thomas Fernegan. Pr. at Clare 1 October 1630.

125. W(R) MARGERY PARKER (N) of Stoke by Clare. 12 June 1630.

A note of those goods that the Goody Margery Parker did dispose of and to whom. To William Hayes the flock bed that is at Cambridge with the bedsteadle that is in Thomas Hayes chamber with a coverlet, 2 blankets, a pair of sheets, a table in the hall, a great chest in the chamber, the least kettle, a posnet and 2 little pewter dishes. To Thomas Hayes a bedsteadle in the lower chamber and another bedsteadle in the chamber above it with a flock bed and bolster, a coverlet, a pair of sheets, two cupboards in the parlour, a table in the best chamber, the middle kettle, a brass pot, two tubs, 2 hogsheads and the dairy with all that belong to it. To Mary Amys a featherbed with a bolster in the parlour, 2 of the best blankets, a pair of sheets, 2 pillows, a mattress, a pair of green curtains, a pair of white curtains, a bed sheet, all her wearing linen, a hutch and a red petticoat. To Margaret her best cloth petticoat and her gown. To Katherine 2 joined stools, the least kettle but one, the bed pan, and a hutch in the parlour. To Ann the great kettle, the livery cupboard in the best chamber, the best chair, a hogshead, a cradle and 18 pounds of wool. The timber in the croft, and the boards over the malt house to go to John Gaskines. All the pewter is to be divided equally between Thomas, Mary, Margaret, Katherine and Ann. Two great chairs the one for Thomas Hayes two boys. All the rest of her goods and chattels she gave to Thomas Hayes and John Ammys, whom she made her exors to pay her debts and legacies. Wit. Daniel Wade, Thomas Bridge. Pr. at Clare 1 October 1630.

126. R(W) JUDITH HATCHET (X) of Wetherden, widow. 5 May 1630.

Commends soul to God and steadfastly believes she will be a partaker of the everlasting joys of the kingdom of heaven.
My body is to be buried at the discretion of Edmund Basse, whom I name exor. I give all my goods to my son John in this manner: within 8 days of my decease they are to inventoried and prized by our minister William Kilborne, John Hovill alias Smyth and William Base if they are living, and if not by their successors as minister and churchwardens of Wetherden. After my will has been proved, my goods are to be sold by my exor with the advice of the aforementioned persons and the money

raised, together with any due to me by bonds or bills, is to be given to John when he is 21. My exor is to deduct from this sum the costs of probate and my funeral, paying my debts and putting my son apprentice to any trade he has a mind to when he is 14. If John dies before he is 21, my exor is to pay £5 to Thomas Hatchet of Haughley, my son's uncle, and to give the remainder of the money at his discretion to any of my kindred that are in true want or to the use of the poor of Wetherden. Supervisor: William Kilborne, clerk of Wetherden, to whom I give 5s for his pains. Wit. William Kilborne clerk, George Rosyar (X), Jane Barnard (X). Pr. at Bury 20 November 1630.

127. R(W) AUGUSTINE UNDERWOOD of Chevington, clerk. 18 November 1629.

Commends soul to safe keeping of God and believes to be discharged from all his sins through merits of Jesus Christ.
I give 10s to the poor of Chevington to be distributed on my burial day, or paid within 1 month to the chief inhabitants to distribute. I give to my wife Katherine for life the freehold messuage in Chevington called Mottes, wherein my son William now dwells, with its land, and after her decease to my son Thomas on condition he pays £20 to my daughter Elizabeth. This is to be paid in 2 instalments, 1 and 2 years after my wife's death, in the porch at the south door of Chevington church. She has power to distrain. I give my wife for life my freehold messuage and land in Thorpe Morieux now occupied by [blank in MS] Stock. After her decease my daughter Elizabeth is to hold this property for 2 years, and then it is to pass to my son Francis. After my wife's decease I give my daughter Mary Whithand, widow, my best kettle with a skillet, and my greatest brass pot. I give 10s each to her children John and Susan to be paid to them when 21. After my wife's decease I give to my daughter Judith, wife of Josias Stammer, my best kettle save one and a skillet to be taken at her choice. I give 20s to her children to be paid to Josias Stammer within a year of my decease. After my wife's decease I give to my daughter Margaret, wife of Robert Hammond, my best kettle save two and I give 20s to her children to be paid as above. I give my daughter Elizabeth £10 to be paid within a year of my death, and immediately after my decease the bedstead with its furniture now standing in the little chamber near the fore door of my parsonage house, the cupboard in the same chamber and my little brass pot. I give my son Thomas my cupboard in the hall. I give 20s to the children of my son Augustine and 20s to those of my son John to be paid as above. After my wife's decease I give my daughter Mary Whitehand the cobirons, firepan and tongs that usually stand and are used in the parlour of my parsonage house, and the 2 carpets and the cushion on the cupboard in the parlour in performance of my uncle's request. I give my son Robert my horse mill with my brewing brass as they are now in the backhouse, the great table and 2 forms in the hall, my bedstead cupboard table and a great chest now standing in the parlour of my parsonage house, and all my books. He

must pay £20 to my daughter Elizabeth within 6 months; if he defaults my exors are to sell the goods left to him and pay the £20 to Elizabeth. I give all my unbequeathed goods to my wife to be given by her amongst my and her children as God shall put into her mind. Exors: wife and son Thomas. I give 20s to the children of my son William and 20s to those of my son Francis to be paid as above, and 20s to my son Augustine. Wit. Robert Paman, George Sparrowe, Christopher Pricke (X) Pr. at Bury 15 December 1630.

128. R(W) HENRY CLYFTE the elder of Mildenhall, yeoman.
5 October 1630.

Commends soul to God and hopes assuredly to be amongst the elect and chosen people of God in the kingdom of heaven.
I give 16d towards the repair of Mildenhall church, and 12d to poor men's box of the parish. I give John my youngest son 2 pieces of copyhold land in West Row field: one of 3 acres between land of Sir Roger North on the west and east with the south end abutting on Charnock way and the north end on Framhowe way; the other piece contains 1 rod lying between the land of Henry Childerston on the east and that occupied by Agnes Craske on the west and with the south end abutting on Bagsholme way and the north end on Charnock way. I also give my son John 3 pieces of freehold land in West Row field: one of 2½ acres with the south end abutting on Framhowe way and the north end on the land of William Eaton and lying between the land of Sir Roger North on the west and of Thomas Bovell alias Lanur on the east; the second piece of 5 rods has the land of Sir Thomas Gee on the east and Broadmeere on the west with the south end abutting on Charnock way and the north on Framhowe way; the third piece of 3 rods lies between the same land as the second piece. I give my eldest son Henry 40s to be paid within 1 year. I give Margaret my wife the bedstead in the middle chamber with all its bedding both linen and woollen, a wicker chair and a joined chair in the hall, a skillet, a hutch and a kettle at her own choice. I give 20s each when 21 to my grandchildren Mary, Margaret and Henry, children of my son Henry. My debts and funeral charges being paid, I bequeath all the remainder of my goods and chattels to my son John, whom I make exor. Wit. John Clyft, Philip Heynor, Nicholas Coates junior. Testator surrendered his copyhold land to the use of his will by the hands of John Clyft and Philip Heynor. Pr. at Bury 6 December 1630.

129. R(W) JOHN COOKE (X) of Little Livermere, yeoman.
1 September 1625.

Bequeaths soul to God.
I bequeath to my wife Elizabeth for life my tenement in Livermere where I now dwell with its outbuildings, yard, garden, orchard, croft and all other ground called the home setting; also a 2 acre piece of arable land at

the Brome and an half acre piece lying in a went called the Breache. After her death all this property goes to my son John, who must pay £6 each to my daughters Anne and Elizabeth and to my sons Edmund, Robert and Thomas. The payments are to be spread over 10 years. I will that my daughter Anne shall have the low room in my tenement where she now usually lies, being on the north side of the house and at the end next to the malt house, until she marries. My son John is to pay a mortgage of £5 and if he fails to do so, 1 acre of the land left to him is to go to my wife. If any of my children to whom cash legacies are left die, my son John is to keep their share. These children have power to distrain. All the rest of my goods and chattels I give to my wife Elizabeth, whom I make sole ex'trix. Wit. John Cooke of Great Livermere, Richard Norman (X). Pr. at Bury 6 December 1630.

130. R(W) JOHN LARGENT (X) of Mildenhall. 10 September 1613.

Bequeaths soul to God.
I give my eldest son Simon the west part of my copyhold tenement with the backyard on the south and half the yard on the north side. I give my daughter Agnes the other part of my tenement and the other half of the yard on the north side. I give 30s to my son William to be paid by my son Simon within one year, and 20s to my son John to be paid by Simon within 2 years. Benefit of survivorship. Simon is to be my exor, and have all my moveable goods to pay my debts and funeral expenses. Wit. Robert Suckerman, Francis Lusher, Thomas Barton. No probate.

Note: John Largent's original will is in the 1613 box and also has no probate.

131. R(W) WILLIAM BRIDGE of Burwell [Cambs], butcher.
20 September 1630.

Bequeaths soul to God trusting to have free remission of sins.
I give my wife Elizabeth for life my messuage in Market Street, Fordham, held of the manor called the Duchy in Soham. I also give her for life 12¼ acres freehold land in Fordham and 2 acres held copyhold of Biggen manor in Fordham. After her decease, I give my son William the 10 acres freehold land which were my father's, and to my son John my house in Fordham, the 2 acres of copyhold and the rest of my freehold land. I also give John my copyhold shop in Newmarket held of Sir Giles Allington's manor. I give my copyhold house in Burwell, held of Mistress Barrowe's manor, to my wife for life and then to my youngest son Robert. I give my son William £5, my son John £3 and my son Robert 40s, all to be paid within a year by my ex'trix. I give 12d each to my godchildren, and 20s to the poor of Fordham on my burial day. The rest of my goods and chattels I give to Elizabeth my wife and make her sole ex'trix. Wit. Thomas Hinson, William Randall, Thomas Sargant (X).
The testator surrendered all his copyhold property to the use of his will as follows: the shop in Newmarket by the hands of Thomas Beniefeild and

John Barrett; the copyhold house in Burwell by the hands of Robert Browne and Thomas Barrow; the copyhold house in Fordham by the hands of Thomas Hynson and William Randall; and the copyhold land in Fordham by the hands of Thomas Seargent and William Randall. All these men were copyhold tenants of the respective manors. Pr. at Bury 6 December 1630.

132. R(W) ELIZABETH GILMAN (X) of Langham, spinster. 8 July 1627

Commends soul to Jesus Christ through whom she is sure of salvation. I give to Mary my nephew [sic], daughter of Ezekias Rose of Langham husbandman, £8 to be put out to good use until she is 21 or marries. I give to Philip, Katherine and Thomas, children of Andrew Gilman my brother, 10s each to be paid within 6 months. I also give 10s each to be paid within 6 months to Margaret, Katherine and Stephen, children of my brother Stephen Gilman. I give to my sister Alice, wife of Ezekias Rose, all my wearing apparel both linen and woollen. I make Ezekias Rose my exor and give him all my bonds and bills and sums of money owing to me. Wit. Thomas Syer junior, Robert Page, William Browne. Pr. at Bury 8 December 1630.

133. R(W) WILLIAM COUNTER (X) of Exning, labourer. 22 January 1625/26.

Bequeaths soul to God and trusts to be saved. To be buried in Exning churchyard.
I give and bequeath to Elizabeth my wife for ever the house in which I dwell with the croft and 1 acre of freehold land in West field in Exning. I give 5s each to my brother-in-law William Wright and to his children Robert, Margaret and Mary to be paid within a year. I give 5s each to my brother-in-law Henry Teball and to his children Henry, John, Elizabeth and Mary to be paid within a year. I give 5s each when 21 to Thomas, William and Clement, sons of Thomas Wright deceased. All the rest of my moveables I give to my wife whom I make ex'trix. Wit. Thomas Fuller, Thomas Sturt. Pr. at Bury 14 December 1630.

134. R(W) THOMAS PATTLE (X) of Mendlesham, husbandman. 3 August 1630.

Commends soul to God.
I give 10s to my cousin Joan, wife of Roger Heath, to be paid within a month. I give 4s to my servant maid Bridget Gunold to be paid within a month. I give to Alice my beloved wife for life all my goods both within and without my house. She is to divide those of my goods left, after paying my debts and funeral charges, into 6 equal parts to be given after her decease as follows: 2 parts to Thomas Raynberd the younger, son of my deceased sister Elizabeth, 1 part each to his sisters Elizabeth,

Thomasin and Cicely, and the last part to the daughter of my deceased brother Adam Pattle. Ex'trix: wife. Supervisor: Thomas Raynberd the younger, who is asked to see that the goods are distributed after wife's death as set out above. Wit. Barnaby Gibson, Robert Ridnall. Pr. at Bury 14 December 1630.

On 1 October 1638 Richard Pitts, husband of Elizabeth Raynberd alias Pitts, took over the executorship as next of kin to Thomas Raynberd.

135. R(W) THOMAS HENGAMES (X) of Thorndon, husbandman. 2 November 1630.

Commends soul to God trusting assuredly to be saved.

I give and bequeath to my nephew Thomas, son of Anthony Hengames, £10 to be paid 1 month after the decease of my wife Margaret. I give £15 to my nephew Anthony Hengames to be paid 6 months after the death of his mother or my wife, whichever happens first. I give £5 each to Anne and Frances Newman, my sister's daughters, and to my nephew Walter Newman; all to be paid a month after my wife's death. I give my sister Joan Newman 20s to be paid within a month of my decease, and to Mabel Casen 20s to be paid within a year. I bequeath to Margaret my wellbeloved wife all my goods, money and household stuff, and make her ex'trix. Wit. John Jessope, Thomas Bishoppe. Pr. at Bury 14 December 1630.

136. R(W) THOMAS NOBLE (X) of Stanton, yeoman. 15 May 1627.

Commends soul to God and trusts to be saved.

I give to Margery my wife for life all my messuages and lands in Stanton and Hepworth. She must not break up or convert to tillage any more of my land than is now tilled. It is lawful for her to lop and fell the wood necessary for her fuel and brewing, and for mending fences and hedges, and to fell timber needed to repair houses and buildings. One month after my wife's decease, my son Thomas is to inherit all the above property on condition he has paid to my son-in-law Thomas Craske the £20 he stands bound to pay him on the due date. If Thomas fails to do this and my wife has to pay Thomas Craske £20, I give her for ever a 3 acre close in Stanton called Undeles. I give to my wife Margery all my moveable goods for ever, and make her ex'trix. Supervisor: William Williment junior of Downham. Wit. William Clarke, Giles Rust (X), Francis Hawes. Pr. at Bury 13 December 1630.

137. R(W) JOHN RAYMENT of Clare, tailor. 2 June 1626.

Commends soul to God.

By an indenture, made 10 January 1610, I sold to my son John a messuage with yard and outbuildings, now in the occupation of John Martyn weaver, situated in Cosford Street in Clare between the highway leading from Clare to Chilton Street on the west and town lands on the east with the south end abutting on Roger Martyn's messuage and the north end on a messuage belonging to the town of Clare. The condition of this sale is that my son John must pay £20 within 40 days of my decease in the south porch of Clare church to my ex'trix my daughter Margery Norfolke widow. If this sum is not paid, the property goes to my ex'trix, who is to sell it within a year and use money as follows: pay 20s to my son John, pay my debts and keep the remainder for her lifetime leaving it to her children. If John pays the £20, my ex'trix is to pay my debts and keep any money left for herself. All my other goods I give to my ex'trix to the intent that she may perform my will. She is to enter into a bond to perform my will with Mr Almott Clench of Much Braxted in Essex, whom I desire to be overseer of my will. Wit. Robert Hutchin senior, Susan Clench, John Barrett. Pr. at Bury 14 December 1630.

138. R(W) JOHN BLOWE of Eye, gentleman. 11 September 1630.

Commends soul to God trusting to have everlasting joy in the world to come.
I give and bequeath to my wife Alice and her heirs my messuage wherein I dwell with its yards and garden. She is to sell it within 2 years of my death with the direction of William Pennynnge of Eye. Out of this money I bequeath £10 each, to be paid a year after the sale, to my children Barnaby, Frances and Elizabeth Blowe and Christian Fassett. I bequeath the rest of my goods and chattels to my wife and make her ex'trix. Wit. Robert Pennynge, Thomas Burges, Nicholas Cullham, William Pennynges. Pr. at Bury 14 December 1630.

139. R(W) ROBERT BEANE of Bury St Edmunds, clothier. 8 July 1630.

Bequeaths soul to God.
I give to the poor people in Westgate Street in Bury 10s to be given to them within a week of my decease. I give to Cicely my daughter, wife of Edmund Tillet, £3 and my great brass pot within 3 months. I give my daughter Dorothy, wife of Francis Baker, £4 within a month. I give my daughter Elizabeth Beane £10 to be paid within a year, and one of my feather beds, a feather bolster, 2 feather pillows, 2 pillowbeeres, my best daunce chest, a pair of my best sheets save one, 6 table napkins, my half-headed bedstead, 1 pair of blankets and a coverlet. All the rest of my goods, debts and plate I give to my daughter Margaret to pay my debts and bring my body decently to the ground, and I make her ex'trix. Supervisor: my brother William Beane and I give him for remembrance a gold ring with a stone in it. Wit. Thomas Biggs, Caleb Browne. Pr. at Bury 14 December 1630.

59

140. W(R) AUGUSTINE SCARFFE (X) of Stanton, husbandman.
6 December 1630.

Bequeaths soul to God.
I bequeath to my wife for life all my land and all my goods. After her decease I give all my land to my son George for his life, and then my freehold land to my grandson George and his heirs for ever. But, if the latter dies before he is 21 leaving no heir, then my grandson, the son of William Wyborough, is to inherit this land. My copyhold land I give to my grandson Augustine, son of my son George. If Augustine dies, this land is to go to my daughter Mary and her husband Roger Rafe. After my wife's decease, I bequeath all my cattle, or the full value thereof as prized in my inventory, to my 2 daughters. All the rest of my household stuff is to be equally divided between my son and 2 daughters. Ex'trix: my wife Elizabeth. Wit. William Brett (X), Robert Fuller, John Sutton. Pr. at Bury 20 December 1630.

141. W(R) MARY CATER (X) of Lidgate, widow. 16 October 1630.

Commends soul to God and hopes to be one of the elect children of God. To be buried in Lidgate churchyard.
I give and bequeath to my son Thomas Cater a flockbed, a bolster, a blanket and a feather bolster. Also I give him a little hutch, a middle kettle, a little kettle, a hogshead, a tub, a cheese press, 6 pewter platters, 3 pairs sheets, 1 pillowbeere, a table cloth, 2 silver spoons, 2 cushions, my little table in the chamber next the stable and a wicker chair. I give to his wife my pillion and pillion cloth. I give to my daughter Katherine my livery cupboard in the parlour, the table and 4 joined stools, one bedstead in the chamber with a flockbed, a flock bolster, a feather bolster, 2 pillows, 1 blanket and a coverlet, my least brass pot, a kettle, a great posnet, 6 pewter dishes, my least pewter candlestick, 2 silver spoons, a chest, 3 pairs sheets, 1 pillowbeere, 1 yard kercher, a table cloth, my linen wheel, a milk keeler, a great barrel, one of my best petticoats, my best hat, a pair of cobirons, a fire pan and a pair of tongs in the parlour. I give to my sister Alice a cloth gown and a petticoat. I give to my sister Elizabeth my best gown and best cloak. I give my brother Thomas Cater my warming pan, a pair of sheets, 1 pillow and 1 pillowbeere. I give my maid Margaret a red petticoat, my white waistcoat, an old hat, a ruff, a coif and a cross cloth, a pair stockings and my best shoes. I give to the poor people of Lidgate 20s to be paid on the day of my burial by my exor. All the rest of my goods I give to my son John whom I make exor. Wit. Richard Evered, Thomas Evered, Richard Halles. Pr. at Bury 20 December 1630.

142. R(W) STEPHEN EVERITT (X) the elder of Wicken [Cambs].
10 December 1630.

In infirmities of old age. Bequeaths soul to God and hopes to be a partaker in a joyful resurrection.

I give my son Robert my 2 lakes with the 3 fishponds at the end of them. I give my grandson Robert Chambers 3 other lakes lying in 3 separate places between the Alder lake and Bayrdsway hill. I also give him a red cow calf. I give all the rest of my goods, my debts and funeral charges being paid out of them, to be equally divided amongst my 5 children: Robert, Joan, Margaret, Anne and Mary. My son Robert and my son-in-law William Chapman are to divide my goods and I appoint them my exors. Wit. Zachary Bentham, William Cassam (X), William Churchine (X).
Memorandum: the 3 lakes bequeathed to Robert Chambers are to be held on his behalf by William Cassam the younger and Robert Everitt. Pr. at Bury 20 December 1630.

143. R(W) FRANCIS SPALDING (X) of Tuddenham. 10 December 1630.

Commends soul to God and trusts to be saved by merits of Jesus Christ. To be buried in Tuddenham churchyard.
I give to my wife Alice £5, to my daughter Anne £5, and to my grandchild Elizabeth Spalding 40s. I give my wife the bedstead and bed in the chamber where I now lie with all its furniture, and the chests, stools, chairs and all other household stuff in the same chamber. I give my son William a boarded standing bedstead in the solar, a flock bed, a bolster, a covering, a sheet and a blanket belonging to it. I give my son Thomas my apparel and one of my scythes. I will that my house be sold after my decease, and my legacies paid after its sale. It is my will, to which my wife Alice has agreed, that she shall make no claim of thirds in the house. I give the residue of the money from the sale of my house to be equally divided between my sons John, William and Thomas. I give the residue of my goods to my son John, whom I make exor. Wit. Henry Claye, Robert Jellye. Pr. at Bury 20 December 1630.

144. R(W) JOHN HALL (X) of Bury St Edmunds, horse bell maker. 6 October 1630.

Commends soul to God.
I will and devise to my loving wife Margaret for life my messuage in Risbygate Street, now in the tenure of Thomas Harrison. She is to keep the house wind and water tight, and after her decease I give it to my son John. If wife fails to keep the house in repair, then it is to go immediately to my son or his guardian, if he is under age. I give to Margaret my daughter £20 to be paid by my son John 2 years after my wife's decease. If she dies before then, the £20 is to be paid to the child my wife is now with if it be a male child, but if a female my son John is to keep this sum. The house wherein I now dwell in the Brackland in Bury is now mortgaged. My mind is that it should be sold by my ex'trix and, after the mortgage has been redeemed, the overplus shall be put out by my wife. The interest is to be used for her maintenance and that of my children

during her lifetime, and after her decease the capital sum is to be equally divided between my daughter Grisel and the child my wife is now with when they are 21. If my wife remarries her husband must enter into a bond to pay my legacies. After my debts and funeral expenses have been paid, I give all the rest of my moveables to my wife Margaret, whom I make ex'trix. Wit. George Ankerson, Henry Bull, Robert Walker. Pr. at Bury 4 January 1630/31.

145. R(W) WILLIAM WELLES of Stowmarket, yeoman. 10 March 1627/28.

Commends soul to God and hopes to live in everlasting happiness.
I give to the poor of Stowupland 10s to be distributed at the discretion of my ex'trices. I give to my son George my house and adjoining 7 acres of land now in the occupation of John Sowgate junior, on condition he pays Alice my wife £10 p.a. in quarterly payments. If George refuses to pay this annuity I give the tenement and land to my wife for ever. I give my son George my house with adjoining 2 acres of land now occupied by Richard Pratt on condition he pays my daughter Joan an annuity of £3 in quarterly payments. After my wife dies, Joan's annuity is to be increased by 5s a quarter. If George defaults, Joan is to have the property for ever. I give to my son George a one acre pightle lying between the land of Robert Byrde to the north and that of Margaret Tyler widow to the south, on condition he pays 20 marks to my ex'trices within 10 months of my decease. If he fails, I give the pightle to my wife and my daughter Anne and their heirs. I give my son George a 2 acre pightle called Newgate, on condition he pays my daughter Anne £33 6s 8d in 4 instalments. If he defaults this pightle goes to Anne. My daughter Anne is to pay 40s each on 1 May 1603 [sic, but must mean 1633] to Alice and William Scotchmer and John Glover in satisfaction of a legacy in the will of my son William Welles. I give my son George a pightle called Plumton, which I purchased of Robert Tedgell, on condition he pays my daughter Joan £4 on 1 May 1631, and my daughter Alice £5 a year after my wife's decease and another £5 3 years later. If George defaults I give this pightle to daughters Joan and Alice. I will that my ex'trices shall hold the pightle called Brasiers until the Michaelmas after my death. All payments by my son George are to be made in the south porch of Stowmarket church. I give all the moveables which were my wife's before we married to her, and all the rest of my goods are to be divided between my ex'trices and daughter Joan. Ex'trices: wife and daughter Alice. Wit. Frances Codde, Thomas Scotchmer. Pr. at Bury 3 January 1630/31.

146. R(W) THOMAS PERKYN of Bury St Edmunds, physician. 16 December 1630.

Bequeaths soul to God.
I give and bequeath to my loving wife Lettice for her life all my houses and lands in Terling and Chelmsford in Essex, and after her decease to

my 2 daughters Rebecca and Mary. I also give my wife all my houses and land in Bury for life, and then to my 2 daughters. I will that my wife has the use of all my plate and bedding for life, and that after her decease they should be divided between my 2 daughters with benefit of survivorship. The residue of my goods, debts and household stuff I bequeath to my wife, whom I make ex'trix. I give my kinswomen Barbara Lawrence and Mary Bryant 20s each to be paid within 2 months of my death. Wit. on 21 December 1630 by John Hyll, Anne Woolverstone. Pr. at Bury 3 January 1630/31.

147. R(W) THOMAS PRETTY of Eye, woollen weaver. 28 October 1630.

Bequeaths soul to God and trusts to have everlasting life.
I give to my eldest son George my messuage in Castle Street in Eye, wherein I now dwell, and all my free and copyhold lands and meadows. And I also bequeath to him a posted bed and a cupboard in the parlour, the biggest brass kettle, a pair of malt querns and a salting trough. I give my son John the loom he works with and a wheel. I give my youngest son Edmund my messuage and yard in the Borough of Eye and now in the tenure of Charles Wade and Grace Swett, and the loom he works with, a wheel standing in the chamber and a pair of warping bars. I give my daughter Jane the long table, the cupboard table and the new kettle. I give all my other goods and household stuff to be equally divided between my sons and daughters: John, Edmund, Elizabeth, Jane and Dorothy. I give my son John £15 to be paid within 6 months of my decease, and £15 to my daughter Elizabeth to be paid within 2 years. I give Jane £15 to be paid within 3 years and Dorothy £15 to be paid within 4 years. These legacies are to be paid in the south porch of Eye church. Within one month of my decease, my son George must be bound in the sum of £100 to my kinsman John Darbye of Gislingham to pay my legacies. I give my daughter Mary £4, which John Brampton gentleman owes me as due from his wife Frances, late wife of John Fulcher of Eye. I give my grandchildren John and Judith Dunkon £2 each: 20s to be paid when they are put out as apprentices and 20s when their time has expired. I give my son George my lease of the Long Meadow, and make him exor. Wit. John Bond, Thomas Gyssinge, John Shene. Pr. at Bury 10 January 1630/31.

148. R(W) GEORGE SPARROWE of Langham, yeoman. 12 December 1630.

Bequeaths soul to Jesus Christ and through faith is sure of salvation. I give to my son George 40s to be paid within 1 year by my exor. I give 40s each to my sons-in-law Thomas Fyrman, George Makyn, Thomas Callowe, Abraham Isaac, John Darkinge and Robert Locke to be paid within 1 year by my ex'trix. I give £20 to Thomas Fyrman to be paid in 2 halves within 2 years, and £10 to Robert Locke within a year as due to him by an obligation. I give to my daughter Margery, wife of John Darkinge, £20 to be paid at 40s p.a. I give £10 to my grandson George Darkinge when he is 21. These legacies are to be paid in my house. I give my son Thomas an arable close in Langham called Castle Ditch and lying between William Browne's land to the west and my son Thomas's land called Castle Ditch [a field east of the church: *VCH*, I, 1911, p. 624] to the east. I also give him the house where he now dwells with yard, garden and orchard and a barn called Tile Barn next to the yard and the land it stands on called Barn Yard. I also give him a little hempland lying at the south end and east side of a piece of pasture next to Langham parsonage and the piece of pasture itself which is next to Langham church; the two together contain 1½ acres. The land left to Thomas is to be in the hands of my ex'trix until the Michaelmas after my decease. I give my son Edward a close called Ryders and an adjoining spong, which lies between the lands of John Lurkyne and William Browne, and a close called Whites; 8 acres in all. Edward must pay my daughter Rebecca £100 a year after my decease or forfeit to her the property left to him. Until this £100 has been paid to Rebecca, Edward must not fell, lop or shred any trees or bushes on this land except what is needed to fence it. I give my son Edward my messuage in Bedfield with barns, stables, garden, orchard and its pasture and arable land now in tenure of Robert Sparrowe of Bedfield. Until the Michaelmas after my decease my ex'trix is to hold this property. To my wife Agnes 2 meadows in Langham called Bockhowse and Margarett at the hawe, and a parcel of arable called Barn Yard and lying next to Langham Hall ground. After her decease my son Thomas is to have Backhowse meadow, except for half an acre next to Margarett at the hawe, which with the latter meadow and the Barn Yard I give to my son Edward. I give my wife Agnes the messuage I live in with its barns, stables, hay houses, garden, orchard, and adjoining croft and a 5 acre arable pightle held copyhold of the manor of Ixworth Priory, and which I purchased from Robert Page. I give this property with a pasture close called Parsons and a piece of pasture called Little Castle ditch to my wife to dispose where she shall think fitting. I give her all my goods and chattels, bonds and money for ever and make her ex'trix. She is not to ask for thirds of my closes called Ryders and Whites, but may do so from the land left to my sons George, Thomas and Edward. Wit. John Frost, William Marketon, Thomas Syer senior (X), Thomas Syer junior. Pr. at Bury 12 January 1630/31.

149. R(W) MARY CARTER (X) of Barningham, widow. 7 August 1630.

Gives soul to God my maker. To be buried in Barningham churchyard. I give my son Andrew a bed as it now stands full furnished in the parlour. I give my son Thomas the bed he lies on and another flockbed in the ceiled chamber. I give my son Nathaniel a bed as it stands at the backside of the chimney and the flockbed that Kent lies on. I give my 2 daughters 2 beds as they stand in the little chamber, and a chest that stands at my bed's head with all its contents to be equally divided between them, and a box in the parlour with all that is therein. I give my daughter Anne a livery cupboard in the hall, and to my daughter Alice a livery table in the parlour. The rest of my goods I give to the payment of £25 to my son Andrew; anything that remains is to be equally divided among my children by my son John whom I make exor. Wit. Dorothy Bobbye. Pr. at Bury 21 September 1630.

150. R(W) ALICE CRICKE (X) of Milden, widow. 15 June 1630.

I give my daughter Margaret's first child Mary 40s, my best featherbed and all that belongs to it, a livery cupboard and 2 joined stools in the white chamber. I give Alice Mayer £5, a warming pan, a spice mortar, a pair of sheets, a pair of pillowbeeres and a joined frame. I give to my daughter Joan's eldest son, Francis Gates, £5 if Alice Mayer dies. I give my daughter Joan a tick flockbed and all that belongs to it. My brewing copper is to be equally divided between my daughters Margaret and Joan. I give my daughter Joan my biggest brass pot. I give my daughter Alice's 2 sons, Michael and John Fowle, 50s each and to John a flockbed and all that belongs to it. I give my daughter Mary the table in the hall, 4 joined stools, the feather bed in my chamber, a great chest and a box that stands on it in a chamber next to the hall; also a brass pot, a posnet, the biggest kettle and smaller ones, and one of the great barrels. The pewter I leave to be parted between my daughters Margaret and Mary, and my linen between all my daughters equally. Exors: Mr James Daniell of Acton and William Clarke of Acton. No witnesses. Pr. at Bury 7 December 1630.

151. R(W) MARY HADLOCKE (X) of Whatfield, widow.
26 November 1630.

Commends soul to God trusting to be made partaker of life everlasting. All my moveable goods are to be sold by my exor and the money used to pay my legacies. I give my sons Samuel and Robert 10s each. I give Beatrice, daughter of my son Samuel, £10 when 21 and £10 when 21 to Alice daughter of my son Robert. If Beatrice dies before she is 21, my son Samuel is to have her legacy. I give 5s to the poor of Whatfield to be paid after probate of my will. Any money left after paying these legacies I give to be equally divided among the children of my son Robert (except Alice) when 21. If Alice dies her legacy of £10 is to be divided amongst her brothers and sisters. Exor: my son Samuel, or if he refuses to act, William Grymwoode of Whatfield. Wit. John Asheley (X), Richard Wyles, James Maye (X). Pr. at Bury 20 December 1630.

152. R(W) NICHOLAS SKEVINGTON (N) of Brandon Ferry.
30 December 1630.

I give to Susan my wife all my moveable goods to pay my debts and the overplus to her own disposing. Wit. Thomas Jeninges, Thomas Scott, Elizabeth Madwell. Let. ad. granted to testator's son Edward at Bury 3 January 1630/31.

153. R(W) THOMAS CASBORNE of Burwell [Cambs], yeoman.
21 December 1628.

Commends soul to God trusting to be saved.
I give to Margaret my wife, until my son Thomas is 24, the messuage
wherein I dwell and all my freehold land in Burwell, my copyhold land
next to the messuage and 4½ acres of freehold land. After Thomas
inherits he must pay my sons William and Robert £40 each at the age of
22 in the north porch of Burwell church. If Thomas defaults, I bequeath
to William my 10 acres freehold land purchased from my late father
Thomas Casborne and from John Parkyn, and to Robert the copyhold
and freehold land on the north side of my messuage. I give my wife 22
acres copyhold land in Burwell until my son John is 24. If John dies
without heirs, I bequeath this land to my 3 youngest children: William,
Robert and Alice. After he is 24 Thomas is to pay my wife £5 p.a. in lieu
of dowry; she has power to distrain. If Thomas troubles my wife about
any legacy left her by the will of his grandfather John Casborne, then she
is to have for life a copyhold meadow called Pricke meadow. My wife is
not to chop or fell any timber trees or wood, except what is needed to
repair buildings and fences. I give my daughter Alice £35 when she is 21
on condition she does not demand from my wife any legacy given to her
by her grandfather John Casborne. I give my son Thomas the framed
table standing in my hall with the form belonging to it, a posted bedstead
in the parlour chamber and the biggest chest but one in the parlour. All
my other goods I give to my wife whom I make ex'trix. If either of my 2
youngest sons depart this life before receiving his portion, the other is to
be his heir. Wit. Ezechiell Parkyn (X), Thomas Butcher, Thomas
Freiston, John Costen. Pr. at Bury 8 January 1630/31.

154. R(W) NICHOLAS CHEESEWRIGHT (X) of Chippenham
[Cambs], yeoman. 1 December 1630.

Commends soul to God.
I give Susan my wife my red heifer, my best bed save one with the
bedding, a coverlet, 2 blankets, a pair sheets, and her board and diet in
my house for 3 months after my decease at the cost of my exor. I give her
£5 p.a. 2 bushells rye, 2 bushells barley and a load of thorns are to be
given to her every year by my exor. My exor is to give my wife security
for these payments, which are to be made quarterly. I give my house and
land, held by copy of court roll of the manor of Chippenham, to my son
John. I give John Fuller, my wife's son, 10s and to her son Thomas Fuller
20s to be paid within 2 years of my decease. I give my sister Agnes £3 to
be paid at 20s p.a. I give my godson Nicholas Cheesewright £5 when he is
21. I give my brother Richard Cheesewright 40s and my cousin Edward
Cheesewright 20s. I give my servants Mathew Norman 20s, William
Gilbert 10s, Thomas Chapman 5s, Elizabeth Corder 20s and Grace Olde
5s, all to be paid within a year of my decease. I give 20s to be paid to the
poor of Chippenham at my burial, and £6 to be a stock; the interest to be

distributed to the poor every year on Good Friday. The rest of my goods I give to my son John whom I make exor., and I make my brother-in-law Thomas Leigh guardian to my son John until he is 21. If John dies without heirs before he is 21, I give my goods to my brothers Richard and William, my sister Agnes and my brother-in-law Thomas Leigh to be equally divided among them. Wit. William Chapman, Mathew Norman. Pr. at Bury 11 January 1630/31.
Thomas Leigh proved the will because John Cheesewright was a minor.

155. R(W) JOHN JEAMES of Polstead, yeoman. 10 October 1629.

Commends soul to God and trusts to have everlasting life.
I give my eldest son John my land called the Brach, with a barn on it, which I purchased from Sir William Waldgrave; and my messuage called Knoppitts with outbuildings, garden and land in Stoke by Nayland, which I bought from John Man. I also give John my messuage in which Henry Goldinge now dwells together with the Leyes and a meadow called Mabbes fen, all in Nayland, and my messuage called Smythes with outbuildings, garden and land in Stoke by Nayland. I give and bequeath to my son John my messuage with buildings, yard, garden, orchard and pasture in Boxford, which I purchased of Robert Sparrowe. I give Thomas my second son towards his bodily maintenance £3 to be paid over 3 years. I give my youngest son Richard my messuage called Berries in Stoke by Nayland with buildings and land, which I bought from John Grymes. I also give him for life my land called Malinges and Malinge fens in Stoke by Nayland, and after his death to be parted between his 2 daughters, Margaret and Mary. I give my daughter Anabel, wife of Edward Barnard, £15 to be paid within a year, and 20s each to her children to be paid within 2 years of my decease. I give my daughter Susan, wife of Jeffery Tanner, £3 and to her children Jeffery, Susan and Mary 20s each, all to be paid within 2 years. I give to Margaret, wife of my son Richard, 40s to dispose of at her own pleasure. All the rest of my goods I give to my son John, whom I make sole exor hoping he will carefully perform my will as my trust is in him. Supervisor: my trusty friend and son-in-law Edward Barnard, to whom I give 20s for his pains. Lastly I bequeath to Mary, wife of John Kingesburye, 10s to be paid within 3 years. Wit. Thomas Ward, Caleb Morris, Richard Robinson. Pr. at Bury 11 January 1630/31.

156. R(W) RICHARD PIRSON the elder of Thelnetham, linen weaver. 19 December 1630.

Commits soul to God.
I give my son Richard, towards paying £40 of debts I owe to several persons, 4 pieces of land and pasture in Thelnetham: 1 acre freehold next to land of William Howchine clerk (sometime Cages) on the south and abutting on the highway to the east; half an acre copyhold of manor of Thelnetham and lying next to the first piece; half an acre held copyhold

of the same manor and lying near Alestones meere, and 5 rods copyhold of Thelnetham rectory, which abutts on the highway to the east and on Abottes Wood to the west. I give and bequeath to Richard my son and his wife Mary all my other land and tenements in Thelnetham after the decease of my wife Avis, to whom they are left for life. Richard must pay £20 each to my daughters Anne and Mary at the rate of £5 p.a. each after my wife's death. The payments are to be made in the porch of Thelnetham church. They have benefit of survivorship and the right to distrain. I give all my goods and chattels to my wife Avis towards paying my debts and funeral charges and proving my will, making her ex'trix. If she refuses to act, I make my son Richard exor and give him all my goods, and if he too refuses to act then my brother William Pirson is to be my exor and have my goods. Wit. William Cordie (X), Richard Woorledge (X), William Payne, John Payne.

Codicil, bearing same date as will: I give to Rose my daughter my 2½ acre pightle called Little Ayers in Thelnetham. She must, when 21, assure to John Wyard of Wattisfield by surrender in the manor court 2 acres copyhold land in a close in Thelnetham which abuts on Brockhold way. Until 1 year after Rose has done this, my wife is to hold the pightle left to her. I will that my wife has right to take firewood from the 4 pieces of land left to my son Richard, and to sell it towards the payment of my debts if she acts as my ex'trix, but not otherwise. If Richard refuses to pay my debts of £40, the 4 pieces of land left to him for that purpose are to go to my ex'trix or exor. Wit. John Payne, Richard Pirson (X), William Payne. Pr. at Bury 10 January 1630/31.

157. R(W) WILLIAM HIXE (X) of Denston alias DENERDISTON.
14 October 1630.

Commends soul to God.
I give to William my son 20 marks to be paid within 3 months on condition he gives my daughter Mary a release and acquittance for all debts owed to me by her husband John Bryde. If my son troubles my ex'trix he is to have but 5s. I give my daughter Mary Bryde all my household goods, ready money, bonds, debts, leases and moveables and make her sole ex'trix. I desire my loving good friend Walter Payne of Boxford, clothier, to be overseer of my will. Wit. Thomas Raye, John Raye. Pr. at Bury 10 January 1630/31.

158. R(W) JOHN CATER (X) of Great Livermere, husbandman.
17 January 1630/31.

Bequeaths soul to God in expectation of everlasting life. To be buried at Great Livermere.
I give and bequeath to my daughter Mary my featherbed whereon I now lie with the bedstead, covering, blanket and sheets now used with it. Also my great chest in the chamber where I commonly lie, my long table in the hall, my brass pot, my mortar, my malt querns, my cupboard and a

joined chair. I give my daughter Margaret my little joined table in the hall, my great kettle, my flockbed and trundle bedstead with the covering and sheets belonging as they are in the chamber where I now lie. All the rest of my goods and chattels I give to my son Ralph, whom I make exor. Wit. John Cooke, William Noble. Pr. at Bury 24 January 1630/31.

159. R(W) STEPHEN BAKER (X) of Hepworth, husbandman.
11 January 1630/31.

Bequeaths soul to God. Body to be buried in Hepworth churchyard.
I give all my moveable goods to my wife Anne according to my promise made to her in consideration that she would be my wife. After her death her daughter Margaret is to have my goods as I promised before I was married to her mother, and in consideration of the pains she has taken with me in my lifetime. Wit. Giles Fuller (X), Richard Barker. Pr. at Bury 31 January 1630/31 to widow.

160. R(W) ALICE JACKMAN (X) of Bury St Edmunds, widow.
15 September 1621.

Bequeaths soul to God and trusts to have remission of sins.
I give Alice Cooper my grandchild when she is 24 or marries a featherbed, a feather bolster, a pillow, a coverlet, a pair blankets, a pair sheets and a posted bedstead as it stands in the vaunce floor, and wherein my son and his wife now lie, and a chest with its contents. I give my god-daughter Alice Bowler 1 pair sheets. All the rest of my goods I give to my son Edmund Jackman, whom I make exor. Wit. John Jewell, Richard Cooper (X), George Baxter (X), Anne Jewell.
Codicil, dated 1 October 1624: I give to my grandsons Richard and George Cooper when they are 24 a flockbed and flock bolster each. Wit. John Jewell, Richard Cooper. Pr. at Bury 20 January 1630/31.

161. R(W) LUKE GRAYE of Fordham [Cambs], husbandman.
20 September 1619.

Bequeaths soul to God trusting to have forgiveness of sins.
I give to Magdalene my wife my messuage and close with half an acre adjoining land held copyhold of the Duchy of Lancaster manor and which I have surrendered into the hands of Thomas Hinson and Edward Graye, both copyhold tenants of the manor. After my wife's decease, I bequeath the messuage and land to my sons Thomas, William and Luke. I give my son John half an acre in Barrowe field lying next to the Green way on the south and with west end abutting on Edward Graye's land; 1 acre in Kettinge Hall field next to Edward Graye's land on east and with south end abutting on Chippenham nether way; and half an acre in Little Hales next to Thomas Hinson's land on south and with west end abutting on Edward Graye's land. I give my son Robert half an acre in Little Hales next to Thomas Chessewright's land on south and with west end abutting

on Edward Graye's land; half an acre in Barrowe field next to Edward Graye's land on east and with south end abutting on Freckenham way; and half an acre in Kettingham field next to Thomas Kinge's land on east and with south end abutting on Thomas Chessewright's land. I give my son Seth half an acre land between meres in Barrowe field next to Thomas Chessewright's land on west and with south end abutting also on his land; half an acre in the same field next to the land of Thomas Gilbert on south and the west head goes over Three Went path; 1 acre in Ketting hall field between Duke of Lancaster's land now occupied by William Randall and with south end abutting similarly; and 3 rods land in Biggyn field next to Edward Graye's land on north and with east end abutting on Exning way. I give my daughter Joan 5 rods land in Ketting hall field next to Robert Page's land on west and with north end abutting on Vicar's land. My wife is to occupy all this land left to my children during her life. I also give her all my goods, corn and household stuff towards her better maintenance and the bringing up of my children. I make her ex'trix. Wit. Thomas Hynson, Edward Graye. Pr. at Bury 26 January 1630/31.

162. R(W) STEPHEN FULLER (X) of Bardwell, husbandman. 22 February 1628/29.

Commends soul to God.
I give my wife Anne for life the tenement wherein I dwell with the homesittings, pightles and yards, and she is to keep the buildings and fences in repair. After her death, I bequeath this property to my son Stephen on condition he pays my legacies to my other children as follows. I give my son Charles £10 to be paid within 18 months, to my daughters Anne and Alice £18 each within 2 years, to my son John £10 and to my son James £15 within 3 years. All have benefit of survivorship. If Stephen defaults the other children are to have the land and pay the legacies. My son James's portion is to be paid into the hands of my cousin William Syllet, who is to give him the money when he is 25. I give all my goods to my wife Anne and make her ex'trix. Wit. William Sillett, Richard Wharton, Henry Daldye, Thomas Onge, Reginald Whitney. On the same day the testator surrendered his copyhold land held of the manors of Wykes and Bardwell Hall to the use of his will by the hands of William Syllett, Henry Daldye and Richard Wharton, all copyhold tenants. Pr. at Bury 7 December 1630.

163. R(W) WILLIAM STRONGE (X) of Mildenhall. 5 December 1630.

Bequeaths soul to God and to his saviour Jesus Christ.
I give my wife Agnes a cupboard, a table, 2 coffers, a form, a kettle, a platter, a roasting iron, a sheet, a coverlet, a pair of bedsteads and a bed. And I give her 2 bushels of barley and a piece of rye growing at Langmere pond, and 2 bullocks to take her choice of one at May Day. I give James Stronge the younger a blage mare and a brindle burlinge with a white back; James Stronge the elder is to have the use of them. All the

rest of my moveable goods, corn and cattle I give to my son Simon, whom I make exor. Within a year of my decease he is to pay my 2 daughters, Joan and Grace, 10s each, and to my son James 5s within 1 month. Wit. Thomas Barton, Robert Grengres (X). Pr. at Bury 24 January 1630/31.

164. R(W) JOHN GROVE (X) of Sudbury, husbandman. 8 April 1629.

Commits soul to God and hopes to be a partaker of everlasting joys in the kingdom of heaven.
I give Philippa my well-beloved wife for her life the messuage in which I dwell in the parish of St Gregory in Sudbury. If she refuses to keep this house in repair this gift shall be void. After her death I bequeath it to my grand-daughter Elizabeth daughter of Daniel Hall. She must pay her sister Thomasine 40s p.a. for 4 years, and must not allow her father or mother to dwell in my house at any time. Remainder to Thomasine if Elizabeth dies. I give my 2 daughters Ellen Hall and Katherine Cannt 2s each. All the residue of my moveables I give to my wife for life and after her decease to my grandchildren Elizabeth and Thomasine Hall. Ex'trix: wife. Wit. Thomas Ingrome (X), Philip Clarke. Pr. at Bury 31 January 1630/31.

165. R(W) THOMAS SWALLOWE of Elmswell, yeoman. 12 November 1626.

Bequeaths soul to God.
I give to my sister-in-law Frances, widow of my brother Edward Swallowe clerk, 6 pieces of land in Northfield in Rickinghall Inferior, mortgaged to me by John Hart on 1 February 1623/24. I give my newphew Edward, son of my late brother Edward, £20 to be paid by my ex'trix when he is 21. I give £13 6s 8d each to my brother's other children, Thomas, Anne, Elizabeth and Francis, when 21. Benefit of survivorship. I give all my household goods, money, plate, debts, cattle and moveables to my sister-in-law Frances Swallowe and make her ex'trix. She is to pay my debts and legacies. Wit. Thomas Kettleborowe, Roger Aggas, John Smyth, Edward Crosse (X). Pr. at Bury 31 January 1630/31.

166. R(W) KATHERINE KENT (X) of Chippenham [Cambs], widow. 16 December 1630.

Commends soul to God hoping to be saved through Jesus Christ. To be buried in Chippenham churchyard.
I give my son Thomas £5 to be paid within a year of my decease. I give my son William £5 to be paid within 2 years. My son John is to bring up and keep my son William until he is 21. I give Margaret Crane all my apparel, except one blue coat, and 10s. All the rest of my goods I give to my son John whom I make exor. I will that he sows with barley seed 4 acres of land for my son Thomas. Wit. James Fyson, William Cheese-write, Richard Clyngdowe. Pr. at Bury 24 January 1630/31.

167. R(W) EDITH GOULDINGE (X) of Cavendish, widow of John Goulding of Cavendish. 8 November 1630.

Bequeaths soul to God and trusts to have sins pardoned through Jesus Christ.

I give to John Goulding my son my best pair of sheets, best pillowbeere, best board cloth, best cushion, 2 of the best pewter dishes, 1 of the best pottengers, 1 candlestick, 1 of the best cupboard cloths, the best featherbed, the best bedstead, 2 blankets, 1 of the best bolsters and a dozen trenchers. I give my son Robert the next pair of sheets in goodness, 2 pewter dishes, 1 pillowbeere and a dozen trenchers. I bequeath my son William 1 pottenger, 2 pewter dishes and a dozen trenchers. I give my son Roger 1 pair sheets, 1 diaper tablecloth, 1 pillow, 1 pillowbeere, 2 pewter dishes, a pewter pottenger, a pewter candlestick, a dozen trenchers, a livery table, a great chest and a buffet stool. I bequeath my son Mark a pair sheets, 1 pillow and 1 pillowbeere, 2 pewter dishes and 1 dozen of trenchers. I give my son Thomas a feather bed and bedstead, a bolster, 2 blankets, 2 pewter dishes, 1 pillow and 1 pillowbeere, 1 pair sheets, a dozen trenchers and a square table. I give my son Richard 1 flockbed and bolster, 1 pair sheets, 2 blankets, 2 pewter dishes, a pillow, the warming pan, a pillowbeere, a cupboard cloth and a dozen trenchers. I give my sons Thomas and Roger a cupboard cloth apiece. I make my son John sole exor. I give my son Robert's children 5s apiece, saving Joan to whom I give my best gown. I give 5s each to the children of my sons William and Mark, and to those of my son-in-law John Jiggins, saving his daughter Edith to whom I give 10s. All the rest of my goods and money, not before disposed of, and whatever else is mine I give to my exor. Wit. Roger Bell. Pr. at Bury 1 February 1630/31.

168. R(W) WILLIAM WIFFIN of Haverhill, yeoman. 1 January 1630/31.

The unprofitable servant of God. Gives his spirit into hands of God and believes that through his only saviour Jesus Christ it will be placed in the company of his heavenly angels and blessed saints.

I give my wife Dorothy, so long as she remains unmarried, the lease of the house wherein I now dwell with the freehold land belonging to it, and all my household stuff. If she remarries, or when she dies, my daughter Mary is to have half household goods and my sons Richard and William are to share the other half. I give my son Richard a 3 acre copyhold pasture close in Haverhill called Cotes Croft, on condition he pays my daughter Mary an annuity of 40s at Michaelmas. If he defaults Mary is to have this land. I make my 2 sons Richard and William exors. Wit. John Hurst, William Myller. Pr. at Bury 7 February 1631/32.

169. R(W) EDMUND MORTLOCK (X) of Brandon, innholder.
14 December 1630.

Bequeaths soul to God in certain hope of life everlasting. To be buried in church or churchyard of Brandon.
I give to my son James and to Elizabeth my wife all the goods and chattels I now have for her widowhood. If she remarries James is to have them all immediately except a posted bedstead standing in the hall chamber with a featherbed, a feather bolster, 2 feather pillows, 2 blankets, a bird coverlet, a pair sheets and a danske chest which was hers, and no more. Wit. Bartholomew Smyth, Thomas Watts. Pr. no place given 7 February 1630/31.

170. R(W) FRANCIS HARDED of Cockfield, tailor. 1 May 1630.

Bequeaths soul to God hoping to be saved.
I give to John my son my copyhold tenement and land on condition he performs my legacies. I give my wife Dorothy free access to all the outhouses, and the right to live in my house and have the benefit of the hall fire. I give her an annuity of £3 to be paid quarterly by my son John, who is also to give her every year half a load of good 2-bond wood and a comb of apples. I give my daughter Abigail £7 to be paid 5 years after my decease, and if she has died to her daughter Katherine Harded. I give my son John my joined table as it now stands in the hall. I give all the rest of my goods to my wife for ever. Exor: son John. Wit. Thomas Milles, Robert Kinge (X). Pr. at Bury 5 February 1630/31.

171. R(W) WILLIAM FROST of Mildenhall, yeoman. 26 January 1630/31.

Commends soul to God and hopes to be amongst the elect and chosen people of God in the kingdom of heaven.
I bequeath to Alice my wife for life the house which I now dwell in with 4 acres adjoining copyhold pasture. After her death this goes to my grandson William Frost. I give Susan my daughter-in-law my freehold messuage in Mildenhall in a place called the Wyldmare for life, and then to her son John. I give my grandson William 2 acres copyhold land in Litley field lying next to the land of John Bowle and Giles Cobbyn. Until he is 30 my son Simon is to receive the profits of this land. I give my son Simon 2 acres copyhold land, lying next to the above piece, for his life and then to my grandson Thomas. I give Simon 2 pieces enclosed freehold pasture, containing 2 acres, and lying next to his land. My wife must deliver to my exors all bonds by which I am bound to her and my son-in-law John Bowle, or forfeit the property left to her. I give my wife Alice 4 of my bullocks and a gelding mare at her own choice, and 2 combs corn. I give her all the moveable goods which were hers before we

married. The rest of my goods, corn, cattle, growing grass and leases I give to my son Simon and make him exor. He is to pay and receive my debts and perform my will. No witnesses. Pr. at Bury 7 February 1630/31. It is noted that the testator died before his will could be read and confirmed by him.

172. R(W) THOMAS MASON of Beyton, yeoman. 30 October 1628.

Bequeaths soul to three persons of Trinity.
I give to my son Francis £20 and to my son Thomas £40 when 21. I give my daughter Mary £60 to be paid within 2 years of my decease. Benefit of survivorship. I give my sister Margery, wife of Richard Baker, 20s. All the rest of my goods I give to my well-beloved wife Sarah, whom I make sole ex'trix. Supervisors: my well-beloved in Christ Jeremy Holt and Thomas Goddard. Wit. Thomas Goddard clerk, Robert Rust. Pr. at Bury 7 February 1630/31.

173. R(W) RICHARD HAWYS of Hinderclay, yeoman. 18 October 1626

Commits soul to God trusting to be inheritor of kingdom of heaven.
I give my wife Frances for life all my tenements and lands in the town and fields of Hinderclay, and she must keep the buildings in repair and cause no strip or waste. After her decease I give my grand-daughter Mary Hobbard the tenement in Hinderclay wherein I now dwell with its land, and to my grand-daughter Elizabeth Hobbard my other tenement and land in Hinderclay that was sometime Worryns. After my wife's death I give my wife's daughter Grace Brett all those moveables that were my wife's before I married her, and all my other moveables I give to my grand-daughters Mary and Elizabeth. Ex'trix: wife. Wit. Gregory Carter (X), Thomas Williamson. Pr. at Bury 7 February 1630/31.

174. R(W) WILLIAM BUTCHER (X) of Lackford, servant to Mr Francis Croftes of Lackford. 13 February 1630/31.

Commends soul to God and Jesus Christ by whose merits he hopes to be saved.
I give to the poor of Lackford 20s to be distributed within 1 month at the discretion of my master Mr Francis Croftes. I give to Roger Butcher my kinsman £7, and to his 3 sisters 40s to be divided between them. I give to my sister's children £4 to be equally divided between them, and to William Butcher 40s. I give to Francis Nunne of Hengrave 4s. I give to the 4 almswomen of Hengrave 8s 6d. I give the money owing to me by John Frost, Miles Redgyn and the widow Anis as follows: 10s each to Edmund and Benjamin Croftes, sons of my master, and the rest to be equally divided amongst my master's maid servants. I give my master Mr Francis Croftes all the money owing to me for my wages. Francis Owles of Hengrave owes me 10s with some interest, which I bequeath to him

and his brother Thomas. I give 5s to Edmund Flaunders, one of my master's servants and to his 4 ploughmen the 5s William Stegell owes me. I give to the widow Land, who hath taken a great deal of pains with me in the time of my sickness, 5s, a pair of breeches and my cloak. I give to Rashe, one of my master's servants, a pair of breeches and to Ambrose Maye, another of his servants, my canvas doublet and a pair of breeches. The rest of my goods I give to William Whitbye of Stoke in Norfolk and to Henry Potter of Ropham in Norfolk and make them exors not doubting that they will faithfully perform my will. Wit. John Cocke, Richard Rogers. Pr. at Bury 17 February 1630/31.

175. R(W) THOMAS LILLY of Stansfield, yeoman. 17 December 1630.

Yields soul to God and hopes to be partaker of eternal blessedness in kingdom of heaven.

I give 20s to the poor people of Stansfield to be distributed at or soon after the day of my burial, and similarly 20s to the poor of Denston. I give my loving wife Margaret for ever, in satisfaction of her claims for dower or thirds, the messuage in Stansfield where I now dwell with buildings, yards, garden, lands and woods, which I bought of my brother-in-law, Francis Westroppe and which is settled on myself and my brother-in-law William Orbell. My exors are to have all that part due to me of the money, goods and personal estate of my wife's late uncle Stephen Ashwell, and all such money and legal charges as shall be ordered to be paid in respect of the suits engaged in by me against the exors of Stephen Ashwell, on which I have laid out much money. Within 3 months of my decease my wife must give a release in writing to Thomas Ashewell of Stradishall of all her rights in the lands and tenements in Stradishall which I lately sold to him. Within 6 months of my wife's decease her exors must pay £100 to such persons as I shall hereafter appoint. I give my wife 7 cows at her choice and my best gelding with sufficient fodder and stover to feed, keep and winter them until next May Day. I also give her all my household stuff and plate, and all other things in and about my house which are needful for her. My brother-in-law William Orbell is to assure to my wife and her heirs the property left to her, and is to pay an annuity of £20 charged on this property and payable to Alice Westrope, widow and mother of Francis Westrope. I give to William Orbell, my exor, for 16 years my lands and tenements, sometime my father's Thomas Lyllie, and lying in Stansfield, Poslingford and Chipley. After this term is up I give all this property to Thomas Lyllie, son of my brother John. All my other land and tenements I give to my exor to sell to pay my debts and legacies; also all my leasehold land and tenements and all my unbequeathed goods and chattels. I give my brother John 10s. I give Thomas, son of William Orbell, £100 to be paid within 4 years of my decease. I give to all my brothers' and sisters' children, except Thomas Lyllie and Thomas Orbell, £10 each to be paid when they are 24. I give to my aunt Coppinge £5 and to her son William 20s. I give to William Treake, who now keeps with me, 10s. Before he pays any of my other debts my exor is to free and discharge himself of several bonds amounting to £600 in which he stands bound with me. I give Sarah Kinge and John Hasted my servants 10s each. Wit. John Cooke, Thomas Wright. Pr. at Bury 14 February 1630/31.

176. R(W) GEORGE BROWNE of Finningham, husbandman. 30 August 1616.

Bequeaths soul to God.
I give my wife Susan for ever the cottage with yard and adjoining orchard at Sarisaneshill in Finningham, and lying on the west side of the tenement and yard of Henry Burges. She must bring up my children in consideration of this gift. I also give her all my goods and chattels and make her my ex'trix. Wit. John Talbott, Henry Burges, John Burges. Pr. at Bury 12 February 1630/31.

177. R(W) RICHARD DIX of Burwell [Cambs]. 4 November 1630.

Bequeaths soul to God.
I will that my wife Susan and my son Oliver shall have their dwelling in the East end of my house during their lives, and that my wife shall have the use of half my lodge with all other easements convenient for her. She shall have yearly one hundred of plain fen straw ready mown and she is to pay for its making. She is to have half my moveable goods. I give my son Richard 12d and my son Thomas 12d. I give my son Oliver my apparel and a flockbed with the bedding belonging to it. I give my daughter Elizabeth 2s 6d. I give my house to my son William and after his death his wife Rachel is to have it for her life. I make William my sole exor, but if he refuses to act my grandson Richard, son of my son Richard, is to have my house for ever. I will that William has free access to the oven to bake and to the cellar to lay corn in without any hindrance from Richard. Wit. Jeffery Vaisse (X), Michael Norman (X). Pr. at Bury 19 February 1630/31.

178. R(W) JOHN CLARKE (X) of Langham, yeoman. 8 February 1630/31.

Bequeaths soul to Jesus Christ through whose death I am sure of salvation.
I give to my nephew Edmund Clarke £15 to be paid within 1 year of my decease; to my nephew George Woodburne 20s within 2 years; to my nephew Robert Clarke £15 within 3 years; to my nephew Charles Woodburne £10 within 4 years; to my sister Anne Woodburne £6 within 2 years; to my nephews [sic] Elizabeth and Sarah Clarke £6 each within 6 years; to Anne and Tabitha Woodburne £6 each within 6 years; and to the children of Richard Lambert of Bury St Edmunds 40s each. I give 20s to the poor of Langham to be distributed at the discretion of the minister and churchwardens upon my funeral day or within 8 days. I make my

nephew John Clarke the elder of Pakenham, yeoman, my exor and I give him the messsuage wherein I now dwell with all my land in Langham, except for a piece of pasture in a close called Walsham Layes, until his son and my godson John Clarke the younger is 24 when he is to inherit this property. The piece of pasture in Walsham Layes I bequeath to my nephew Edmund Clarke together with all writings and scrolls belonging to it. I bought this land from William Hubbard of Occold. Within a month of my decease my exor is to enter into a bond of £200 with Thomas Syer the elder and William Browne, both yeomen of Langham, to pay my debts and legacies and perform my will. If my exor refuses to act or to enter into this bond, then my nephew Edmund Clarke is to be exor and receive the property left to John Clarke. Wit. Thomas Syer senior, William Browne, Thomas Syer junior. Pr. at Bury 17 February 1630/31.

179. R(W) JOHN ALDHAM of North Cove [formerly of Sapiston], gentleman. 1 January 1626/27.

Commends soul to God in full hope of redemption.
By a deed of feoffment, dated 7 December 1626, I have granted to Christopher Mutton and his son John, to the uses and purposes expressed in this my last will and testament, all my lands, manors, messuages, parsonages, mills, dove houses, lands and woods with appurtenances. All this property is to be to the use of my loving wife Jane during her life and after her death to that of my loving cousin and son-in-law Thomas Aldham of North Cove gentleman and his heirs. By an indenture, dated 4 December 1626, I sold to Richard Gurlinge a 99-year lease of the manor of Sapiston Grange, formerly in the possession of the dissolved Ixworth Priory, together with Sapiston rectory and the advowson of the vicarage, and all the buildings and land in Sapiston, Honington and Bardwell which lately belonged to my brother Thomas Aldham of Sapiston, gentleman and which was inherited by him from our late father Thomas Aldham gentleman. Richard Gurlinge is to hold this property to the use of my brother Thomas Aldham during the term of the lease made to the latter by our father. Thomas Aldham must permit my wife, and my cousin Thomas Aldham to enjoy the messuage and 2 acres adjoining the house, which I purchased of Hunt, and also 3 pightles which I have by an agreement set down by Sir William Spring and Sir Edmund Bacon. After the decease of my brother, this house and land are to remain to the use of my cousin Thomas Aldham for the remainder of the 99-year lease. I give 20s to the poor of North Cove, and of Worlingham and of Barnby, and £5 to the poor of Beccles. I give 20s to the poor of Sapiston and 40s to the poor of Wormegay in Norfolk. I give to Jane my dear and espoused wife for life all my lands and tenements in North Cove, Great and Little Worlingham, Ellough and Henstead. I also give her for life all my plate, household stuff, cattle, corn, implements of husbandry, carts and tumbrils. An inventory is to be made of all these goods, which are to pass

to my son-in-law Thomas Aldham and his wife Jane after my wife's decease. As she will have to pay great annuities and legacies, I also give my wife for life the land and tenements in Sapiston, which I purchased of Hunt and also all my houses and lands in Wormegay. She must keep the buildings in repair and cause no waste. My brother Thomas Aldham pays me a yearly rent of £40 at Michaelmas; if he pays my wife 20s p.a. he may keep the rest. He must allow my wife peaceably to enjoy the part of the tenement and 3 pightles now occupied by John Goodaye and all other property bequeathed to her and my son-in-law. If my brother troubles them, then the whole rent of £40 p.a. immediately becomes payable. My wife is to give my son-in-law and her dear daughter their board with that for 2 maids and 3 horses. I give my sister Wildes an annuity of £6 6s 8d, and her dwelling in part of the house she now lives in. If she tries to sell her annuity it shall cease. I give to her daughter Elizabeth Wyldes an annuity of £3, and to Nan and Edward Wildes annuities of £3 each. I give Thomas Wildes an annuity of £6 6s 8d, but if he is not content with it he will lose it. After his mother's decease he is to have her annuity as well as his abode in the same house if he thinks good. After my wife's death, the annuities to Elizabeth, Nan and Edward Wyldes shall cease, and my son-in-law Thomas Aldham is to pay them 100 marks each. He must also, within 3 years of inheriting, pay £30 each to the daughters of my sister Wether: Alice, Margaret, Elizabeth and Frances. After my wife's decease Thomas Aldham must pay an annuity of £3 to my godson William son of Henry Aldham. There came into my hands about £10 of goods belonging to Nan, wife of Francis Harper, for the bringing up of her 3 daughters. Although this sum is not sufficient for the purpose, I give them £5 each when 20. I give £5 each to Nan Suthese, John Poyner and to Wellin, and 40s each to John Page and Thomas son of Thomas Page. I give to those servants that shall be with me at the time of my death, and that have no other gift, 10s apiece. I give my daughter Joan a gold ring worth 10s and the same to my Valentine old Mistress Beere and to my niece Mary Aldham, who is here in the house with me. I give the like rings to my niece Mary Harne, to my sister [sic] Thomas Aldham and to Mary Goodaye. To my godson John Goodaye I give 10s, and to my godson John Harvey a piece of plate or 2 silver spoons of 20s value. I give John Elcocke my old servant £5. I will that my 3 sisters Mary, Christian and Margaret shall have gold rings worth 10s, and the posy that shall be engraved on them shall be 'the gift of a friend'. I give a like ring to Mrs Mutton. If Mr Reyner preaches my funeral sermon he shall have 20s, and I give to the reverend father Mr Davies 20s. Four coats of coarse black cloth shall be provided for the 4 poor men that shall be appointed to carry me to church, and 2 gowns for the poor women that shall wind me. I give to Beame's wife of Sapiston 10s. I give to John Goodaye a ring of the same price and engraven with the same posy as the others. My daughter Jane is to have her £100 as soon as it may be raised, and my son Aldham a seal of arms given him worth some 40s. When my estate comes to my son-in-law, he is to give an annuity of £20 to Henry Aldham of Wangford and after his death to his wife. I will that Jane my dear wife be sole ex'trix

of this my last will and testament, written with my own hand. Wit. Robert
Rayner, Charles Pangham, Philip Richardson (X), Christopher Mutton,
John Mutton. Pr. of will of John Aldham, formerly of Sapiston, at Bury
21 February 1630/31.

180. R(W) ALICE LEGAT (X) of Icklingham St James, widow.
1 January 1630/31.

Commends soul to God and hopes to enjoy salvation. To be buried in
Churchyard of St James, Icklingham.
I make my son Francis Parre my exor to pay my debts and bring my body
decently to the ground. I give my son John Parre 10s within a year, my
son Henry Parre 10s to be paid within 2 years and my son Robert Parre
10s within 3 years. I give my daughter Anne Mayhew and my grandson
Robert Mayhew 10s each within 4 years. I give my grandchildren John
and Elizabeth Bowman 10s each when 21. All the rest of my moveable
goods I bequeath to my son Francis Parre. Wit. John Fyrmage, William
Parson (X). Pr. at Bury 7 March 1630/31.

181. R(W) EDWARD SPALDING of Exning. 19 October 1630.

Bequeaths soul to God. To be buried in Exning churchyard.
I bequeath to Martha my wife for life all my house, land, corn and cattle.
After her decease I give to William my son the barn and the croft, and to
my son Richard all my lease lands sometime in the use of Thomas
Torladie, carpenter. I give to my son Edward my house that Johnson
dwells in, standing on the north side, and the shop with 3 rods land I
bought of John Redewlon and lying on the Mellhavens for life, and then
to my son William and his heirs. If my son Richard dies, his land is to be
divided between Edward and William. For paying rent capons, Edward is
to pay 2 and William 4. I give my daughter Margaret £10 within 2 years
and another £5 if my sons Richard and William have no heirs, to be paid
by the longer liver of them. I give to Margaret the bed and bedstead that
stands in the parlour with all that belongs to it, and the chest and little
table in the same room. I give my daughter Elizabeth 12d. Exors: wife
and son William, who are to keep my house in good repair. Edward is to
keep the house left to him in repair, and if he does not live there he is not
to put in a tenant to disturb the dwellers in the same yard, but my son
William is to pay him rent for the house, shop and 3 rods of land. Wit.
Peter Johnson, Richard Sherman. Pr. at Bury 1 March 1630/31.

182. R(W) RICHARD BARNARD of Nayland, tailor. 6 February
1630/31.

Commits soul to God and hopes to have eternal life.
I give my son Richard all my lands and tenements now in my possession,
and those that shall descend to me after the decease of my mother

79

Elizabeth Barnard. Until Richard is 21 my exor has full power to let the land and tenements and to receive the rents. In consideration of this, I bequeath my son to my exor to bring him up with meat, drink and apparel. When he is 21 my exor must give him an account of the surplus and pay it to him. I give my exor £20 for his pains to be taken in the bringing up of my son to write and read and make sufficient evidence between man and man. If my exor dies before my son is 21 he is to put himself out apprentice to some good trade. I give my son Richard 4 silver spoons, a jewel to wear about his neck, 2 silver whistles and my black suit of apparel. I give my exor my best jerkin and cloak, and my best stockings in token of my love and for the better usage of my son. All the rest of my goods I give to William Gattenward, clerk of Nayland, whom I make exor and in whom I repose my trust. Wit. Richard Coppine, Martin Taylor. Pr. at Bury 2 March 1630/31.

183. R(W) ELIZABETH SHEPPARD of Mendlesham, widow.
16 October 1630.

Commends soul to God and hopes for remission of sins.
I give my eldest son John all my goods and chattels on condition he, with all care and conscience, performs his father's will in seeing his brothers and sisters well brought up, paying their portions and does what I should have done as ex'trix of his will. I will that he pays my daughter Elizabeth £50 at the age of 19 when she is to receive her legacy of £350, and gives her the bedstead with 2 beds whereon I now lie with the curtains, hangings, coverlets, blankets, sheets, pillows and bolsters belonging to it, and all the linen I have made since my husband's death and all my flaxen yarn. John is to pay £9 each within a year to my 4 sons Edmund, William, Francis and Ambrose in place of their share of the household goods over and above the bedding and linen given to them by will. I will that John pays £5 each, within a year, to my sons Edmund and Thomas, and 15s p.a. for 4 years to my son William. John is to give 30s each to my sons Francis and Ambrose to buy themselves a piece of plate. Within a year he is to pay my daughter Elizabeth 40s and 20s each to my god-daughters Elizabeth and Dorothy Gibson. He is also to pay 20s to my sister Cooke, and 10s each to my old cousin Dunkon and to her daughter Susan Dunkon, to the widow Seaman, my cousin Wealey, Goodwife Nasy, Goodwife Beale and Goodwife Fayerweather, and 5s to Mary Nicholas. John is to give my sister Kempe my new gown, and to Mary Landemer and Philippa Brame, my former servants and now my son's, all my workday apparel to be parted between them at my exor's discretion. John is to pay 40s to Mary Landemer. I make him exor. Wit. Charles Gibson, Alice Bell, Barnaby Gibson, Thomas Sheppard. Pr. at Bury 2 March 1630/31.

184. R(W) RICHARD ELLIGOOD of Hitcham, cook. 28 February 1629/30

Commends soul to God and trusts to be in heaven for ever after the resurrection. To be buried in Hitcham churchyard.

I give and bequeath to Jane my loving wife for life my copyhold tenement in Hitcham called Sabardes and held of the manor Hitcham. It is divided into 2 parts occupied by Thomas and John Wright; I bought it of the former. If it pleases God to strike my wife with poverty so that the rent of the above tenement is not sufficient to maintain her, then I give it to her for ever. After my wife's decease the part of the tenement occupied by John Wright I give to my daughter Alice, wife of Robert Wood, for life. She must pay her daughter Anne Goodinge 16s p.a., and after Alice's death Anne Goodinge inherits the tenement. Within 2 years of my decease my wife is to sell a 1 acre piece of land in Buxhall called Grove, and pay my daughter Alice Wood 40s from the price. The rest of the money and all my goods I give to my loving wife and make her ex'trix. Wit. George Frenche. Pr. at Bury 20 November 1630.

185. R(W) ELIZABETH CROPLEY (X) of Bury St Edmunds, widow. 17 September 1630.

Commends soul to God.

I give 40s to the poor of the parish of St James to be distributed at the discretion of my exor. I give £5 each when 21 to my grandchildren Michael, Elizabeth, Jeremy and Henry, children of my son Henry Cropley, and to Elizabeth, Alice, Thomas and William, children of my daughter Elizabeth Payne. I give to Elizabeth, wife of my son Henry, my best tapestry coverlet in the great chamber. I give £55 each to my children Henry and Thomas Cropley and Elizabeth, wife of William Payne, to be paid within a year. I give £20 when 24 to Thomas, son of my deceased son Edward. I give 40s to Henry Heigham, 20s to John James, and 10s each to Mathew Ogden my ostler and to Christopher my servant, and to Anne Woodburne my servant. I give my daughter Payne all my apparel, both linen and woollen, 3 pairs sheets and 3 pairs pillowbeeres. The residue of my goods I give to my son Thomas and make him exor. Wit. Henry Adames, James Coppinge. Pr. at Bury 24 November 1630.

186. R(W) WILLIAM GAME (N) of Stanton, innholder. 5 December 1630.

He willed Susan his wife, within 2 years of his decease, to purchase a house to the value of £30 for his daughter Mary and her husband John Peck; this is to descend to their son William who must pay his sister Susan £5. He gave his daughter Frances £37 6s 8d when 21 on condition she assures to her brother Robert a backhouse belonging to the house late Mr Clynch's. When she has done this, Robert must pay Frances 20 marks. He willed that his horse mill, copper and brewing vessels should remain with his house, and he bequeathed them to his son Robert after his wife's decease. He gave all the rest of his goods to his wife Susan and made her ex'trix. Wit. Edward Feast, John Greene, Robert Fuller. Pr. at Bury 10 January 1630/31.

187. R(W) JAMES MIDGELY senior (X) of Brandon Ferry, shoemaker. 23 November 1630.

Bequeathed soul to God.
I give my son James my cloak and 2 cushions, one of tapestry work and one of darnacke. I give his 3 children 10s to be divided between them within 1 month of my decease. I give to James son of Thomas Fytt 10s within 1 month. I give my son Joseph a joined work bedstead with the bedding as it stands in the parlour next the entry. I give my son William the other bedstead in the same parlour with its bedding. The rest of the joined work stuff in the parlour is to be divided between my 2 sons Joseph and William, and I give them one of my best cushions each. I give Joseph the bedstead ready furnished in the chamber where I usually lie, and the other in that chamber to William. I give my daughter Margaret Thurston a tapestry work cushion. I give my son-in-law Thomas Fauxe all my wearing apparel except the cloak given to my son James. I give my sons Joseph and William all my horse beasts, mares and colts, all my milk cows and swine, and all my other goods to pay my debts and legacies. If Joseph wishes he may pay William the value of his share of my goods as they are prized. I give my daughters Amy and Faith 30s each. Supervisor: John Ransome. Exors: sons Joseph and William. Wit. Thomas Jeninges, Richard Fothergell. Pr. at Bury 10 January 1630/31.

188. R(W) GEORGE MILLS (X) of Cockfield, husbandman. 19 November 1630.

Bequeaths soul to God and hopes to be saved.
I give 20s to the poor of Cockfield to be distributed where most need is at my burial or on the next Sabbath day. I give John Mills my brother my copyhold tenement with the outhouses and 9 acres land, on condition he pays my legacies. Legatees have power to distrain. I give 10s each when 21 to John, Richard, Elizabeth and William the children of my brother Anthony Mills, and £5 each when 21 to John and Agnes, children of my brother John Mills. I give my sister Diana Hall my bed whereon I now lie with all its furniture, and all my apparel except my leather suit. I give my brother-in-law Richard Hall £12 to be paid over 2 years, and £3 10s 0d to each of his children now living when they are 21. I give my godson George Folker £3, John Folker 6s, Alice and Joan Game 6s each when 21. The rest of my goods and chattels I give to my brother John Mills and make him exor. Wit. John Nutkinge (X), Thomas Milles. Pr. at Bury 7 March 1630/31.

189. R(W) DANIEL ELYE of Stanstead, yeoman. 10 February 1630/31.

Gives soul to God.
I give my brother Francis Elye £80 to be paid within a year of my decease, and all my apparel except my cloak which I give to Augustine Coppen, my brother-in-law. I also give the latter such sums of money as he owes me, and £31 to be paid within a year. I give Agnes Frost my sister £4 within 2 years, and Rose Kinge 30s to be paid within 3 months. I give the wife of John Carter 20s within a year, and 40s to Mary Coppen, daughter of my sister Martha, to be paid within 2 years into hands of her father Augustine Coppen. All the rest of my goods, money and debts I give to my brother-in-law William Palsie, whom I make exor. Wit. John Woodcocke, William Daye. Pr. at Bury 7 March 1630/31.

190. R(W) EDWARD FOREDOM of Rougham. 3 March 1630/31.

Commends soul into hands of God.
All my worldly goods I give and bequeath to my wife Joan absolutely, and my lands and tenements to her for term of her life to pay my debts and funeral expenses. On her decease I give my daughter Dorothy a backhouse or tenement, now in the occupation of Robert Ashele, with a little yard at the east end of the house being 3 yards long and the width of the house. She is to have free entry to the house and access to the usual place where water is taken. The rest of my land and houses I give to my son Anthony on condition he pays my daughter Anne £5 within 3 years of my wife's decease. Remainder to Francis son of Anthony. If Joan my wife dies within 5 years of my decease, Anthony is to pay her exors £20 within 2 years. Ex'trix: wife. Wit. William Goddard, Frances Roote. Pr. at Bury 9 March 1630/31.

191. R(W) EDMUND FRANKE (X) senior of Mildenhall, waterman. 31 October 1630.

Commits soul to God and hopes to receive remission of sins. To be buried in Mildenhall churchyard.
I give my son Edmund 10s to be paid within a year. I give my son John my boat on condition he gives my son Thomas and my daughter Judy 10s each within a year. I give to Margaret my wife, whom I make ex'trix, all my goods, debts and monies. Wit. John Flower (X), William Haylock (X). Pr. at Bury 21 March 1630/31.

192. R(W) NICHOLAS CHURCHMAN (X) of Wickham Skeith. 3 January 1630/31.

Commends soul to God and hopes to have remission of sins. To be buried in Wickham Skeith churchyard.
First I give my son Samuel my best doublet and breeches, a post axe, a great mortice wimble with a whipple tree wimble, a draught hook, a

sickle, my grindstone and my longest hagg saw. I give my daughter Hope a posted bedstead with the bed belonging and the blankets, coverlet and a pillow, a framed table, 2 joined stools, a great chair, a coffer which was my wife's before our marriage, a brass warming pan, my biggest new kettle, my brass posnet, my biggest skillet and a trevet, my shortest hagg saw and my shortest hand saw, a brass candlestick, a wimble, a spit, a percer with a bit, a boulting hutch, my least wooden bottle, and a pair of mustard querns with the stock of stone. I give to my daughter Elizabeth my cupboard with the cloths that lie on it, my great chest and coffer wherein we usually lay linen, a brass pot, 2 kettles and 1 hake, a fire pan and tongs, a pair of andirons, a roasting iron, a brass skillet, a feather bed with the coverings and blankets belonging to it, a truckle bed as it now stands, a feather bolster and a pillow of feathers, my stock cards, my fan and my scales with the weights. I also bequeath to my 2 daughters, whom I make ex'trices, all my linen, pewter and other goods to be divided between them at the discretion of my assured and well-beloved friend John Hawes of Wickham Skeith. If my son Samuel questions my will in any way the gifts made to him shall be void and given to my 2 daughters. Wit. John Hawes, Robert Parker. Pr. at Bury 15 March 1630/31.

193. R(W) THOMAS GAGES (X) of Drinkstone, yeoman. 18 January 1630/31.

Bequeaths soul to God trusting to be saved.
I give my wife Anne for life the messuage in Drinkstone wherein I now dwell with all free and copyhold land lying together on its west side, and after her death to my son Richard. I also give my wife for life 3½ acres land lately purchased of Leonard Tyllet gentleman, a piece of land in Drinkstone called Ferthadge hill, and 9 acres arable land abutting on the highway leading to Woolpit and lying between the lands of Mr Burrowes; and after her death to my son Richard. I give my wife all the land in Bradfield which I purchased of George Howe until my son Humphrey is 21. If he dies without issue, I give this land to my son Theodore. Until Humphrey is 21 I give my wife the following to use the profits for his education and upbringing: 3½ acres pasture in the long close next to the smith's shop in Drinkstone, wherein Henry Nunne now dwells, the smith's shop, a 1½ acre meadow called Bood meadow, a 1 acre meadow next to Long Close and between the land of Edward Page and Drinkstone town, 2½ acres copyhold pasture in Broome close held of Mr Motham, 2½ acres arable called Damland and 5½ acres copyhold arable in Shipp close; both the last 2 held of the manor of Drinkstone Hall. If Humphrey dies without heirs before he is 21, all this land is to go to my son Richard. Anne my wife must keep in good repair the messuage where I now dwell and all its outhouses. I give my wife until my son Theodore is 21 a copyhold tenement standing near Drinkstone Green, which I bought of [blank in MS] Cotton and a 4 acre close of pasture, both occupied by William Hall, and 1 acre of freehold meadow lying in Farthinge hill in Drinkstone, which I purchased from Leonard Tillet gentleman. My wife

is to use the profits of this land to educate and bring up Theodore in the fear of God and to allow him sufficient food and clothing. I give my son Richard my close in Drinkstone called Cross a Hand and containing meadow, pasture and arable, on condition he pays £40 each when 21 to my daughters Margaret and Susan. Benefit of survivorship and power to distrain. Until the elder of my daughters is 21 my wife is to take the profits of this close towards their maintenance and upbringing. I give my son Richard towards his maintenance all the Broome hill, both free and copyhold, Cordells and Hindes close, 7 acres close and a piece of land called Husselgate Slinke meadows in Drinkstone. He is to allow my wife peaceably to enjoy the land given to her for life. After the decease of my wife Anne I give to Richard the copper in the backhouse, a long table in the hall with all the buffet stools there used, a great cupboard in the hall, a featherbed with all its furniture in the hall chamber and my silver gilt salt. My wife is to have the use of these things during her life. I give my daughter Margaret another feather bed in the hall chamber with a whole tester and all its furniture when she is 21. I give my son Theodore when 21 a posted bed with a feather bed and all the furniture, and to my son Humphrey after my wife's decease a featherbed with its furniture that was hers. All my other household goods I give to my wife for life, and then to be equally divided among my children Richard, Margaret, Susan, Theodore and Humphrey and Anne Taylor my wife's daughter, to whom I give £100: £60 to be paid when she is 21 and £40 at my wife's death. My wife is not to fell any timber or top or crop any trees except what is needed to repair buildings and mend fences, and to provide her with 12 loads of firewood a year. I give my wife all my corn and cattle, such as neats, horses, bullocks, hogs and sheep, and all my husbandry utensils to pay my debts, legacies and funeral charges. I make my well-beloved wife Anne ex'trix and will her to distribute £3 among the poor people that shall resort to my burial. Supervisor: my brother-in-law Thomas Shreve and my son Thomas, and I give them 30s each to buy a ring. My wife is to be bound to my supervisors in the sum of £300 to perform my will. Wit. John Muninge, Stephen Goddard, Stephen Bulbrock (X), Richard Barker, Henry Mickelfeilde.

Codicil, bearing same date as will. In addition to the bequests already made to my wife Anne, I give her a meadow called Heardes, 2 pieces of land in Tycers field, and a piece of land called Hindes; all in Drinkstone. I also give her all my unbequeathed goods and chattels. Wit. Isaac Motham, John Muninge, Henry Micklefeild. Pr. at Bury 16 March 1630/31.

194. R(W) JOHN BAKER the elder of Great Ashfield. 14 January 1627/28.

Commends soul to God trusting to be saved.
I give to Elizabeth my wife for life my house in Bradfield St George, in which Luke Cocksedge dwells, with 2 adjoining orchards containing 2

acres; an arable and pasture close called Pages; Pages Brook with a barn standing on it; a 9 acre close of pasture and meadow called Blacka-moores; a 13 acre pasture close called Bradcar field; and 3 pieces of pasture totalling 9 acres lying together and called Longkar field, Littlekar field and Birche close. All this land lies in Bradfield St George and Bradfield St Clare. After my wife's decease all this land is left to my son John on condition he pays £20 each at yearly intervals to my children William, Elizabeth, Richard, Anne, Sarah, and Mary. All have power to distrain and benefit of survivorship. I give my son John my other tenement in Bradfield St George where John Rydnall dwells with all my other land in that parish and in Bradfield St Clare; and 1 acre copyhold pasture being part of the Carre and held by lease of Sir Robert Jermyn, late of Rushbrook. John must, starting 1 year after my death, pay £20 each to my children in the following order: Elizabeth, William, Richard, Anne, Sarah and Mary. When this is done he must pay them another £20 each in the same order as before, but William precedes Elizabeth. All have power to distrain. I give my son John the bed wherein he now lies with the bedstead and bedding, a brass to brew in, 3 milk kyne, the bald nag and a heifer. I give my daughter Elizabeth 2 milk kyne, and my son Richard a bed and bedding. All my unbequeathed goods I give to Elizabeth my wife and make her sole ex'trix. Wit. Mirabel Smyth alias Hovell (X), Thomas Peake. Pr. at Bury 14 March 1630/31.

195. R(W) ROBERT WESTLEY the elder of Barnardiston, husbandman. 16 February 1630/31.

Commends soul to God trusting to be saved.
I give my eldest son Henry the house where I now dwell with yard and appurtenances except such moveables as hereinafter mentioned. I give my second son Robert 12d. I give my youngest son John when 21 my biggest table and frame, a form, the flockbed I usually lie on with a coverlet, blanket, bolster, a great pillow, a pair sheets and the bedstead, and a little form by it but not the hangings over it, my biggest hutch, 2 fair pewter platters, 2 pewter spoons, a broad saucer, a salt cellar, my brass pot, my least kettle but one and £4. I give my youngest daughter Sarah, when 21, 3 fair pewter dishes, a little pewter dish, a pewter salt cellar, 2 pewter spoons, a pewter candlestick, the best coverlet I have, an old hutch, a little box, my least kettle but two, a little barrel and £4. I give my eldest daughter Mary my cupboard standing in my lower chamber, a flockbed lying on a trundle bed with the trundle bed, 2 blankets, a pillow and a bolster, a new hutch or chest, my best kettle, £3, 2 long pewter dishes, 4 saucers, a salt cellar and 2 pewter spoons to be given to her within 1 year of my decease. I give my second daughter Thomasine, when 21, a framed table in my chamber, a frame in the chamber above, my best kettle except one, by best chest, 2 pewter dishes, a deep saucer, a salt cellar, 3 pewter spoons and £3. All, with the exception of Robert, have benefit of survivorship. All the rest of my goods I give to my son Henry and make him exor. He must maintain my

2 youngest children until they are 21. If Henry refuses to act as exor, the churchwardens and overseers of Barnardiston are to have my tenement and the goods bequeathed to him to maintain my children until the youngest is 21. Wit. John Westley clerk, Robert Webb, Robert Butten. Pr. at Bury 14 March 1630/31.

196. R(W) GEORGE SHAWE (X) of Stanstead, shoemaker. 3 March 1630/31.

Bequeaths soul to God.
I give my brother Roger an annuity of 10s to be paid by my wife Grace or, if she dies, by my brother George or his son John out of the profits of my land in Stanstead. If Roger sells this annuity it becomes void. I give my wife Grace for her life my house in Stanstead wherein I now dwell with all its land, and after her decease to my brother George and his son John. George must pay £85 as follows: to Agnes Frost my sister-in-law £4 within 6 months of my decease; to her daughter Lettice £20, half within 1 year and the other half within 2; £5 each to Thomas, Susan and John, children of my deceased brother Thomas; 40s each to Thomas and Elizabeth, children of my late sister Elizabeth Warman, and to Edward, son of my deceased sister Frances Soles; 20s each to Bridget and Susan Soles; £5 each to Elizabeth, Anne, Mary and Bridget, daughters of my sister Agnes Frost; £3 each to George, Robert and Thomas, sons of my late sister Joan Marshall; 40s each to her daughters Sarah and Anne; and lastly £5 to my sister Anne Shaw. These payments are spread over 8 years, and the legatees have power to distrain. The gifts to Thomas and Susan Shaw are legacies left to them by my uncle John Daye of Lavenham. I give Anne Frost my warming pan and Lettice Frost my cupboard after my wife's decease. All the residue of my moveables I give to my wife Grace. Exors: my brother John Shawe and his son George. Supervisor: my kinsman William Daye. Wit. John Hamond, William Daye. Pr. at Bury 14 March 1630/31.

197. R(W) WILLIAM MARSHALL of Stanstead, cloth worker. 15 April 1630.

Bequeaths soul to God trusting to be saved.
I give to Susan my wife for her life my house wherein I now dwell. After her decease it is to be sold and the money divided among my 5 children: William, John, Susan, Anne and Mary, whom I appoint to sell it. I give my wife my counter and all my shop stuff, and all the rest of my goods, which are to be divided equally among my children after her decease. Ex'trix: wife. Wit. Rose Dutton, Anne Elson, William Daye. Pr. at Bury 14 March 1630/31.

198. R(W) JOAN MANINGE (X) widow of William Maninge of Great
Saxham. 14 December 1625.

Commends soul to God and hopes it will be received into heaven.
Remembering that all those children it pleased God to send my husband
and me, except our unmarried daughter Mary, have had portions
bestowed on them by my husband or since his death by me, and desiring
to provide for Mary I make my will. I give 5s to be distributed by my
ex'trix amongst the poor folks of Saxham within a month of my decease. I
give all my goods and household stuff to my daughter Mary and make her
ex'trix. Wit. Clement Paman, Robert Frost. Pr. at Bury 14 March
1630/31.

199. R(W) RICHARD FULLER (X) of Mildenhall, yeoman.
19 December 1629.

Commits soul to God hoping to obtain pardon of sins and kingdom of
heaven.
I give 3s 4d to poor man's box of Mildenhall, and towards repair of parish
church 3s 4d. I give to my well-beloved wife Agnes for her life the
copyhold messuage wherein I dwell being in Beck Street or Rowes in the
parish of Mildenhall, and after her decease to my eldest son Richard
according to the custom of the manor. I also give my wife for life, and
then to my son Richard, 2 acres copyhold arable land sometime part of 5
acres lying in Stapenhowe field in Mildenhall with the freehold land late
John Ealsinge's on the west, the rest of of the 5 acres on the east and
abutting on Stapenhowe way at the north end and on land of Richard
Tabbut alias Burges at the south end. I give my second son Robert 3
acres copyhold land sometime parcel of 5 acres of arable and pasture
called Hardies in Stockfeild, which I bought from the late Henry
Childerstone. Until Robert is 21 my wife is to hold this land. I give
Robert immediately after my wife's decease a 1 rod piece of copyhold
meadow with a house built on it being near Stockford in Mildenhall. I
bought it from the late Thomas Childerston gentleman. I give my
youngest son Francis 3 acres copyhold arable land in Beckfield next to
Henry Pechie's land on west and land late of Henry Taylor on the east
with the north end abutting on Stockpath and the south end on
Stapenhowe way. Until my wife dies she is to hold this land and take its
profits. My 2 acre piece arable land at Hardesse in Mildenhall, being part
of 5 acres late purchased of Henry Childerston, I give to my daughters
Anne and Frances. Anne is to have her share at once and Frances when
she is 21, until which time my wife is to hold it. I give to my youngest
daughter Margaret, after my wife's decease, 3 rods copyhold in Stapenhowe field, which I bought from the late Thomas Pechie. I give my son
Richard my copyhold close called Stock close, which I inherited from my
father Richard Fuller, on condition he pays my wife £14, half within 6
months and half within 1 year of my decease. If he defaults, I give Stock
close to my wife for ever. In order to pay my debts my ex'trix is to sell 2

acres copyhold arable in Stapenhowe, which I bought of Richard Currey. I give my daughter Margaret £5 when 21. I give the cupboard standing in my parlour to my son Richard after my wife's decease; also the long table in the hall and the black chest in the parlour chamber. I give my son Robert after my wife's decease my posted bedstead in the hall chamber, my long table in my parlour and my greatest brass pan. The residue of my goods and chattels I give to the use and discretion of my wife Agnes, whom I make ex'trix. She is to pay my debts and legacies and see my body honestly buried. Wit. Francis Winge (X), William Dallyson.

Memorandum that I have surrendered to the use of my will all my copyhold land by the hands of Robert Fuller and Francis Wing, copyhold tenants. Pr. at Bury 21 March 1630/31.

200. R(W) ALICE WARWELL (X) of Lavenham, widow. 11 March 1630/31.

Bequeaths soul to God hoping to find access to his glorious presence.

I give my daughter Anne a trundle bedstead, a flock bed and bolster, a blanket, a coverlet, 2 pairs sheets, 2 pillows, 2 pillowbeeres, a kettle, a brass kettle without a band, a pot brass posnet, a brass skillet, 4 pieces of pewter, a brazen candlestick, a tramell, a peel, a spit, a roast iron, a chest, a hutch, 2 buffet stools, and a beer vessel. I give my daughter Rachel a posted bedstead, a flock bed, a boarded bedstead, a blanket, a coverlet, a pair sheets, a great brass kettle, a brazen candlestick, 3 pieces of pewter, a table, a buffet stool, a hutch, a cupboard, a stained cloth, a kneading trough and a beer vessel. I give my daughter Rose my middle brass kettle or 9s in money, whichever she chooses. If she takes the money, 5s is to be for herself and 4s for her sons Henry and William Smyth. I give my grandchild Marabel Warwell a feather bed and bolster, a brass pot and my greatest brass candlestick. Exor: my son James Warwell. Wit. Richard Tyler, Anne Cason. Pr. at Bury 21 March 1630/31.

201. R(W) ELIZABETH PEPPER (X) of Lavenham, widow. 11 November 1630.

Commits soul into hands of God.

I give to John Pratt and Thomas Hornsbie, exors of this my will, £46 to be used within a year to buy a house for my grandson John Coult. If the house costs less than £46, the remainder is to be paid to Elizabeth Coult my daughter who is to have the house until John is 21. All the rest of my household goods and corn I give to Elizabeth Coult my daughter. Wit. Walter Sheader, Jane Sheader (X), John Pratt, Thomas Hornisbie. Pr. at Bury 21 March 1630/31.

202. R(W) RICHARD MEENE of Ixworth, tailor. 24 February 1630/31.

Commends soul to God in hope of joyful resurrection to eternal life.
I give my wife Katherine my house wherein I dwell for 10 years if she live so long. She is to keep it in repair. I also give her an acre of copyhold meadow in Badwell Ash, which belonged to Gilbert Hill deceased. After 10 years, or after my wife's decease if earlier, my tenement is to be sold by my loving brother-in-law John Jewell clerk, my brother James Meene and my cousin Edward Smyth of Rougham. From the money arising from this sale I give 30s each to the 6 children of my brother Edward Meene and to his daughter Anne 50s. I give 30s each to my brother George Meene and his 3 children, and £4 to Thomas, son of my kinsman Thomas Meene, and 20s each to his 2 daughters. I give all my wearing apparel to my brother George, and all the rest of my goods to my wife, whom I make ex'trix. Testator surrendered all his copyhold land held of Bardwell Hall into hands of John Craske in presence of Henry Daldie, copyholder of the manor. Wit. John Syer, John Craske, Henry Daldye, Ralph Whitney. Pr. at Bury 17 March 1630/31.

203. R(W) JOHN FULLER (N) of Hepworth, singleman. 27 January 1630/31.

I do give and bequeath to Margaret Baker all my moveable goods both within and without the house, and make her my ex'trix. She is to bring my body decently to the ground and pay my debts. Wit. William Baker, Richard Baker. I William Baker will testify willingly upon oath whensoever it please God to enable me to come to Bury St Edmunds. Pr. at Bury 22 February 1630/31.

204. R(W) JOHN BIGG (X) of Little Cornard, yeoman. 19 November 1630.

Bequeaths soul to God and hopes to be saved through Jesus Christ.
I give to my 3 young sons Robert, Henry and Thomas a 1½ acre close called Weddie close, a 1 rod pasture pightle called Stoners and 1 rod of meadow in Alfleet meadow. My wife Katherine is to receive the rent of this land until my children are 21, when the land is to be sold by the churchwardens and overseers of the parish and the money divided amongst my 3 sons. If my wife dies before my sons are 21, my son Robert is to hold the land and use the profits to maintain and bring up my children. I give my wife the best shoate I have, and the best skep of bees in my yards at her own choice. I give my son Robert my best cloak and hat, and my son John my best pair of breeches. I give my daughter Mary all the linen and woollen apparel that was my late wife's. The rest of my moveable goods, corn and cattle I give to my wife whom I make ex'trix and I give her all the debts due to me and charge her to pay what I owe. The overplus of my goods is to be divided between my 4 youngest children. If my wife neglects to prove my will within 3 months, then I

appoint my son Robert as exor. For 4 years my wife is to have my tenement Obyes with 4 pieces of arable land (2 being in Wetchmare) towards bringing up my 3 youngest children. During this time she must pay my son John 40s p.a. and after 4 years he is to have this tenement and land. Wit. Henry Underwood, Thomas Levett (X), Matthew Howe. Pr. at Bury 1 March 1630/31.

205. R(W) SUSAN LADYMAN (X) of Lidgate, widow. 12 November 1630.

Bequeaths soul to God trusting to be saved.
I give all the money owing to me by bond to my 6 youngest children to be divided among them in equal portions as they come of age. I give my daughter Elizabeth my best coverlet and my posted bed in the hall chamber at Whelnetham. I give my daughter Susan my green bed in the parlour chamber at Whelnetham. I give my daughter Frances my 2 beds at Lidgate and all other things of mine there not otherwise disposed of. I give a bed each to my sons Benjamin, Ezekiel and Nathan. I give my daughter Elizabeth my gilt salt at Whelnetham; my daughter Susan my silver salt at Whelnetham; and my daughter Frances my gilt salt at Lidgate. I give my sons Benjamin and Nathan my 2 silver tankards and my son Ezekiel my silver tunne. I give my biggest ring to Elizabeth, the next to Susan and to Frances that which was her uncle's. I give a pair sheets each to Benjamin and Nathan, and 3 pairs each to my 3 daughters. I give my son Joseph my great brass candlestick, and to my daughter Susan my biggest brass pot. I give my daughter-in-law Anne my carpet at Lidgate, and my bason and ewer. I give my grand-daughter Anne my little gold ring. I give Alice, my daughter-in-law, 6 porrengers which were her father's and 6 pewter dishes at Lidgate, and the bed which her father gave her should be delivered to her. I give my sister Cornishe my still. I give 10s each to my 3 sisters: Cornishe, Moore and Emduce. The £20 my son Gabriel owes me and for which I have no bond is to be used by him to help bring up my sons Ezekiel and Nathan. My exors are to divide the rest of my goods amongst my 6 youngest children as they come of age. Benefit of survivorship. Exors: my brother-in-law Thomas Cornishe and my son Gabriel Catchpoole. Wit. John Smyth, John Clerke (X). Pr. at Bury 7 February 1630/31.

206. R(W) MARY CHURCHE (N) of Elveden, widow. 14 September 1630.

She gave and bequeathed all her moveable goods to her godson William, son of William Fuller. Wit. Thomas Robertsonne, Anne Batement, Joan Lusher. Let. ad. granted to William Fuller senior at Bury 4 October 1630.

207. RICHARD BULLOCKE of Sudbury, say maker. 13 September 1630.

Bequeaths soul to God trusting in Jesus Christ for eternal salvation.
I give my wife Dorothy for ever all such moveable goods as she had when we were married, and the bed, bedstead, bolster, pillow and all other furniture belonging as it is daily used and wherein I now lie, and 20s p.a. I give my daughter Joan, wife of William Frenche, the messuage in Cavendish now let to Thomas Chrisenwheate. If she dies without heirs, my other children are to sell the messuage and share the money. I give my daughter Elizabeth the house in Cavendish wherein Francis Elsden now dwells. I give my daughter Margaret, wife of Mathew Sterns £10 and to Jeffery my son 12d. My exors are to sell the messuage in Cavendish wherein Mr Gilbert dwells to pay my debts and legacies. I give my brother Robert Bullocke for life the messuage in Cavendish now occupied by widow Thetford, and after his decease to my son Ralph. I give all the rest of my goods to my sons Ralph and Thomas and make them exors. No witnesses. Pr. in church of St Peter in Sudbury 2 October 1630 when William Musant said the testator sent for him to make his will and he wrote it at his instructions. Testator died before will was brought for him to sign. Wit. Cecily Ralphe.

208. W(R) FRANCIS ADAMS (X) of Little Whelnetham, yeoman. 20 December 1630.

Commends soul to God hoping to be saved by merits of Jesus Christ. I will that Martha my loving wife shall have all my land in Burnt Bradfield [Bradfield Combust] for her life as her jointure. After her decease my daughter Martha is to have this land. I give to Amy Howe my sister £5; to Robert Adams my brother and to Ann his wife £5; to John Adams my brother and Rachel his wife £5; all to be paid within a year of my decease. I give John Adams, my godson and son of my brother Robert, 20s when 21, and 20s to Frances Adams, my god-daughter and daughter of my brother John when she is 21. I give 20s when 21 to my godson William, son of my sister Amy. The residue of my moveables I give to my wife, whom I make ex'trix and who is to pay my debts and legacies. I give 20s to Robert Adams, son of my brother Robert, when 21. Wit. Robert Adams, Alexander Pistor, John Clarke, Richard Parker. Pr. at Bury 28 March 1631.

209. W(R) JOHN MAKYN of Rattlesden. 9 February 1628/29.

Commends soul to God and hopes to be saved through Jesus Christ. I give my son John my posted bedstead and my framed table, and my best chest at my brother Heigham's. I give my daughter Anne a coffer of linen and all things therein standing in the firehouse where I now dwell. I bequeath £40 to my son John when 24. My exors are to put this sum out to the best profit and pay John the interest on it from his age of 21. I give my sons Henry and Peter and my daughter Anne £35 each to be paid when they are 21 by my exors, who are to put these portions out to the best profit towards the bringing up of these children. I give my daughter Anne her mother's stamell petticoat and taffeta apron. Benefit of survivorship. The rest of my unbequeathed goods, after my debts and funeral expenses are paid, I give to be equally parted between my 4 children. Exors: Edmund Baker, tanner, and Robert Muriell. I give them 40s apiece for their pains. Wit. John Underwood the elder, John Underwood his son. Pr. at Bury 28 March 1631.

210. R(W) ANDREW WRIGHT (X) of Thurston, yeoman. 25 January 1625/26.

Commnends soul to God and hopes through faith to be saved. To be buried in church or churchyard of Thurston.
I give my son John my freehold meadow with the pightle belonging to it lying in Thurston and containing 3 acres. I give my son Andrew my 3½ acre close in Thurston and Rougham called Nettlecroft. I give my sons John and Andrew all my goods and chattels to be equally divided between them, and I make them exors. Wit. Thomas Clarke, Eme Clarke. Pr. at Bury 31 March 1631.

211. R(W) THOMAS MORLEY of Lakenheath, labourer. 28 February 1630/31.

Bequeaths soul to God.
I give my son Edmund my copyhold tenement in Lakenheath. I give my son Thomas 50s to be paid within a year of my decease. If Edmund refuses to pay this sum, Thomas is to have my tenement for 2 years in lieu of his legacy. I give my son John 50s to be paid within 2 years on same terms. I give my grandson John Morley 20s to be paid within a month. I give all my goods and chattels, except a pair of fine sheets given to Thomas, to my 3 sons whom I make exors. Testator surrendered his copyhold land to his son Edmund to the use of his exors in the presence of Thomas Halman, Edward Man, John Lewis. Pr. at Bury 12 April 1631.

212. R(W) JOHN BUDLEY of Bury St Edmunds, gentleman. 14 March 1628/29.

Commends soul to God.
I give to my loving wife Elizabeth my messuage in Eastgate Street, Bury, wherein Edmund Clarke now lives, and all my land in Glemsford now in the tenure of [blank in MS] for her life and then to my son John. I also give to my wife absolutely all my land anywhere in England, and all my goods, chattels, plate, jewels and household implements. I give to my son John 20s for a remembrance to make him a ring, or a gold ring worth 20s at the discretion of my ex'trix. I make Elizabeth my wellbeloved wife sole ex'trix. Wit. Edmund Clarke, Robert Skynner, Henry Skynner. Pr. at Bury 11 April 1631.

213. R(W) WILLIAM VALE (X) the elder of Groton, cooper.
26 November 1630.

Bequeaths soul to God hoping for salvation through Jesus Christ. To be
buried in Groton churchyard at cost of my ex'trix.
I give Elizabeth my wellbeloved wife my copyhold tenement wherein
Michael Beamont dwells with its buildings and yards, on condition she
pays the following legacies: £4 to my eldest daughter Joan when 24; £4
each to my daughters Ann and Mary when 21, and £4 to my daughter
Susan when 16. Benefit of survivorship. If my wife fails to pay these
legacies, the gift to her is void. I give John my eldest son half my working
tools and the other half to my son Thomas. I also give them 5s each. I
give my son William 20s when 21. All the rest of my goods I give to my
wife towards paying my debts and legacies, and I make her sole ex'trix.
Supervisor: my good friend and neighbour John Piper the elder of
Boxford, grocer. Wit. William Leigh, curate, John Piper, John Sawen
(X), Richard Payne (X). Pr. at Sudbury 15 April 1631.

214. R(W) BENNETT GRYMWOOD (X) of Lindsey, husbandman.
4 December 1630.

Commends soul to God and hopes to have remission of sins. To be buried
in Lindsey churchyard.
I give George, son of John Daye of Lindsey, 10s to be paid within 6
weeks. I give to John, son of my brother John Grymwood of Assington
husbandman, 20s to be paid within 2 months of my decease. I give his
brother Thomas 10s to be paid within 3 months. All the rest of my
moveables I give to my brother John, whom I make exor. Wit. William
Greene (X), Joseph Willasonne (X), John Bluett. Pr. at Sudbury 15 April
1631.

215. R(W) RALPH DOWNSDALE of Nayland, yeoman. 13 November
1630.

Bequeaths soul to God my maker and to Jesus Christ his redeemer by
whose passion I hope to be saved.
I give Priscilla my wife for life all my free and copyhold lands and
tenements in Stoke by Nayland and Nayland, and after her decease to my
son William for his life and no longer towards the decent bringing up of
his children and their preferment to service in trades or handicrafts. But if
he wilfully neglects his children, then the churchwardens and overseers of
Nayland are to receive the rents and profits of my land and use them to
educate, bring up and maintain my grandchildren as the duty of their
father should have done. If my son neglects the education of his children,
he shall have to his use the tenement wherein he and the widow Webb
now dwell. After my son's death I give my grandson Ralph Downsdale
my tenement and dwelling houses in Nayland called Weepinge hill with
yards and orchards, and my tenement and dwelling house wherein Mr

94

Man Clarke now lives. I give my grandson William, after his father's decease, my dwelling house and land in Stoke by Nayland, and the copyhold tenement in Nayland which I lately purchased and is now occupied by Edward Nebbett. I give my grandchild Roger my 2 tenements in Court Street, Nayland, now occupied by William Sewell and Thomas Nicholson. If any of the persons to whom I have left houses neglect to repair them for one whole year, then the next heir is to have the property. All my goods and chattels I give for life to my wife, and after her decease they are to be divided between the children of my son William by the churchwardens and overseers of Nayland, or any 3 of them. The children are to choose their share in descending order of age. I make my wife Priscilla ex'trix; she must prove my will within 2 months. Supervisor: Thomas Blythe the elder, gentleman of Nayland, to whom I give 20s. Wit. John Pearelye, Joseph Cutler (X), Mathew Howe, who wrote this will. Pr. at Sudbury 15 April 1631.

216. R(W) EDWARD SNOWDEN of Bury St Edmunds. 26 April 1628.

Bequeaths soul to God in sure hope of joyful resurrection.
I give my father-in-law, John Lorkyn of Glemsford, all my linen and woollen which is at my master's. I give his son, my brother John Lorkyn, a meal sack, my feather bed tick and bolster with the feathers. I give my hutch and all the money I leave behind me, after paying for a decent burial, to John Lorkyn the younger when he is 21; the money to be paid to him by Thomas Sandell of Cavendish. I give my cloak to Jeremy Hasell of Cavendish, and the rest of my apparel that I do wear I bequeath to Francis Edwardes of Bury. I give Thomas Sandell of Cavendish my bible, and Mathew Abbut of Cavendish my testament. The cost of proving my will is not to be at the charge of my exor, but is to be paid to him by Thomas Sandell who has my money in hand. Exor Clement Chaplyne of Bury. Wit. Gyles Steward (X), William Maning (X). Pr. at Bury 27 April 1631.

217. R(W) ROGER SHARPE of Bury St Edmunds, maltster. 4 September 1630.

Commends soul to God and trusts through Jesus Christ to have remission of sins and be received into his blessed kingdom.
I give to the poor people of the parish of St James in Bury £5 to be distributed within a month of my decease at the discretion of my ex'trix. I give my son Jasper £5 within 3 months, and my son Roger £100 when 24. I give £100 each to my sons Robert, Henry and John when 24, and £100 each to my daughters Margaret, Anne and Phoebe when 21 or on their marriage days. Benefit of survivorship. I give my daughters Grace, wife of Henry Spalding, and Elizabeth, wife of Christopher Sudburie, and Joan, wife of John Meadowes, a piece of plate worth 40s each to be delivered within 3 months. I give my grandson Roger Spalding 40s when 24, and my grandchildren Grace, Elizabeth and Anne Spalding 20s each

when 21. I give my grandson John Meadowes 40s when 24. I give and demise to my loving wife Grace for life the messuage wherein I now dwell in Bury, and the next door messuage now occupied by Richard Copsey, baker and which I lately purchased of John Bryant. After my wife's death my sons Roger, Robert, Henry and John are to sell my tenements and equally divide the money between them. All the rest of my goods, money and household stuff I bequeath to my wife Grace whom I make sole ex'trix. Wit. Frances Wragg, Charles Greene, Robert Walker. Pr. at Bury 28 April 1631.

218. R(W) RICHARD FREND (X) of Sudbury, clothier. 23 April 1631.

Bequeaths soul to God trusting in Jesus Christ for eternal salvation.
I bequeath to Ralph Wheeler of St Gregory [Sudbury parish], my kinsman dwelling in Sudbury, for life my messuage wherein I now dwell within 3 months of my decease; also my long table in the hall. After his death I give the house and table to my kinsman Thomas, son of John Frend of the parish of St Gregory. Ralph Wheeler must pay my exors 40s within 14 days or my exors are to have the messuage for 4 years. I give Susan Bushe, my kinswoman now dwelling with me, her dwelling in my house for 3 months after my decease without molestation. I also give her my feather bed with 2 feather bolsters, a feather pillow, a coverlet, 2 blankets, 1 pair of my best sheets and the bedstead wherein I usually do lodge. Also my best cupboard, my best chest, my best brass pot, 2 kettles and 1 posnet which she will make choice of, and my great bible. I give Susan Bushe for ever all my messuage and tenement in Wigen End in the parish of St Peter in Sudbury and which I purchased of John Lord of Sudbury. I give Susan, wife of Daniel Stranger, for ever the messuage in the parish of St Gregory in which widow Foster now dwells. I give Rose, daughter of my brother Roger Frende, the messuage in St Gregory's parish in which widow Harbor now dwells for Rose's life and after her decease to John Hedge her first husband's son. I give Mary, daughter of my brother George Frend, for ever the messuage in the same parish in which one Profyte now lives. I give Sarah, my sister Christian's daughter, my messuage in the same parish in which Valentine Lay lives for her life and then to her first husband's sons. I give my cousin Joseph Frend of St Peter's parish in Sudbury the messuage in St Gregory's parish in which Bretton now lives and in which Goodey lately dwelt for his life and then to be divided among his children. I give the rest of my goods to be divided between Joseph Frend, Susan wife of Daniel Stranger and Susan Bushe, who now dwells with me. I give my cousin Roger Frend of London 12d, and to my kinsman John Frend dwelling in the parish of St Gregory 12d. I give all my tenants their dwelling rent free for 3 months after my decease. Exors: Daniel Stranger of Sudbury, weaver, and Susan Bushe. Wit. Israel Woolstonne, Arkknoll Browne, Daniel Goode. Pr. at Bury 29 April 1631.

219. W(R) ANNE CHAPLIN (X) of Semer, widow. 26 January 1629/30.

Commends soul to God and steadfastly believes to have remission of sins.
I bequeath to my kinsman James, son of my brother Ralph Cloptone, £10
on the day of his marriage. I give Susan, daughter of Brian Stevens, 50s
when 21 or married, and 40s to her brother Henry when 24 and 50s to her
brother Richard when 21. I give Anne, daughter of Robert Parke, 50s
when 21 or married, but if she dies I give this sum to her brother and my
godson William Parke. I give 50s each when 21 to William and Robert,
sons of my son-in-law Robert Smeth, and to Francis and Robert, sons of
son-in-law Robert Chapline. Benefit of survivorship. I give Judith,
daughter of my kinsman James Frost, 20s when 24, and 20s when 24 to
Anne, daughter of my kinsman Francis Cloptone. I give 10s to the poor
people of Semer, and 40s to the poor of the town where I am buried, to
be distributed by my exor. I give my son Richard Chaplin my lease of a
farm called Wally and lying in Postwick, on condition he pays my legacies
and I make him exor. Wit. John Brunning, Stephen Goymer (X). Pr. at
Bury 6 May 1631.

220. W(R) MICHAEL KINGE of Chedburgh, clerk. 13 June 1623.

Bequeaths soul to God and trusts to be saved through Jesus Christ.
I give my son Richard all my free and copyhold land and pasture in the
fields of Hingestone [Cambs], and £5 to be paid within 6 months. I give
my younger son Michael my land and pasture in Chedburgh called Ladies
Hedges. As my son Michael cannot have this land during lifetime of my
wife Anne because of an enfeoffment to her and my mother-in-law, I give
him my free and copyhold tenement called Winters which I lately bought
of Henry Sparrowe with a copyhold pightle called Brundish. Michael
must pay Richard £5 within 2 years of my wife's decease, and £5 to my
grandchild and godson Michael Nunne when he is 21; both have power to
distrain. All the rest of my goods, books and ready money I give to my
exor, who is to pay out of them within a month £5 to my sister Ellen as
part of the portion of £10 I gave her when she married to help towards
paying a fine on taking up a copyhold in Stanningfield which is her
jointure. Exor: my son Michael. No witnesses. Pr. at Bury 6 May 1631.

221. R(W) EDMUND SHEPPARD (X) of Redgrave, wheelwright.
11 January 1630/31.

Commits soul to God hoping to be an inheritor of the kingdom of
heaven.
I give my son Richard the cottage I lately built, situated between my head
tenement and that lately Henry Groom's, and the hempland belonging to
it. I also give him 17 foot of land from the Rowe belonging to the
hempland and extending the length of the row into my blye close, and a 3
rod piece of land in the Back field of Redgrave abutting on Edward
Fisher's land called Broome close to the east. I give my son John the

tenement in which I now dwell with barn, stable and adjoining land except 3 rods in Back field which abut on Redgrave fen. John must pay the following legacies: to my daughter Elizabeth £5 within a year of my decease; to my son Edmund £10 within 2 years; to my son Thomas £5 within 3 years; and to my grandson William, son of Thomas, £5 when 21. All payments to be made in my house, and legatees have power to distrain. I give my son William the 3 rods in Back field excepted above. I give my son Richard the featherbed on which he now lies with the bolster, 3 blankets, a covering and the bedstead on which they lie in my chamber; also my biggest brass pot, my 3 middle kettles and my long table in the hall. I give my son John the bedstead in the parlour wherein I now lie with the feather bed, bolster, covering and 3 blankets, my table standing at the bed's foot, my biggest and my smallest kettle, my smallest brass pot and my trevet. Exors: sons Richard and John. Wit. Robert Shornebise, Thomas Williames (X), William Jasper (X). Pr. at Bury 7 May 1631.

222. R(W) BARBARA FLOWER (X) of Mildenhall, widow. 29 March 1631.

Bequeaths soul to God and body to earth.
I give my son Henry a brown cow and a great chest, the best hutch and the cupboard in the hall. I give my son Francis the bed in the chamber with its bedding, a black cow, the table with frame in the hall and a hutch. I give my daughter Margaret a red cow, the cupboard in the chamber, 2 pillows, a pair of the best sheets in my house, the bearing cloth, a napkin, a towel and part of the great kettle. I give my daughter Elizabeth a brown cow, the table in the chamber, 2 pillowbeeres, a napkin, a towel, part of the great kettle with her sister Margaret and a kercher. I give my daughter Barbara a red cow, the brass pot, a kettle and a table that is to make. I give my daughters Elizabeth and Barbara 3 pewter platters and a pewter candlestick, and to Barbara 2 joined stools and a joined chair. I give my daughter Margaret my cloak and a waistcoat. I give my son Robert 10s. I give my 3 daughters the bed wherein I now lie as it stands, but I give it all to Margaret if the other two marry or depart. The rest of my goods I give to my son Henry and make him exor. Wit. Philip Hynard (X), Nicholas Mynett. Pr at Mildenhall 13 April 1631.

223. R(W) JOHN BARON (X) of Burwell [Cambs], husbandman. 24 February 1630/31.

Commends soul to God hoping for everlasting life. To be buried in Burwell churchyard.
I give my eldest son John a rod of copyhold land in Millfield with Stephen Warren's land on east and Thomas Fryston's on west. I give him 1 acre of land I hold of Goodman Pamplyn to sow barley this year. I give my daughter Grace the posted bed in the parlour, and a rod of saffron

ground in Mill field near Sapleon way. All the rest of my goods and chattels I give to Grace my wife, whom I make ex'trix and charge to see my children brought up. After my wife's decease I give my copyhold house in Burwell to my eldest son then living, and he must pay £30 to be equally shared amongst the rest of my children within 2 years or the house shall be given to my other children. Wit. William Rogers, Robert Browne, Robert Baron, Daniel Livermore. Pr. at Mildenhall 13 April 1631.

224. R(W) HENRY STEELE (X) of Herringswell, husbandman. 6 February 1630/31.

Bequeaths soul to God looking for salvation through merits of Jesus Christ. To be buried in Herringswell churchyard.
I give my eldest son Henry my copyhold house and land in the fields of Herringswell when 24, until which time my wife Rachel is to receive the rents and profits. She must pay my younger sons Thomas and Edward £10 each when 18. My wife is to have for life a house called Younges with the adjoining croft and 6 acres arable land, that is 2 in each shift. When Henry reaches 24 he is to pay my other 4 children £10 each at the rate of one a year. They have power to distrain and benefit of survivorship. My wife Rachel is to have the use of all my household stuff until Henry is 24 when these goods are to be divided between the two of them. Wife sole ex'trix. Wit. Thomas Cabeck, clerk, John Pleasannce. Pr. at Mildenhall 13 April 1631.

225. R(W) JEFFERY TANNER (X) of Bures, yeoman. 1 March 1630/31.

Bequeaths soul to God hoping to be redeemed by Jesus Christ. To be buried in churchyard of Bures St Mary.
I give the curate of Bures 10s to preach at my burial and to the poor people there 10s, and to the poor of Assington 10s. I give my sister Katherine 10s and her daughter Mary 20s. I give my godson, son of Anne Ball, 20s and 10s to Henry Cooke's daughter. I give my son John my 4 crofts called Higgins, Kytles pightle, Hagbushe and Bawlehill, and containing 12 acres and lying in Bures St Mary; also all my house and land in Bures St Mary and Little Cornard. I give my grandson, Jeffery Tanner, my freehold and leasehold land and houses in Boxford in full satisfaction of his rights in my land; if he refuses to accept this I give this legacy to my son John. I give Jeffery Tanner 10s in lieu of any right of his in my goods and chattels. I give my daughter Amy, wife of John Nevell, in full satisfaction of all sums of money due to her by bond from me, my messuage and land of old called Layes and situated in Bures St Mary, and 3 pieces of land called Great, Middle and Little Brettes and containing 3 acres, and 2 acres land in Bradfield. I give my son John all my copyhold land and tenements in Assington held of Brampton Gurdon, esquire, and my lease land in Assington devised to me by Robert Gale. I give £10 to

my grandchild Alice, daughter of my late son Jeffery, when she is 21 or marries. The residue of my lands and goods I bequeath to my son John to pay my debts and legacies, and I make him exor. Wit. Henry Colman, Richard Mather, William Rudland (X). Pr. at Sudbury 15 April 1631.

226. R(W) JOHN KINGSBERIE (X) the elder of Great Cornard, yeoman. 14 February 1630/31.

Commends soul to God trusting to be saved throught Jesus Christ. To be buried in Great Cornard churchyard.
I give my eldest son John the house wherein he now dwells, all my other copyhold land and houses, and a piece of freehold land in Great Cornard called Clogges hill. He must pay my daughters Joan and Alice £40 each: to Joan on her marriage and to Alice 1 year after my decease. Power to distrain. I give my second son Robert a piece of land called Crowe meadow and the adjoining Dickmans croft. I also give him 2 pieces of arable land in Brooke field lying next the Kell and abutting on the way leading to it, and the house I lease from Mr Danyell for the remainder of the term of years. I also give Robert all my cattle, corn and household stuff except a cow, a horse called Dicke and a brass pot which I give to my son John; and a flockbed which I give to son William; and a feather bed standing in Stoanes chamber and the least kettle which I give to my daughter Alice. I give my third son William a 2 acre piece of land in Brooke field abutting on Pedgate, and a piece of land called Hatters croft abutting on the highway next to Marittes barn and 3 pieces of meadow lying in Shawford. My son Robert must give my daughters Joan and Alice £10 each on their marriage days. The residue of my goods I give to my son Robert, whom I make exor and who is to pay my debts and legacies. Wit. Henry Tanner and me Robert Kingsberie. Pr. at Sudbury 15 April 1631.

227. R(W) HENRY LOKER (X) of Bures St Mary in Essex, glover. 22 February 1630/31.

Bequeaths soul to God and looks for resurrection on the last day. To be buried in Bures St Mary churchyard.
I give Elizabeth my wife all my goods for life if she remains single, but if she remarries my eldest son Henry is to have my great brass kettle with a little table standing in the parlour, and my son John is to have the long table in the hall and the best barrell. I give my daughter Bridget a flockbed, a coverlet, a blanket, a bolster, 1 pair of sheets and a deal hutch. I give my younger daughter Ann the best cupboard, 1 of the biggest barrels and a little barrel. If my wife remains single, she shall have the use of these goods during her life. From my stock I give my wife Elizabeth £12, my son Henry £12, my son John £10 and £4 each to my daughters Bridget and Ann on their marriage days or after my wife's decease. Benefit of survivorship. My wife and sons are to share the use of my household stock, but if a son marries he is to have half his cash legacy

at once. I give my daughter Bridget 20s due to me from John Mathew, shoemaker of Bures. Exors: wife and son Henry. Wit. Joseph Isaack, Jeffery Hust, John Parmiter. Pr. at Sudbury 15 April 1631.

228. R(W) JAMES MOUNTECUTE of Edwardstone. 14 January 1630/31.

Being mindful of mine end and careful of the peace and welfare of my wife and child. Bequeaths soul to God steadfastly believing in remission of sins and fullness of redemption.
I give Mary, my well-beloved wife, my dwelling house where I now live in Edwardstone with buildings, yard and orchard, to use at her will and pleasure. I also give her all my shop stuff and my press belonging to it, and anything else belonging to be used by her, and all my tasell growing in Groton on land of Mr Thomas Gostlyn of Groton Hall. I give my daughter Mary £15 when 18 or married. The money is to be put out at interest of 15s p.a. which is to be kept by my supervisor to pay to Mary when she is 18; the last 2 years' interest he is to keep for himself. If Mary dies, I bequeath her legacy as follows: 40s each to my kinsman John, son of my brother John Mountecute of Mount in Essex; to William Huiston the younger, son of my well-beloved brother-in-law William Huiston of Edwardstone; and to John Tompson the younger son of my brother-in-law John Tompson of Nayland; and the remaining £9 to my wife. I give my daughter Mary, after my wife's decease, my biggest bible, my long table in the hall, the best bedstead in my chamber and my desk. I give my own mother 20s to be paid 1 month after the sale of my house. I give my well-beloved kinsman John Mountecute the younger my little bible. All the rest of my moveables, my wood, hogs, fowls and debts I bequeath to my well-beloved wife towards paying my debts and the decent and comely burial of my body. Ex'trix: wife. Supervisor: my well-beloved brother-in-law William Huisham of Edwardstone, and I give him 10s. Wit. Arnold White, William Huisonne, Thomas Deareslie. Pr. at Sudbury 15 April 1631.

229. R(W) ELLEN GOODAYE (X) of Bradfield St George, widow. 27 August 1630.

Commends soul to God trusting to be saved.
I give to George Hunt of Bradfield St George, my kinsman and son of late George Hunt of Bradfield St Clare, a tenement with 2 acre croft held copyhold of the manor of Bradfield St George after the decease of John Posford and Joan his wife and my niece. I give Rose Hunt, my kinswoman now dwelling with me the narrowest of my 2 great chests standing under the window and the linen in it; my will is it should be parted equally betwixt the 3 sisters Rose, Ellen and Elizabeth Hunt. My other biggest chest standing by the first, I give to my kinswoman Ellen Hunt and also my best kettle but one. I give Elizabeth Baley of Brettenham my gown and my black petticoat. I give my niece Joan

Pasford my red petticoat. I give Rose Hunt my best kettle, my brass pot, my warming pan, my skillet, my pestle and mortar. All the rest of my brass I give to her sister Elizabeth. All my pewter is to be parted between the 3 Hunt sisters. I give Ellen Hunt my joined form. I give Rachel, my kinswoman and daughter of Henry Write, a trundle bedstead with a flockbed, a blanket, a bolster, a coverlet, and a pair of sheets with a mat and bed line. My upper bed in the parlour I give as it stands complete to Rose Hunt. All the rest of my unbequeathed goods and debts I give to Rose Hunt, whom I make ex'trix. Wit. Samuel Crossman clerk, William Jollye. Pr. at Bury 25 April 1631.

230. R(W) JOHN BARKER (X) of Saxon Street [Saxham Street in Stowupland]. 10 February 1630/31.

Bequeaths soul to God.
I give Elizabeth my sister a posted bedstead with a flock bed and all that belongs to it except the coverlet. I give Alice Smith my sister a gown and a table. I give Anne Wymark a coverlet and a cupboard. I give Margaret my sister a petticoat, a kettle and the best ruff. I give my brother Christopher my best suit of apparel and all my carpenter's tools. I give Christopher Wymark, my kinsman, my second best suit of apparel. I give my brother Henry Smith my best stockings and to Alice my hat. I give Anne an apron; my least hutch to Elizabeth; and my biggest hutch to Alice. I give my father Christopher Barker all my goods and make him exor. My meaning is that my father and Anne my mother should have my house and ground for their lives, and afterwards they should go to William Wymarke the younger. If he is not of age, John Barker is to hold it. Wit. Thomas Kilborne, John Potter (X), Henry Reeve. Pr. at Bury 2 May 1631.

231. R(W) LAWRENCE HEMPSTED (N) of Rougham, husbandman. 23 April 1631.

Upon Saturday at night about twelve of the clock Lawrence Hempsted made and declared his will. He gave Reuben his son a cupboard; a long table in the hall to his daughter Constance; a little round table to his daughter Elizabeth; a long chest in the chamber to his daughter Anne; and the bed he lay in to his daughter Abigail. The residue of all his goods and his lease he gave to his wife Susan towards paying his debts and educating his children. He made her and Nicholas Adiold of Bury St Edmunds exors. If his wife dies before Reuben is 21, Nicholas Adiold is to have his lease and educate his children until Reuben is 21. Wit. Edmund Clarke, John Tillett (X). Let. ad. granted at Bury 2 May 1631 to exors.

232. R(W) DOROTHY BUCKSTON (X) of Shimpling, widow.
18 March 1630/31.

I give Robert Plampyn my brother all my household goods in his hands and I forgive him the £30 he owes me. I give £10 each to his 2 children Robert and Frances when 21. I give £10 each when 21 to John, Dorothy, Elizabeth, Anne, Dorcas, Mary and Frances, the children of my brother John Plampyn. Benefit of survivorship. I give all my plate, linen, brass and pewter to be equally divided between John Plampyn's 7 children. I bequeath all my household goods to my brother John Plampyn, and after his death to his children. I give 2 silver spoons of 20s price to Robert my godson, and a silver spoon of 10s to Frances, the children of my brother Robert Plampyn. I give 2 silver spoons of 20s to Frances daughter of John Plampyn; a 10s silver spoon each to my godchildren Lawrence, son of William Sterne, and Mary Golding. I give silver spoons of following values to: 8s to my god-daughter Elizabeth Clarke; 8s to Dorothy, daughter of Philip Sterne; 5s to my god-daughter Dorothy Johnsonne; and 5s to my godchild Dorothy, daughter of Edward Johnsonne clerk. I give my kinswoman Frances Hunt 40s, to my brother John Plampyn's 2 maid servants 5s each and 3s each to all his manservants. I give John Hamblyn 2s. I give all the residue of my goods to my brother John Plampyn, whom I make exor. Wit. Michael Pilborowe (X), Thomas Wright. Pr. at Bury 2 May 1631.

233. R(W) WILLIAM INGLISHE (X) of Bury St Edmunds, joiner.
8 August 1630.

Commits soul to God trusting to be saved through Jesus Christ.
I give my well-beloved wife Joan my messuage wherein I now dwell for her life, and also all my moveable goods and household stuff. After her decease my daughter Elizabeth is to have my messuage provided that within a year she pays £5 to my daughter Mary, wife of William Johnson. If Elizabeth refuses to pay £5 Mary is to sell my house and take her £5 out of the price before giving the rest to Elizabeth. Wife sole ex'trix. Wit. Thomas Biggs, William Brightwell, James Jennings. Pr. at Bury 5 May 1631.

234. R(W) WILLIAM FREND (X) of Great Saxham, yeoman. 13 April 1630.

Bequeaths soul to God trusting to be saved eternally through Jesus Christ. Being of great age.
God has bestowed on me a loving and comfortable wife with whom I have lived in married estate since our youth, praised be God for it. Notwithstanding that I have provided for her an allowance of £12 p.a. to be paid by my son-in-law Charles Shawe out of the profits of the land he will inherit after my decease, I give my wife Elizabeth 40s to be paid to her within a month, and all her linen to do with as she shall think best.

103

She shall live in the house and chamber where we now continue, and have the use of the bedding and other necessary things which she now uses in the chamber for her life if she remains in my son-in-law Pittes house; my mind is that none of these things shall be removed from that house. After my wife's decease, I give my bedding and household stuff in the house where I now dwell to Simon Pitts and his wife Elizabeth. As my daughter Katherine had a far larger dower of land than I was able to give to Elizabeth, the former's husband, Charles Shawe, was bound in £200 to pay £100 to Simon Pittes after my decease. Since that time I have paid £100 out of my own goods to Simon Pittes, so the bond no longer stands. At my breaking up of house, intending to spend the rest of my life sojourning, I gave into the custody of Charles Shawe some of my cattle and almost all my household stuff. I now give him and his wife all these goods and also that part of my household goods remaining in several rooms in the house from whence I went, and the posted bedstead I had reserved for my own use but is now in his house. In a former will made about 2 years ago I bequeathed the following sums to the children of Charles and Katherine Shaw: £5 to Francis (to whom I had already given £10), £10 each to Edward, Charles, Simon and Susan. I have already paid the first 3 their legacies, and paid £10 into the hands of Peter Baxter with a bond to pay this sum to Susan. I give Simon £10 to be paid a month after Michaelmas next, which I will give him with my own hand if I live so long. I have also given my daughter Katherine £5 and a legacy to her sixth child Anne, as well as giving as much as I intended to Francis Mills and to William and Avis, the 2 children of my daughter Pyttes. The residue of my goods and chattels I give to Simon Pyttes and make him exor. Wit. John Eldred clerk, Edmund Gates senior. Pr. at Bury 9 May 1631.

235. R(W) ROBERT WEETINGE of Redgrave, linen weaver.
15 February 1630/31.

Commits soul to God and hopes for remission of sins.
I give Alice my well-beloved wife all my lands and tenements for life, but if she remarries the 2 pightles called Chapmans shall be let by my son Robert and the rents divided amongst my children. I give all the property bequeathed to my wife to my son Robert after her decease. I give £80 to be paid in equal portions to my children John, Nicholas, Stephen, Jonathan, Joseph, Alice, Mary and Elizabeth at age of 26. Benefit of survivorship and power to distrain. If any of these children are 26 when my wife dies, then Robert is to pay their legacies within 2 years. I give my son Robert my best pair of looms and all my slayes and other implements belonging to my trade, except for my other looms. I give my sons John and Nicholas my next best pair of looms to be parted between them if they are sold or otherwise at their discretion after my wife's decease. I give my 3 sons Stephen, Jonathan and Joseph a pair of looms each after my wife's decease; the eldest to have first choice. I give Robert my best table in the hall, my cupboard in my lodging chamber, and the bed

complete whereon I now lie on condition that within 6 months of my wife's death he pays my daughters Alice and Mary 10s each and my daughter Elizabeth 20s. If he defaults I give all my household stuff bequeathed to him to my 3 daughters. I give my daughter Alice my posted bedstead with feather bed and bedding and now standing in my chamber. I give my daughter Mary my best chest and my daughter Elizabeth my next best chest. These gifts are to be delivered after my wife's decease. All the rest of my goods and chattels, cattle and corn I bequeath to my wife Alice and make her my ex'trix, desiring her to bring up my children in good education and the fear of God. Wit. William Greenewood, who wrote this will, Richard Welton (X). Pr. at Bury 9 May 1631.

236. R(W) ELIZABETH PEIRSON (N) of Little Saxham, widow. October 1630.

She was keeping at the house of William Dawson when she declared her will as follows: she took a cushion into her hand and said to William Dawson I give you this cushion and with it all the rest of my moveable goods on condition that when I die you shall see me decently buried. I desire that, if it may be spared, you shall give my son Abraham Peirson, a flockbed, a flock bolster and a bird coverlet. Wit. John Wymark, Roger Emyns (X). Let. ad. granted in John Jewell's house in Bury on 16 May 1631 to William Dawson.

237. R(W) EDMUND FROST (X) of Cockfield, joiner. 2 December 1630.

Commends soul to God and hopes to be saved through Jesus Christ.
I will that my wife Anne has for life my half of the messuage wherein I dwell with outhouses, yard and orchard, and all belonging except what I have lately conveyed to Francis Bumpsted. After her decease it is to be equally divided between my sons Thomas and Gabriel. If at any time during her life my wife is in need and she is still a widow, she may sell the messuage. I give my son Thomas all my tools belonging to the trade of joining. I give all my unbequeathed moveables to my wife and make her ex'trix. Wit. Gabriel Warner (X), John Smyth. Pr. at Bury 16 May 1631

238. R(W) JOHN SARGENT of Stradishall, husbandman. 2 April 1630.

Commits soul to God in name of my only saviour Jesus Christ.
I give my son John 30s, and my 2 daughters Anne and Elizabeth £4 each within a year of my decease. All the rest of my goods and chattels I give to my wife Phyllis, whom I make ex'trix. Wit. Richard Bucher (X), John Webb, who wrote will. Pr. at Bury 23 May 1631.

239. R(W) STEPHEN GILLMAN (X) of Stanton, timber master.
25 March 1631.

Commends soul to God.
I give my wife Margaret all my lands and tenements in Stanton for life, and after her decease to my son Stephen. I give £10 to my daughter Katherine, and £5 to my daughter Margaret to be paid by Stephen at £5 p.a. after he inherits my land. Power to distrain. I give Stephen, after my wife's decease, a chest, a chair table, a cupboard and the posted bed that stands in the parlour with all its bedding. I give my daughter Katherine a framed table, a joined chair and a bedstead standing in the hall chamber with all its bedding after my wife's decease. All the rest of my moveables I give to my wife for ever, and make her ex'trix. Wit. John Dawson, Jane Hawis (X), Robert Fuller. Pr. at Bury 23 May 1631.

240. R(W) WILLIAM PEACHIE (X) of Mildenhall, shepherd. 13 April 1631.

Bequeaths soul to God.
I give my son William my best suit of clothes, my boots, shoes and my best hat, my hutch standing at the bed's foot next to the wall, half my working implements and tools, a long table and a wicker chair standing in the hall, a pair of bedsteads lying aloft on rafters and the bullocks loft in the yard. I give my daughter Agnes a hutch standing in the corner behind the window in the bed chamber, the feather bolster I lie on with 2 pillowbeeres and 2 pairs sheets and my best coverlet. I give my daughters Agnes and Elizabeth all the pillows on the bed I lie on to be divided between them, and all the pewter in my house. I give Agnes the cupboard, which was mine before I last was married and my best kettle but one. I give my daughter Elizabeth my 3 milk bullocks, the biggest chest in the bed chamber, the bedstead I lie on with its bedding except the pillows, my new cupboard, the rest of my kettles and my smallest brass pot. I give my wife Elizabeth my midsummer quarter's wages, which I am to receive of Mr Cotes, to pay her rent, an acre of barley and all my tubs, dishes and spoons. All the rest of my goods I give to my son Nicholas, whom I make exor. Wit. Nicholas Coates, Henry Johnson (X). Pr. at Bury 26 May 1631.

241. R(W) EDWARD REEVE (X) of Hundon, miller. 21 December 1630.

Commits soul to God.
I give my wife Margaret for life my lease of the windmill in Hundon, which I hold by indenture from the late William, Earl of Devonshire, on condition she keeps the windmill in good repair and also keeps the stones, hopper, goeing gear and other implements in as good condition as they now are. She must pay my children £4 each at one a year in the following order: Mary my eldest daughter, Avis my second daughter, my

son John, and my youngest daughter Elizabeth. After my wife's death, I give the lease of my windmill to my son John, who must pay my 4 daughters £4 each at one p.a. in this order: Mary, Avis, Anne, Elizabeth. All my other goods I give to my wife towards bringing up my children and paying my debts; I make her ex'trix. Wit. Robert Pledger, William Kinge. Pr. at Clare 14 April 1631.

242. R(W) THOMAS BAKER (X) of Hepworth, tailor. 14 March 1630/31

Bequeaths soul to God.
I give my son Edmund all my houses and grounds in Hepworth and Barningham for life to him and his wife Lydia and then to their son Thomas. I give the following legacies to my daughters to be paid one a year: 30s in 3 instalments to Elizabeth, 10s to Joan, 10s to Margery and 10s to Margaret. If Edmund refuses to pay any of these legacies, the legatee has right to distrain on my close in Barningham. I make my son Edmund exor. He is to bury my body decently and to pay my debts and legacies. I bequeath to him all my moveable goods within and without my house. Wit. John Baker (X), Richard Frost, Samuel Pett. Pr. at Ixworth 20 April 1631.

243. R(W) JOHN SMYTH (N) of Redlingfield. 14 December 1630.

I give to my wife all those things that were hers and 1 pair of sheets of the best sort, a board cloth and £30 and 'you I do intreate to pay her'. I give to her the profits of my land according to your bargain and mine. My son Reginald and his wife are to stay with her as they do now. I give Reginald all the residue of my goods. I make my wife and my son John exors. He made his will by word of mouth and did pull his hankerchief out of his pocket and gave it to his wife to put her in possession of his goods. Wit. William Bartlett, William Warne. Pr. at Bury 24 May 1631.

244. R(W) SAMUEL ONGE (X) of Bardwell, labourer. 18 May 1631.

Commends soul to God and trusts Jesus Christ will save him. To be buried in Bardwell churchyard.
I give Rose my wife for life my tenement and land in Bardwell as now divided from my brother Thomas's part, and after her decease to my son Samuel. I give my son John my acre of land in Willowmeere in Bardwell and £4 to be paid by Samuel at £1 p.a. after my wife's decease. All my moveable goods and chattels I give to my wife Rose towards bringing up my children and paying my debts. Wife ex'trix. Wit. John Sillett, Thomas Wyndout. Pr. at Bury 30 May 1631.

245. R(W) OLIVER HOWLET of Exning, yeoman. 9 May 1631.

Bequeaths soul to God and hopes to be saved through merits of Jesus Christ. To be buried in Exning churchyard.
I give my wife Rebecca for life the lease of my house with adjoining close, totalling 5 rods and lying by Watering Lane, and 9 acres free land lying dispersed in Exning fields. After her death I give the remainder of the lease to my son Henry, and the 9 acres to my son Edward. I give my 2 daughters £10 each to be paid by Henry 3 years after he inherits my house. I give my daughter Elizabeth my new house which I built in the orchard with all the rooms therein and the adjoining orchard after my wife's decease. I give my wife all the bedding and household stuff belonging to the parlour and the bed and bedding in the chamber over the parlour which she lies in, and 2 of the best cows. I give my daughter Philippa £4 to be paid by my exors within 4 years of my decease. I give my grandchildren 10s each to be paid within 10 years. The rest of my goods I leave to Rebecca my wife and Edward my son, and I make them exors. Wit. John Westhorpe, William Folkes. Pr. at Bury 23 May 1631.

246. R(W) PHILIP FOOKES (X) of Lakenheath, shepherd. 28 January 1627/28.

Bequeaths soul to God and Jesus Christ and hopes to be partaker of heavenly joys promised for elect people of God.
I give Edward and Philip, sons of John Largent, £12 each to be paid 1 year after the decease of my wife Elizabeth. I give my godchild Philip Fookes £3 when 21. The residue of my goods and chattels I bequeath to my wife and make her ex'trix. Wit. Thomas Halman, Thomas Brewett, Edmund Morley. Pr. at Bury 26 May 1631.

247. R(W) ROBERT RUMBELOWE (X) of Dalham, singleman. 27 January 1630/31.

Commends soul to God trusting to be saved by merits of Jesus Christ.
I give my uncle Edmund Hibble £30 to be paid within 1 year of my decease. I give my kinsman John Pettit £5 and my servant Frances Cutmer 40s, both to be paid within 1 year. I give my kinswoman Mary Whiffine, one of the daughters of my uncle John Pettit £5 and my kinswoman Bridget [blank in MS] daughter of John Pettit £5, both within 2 years. I give my kinswoman Esther Pettit £5; I give Anne, daughter of Thomas Rumbelowe, £5; I give my kinsman Thomas Cobb £5; and £5 to Jonas Cobb; all to be paid within 3 years. I give my servant Thomas Cutmer 20s to be paid when he is 21. I give 20s to the poor of Dalham and 10s to the poor of Hinderclay. The residue of my lands and goods I give to my brother John Rumbelowe and make him exor. Wit. Edmund Hebble, Thomas Wakefeild. Pr. at Bury 9 May 1631.

248. R(W) ALICE BOWTELL (X) of Haverhill, widow. 4 May 1629.

Commends soul to God hoping through merits of Jesus Christ to be a partaker of eternal life and to be amongst the company of the heavenly saints in glory for ever.

I bequeath to my 2 daughters Margery, wife of Francis Penny cutler of Cambridge, and Elizabeth, wife of Henry Fann wool driver of St Ives in Huntingdonshire, my messuage in Haverhill called the Crown with outhouses, stables and gardens now occupied by John Sale. Margery must pay £5 to my grandchild Barbara Clarke, and Elizabeth must pay £5 to my grandchild Emma Clarke. Both payments are to made in the south porch of Haverhill church one year after my decease. Benefit of survivorship, and in case of default the legatee is to inherit the defaulter's share of the Crown. Elizabeth and Margery must allow my grandson Robert Clarke free access into and through the yard of the Crown to fetch water from the well and to bring in and out carts carrying wood, timber or straw. I give my daughter Margery Penny 6 silver spoons and a silver beaker. I give my daughter Elizabeth Fann 6 silver spoons, a mortar, a pair of iron racks and a great cobiron. I give them all my linen, brass and pewter to be equally divided between them. I give my grandson Robert Clarke my lately built messuage wherein I dwell, which is next to the Crown and is called the Shop, with yard, shops and stable belonging to it. I also give him the great chest in the chamber over the gatehouse, and all my moveable goods in the chamber where he now lies, that is a posted bed and trundle bed with all their bedding, 2 livery cupboards, 2 chests, a wicker chair, 2 green chairs and a glass case. I give my grandchild and god-daughter Barbara Penny all my household stuff in the chamber next to the street where I lie, that is a bed and bedding, a table, 8 buffet stools, 1 chair and a livery cupboard. I give my grand-daughter Emma Clarke the best chair, a table and 8 buffet stools in the chamber over the gatehouse. All the unbequeathed goods in this chamber I give Alice, daughter of my grandson William Clarke. I give 20s to the poor people of Haverhill to be paid to the overseers of the poor and laid out in wood for the poor against the winter after my decease. I give all my unbequeathed goods to my grandson Robert Clarke and make him exor. Wit. John Clarke, George Austyne, William Clarke. Pr. at Bury 24 May 1631.

249. R(W) ABIGAIL BOOTHE (X) of Chelsworth, singlewoman. 10 March 1627/28.

I give £5 each to my cousins Robert and Elizabeth, eldest son and daughter of my brother Robert Booth. I give his son Thomas £10 and his daughter Mary £5. These legacies are to be paid within 4 years. I give £5 each when 21 to the following children of Robert Booth: Richard, Henry, Nathan, John and Abigail. Benefit of survivorship. This sum of £50 was left to me by the will of my father Robert Booth and is now in the hands of my brother Robert, who has mortgaged to me 8 acres freehold land as surety for the performance of my will. I make my cousin Thomas Booth exor, and give him all my moveables. Wit. Robert Boothe, John Mynnes, Judith Mynnes (X), Anne Rosse (X). Pr. at Bury 6 June 1631.

250. R(W) ROBERT MYNIT of Ashley [Cambs], husbandman.
14 March 1630/31.

For her long and faithful service to me I give my servant Margaret Pepper widow all the money in my house at the time of my death and all my household stuff, except a cupboard and a feather bed which I have sold to Mistress Norridge, and which Margaret Pepper is to give to her after my death. My gift to Margaret Pepper is void if she does not remain my faithful servant until the day of my death. Wit. John Norridge senior, John Norridge junior and others. The testator lived until 22 April 1631. Pr. no place given on 1 June 1631.

251. R(W) EDWARD MUSKET (X) of Harleston, yeoman. 23 April 1631.

Commends soul to God hoping to be made a living member of Jesus Christ.
I give my son Robert and his wife Mary a parcel of land called Longhand and held copyhold of Harleston manor, and 2 closes called Sumings and held copyhold of Haughley manor. I give the messuage wherein I now dwell with its land to my son Robert for ever, and if he has no heirs to my son William after his decease. Robert is to pay William £30 at £5 p.a. out of the profits of the 5 acre close called the close before my gate with its east end abutting on Sheepe Coate Green in Harleston and the west end on my messuage. William has power to distrain. I give William 4 pairs of sheets and all my pewter, and all my household goods in his possession at the time of my death. I give his children, William and John, 40s each when 21. All my other goods I give to my son Robert and make him exor, but if he refuses I appoint William exor. Wit. Edmund Leywarde, Anne Heyward. Pr. at Bury 7 June 1631.

252. R(W) WILLIAM BARTLETT (X) of Redlingfield, yeoman.
20 May 1631.

Commends soul to God and trusts to inherit life everlasting.
I give Katherine my wife £40 in value of my goods and chattels to be taken at her choice, and appraised by 2 indifferent persons. If she does not remain in my house and farm where I now dwell, she is to have 12 loads of wood for her fuel. I give her £5, and all my land in Redlingfield for life, and after her decease to my son Edmund on condition that within 1 year he pays £100 as follows: £10 each to Katherine and John, children of my son William; £20 each to my sons James, John and Robert; £5 each to my daughters Margaret and Anne; and £5 each to Edmund and John,

children of my son Edmund. Legacies are to be paid to heirs of any legatees who have died. If Edmund defaults on any of the above payments, my good friend and landlord. Francis Bedingfeild esquire of Redlingfield, is to sell all my land in that parish and Horham and, after paying my legacies, is to give the remaining money to my son Edmund. I give my son John £20 to be paid within a year and £20 within 2 years of my decease. I give my son William £13 6s 8d and my son James £10, both to be paid within 1 year. I give Anne, daughter of my son James, 40s within a month of my wife's death. I give my daughters Margaret and Anne £35 each within 2 years of my decease. I give my wife all my timber towards repairing my house. I give my son Edmund £5. Exors: my especial good friend Francis Bedingfeild, my wife and my son Edmund. I give my wife my unbequeathed goods and chattels. Wit. William Deane, Roger Barker, Thomas Easton, who wrote this will. Pr. at Bury 14 June 1631.

253. BENJAMIN PAYNE of Burwell [Cambs], yeoman. 2 April 1631.

Gives soul to God and steadfastly believes to be saved by Jesus Christ.
I give my son Stephen the messuage wherein I now dwell with a meadow and 3 acres of arable land, which I bought from Timothy Hutton. Stephen must pay the legacies in this will. I give my grandsons John, Benjamin and William Sowth £5 each when 21 or married. I give my grandchild Mary Sowth when 21 or married a posted bedstead with a feather and a straw bed, a coverlet, a blanket, the curtains and rods, a bolster and a pillow as it now stands in the upper chamber. I give my grandchild Agnes Sowth a bullock or 40s at her choice when she is 21 or marries. I give my grandson Benjamin Canford when 21, 1 acre copyhold arable near Halledgate and half an acre near where Thomas Pamplyne's windmill stands; this 1½ acres is part of the land I bought from William Gilbert. I give 1 acre of the same land to each of my grandsons Richard and Robert Canford when 21. I give my grandchild Alice Canford when 21 or married one Thurdale rod of arable land purchased from Barnabas Turner. I give my daughter Alice Canford 3½ acres arable late Gilbert's and the Thurdale rod until her 3 children reach the age of 21. I give my son-in-law Richard Canford the crop of the 2 crofts now sown, and £20 to be paid 6 months after my decease. I give Benjamin, Richard and Robert Canford 20s each to be put out to the best profit by their father until they are 21. I give my grandchildren Benjamin and Elizabeth Hymer 40s each when 21 or married. I give Benjamin, son of my son John, £5 and 40s to Elizabeth, daughter of my son Stephen, within 1 year. I give the latter my wife's black gown and her best petticoat. I give 20s each to the rest of my son Stephen's children to be paid within 1 year. I give my grandson Benjamin Canford a pightle abutting on the Common Lane and lying between Hall close and Cunny close. I give all my household stuff to be equally parted between my son Stephen and my daughter Alice Canford. I give 20s to the poor of Burwell to be dealt out at my burial. All my unbequeathed goods and chattels I give to my son Stephen and make him

exor. Wit. John Wilkyns, Richard Bulman (X).

Memorandum that I have surrendered all my copyholds held of the manor of Ramsies to the use of my will into hands of John Wilkyns and in presence of Richard Bullman, both tenants of the manor. Pr. at Bury 6 June 1631.

254. R(W) RICHARD JACOB of Great Fakenham, yeoman. 23 January 1629/30.

Commends soul to God in sure hope of everlasting life.

I give the poor people of Great Fakenham 5s. I give my wife Agnes for life all my lands and tenements; she must keep them in repair with claying and thatching. After my wife's decease I give my land and tenements to my son Philip. If he dies before my wife, she must pay his wife Mary £6 p.a. for her maintenance and bringing up her children. If my wife refuses to do this, the property goes to Mary. After my funeral and probate expenses and the 10s left to my supervisor are paid, I will that my wife shall have for life the use of my household stuff, corn, cattle, poultry and implements of husbandry on condition she is bound in surety to preserve these goods and deliver them to her exors. After her decease I will that her son William Gooch shall have all the household stuff she brought to me at our marriage. I will that my wife Agnes pays my daughter Elizabeth £5 within 6 months; power to distrain. I give my daughter Elizabeth £50 to be paid at £10 p.a. starting 2 years after my wife's decease, and I give her daughter Anne Marten £10 a year after my wife's death or when she is 21. If my son-in-law John Marten does not pay my son Philip the various sums of money he owes him, then the legacies to Elizabeth and Anne Marten shall be void. The rest of my goods and chattels I give to my son Philip and make him exor. Supervisor: my brother Grigge of Bury St Edmunds to whom I give 10s. Wit. Henry Rewse, Simon Rewse. Pr. at Rickinghall Inferior 17 June 1631.

255. R(W) HENRY STEELE the elder of Bury St Edmunds, bricklayer. 29 March 1631.

Commends soul to God and trusts through Jesus Christ to have remission of sins.

I give my son Robert 2s 6d and my son William 5s. I give my son Henry 4s and my daughter Martha 12d. I give my daughter Barbara 20s and a posted bedstead furnished as it stands in the parlour or shop in the house where I now dwell. All these legacies are to be paid within a year of my decease. All the rest of my goods and chattels I give to Alice my loving wife, whom I make ex'trix. Wit. Edward Fletcher, Robert Walker. Pr. at Bury 14 June 1631.

256. R(W) THOMAS BAXTER (N) of Flempton. 24 April 1631.

He made his father Peter Baxter exor and gave him all his moveable goods, except that he gave his wife Marian her linen and woollen apparel. The reason why he did this is that his father stands bound for him for some debts, and his wife has more than £10 p.a. to live on. Wit. John Layman, Richard Reeve. Let. ad. granted to exor 27 June 1631. No place given.

257. R(W) SUSAN SAER (N) of Groton. 1 June 1631.

Bequeathed soul to God.
She gave Mary, daughter of Robert Goulston of Groton, a lamb worth 5s and another to Mary, daughter of John Blewet of Groton. She gave 10s to Nathaniel Blewet of Groton widow [sic], and a 5s lamb each to his daughters Sarah and Elizabeth. She gave lambs worth 5s each to Elizabeth, daughter of Francis Browne of Groton, and to all 4 children of Stephen Kinge of Groton. All the remainder of her goods she gave to Annabel wife of Stephen Kinge. Wit. Elizabeth, wife of Austen Scofen, Mary Goulston. Pr. at Bury 16 June 1631.

258. R(W) RICHARD CRADOCK of Barrow, clerk. 18 March 1629/30

Bequeaths soul to 3 persons of Trinity and hopes for resurrection.
I give to my loving son John Cradock of Redgrave, bachelor of Divinity, all my books and papers in my study, and the chair, table and pictures in the hall on this date. I also give him my best bed and featherbed with rug, blankets, 2 bolsters, 2 pillowbeeres, 2 pairs of best sheets and the curtains. I give him all the hewn timber in my possession and a skep of bees. The rest of my goods and chattels are to be divided into 2 equal parts. My loving daughter Priscilla, wife of Richard Thache of London, is to have one part and the other is to be divided between my loving daughters Crabtree and Baker. I give all my daughters a skep of bees each. I give my loving son Mr Baker of London, bachelor of Divinity, 30s to make a ring in token of my love to him. I give my loving cousin John Cradock, bachelor of arts, Mr Eastye his works and a skep of bees. I give £20 to be paid out of my ready money, before anything else is paid, to my poor blind cousin Mary Cradock now with me towards her placing and settled maintenance. I give £13 6s 8d to the poor of Barrow to be paid at 13s 4d p.a. at Christmas. I give Mr Arthur Heigham gentleman of Barrow Hall the book in my study entitled Dr Whitakers against Stapleton in folio. I give my godson Timothy Auckland living in Nottinghamshire 20s if so much remain after my other legacies have been paid. I give my faithful servant Judith Chapman now dwelling with me 40s if so much remain. I give Goodwife Isbell a comb of malt and a bushel of wheat. I give my cousin Mary the old flockbed in the servants parlour with some

113

old caverings, an old pair sheets and a trundle bedstead. I give Judith Chapman a skep of bees. Exor. John Cradock. And now farewell vain world and come Lord Jesus and welcome Amen. Come quickly Amen. Wit. Anthony Disborowe, John Cradock, Judith Chapman. Pr. at Bury 9 May 1631.

259. R(W) THOMAS SYMONDES of Hinderclay. 6 January 1628/29.

Gives soul to God.
I give John my son all my tenements and lands in Hinderclay, on condition he pays my debts and legacies and shall be bound within 6 weeks of my decease to Richard Elcocke, rector of Westhorpe and Thomas Hart gentleman of Westhorpe to pay my wife Thomasine £10 p.a. During her life my wife is to have so much of my household stuff as the above two persons shall think fit and convenient. I give William Craske of Bardwell, my son-in-law, 20s and all my wearing apparel both linen and woollen. I give my daughter Elizabeth 20s and all my books for the benefit of her children. I give her 3 children: John, William and Elizabeth Craske 20s each to be paid 1 year after my burial. All the rest of my goods and chattels I give to my son John now rector of Gislingham and make him exor. Wit. Richard Elcocke, Thomas Harte, Robert Foxton. Pr. at Bury 20 June 1631.

260. R(W) JOHN SCOTT (X) of Hawkedon, labourer.

Resigns soul to God. To be buried in Hawkedon churchyard.
I give to William my eldest son 12d and to Edward my second son my hatchet, my spade, my shovel, my scythes and all that belongs to them. I give Martha my daughter 12d. All the rest of my goods and chattels I give to my wife Mary and make her ex'trix. Wit. Robert Raye, clerk, Nathaniel Ray. Pr. at Stanfield 25 June 1631.

261. R(W) MIRABEL REVELL (X) of Chevington, widow. 13 May 1631.

Commends soul to God hoping to be received into heaven.
I give all my goods and chattels and ready money to my loving daughter Martha Revell of Chevington singlewoman and make her ex'trix. Wit. Joshua Waad, Anne Sparrowe (X), Elizabeth Claydon (X). Pr. at Bury 11 July 1631.

262. R(W) MARGARET BEDINGFEILD (N) of Gazeley, widow. 25 June 1630.

She gave Jervis Barret, yeoman of Needham in the parish of Gazeley, her book of the New Testament. She gave his son John her ewe sheep, and his daughter Anne all the rest of her goods and chattels. She made Jervis Barret her exor. Wit. Martha (X) wife of Edmund Gatteward. Pr. at Bury 11 July 1631.

263. R(W) THOMAS LOWE (X) of Norton, yeoman. 28 June 1631.

Commits soul to God. To be buried in Norton churchyard.
I give my wife Ellen for life my land with tenements and a pightle lying in Norton and Thurston. After her decease I bequeath to my son Thomas my house wherein I now dwell with barn, stable, yard and a pightle lying between Edmund Cartwrite's land on the east and William Gage's to the west. I give my son William, after my wife's decease, a 2 acre meadow at Norton bridge with Thomas Browne's land to the south and Norton bridge close to the north and abutting on the river towards the east. I give my son Benjamin £20 to be paid by William a year after my wife's decease. Power to distrain. My wife is to keep my house and buildings in good repair with the help of my son Thomas. My wife is to have all my moveables within and without my house, and is to pay my debts. I make her ex'trix. Wit. Jeffery Lord, Richard Loft. Pr. at Bury 11 July 1631.

264. R(W) ROBERT ALDERTON of Great Ashfield, yeoman. 6 April 1631.

Commends soul to mercies of God trusting to be saved as one of elect.
I will that Elizabeth my wife has all the household goods she brought unto me. I give her 1 milk cow out of my dairy which she is to choose after 2 others have been chosen. I give her all the wood standing in the yard on the south side of the messuage wherein I dwell at time of my decease, and 1 cart load of brend wood yearly to be laid in a convenient place near my messuage by my son John as long as my wife remains a widow. I give her 4 of the best cheeses in the house at her choice, and half a firkin of butter to be given to her by John within 4 days of my decease. I give my son John my messuage wherein I dwell in Great Ashfield with its buildings, yards, orchard, the adjoining hempland and the croft with a barn on it on the north side of the messuage. The croft and hempland together total 2 acres. I also give him an adjoining 2 acre enclosed pasture called short crofte and a half acre pightle at the end of it called the Nabb. Also an enclosed field with an adjoining parcel of wood totalling 8 acres. I give my son John the reversion of a 5 acre close in Ashfield called Sallow close and that of a 3 acre close called Hustowe. I also give him a 12 acre enclosure now divided with a Bowe into 2 parts and called Lound field, which I bought of Richard Hovell gentleman. Whereas it is unknown to me whether my son Thomas is still living, my son John is to hold a 10 acre pasture close called Springe close in Ashfield until such time as Thomas comes to my messuage and shows himself to 3 witnesses and claims anything left to him in my will. I give my grandson called Henry my tenement in Ashfield called Cobbes with adjoining 8 acres of pasture and a 3 acre piece of land in Lounde field. I also give him a posted bed in the hall chamber and the featherbed on it whereon my son John now lies, together with the bolster, a coverlet of the best sort, 2 blankets, 2 pairs sheets and a pillow of the best sort at his choice with a pillowbeere. I give him two milk neates, one at his choice and the other

chosen by my son John. I give Henry one of my best horse collars and a pair of traces for 1 horse. I give my grandchildren Robert and Rose Alderton 40s to be paid to them when 24 by their brother Henry. All the rest of my goods and cattle I give to my son John to pay my funeral charges and perform my will. Exors: my loving friend and brother-in-law Robert Newman of Haughley and my son John. I give the former 10s for his pains. Wit. William Stokes, Robert Growse, John Deverex. Pr. at Bury 14 July 1631.

265. R(W) ROBERT TWYNE of Glemsford, clothier. 23 June 1631.

Resigns soul into hands of Jesus Christ who shall come to judge the quick and the dead. To be buried in Glemsford churchyard.

I give my wife Anne £4 p.a. for 12 years towards bringing up my children. She is to have the chamber over the butteries and room in the hall of the messuage where I dwell with free access to the fire until such time as the tenement where my brother George lives becomes empty. I bequeath her this tenement for life, and she is to have liberty to take water from the best ponds or springs belonging to the messuage where I dwell. I give her one of my best cows and £5 to be paid by my son Robert one year after my decease, and all such goods as were hers. I give £5 each to my 3 youngest sons Henry, Francis and Ambrose to be paid out of my house and land called Tylnes hall at rate of one p.a. I give my son Robert my manor house called Tylnes hall wherein I now dwell, a piece of arable and 2 pieces adjoining enclosed pasture and a green called Tylnes green. He must pay the above legacies and others to be paid out of the profits of this house and land. Robert is to pay £10 each when 18 to my youngest daughter Jane, my son Jerome and my daughter Sarah. Benefit of survivorship. I give my daughter Alice £10 to be paid by my exors within 6 months of my decease, and a chest standing by her bed. I give my daughter Martha £10 within a year. I bequeath to my son Thomas 2 pieces of land in Oxden field, a piece of land called Tylnes wood and a piece in Mill field, all of which are part of Tylnes manor, and a piece of land called Houbrooke. I give my son Edward my right in a piece of arable lying in Longland field and part of same manor, and £10 within a year. I give £10 each to my children John, Charles and George to be paid one a year starting 2 years after my decease. Benefit of survivorship. I also give these 3 sons some enclosed land called Cobbes croft or Claydons, but until their legacies have been paid my son Thomas is to hold this land. During this time he must pay 20s p.a. each to Sarah, Jane and Jerome towards their maintenance. My wool, cloth, corn and cattle are to be used to pay those legacies which my exors are to pay. The rest of my goods I give to be equally shared by Anne my wife and my children. Exors: sons Robert and Thomas. I give £5 to the child Anne my wife now goeth with. Wit. William Cannam, Richard Gardner. Pr. at Glemsford 6 July 1631.

266. R(W) ROBERT HAMAND of Long Melford, yeoman. 24 January 1628/29.

Commends soul to God hoping to be saved by merits of Jesus Christ.
I make my brother-in-law Abraham Hamond of Staningfield and my brother John Hamand of Melford my exors, bequeathing them all my goods to discharge my debts and funeral expenses. I also give them my 2 pieces copyhold land called Sheppards Croft and John Wright's piece, which are part of my tenement Hills. The former lies within the lands of Abraham Wright and the latter between the land of William Brand and that of Sir Robert Roockeard. If my moveable goods and these 2 pieces of land will not pay my debts, my exors are to hold my freehold land and houses until they are paid. I give my wife Susan for life the rest of my copyhold land, and my freehold land after my debts have been paid towards bringing up my children. If she remarries my exors are to take my land and pay her 40s p.a. and use the rest to bring up my children until they are 21. Wit. Abraham Wright, Robert Hamond, Philip Hamond. Pr. at Bury 18 July 1631.

267. R(W) THOMAS NEGUS the elder of Stanstead, clothier. 22 April 1631.

I give my wife Frances £30 in satisfaction of her rights of dower or thirds in the freehold land and tenements in Hartest and Stanstead which I bought from Richard Frost, and which are now occupied by Sarah, widow of my son Richard. I also give my wife half my household stuff and cattle on condition she gives Sarah a full discharge of her rights in the above property. If she refuses, her legacies are to be given to my exor. I give my son John and his wife Mary, after my wife's decease, the messuage wherein I dwell with its land in Stanstead called Punges totalling 10 acres and now occupied by myself and George Abbott. I give my son Thomas my messuage in Stanstead called Sheppards and occupied by William Sharpe with an adjoining 4 acre pasture close now occupied by George Abbott, on condition that within 6 months he discharges my exor of any obligation for debts for which I and Thomas stand charged. Failing this I give this tenement and land to my exor. I give my son Henry, after the decease of my wife, my messuage and adjoining 2 acre piece of land late Andrew Walter's in Stanstead and now occupied by Thomas Evered, and £10 to be paid within a year of my decease. I give 20s to the poor of Stanstead. The rest of my goods and estate I give to my son John, whom I make exor. Wit. Thomas Wright, Richard Gardner. Pr. at Bury 8 August 1631.

268. R(W) KATHERINE CATLIN (X) of Culford, widow. 6 July 1631.

Commits soul to 3 persons of Trinity to attend resurrection of all those that depart in true faith.
I give my house and lease land in Culford, which I had by gift of my late husband William Browne and by the will of my son Isaac Browne, to my

exor to sell and distribute the money as follows: to my daughter Susan Reynolds £10 to be paid to John Coxsage of Fornham St Martin to my daughter's use. I also give her a silver and gilt spoon and a pair of my best sheets. I give her son Thomas Page £10 and her daughter Katherine £30. both to be paid within a year. I give £20 when 21 to James, son of my late deceased daughter Mary Skinner, and a silver spoon. I give his sister Martha £20 when 20 and a silver and gilt spoon. When my daughter Anne married John Coxsage I became bound with my brother Abraham Chaplyn to pay a marriage portion of £100. My exor is to pay this sum out of money my lease land is sold for. I give my daughter Anne Coxsage a silver salt, a gilt spoon, a pair of my best sheets, 12 table napkins, a great chest and my largest brass pot. I give 40s to Abraham, son of my brother John Chaplyn sometime of Capel deceased. I give 6s 8d each to James, Abigail, Susan, Sarah, Margaret and Anne, the children of my sister Susan Wolfenden. I give 5s each to my brother Joseph Chaplyn, my sister Sarah Brett and my sister Rachel Bentlie, and 10s to the poor of Culford to be paid on the day of my burial. I give my exor for his pains £3, and he is to dispose of any surplus of my goods, after paying my legacies etc, amongst my children's children. I make my brother Abraham Chaplyn of Kedington my exor. Wit. James Worwell, Richard Summer. I give Francis Skynner, my son-in-law £10. James and Martha Skinner are to have benefit of survivorship. Pr. at Bury 9 August 1631.

269. R(W) THOMAS VINCENT (X) of Bacton, blacksmith. 17 March 1630/31.

Commends soul to Jesus Christ through whom he trusts to be saved.
I give my wife Margaret my cupboard standing in the parlour and a keep for glasses, a table with a frame and a joined form belonging to it, a buffet stool, 2 posted bedsteads with 2 featherbeds and 4 bolsters belonging to them, 4 pillows, a green rug, 3 coverlets, 2 pairs blankets, a trundle bedstead, 1 bed stool, a great chest, 3 coffers, 4 chairs, a wicker chair, a pair of cobirons, 2 spits, 2 pairs tongs, a hale, a gridiron, a trevet, 2 fire pans, all my brass and pewter, all my linen and woollen, a boulting hutch, a cheese press, cheese vats, bowls, keelers, milk pans and anything belonging to the dairy, all my beer vessels, 9 cushions, a bible, a warming pan, a latten candlestick, a pewter candlestick and all my other household goods. I make my wife ex'trix and she is to receive and pay my debts, and see my body brought decently to the ground. Wit. John Symonds (X), John Watchance, who wrote this will. Pr. at Bacton 3 August 1631.

270. R(W) OSBORNE STUBBS (X) of Sapiston, labourer. 12 April 1630.

Commends soul to God who made him and who through merits of Jesus Christ will save him.
I give my wife Mary for life my tenement and lease lands and my freehold land in Sapiston and Great Fakenham, and after her decease to my

youngest son William. I give my son John £8 to be paid by William in 3 instalments starting 1 year after my wife's decease. I give my son Thomas 40s to be paid by William 4 years after my wife's death, and my daughter Katherine £5 to be paid by him in 2 portions starting 5 years after my wife's decease. My son Richard shall freely have his dwelling in the house where I now live for his lifetime, and from the decease of my wife William shall pay him 13s 4d p.a. I give Richard a flockbed, a pair sheets, a coverlet and a bolster. If William fails to pay Richard his annuity, latter is to enter Clint pightle until the money is paid. All the rest of my moveable goods I give to my wife whom I make ex'trix. Wit. Thomas Aldham, John Bland, Thomas Wyndout. Pr. at Bury 1 August 1631.

271. R(W) PHYLLIS SERIANT (X) of Stradishall, widow. 26 July 1631.

Commends soul to God in name and merits of Jesus Christ.
I give my son John Seriant £3 to be paid within a year. I give my daughter Elizabeth, wife of Thomas Hamond, the low bedstead in the chamber wherein I now lie with all its bedding, that is a flockbed, 2 flock bolsters, a straw bed, 2 blankets, a covering and a pair sheets, the hutch standing at the foot of the bed, the best kettle save one, the middle tub and £3. The rest of my goods and chattels I give to my daughter Anne Seriant, whom I make ex'trix on condition she pays my debts and legacies. I make my loving friend in Christ Richard Butcher, yeoman of Stradishall, supervisor. Wit. John Webb, Richard Butcher (X), Anthony Pettiwate. Pr. at Bury 15 August 1631.

272. R(W) GEORGE SKEPPER (X) late of Thurston, yeoman.
28 December 1627.

Commends soul to God trusting through Jesus Christ to have his sins forgiven.
I give my copyhold messuage at Woodend in Thurston called Walters and occupied by Henry Sawer with 20 acres copyhold land all held of the manor of Littlehaugh to my wife Constance for life, and then to my son John on condition he pays following legacies: £20 each to my sons George and Peter 1 and 2 years after my wife's decease in the south porch of Thurston church. Power to distrain. Because I have been at great cost in the education of my son John at the University of Cambridge (whose studies and proceedings in learning I pray to God to bless and prosper), and because my sons George and Peter have carefully bestowed their labour and time in my service as servants to me without any recompense, I desire John to pay his brothers their legacies of £20. I give George my 2 closes of arable and pasture containing 14 acres and lying together in Thurston in a field called Black field and held copyhold of the manor of Netherhall. Also 8 acres in Alton meadow in Thurston, which is partly copyhold, part freehold and part leasehold of same manor. I give my son Peter my 1 acre pasture pightle in Thurston with its north end abutting on Bally way, and which I bought from John Verbye, 4 acres freehold

pasture called Footestande, and 14 acres arable lying dispersed in the fields of Rougham (4 acres in Mell field and the rest in St Edmunds field) held copyhold of Barton Hall manor. Peter is to have right of access with horse and cart to Footestande over 3 rods pasture on the south side of Baylie field doing as little damage as possible to the grass. I give my daughter Sarah. wife of Anthony Mapole, £40 to be paid in 2 halves at Michaelmas 1629 and 1630. I give Constance my wife a coffer or hutch in the parlour chamber with all the linen in it, a cupboard in the little parlour, a half-headed bedstead with a feather bed as it stands complete in the little parlour, a framed long table in the great parlour chamber, a little square framed table in the great parlour, a new chair and another great new chair, a buffet stool, the biggest brass kettle save one, the lesser brass pot, a fustian and a tick pillow, and 4 pewter dishes, 2 of the greatest size. I also give her all my household stuff in my messuage at Wood Ende, a latten mortar, my 2 silver spoons, 2 beer barrels to be chosen by her, 1 dozen trenchers, 6 hens and 2 shoats at her choice, a kneading trough, a boulting tun, 4 milk neats at her choice and 2 ewes. The residue of my goods and chattels, corn and cattle I give to my exors to pay my debts and legacies, and £12 to Henry Sawer and his wife Anne at Michaelmas next. Exors: sons George and Peter. I charge them to agree together in brotherly love. Wit. William Rushbrooke, John Sibbs, Thomas Bryant, Thomas Sibbs, Thomas Salsburye, Robert Bulwer. Pr. at Bury 15 August 1631.

273. R(W) EDWARD SPOONER (X) of Saxton Street in the parish of Wood Ditton [Cambs]. 11 February 1627/28.

Bequeaths soul to God trusting to be saved by Jesus Christ.
I give my son Thomas Spooner of Newmarket my free tenement where I now dwell with adjoining barn and ½ acre orchard in Saxon in Wood Ditton 6 months after my decease on condition he pays my 2 daughters Elizabeth and Mary £10 each within 2 years. Benefit of survivorship. If Thomas fails to pay this legacy, the tenement goes to my 2 daughters, who must then pay Thomas £20 within 4 years of my decease. My 2 daughters are to occupy my tenement for 6 months after my death. I give my daughter Agnes 5s. The rest of my goods and chattels I bequeath to my 2 daughters Elizabeth and Mary, and make them ex'trices. Wit. John Adams (X), Robert Gumer. Pr. at Cheveley 1 June 1631.

274. R(W) ANN SHEEP (X) of Burwell [Cambs], widow. 9 January 1629/30.

Bequeaths soul to God and steadfastly believes to be saved through Jesus Christ.
I give my daughter Anne £12 to be paid as follows: £11 on 1 November 1630 and 20s on 29 November 1631 into the hands of my kinsman Thomas Freston, who is to put money out until Anne is 21 or marries. I give my son John £12: £9 to be paid on 29 September 1631 and £3 on 29 September 1632 to Thomas Freston as above. John is to have his money when 21. I

give my son Thomas £6 and my daughter Elizabeth £6 to be paid by my exor on 29 September 1632. I give my son Henry £3 to be paid within 3 years of my decease if he comes to demand it, but if he does not come or it has pleased God to take him out of this world, 20s is to be paid to Thomas Sandewige of Bury St Edmunds where Henry owes for his wife's gown, and 40s to my daughter Anne. I give her all my household stuff both linen and woollen and my apparel and all my other goods except 40s, which I give to Thomas Freston to see my body decently buried and my will proved. Exor: Thomas Freston. Wit. John Wilkyns, Thomas Fuller, John Baron, Robert Baron. Pr. at Burwell 2 June 1631.

275. R(W) JOHN TABRAM of Soham [Cambs], blacksmith. 20 April 1631.

Bequeaths soul to God trusting to have sins forgiven through Jesus Christ.
I give Agnes my wife all my moveable goods. She must pay my daughter Anne £13 when 18. I give my daughter Margery 40s within a year of my decease. I give my daughter Elizabeth my freehold tenement and ground. I give my daughter Anne 3 rods arable lying in Fordham Hales and called Little Hales. I give Agnes my wife for her life my freehold tenement in Soham where I live, and make her ex'trix. I have surrendered my copyhold land to the lord of Netherhall Wigorns manor by Thomas Wilken and in presence of John Hodgkine, and my copyhold held of Soham manor into hands of Thomas Bugge and in presence of John Hodgkine. Supervisors: Thomas Bugge and Thomas Wilken. Wit. Thomas Bugge, Thomas Wilken, John Hodgkyn and me William Howe. Pr. at Soham 2 June 1631.

276. R(W) JOHN READE (X) of Soham [Cambs], husbandman. 3 April 1631.

Commends soul to God not doubting to be saved through Jesus Christ.
I give my eldest son John 10s to be paid by my ex'trix within 1 year of my decease. I give my second son Thomas my copyhold tenement wherein I live. I give my third son Robert £4 when 21 and my son Edward £4 when 21. I give my daughter Elizabeth £4 within 1 year. Benefit of survivorship. The money to pay these legacies is to be put out at interest by supervisors of will until they are due; the interest is to be paid to my ex'trix. I give Margaret my wife all my moveables and stock to pay my debts and legacies, and make her sole ex'trix. Supervisors: Thomas Cheavelye the elder, yeoman of Soham and his son Thomas Cheavelye the younger. Wit. Thomas Wylkins, Robert Petchey, Henry Petchie and me William Howe.
Memorandum: my daughter Elizabeth is to have the cupboard in the hall house. The testator surrendered his copyhold tenement to the lord of Netherhall Tendalls formerly Paynes manor into hands of Thomas Cheavelie in the presence of Benjamin Cropley, both copyholders of the manor. Pr. at Soham 2 June 1631.

277. R(W) RICHARD GIPPES (N) of Horringer, husbandman. 23 April 1631.

He willed that his debts should be paid, and his personal estate divided into 2 parts: one to his eldest son Thomas and the other to his wife Elizabeth for life, and after her death to his daughter Rose. Thomas and his wife are to pay the other 2 sons Miles and Simon 20s each after decease of testator's wife. Wit. John Longe, Holyfernus Towler. Let. ad. granted to Elizabeth Gippes on 23 May 1631. No place given.

278. R(W) JOHN STEGALL (N) of Elmswell, husbandman. 3 August 1631.

He gave all his goods and chattels to his wife Unita. Wit. William Crowe, William Ryce. Let. ad. granted 15 August 1631 to widow. No place given.

279. R(W) FRANCIS BRADNHAM (X) of West Stow, yeoman. 9 August 1631.

Bequeaths soul to God trusting to have remission of sins through Jesus Christ.
I give my daughter Dorothy £5 to be paid by my ex'trix when she is 20 or marries. The rest of my goods and chattels I give to my wife Mary and make her ex'trix. If she remarries, Dorothy is to have £5 more. Wit. Robert Webb, John Layman. Pr. at Bury 22 August 1631.

280. R(W) JOAN BRACKE (N) of Bury St Edmunds, widow. Saturday 27 August 1631.

She gave each of her 2 nephews Robert and John Doe 20s, and a flockbed or transome or bolster, a sheet, a blanket and a pewter dish. She gave 10s each to the 3 children of John Doe and £5 to her sister Kempe. The rest of her goods and chattels she gave to her nephew Thomas Kempe, and made him exor. Wit. Henry Kempe, Elizabeth Nodson (X) singlewoman, Katherine, wife of Nicholas Kempe. Let. ad. granted to exor at Bury 29 August 1631.

281. R(W) RICHARD HOWLETT (X) of Thurston, yeoman. 25 October 1627.

Bequeaths soul to God and hopes to be saved through merits of Jesus Christ.
All my copyhold land and tenements in Hargrave are to be sold by my brothers-in-law Andrew and Bennett Wright of Thurston, or by their eldest sons if they have died. They are to use the money to pay my legacies. I give my brother John £5; my godson Thomas Hindes £10; £10 to be divided amongst the children of my cousin Anne Hindes; £10 to my cousin Francis Hindes; £14 to be divided amongst the children of my

cousin Margery Sparrowe; £10 to my cousin Alice Sparrowe; £10 my cousin Audrey Sparrowe; £10 to my kinswoman Judith Linge; £3 to Elizabeth, daughter of Thomas Austine; £5 to Anne, daughter of my kinsman Bennett Wright; £8 to her sister Sarah; £3 to her sister Rachel; £3 to her brother John; £9 to be divided between John, Andrew and Barbara the children of Andrew Wright; and £10 to be divided amongst the children of my cousin John Hindes. Legatees have benefit of survivorship, and all the legacies are to be paid within 18 months of my decease. I make John and Sarah, children of Bennett Wright, my exors. Supervisor: William Wright. Wit. Nathaniel Craske, James Margerie. Pr. at Bury 7 September 1631.

282. R(W) JOHN BARLYMAN (X) the elder of Barningham, yeoman. 26 July 1631.

Bequeaths soul to God my creator, sanctifier and redeemer.
I give my wife Anne for life my tenement in Barningham where I now dwell and all my land in Barningham and Hepworth, and after her decease to my kinsman Robert, son of Thomas Barlyman, on condition he pays my legacies. I give £40, to be paid in 4 instalments, to my kinsman Timothy Shippe of Catlidge [Kirtling, Cambs]; £20 to be paid 5 and 6 years after my wife's decease to my kinswoman and servant Anne Barlyman; £10 to my kinsman John, son of Robert Deye of Hepworth; £5 to my kinsman John Deye of Kenninghall; £5 to my servant Rose Gates; and 50s to Mary, daughter of John Hawkes. Last 4 legacies to be paid within 1 year of my decease, and all to be paid in Barningham church porch. I give Robert Barlyman, immediately after my decease, my tenement and land in Weston [Market]. All my moveables I bequeath to Anne my wife and make her ex'trix. Wit. John Deye (X), Henry Spurgen, who wrote will. Pr. at Bury 8 September 1631.

283. R(W) RICHARD HOWE of Cockfield, yeoman. 12 July 1631.

Bequeaths soul to God steadfastly hoping and believing to be saved by Jesus Christ.
I give my wellbeloved wife Joan an annuity of £6 to be paid out of my lands and tenements in Cockfield. She has power to distrain. Joan shall have her dwelling in my mansion house where I now inhabit, but if she dislikes this she is to live in my adjoining dwelling. I give my eldest son John an annuity of 20s during my wife's life and one of £5 after her decease. I give my youngest son Daniel all my lands and tenements in Cockfield. Also my best cupboard and my great chest in my chamber, my best bed and bedstead with its furnishings standing in my chamber, my best framed table now in my hall house, my 2 best kettles and a brass pot. I give my son John a half-headed bedstead with bedding in my furthest house. I give my wife 3 loads of wood yearly. The residue of my goods I give to my wife Joan and make her ex'trix. Wit. Bennett Howe (X), Peter Marshall, who wrote will. Pr. at Cockfield 20 July 1631.

284. R(W) THOMAS CRANE (X) of Barnardiston, yeoman. 25 August 1631.

I give my wife Anne all my household stuff and moveables now in the house where I dwell for her life, and after her death to John Rowneing, husbandman of Barnardiston. However, if my wife becomes very much aged and falls into want she may use any of my goods for her needs as she thinks fit by selling them. Ex'trix: wife. Wit. William Kinge, John Haxall (X). Pr. at Clare 27 September 1631.

285. R(W) WILLIAM BANISTER (X) of Chevington, singleman and son of James Banister late of Chevington. 13 June 1631.

I give my messuage called Cocks and 10 acres land with a copyhold ditch, and a 7 acre close called Pease close and Awces in Chevington to my good and loving mother Rose Banister, widow, and I make her ex'trix. Wit. John Underwoode, Robert Underwoode, Robert Paman. Pr. at Bury 19 September 1631.

286. R(W) RICHARD COOKE (X) of Barrow, yeoman. 14 August 1631.

I bequeath my soul to God in Christ who hath redeemed and loved it, and my body to the grave to rest in assurance of resurrection and eternal life.
I give my loving wife Katherine for life all my land and tenements in Barrow and all my household stuff, and after her decease to my loving son Timothy. I give my loving son James all my horses, sheep, corn, hay and implements of husbandry. I give my daughter Abigail £20 to be paid 1 year after my wife's decease; power to distrain. I owe my son Robert some money and I give him so much as will make up £14 to be paid by my son James within 2 years of my death in consideration of the gift made to the latter. James is also to pay my debts and give my wife 4 combs of rye and wheat every year. I give my wife 3 cows, a bull and 2 hogs, and make her ex'trix. Wit. John Cradock. Pr. at Bury 19 September 1631.

287. R(W) WILLIAM EMYNS (X) of Westley, yeoman. 2 September 1631.

Commends soul to God hoping to be saved through merits of Jesus Christ.
I give my wife Mary £5 to be paid within a month of my decease, and she is to have the household stuff she brought to me when we married. All my other moveable goods, after my debts and funeral expenses are paid, I bequeath to be divided between my 2 daughters Susan and Elizabeth. I entreat Robert Cotton gentleman of Horringer and my brother Robert Emyns of Westley to choose 2 honest men to part my goods. Ex'trix: my daughter Susan. Wit. Robert Cotton, Robert Emyns. Pr. at Bury 12 September 1631.

288. R(W) ROBERT EDMOND (X) of Cheveley [Cambs], husbandman. 13 August 1631.

Bequeaths soul to God. To be buried in Cheveley churchyard.
I give my wife Anne my house and ground in Ashley [Cambs] to be sold, and all my moveable goods. Wit. Reuben Bridge, who wrote will, Nicholas Santey, Edward Payne (X). Pr. at Bury 21 September 1631.

289. R(W) EDWARD WYMARKE (X) of Lakenheath, blacksmith. 25 September 1631.

Bequeaths soul to God who gave it me.
I give my wife Dorothy all my goods, and she is to pay my debts and bring my body decently to the ground. I make her ex'trix. Wit. William Troyse, Nicholas Orgell (X), Anthony Childerston. Pr. at Bury 3 October 1631.

290. R(W) JOHN MAN of Lakenheath. 23 September 1631.

Commits soul to God.
I give Margaret Turner, my mother, my house and land for life and then to Mary Drinkmylke and her heirs, but if she has none to my brother-in-law Gregory Drinkmylke. All my unbequeathed goods I give to my mother, whom I make ex'trix. I have surrendered my house and land into the hands of John Roper tenant of the manor in presence of Henry Crane and Edward Man. Wit. John Allen, Edward Man, Henry Crane, John Roper. Pr. at Bury 3 October 1631.

291. R(W) MARGERY CUNOLDE (X) of Old Newton, widow. 6 August 1631.

Commits soul to merciful goodness of God being assured of free pardon of sins through Jesus Christ.
I give my messuage with all its land in Stowupland, which I purchased from Philip Garrade, to my son Nicholas. My son John is charged with paying me an annuity of which he owes me £23, and I give his children John and Frances £10 each when 12 from this sum. I give my grandson John a long table standing in my parlour, a candlestick, 2 cushions, a spit, a dripping pan, and a pair cobirons; all these goods are in the hands of my son John. I give him a featherbed, 2 beer vessels and a salting trough already in his hands. My son John is indebted to me for cattle and other commodities he bought from me to a total of £39 10s 0d. He is to pay £20 of this sum to my son Nicholas to pay my debts and funeral expenses. I also give Nicholas a featherbed, a pair blankets, a coverlet, my best trunk, another bed and a cheese press; all in John's house. All my other goods in John's house I bequeath to him together with the remainder of the money he owes me. All my other household stuff, corn and cattle I give to my son Nicholas, whom I make exor. Wit. John Osborne (X), Edmund Heyward, Jeffery Keble. Pr. at Stowmarket 5 October 1631.

292. R(W) AMBROSE PRICK (X) of Lavenham, felt maker.
16 September 1631.

Bequeaths soul to God. To be buried in Lavenham churchyard.
I give my wife Anne for life the dwelling house in Church Street in Lavenham wherein I now live, and then to my son Ambrose. I also give her my tenement in Kettlebaston now occupied by William Grove of Kettlebaston for life and then to my son Ambrose. I give all my wares, shop stuff, working tools and household stuff to my wife and make her ex'trix. Wit. Robert Wright, Christopher Harper and me Thomas Tayler.
Pr. at Bury 10 October 1631.

293. R(W) REUBEN DEARMAN (X) of Lidgate, blacksmith.
12 September 1631.

Commends soul to God trusting to be saved through Christ Jesus.
I give my son Henry my cottage, which belonged to my late father Reuben Dearman, but my son William is to receive its rent for 3 years after my decease. William must pay the entry fine and rent to the lord of the manor, and keep the cottage in repair. I give my son Robert my house and land late Thurstons, but William is to have rents until Robert is 21 on the same terms as above. William must pay £10 to Henry when 24 in Lidgate church porch, but if Robert molests William's receiving of rent then Robert is to pay this £10 to Henry. I give my 2 daughters Prudence and Thomasine £30 each when 21. I one dies her portion is to be divided between the other and my 2 younger sons Henry and Robert. I give my son William my freehold house where I now dwell with 1 rod of land on condition he pays my daughters' legacies. If he fails, the property goes to my other 2 sons and if they refuse to pay then my daughters are to have it. All my unbequeathed land, goods and chattels I give to my son William and make him exor. Wit. Henry Paman (X), Thomas Wakefield.
Pr. at Bury 3 October 1631.

294. R(W) JOHN FROST of Whepstead, yeoman. 10 September 1631.

Commends soul to God.
I give out of my close called Blackmans close in Chevington £5 to be paid by my son John to the poor people of Whepstead in 5 equal payments on successive Ash Wednesdays. I give my son Robert my copyhold tenement at Stone Cross in Whepstead with my free and copyhold land and a piece of meadow held by lease. This land is occupied by my son Robert and I bought it from various persons: Thomas Goodchilde, Roger Frost, Thomas Cooke, John Nunne, Thomas Lyllie, Anthony Cooke and Richard Mayhewe. I give my son Robert my copyhold tenement in which Francis Last now lives. I give Marion my wellbeloved wife for life my freehold tenement in Whepstead, which I bought from Agnes Byrd widow and her grandson Thomas Byrd. I give my daughter-in-law Frances, wife of my son John, for life my copyhold land totalling 20 acres

in Smythes field, Blackman croft, Stubbinges foule feilde and Osebredge. I give for ever to Alice, wife of my grandson Christopher Bedford, my copyhold tenement at Hay green which I had of James Silvester with an adjoining piece of freehold land in Chevington, which my uncle Henry Pament gave me in his will. I give Marion my wife all my goods and chattels and make her ex'trix. Wit. Thomas Godfrey, Robert Nunne, John Olie. Pr. at Bury 14 October 1631.

295. R(W) MARTHA MANFEILD (X) of Sudbury, widow.
4 September 1631.

Bequeaths soul to God trusting only to Jesus Christ for salvation.
I give my daughter Martha, wife of Richard Hasfeilde, my bed and bedstead which I do now lodge in with all its furniture, a great brass pot, a great kettle, a dozen pieces of pewter, my bullock and 2 pairs of sheets. I give my daughter Thomasine, wife of John Clarke, a great brass pot, a kettle, a flockbed and bedstedle in the upper chamber and 40s. I give my daughter Jane, wife of John Bird, a great brass pot, a kettle, a flockbed and bedstedle in the upper chamber and 40s. I give my grandson John Bird £3 to be employed to the best advantage by my exor until he is 21. All the rest of my goods I give to William Wollaston, my son-in-law, and make him exor. Wit. Francis Longe, Robert Howe and me William Mayzante. Pr. at Bury 17 October 1631.

296. R(W) EDWARD DARBEY of Bury St Edmunds, gentleman.
10 August 1631.

Commends soul to God trusting through Jesus Christ to have everlasting happiness with the blessed saints in heaven.
I bequeath to the poor of St James parish £6 to be bestowed as my exor thinks fit. I bequeath my brother Henry all my free and copyhold houses and land in Bury for his life and then to his daughter Mary and after her decease to my nephew Charles Darbey, one of the sons of my deceased brother John. I give my nephew Edmund, another son of my brother John, all my title and interest in a messuage in Ipswich, in which Henry Buckenham and later Robert Cooper lived, mortgaged to me by his mother Elizabeth Darby widow for £200 due on a day long since past. If she will pay £200 to Edmund within a year of my decease he shall accept this in lieu of my bequest. I give my niece Mary Darbey £500 to be paid within 2 years, and £200 each to my brother Henry's other 2 daughters: Beatrice, wife of John Knapp gentleman of Barton, and Elizabeth, wife of Thomas Keble gentleman of Newton. The £200 given to Beatrice is to allowed out of the debts and monies owed to me by her husband. I give my nephew Charles £100 a year after the decease of myself or of my brother Henry, whichever happens first, on condition he allows my niece Mary quietly to live in my house in Northgate Street where I and my brother Henry now live with its buildings, yard, garden and orchard lying between the lane called [blank in MS] on the south and Samuel Wyllis's

127

pasture close on the north and west with Northgate Street on its east side. Mary is to live there for 1 year after both I and my brother have died. I give my 2 nieces Susan and Mary, daughters of my late brother John, £100 within 2 years. I give £100 to Mary and £50 to Joan, my nieces and daughters of the late Mr Henry Gippes of Bury, within 2 years. I give my nephew Mr Thomas Gippes of Bury £50 within 2 years. I give Mr Henry White, preacher of St James parish, £10 to be paid within a month. I bequeath £10 to Anthony Beale of Ipswich, and £5 each to John Maies the elder and Roger Halstead the elder, both of Bury, within a month. I bequeath £300 to the alderman and burgesses of Bury St Edmunds on condition they give security to pay yearly £17 6s 8d towards maintaining catechising and instructing the poor people in St James parish every fortnight in such manner as is already being used. 13s 4d is allotted for each fortnight: 10s to be bestowed in wheat bread of which there will be 70 loaves: 65 for that number of poor folk and 5 for the clerk and sexton to share. The remaining 3s 4d is to be for the ministers. 53s 4d may be given to the ministers in advance. Exor: my brother Henry Darbey to whom I bequeath the residue of my goods and chattels. Wit. Isaac Wragge, William Wragge. Pr. in Prerogative Court of Canterbury.

297. R(W) MARY JASLYN of Newton, spinster. 15 September 1631.

Bequeaths soul to God.
I give my uncle Thomas Howsen of Polstead all my goods and chattels, my rights and credits and £10, which was my share of the goods of my grandfather Thomas Howsen of Raydon. I and his wife were ex'trices of his will. Exor: my uncle Thomas Howsen. I give my brother Philip my coat, and my sister Anne my suit of apparel in the parsonage in Hadleigh, a pillowbeere and a casting kercher. I give my sister Rose 2 coats and a waistcoat. Wit. Robert Colle, John Hardey. Pr. at Sudbury 28 September 1631.

298. R(W) ADAM PRIGGE (X) of Stradishall, tailor. 5 September 1631.

Bequeaths soul to God and Jesus Christ my only saviour.
I give my wife Constance for life the house wherein I live with about 1½ acres land. She must pay the legacies due to be paid by the will of her father Edmund Prigg. I also give her all the houses and ground I bought from Nathaniel Paske to sell towards repairing the house I now dwell in and bringing up my children. I give her all my moveables and make her ex'trix. After my wife's decease my son Adam is to have the house where I now dwell on condition he pays £4 each to the rest of my children. Wit. John French, Thomas Pratt, Henry Prigg, Charles Burroughe. Pr. at Clare 27 September 1631.

299. R(W) THOMAS PARTRIDGE of Long Melford, clothier.
9 August 1631.

Bequeaths soul to God who gave it me.
I give my eldest son Thomas a pair of broad looms with a treadle and all
its appurtenances, a cupboard, a table and a form in the hall. I give my
kinsman Thomas Partridge a pair of narrow looms with a trundle. I give
my son Thomas my 4 acre copyhold field purchased out of High field, on
condition he pays my youngest son John £20 if he comes to demand it,
but if he does not this sum is to be paid to my godchild and grandson
Thomas son of my son Thomas. Within a year of the decease of my wife,
my son Thomas is to pay the following legacies: £10 to my kinsman
Thomas Partridge of Melford, 10s to John Partridge weaver of Melford,
3s 4d to Gabriel Gates cooper of Sudbury and 3s 4d to Alice daughter of
my kinsman Thomas Partridge. All my other goods and chattels I give to
my wife Elizabeth, who is to pay my debts and I make her ex'trix.
Supervisor: John Deekes of Melford clerk to whom I give 10s for his
pains. Wit. Robert Howe, Richard Mylles, John Deeks. Pr. at Long
Melford 28 September 1631.

300. R(W) THOMAS WHITHEAD (X) of Kedington, yeoman.
No date.

Commits soul to God in sure hope of salvation. To be buried in
Keddington churchyard.
God has given me a faithful and loving comfort in my loving and
wellbeloved wife Margaret, whom I commit to the merciful providence of
God as the principal part of my substance on earth. I make her sole
ex'trix. I give my brother Robert an annuity of 20s to be paid at Easter
out of my lands and tenements, and one of 20s to my sister Mary, wife of
Henry Jelson. I give 10s to be distributed to the poor of Keddington on
my burial day by the churchwardens. I give my land and tenements to my
wife for life and then to my wellbeloved grandson Thomas, son of my
deceased son Thomas. I give all my goods and chattels to my wife. Wit.
Philip Lagger, who wrote will, Edmund Bettes (X), William Fitch (X).
Pr. at Clare 27 September 1631.

301. R(W) MICHAEL BOBYE of Stowupland, husbandman. 18 August
1631.

Commends soul to 3 persons of Trinity.
I will that Anne my wife and Christopher my son shall together have the
use of all my goods and chattels, except for one calf given to my daughter
Anne. After wife's death Christopher is to keep my goods and pay my
other children's legacies: 20s each within a year to my sons Nicholas and
Robert and to my daughter Helen, wife of Humphrey Clarke. The

weaned calf given to my daughter Anne is to be kept by my wife and son Christopher until it is 2 or 3 years old, and I give her 20s to be paid 2 years after my wife's decease. Exor: my son Christopher. Wit. Christopher Bobie senior (X), John Goddard. Pr. at Stowmarket 5 October 1631.

302. R(W) JOHN FRENCH of Stradishall, clerk. 18 January 1630/31

Commends soul to God. To be buried in the chancel of Stradishall church.
I give 40s to the poor of Stradishall to be distributed by my exors on the day of my burial. I give my wife Margaret for life my 2 houses called Greenes and Calice with their 14 acres of land, which I purchased from John Ockley. I also give her for life a 3 acre pasture close called Stepenfeild, a 7 acre close called Brady meadow, a 11 acre close called Hamells, a 17 acre copyhold close with a grove called Dawes Horne, and a tenement called Jermyns with 2 acres which I bought from my brother George. All this land is in Stradishall. After my wife's decease I give all this land to Christopher Goodyn of Stradishall. I give my wife all my moveables for life and after her death to be divided between Nicholas Fenton, Barbara French, Elizabeth Goodyn and all my godchildren who are sons or daughters of my kindred. Exors: my wife and Christopher Goodyn. Wit. Elizabeth Goodyne, Richard Goodyne. Pr. at Bury 10 October 1631.

303. R(W) BENNET WRIGHT (X) of Thurston, yeoman. 21 April 1629.

Bequeaths soul to God and has faith to be saved through Jesus Christ.
I give my wife Sarah for life my house where I now dwell with all its land, which I bought from Thomas Clarke, and then to my son John, who must pay £5 each to my daughters Sarah and Rachel within a month of my wife's decease. After my wife's death Rachel is to have the chamber over the parlour with free access as long as she remains unmarried. I give my son William my tenement and land now in the possession of my brother Richard Howlett after the latter's death. I give £30 each to be paid to my daughters Sarah and Rachel on their marriage days or at their mother's decease whichever happens first. I give 10s to the poor of Thurston. I make Sarah my wife ex'trix and give her all my moveables towards paying my legacies. Wit. Richard Howlett (X), Thomas Clarke. Pr. at Bury 3 October 1631.

304. R(W) THOMAS MANNYNGE of Beyton, yeoman. 24 January 1617/18.

Bequeaths soul to God.
I give Mary my wellbeloved wife my messuage with its land for life, but not my shop, and after her decease to my son William, but if he has no heirs to descend to my eldest son Thomas. William must pay £6 13s 4d

each to my daughters Elizabeth, Joan and Susan one a year starting a year after my wife's decease. Benefit of survivorship. William must pay Thomas £20 in 3 instalments starting 4 years after my wife's decease. If Thomas dies his children are to share his legacy. All legacies to be paid in my messuage in Beyton, and legatees have power to distrain on 2 closes called Abells croft and Church close. I give my son William my shop immediately after my decease. I give my youngest son Thomas £13 6s 8d when 21. I give my daughter Margaret £6 13s 4d when 21. Benefit of survivorship. All my goods and chattels I give to Mary my wife to her own use and to pay the last 2 legacies and bring my body decently to the earth. I make her ex'trix, and my brother-in-law John Mason supervisor; I give him 5s. Wit. Thomas Rockett, John Mason, Thomas Wright. Pr. at Bury 17 October 1631.

305. R(W) ELIZABETH MUNNINGE of Brettenham, widow of Humphrey Munninge clerk and minister of Brettenham. 8 March 1624/25.

I give my soul to God in hope of a blessed resurrection.
I give £5 each to my daughter Elizabeth, wife of George Salter, and to my sons Richard, Theophilus and William. I give my daughter Anne £10 to be paid within 2 years. I give £18 each to my children Ellen, Humphrey, Abigail, Katherine and Leonard. Those who are 21 two years after my decease are to receive their legacies then, and the others as they reach that age or marry. All my legacies, debts and charges are to be paid out of my goods and chattels and tenements. I give authority to William Chaplyn of Hitcham and my brother-in-law Henry Manning to sell the land and tenements in Brettenham and Bildeston left me in my late husband's will, and they are to divide any money left over between my children. I make them exors. If one of my exors dies before my land is sold, I appoint Mr Humphrey Morgane, minister of Bildeston, to act with the surviving exor. Wit. John Underwoode, William Janinges, William Makeinges (X). Legacies of any of my children who die are to be paid to their children if they have any and, if not, shared amongst my other children. Pr. at Bury 17 October 1631.

306. R(W) ROBERT HOWLETT (X) of Ixworth Thorpe, yeoman. 1 April 1626.

Commits soul to God trusting through Jesus Christ to be made a partaker of joys of heaven.
I bequeath my wife Margery an annuity of £3 to be paid by my exor as long as she remains a widow, and another 20s a year to rent a house. Even if she and my son Sylvester agree to live together he is to pay her this sum to bestow or keep at her pleasure. I give my wife a load of wood yearly to be laid in the yard where she lives. If she remarries all these gifts are void and I give her 40s p.a. instead. I give my son Sylvester my copyhold land and tenement in Walsham in the Willows, and my tenement called Laights in Ixworth Thorpe where I now dwell and which

contains 3 rods. I also give him my copyhold land in Ixworth and Ixworth Thorpe, and my freehold land lying in divers pieces in the fields of Honington, which I bought from William Ives, and 2 acres 1½ rods copyhold land sometime John Greene's of Thorpe deceased. I give my grandson Robert, son of my lately deceased son Thomas, my 3 rod copyhold tenement called Masons in Honington. He must pay my wife Margery 20s a year until he is 21. I also give my grandson Robert my shop tools belonging to the craft of a smith, which were used by his father, except for the largest stithe and a pair of smith's bellows. I give my son Sylvester my posted bedstead in the chamber with its tester, mat, bedline, flockbed, a pair of blankets, a pair sheets, a coverlet, a bolster, 2 large pillows and 2 pillowbeeres for them. Also my best joined table and a joined chair. I give Sylvester immediately after my decease all my horse cattle that is horses, geldings, mares and colts; my carts, tumbrels and ploughs; harness for cart and plough; my harrows, a swathe rake, a cart rope and a pitch fork. I give to be equally divided between my wife and my son Sylvester all the corn growing in my fields or in the barns at the time of my decease; all my hay; all my household provision in malt, meal, bread, drink or any victuals except butter. I also give them all the wood in the yard and all my neat cattle and swine. The residue of my goods and chattels I give to my wife Margery. Exor: my son Sylvester. My wife is to enter into a bond of £80, before she receives any of my goods, not to demand any dower or thirds. If she does, or disputes my will all gifts to her are void. Wit. Ran. Whitney, Thomas Whitney. Pr. at Bury 17 October 1631.

307. R(W) RICHARD CARTER (X) of Walsham le Willows, yeoman. 18 September 1631.

I give my soul to God hoping to inherit life everlasting.
I give my wife Marian a 4 acre pightle in Walsham called Priary for her life and then to my son Edward, who must pay £5 to William, eldest son of my son-in-law William Grome, when he is 24 in the porch of the parish church. Power to distrain. I give my son-in-law William Grome £10 and £10 to my other son-in-law John Powlyn, both to be paid within a year. I give my son Edward a table, a cupboard and a bedstead and bed complete standing in the chamber where I now lie. I give all the rest of my moveables and cattle to my wife, and make her ex'trix. Wit. Thomas Rampley, John Page, Stephen Windout. Pr. at Bury 24 October 1631.

308. R(W) GUY MAN of Stanton. 1 November 1631.

Commits soul to God and body to earth.
I will all my land and houses to my brother-in-law Robert Beales, who is to be my exor and pay my debts. I give my sister Margery Ransome £5 to be paid 2 years after my death, and £5 to my sister Ann Aierese to be paid 2 years later. I give £5 to Thomas Musscit, 40s to James Lavnder and

£10 to the eldest son of Robert Beales. I give all my moveables to Robert Beales and Thomas Ransome, my brothers-in-law, to be equally divided between them. Wit. John Waller, Emma Steggell, Mary Pattrage. Pr. 9 November 1631. No place given.

309. R(W) ELIZABETH LINGE (X) of Hepworth, widow. 14 March 1631/31.

Commends soul to God.
I give my daughter-in-law Susan my best cloak and riding kirtle, and my lesser copper kettle. I give my daughter Margaret Trapet all the rest of my clothes and all my body linen. All the rest of my goods and chattels I bequeath to my son Thomas and make him exor. Wit. James Fuller (X), Robert Fuller. Pr. at Bury 12 May 1631.

310. R(W) (In.) MARY BALLYE (N) of Chelsworth. January 1630/31.

She gave all her goods and chattels to her son Edward and to her daughter Mary, wife of Mark Webbe.
Wit. Isaac Abbott, Abraham Greene. Let. ad. granted 21 July 1631 to Mark Webbe in his wife's name. No place given.

Note: As Mary Ballye is the only testator in this volume whose inventory survives, it is printed here. It was made on 23 April 1631. 'Item Her wareing parell and muney in her purse £2 2s 6d. Item In the fyer rume. Item Cuberde and pres 13s 4d. Item an oulde amere 2s. Item i ould trofe and a lyd 2s. Item fyve peces of peuter 4s. Item i eyerne poot 2s. Item brasen marter A pestel 1s. Item i oulde cetell 1s. Item i posnet 1s. Upon the chamber. Item i cetel 6s 8d. Item i bedsted ande oter lumber 12s. Item i ould flocke bed with that belonginge to it 8s 6d. Sume £3 15s 6d.'

311. R(W) GEORGE BROWNE (N) of Cockfield, husbandman. 20 May 1631.

He gave his son John 20s, his son Isaac 20s and a hagg saw, his son Robert 40s and all his wearing apparel, and his daughter Revell or her children 20s. The rest of his goods and chattels he gave to be equally divided between Anne his wife and Mary his daughter. Wit. Stephen Pattrick (X), Stephen Bemond. Let. ad. granted to widow 20 July 1631. No place given.

312. R(W) PHILIP SMITH (N) of Whatfield, yeoman. 16 or 17 March 1630/31.

He willed that his wife Anne should have all his goods and chattels for life and pay his debts. After her decease, goods to be equally divided among his children. Wit. George Carter, Richard Wyeles. Let. ad. granted to widow 21 July 1631. No place given.

313. R(W) RICHARD SMITH (N) of Stoke Ash. 14 September 1631.

He gave his wife Elizabeth all his goods and chattels. Wit. Robert Crowe (X), Mary wife of Robert Crowe (X), Anne wife of Roger Wynke (X). Pr. at Bury 10 October 1631.

314. R(W) FRANCIS REEVE (X) of Hepworth, singleman. 30 July 1631.

Bequeaths soul to merciful hands of God.
I give my sister Margaret my house and all my meadow and pasture land in Hepworth. I give my sister Margaret Reeve all my moveables and make her ex'trix. Wit. William Baker, Joseph Baker, Richard Baker. Pr. at Bury 24 October 1631.

315. R(W) THOMAS WYMARKE (N) of Denham, yeoman. 15 October 1631.

He gave to 6 poor houses in Denham 5s each: to Thomas Crosse, Mathew Tompson, Clement Crowe, William Titterell, Margaret Bird widow and Martin and Mary Bellman. He gave his father Henry £10. He gave his servant Edward Kempe one of his suits of clothes, to his other servant James Bulbrooke a cloak and a suit of clothes, and to his maid servant Susan Bird 10s. All the rest of his goods and chattels he gave to his wife Helen, making her ex'trix. Wit. Mr Timothy Oldmayne alias Pricke, William Smyth. Let. ad. granted 24 October 1631 to ex'trix in John Jewell's house in Bury.

316. R(W) JOHN BENNET (X) of Polstead. 28 September 1631.

Bequeaths soul to God and Jesus Christ by whom I hope to be saved. To be buried in Polstead churchyard.
I give my son Andrew 40s, my cloak and all my cooking tools i.e. a great knife, a cleaver, a ladle and all my moulds. I give my daughter Scereine, wife of Robert Beetes, a joined chest with its contents, a brass pot, a copper kettle and another kettle. I give her 3 children Katherine, John and Seereine 20s each. I give my grand-daughter Seereine a posted bed furnished as it now stands with a feather bed, 2 bolsters, 2 pillows, 2 blankets and 2 coverlets but no sheets. I give Humphrey, Mary, Anne, Denis and Susan, children of my son Andrew, 20s each and 10s each to his 3 children John, Andrew and Christian. I give my daughter Beetes the house wherein I now dwell with the field, buildings, orchard and garden for 12 years, and then to her son Joseph. I give my maid Rose Benson £4, a trundle bed, a bolster, a pillow, 1 pair sheets, 1 coverlet, 1 bolster, the bed she lies on and a small kettle. I give 10s to the poor of Polstead. I give my sister Rachel Honyball 5s. I give Rose Benson a little joined

134

table, 2 pewter platters, an old chest and the wheel she spins on. I give John Hall £3 and my halberd. The money that Mistress Brand owes me is to be used to pay my legacies within 8 months of my decease. Wit. Em. Hanham, James Shelley (X), Robert Thirstone (X), John Larke (X), Christopher Hanham. Pr. at Bury 1 November 1631.

317. R(W) JOHN GOODERICHE of Bacton, physician. 7 January 1630/31.

Commends soul to God and hopes to be saved by Jesus Christ. To be buried in Wyverstone churchyard.
I give my well-beloved niece Eunica, wife of Robert Spencer, my messuage and land in Bacton bought from John and Mary Symonds. I give Eunica, only daughter of Robert Spencer, £100 to be paid at £10 p.a. starting a year after my decease. Power to distrain. No trees are to be felled on my land except what are needed to repair my tenement. If any others are cut down, 40s over and above the value of the tree will be forfeit to Robert son of Eunica and Robert Spencer. After my niece dies, her husband is to have £10 p.a. out of the lands left to her provided that he reads every day 2 chapters of the sacred word of God and that he brings up his son in learning, and both his children in the Catholic religion. If these children die without heirs, I will that my land passes to the nearest of my blood and name that is of the Catholic religion. I give John Gooderiche, son of my deceased brother William, a 2 acre freehold grove in Wetherden if I do not fell or sell it in my life time. I give 20s to poor of Bacton within 2 days of my decease. Exors: my niece Eunica and her son Robert. Wit. Thomas Hart, James Walton, William Meadowe (X). Pr. at Bury 4 November 1631.

318. R(W) WALTER ROSIER (X) of Wetherden, yeoman. 30 July 1631.

Commends soul to God in full assurance of free pardon of sins.
I give my wife Alice for life all my copyhold land and tenements held of the manors of Wetherden Hall and Pulham Hall, and after her decease to my son William, on condition he pays following legacies: £10 to my son Thomas within 1 year of my wife's death, £6 13s 4d to my daughter Anne within 2 years, £6 13s 4d to my daughter Mary within 3 years and £6 13s 4d to my daughter Alice within 4 years. Benefit of survivorship. If William defaults, my land goes to my son Thomas on the same conditions, and if he defaults the legatees have power to distrain. All my personal estate I give to my wife Alice and make her ex'trix. Wit. William Kilborne clerk, Thomas May (X), Robert Brett. Pr. at Bury 14 November 1631.

319. R(W) ROBERT CLARKE (X) of Mildenhall, yeoman. 26 October 1631.

Commits soul to God hoping assuredly through Jesus Christ to obtain kingdom of heaven.
I give 3s 4d to the poor man's box of Mildenhall and 3s 4d to the repair of the parish church. I give Anne my wellbeloved wife for ever 7 acres copyhold arable lying in 1 piece in Beckfield with the south end abutting on land called Wonge, late of Richard Childerston, gentleman. I also give her for ever my reversion to all the copyhold land lying in various pieces in Beckfield and which should come to me on the decease of my mother Margaret Clarke. She is to pay my debts and educate and bring up my children. I give my wife all my moveables and make her ex'trix. Wit. Francis Bugg, Robert Knight (X), John Clarke (X), William Dallison. Testator surrendered his copyhold land to the use of his will into the hands of John and Richard Peachie, copyhold tenants of the manor. Pr. at Bury 14 November 1631.

320. R(W) ROBERT CHALLICE (X) of Little Bradley. 20 October 1631.

Commends soul to God hoping to be saved by merits of Jesus Christ.
I give Jane my wife all my goods and chattels for life and then to my son Robert, my 2 daughters Grace and Elizabeth, my eldest son Henry and my 3 youngest sons James, Richard and Stephen. After his mother's decease I give my son Robert the bed whereon I now lie with all that belongs to it and 2 chests: one he has already and the other he shall choose. I also give him my cloak and all the rest of my wearing apparel that is fittest for him, and my husbandry tools. I give my daughter Grace the bed whereon she now lies with its bedding, a brinded bullock, my brass pot which she likes best and a little framed table. I give my daughter Elizabeth, after her mother's decease, a bed with bedding, a brass pot and a cow or bullock. I give 20s each to my sons Henry, James and Richard. I give my son Stephen £10 after his mother's death to be paid into the hands of my son Robert if they agree that latter shall have use of the money and his brother's labour for Stephen's maintenance. Exors: my wife Jane and my son Robert. Wit. Edward Paine, Thomas Claydon (X) Pr at Bury 16 November 1631.

321. R(W) JOHN HARVIE of Wissington, husbandman. 13 January 1624/25.

Commends soul to three persons of Trinity trusting to come to everlasting life. To be buried in Wiston [Wissington] churchyard.
I give 10s to the poor people of Wiston to be distributed at the discretion of my reverend good friend and minister Mr John Le Gris. All the rest of my household stuff, cattle and money I give to be equally divided among my 4 children: John, Thomas, Grace and Bridget. Exor: my son John. No witnesses. Pr. at Bury 15 November 1631.

322. R(W) NICHOLAS FRANCIS (X) of Bury St Edmunds, cloth worker. 2 October 1631.

Commends soul to God and body to the earth.
I give Katherine my loving wife all my goods and chattels to dispose of at her pleasure, and I make her ex'trix. Wit. William Beane, Oliver Johnson. Pr. at Bury 15 November 1631.

323. R(W) GEORGE WARREN (X) of Kirtling [Cambs], yeoman. 24 August 1631.

Commits soul to God hoping to be made partaker of everlasting life through merits of Jesus Christ.
I give Rose my wife an annuity of £10 in satisfaction of her dower to be paid out of my lands in Kirtling, except those mortgaged to Thomas Dillamore and his wife Frances. I also give her the best bed and bedding with its frame, 2 of the best chests, a cupboard, a table and 2 stools belonging to it in the parlour chamber of my dwelling house. Rose is to have the use of the parlour chamber and the chamber over it with free access to these rooms, and half the fruit in the orchard. I give my eldest son Thomas my dwelling house with outbuildings and the land that was mortgaged with the house to Thomas and Frances Dillamore, that is a 5 acre close called Good grounds, 5 acres of arable called Gippes croft, 6 acres arable lying in a close called Broadlands, 5 acres arable lying in Crowell field and called Crowell Layes, 6 acres arable in Flockett field, 1 acre meadow in Walthorne meadow and 5 rods meadow called Buckes hooke and abutting on Crowell field. Thomas is to pay £140 to Thomas and Frances Dillamore at the day and place named in the mortgage. I give my son Thomas all my other land in Kirtling, either bought by me or inherited from my father Thomas Warren, on condition he pays my legacies and my wife's annuity. I give my son George £50 to be paid within a year of my decease. I give my son John £10 to be paid within 3 years, but if he disturbs Thomas in his occupation of my land this legacy is void. I give my son Francis £40, of which £10 is to be paid within 3 months of my death to put him forth as an apprentice, and the other £30 is to be paid within 8 years. I give my daughter Christian, wife of Henry Payne, £20 to be paid within 5 years, and my daughter Rose £40 to be paid within 4 years. I give 5s each within 1 year to the children of my daughter Alice, the late wife of John Sharpe. I give all my other goods and moveables to my son Thomas. Legatees have power to distrain. Exors; wife Rose and son Thomas. Wit. Henry Stearne, George Warren junior, Robert Evered. Pr. at Bury 14 November 1631.

324. R(W) HENRY WARD (X) of Hawstead, yeoman. 28 October 1631.

Commends soul to God hoping through merits of Jesus Christ to inherit the kingdom of heaven. To be buried in Hawstead churchyard.
I give my wellbeloved kinswoman Susan, wife of Ezechiel Edgar clerk,

my brown bay nag. I give my brothers John and Richard Ward £5 each to be paid within 3 months. I give my brother Robert Ward 40s and my kinsman Mr William Warde £5, both to be paid within 3 months. I give the poor of Hawstead 14s to be distributed by the churchwardens and overseers of the poor to those that have most need 12d each. I give my kinswoman Susan Edgar a chest with its contents and a bed with its furniture now in my chamber at Hawstead Place. All the rest of my personal estate, my debts and legacies being paid, I give to be equally divided between my loving kinsman Ezechiel Ward and Timothy Ward, and I appoint them exors. Wit. George Scarpe, Thomas Cracheroke. Pr. at Bury 22 November 1631.

325. R(W) WILLIAM YMMINSON (N). No place given. 3 September 1631.

Memorandum that we Gilbert Wymberley, doctor of divinity, and Ambrose Chapman clerk, being with William Ymminson in his sickness did ask him, if it should please God to take him to his mercy, how he would dispose of his goods and provide for his young son. He answered that his will was to leave all his estate to his wife on condition she paid £40 to his son Henry and educated and brought him up well, which he did not doubt she would do. Wit. Gilbert Wymberley, Ambrose Chapman, Henry Ymminson the elder (X). Let. ad. granted to widow, Mary Ymminson, on 20 September 1631. No place given.

326. R(W) HENRY YEOMANSON (X) of Stanningfield, yeoman. 9 July 1631.

Commits soul to God who hath redeemed me from captivity of sin through Jesus Christ by whose passion I trust to be saved. To be buried in Stanningfield churchyard.
I give 5s to the poor of Stanningfield to be paid by my exor within a month of my decease. I give my grandson Henry, son of John Raye, £10 when he is 21. I give my grandchild Henry, son of my son William, a bedstead, a flockbed, a flock bolster, a featherbed, a feather bolster, 2 pilllows, 2 pillowbeeres, a blanket and 3 coverings, a press with 2 cupboards in it and all that is in them, a chest, 2 chairs, 2 stools, a little drawing table, a desk, a pot shelf, a warming pan, a brass pot, a pewter bason or bowl and £5. All these gifts are to be given to him when 21, or sooner if need be. If Henry dies before he is 21 my exor is to pay £5 to Henry Raye. I give the poor of Shudy Camps [Cambs] 5s to be paid within a month of my death. I give 6s 8d to John Mason of Stanningfield, and 10s to Margaret daughter of Isaac Webb, both to be paid within a month. I give my son-in-law John Raye 20s to be paid within 3 monhts, and my son William 20s. All the rest of my goods and chattels I give to my son William, whom I make exor. Wit. Richard Wakelin, John Clayton, who wrote will. Pr. at Bury 25 October 1631 to Mary, widow of William Yeomanson exor of will.

327. R(W) ROBERT GRAVE (X) the elder of Fordham [Cambs], yeoman. 6 January 1630/31.

Commits soul into hands of God hoping through merits of Jesus Christ to have pardon of sins and to be associated in kingdom of heaven among the elect and chosen people of God.
I bequeath to Susan my wellbeloved wife £18 to be paid in 4 instalments over 3 years. My son Robert, whom I make exor, must a week after my decease enter into a bond to pay my wife this sum, and she must give him a deed releasing all her rights in my dwelling house and freehold land or forfeit this gift. I give my wife 3 of my milk cows at her choice, and all the household stuff she brought to me at our marriage and which was left to her by her husband Eaton. I give her 2 bushells of wheat and 2 of barley to be given to her out of my crops in the barn, and the same quantity again the following year. I give Thomas Bretten my son-in-law my mare and her colt. I give his wife and my daughter Elizabeth 20s. I give my grandson Robert, son of my son William, £20 to be paid in 10 instalments at Lady Day and Michaelmas. I also give him 20s and 2 bushels barley. The residue of my goods and chattels I give to my son Robert, whom I make exor. If he refuses to prove my will, I make my son William exor. Wit. William Hill, Richard Ballard (X), William Wooll, who wrote will. Pr. at Bury 28 November 1631.

328. R(W) ROBERT RIDNALL (X) the elder of Mendlesham, yeoman. 7 November 1631.

Bequeaths soul to holy and inseparable Trinity trusting assuredly to have sins pardoned.
I give my nephew Robert Ridnall my freehold land and tenements in Buxhall called Howletts and containing 14 acres for his life and then to his sons Robert and John. I give John, son of Robert Ridnall, 3 pieces copyhold land in Buxhall: 2 pieces held of Buxhall manor and 1 of the manor of Cockereels. I give Robert, son of Robert Ridnall, my freehold pightle in Woolpit called Brightes close. This pightle pays a half penny rent p.a. to the house at the chancel's end, which was Robert Wade's, if it is demanded. I give Anne and Elizabeth, daughters of my nephew Robert Ridnall, £20 each on their marriage days. Benefit of survivorship. I give my nephew William Ridnall and my nieces Margaret Lock and Alice Curtis 5 marks each within 6 months of my decease. I give Richard, son of my nephew Robert Ridnall, 20s within 6 months and 20s to Anne Beutton. I give Anne and Elizabeth Ridnall all my household stuff to be divided between them. The rest of my goods, bonds and ready money I give to my exor towards the payment of my legacies, and I make my nephew Robert Ridnall my exor. Wit. Francis Harssante (X), John Phenexe (X). Pr. at Bury 5 December 1631.

329. W(R) EDWARD KEMPE of Denham, yeoman. 25 September 1629.

Bequeaths soul to God trusting to be saved through Jesus Christ.
I bequeath to my wife Susan the £15 bequeathed to her by her brother James Glover. I give £10 each to my 4 sons Edward, William, John and James on their marriage days. When they have received their legacies they must pay 10s p.a. to my wife during her widowhood. Benefit of survivorship. I give my son Robert £12 on his marriage day. The residue of my goods and chattels I give to my wife whom I have always found a kind and loving help to me, and I make her ex'trix. Wit. Timothy Oldmayne alias Pricke, Simon Pittes. Pr. at Bury 12 December 1631.

330. W(R) JOHN COWPER (X) of Old Newton, yeoman. 12 November 1631.

Commits soul to God hoping to have free pardon of sins through Jesus Christ.
I give the backhouse where widow Neale now dwells, the milkhouse and the horse mill standing on a little piece of ground at the end of the little house to my son Robert, who is to have free access to these buildings through the yards belonging to the messuage where I now dwell, and the liberty to set up ladders and make repairs to his buildings. My wife Anne is to have the use of the horse mill, and I bequeath her for life my messuage and all its land. After her decease I give them to my son John. He must pay my son James £30 at £10 p.a. starting one year after my wife's decease, and £10 to my grandchild Anne, daughter of my son Thomas, 4 years after my wife's decease, or if Anne has died to my son Thomas. Legatees have power to distrain. I give my son Thomas £20 to be paid within 2 years of my death, to my son Robert £20 within 6 months and to my son Edward 10s within 6 months. I give my daughter Joan, wife of Francis Holbage, £10 within 6 months and to my daughter Anne £20 when 22. These legacies are to be paid by my wife Anne. All my moveables, corn and bills I give to my wife towards paying my legacies and make her ex'trix. Wit. Thomas Eley, Edmund Heyward. Pr. at Bury 20 December 1631.

331. R(W) JOHN HAXOLL (X) of Long Melford, comber. 25 July 1629.

Bequeaths soul to God expecting resurrection.
I give my copyhold tenement where I dwell with its croft to my loving wife Susan and her heirs. I also give her all my goods and chattels and make her ex'trix. Wit. Thomas Partaredge, Thomas Axreed (X), Thomas Lee, who wrote will. Pr. at Bury 28 December 1631.

332. W(R) WILLIAM GOODRICH of Hessett, yeoman. 4 April 1631.

Commends soul to God trusting to have remission of sins through Jesus Christ.
I bequeath my son John all my houses and land in Hessett. He must pay legacies to my other children: £16 to my son William to be paid in 3 instalments 1, 4 and 7 years after my decease; £8 to my daughter Elizabeth, wife of Philip Clarke, in 2 halves 2 and 5 years after my death; and £8 to my daughter Susan, wife of John Beamonds, in 2 parts 3 and 6 years after my decease. Power to distrain. Exor: son John. Wit. John White, Richard Sharpe (X), John Bawley (X), John Topley (X). Pr. at Bury 2 January 1631/32.

333. R(W) JOHN ROBSON (X) of Soham [Cambs], yeoman. 29 December 1631.

Commits soul to God trusting through Jesus Christ to be saved. To be buried in sanctuary of Soham church.
I give my daughter Emma, wife of Stephen Hill, £10 6s 8d and a bill in my hands that she owes me to be given to her before the 29th September next after my decease. If she has died, the money and the bill are to be shared by my other 2 daughters. I give Robert Peachey, husband of my daughter Katherine £20 9s 4d due to me by bond, which he is to collect as soon as it is due. I also bequeath to him the bed, bedstead and bedding, both linen and woollen, in the chamber where I lie, and 2 pillows. I give Mary, daughter of Katherine Peachey, my least table in the hall and to her sister Katherine one of the 2 brazen candlesticks standing in the hall. I also give 20s to be divided between these sisters to be paid by Thomas Wilkin in lieu of certain brass that was mine. I give Robert Peachey my best cloak, jerkin, doublet, breeches, stockings and a shirt, and 40 stone of hemp. I give my daughter Elizabeth, wife of Thomas Wilkyn, my freehold messuage wherein I dwell in Sand Street in Soham abutting on the street to the west and with James Tirrill's hempland to the east. I also give her my copyhold tenement with its land in Soham abutting on the highway leading from Sand Street to Brook Street, and now occupied by John Longe. I give John Wilkyn my mare. I give my daughter Elizabeth all the rest of my goods and chattels. She is to bear half the cost of my burial and of proving my will, and Robert Peachie, whom I make exor, is to pay the other half. The bonds due to me from Edward Daye and Richard Cropley are to pay my daughter Emma's legacy. I give my exor a £20 bond of his in my possession. Wit. Richard Brand (X), Thomas Smith and me Robert Carlton. The testator surrendered his copyhold tenement to the use of his will. Pr. at Bury 10 January 1631/32.

141

334. W(R) ELIZABETH JENNINGES of Stoke by Clare, widow.
No date.

Bequeaths soul to God hoping to be saved by death and passion of Jesus Christ and to inherit kingdom prepared for me.
I give my daughter Elizabeth Wyate my featherbed and bolster, the bedstead, the little covering, a chair without a bottom, 2 pairs sheets (one of the little and one of the other), my second ruff, a pillow and a pillowbeere, a kerchief, a gown, a deroye petticoat and a little barrel. I give Francis Jeninges the younger a pewter platter, and Francis Jeninges the elder my husband's little chest and my middlemost barrel. I give Susanna Jeninges my hat and my warming pan. I give my son Samuel Jeninges my cow and all my unbequeathed things and I appoint him exor. Wit. Organ Edes, John Bryant (X). Pr. at Clare 17 September 1631.

335. W(R) THOMAS DOWNHAM (X) the elder of Assington.
13 September 1631.

Desired Lord to receive his soul.
I make Elizabeth my wife sole ex'trix. I give my son Thomas a house with yard in Bures hamlet, now occupied by Arthur Fuller, tailor. I give my daughter Jane, wife of William Upcher husbandman of Bures, £5 to make up what she has had already to £20. I give my daughter Joan, wife of Stephen Cage, £5. I give my 3 eldest children by my wife Elizabeth £10 each: to John, Joseph and Bridget. I give my 3 younger children the following legacies: £15 to James, to Samuel a house in Wissington which Charles Smith has hired and which cost me £15, and to Elizabeth £15. My son Thomas is to have his house immediately after my decease, my daughters Joan and Jane are to receive their legacies within 12 months and the rest at the discretion of my wife. I give the poor of this parish 10s. I give Mr Rogers towards his enlarging of the vicarage house 10s. I give Mr Jacie 20s in consideration of his pains. Wit. Henry Jacie, John Day (X), Susan French (X). Pr. at Sudbury 28 September 1631.

336. W(R) GEORGE OLLYE (N) of Whepstead, sawyer. St Luke's Day 18 October 1631.

He gave his 3 sons John, George and Robert a box each, and George to have the biggest. All the rest of his goods he willed to his wife Elizabeth. He confirmed his will on 27 October. Wit. Bridget Steward widow, George Frost and Elizabeth the testator's wife. Let. ad. granted to widow 28 December 1631. No place given.

337. W(R) FRANCIS PATTELL (X) of Barrow, husbandman. 20 March 1628/29.

Bequeaths soul to Jesus Christ by whose merits he hopes to be saved. To be buried in Barrow churchyard.
I make my daughter Margaret sole ex'trix. I give my son William my red bullock now about a year old. In a former will, which I now renounce, I made my daughter Elizabeth, now wife of William Crowne, one of my ex'trices and gave my goods to be divided between her and my daughter Margaret. Since that time I have, with the help of my good friends, arranged for her a marriage with a good portion, so I now give her the featherbed she lies on with all things belonging except the linen. All the rest of my goods I give to my daughter Margaret, who is to pay my debts and bring my body decently to the ground. In order that no difference may arise over the payment of my debts I have caused them to be set down: 7s to John Linge, 20s to Alice Simpson, 6s to Richard Harte, 20s to John Wymarke, 18s to William Crowne, 40s to one that William Pattell gave his word for me. Wit. Thomas Seargeant, John Dersly. Pr. at Bury 12 December 1631.

338. R(W) THOMAS COSSEN (X) the elder of Whatfield, husbandman. 10 December 1629.

Commends soul to God believing to be saved by merits of Jesus Christ. To be buried in Whatfield churchyard.
I bequeath to my wife Katherine for life all my moveable goods, corn and cattle. After her decease I give my youngest son Thomas a cupboard standing in the chamber where I usually lie, and the best bedstead with a flockbed on it, a feather and a flock transome, 2 feather pillows, a birded coverlet, 2 blankets, a pair of the best sheets and a stained cloth over the bed. All the rest of my goods, corn and cattle are to be divided between my 2 sons Robert and Thomas after my wife's decease. My copyhold house and land, which I hold of the manor of Barrardes in Whatfield, my youngest son Thomas is to take up at the next court held after both I and my wife have deceased, on condition he pays my eldest son Robert £40 on 3 consecutive Michaelmas days in the south porch of Whatfield church. If Thomas defaults on payments, the property passes to Robert. From the death of the longest liver of myself and my wife until the following Michaelmas my 2 sons are to share the profits of my house and land, and then for one whole year Robert is to hold the property paying 50s to Thomas. Ex'trix: wife. Wit. George Carter, William Grymwood. Pr. at Bury 14 November 1631.

339. W(R) JANE HALLAWAYE (X) of Stowmarket, widow. 1 June 1631.

Bequeaths soul to God hoping to have eternal salvation through Jesus Christ. To be buried in Stowmarket churchyard.
I give £8 to Christian, wife of Stephen Ward, my dame whom I have some years yet to serve as an apprentice, if it please God that I depart this life in her service and before my term of years has expired. This money is in the hands of John Duncon, tanner of Mendlesham, and other inhabitants of that place and is to be paid to Christian Ward by my exor one week after he receives it. She is to see my body decently buried if I die in her service. I make Richard Ryvette, worsted weaver of Stowmarket, my exor. Wit. John Broome and me Philip Barne. Pr. at Bury 9 January 1631/32.

340. W(R) THOMAS DAYNES (X) of Bacton, yeoman. 26 December 1631.

Commends soul to God hoping through Jesus Christ to live eternally in his everlasting kingdom.
I bequeath to Dorothy my wife for life all my lands and tenements in Bacton and Cotton. She must educate well and bring up my children until they are 21. I give my 3 daughters Alice, Mary and Susan £40 each when 21. Until then this money is to remain in my exor's hands and the interest paid to my wife. I give my daughter Alice a red cow immediately after my decease, and £5 to be paid by my wife when she is 21. I give my wife all my goods for her life. After her death I give all my land and tenements to the child that she is now great with if it is a son, but if it is a girl my land and tenements are to be divided amongst my 4 daughters. If the child is a son, my 3 daughters are to share my goods and chattels after my wife's decease, but if a girl all 4 are to divide them. Benefit of survivorship. My wife is to keep my house in repair. If she remarries, her husband is to be bound in the sum of £100 to my exor not to consume any of my goods. If my wife dies before all my children are 21, then my brother John Daynes of Bacton is to educate and bring them up until they are 21. Exor: my brother John Daynes. Wit. Stephen Keble, Nathan Keble, Robert Bugge (X). Pr. at Bury 9 January 1631/32.

341. W(R) THOMAS BARTON of Mildenhall. 24 December 1631.

Bequeaths soul to God and body to the earth.
I give my wife Elizabeth for life my house wherein I dwell which she must keep in repair with thatching and claying, and after her decease I give it to my son Thomas. I also give him £20 when 21. I give my sons John and Robert £20 each when 21. Benefit of survivorship. The residue of my goods and chattels I give to my wife towards the performance of my will and I make her ex'trix. Wit. Thomas Pechey, Francis Lusher (X), John Bird, Richard Bull. Pr. at Bury 9 January 1631/32.

144

342. W(R) ROBERT JOHNSON (X) of Gislingham, yeoman.
22 November 1631.

Bequeaths soul to God hoping to have remission of sins through Jesus Christ. To be buried in Gislingham churchyard.
I have mortgaged my tenement and freehold land in Gislingham to William Smeare of Gislingham, and my copyhold land in Gislingham to John Hubberd the elder of Gislingham. My wife Elizabeth is to redeem these mortgages and I give her full power to do anything necessary such as selling some of the land so that she can repay the capital sums and interest. The remainder of my land not sold shall descend to my son Robert after my wife's decease. If she dies before my land is redeemed, my brothers-in-law William Bedwell, Thomas Garland and Barsheborne Cooper shall have the same power to act as I have given my wife. I give Elizabeth my wellbeloved wife all my moveable goods to pay my other debts, and I make her ex'trix. Wit. John Symonds, John Hubberd (X), Robert Brett. Pr. at Bury 9 January 1631/32.

343. W(R) ADAM HALLS (X) of Poslingford, yeoman. 24 January 1630/31.

Commits soul to God hoping through Jesus Christ to be partaker of everlasting life.
I give my wife Mary for life my 2 tenements, wherein John Collin and William Norfolke now dwell, with their yards and orchards in Poslingford, and after her death to my son John. If John dies before he marries, the tenements are to go to my son Giles and if he dies to my son Nicholas. My wife is to keep the tenements in repair; if she does not the son who will inherit them is to find 2 honest men to estimate what needs to be done, and if my wife refuses to carry out the work this son has the power to do so. I give my son Giles £10 to be paid by John a year after my wife's decease, and my son Nicholas £10 to be paid by John 2 years after. Power to distrain. I give my sons Giles and Nicholas £20 each to be paid by my wife 1 and 2 years after my death. If my wife remarries before these legacies are paid, she is to enter into security to my sons to pay them. Sons have benefit of survivorship. All my goods and chattels I bequeath to Mary my wife to pay my legacies, and I make her ex'trix. Supervisor: Stephen Halls my brother. Wit. Walter Derisley, Francis Derisley, John Metcalfe (X). Pr. at Bury 10 January 1631/32.

344. R(W) WILLIAM SPEARMAN (X) of Wicken [Cambs].
23 December 1631.

Bequeaths soul to God hoping to be saved through Jesus Christ. To be buried in Wicken churchyard.
I give my son William my coat and breeches. I give my son Robert 40s to

be paid when he is 21. I give my daughter Elizabeth 40s when 18. I give the rest of my children 12d apiece. All the rest of my goods I give to my wife Elizabeth, whom I make ex'trix. Wit. Nicholas Cowper, Zachary Bentham, Edmund Haylock (X). Pr. at Bury 23 January 1631/32.

345. W(R) THOMAS UNDERWOOD (X) the elder of Hartest, yeoman. 19 September 1629.

I give the poor people of Hartest 20s to be paid to the churchwardens and overseers of the poor within a month after my decease for distribution amongst the most aged and needy poor of the parish. I bequeath my eldest son Thomas 20s, and his eldest son Thomas 20s when 21. All the residue of my goods and chattels I give to my son John and make him exor. He must pay my wife Anne an annuity of £5 in equal portions on the 4 quarter days in my dwelling house in Hartest called the Hatch. To assure this annuity John must enter into a bond of £40 within a month of my decease to my loving friends Daniel Copping yeoman of Hartest and John Copping yeoman of Brockley. If John refuses to do this, he must pay my wife £40 in recompense for her annuity. Wit. Daniel Copping (X), Thomas Wright. Pr. at Bury 23 January 1631/32.

346. W(R) VINCA ELLIS (X) of Cotton, widow. 4 April 1631.

Commends soul to God with an assured faith of receiving remission of sins through Jesus Christ.
My late husband, Nicholas Elles yeoman of Cotton, devised by his will that his son William should pay me an annuity of £10, the first payment of which was to begin in or about the 1611. The annuity has not since 1611 been paid fully every year. My son Thomas, yeoman of Cotton, by a deed dated 14 January 1605 granted an annuity of £15 to my late husband and myself to be paid out of the lands held by him. Since my husband's death the annuity has not been paid to me, but has been most unnaturally detained from me in my great necessity in which I might have perished had not my wellbeloved son-in-law Thomas Bartropp, yeoman of Cotton, not succoured me. All the arrears of the 2 annuities due to me at the time of my death are to be equally divided between Vinca and Mary, daughters of Thomas Bartropp, when they are 21. Benefit of survivorship. All the rest of my goods and chattels I bequeath to Thomas Bartropp and make him exor. Wit. Randolph Carliells, Edward Fryer, Thomas Younges. Pr. at Bury 23 January 1631/32.

347. W(R) MIRABEL HOVELL alias SMYTH (X) of Great Ashfield, widow. 5 April 1631.

Commends soul to God trusting assuredly to be saved by death and passion of Jesus Christ. To be buried in parish of Great Ashfield.
I give 20s each to the 8 children of my son John Smith: John, Martha, Elizabeth, Mary, Simon, Rachel, Olive and William. I give 20s each to

the 5 children of my son Edmund Smyth: Elizabeth, Mary, Robert, Abigail and Lydia, and 10s each to the 3 children of my son Thomas Smith: Elizabeth, Deborah and Hannah. All these gifts are to be paid by my ex'trix as the children reach 21. Benefit of survivorship. I give Robert, eldest son of my son Robert Smyth, a great brass copper hanging in the backhouse, and a long table in the hall with 2 table forms, and a horse mill with the stones and all other parts of it, on condition he pays his sister Elizabeth Gibbon widow £3 immediately after my decease. If he refuses, Elizabeth is to take the table and forms and the horse mill to pay herself. I give my daughter Baker's children, being 7 in number, 40s each: John, Elizabeth, William, Richard, Anne, Sarah and Mary; all to be paid by my ex'trix when 21. Benefit of survivorship. I give the poor of the parish of Great Ashfield 40s: 10s to be distributed at my burial and 10s at each of the next 3 Christmases at the discretion of Mr Peake, minister of the parish. I make my daughter Elizabeth Baker, widow, ex'trix and I give her all my unbequeathed goods. Wit. William Blumfeilde (X) Audrey Barnes (X), Thomas Peake. Pr. at Bury 23 January 1631/32.

348. W(R) BRIDGET CLARKE (N) of Exning, widow. 31 January 1631/32.

I give to Bridget Cropley my daughter a featherbed, a feather bolster, a feather pillow, a pair of blankets, a coverlet, a quilt, a pair sheets, a gown, 2 under petticoats, 1 red petticoat, 2 aprons, a bolt of new cloth and a waistcoat cloth of my new web. I give her in money £13. I give Robert Linwoode my grandchild 40s, and to Simon Cropleye my grandson 20s. I give 20s to the child my daughter Cropley is now with. I give my grandson William Cropley 20s. Benefit of survivorship. Wit. Charles Chenerye, Richard Shearman. Let. ad. granted 4 February 1631/32 to Richard and Bridget Cropley. No place given.

349. W(R) ALICE KEDGE (X) of Boxford, widow of Richard Kedge of Boxford. 22 February 1626/27.

Bequeaths soul to God believing to have pardon of sins and everlasting life through Jesus Christ.
I give my eldest son John my tenement or dwelling house in Boxford wherein he now dwells with its yard extending in length from the house to the yard of Goodman Watson sometime William Parson's, and in breadth from Richard Dunnyngham's yard to the lodge belonging to the house wherein I dwell; it is divided by posts from the yard of this latter house. John must pay my daughter Elizabeth 20s within a year and a month of my decease. If he fails Elizabeth is to have the house for 2 years. I give my youngest son William the house in Boxford where I now live and which adjoins my other house. He must pay my daughter Elizabeth 40s on the same terms as above. If William dies without heirs, I bequeath my house to my daughter Elizabeth. If she dies unmarried William is to have the 40s bequeathed to her. I give my son John 5s which I lent him and

which he doth yet owe me. I give my son William my copper kettle, my brass pan, my 2 posted bedsteads, my featherbed, my worst flockbed, my new kettle, my skillet, my candlestick and my cupboard. I give my daughter Elizabeth 2 other bedsteads, my 2 best flockbeds, my best covering, a blanket, my brass cauldron, my brass kettle, my little kettle, a little posnet and a mortar and pestle. All my other household goods and moveables I give to be equally divided between William and Elizabeth and I make them exors. Wit. Thomas Cole, John Parson, Thomas Dearslye. Pr. at Bury 6 February 1631/32.

350. W(R) JOAN ELDRED (N) wife of John Eldred of Great Saxham, clerk. November 1627.

She made her will with the consent of her husband. She gave to her mother a stammell petticoat, to her sister Kempe her high hat and a petticoat, to her sister Franke her riding suit, to her sister Mary a pair of gloves, to her sister Catherall a petticoat and waistcoat, to her sister-in-law her best dressing for her head and to Elizabeth Gilman her servant her red stammell petticoat. She further willed that the £15 given to her by her father by his will should be paid to her husband John Eldred to be shared between her children John and William when of full age. Witnesses not named. Let. ad. granted to John Eldred 8 February 1631/32. No place given.

351. W(R) FRANCIS ABBOTT the elder of Cavendish, clothier. 27 August 1630.

Commends soul to 3 persons of Trinity. Very aged.
I give 20s to the poor of Cavendish to be distributed by the minister, curate, churchwardens or overseers the sabbath after my burial. I give my eldest son Francis an annuity of £4 to be paid out of the profits of my messuage in Cavendish called Wardes and the 6 acres pasture belonging to it. During the life of my wife Abigail he is to be paid only 40s p.a., and after her decease £4 p.a. at the 4 usual quarter days. Power to distrain. I give to my wife Abigail for her life my messuage called Wards with its yards, orchards, outhouses and the 6 acres pasture, and after her decease to my youngest son Abraham. Within a year of my decease Abraham must pay £30 to my eldest daughter Abigail, and £30 to my youngest daughter Susan within 2 years. Payments to be made in the south porch of Cavendish church and legatees have benefit of survivorship. If Abraham does not pay these legacies the bequest to him of my messuage and land is void, and they are to be given to Abigail and Susan instead. All my household stuff and implements I give to my wife for life, and she must leave them in as good repair as she receives them. After her decease I give them to be equally divided betweeen my 3 children: Abraham, Abigail and Susan, and they must pay £2 13s 4d to my son Francis within 6 months of my wife's decease. I give my wife my 3 milk kine and all the hay, grass and corn in my possession at my death. I give my son Abraham

my gelding with bridle, pack saddle and road saddle and all belonging to him except women's furniture for a horse. I also give him all my wool, yarn, cloth, tools and implements belonging to the trade of a clothier. The residue of my goods and chattels I give to my son Abraham whom I make exor as my special trust and confidence is in him. Wit. Henry Cutts, Mathias Dyke (X), Richard Walkinson. Pr. at Bury 18 March 1631/32.

352. W(R) THOMAS COATES (N) the younger of Mildenhall, husbandman. 17 December 1631.

I give to Thomas my son my copyhold tenement I now dwell in. I give Mary my daughter 3 acres of freehold land in 2 pieces against Peter Buroughes I give my daughter Agnes 2 acres pasture at the hearst. I give my daughter Ellen 3 acres arable in the town field. I give my son Thomas the close at the hearst that the house stand in. My wife is to hold all this land left to my 3 children until they are 21. I give Mary my wife my freehold tenement now in the tenure of John Wythers for life and then to my son Thomas. I make my wife ex'trix to pay my debts and bring my body to the ground. No witnesses. Let. ad. granted to ex'trix 11 January 1631/32. No place given.

353. W(R) WILLIAM BARBER (N) of Mildenhall, husbandman. 13 January 1631/32.

He gave Anne his wife all his goods whatsover towards the payment of his debts. Wit. Thomas Spark, Anthony Sparhawk. Pr. at Bury 30 January 1631/32.

354. W(R) THOMAS GISLEING (X) of Eye, husbandman. 10 November 1630.

Commends soul to his maker trusting through his redeemer to have everlasting life.
I give my wife Anne for life my 1 acre piece of meadow held of Netherhall manor and lying in a meadow called Swans hill and then to my youngest son Nicholas. I give my eldest son Anthony, after my wife's decease, my half acre piece of copyhold held of the manor of Cranley Hall and on which a barn stands. I give my second son Thomas half an acre copyhold land held of Cranley Hall manor after my wife's death. Anthony is to maintain the ditch separating his piece of land from Thomas's, and Thomas is to maintain that between his land and Nicholas's. If any of my sons wishes to sell his land, he is to offer it first to his brothers. I give my wife Anne all my goods and chattels. Any hop poles on the land left to my wife that are there at her decease are to remain on that land. I make my wife sole ex'trix. Wit. James Frary, John Hall, John Harvey. Pr. at Bury 9 January 1631/32.

149

355. W(R) JOHN BRIDGE of Stoke by Clare, glover. 22 June 1631.

Commits soul to God trusting through Jesus Christ to have remission of sins and be raised up to life everlasting.
I give to Margaret my loving wife the tenement wherein I now dwell with an adjoining pasture pightle for life, and then to my son Reginald. I give my wife another pasture pightle abutting on Rentford Green and containing 1 acre until my son Reginald is 21 when he is to have it. I give my son Reginald a great book called Mr Foxes book of martyrs. All my sheep combs and household stuff I bequeath to my wife to dispose of at her pleasure. All the money owing to me by my brother-in-law Ralph Turner is to be paid to my brother Ralph Bridge, who is to employ it to the best profit. The interest is to be given to my wife towards bringing up my 2 children Reginald and Elizabeth until they are 21 or the latter marries. I give out of this money £6 13s 4d to be paid to my daughter Elizabeth by Ralph Bridge when she is 21 or marries. All my other unbequeathed goods I give to my brother Ralph, whom I make exor. Wit. Thomas Bridge, William Bareham (X), Thomas Dennell. Pr. 25 October 1631. No place given.

356. W(R) ROBERT SANCTY (X) the elder of Wickhambrook, yeoman. 26 November 1631.

Bequeaths soul to God and Jesus Christ.
I give my son Robert my long table in my hall with a joined form belonging to it, one of my joined stools standing under the table, my cupboard in my chamber where I usually lie, my posted bedstead standing there and the coverlet lying on it. I also give him my greatest posnet together with my brazen mortar and its pestle. I give my son Thomas my greatest joined chest in my chamber, my greatest kettle, my brewing tub, a feather bolster and a feather pillow and 1 of my joined stools. I give my son John my flockbed on which I lie together with a feather bolster and feather pillow used with this bed. I also give him my yellow coverlet, my greatest brass pot and 1 of my joined stools. I give my son Joslas 2 of my boarded hutches, a trundle bedstead, my greatest chair, a joined stool and 2 barrels. I give Lydia Guest, my daughter, my featherbed, a feather bolster and a joined stool. In requital of her diligent attendance and great pains about me, Bridget Sadler shall dwell in the chamber where I lie as long as she lives, with free access through my hall house and liberty to make a fire in the chimney of the hall house. She shall have the use of my garden with access to it through the yard. The chamber and garden are not to be let to any stranger during her lifetime. After my debts and funeral charges have been paid the residue of my goods are to be divided amongst my children. Exor: my son Robert. Wit. Margaret Sadler, Charles Burrough. Pr. at Bury 13 February 1631/32.

357. W(R) GILES WOOD of Oakley, clerk. 21 November 1628.

Commends soul to God trusting through Jesus Christ for resurrection.
I give Mary my wellbeloved wife £10 to be paid in the porch of Oakley church immediately after my decease. I give my son Gregory all my messuages and land in Oakley. He must pay my wife £12 p.a. in lieu of dowry; the payments to be made quarterly in the church porch. I give my sons Peter, Giles and John £10 each and my daughters Elizabeth and Margaret £10 each immediately after my decease. I give my wife Mary the featherbed I lent to my son Giles, the best bedstead in the parlour chamber and a flockbed there, a table and a cupboard in the hall, 6 buffet stools, a chair in the hall and another in the parlour, a chest, a press, a little short form in the parlour, a coffer, a desk, a little framed table in the parlour chamber, half the linen she has in her custody, half the pewter and brass excepting the copper, 6 of the smaller beer vessels, 6 milk bowls, a cheese press, a firepan here at the parsonage, a pair tongs, 2 pairs cobirons, a roasting iron, a frying pan and 2 spits. I give my daughter Elizabeth a feather bed and bedstead in the parlour ready furnished. I give my son Giles a framed table in the parlour, a ceiled bedstead with all its furniture as it now stands in the buttery chamber, 2 forms in the hall and a pair sheets. I give my son John a feather bed and a trundle bedstead in the buttery chamber well and decently furnished. I give the parishes of Oakley and Brome 20s to be equally divided and distributed among their poor people. My son John is to have some part of the books in my study. The residue of my goods and chattels I give to my son Gregory, whom I appoint exor. Supervisor: Thomas Wood gentleman of Sandon, Essex to whom I give 40s and to Anne his wife 20s to make rings in remembrance of me. Wit. Richard Murrell (X), Thomas Balles. Pr. at Bury 13 February 1631/32.

358. W(R) PHILIP HAMOND of Boxted, clothier. 20 December 1631.

Commits soul to God and body to earth steadfastly believing to be made partaker of everlasting blessedness in kingdom of heaven.
I give to Elizabeth my wife for life all the land in Hawkedon and Somerton which I lately purchased from George and Henry Browne, so that she may keep my son Robert with meat, drink and apparel. After her decease I give this land to my second son Philip, but an annuity of £20 is to be paid to Robert out of this land after my wife's decease during Robert's life and for 1 year after. Power to distrain. I give my eldest son Thomas the money owed to me by Mr Thomas Cutter of Stanstead for which I have land in Stanstead and Shimpling mortgaged to me; it is called Gatefeild and Weifes meadows. I also give Thomas £128 to be paid within 6 months of my decease and £360 to be given to him within 3 months of the death of my ex'trix. I give my daughter Anne £260 to be paid as follows: £150 when she is 21 and £110 within 6 months of the death of my ex'trix. I give to Anne, daughter of my son Philip, £10 6

months after death of my ex'trix, but to be paid to her father if she is not of age. If she dies, her father is to have the £10. I make Elizabeth my wife my ex'trix and give her all my goods and chattels to perform my will. Wit. William Hall, John Spalding. Pr. at Bury 20 February 1631/32.

359. R(W) THOMAS MEADOW (N) of Brent Eleigh, blacksmith. About All Saints 1631.

He gave his son George all his goods and chattels. Wit. Edward Hitchcocke, William Laye. Let. ad. granted to George Meadow 18 February 1631/32. No place given.

360. W(R) HENRY JOHNSON (X) of Mildenhall. No date.

Bequeaths soul to God.
I give my wife my house and my acre of land for her life, and then my house to my son Simon, who must pay my daughter Grace 40s within a year of his mother's death. My acre of freehold land lying by Church way and abutting to the north on the Styeway and to the south on Old way I give to my son Henry, who must pay my daughter Mary 40s within a year of my wife's decease. I give my wife all my moveables to pay my debts and make her ex'trix. Wit. Robert Barber (X), Joseph Smethe (X), Thomas Raye. Pr. at Bury 26 February 1631/32.

361. R(W) HENRY SCROOPE (N) of Mildenhall, husbandman. August 1631.

He gave to Anne his wife all his goods and chattels, except a birding piece, which he gave to his eldest son John. He appointed his wife ex'trix. Wit. William Curtis, Charles Lumpkyn. Let. ad. granted to widow 12 December 1631. No place given.

362. R(W) EDMUND BROWNE of Risby, yeoman. 24 January 1631/32.

Commends soul to God hoping to be a partaker of the kingdom of heaven prepared by Jesus Christ for his elect.
I bequeath to Joan my beloved wife the remainder of the lease of the house and land in Risby, which I rent from the Lord Rivers. She must pay the rent. I give her all the corn at home in my barns or sown in my fields, and all my hay and fodder. I give her all my horses and cows, and all my household goods and chattels and my instruments of husbandry. She must pay all my debts and I make her ex'trix. Wit. Anthony Disborowe, Andrew Wrighte. Pr. at Bury 18 February 1631/32.

363. R(W) THOMAS SHEENE (X) of Chippenham [Cambs], yeoman.
7 December 1631.

Bequeaths soul to God. To be buried in Chippenham churchyard.
I give my son John 4 acres arable lying in several pieces in the fields of
Chippenham: a 3 rod piece lying between the lord's land occupied by
John Tetsole on the east and John Turner's land to west and with north
end abutting on Ditched way; the second piece in the same field and
furlong next to Thomas Delamare's land on west with north end abutting
on ½ acre of my own land; 1 acre in Mill field next to the Lord's land
occupied by Thomas Howes on the north and with west end abutting on
Moulton way; 1 acre in Sand field next to Thomas Delamare's land on the
west and with north end abutting on Bells Crofts and south end on the
lord's demesne; and 1 acre in the West field next to the land of John
Francis on the west and with south end abutting on the lord's land
occupied by John Tayler. I give my house and adjoining ground and all
the rest of my land held copyhold of the manor of Chippenham to my son
Thomas, who must undertake the execution of my will and pay my debts
and legacies. If he refuses to do this, I give all my land in Beck field and
West field to John Bentlie of Chippenham to sell and pay my debts and
legacies. I give my daughter Elizabeth a little black cow to be given to her
one week after my decease, and 40s to be paid within a year. I give my
daughter Margaret a garled cow and 40s at same times as her sister. I give
my daughter Anne a kirtle or waistcoat to be provided within a month,
and £10 within 3 years. I give my brother William Sheene 20s within a
year, and my brother-in-law Robert Tayler 20s within 2 years. I give 6s 8d
to be distributed amongst the poorest people of the parish of Chippenham on the day of my burial. All my unbequeathed goods I give to my
son Thomas whom I make exor. Wit. William Chapman, John Bentlie,
William Sheene, John Norman the younger, Martin Hilles. Pr. at Bury 16
January 1631/32.

364. R(W) JOSEPH SMYTH of Polstead. 2 February 1630/31.

I appoint my wife Alice and my son Fabian my exors. My mind is that
they shall sell my land to pay my debts and legacies. I give my son Fabian
£80, my son Soffiny [sic] £45, my son John £15, and my daughters
Elizabeth and Alice £25 each, all to be paid one year after my decease. If
my land is sold for £40 more than these legacies my wife is to have the
money, but if not this sum is to be deducted from my legacies so that my
wife has £40. Wit. John Gostlin. Pr. at Bury 31 January 1631/32.

365. R(W) ROSE SOWTER of Horringer, widow. 22 March 1627/28.

Bequeaths soul to God.
I give my sister Mayhew my best hat and my best waistcoat. I give my
cousin Thomasine Wright my linsey wolsey cloak. I give the wife of
Richard Cooper my red petticoat, my other hat and my cloak. The

residue of my goods I give to my son Edmund Sowter, whom I make exor. Wit. William Bedell, Robert Mayhew, Andrew Wright. Pr. at Bury 19 March 1631/32.

366. W(R) FRANCES EDWARDS (X) of Bury St Edmunds, singlewoman. 4 January 1631/32.

Commits soul to God trusting to be saved by Jesus Christ.
I give my brother Nicholas Edwards 40s, my sister Elizabeth £3, my eldest brother Thomas 40s and his son Thomas 20s. I give my sister Margaret Tompson widow £3. All these legacies are to be paid within 6 months of my decease. I give Margaret Tompson my stammell petticoat and my cloth gown. I give my best gown to my sister Elizabeth, and my best ruff to Audry, wife of my brother Nicholas. All the rest of my goods and estate, my funeral charges and expenses of proving my will being paid, I give to Nicholas and Elizabeth Edwards and make them exors. Wit. Thomas Gippes, William Turnor, William Sarson. Pr. at Bury 7 March 1631/32.

367. W(R) ROBERT IGNES of Bury St Edmunds, goldsmith. 1 March 1631/32.

Bequeaths soul to God trusting to have remission of sins through my saviour Jesus Christ and expecting to reign in glory for evermore at last day.
I give my daughter Margaret, wife of George Groome all my copyhold and lease lands and tenements in Rattlesden and Woolpit. I give my daughter Elizabeth, wife of Thomas Chaplyn, all my messuages and land in Wyverstone. I give my son-in-law Thomas Chaplyn £50 already in his hands as a debt he owes me. I give my daughter Abigail and her husband Richard Scott of Braintree [Essex] all my messuages and lands in Hitcham. If she and Richard have no heirs this property is to descend to my other 3 daughters Margaret Groome, Elizabeth Chaplyn and Sarah Chaplyn. The gift of these messuages and land to Richard Scott for his life is dependent on him conveying to my daughter Abigail an estate for life of his messuages and land in Braintree. I give my daughter Sarah, wife of Clement Chaplyn, my messuage wherein John Maies now dwells, being near the Northgate in Bury. I also give her £460: £250 already in her husband's hands, £160 in the hands of my son-in-law George Groome and £50 in the hands of William Chaplyn of Hitcham, brother of Clement Chaplyn. I give my son-in-law Clement Chaplyn for ever my messuage in Churchgate Street in Bury in which widow Turle now dwells. I give the 5 children of George and Margaret Groome £5 each to be paid to their father for their use within a year of my decease. I give the 5 children of Thomas and Elizabeth Chaplyn £5 each on the same terms. I give Henry Tylar of the parish of John Zacharie in Foster Lane in London and his sister Margaret, wife of Robert Bawlye of Norton, £5 each within 3 months of my decease. I give 50s each within 3 months to Philip Clarke of

Norton, to the wife of William Cooke dwelling in Foster Lane, to Lydia wife of Richard Turner living in [blank in MS] and to Joan Fiske, all four being my sister's children. I give £6 to the poor people of Bury, £3 to be distributed in each parish by my exor within a month of my death. All the residue of my goods and chattels, jewels, money and plate I give to my son-in-law Thomas Chaplyn towards the performance of my will and I make him sole exor. Wit. John Jewell, William Cropley. Pr. at Bury 9 March 1631/32.

Note: Robert Ignes always signed his name thus, but in other documents it is often spelt Hindes.

368. W(R) LAWRENCE RAYNBERD the elder of Walsham the Willows, yeoman. 17 November 1631.

Commends soul to God believing that he will enjoy life everlasting.
I give 10s to the poor of Walsham in the Willows to be distributed by my exor on the day of my burial or on the next Sunday. I give my eldest son William my ancient [former] messuage wherein I lately dwelt called Fullers with its yard, orchard, garden and 2 adjoining pasture closes containing 10 acres. I also give him a close called Pyes close with its west side abutting on the common way leading from Church bridge to Pallmer street, and a 3 acre close called Peppers lying on the backside of my tenement and next to the land of Reginald Rise on the east, as well as all the pasture ground on the north side of my messuage known as the pightles and divided into 4 parts. They lie next to the tenement and land sometines William Rise's and abut on those belonging to my son Lawrence; they belong to the tenement called Raunds. I give my son Lawrence my messuage in Walsham in which he lives with its yard, orchard, garden and an adjoining 3½ acre pasture croft called Leves or Raunds. It lies on the south side of Raunds tenement next to Whartust lane, and the north side of this tenement abuts on Jollicote hill, I give my daughter Mary, wife of Reginald Johnson, £5 to be paid within a year. I give my son William all my household stuff remaining in the house where he lives. I give my son Lawrence all the rest of my household goods to pay my debts and legacies, and I make him exor. Wit. John Page, Samuel Canham, William Raynberd. Pr. at Bury 5 March 1631/32.

369. R(W) JOHN NORMAN (X) of Burwell [Cambs], tanner. 27 October 1630.

Bequeaths soul to God and steadfastly believes to be saved by death of Jesus Christ and by no other means.
I give my daughters Elizabeth, Phyllis, Marian, Theoder and Frances £3 each when 21. I give my son John £5 when 21. If any of my children die

155

before receiving their legacy it is to be paid to my daughter Phyllis. All my other goods I give to be equally divided between my wife Phyllis and my son Robert, on condition they provide for the bringing up and maintenance of my children until they are 21. I make them exors. Wit. John Wilkyns, Thomas Steward, Robert Heromer (X). Pr. at Bury 5 March 1631/32.

370. W(R) ANTHONY SPARROW (X) of Chevington, yeoman. 15 February 1631/32.

Humbly commends soul to God trusting through Jesus Christ to be received into celestial joys. To be buried in Chevington churchyard.

Before my marriage with my loving wife Anne I made her a jointure of half the messuage wherein I dwell and of half my land, except for 3 closes. She is to have jointure and the 3 closes until my son Anthony is 15 towards his maintenance and bringing him up in learning, and towards maintaining my daughter Margaret. I give my son Anthony my wife's jointure land in Chevington and Whepstead after her decease, and the rest of my land immediately after my death. I give my daughter Margaret £60 which my exor is to pay within a year to my loving brothers George Sparrow and John Gooday in trust for her. I earnestly desire my brothers to put this sum to the best use by buying land or doing what they think most fit with it. The profit is to be added to the principal until my daughter is 21 or marries. If Margaret dies, this money goes to Anthony, but if both children die to my wife Anne if she is still living, but if she has died it is to be divided between my brothers George Sparrow and John Gooday. I give my loving wife Anne all my moveables, hay and stock of cattle, but not my bonds and bills or the debts owing to me. Within 10 days of my decease she must enter into a bond of £40 to my exor to pay my daughter Margaret £20 when 21. If she refuses this bequest goes to my exor. I give my son Anthony, after my wife's decease, a posted bedstead with curtains and valance and curtain rods, the featherbed, feather bolster, blankets and coverlet lying on it as it now stands in my parlour chamber, a livery cupboard and a framed table in the same room. I give my daughter Margaret when 21 or married a livery cupboard, a featherbed and a silver spoon (all of which were once my mother's now deceased), a great framed table in my parlour and a great framed chair in my parlour chamber. I give Michael Kinge, yeoman of Rede, 21 lambs now in my pasture and all my bonds, bills and debts towards paying my debts and legacies and proving my will. I make him my exor. Wit. Joshua Wade, Thomas Pleasaunce, John Baylye (X). Pr. at Bury 19 March 1631/32.

156

371. W(R) ELIZABETH RAFFE (X) of Hitcham, widow. 3 March 1616/17.

Bequeaths soul to three persons of Trinity.
I bequeath to my daughter Anne Raffe £20 to be paid by my exor as follows: £10 is already due to her by bond and my exor is to pay the other £10 within a year of my decease. But if she marries James Dawling, carpenter of Hitcham, the second £10 is never to be paid to her. I give 40s to Elizabeth, wife of Thomas Percifall, and 20s to my son Simon, both within a year. All the rest of my goods and chattels, bonds and ready money I give to my son Thomas whom I make exor. Wit. John Rushe (X), Barnabas Salter. Pr. at Bury 22 March 1631/32.

372. W(R) FRANCES GARNET (X) of Wicken [Cambs], widow. 28 January 1630/31.

Gives soul to God who gave it her not doubting that his son Jesus Christ will place it in the company of the heavenly angels and blessed saints.
I give my grandson James Hales £40 to be paid by my exor within a year into the hands of my cousin Henry Payne gentleman until James is 21. If James dies before then the money is to be divided among my grand-children as follows: £20 to Richard Hales, £10 to Anne Hammerton and £5 each to Mary and Joan Hammerton. I give my grandchild Susan Roote 40s within a year of my decease. I give Francis Webber 12d, Margaret Gatward 6d, and 8d each to John Mounsey and Anne Sherman, and 6d each to the rest of the poor folk dwelling in the almshouses. All the rest of my goods and chattels I give to my grandson Richard Hales, provided he behaves well to my supervisor and sees my body buried in Wicken church according to the rites of the church. I give to a gentleman to preach at my funeral 10s, and 20s to be distributed to the poor at my burial. Exor: Richard Hales. Supervisor: my cousin Henry Payne, whom I ask to assist my exor with his best counsel and advice, and I give him the use of the £40 left to James Hales until he is 21. I also give him all my pictures, a long cushion and a cupboard cloth of green kersey. I desire him to give a suit of apparel to James Hales. I give to Mistress Cooper the posted bedstead I lie on with its curtains and valance. I give Fisher my servant the great chest in the parlour and the hutch in the chamber. Wit. John Tabraham (X), and me William Hopwood. Pr. at Bury 15 December 1631.

373. R FRANCIS SPENCER (N) of Flempton, clerk. 28 March 1630.

He said his wife should have his house in Bury during her life and a room in his house at Fornham, and half the fruit in the orchard. His daughter to have half his household stuff and all his brewing vessels and the brass belonging to them; also half the debts due to him and the half the corn sown on his glebe land, and half his money now in his house. His wife was to have the other half of all these things and to be his ex'trix. He said he would give nothing now to his son as he had already bestowed a large portion on him. Wit. Robert Webb, John Bryant (X). Let. ad. granted to ex'trix and Francis, son of the testator, on 14 June 1631. No place given.

374. W(R) WILLIAM PEIRSON (N) of Wangford, husbandman. 20 June 1631.

On Monday 20 June 1631 in the morning about eight of the clock and about 6 hours before his death speaking to Lucy his wife, being then with him, he said sweetheart I do give thee all that I have paying my debts or words to that effect. Wit. William Cappe, Robert Cappe (X), Rose Milles (X). Pr. at Bury 5 July 1631.

375. W(R) THOMAS COOKE (X) the elder of Bures St Mary, ploughwright. 29 July 1614.

Bequeaths soul to God steadfastly believing to be saved through Jesus Christ. To be buried in Bures churchyard.
I give Elizabeth my wife for life my tenement wherein I dwell with yard, garden, orchard and land in Bures and after her death to my son William. I give my wife for life the use of my goods and chattels. She is to leave them in as good state as she received them or replace them. After her decease I leave them all to my son William. I give my son John £10 to be paid out of my land by William 1 year after my wife's death. I give my sons Thomas and Robert £10 each to be paid in the same way, and I give Robert my best bird coverlet. I give my daughters Elizabeth, Rose and Mary £10 each to be paid by William 18 months after my wife's decease. I will that William allows Elizabeth to have sufficient room in my tenement to set a bed and abide there, or hire her some convenient room nearer the church, and I give her a flockbed furnished and a joined cupboard. Legatees have power to distrain. If my son William, whom I name sole exor, does not prove my will within 3 months of my decease I make John exor and give him my tenement and land for 3 years. Wit. Philip Barker, Nathaniel Cooke (X), John Gryme (X). Pr. at Little Cornard 28 July 1631.

376. W(R) JOHN CAPP (X) of Brandon Ferry, labourer. 12 April 1629.

Bequeaths soul to God hoping to be saved through Jesus Christ.
I give Anne my wife my house I now live in and after her death to my son John, on condition he pays my son Thomas £3 within 2 years of my wife's decease. My wife must keep my house in repair. Wit. Thomas Webb, Peter Smyth, William Gryme. Pr. 13 June 1631. No place given.

377. R(W) EDWARD HOWE the elder of Soham [Cambs], tailor.
8 January 1631/32.

Commends soul to God trusting to be saved through Jesus Christ. To be
buried in Soham churchyard.
I give Anne my wife all my goods and chattels on condition she pays my
son Edward £5 within a year and my son John £5 within 2 years of my
decease. My wife is assured for life of my copyhold tenement held of the
manor of Soham rectory, and after her death I bequeath it to my
youngest son Thomas, but if he dies without heirs I give it to my 2 elder
sons Edward and John. I make my wife Anne sole ex'trix, and nominate
my loving cousin Oliver Potter as supervisor. I have surrendered my
copyhold to the use of my will by the hands of Richard Pechey and in the
presence of John Lowes, both customary tenants of the manor of Soham
Rectory. Wit. Richard Pechey, John Lowes (X) and me William Howe.
Pr. at Bury 30 January 1631/32.

378. R ROBERT JELLEY (X) of Tuddenham. 16 May 1631.

Commends soul to God trusting to be saved by Jesus Christ. To be buried
in Tuddenham churchyard.
I give my wife Mary my house and land for life, and then to my son
William, to whom I give my apparel. All the residue of my goods I give to
my wife and make her and my son William exors. Wit. Roger Steward
(X), Thomas Pricke. Pr. 3 June 1631. No place given.

379. R(W) MARGARET BARRET (X) of Cavendish, widow. 20 May
1627.

Commends sinful soul to God trusting to have sins forgiven through Jesus
Christ.
I give 20s to the poor of Cavendish to be distributed by my exors on the
day of my burial. I give and bequeath to my eldest son Roger 1 pair
sheets, 1 pair holland pillowbeeres, 3 diaper table napkins, a towel, a
chest bound with iron, a hutch standing next the chimney in my chamber
and 10s. I give my son Thomas one trundle bedstead drawn with lines, a
feather bed, a feather bolster, a feather pillow, 2 blankets, 1 pair sheets,
2 pillowbeeres of holland and 1 other coarse pillowbeere, a red coverlet,
a hanging coverlet, 3 diaper and 1 wrought holland table napkins, a chest
standing in the hall chamber by the bed, 6 pewter dishes, a pewter saucer,
a pewter porrenger, a pewter chamber pot, a brass pan with a long steel,
a great chair in my bed chamber, my bible, a book called The General
Epistle of St Jude and 40s. I will that my great carved chest standing in
my bed chamber be sold for the best price and the money from the sale
equally divided between the children of my son Henry. I give my
grandson Thomas Woodsyde 5s, and my grandchild Dorothy Woodsyde a
book called The Plain Man's Pathway to Heaven and 5s. I give Mary my
daughter my best gown and petticoat and the overbody to it, a little chair

of bull rushes and a pint pewter bottle. All my linen great and small, not otherwise disposed of, is to be equally divided between my daughters Mary and Margery. I give John Sowter, husband of my daughter Mary, all the debts he owes me by bond or otherwise provided that he gives his children 5s each within 3 months of my decease as a legacy from me. I give Margery Barrett, daughter of my late son-in-law George Barret, a trundle bedstead with a boarded bottom, a flockbed, a flock bolster, a feather pillow, 2 old blankets, a white coverlet, a coverlet of damask, a little form, the stained cloths and the hangings about the bed, 1 pair sheets, 1 pair coarse pillowbeeres, 2 coarse napkins, 2 yard kerchers of holland, a long wheel, a reel and the great cupboard in my chamber. I give my daughter Margery the tables in the hall where I am now dwelling, the benches in the hall, the shelves in the milk house, the cheese press and forms in the dairy, my great tub, the long rake for barley, the two-handed saw, all the shelves in the buttery, the powdering trough, the mustard querns, the beer stools, a little brass pot, a skillet pan, a little pair of cobirons, a pair tongs, an old chair, a great spalter, a posted bedstead standing in the chamber and all the wimbles and ladders. I give my grandson Ambrose More 5s and my book called David's Blessed Man, and to all the rest of my daughter Margery's children by her husband More 3s 4d each to be paid within 2 months of my decease. I give Edward Collyn my son-in-law 20s, and 2s 6d each to his 4 children within 2 months. I give the present wife of my son Woodsyde 20s and 2s 6d each to her 2 children within 2 months. Exors: son Thomas and son-in-law John Sowter. I give them £3 to spend on my burial and 10s for a sermon at my funeral. I give my book of the New Testament to Michael More my grandchild, my service book to my grandson John More and my book of sermons made by Mr Henry Smyth to my grandchild Margery More. My daughter Collyns is to have the use of the service book and the book of sermons during her life, and I give her all my woollen apparel and cloaks not otherwise disposed of. Wit. Roger Bell, Thomas Revell. Pr. at Bury 25 March 1632.

380. R(W) ALICE TURNER (X) of Kirtling [Cambs], spinster. 21 March 1631/32.

Bequeaths soul to God hoping that Jesus Christ will receive me into glory.
I give my copyhold tenement in Kirtling, which I have already surrendered to the use of my will, to my nephew Simon, son of my brother Bartholomew Turner. I give his daughter Alice £12 which my brother has in his hands and borrowed from me, £7 at one time and £5 at another. He is to pay this sum within a year of my decease. The sum of £10 in the hands of my brother Bartholomew is a legacy left to me by my father to be paid to me when I married. I would be willing it should be given to my niece Alice although I never married, but I leave this £10 to her father hoping he will be more mindful of her in regard she is his child. I give 40s each to Martin, Alice, Simon, George and Samuel, the children of my brother Bartholomew. I give to my brother Blackaby's children the £5 he

160

owes me to be divided 20s apiece. I give 40s apiece to the children of my sisters Flack, Miller and Mast. All these legacies to be paid within a year of my death. I give 4 nobles each to the children my master George Stearne had by his second wife; with which master I lived many years. I give my 3 sisters Blackaby, Mast and Flack my wearing apparel. I make my very loving friend Mr Henry Sterne my exor and bequeath to him all the residue of my goods and chattels to perform my will. Wit. George Stearne, Bartholomew Turner's wife (X), Anne Taylor (X) widow. Pr. at Bury 16 April 1632.

381. R(W) JOAN ENGLISHE (N) of Bury St Edmunds, widow. 20 March 1631/32.

She gave her daughter Mary a brass posnet and 2 pillowbeeres and a fine sheet. All the rest of her goods she gave to her other daughter Elizabeth. Wit. Margaret Cullam (X) wife of Andrew, Mary Browne (X) wife of Caleb, Thomas Biggs. Pr. at Bury 26 March 1632.

382. R(W) ROBERT KNIGHT (X) of Mildenhall, yeoman. 3 March 1631/32.

Commits soul to God.
I give James my son and heir apparent all my messuages and lands both free and copyhold in Mildenhall. I give £5 each to James and Joan, children of my brother James, to be paid into his hands to their use until they are 21. I give my kinswoman Anne Bell £20 to be paid within 6 weeks of my decease. I give 40s each to Thomas, William, Zachary, Joan, Robert and Mary the children of my brother-in-law Thomas Bell to be paid into his hands at midsummer after my decease. I give Richard Rickard my servant 10s to be paid into the hands of Thomas Bell to the profit of Richard until he is 21. The residue of my goods and chattels, after payment of my debts, legacies and funeral expenses, I give to my son James and make him exor. I give 10s towards the repair of the parish church of Mildenhall. Wit. John Blower, Robert Peachie draper, William Gault (X) and me William Dalleson. I have surrendered to the use of my will all my copyhold tenements into the hands of Robert Peachie and William Gault copyhold tenants of the manor. Pr. at Bury 3 April 1632.

383. R(W) WILLIAM PARKER (X) of Barnardiston, husbandman. 30 March 1632.

Bequeaths soul to God by whose mercies through Jesus Christ I hope to be saved. To be buried in Barnardiston churchyard.
I give my eldest son Thomas all my woollen apparel and shoes, and all my working tools except my hatchet, a bell, a spade and a shovel. I give 20s to my other son William to be paid by my ex'trix when his time as an apprentice is out. I give my daughter Anne a yearling bullock. All the rest of my goods I give to Alice my wife, whom I make ex'trix. Wit. Robert Webb, Robert Butcher. Pr. at Clare 4 April 1632.

384. R(W) GEORGE WARD of Creeting All Saints, miller.
23 February 1618/19.

Commits soul to God my maker, redeemer and sanctifier.
Alice my wife holds copyhold houses and land in Needham Market and
Barking which revert to me after her decease. In consideration of this I
bequeath to my son George the messuage with yard in Needham Market
now occupied by Samuel Lucas, John Hill, James Brundishe and John
Wood; and to my son John my 4 acre piece of land in Needham field now
let to Stephen Betts; and to my daughter Margaret Wood a little cottage
with yard in Needham Market in Church Lane and now occupied by
Thomas Nobbett. I also give Margaret my half acre piece of copyhold
land lying near Church Lane in Needham Market and occupied by
Edward Smye and mortgaged to Samuel Grymwood. She is to have this
land after the mortgage is redeemed. If my sons try to prevent Margaret
from having this land, she is to have £30 out of the property left to them.
I give my daughter Margaret Wood £15 to be paid by my son George in 3
annual instalments starting 3 years after the decease of my wife Alice.
She has power to distrain. I give my wife all my goods towards the
bringing up of my children and the payment of my debts. Exors: wife and
son George. Wit. Thomas Coulchester, John Martyn, Thomas Wood and
me Nicholas Bubbe. On the same day the testator surrendered his houses
and land held copyhold of Barking manor into the hands of Thomas
Wood and in the presence of Nicholas Bubbe, both copyhold tenants of
the manor. Alice Ward widow and ex'trix appeared before the probate
court on 11 October 1619, but probate was granted at Bury on 17 April
1632.

385. R(W) EDMUND SMYTH of Rushbrooke, yeoman. 6 March
1631/32.

Commends soul to God trusting through merits of Jesus Christ that my
soul will attain to celestial joys prepared for me and all the elect of God.
I give my brother Edward for life all my lands and tenements in
Wramplingham, Norfolk, which I purchased of John Berton minister and
Thomas Clover miller, both of Wramplingham. I also give him 1 rod
pasture in Wramplingham, which I hold by lease for many years to come.
After Edward's decease I leave all this land to Robert, one of the sons of
my late brother William with remainder to his brothers John and
Lancelot if Edmund has no heirs. He who holds my land at the time the
following legacies are due must pay them: £6 to my nephew John Smyth
within 2 years of my decease; £3 each to his brothers Lancelot and
Edward within 3 years; 50s to Elizabeth, wife of John Wright and 40s to
Mary, wife of John Hamond of Bury, within 4 years; 40s to the daughters
of my brother Edward within 5 years; 50s within 6 years to Barbara, wife
of William Cuslinge and one of the daughters of my late brother Thomas;
40s within 7 years to Alice, wife of Edmund Wright and one of the

daughters of Francis Burgis my late brother-in-law which he begot on the body of Anne his late wife and my sister. I give Mr Benton, minister of Wramplingham, 10s to be paid within a year, and 3s 4d to the poor people of Wramplingham. I also give 10s to the poor of Forncett [Norfolk], 5s to each parish, and to the poor of Rushbrooke 10s to be disposed of by Mr Heley. Legatees have power to distrain. I give my brother Edward my broad wooden chest with all my tools, the lesser trunk in my chamber with all things therein, my turned chair, my wicker chair, my close stool, my saddle, bridle, boots and sword, with my best cloak and best suit of clothes. I give my nephews Lancelot and Edward my livery cupboard and the little table standing on it and my carved chest. My will is that they sell them and part the money equally between them. I also give Lancelot my everyday suit and my old cloak. The residue of my goods and chattels I bequeath to my brother Edward whom I make exor. Supervisor: my ancient friend John Spaldinge of Great Horningsheath [Horringer], praying him to assist my exor with his best advice and I give him 10s for his pains. Wit. John Scott, William Baggott, John Spaldinge. Pr. at Bury 16 April 1632.

386. R(W) JOHN OXE (X) of Bury St Edmunds, husbandman. 5 April 1632.

Bequeaths soul to God believing to have remission of sins through Jesus Christ.
After my debts, probate and funeral charges are paid, I bequeath all my personal estate to my son John. I make my loving brother Roger Hawsted exor, desiring him to take charge and care of my son. My desire is that my goods which are fit to be sold should be so, and the money, together with any owing to me or of which I am possessed, put to the best use for the benefit of my son and paid to him at the age of 21. Wit. Mary Corder, Philip Morse. Pr. at Bury 16 April 1632.

387. R(W) RICHARD RAYE (X) of Stradishall, yeoman. 3 April 1632.

Bequeaths soul to God and Jesus Christ.
I give Susan my wife the annuity of £12 bequeathed to me by the will of my late deceased brother John, and after her decease I give it to my daughters Mary and Susan, who are to pay out of it 20s p.a. to my son John. All the residue of my goods I give to my wife Susan whom I make ex'trix. Wit. Robert Bun, Charles Burroughe. Pr. at Bury 23 April 1632.

388. R(W) PETER COCKE of Thorndon, gentleman. 8 October 1624.

Bequeaths soul to almighty God and body to earth.
I will that Anne my wellbeloved wife shall have the use and profit of all my messuages and lands until such time as my 2 sons John and Peter come to the age of 21. I give my eldest son John when 21 my messuage in Kesgrave, my best table, my best bedstead with the bed, bolster,

coverings and blankets. I give my second son Peter when 21 all my land in Trimley St Martin and St Mary, the long table in the parlour, my best bedstead save one with the bed, bolster, blanket and coverings. I give my wife Anne in consideration of her dower an annuity of £30 to be paid half each by my sons after they inherit their land. This annuity is to be paid half yearly in the house of Jeremy Fyske in Laxfield. Power to distrain. If my wife claims dower from my lands the gift of this annuity is void. I will that my wife shall have the custody and use for life of all my plate and household goods, except those already bequeathed to my 2 sons, and after her decease I give them to my 4 daughters Anne, Elizabeth, Alice and Mary. I will that my exors sell my corn, cattle and outside goods with all convenient speed after my decease. This money, together with that I have already and what is due to me by bonds and mortgages, is to be paid by my exors as portions to my daughters when 21 or on their marriage days whichever happens first. My funeral and other necessary charges are first to be deducted from this money. My wife is to use the profits of my lands and goods to keep all my children and provide them with all things necessary for a good and virtuous education until such time as they receive their legacies. I give Jeremy my youngest son £300 to be paid to him by my other 2 sons as follows: John is to pay him £200 when he is 21 and Peter £100 40 days after Jeremy is 21; these payments are to be made in the porch of Kesgrave church. I will that Anne my wife educate and keep Jeremy until John and Peter are 21 when they are to pay £5 p.a. each to my wife during the rest of Jeremy's minority. Wife and Jeremy have power to distrain for failure to pay legacy or annuity. When 21 John is to give Peter an assurance of his land and Jeremy is to do the same for Peter or forfeit the £100 due to him from Peter. Exors; Jeremy Fyske, my father-in-law, and Anne my wife. Wit. Henry Gardner, Gualcher Peirson, Lionel Peirson (X). Pr. at Stowmarket 11 April 1632.

389. (W) JOHN WATCHAM of Bacton, yeoman. 4 April 1632.

Commends soul to God my heavenly father.
I give Elizabeth my wife all my implements of household: brass, pewter, linen, woollen, bedding and bedsteads, tables, coffers, stools, chairs, forms and all other things whatsoever. Ex'trix: wife, who is to take and pay my debts and see my body buried in Christian burial. Wit. John Muskett, William Watcham, Thomas Watcham (X). Pr. at Stowmarket 11 April 1632.

390. R(W) PHILIP WARDE (X) the elder of Bradfield Combust, yeoman. 17 March 1631/32.

Bequeaths soul to God who gave it hoping for salvation through Jesus Christ.
I give my eldest son John 10s to be paid within a year of my decease. I give Bridget my wife all the rest of my goods and chattels for life, and

after her death to be equally divided between my children Philip, Elizabeth and Susan. Within 2 months of my decease my wife is to enter into a bond of £100 with 2 men named by my above 3 children to perform my will. Wife sole ex'trix. Wit. Edmund Clarke, Robert Burde (X). Pr. at Bury 16 April 1632.

391. R(W) LEONARD WACE (X) of Ixworth Thorpe, yeoman. 31 May 1628.

Commends soul to God.
I give my son James my tenement in Chevington which I hold by copy of court roll of the manor of Chevington, and the copyhold land I hold of the manor of Chedberg with Armborowes, and after his decease to the heirs of him and his wife Anne according to the custom of the manor. I will that my tenement and adjoining croft in Mildenhall, now occupied by James Lusher, be sold by my sons James and William within 2 years of my decease, and the money used as follows: £10 paid to Francis Sowter my son-in-law within 3 years of my decease, and the residue divided between my sons James and William. I give my wife Mary all the household stuff which was her's before I married her. I give her all my cows and beasts, and all my corn and hay growing in Ixworth Thorpe on condition she pays my son James £10 within 6 months in Thorpe church porch. With 6 days of my decease she is to give him a bond of £20 to assure the payment of this £10. If she refuses James is to have the cows, beasts, corn and hay. I give my youngest son William the bed wherein I now lie with all that belongs to it, and all the household stuff I have at Great Livermere, except the round table and 1 joined chair. All the rest of my goods I give to my son James, whom I make exor. Wit. John Ward, John Fletcher. Pr. at Bury 2 May 1632.

392. R(W) FRANCIS FRANCIS alias FARROWE (X) of Botesdale, labourer. 12 April 1632.

Commends soul to God in certain hope of resurrection to eternal life.
I give my son Edmund all the sums of money he owes me, a flockbed, a feather transome, a pewter dish, 1 sheet, 2 blankets, a trundle bedstead, the kettle and skillet under my bed, and my best doublet and breeches. I give my daughter Anne Jasper the bed complete whereon I lie together with all my brass now in her own use, a pewter dish, a saucer, and all my hemp lying in the barn. She is to pay my daughters Elizabeth Harvey and Rebecca Smyth 20s within 3 months of my decease, and give them a sheet each. If Anne refuses to pay these legacies, my gifts to her are void and go to my son Edmund, who is to pay the legacies. I give my son-in-law Henry Jasper my cloak. I give 12d each to all the children of my daughter Rebecca to be paid within a month. I give Henry Jasper my grandchild a pewter dish marked with 2 letters for his name, a chair and my best jerkin. I give my grandchild Ruth the other pewter dish fellow to the one I gave her brother, and a buffet stool. I give my son-in-law John Harvey

165

my white doublet, my son-in-law Henry Jasper my best chest and my son Edmund my other great chest. All the rest of my goods and chattels and money I give to my exors: son Edmund and son-in-law Henry Jasper. Wit. William Greenewood, Michael Baldre (X). Pr. at Bury 17 April 1632.

393. R(W) GEORGE COLE (X) of Great Thurlow, yeoman.
19 December 1630.

Bequeaths soul to God trusting to be saved through merits of Jesus Christ. To be buried in the churchyard of Great Thurlow.
I give William Smyth my son-in-law 12d to be paid within half a year of my decease. I give all my moveables to Elizabeth my wife and John my son to be equally divided between them. I give Peter Lyvermer and Henry Martyn, my sons-in-law, 12d within 6 months. All the rest of my goods are to be divided between my wife and my son John, whom I make exors. Wit. Jeffery Deareslye, John Clayton. Pr. at Clare 4 May 1632.

394. R(W) JOHN GOODERICH (X) of Bury St Edmunds, clothier.
14 April 1632.

Commends soul to God steadfastly believing through merits of Jesus Christ to have forgiveness of sins and be made a partaker of the joys of heaven.
I give Margery my wife for life my house in Bury wherein I dwell and my lands in the fields of Horningsheath [Horringer], and after her decease to be equally divided among my 4 sons William the elder, William the younger, John and Jeremy. I give my son John my house and land in Hessett, and my wife shall take the profits until he is 21. If he dies before he is 21, his 3 brothers are to have this property. I give my sons William the elder, William the younger and Jeremy £100 apiece to be paid by my ex'trix when 21. Benefit of survivorship. My wife is to manage my sons' portions until they are 21 and use the increase for their education, maintenance and binding them forth as apprentices; any residue to be paid to them when 21. If any of my children prove rebellious, stubborn or disobedient and refuse to be governed according to my wife's discretion, then the increase of their portions shall go to those of my sons who are dutiful and obedient. My wife must pay all the legacies in my father's will not yet paid by me. I give Margery, daughter of my brother Henry, £5 when 24 and her brother William £5 at same age. Benefit of survivorship. I give 40s each when 24 to the 2 youngest children my sister Susan had by her first husband John Lock. Benefit of survivorship. I give to the poor of the parish of St Mary in Bury 40s to be distributed within a month of my decease at the discretion of ex'trix and supervisors. I give to my poor

166

spinners of Drinkstone 20s to be distributed as above. All the rest of my goods and chattels, wares and stock, after my debts and legacies have been paid, I bequeath to my wife whom I make sole ex'trix. Supervisors: Thomas Chaplyne mercer, his brother Clement Chaplyne grocer, Jeremy Stafford mercer and my cousin Robert Gooderich, all of Bury. I give them each 40s for their pains. If my wife dies before my will is fully performed and has not nominated a person to act in her place, then my supervisors are to undertake the performance of my will as my wife should have done. They are to pay themselves any expenses incurred. Wit. Richard Cooper (X) shearman, Robert Brightall (X), Philip Crowe. Pr. at Bury 16 May 1632 to the 4 supervisors, who are called exors, and to the ex'trix.

395. R(W) RICHARD HALLYDAYE (X) of Preston, yeoman.
15 January 1630/31.

Bequeaths soul to God believing to have free remission of sins through Jesus Christ and in certain hope of a joyful resurrection.
I give 20s each to the poor of Preston to be distributed by the overseers of the parish within a month of my decease. I give towards the leading and repairing of Preston church 20s to be laid out by the churchwardens within 6 months. I give my wife Helen £30 to be paid over 3 years, and she is to have her abode in the house where I now dwell for 2 months after my decease. I give to Thomas Leaman, yeoman of Westley, my tenement in Preston where I now dwell with all its land towards performing my will and paying my legacies. I give an annuity of £12 to my daughter Elizabeth, wife of Edward Ranston labourer of Preston. If the half yearly payments are 40 days overdue I give her my tenement and land left to Thomas Leaman. I give Thomas Leaman my freehold tenement in Hessett to pay the following legacies: £5 to my sister Anne Brooke, £5 to her daughter Lea Brooke, £5 to John Leaman of Stanstead, £5 to his sister Agnes Seawell, £5 to Francis Leaman of Stowmarket, £5 to Margaret daughter of my eldest brother John, £5 to John Hallydaye glover of Sudbury and £5 to the daughter of my youngest brother John, being lame and a singlewoman dwelling in Sudbury. All these legacies are to be paid within a year of my decease. I charge and require Thomas Leaman to receive, educate and bring up Elizabeth the supposed daughter of my son John until she is 21 when he is to pay her £10. I give to Mr Thomas Wyllis, our minister here at Preston, 10s and desire him to preach at my funeral. All the rest of my goods and chattels, after my debts and legacies are paid, I bequeath to Thomas Leaman and make him exor. I give thanks to almighty God for his goodness in giving me leave to finish this my last will. Wit. Edmund Rose, Joshua Blower, Robert Ryece. Pr. at Bury 19 May 1632.

396. R(W) WALTER READE (X) of Stoke Ash, husbandman. 29 November 1630.

Commends soul to mercies of God purchased through merits of Jesus Christ.
I give and bequeath all my goods and chattels, money and debts to Mary my wellbeloved wife towards paying my debts, educating my children, proving my will and for the relief of Ellen Reade widow, my mother. Wit. Ellis Clarke, Thomas Cullam, Ellis Clarke junior. Pr. at Stowmarket 11 April 1632.

397. R(W) ANDREW TANNER of Benningham in Occold. 4 June 1631.

Bequeaths soul to God my creator and Jesus Christ my redeemer in whose name I hope to be saved.
I give my son John my house wherein I dwell and all my lands in Beningham in Occold on condition he pays my debts and legacies. I give my son Robert £20 to be paid within 3 years. I give my son Richard 40s a year for life to be paid at Lady Day and Michaelmas. I also give him the bed he lies on in my hall chamber with free access to this chamber for life. I give my son William £20 to be paid within 4 years, and my daughter Grace £20 within 5 years. I also give Grace the bed standing in my parlour with all its furniture, my greatest dansk chest, a little cupboard table, 2 joined stools and a little joined stool all being in the parlour, my middle brass pot, and half my dairy vessels to be equally divided between her and my son John. I give my grandchild Andrew, son of John, my greatest brass pot, and to Elizabeth Tanner my lesser danske chest. I bequeath to Andrew and Philip Tanner, if they live to the age of 24, 20s each. All the rest of my unbequeathed goods and household stuff I give to my son John and make him exor, not doubting by the great trust I have in him that he will carefully and dutifully perform my will. Wit. William Alldehowse, William Hubberd, John Jessopp. Pr. at Stowmarket 11 April 1632.

398. R(W) JOHN PLAYFERE of Depden, clerk and parson of Depden. 10 April 1632.

I bequeath my soul and body to Jesus Christ who hath loved me and given himself for me, and whose faithful servant I have endeavoured to prove myself in the ministry of his gospel.
I will that all my debts be paid by my ex'trix. I give the poor of the parish of Depden 10s to be distributed at my burial. I give my loving and faithful wife Margaret all my household stuff, books, corn, hay and goods towards payment of my debts, and for her use and benefit in the education and maintenance of my 5 daughters Abigail, Sarah, Susan, Dorothy and Dorcas and my youngest son Anthony. For the same purposes I also give her my house in Depden built on a plot of ground

called Howes garden with all the outhouses and 12 acres adjoining pasture, which I bought of Thomas Coell, gentleman of Depden; and 7 acres pasture and meadow called Davidges and lying near Depden Green, which I bought from Thomas Jermyn esquire late of Depden. She is to have all this property for her life for her maintenance and the sustenance of my children, most of which are little and young. After her decease, I give my house and land to my eldest son Thomas, who must pay my legacies to my other children. I give my younger son Anthony 100 marks, and £30 each to my 5 daughters, all to be paid when 22 except that if any reach that age during the life of my wife they are to receive their legacies within 1 year of her decease. Legatees have benefit of survivorship and power to distrain. After the decease of Margaret my wife, my son Thomas is to have the care and education of those of my children who have not attained the age of 22. Ex'trix: my wife. As my daughter Abigail is of more years than any of my other daughters, I desire my wife to pay her £20 of the £30 bequeathed to her as soon as she can conveniently raise it. Wit. Robert Paman, Ralph Wymark (X). Pr. at Bury 14 May 1632.

399. R(W) JOHN CHANTER of Bury St Edmunds. 19 April 1632.

To the Lord I commend my soul.
To my daughter Elizabeth I give £10, a bedstead complete as it now stands in the chamber, and the cupboard in the house. I bequeath to my son Robert all my debts due to me. The brass and pewter are to be equally divided between my son and my daughter. I give my son a bed in the house, and my daughter my wife's linen. Also to my son I give my woollen and to my daughter a great chest and a box, and to my son 2 hutches and a table. All the rest of my moveable goods in the house are to be divided between my son and daughter, and the shop stuff I leave to my son alone. The cost of paying my debts and of my funeral are to be equally shared between my son and daughter. Exors: Elizabeth and Robert Chanter. Supervisor: Stephen Borrows. Wit. Thomas Rayniad, Stephen Burrowe, Francis Glover. Pr. at Bury 24 May 1632.

400. R(W) JOHN MALLETT (X) of Stoke by Clare. 21 May 1629.

Bequeaths soul to God my most merciful saviour and redeemer. To be buried in Stoke by Clare churchyard.
I give Katherine my wife all my household stuff and money. I give 4 of my kindred 12 pence apiece: to Elizabeth Cartner, Mary Grove, Thomas Waters and Francis Waters to be paid within a year of my decease at the house where I now dwell in Stoke. Ex'trix: my wife. Wit. John Lemon (X), Joseph Jackson (X), William Matthew. Pr. at Clare 4 April 1632.

401. R(W) FRANCIS COOKE (X) of Braiseworth, yeoman. 16 March 1631/32.

Commends soul to God and Jesus Christ hoping to have pardon of sins.
I give my wellbeloved wife Christian all my goods and chattels on condition she brings up my children George, Edward and Ellis and puts them to trades when they are fit for it. I give my eldest son Alexander my copyhold tenement and land in Braiseworth on condition he pays my son George £20 1 year after my wife's decease, my third son Edward £20 within 2 years and my fourth son Ellis £20 within 3 years. My son Alexander shall also pay another £10 each to my other 3 sons within 3 years of the first payments and in the same order. If Alexander refuses to pay these legacies, George is to have my land and pay them. Ex'trix: my wife. Wit. William Coleman, Robert Colman, John Cotton, Alexander Brome (X). Pr. at Stowmarket 11 April 1632.

402. R(W) CHRISTOPHER JARVIS of Wicken [Cambs], yeoman.
18 May 1632.

Bequeaths soul to God hoping to be saved through merits of Jesus Christ. To be buried in the church or churchyard of Wicken.
I give £5 to the use of the poor of the parish of Wicken to remain in the hands of my exors during their lives, and of the churchwardens after their decease. The profit is to be distributed to the poor yearly on St Thomas's Day. I give my son John 40s to be paid 1 year after my decease. I give my daughters Mary, Anne, Elizabeth, Alice and Christian £20 apiece to be paid when 21. I give all my godchildren in Wicken 12d each to be distributed within 2 months of my decease. The rest of my unbequeathed goods I give wholly to Mary my wife, whom I make ex'trix. I give my wife for life 5 acres copyhold land which I purchased from Elias Jarvis, a messuage with 10 acres arable and fother ground late Simon Clark's gentleman, 1 acre arable after the decease of John Talbutt of Wicken who holds it for life, 1 acre fother ground late John Hodgkyn's of Chippenham, 8 acres 1 rod of arable and fother ground late William Roote's and 14½ acres arable late John Tyler's gentleman of Soham. After my wife's decease my land is to be equally divided among my 5 daughters. I have surrendered my land, tenement and fother ground into the hands of the lord of the manor of Wicken by the hands of Nicholas Cowper and Robert Fletcher, both customary tenants, to the use of my wife for life and then to my daughters and their heirs. Wit. Nicholas Cowper, Robert Fletcher, John Jarves (X). Pr. at Wicken 31 May 1632.

403. R(W) JOHN GAINFORD of Icklingham, yeoman. 28 April 1632.

Commends soul to God hoping to enjoy salvation through death and resurrection of Jesus Christ.
I give Thomas Gainford, second son of my brother Thomas, my house and all my land in Icklingham, except what is otherwise bequeathed. If he

has no heir my house and land are to pass to my next heir. I give my sister for life the meadow of Gabriel Gainford, and the south end of my house which she now holds together with the lodge and free access to draw water at the well belonging to my messuage, and after her decease to her son William, son of my late brother Gabriel. After William's death, the end of the house, the lodge and meadow are to return to my nephew Thomas and his heirs. I give Gabriel, eldest son of my brother Thomas, 3½ acres arable in Cowpit field in the up and downes near to Sewenshanden way with the east head on Bernes land, Michael's to the north and with the south head abutting on Bearners. I also give him half a 3 acre piece of land abutting on the highway to Lackford bridge, that is at the west end of this piece. I also give him 3 rods of infield land abutting on the highway to Lackford bridge with Michael's land to the north, and a rod of infield land lying in Ospit. I give John, son of my late brother Peter, my bible and 40s. I give my sister, the widow of Gabriel Gainford, 40s, and Gabriel, son of my brother Thomas, 20s. All to be paid within a year of my decease. I give Anne, daughter of my brother Thomas £10 to be paid within 1 year and 8 months. Benefit of survivorship for all legatees. I give to the grandchildren of Rose, my deceased wife, £10 to be divided between them within a year. I give 10s to the poor of West Stow, 10s to the poor of Icklingham All Saints and 6s 8d to the poor of Icklingham St James to be paid into the hands of the overseers of the poor of each parish within 1 month of my decease. I give my sister Margaret Plumbe of Bury 40s, and the widow of my brother Thomas 40s, both to be paid within a year. I discharge the exors of my later brother Peter and the widow my late brother Gabriel of all debts due to me from them. My will is that all my unbequeathed goods including leases, sheep and great cattle be sold by my exor to the best advantage within 1 year and the money, after paying my debts and funeral charges, is to be divided equally among all the children of Thomas, Peter and Gabriel Gainford and of Margaret Plumbe except for the legacies I give to my exor and supervisor. I make Thomas Craske of Icklingham my exor giving him £10 to perform my will, and allowing him all the costs of his executorship. I appoint John Gaynford the elder of Ingham supervisor and give him £4 to be paid within 20 months of my decease. Wit. George Stanton clerk, John Goslinge. Pr. at Bury 21 May 1632.

404. R(W) WILLIAM SMITH (X) of Burwell [Cambs], husbandman. 10 May 1632.

Gives soul to God that gave it me and steadfastly believes to be saved through death and passion of Jesus Christ and by no other means.
I give my wife Lucy for life my house where I now dwell, which I had by surrender of Christopher Rowe, and after her decease to my son William, but if it pleases God to take him out of this life leaving no heirs before my wife dies then my house shall remain to her and her heirs. I give my son William my house which I hold by surrender of Peter Taylor and which belongs to the manor of Dullingham. All my worldly goods and chattels I

171

give to be equally parted between my wife and son, and I make them exors. Wit. John Wylkins, Robert Casburne, John Cropley.

Memorandum that I have surrendered my copyhold tenement belonging to the manor of Burwell Ramsies to the use of my will into the hands of John Wilkins in the presence of Robert Casburne, both tenants of the manor. Pr. at Burwell 31 May 1632.

405. R(W) ROBERT HEYWARD of Whatfield, yeoman. 11 February 1623/24.

Commends soul to God believing to be saved only through passion of Jesus Christ.

To pay my debts and legacies Martha my wife shall sell all the land left to her. I give her all my lands and tenements in Semer, Whatfield and Nowton, lately bought of Randall Greeton and his wife Avis. I also give her £100 in lieu of her thirds, my standing bed and trundle bed in the chamber over the hall and all their beds and bedding. If my wife does not sell my land within 2 years of my decease, I give it to my eldest son Robert. I give him £20 to be paid when he is 23. The remainder of my goods and chattels I give to be equally divided among my sons Robert, John and George when 23. Ex'trix: wife. Wit. John Kinge, Thomas Colman. Pr. to widow at Bury 28 May 1632.

406. R(W) THOMAS TAYLER (X) of Burwell [Cambs], mason. 14 May 1632.

Bequeaths soul to God and steadfastly believes to be saved through Jesus Christ and by no other means.

I give my wife Frances all the household stuff she brought to me, 2000 turves and 500 hassocks laid to dry in the yard and 2s, on condition she makes no claim on any other part of my goods. I give my daughter Grace £10 when 21, and in the meantime 20s p.a. until she is 18 and then 10s a year until she reaches 21. I give my son Thomas my dwelling house on condition he pays my daughter Grace her legacies. If he fails, Grace is to hold my house for ever. All the rest of my worldly goods I give to my son Thomas whom I make exor. Wit John Wilkyns, Thomas Freiston, Robert Casburne. Pr. at Burwell 31 May 1632.

407. R(W) THOMAS SPARROWE (X) of Great Saxham, husbandman. 10 February 1631/32.

Bequeaths soul to God trusting to be saved through merits of Jesus Christ.

I give my copyhold and freehold estate at Tuddenham to my son George together with my timber lying there and all my timber at Saxham and Rede towards the repairing of his houses there. I also give him my malt querns. I owe William Sparrowe £3 and I will that my cart be sold to pay this debt. I have lately sold my land at Rede for £106 and after my expenses in this my extremity, my debts and the charges of my burial and proving my will have been paid, I give the residue to be equally divided between my 2 daughters Margaret and Alice when 21. Until then the money is to remain in my brother Goodaie's hands for their benefit, and I entreat him to be careful for their education. Benefit of survivorship. I give my daughter Margaret my best cupboard, my biggest kettle and the wainscot hutch. Whereas there is a legacy due to be paid by William Sorrell of Cavenham to me or my son after the death of an old woman whose name I know not, so far as I have power to dispose of it I will that my 2 daughters shall each have £7 of this legacy. The residue of my goods is to be equally divided among my 3 children. Exor: son George. Supervisors: brother-in-law John Goodaye and my neighbour Simon Pittes, whom I entreat to advise my children and especially my exor. Wit. William Maninge, Alice Gilman (X). Pr. at Bury 11 June 1632.

408. R(W) JOHN BLOGGETTE (X) of Stowmarket, innholder.
17 February 1631/32.

Bequeaths soul to God hoping to have pardon of sins and eternal salvation through Jesus Christ. To be buried in Stowmarket churchyard.
I give my brother Thomas my best breeches, my hat and my best petticoat to be delivered to him within a month of my decease. I give John Bloggette my chest standing in the little parlour and all that is in it, and £5 within 3 months. I give Alice Crosland my maid servant 10s within 3 months. All the rest of my goods and chattels I give to Anne my wellbeloved wife who is to pay my debts and legacies and see me decently buried. I make her sole ex'trix as my trust is in her. Wit. Jonathan Speere and me Philip Barne. Pr. at Bury 4 June 1632.

409. R(W) THOMAS BLAND (X) of Ampton, tailor. 23 May 1632.

Commits soul to God. To be buried in Ampton churchyard.
I will that Susan my wife be sole ex'trix. My will and pleasure is that she shall enjoy all my goods for her life, paying my debts. After her decease the remainder of my goods is to be equally divided among my children Thomasine, wife of Thomas Rose, Robert, Mary, Stephen, Susan and Anne or as many of them as shall be then surviving. Wit. Robert Stafford, Edmund Bryce, Richard Payne. Pr. at Bury 4 June 1632.

410. R(W) RICHARD PECOK (X) of Pakenham, yeoman. 19 May 1631.

Commends soul to God trusting assuredly to have sins forgiven through Jesus Christ. To be buried in Pakenham churchyard.
I give my nephew Robert Pecok 40s within a year and my bed complete as it stands. I give my nephews Thomas and John Pecok 40s each within 2 years. I give Richard Forman 40s and Anne Baxter 20s. I give Anne and

Elizabeth Wright 10s each. I give the poor of Pakenham 13s 4d to be paid within 2 months. I give George Wright, whom I appoint exor, all my bonds and debts and the residue of my goods to pay my legacies and bring my body to the ground. Wit. William Prior (X), Richard Goodaye (X), John Cage. Pr. at Bury 4 June 1632.

411. R(W) JOHN GRIMMOD (X) the elder of Assington, husbandman. 25 May 1632.

I bequeath my soul to God and Jesus Christ by whose merits I steadfastly believe to be saved. To be buried in Assington churchyard.
I give to Elizabeth, wife of Thomas Porter, £5 within a year of the decease of the longer liver of myself and my wife Elizabeth. I give to Jane, wife of Simon Browne, £5 to be paid at the same time. I give my daughter Jane Browne a hanging cupboard, a brass pot, a tramell and 2 chairs with rush bottoms. I give my eldest son John a posted bedstead with a flockbed, 2 flock bolsters, 2 blankets, a covering, 2 pillows, a trundle bed with a flockbed, bolster, blanket and covering. I also give him a cupboard in the hall and a pestle and mortar. I give my youngest son Thomas a posted bedstead with a hanging on it, a featherbed, a bolster with a green covering, 2 pillows, a half-headed bedstead, a latten chafing dish and my biggest grindstone. I also give him a table and form in the hall and the middle kettle. My 2 sons shall choose 2 honest men to divide the residue of my goods between them. My wife Elizabeth is peaceably to enjoy all my goods during her life and if my 2 sons in any way molest or trouble her my will shall be void. Exors: sons John and Thomas. Wit. Peter Parson, Edward Neale (X). Pr. at Assington 23 June 1632.

412. R(W) PRISCILLA CLOPTON (X) of Boxted, widow. 1 May 1632.

Bequeaths soul to God in certain hope of salvation and eternal life through Jesus Christ.
I make my daughter Bridget sole ex'trix and give her in ready money £20. I give her all my household stuff and apparel only excepting my stammel petticoat, which I give to my niece Bridget Horman. Wit. Theodore Beale, Roger Browne. Pr. at Groton 27 June 1632.

413. R(W) HENRY SMYTH (X) of Shimpling, yeoman. 2 February 1626/27.

I give my daughter Mary all my goods and chattels and make her ex'trix. Wit. Thomas Smyth, George Death, Thomas Wright. Pr. at Bury 25 June 1632.

414. R(W) ELIZABETH NOOTHE (X) of Stoke by Nayland, widow. 26 May 1632.

Commends soul to God and Jesus Christ my alone saviour and redeemer. I give to my eldest son Hugh my cottage wherein I now dwell with yard and orchard in Stoke by Nayland, on condition he pays my legacies to my children and grandchildren: to my son Thomas 40s within 1½ years; to my daughter Bridget 20s within 3 years; to my daughter Margaret 20s within 4½ years; to my daughter Elizabeth wife of William Inman 30s within 6 years; to my son Robert £3 within 7½ years; and to my grandchildren Anne, Mary and William Noothe 13s 4d each when 21. I give my daughter Bridget the bed whereon I lie with the bedstead fully furnished, a warming pan, a framed table in my bedchamber and a little posnet. I give my daughter Margaret a cupboard, a chafing dish, a brass kettle, 2 pewter dishes, a latten candlestick and a hutch that was my husband's. I give my son Thomas a little flockbed and a pan kettle. All the rest of my moveable goods I give to my son Hugh towards payment of my debts and legacies, and probate of my will. I make him exor hoping he will carefully perform my will. Wit. Edward Barnard (X), William Gatteward. Pr. at Stoke by Nayland 22 June 1632.

415. R(W) GEORGE PLEASANCE of Barrow, yeoman. 24 May 1632.

Bequeaths soul to God when it shall please him to call it out of my body and I believe to be saved through merits of Jesus Christ. To be buried in Barrow churchyard.
I give Alice my beloved wife for life my house in Barrow called Halles and 10 acres arable lying in the several shifts of the fields of Barrow, and after her decease to my eldest son John with remainder to son William and only daughter Judith if no heirs. I give John my biggest brass pot, a mustard quern, a malt quern and the cupboard in the hall. I give my second son William £10 to be paid by my son John within 4 years of the decease of his mother. I give my daughter Judith £10 to be paid by John within 2 years of my wife's death; both legacies to be paid in 2 annual instalments. I give my corn now growing, my hay, fruit and moveable goods to my wife Alice to pay my debts and bring up my children during their minorities. I appoint my wife sole ex'trix. Wit. Arthur Heigham, Andrew Heyward.
Codicil: my house and ground are to stand surety for the legacies to my son William and daughter Judith, and it shall be lawful for each of them in turn to hold them for 2 years. Benefit of survivorship. Wit. Arthur Heigham, Richard Prick, Francis Heigham. Pr. at Bury 28 June 1632.

416. R(W) WILLIAM BENSTED of Rattlesden. 12 May 1632.

Bequeaths soul to God my creator and Jesus Christ my merciful redeemer, and my body to earth in hope of joyful resurrection.
I give my wife Frances all my money and moveable goods for life towards

bringing up my children. If she marries again she must be bound to my brother Robert that my money and goods in her hands at her death shall be left as appointed in my will. After her decease my money and goods are to be divided among my children: William, Zachary, Robert, Francis and Peter. If it can conveniently be done the money I leave is to be used to buy land for my wife during her life and then to my children. Exors: my wife and Peter Deverux minister and my father-in-law. Wit. Robert Bensted, Thomas Barly (X) Pr. at Rattlesden 14 June 1632.

417. R(W) THOMAS CHAPMAN (X) of Burwell (Cambs). 15 April 1631.

Bequeaths soul to God.
I will that my sons Thomas and Richard sell all my goods and pay my debts; any surplus is to be equally divided among my children. Wit. Richard Chapman (X) and I Richard Iveson. Pr. 16 July 1632. No place given.

418. R(W) WILLIAM BUNTINGE of Burwell [Cambs], chandler. 4 August 1631.

I render my spirit to my God and creator nothing doubting that he will receive my soul into his glory and place it in the company of heavenly angels and blessed saints.
I give my brother Richard all my copyhold arable land, and £20 to be paid within 2 years of my decease. I give my brother Thomas all my freehold messuages and land on condition he pays £30 to John Caseburne to redeem the mortgage on my copyhold land. If he refuses, Richard is to have my freehold land. I give £5 to be paid to the churchwardens within half a year; the interest to be paid to the poor people of these parishes [sic] for ever. I give £5 to my uncle Richard Buntinge's daughter Anne to be paid within 4 years, and to William Cooper's daughter and my godchild £5 within 5 years. I give William Hopwood all the money he owes me, and to Henry Cooper all the money due unto me by my book. All the rest of my unbequeathed goods I give to my brother Thomas whom I make exor. He is to spend 25s at my burial and pay my debts and legacies. I give 20s to my brother John's son a year after my decease. I have surrendered my copyhold land to the use of my will by the hands of John Barton and in the presence of Thomas Vyse, tenants of the manor. Wit. John Casburne, John Barton (X), Thomas Vice, William Hopwood. Pr. at Bury 10 July 1632.

419. R(W) HENRY GRIMWADE (N) of Bildeston, clothier. Saturday 14 July 1632.

He gave his brother Richard all his goods and chattels. Wit. John Gault, Bartholomew Allen and the testator's wife. Let. ad. granted 23 July 1632 to Richard Grimwade. No place given.

176

420. R(W) THOMAS SMYTH of Sudbury, gentleman. 27 May 1632.

Bequeaths soul to God being persuaded all my sins will be forgiven through Jesus Christ my saviour and redeemer. To be buried in Churchyard of St Gregory in Sudbury.
I am seized in demesne as of fee of the manor of Otton Belchampe [Essex] held by knight service of the king's manor of Clare as appears by many ancient records. I will the custody and wardship of the body and lands of my son Thomas to my loving friends and kinsmen by the mother's side Richard Wyffen yeoman of Pentlowe [Essex] and William Wyffen citizen and skinner of London, together with all my other lands and tenements in Sudbury, Cornard, Bulmer [Essex] and Stanningfield, hoping that the Master of the Court of Wards and Liveries will grant my lands to my above friends, whom I appoint exors. I desire these kinsmen, in whom I put my special trust, to be very careful both for the lands and personal estate of my son. They are to use the profits of the manor of Otton Belchampe to pay for the composition of wardship, and the residue is for the use of my son. My wife Sarah is to have an annuity of £30 out of the profits of the manor of Otton Belchampe and of some other land which I had by my marriage with her. The residue of my goods and household stuff I give to my exors during the minority of my son Thomas, who is to have them when 21. I give Mr John Harryson, minister of St Peter's in Sudbury, 10s for a sermon to be preached at my funeral. Wit. Richard Houlbrughe, John Fothergill, Henry Colman. Pr. at Bury 17 July 1632.

421. R(W) NICHOLAS ADWELL (X) of Bury St Edmunds, cooper. 29 May 1632.

Bequeaths soul to God trusting to have remission of sins through Jesus Christ.
I make John Kinge yeoman of Rushbrooke and Richard Nunne maltster of Bury my exors. I give Mary my loving wife half of all my goods and chattels, timber, wares, debts and money; and the other half I give for life to my daughter Mary, wife of Richard Wood. My exors are to sell my goods to the best advantage unless my wife and daughter think fit to keep them. The money raised from the sale I desire my exors to put out with good security towards the maintenance of my wife and daughter. After the death of my daughter Mary, her share of my goods or the money raised by their sale is to be equally divided between her children Mary, Esther and Nicholas. If my daughter's husband, Richard Wood, comes again and makes sale of or embezzles away any of her goods or molests my exors about money or goods given to Mary, then my exors and supervisor may recover any goods sold by him and keep them to the use of my daughter and her children. My exors and my supervisor, Edward

Cock alias Chase cooper of Bury, are to make sale of such of my goods, timber and ware as my wife and daughter do not want to keep. I give them for their pains 13s 4d each. They are to deduct out of my estate all debts due by me and all the charges they have to pay. Wit. John Jewell, Giles Steward (X) and his wife. Pr. at Bury 24 July 1632.

422. R(W) JOHN EDGLEY (X) of Stanstead. 16 July 1632.

Bequeaths soul to God hoping to be saved by Jesus Christ.
I give William Freanch all my moveable goods except bills and bonds, which I give to my exor to pay my debts, prove my will and bring my body to the ground. Exor: my neighbour William Stebbinge. Wit. Henry Bowser, John Carter. Pr. at Bury 30 July 1632.

423. R(W) EDMUND GREENGRASSE (X) of Troston, yeoman. 16 July 1632.

Bequeaths soul to God.
I give my wife Susan all my arable and pasture lands which are not in her jointure until my son Edmund is 21 when he is to have them. I give Elizabeth Russells my sister 40s to be paid by my wife within 2 years of my decease. If my son Edmund dies without issue my will is that my kinsman Edmund Andrewe shall have my house and land. I give my kinswoman Ellen Kelner 10s. I give Elizabeth and Sarah, daughters of Ellen Kelner, 5s each when 21. I give Ellen and Elizabeth Hill of Bardwell 5s each within 3 years of my decease. I give my kinswoman Christian, wife of William Yonges, 5s to be paid by my wife 4 years after my decease. I give my wife all my goods and chattels and make her ex'trix. Wit. James Hodson, Roger Greenegras, Henry Sewell (X). Pr. at Bury 30 July 1632.

424. R(W) THOMAS KENT (X) of Barrow. 13 March 1631/32.

Bequeaths soul to God and body to be buried in Barrow churchyard.
I give my wife Anne, whom I make sole ex'trix, all my goods and chattels at Barrow to pay my debts and bring my body decently to the grave. I give my son Nicholas my mill on condition he pays my wife the third part of the rent during her life. If he defaults, my wife is to have the mill for her life. Wit. William Smith, George Pleasannce. Pr. at Bury 16 April 1632.

425. R(W) JOHN TOLWARDYE (X) of Exning, shepherd. 1 September 1631.

Bequeaths soul to God and body to be buried in Exning churchyard.
I give my son John a cupboard which he already has in his possession and all my other household stuff that he has in his custody. I also give him all my hewn timber in my barn and the 2 ladders on condition he pays my

grandson John Garret 10s when 15. I give my son John my house which I hold by lease with 1 acre called Diggeons lying on south side of the house and with the west part abutting on Broad way. I purchased the lease of Sir John Cotton and his wife Elizabeth, lords of the manor. My son John must pay £10 each to my 3 daughters Judith, Frances and Agnes at one a year. Benefit of survivorship. If John dies before their legacies are paid his exors are to pay them, and if he refuses to pay them Frances is to have my house and land and pay her sisters' legacies. If she refuses, Ambrose Tolwardye my brother, whom I make supervisor, is to sell my house and land and divide the money between my 3 daughters. I give my daughter Judith my table in the hall and the bed I now lie on with the bolster, pillow and a blanket, one of my best tubs, my best chair and my best cow. I give my daughter Frances my cupboard standing in the hall, my best bedstead and my best featherbed. I give my daughter Agnes my trundle bed in the chamber with the flockbed, a yellow blanket and all other things lying on the bed, my best chest, one of my best tubs, my kneading trough with the moulding board and my best heifer. All the rest of my goods I leave to my daughter Frances, whom I make sole ex'trix. Wit. John Curtys, Edward Fysher (X), Richard Spaldin (X). Pr. at Newmarket 7 April 1632.

426. R(W) AGNES DARBYE (X) of Burwell [Cambs], widow. 30 December 1631.

Gives soul to God that gave it.
I give my kinsman John Rogers £12 to be paid within a year of my decease. I give Richard, son of my brother Richard Canforth, 40s within a year. I give 5s each to the 5 children of Lucy, now wife of Thomas Wenham, within a year. I give Anthony Bradley 5s within a year. I give the poor widows of the parish of Burwell 10s on the day of my burial. All the rest of my goods I bequeath to my sister Isabel, wife of Richard Canforth and make them exors. Wit. Stephen Payne, Barnaby Garner, Richard Iveson. Pr. at Newmarket 7 April 1632.

427. R(W) THOMAS DOVE (X) of Chippenham [Cambs], singleman. 31 March 1632.

Bequeaths soul to God my saviour and body to be buried in Chippenham churchyard.
I give Anne Dove my sister 40s and my brother Richard £3, which is in the hands of Leonard Cambridge and Austin Scott, and all my apparel. I give 10s each to Robert Tebett, Gerard, Anne and Elizabeth Gune. I give the poor of Chippenham 10s to be given at my burial. I give Thomas Norman of Wicken 12d. I give 12d each to Thomas Tayler, Robert Francis, John Betes and Elizabeth Read, my fellow servants in the house where I dwelled. I give Mary Francis 12d and 12d each to the 4 children of John Francis the younger. All the rest of my goods I give to William Dabre, whom I make exor. Wit. John Francis the elder, Austin Scott. Pr. at Newmarket 7 April 1632.

428. R(W) HUGH LARGENT (X) of Kirtling [Cambs], husbandman.
8 April 1628.

Commends soul to God trusting to be saved by Jesus Christ.
I make my son Robert heir to my copyhold tenement in Kirtling called
Lightfoote and the buildings belonging to it. He must pay all my debts
and legacies. I give my wife Anne 20s p.a. to be paid quarterly, in the
south porch of Kirtling church. I give my daughter Margaret 40s within 2
years and my daughter Alice 40s within 3 years of my decease. Benefit of
survivorship. I give my son Richard £4 to be paid 4 and 5 years after my
decease. I give my daughter Frances 40s 6 years after and my daughter
Mary 40s 7 years after my death. I give the children Thomas Darbie had
by my daughter Philippa 40s among them to be paid one at a time starting
8 years after my decease. All legacies are to be paid in south porch of
Kirtling church. Legatees have power to distrain. I give my wife Anne the
bed we lie on with all that belongs to it with a flockbed, a pair sheets, 1
bolster, a pillow and a coverlet. I also give her a little kettle, a little
posnet and all her apparel. I give my daughters Alice and Margaret the
bed they usually lie in with a flockbed, bolster, pair sheets and coverlet to
be equally divided between them, and a cupboard each. I give Margaret
the brass kettle and the brass posnet, and Alice the other brass kettle, a
posnet and a pewter dish. I give Alice a hutch that was mine when I was a
singleman. I give all my unbequeathed goods to my son Robert and my
daughter Margaret and make them exors. Robert is to bear the cost of
proving my will and of my burial. Wit. Robert Astes (X), Robert
Borbart. Since the last court held at Kirtling I have surrendered to 2
customary tenants all my land to the use of my will. Pr. at Newmarket 7
April 1632,

429. R(W) ADAM MUNNS (X) of Stanton, yeoman. 10 November
1608.

Commends soul to God and body to Christian burial.
My will is that Agnes my wife shall have all my houses and land in the
fields of Stanton until she marries again or the day of her death,
whichever it shall please God first to happen. Afterwards I give my house
and land to my son John on condition he pays my daughter Elizabeth £10
when 21 or on her marriage day. If John dies without heirs, I bequeath
my house and land to Elizabeth. I give her £10 to be paid to her by my
ex'trix on her wedding day. The residue of my goods I give to my wife
and make her ex'trix. Wit. Robert Brooke, Robert Ropp. Pr. at Ixworth
to widow Agnes 7 April 1632.

180

430. R(W) WILLIAM SYER (X) of Great Ashfield, butcher. 10 January 1631/32.

Bequeaths soul to God trusting to have remission of sins through Jesus Christ. To be buried in Great Ashfield churchyard.
I give my wife Katherine for ever my house and land that I purchased from John Newton and his wife Katherine. I give my wife all my household goods and cattle, and make her ex'trix. Wit. Edmund Terolde, Thomas Woode. Pr. at Bury 14 June 1632.

431. R(W) ROBERT GAULT (N) of Little Saxham, shepherd. 4 June 1632.

He gave his goods and chattels to Mary his wife. Wit. John Wymarke and testator's wife. Pr. at Bury 25 June 1632.

432. R(W) THOMAS BIRD (X) of Stowmarket, shoemaker. 26 June 1632.

Bequeaths soul to God and body to earth trusting through Jesus Christ to be a partaker of eternal bliss.
I give the messuage wherein I dwell in Stowmarket to Anne my loving wife for life, she allowing my son Thomas to dwell in and use the shop next to the street where I work, the chamber over it, the hall chamber and the kitchen or room now used as a kitchen. He is also to have free access to the yards and garden belonging to my tenement. After my wife's decease I bequeath my messuage to Thomas on condition he pays my 2 daughters Anne and Phoebe £4 each within a year. I also give my daughters £6 each to be paid by my exors within a year of my decease. Benefit of survivorship. I give to each of my 3 children a flockbed. All my other goods and chattels I give to my wife whom, together with my son Thomas, I make exors. Wit. John Williames, Thomas Osborne (X). Pr. at Stowmarket 24 June 1632.

433. R(W) LAWRENCE GILDERSLEAVE (X) of Wetheringsett, ploughwright. 6 May 1629.

Commits soul to God craving pardon for my sins and in certain hope of resurrection to everlasting life.
I give Susan my wife the yearly profit of £60 now in the hands of Mr Buttes my feoffee in trust. After my wife's death I give the yearly profit to my daughter Susan Collyn towards bringing up her children; after her decease the £60 is to be divided among these children. I give John Hershame my bed I lie on with the sheets, coverlet, bolster and a pillow. I give all the rest of my goods and chattels to be equally divided between my wife and my daughter Susan Collyn. I make William Withers, clerk, my exor. Wit. George Brame, Anthony Aldrich, John Gotheram. Pr. at Bury 12 July 1632.

434. R(W) THOMAS PARKER of Walsham le Willows, gentleman.
7 June 1630.

Commends soul to God in assurance of a joyful resurrection.
I give to the poor people that shall be present at my burial £4. I give everyone of my godchildren 6s 8d each. I give Richard my only son all my tenements, lands and messuages, both free and copyhold, in Walsham in the Willows on condition he pays my daughter Alice £300 as follows: £100 within 3 years of my decease and £33 6s 8d p.a. for 6 years. Richard must also pay Alice £10 p.a. for the 3 years before he pays her £100. Alice has power to distrain. If Alice marries contrary to the good liking and approbation of my loving friend Mr Robert Cotton of Horringer and my brother Augustine Parker, whom I earnestly entreat to assist her with their good counsel and advice, then all the bequests made to her shall be void and Richard instead is to pay her £150 as follows: £100 within 3 years of my decease and £50 3 years later. I give Margery Swift my servant 40s to be paid within a year. All my household stuff and stock of hay, corn and cattle I give to my son Richard whom I make sole exor. If he fails to prove my will within 6 weeks of my decease, my bequest to him of my personal estate is void and I give my moveables to Alice instead to pay the charges of my funeral and probate, and the legacies to the poor and my godchildren, and I make her ex'trix. Wit. Gregory Hawes, John Hawes, James Neele (X). Pr. at Walsham 5 July 1632 to Richard as exor.

435. R(W) ANTHONY BONNER (X) of Haverhill. 26 May 1632.

Bequeaths body to earth and soul to God.
I make Mr Jaggard of Haverhill my exor. I give Stephen, son of Stephen Dowghtie, of Bury 40s. I give 10s to the minister that preaches at my funeral. I give Mr Burdett 6s. I give my wife Anne all the rest of my goods to pay my legacies. Wit. Godfrey Turells, Rebecca Shary. Pr. 18 July 1632. No place given.

436. R(W) MARGARET KENT (X) of Bury St Edmunds, widow.
24 July 1632.

Commends soul to God trusting to be saved through Jesus Christ.
I give 20s each within a year of my decease to the 6 children of my brother Nicholas Baker: Samuel, Nicholas, William, Mary the wife of Mr John Seller, Anne the wife of John Normanton and Martha. I give my brother Martin Baker 40s and his son Samuel 40s, both to be paid within a year. I give Rebecca, daughter of my deceased brother John Baker, my best chest and the desk that stands on it and all the linen in them; also my trunk and my wearing apparel in it. My brother Nicholas Baker is to give Rebecca these things when she is 21. I also give her £10 when 21. I give my brother Abraham Baker £4 within a year. I give Bridget, wife of

Thomas Newham, and Elizabeth Brettam my old servant 10s each to be paid within 2 months of my decease. The rest of my moveables and money I give to my brother Nicholas whom I make exor. Wit. Thomas Fox, William Brightwell, William Sarson. Pr. at Bury 13 August 1632.

437. R(W) ANNE SPARKE (X) wife of John SPARKE of Rougham. 18 June 1632.

Bequeaths soul to God trusting to be saved by merits of Jesus Christ.
I give my brother John Tillett the freehold land in Elmswell and Wetherden given to me, during the minority of my son Edmund Tillet, by the will dated 28 April 1625 of my late husband Edmund Tillet. John Tillet must maintain my son Edmund and my daughter Anne Tillett with meat, drink and clothing and bring them up to school. He must account to Edmund when he is 21 for the rent of the land, and any surplus from the expenses of my children's upbringing is to be equally divided between them when 21. I give all the moveable goods, given to me by the will of my late husband, to my children Edmund and Anne immediately after my decease. If my husband John Sparke will give security for the safe delivery of these goods to my children when they are 21 or marry, he may have the use of them as long as he lives in Rougham. If he refuses to give security, my brother John Tillet is to keep the goods. I make him exor and desire him to have especial care to see my children are brought up in the fear of God and in education, as he will answer for it at the dreadful day of judgement. I entreat him to put my daughter Anne to be educated by my sister Morris and to pay for her diet and clothing until she be fit to go to service. Wit. Margaret Tillett (X), Margaret How. Pr. at Bury 13 August 1632.

438. R(W) JOHN LYLLIE (N) of Westley, yeoman. 30 July 1632.

Commends his soul to God and body to earth.
He gave all his goods and estate to his father, Barnabas Lillie, towards the bringing up of his child, and his father to dispose of the remainder as he thought fit. Wit. William Steele of Bury St Edmunds, bricklayer, John Rogers of Bury, labourer. Let. ad. granted at Bury 2 August 1632 to Barnabas Lillie.

439. R(W) BENNETT BARKER of Bury St Edmunds, gentleman. 21 January 1631/32.

Bequeaths soul to God expecting a joyful resurrection and to be raised up at the last day to reign in glory for ever with Jesus Christ.
I give and bequeath to Katherine my loving wife for life the messuage I now dwell in with its yards, orchard and garden, and all the brewing vessels, copper and casks belonging to my brewing office, my horse mill and all implements used in brewing. After the decease of my wife I give

all this to my son Francis. I give my wife all my linen to dispose of at her pleasure, and all my household stuff and plate for life, and after her death to my son Francis. I give my wife all my wood lying in the stable and chair house and in the vaunce floors and kiln house of my messuage. I give her an annuity of £7 to be paid quarterly. I give Thomas Cleere of Ipswich gentleman and his wife Katherine 5 marks to make each of them a gold ring. I give Edward Lelam gentleman and his wife Margaret 5 marks to make them gold rings. I give Mary, daughter of Thomas Cleere, 10s to be paid within a year of my wife's decease to make her a ring. I give the other children of Thomas Cleere: Thomas, Bennett and Katherine £5 each to be paid in age order starting the second year after my wife's decease to buy plate for them. Benefit of survivorship. I give £25 each to my grandsons Bennett and Thomas, sons of Edward Lelam, to be paid 5 and 6 years after my wife's death. Benefit of survivorship. If all Edward Lelam's children die, these legacies are to be paid to his wife and my daughter Margaret. I give £4 to the poor of St James and St Mary in Bury, 40s to each parish to be distributed by the overseers of the poor to such as are sick and in most want. I give to the poor of Hopton, where I was born, 13s 4d. The residue of my goods and chattels, debts, corn and hay I give to my son Francis towards payment of my debts and performance of my will, and I make him exor charging him in holy fear of God and in filial respect and reverence to me his father carefully to perform my will and to carry himself with all due regard towards his mother. Wit. Edward Lelam, John Baker (X), John Newham. Pr. at Bury 25 August 1632.

440. R(W) HELEN KIRKE (X) of Risby, widow. 28 June 1631.

Commends soul to God. To be buried in Risby churchyard.
I give my son Richard Buckle 40s, my silver cup wherein I drink, 3 silver spoons, the bed and bedstead wherein he lies, 2 pairs sheets and a pair of blankets. I give my grandchild George Whiter £10, my silver salt, 2 silver spoons, the bed and bedstead wherein I lie, 1 pair sheets, 1 coverlet, 1 pair blankets, 1 feather bolster and a feather pillow. I give my grandson Richard Whiter £10 when 19, my bedstead and feather bed as it stands in the hall chamber of the house of my son-in-law George Whiter, my great trunk in the same chamber and 3 silver spoons. I give my grandson John Whiter £10 when 20, a posted bedstead in my kitchen chamber, a feather bed, a coverlet, a pair blankets, a feather bolster, a feather pillow, a pair sheets, my great trunk in my pantry and 3 silver spoons. I give my grandchild Margaret Whiter £80 to be paid within 1 week of my decease. I will that the £40 which my late husband Edward Kirke clerk, gave her in his will be paid to Margaret by my exors within 6 months of my death. I also give her a posted bedstead and feather bed in my parlour, a trundle bed there with what belongs to it, a long table, a cupboard, 3 chairs, 4 buffet stools, 1 pair cobirons, a chest in which my apparel lies, a silver cup gilt, 3 silver spoons, my great brass pot, my middle kettle, a great candlestick, my bason and ewer and a great skillet. I give Helen Whiter

my grandchild £80 to be paid within a week of my decease. I also give her a cupboard and the long table and forms in the hall of my son George Whiter, and the brewing brass there after the death of my exors. Also a silver cup, 3 silver spoons, a bedstead and feather bed, a feather bolster, a feather pillow, 1 pair blankets, 1 table and 2 chairs in my parlour chamber, 3 buffet stools, a brass pot, a great cauldron, a great candlestick, a skillet, 2 kettles, 2 pairs cobirons and a warming pan. The £40 given to Helen Whiter by Edward Kirke in his will is to be paid to her by my exors within 6 months of my decease. I give John Whithand my kinsman £5 to be paid within 3 months, a flock bed, a feather bolster, a feather pillow and a pair sheets. I give 20s towards the enlarging of the communion cup of Risby. All the residue of my goods, corn, cows, sheep and hogs I give to my son-in-law George Whiter and his wife Margaret and make them exors. The £40 my late husband gave in his will to George Whiter is to be paid to him by my exors within 6 months. Wit. Thomas Yeardlie, James Seley (X). Pr. at Bury 27 August 1632.

441. R(W) WILLIAM LOVES (X) of Soham [Cambs]. 20 May 1632.

Gives soul to God that gave it me expecting to be a joyful inheritor of the kingdom of heaven.
I give my grandchildren Sarah, Joan and William, children of Margaret Loves of Littleport in the Isle of Ely, 40s each when 21. Benefit of survivorship. I give my son Matthew Loves of Littleport £3 to be paid within a month of my decease, and my brown mare with her foal. I give Love Torell my grandchild a pied bullock at once and £4 when 21. I give Margaret, Sarah and Ellen Torell, my grandchildren, 40s each when 21. Benefit of survivorship. I give my daughter Sarah Torrill a red bullock. I give my wife Anne £6 10s 0d on condition she gives up her right of thirds in my house. I give James Turrell my freehold house to pay my legacies. I give my wife Anne my cupboard, a pair of bedsteads, my coffer, a stool and a skillet. All the rest of my goods I give to James Torrell, whom I make exor. Wit. Roger Voyce, John Bridge (X). Pr. at Bury 28 May 1632.

442. R(W) SAMUEL BENNETT (X) of Kersey, yeoman. 2 June 1632.

Bequeaths soul to God in hope of joyful resurrection to eternal life. To be buried in Kersey churchyard.
I give to Anne my dear and loving wife all my worldly goods for life. After her decease my son Thomas is to have £4 of my goods, my daughter Mary £10 and my daughter Anne £10; the overplus to be equally divided among my children. Ex'trix: wife. Supervisor: my good and faithful friend Thomas Allablaster of Hadleigh. Wit. Thomas Seffray, Jonas Rowe (X). Pr. at Bury 10 July 1632.

443. R(W) TITUS SPARROWE (X) of Rede, yeoman. 28 March 1632.

Commends soul to God.
I give my wife Anne for life my tenement where I dwell with the land belonging to it. If she remarries or when she dies my son John is to have this tenement with its land called the Canggle. If my wife remarries John is to pay her £4 p.a. I give my daughters Anne, Susan and Mary my close called the Sleppe to be sold after my wife's decease and the money equally divided between them. If any of my children can buy the others' share they may do so if they give as much as any other man would. My brother William Sparrowe shall have the use of the chamber in my tenement where he now lies for life if he shall think good to accept it. I give my wife Anne all my moveable goods and chattels on condition she pays all my debts, and I make her ex'trix. Wit. William Pitches, John Sparrow. Pr. at Bury 9 April 1632.

444. R(W) GEORGE SCOTT (N) of Wissington, husbandman. 15 June 1632.

He gave all his goods and chattels to be equally divided among his children. Wit. Robert Jenor, Christopher Scott, John Newman. Let. ad. granted to son John 23 June 1632. No place given.

445. R(W) JOHN CHINNERIE of Cockfield. 20 June 1632.

Bequeaths soul to God. To be buried in south porch of Cockfield church. I bequeath to my dear and tender loving mother Chinerie all my land, being about 2½ acres in Cockfield with north end abutting on Wendshoe Green and south end on land of William Dednam. I give my wellbeloved nephew John Custofer, son of William, £10 when he is 21; until then he is to receive the interest on this sum. I give my wellbeloved nephews Thomas and William, 2 other sons of William Custofer, £10 on the same terms as their brother John. I give my beloved nieces Mary and Martha, daughters of William Custofer, £5 each in the same way. All these children have benefit of survivorship. I give my wellbeloved sister Anne, wife of John Heyward, £20 to be used by my exors to buy a house for her as speedily as may be after my decease. After her death this house is to be sold and the price divided among the 3 youngest of her children then living. I give £5 each to John, son of John and Anne Heyward, and to his 2 brothers and sister Hannah to be paid in same way as the legacies given to my sister Custofer's children. I give my dearly beloved sister Thomasine Chinierie £10 on her marriage day or when she is 21; until then she is to receive the interest. I give my god-daughter Mary, daughter of John Snell the younger, 13s 4d to be paid within a year of my decease. I give 40s to the poor of Cockfield, 20s to be distributed by the minister and churchwardens on the day of my burial and 20s on the same day 12 months later. I appoint William Chinerie, my most loving and beloved father, exor and of whose faithful performing of my will I have not the least shadow of fear. No witnesses. Pr. at Bury 9 July 1632.

446. R(W) GEORGE HARVIE (X) of Hopton. 1 June 1632.

I give and bequeath to Bridget my wife all my moveable goods to pay my debts and legacies. I give my daughter Mary a brass pot, 1 pair sheets, a 2-year old brown bullock and a brown calf. Ex'trix: wife. Wit. John Muryell, Elizabeth Howse. Pr. at Hopton 4 July 1632.

447. R(W) JOAN PARKIN of Hopton. 9 September 1621.

Bequeaths soul to God.
I give Elizabeth Croxson, my kinswoman, immediately after my decease my messuage wherein I now dwell with all my land. She must pay £3 to my brother Francis Peirse within 3 years of my decease. If she does not do so, I give my messuage and land to my kinsman Henry Croxson on same conditions. If he fails to pay £3 my property is to go to his brother John. Payment to be made in south porch of Hopton church. I give all my goods and chattels to Elizabeth Croxson. Exors: my brother Francis Peirse and Elizabeth Croxson. Wit. Thomas Goddard, Thomas Astie, Henry Knock. Pr. at Hopton 4 July 1632.

448. R(W) THOMAS COLDOM of Knettishall. 4 May 1632.

I give my beloved wife all my free and copyhold tenements and land for life, and all my moveable goods to bring my body to the ground, prove my will and pay my debts. I give 20s to the poor of Knettishall and 40s to the poor of Coney Weston to be paid 1 year after my wife's decease. I give Richard Hardie's 2 children 20s each and my godson Andrew Hasted 20s. I give 20s each to Robert Crem, Thomas Rede and Edward Write. I give Edmund Sargent's children 10s each. All these legacies are to be paid by my exors within 1½ years of my wife Grace's death. After her decease I give John Muryell of Hopton my free land in Knettishall and my copyhold house and land in Blo' Norton [Norfolk]; he is to pay my legacies. Exors: John Muryell and my wife. Being visited with the hand of God I desire good people to pray for me. Wit. William Rogers, Thomas Rogers. Pr. at Knettishall 4 July 1632.

449. R(W) WILLIAM STAFFORD (X) of Gislingham, yeoman. 23 June 1632.

Commends soul to God hoping to be saved by Jesus Christ. To be buried in Gislingham churchyard.
I give to Richard Johnson my son-in-law, now living in Bricett, my mill with all things belonging to it, a brass copper, the best standing bedstead, the long table with a frame and the best cupboard standing in my parlour after the death of my wife Elizabeth, who is to have the use of these things during her life. I give Margaret Barker my daughter my worst standing bedstead with the featherbed, bolster and coverlet lying on it and my cupboard and table in the hall after my wife's death; she is to

187

enjoy them during her life. I give my daughter Katherine Maninge 20s within a year of my decease. I give the poor of Gislingham 20s, 10s to be given them the Sabbath after my burial and 10s the same day twelve month. My wife is to pay this 20s. I give my wife Elizabeth all the rest of my goods and chattels. Exor: son-in-law Richard Johnson. Wit. John Symonds, Elizabeth Offwood (X), Joan Richardson. Pr. at Gislingham 3 August 1632.

450. R(W) HENRY GOOCHE (X) of Langham, yeoman. 3 May 1631.

Bequeaths soul to Jesus Christ through whose death and passion I am sure of my salvation.
I give my children Dorothy, Thomas, Margaret, Anne and Henry £5 each within a year of my decease. My exors are to pay my wife Dorothy an annuity of 40s to be paid half yearly in lieu of her thirds. I give my son Edmund my great cupboard, a cheese press, a great tub, a beer barrel and a churn. I give my daughter Dorothy 2 of my best pewter dishes and the best brass kettle save one. I give my son Thomas my great brass pot and my great hutch. I give my daughter Margaret my posted bedstead and my flockbed complete. I give my daughter Anne my trundle bedstead and a flockbed complete, my little brass pot and my chest which I have for my own use. I give my son Henry my great table in the hall and the joined form, a new pewter dish and my pestle and mortar. My children are to receive these gifts after my decease. I give all the rest of my goods to my wife Dorothy for life, and after her decease they shall be equally parted among my children. I make my son Edmund sole exor, and give him all my free and copyhold land in Langham. I will that my exor buries me in a decent and comely manner and discharges my funeral expenses. Within 10 days of my decease my exor is to enter into a bond of £60 with Thomas Syer the elder and William Brown, both yeoman of Langham, to pay all the sums of money bequeathed in my will. If Edmund refuses to act as exor and enter into a bond, I make my son Thomas exor and leave him all my land on same terms and give Edmund the £5 Thomas should have had. I will that my legacies be paid in the porch of Langham church and my wife's annuity paid at her dwelling house. Wit. Thomas Syer senior (X), William Browne, Robert Symonds (X), Thomas Syer junior (X). Pr. at Bury 17 September 1632.

451. R(W) RICHARD DOWE (X) of Soham [Cambs], blacksmith. 23 July 1632.

Gives soul to God believing through Jesus Christ to be a joyful inheritor of the kingdom of heaven.
I give my son Thomas when he comes to age of 14 years £10. Until then the money is to be put out and his mother is to have the use of it towards bringing him up. When he is 24 I give Thomas all my shop and working

tools. I give my sister Anne Dowe 30s and my apprentice Bartholomew Write 13s 4d within 3 months of my decease. All the rest of my goods I give to my wife Anne whom I make ex'trix. Wit. John Cheavefly (X), John Brand (X), Roger Voyce. Pr. at Bury 21 September 1632.

452. R(W) GEORGE KERITCH (X) of Saxtead, singleman. 7 April 1632.

Commits soul to God relying wholly on his mercies in Jesus Christ for my salvation.
I give my brother Robert 30s, 20s to his wife and 20s to his son Charles. I give my brother William £10 and 20s each to his children: Elizabeth, Margery, Silvester, Susan, William, Thomas and John. I give my sister Katherine Browne widow £4 and 20s each to her children: Thomas, George, Robert, Mary, Richard, Alice and William. I give my sister Mary, wife of John Jesop, 30s and 20s each to her children Anne and John. I give my nephews and niece John, Thomas and Katherine, children of my brother John Keritch, 10s apiece. I give my sister Alice Keritch 20s, and my brother Giles 40s besides £6 which he owes me. I give his wife 20s and his children Dorothy, John and Samuel 20s apiece. I give my brother Thomas 20s, his wife 20s and 10s each to their children: William, Robert, Philip and John. All these legacies to be paid by my exor within 1 year of my decease. Legatees have benefit of survivorship. If any of my nephews and nieces are not 21 when their legacies are due, the money is to be paid into the hands of their father or mother. I give my brother William my coffer, my cloak, my best suit and my worst suit in doublet and breeches, my best hat, my best girdle, 3 bands, all my shirts, 2 pairs blue stockings, 2 pairs shoes and a pair boots. I give my brother Giles my breeches that are at his house and my leather girdle. I give my nephew George Browne my lac't bond [sic] which I formerly bought of him. I give my niece Alice Browne my desk. All these legacies are to be delivered within a month of my decease. For the great assurance and trust I have in John Jessopp, my kind and loving brother-in-law, I make him sole exor of my will and give him 30s for his pains. In addition I bequeath him my hatchet, my hook, my leather apron and my hedging gloves. My debts, legacies and burial expenses being discharged, I give all my other goods and chattels to my exor towards performing my will. Wit. Edward Moulton, William Wyeth. Pr. at Bury 10 September 1632.

453. R(W) JOHN BARRET (X) of Dalham. 10 November 1631.

Commends soul to God and Jesus Christ hoping to be saved through latter.
I give the poor of Dalham 10s to be paid to the churchwardens and overseers of the poor within a month of my decease and to be distributed at their discretion. I give my son John the messuage in which I dwell with the malt house, barn and stable, and the land belonging to it. He must pay Elizabeth my beloved wife £12 p.a. to be paid quarterly. My mind is

that she shall have her dwelling in my parlour, in which I lately built up a chimney, and access through the hall. I also give her my posted bedstead with featherbed, bolster and all its other bedding as it now stands in the parlour, and the bedstead in the chamber over the parlour with featherbed, bolster and other bedding. After my wife's decease my son William is to have the bedstead and bedding in the parlour. I also give my wife my cupboard now in the hall, one of my best chests, 6 pairs of the best sheets, 4 pairs of the best pillowbeeres, one of the best table cloths, a dozen of the best table napkins, a brass pot, 2 kettles, a posnet and 6 pieces of pewter to be chosen by her. Lastly I give her half of all the firewood in my house and yards at the time of my decease. I give my daughter Elizabeth £70 to be paid by my exor as follows: £10 a year after my death and £15 p.a. for the 4 years following. If she dies before the whole legacy has been paid and she has married leaving children, the remainder is to be paid to them. I also give her 2 of my milk cows to be taken by her within a month of my decease. I give my son William my tenement in Ousden with all its land, and £40 to be paid by my exor as follows: £20 when he is 16 and £20 when he is 21. I also give William 2 of my best milk cows within a month of my decease. He is to choose his cows before my daughter Elizabeth does. I give my 2 children Elizabeth and William all the household stuff that was my father Barrett's to be equally divided between them within a month, except a cupboard now in the dairy which my son John shall have. I give Margaret Pond my servant and kinswoman a boarded bedstead, a flockbed, a bolster, a pair sheets, a pair blankets and a coverlet within a month of my decease. I also give her 20s to be paid within a year. The rest of my goods and chattels I give to my son John whom I make exor. Supervisor: Edward Pond my brother-in-law. John is to enter into a bond of £300 to my brother Pond for the performance of my will, and if he refuses I make Edward Pond my exor. Wit. Henry Russelles and me William Parkyns. Pr. at Bury 21 September 1632.

454. R(W) JOHN MALTE (X) of Santon Downham, shepherd. 21 August 1632.

Bequeaths soul to God trusting to be saved by the merits of Jesus Christ. I give Mary my wife for ever my tenement and land held of the manor of Monkes Hall or of Mayses, on condition she gives my sister Avis, wife of John Yaxley, £5 to be paid at 20s p.a. starting 1 year after my decease. She must also pay £4 to Henry and Elizabeth, children of my sister Susan, wife of Richard Button, as follows: 40s to Henry when he is 9 and 40s to Elizabeth when 11. Benefit of survivorship. I give all my goods to my wife Mary unto whom for weighty causes I have given my estate and whom I make ex'trix. Wit. John Rowse clerk, Edward Hall, John Coward. Pr. at Bury 8 October 1632.

455. R(W) RICHARD PEAKE (X) of Fordham [Cambs], yeoman.
30 June 1632.

Commits soul to God trusting through Jesus Christ that it will be saved
and rest in heaven.
As one having a feeling of the want of the poor, I firstly give to the poor
of Fordham 20s to be distributed on the Sabbath day after my decease. I
give the poor of Hargrave 10s. I give my sister Marian Frost for life my
copyhold tenement held of the manor of Netherhall Tyndalls and 5 rods
of land adjoining it. I also give her my 6 pieces of arable land in Fordham
in the field called Biggen field, totalling 3 acres and which I purchased of
one Stebben. I also give her 2½ acres and half a rod land in Kettingale
field in Fordham, sometime belonging to one Jacob. After my sister's
death I give my tenement with 5 rods land to Henry Russell, who must
pay his sister Rebecca £3 within a year of my sister Marian's death. I give
Marian my wife 2 acres 1 rod in Isleham field for life and after her
decease to Thomas Peake, to whom I also give 1 acre copyhold land in
Fordham Church Crofts on condition he pays Anne, daughter of John
Peake, £3 within a year of my decease. If he refuses Anne Peake is to
have this acre of land. My wife is not to make any claim of thirds on my
land. I give Thomas Peake my tenement standing at Dunnes Green in
Fordham on condition he pays Marian, one of his brother William
Peake's daughters, £3 within 2 years of my decease. I give Thomas
Sergent the reversion of the estate in fee simple of the 3 acres arable land
left to my sister Marian after her decease. He must pay 40s to his brother
William within 2 years of Marian's death and 40s to Rebecca Russell
within 3 years. I give 20s towards the repair of Fordham church. I give to
the persons that ring at my burial 3s 4d. I give John Peake, grandson of
my brother John, 3s 4d. I give Henry Frost son of my sister 20s. I give the
reversion of 2½ acres half a rod left to my sister Marian to her 3 sons
George, Henry and Robert Frost. If their kinsman Thomas Peake will
buy this land, they are to let him have it as reasonable as any man. I give
20s each to be paid within 2 years of my decease to Robert Frost,
Margery and Ellen daughters of my brother Robert Peake, William
Sergent, George Frost, and Margaret and Anne daughters of my sister
Marian Frost. I give Richard, son of John Hinsone, 2 acres of copyhold
purchased of Giles Bridge and held of the manor of Coggeshalles, 2 of my
best horses and 1 mare at his own choice, my best cart and cart gears,
plough and plough gears, a cupboard which I bought of one Daynes, my
great chest, a birded coverlet, a half-headed bedstead with the bedding
standing in the chamber he lies in, 1 comb each of wheat, rye and barley,
and £5. The goods are to be delivered to him 20 days after my decease
and the £5 within a year. I give Anne, one of the daughters of John
Hinsone, 20s to be paid within a year and to her sister Margaret £5 within
a year and a milk bullock immediately after my decease. I give William,
another son of John Hinsone, 20s within a year and a bullock immediately, and to his brother Thomas 40s within a year. I give Marian,
Elizabeth and Mary, daughters of John Hinsone, 20s each within 3 years

191

of my decease. I give my son-in-law John Hinsone and his wife Rose 10s each; Henry and Rebecca Russell my sister Elizabeth's children 20s each to be paid within 4 years. I give Robert Frost, my sister's son, 4 hogget sheep or 20s as my ex'trix thinks best within 40 days of my death. I give each of my servants 12 pence. All my goods and chattels and stock I give to my wife Marian to pay my debts and legacies, funeral and probate expenses, and I make her ex'trix. Supervisor: John Hinsone. I have surrendered my copyhold land and tenement to the lords of the manors from whom they are held. Wit. John Peachie, Robert Carlton and me William Howe. Codicil dated 15 August 1632. I revoke the bequest to Thomas Peake of 1 acre in Church Crofts in Fordham and instead give it to Rose, wife of my son-in-law John Hinsone, on condition she pays Anne Peake £3 within a year of my decease. Anne has power to distrain. Wit. William Hill and me William Howe.

Memorandum: I have surrendered to the use of my will my copyhold land held of the manor of Coggeshalles by the hands of Robert Jeffe and in the presence of John Jeffe, customary tenants of the manor. I have similarly surrendered my land held of Netherhall Tyndalls manor by the hands of Thomas Cheavelie and in the presence of Edward Wake, both customary tenants of the manor. I have also surrendered my land held of Feltons manor into the hands of William Randall and in the presence of William Reve, customary tenants of the manor. Pr. at Bury 1 October 1632.

456. R(W) THOMAS CAMPLIN (X) of Wicklewood [Norfolk].
25 August 1632.

Bequeaths soul to God trusting through Jesus Christ to have life everlasting.

As concerning my estate which it has pleased God to confer on me by the death of my father William Campill alias Camplyn being his heir at common law, I give to my loving master Mr Richard Ryche, in consideration of the kind use I have received from him and of some money I owe him, my tenement with all its land and the houses on it called Carries in Wicklewood and now occupied by my father-in-law Thomas Lee. My master is to sell the house and land to my father-in-law for £50, of which £20 is to be paid to him and £30 distributed among my 5 sisters and my brother John in equal portions. To ensure these payments my beloved master is to tie the land so that in event of default my brother and sisters have power to distrain. Exor: my loving master Mr Richard Ryche. Wit. Oliver Theobols, Mary Theobols (X). Pr. at Bury 1 October 1632.

457. R(W) MARIAN PARSON (N) of Tuddenham, widow. Monday 8 October 1632.

She gave all her goods and chattels to be equally divided between her son Nathan Lummis and her daughter Agnes Lummis. Wit. Roger Phillippes, and his wife Mary. Pr. at Bury 12 October 1632.

458. R(W) ELIZABETH BUMSTED of Sudbury, widow. 1 May 1632.

Bequeaths soul to God craving pardon and remission of sins.
I give my son John Bumsted of Melford 5s and no more because he has been chargeable to me in divers way already. I give my son Thomas Bumsted, joiner of Ipswich, a silver and gilt salt, and I give my son Robert Bumsted of London 2 silver spoons. The residue of my money, plate and household stuff I give to Elizabeth Bumsted my loving daughter and make her ex'trix. Wit. Daniel Biat, John Hotchkins notary public, Thomas Bumsted. Pr. at Sudbury 5 October 1632.

459. R(W) WILLIAM APPLETON of Wissington miller. 25 August 1632.

Commends soul to 3 persons of Trinity hoping to be saved through merits of Jesus Christ.
I give all my goods and chattels, household stuff, muniments and ready money to my wife Rachel to see my children brought up decently according to their degrees and in the fear of the Lord God, on condition that she pays all my children: Hannah, Catherine, Margaret, Mary, Rachel, Priscilla and William 10s each for a remembrance of me without fraud or guile. Ex'trix: wife Rachel. Wit. Wheatly Arnold, William Wharton. Pr. at Sudbury 5 October 1632.

460. R(W) MARY SMITH of Elmsett, widow. 18 July 1632.

Commends soul to God believing to be saved through Jesus Christ.
I give Robert Smith my grandchild my posted bed in the parlour, a flockbed, a pair blankets, a green coverlet, a flock bolster, 2 pillows, my trunk in the chamber with all that is in it, 6 silver spoons, a silver and gilt bowl, a tipped pot, a tipped can, half a score pieces of the best pewter and 2 kettles in the hall chamber. I give my son Matthew Smith my horse and my cow and all my unbequeathed moveables including my corn on the ground, my sheep and lambs, and my swine and poultry. Exor: son Matthew. Wit. George Carter, Margaret Carter. Pr. at Sudbury 5 October 1632.

461. W(R) ROBERT HOWE of Sudbury, gentleman. 23 May 1632.

Commends soul to God trusting to be saved through Jesus Christ. My body is to be buried near unto the place where my late father Robert Howe lies buried.
I give Judith my loving and wellbeloved wife for life my messuage and land in Middleton [Essex], and my messuage, yard and garden in Sudbury near the bridge foot sometime called Ballingdon bridge and formerly occupied by my father. If my wife happens to be with child at the time of my decease I bequeath my houses and land to that child after my wife's death, but if she has no child or it dies without heirs before the age of 21, then I give my messuages and land to Judith my wife for ever. I also give

her all my moveable goods and chattels and household stuff for ever. I give £200 each to my brothers John and Thomas and to my sister Elizabeth wife of John Fothergill, and £100 to their daughter Elizabeth Fothergill. These legacies are to be paid out of the profits of my capital messuage called the Friers and the land belonging to it. If my wife has a child I bequeath to it my messuage called Friers with its outbuildings and land, and the messuage adjoining the wall of the Friers and lately let to John Hibble carpenter and now occupied by several persons; it is held to be part of the messuage called Friers. My wife is to educate and bring up my child and receive the profits of the houses and land bequeathed to it until it reaches the age of 21. My wife is to pay the legacies given above out of these profits. The legacy to my niece Elizabeth Fothergill is not to be paid until she is 21 or marries, and if she dies before then her £100 is to be paid to my sister Fothergill. The legacies to my brothers and sisters are to be paid at the rate of £50 p.a. over 12 years starting 1 year after my decease. Benefit of survivorship and power to distrain. If my wife has no child or bears one that dies without heirs before it is 21, then my brother John is to have my messuage called Friers and its land, and must pay my wife Judith the £200 he would have received as a legacy, and also pay the other legacies chargeable on Friers. So much of my wife's marriage portion as remains in the hands of my father-in-law John Harrison shall be taken and enjoyed by my wife. If Friers comes to my brother John and my wife then attempts to claim dower from it, all bequests of messuages and land to her will become void. If my brother John attempts to dispossess my wife of the messuages and lands given to her in Middleton and at the Bridge foot, then all the legacies of money and land given to him will be void and I give them to my wife. I give William and Anne, two of the children of my brother-in-law Skynner of Bocking in Essex and of my deceased sister his late wife, 20s each to buy them a gold ring each within a month of my decease. I give my brother-in-law John Fothergill, exor of my will, £30 to be paid to him by my wife within 6 months of my decease to pay my debts and the legacies I have charged him to pay. He is to give an account of this to whoever possesses my capital messuage Friers. I give the minister appointed by my exor to preach at my funeral 20s. I give 30s to the poor people of the parish of All Saints in Sudbury, and 10s to the poor of each of the following parishes: St Peter and St Gregory in Sudbury and the hamlet of Ballingdon in Essex. These legacies are to be given to the poor by the ministers on the day of my funeral. Exor: my brother-in-law John Fothergill. I give him all debts and sums of money due to me towards paying my debts and the charges of my funeral and proving my will, and paying my legacies to my brother-in-law Skinner's children, to the minister and to the poor people of the various parishes of Sudbury and Ballingdon. Wit. Mark Sallter, William Gunton and me Abraham Alston. Pr. at Sudbury 5 October 1632.

Note: The house called the Friery was built c.1540 on the site of the dissolved Dominican Friary in Friars Street, Sudbury. Robert Howe (either the testator or his father) bought it in 1621. The house was demolished in 1820.

462. W(R) WILLIAM FISON (N) of Kennett [Cambs], bachelor.
7 August 1632.

He willed all his goods and chattels, his debts and funeral charges deducted, to be divided into 3 equal shares to be given to his brother John, to his sister Elizabeth wife of James Fison and to Stephen son of Stephen Warren and his wife Margaret, sister of the testator. Stephen must pay his mother the interest money from his share for her maintenance. Wit. Elizabeth wife of James Fison and Margaret wife of Stephen Warren. Let. ad. granted 27 August 1632 to testator's brother John. No place given.

463. W(R) THOMAS ELDRED (X) of Santon Downham. 16 September 1632.

Commends soul to God desiring holy spirit to sanctify me during remainder of my life and to receive me into his heavenly kingdom for the sake of Jesus Christ. To be buried in Downham churchyard.
I give Elizabeth my wife all my land and tenement in Weeting [Norfolk] until my son Thomas is 21, to help towards the education and upbringing of my children. I also give her all my goods and chattels to pay my debts and to pay my son Thomas £5 as follows: 20s when he is 16 and 20s p.a. until the whole sum is paid. I give my son Thomas my land and tenement in Weeting when 21 on condition he pays my son William £20 when he is 21. If this sum is not paid within 6 months of the due date, William is to have my land and tenement for ever. My wife is to keep my houses and tenement in repair. Ex'trix: wife. Wit. John Page, John White (X), Thomas Muninge. Pr. at Bury 5 October 1632.

464. W(R) ROBERT GIPPS (X) of Fornham All Saints, yeoman.
6 August 1632.

Bequeaths soul to God hoping to be saved through Jesus Christ.
I give my servant Thomas Gipps £5 to be paid within 12 months of my decease. I give Rose Gipps my man's sister 20s within a year. I give Robert, son of Richard March, 20s when 21. I give Benjamin Lovenes of Great Saxham 10s within a year. I give Joan my beloved wife and Elizabeth my daughter all my moveable goods, corn and cattle to be equally divided between them and I make them ex'trices. Wit. Oliver Phillipps, Thomas Godbold. Pr. at Bury 17 September 1632.

465. W(R) EDWARD COMBES of Bacton, gentleman. 21 November 1631.

Commends soul to God hoping to be made a partaker of life everlasting through Jesus Christ.
I give my sons Edward and John during my wife's life the tenement called Herberts in which Jeremy Betteney now lives with its orchard, garden and homestall totalling 1½ acres; 2 adjoining closes containing 6 acres; a 1½ acre little pightle abutting to the south on the tenement of Nicholas

Daynes; a 9 acre close of pasture going out of Rushcroft pasture alias Thistle close, part of which is called Drakes and a little half acre pightle called the Park pightle lying between the land of Nicholas Daynes to the east and of Mr Edward Cropley to the west. I also give them another 3 acre pasture close called Horsecroft with Mr Cropley's land to the west and Rushcroft to the east; part of this land is copyhold of the manor of Bacton alias Breisworth New Hall in Bacton. Also I give them 2 pieces of meadow lying in the Carr, containing 2 acres and being in Bacton and Westhorpe. After my wife's decease I give the tenement Herberts and all the above land to my son John together with Long meadow containing 8 acres and lying in Bacton. Edward has benefit of survivorship. My will is that all my writings, charters and evidences of title to land in Bacton, Wyverstone and Westhorpe shall remain in the custody of my brother John Combes and my cousin William Raynberd of Walsham le Willows until my sons Edward and John are 21, when they are each to have the title deeds of their land. In the case of deeds relating to property held by both sons, Edward is to hold them and John is to have copies. My wife is also to have copies of evidences of title if her friends think good, and a schedule of these documents to the end that they may have assurance that due care is had for her jointure and the good of my little ones. My ex'trix is to have a care of the goods and chattels which came to me by the will of my grandfather Mr Raynberd, whose debts and legacies I have long since discharged. I have a more than sufficient personal estate for the payment of my debts, which my ex'trix is to do. I give the remainder of my goods and chattels, after debts and other charges have been paid, to such other child or children besides my sons Edward and John as I shall have at the time of my decease. If I have no such children, my above sons are to have my goods and chattels, or my ex'trix may pay them a reasonable sum of money in lieu. I commit to my wife Margaret the guidance, tuition and government of my sons Edward and John and the letting of the lands left to them until they are 21. If my wife dies or remarries before my sons are 21, their guardianship and the management of their lands is to be undertaken by my brother John Combes and my cousin William Raynberd. The profits of my sons' land are to be used for their education and maintenance. I do not wish to estrange my sons from their own mother, but if she remarries and puts herself in the power of another neither I nor she may be certain what measures my little ones may receive at his hands. But I hope for the best and beseech God to bless and direct my wife in all her actions, and I commend her and my little ones to his merciful goodness and protection. I make my wife sole ex'trix. Super-visors: my brother Combes and my cousin Raynberd, desiring them to give my wife their best assistance. I give my wife a gold ring of remembrance of 20s weight; one of 15s weight to my brother Combes and one of 10s weight to my cousin Raynberd. My son Edward is to have my seal gold ring with my arms, my other seal gold ring with my grandfather's arms and my great picture in the parlour. Wit. Richard Rodwell (X), Jeremy Bettony (X), William Thurban (X), John Combes. Pr. at Bury 22 October 1632.

196

466. W(R) RICHARD HEYWARD (N) of Brockley, gentleman. In the month of October or November 1631.

He bequeathed to the wife of Robert Cole all his moveable goods in his house at Brockley in regard of the pains Robert Cole and his wife did take about him in the time of his sickness. Wit. John Frost, Robert Frost. Let. ad. granted 29 October 1632 to Anne, wife of Robert Cole. No place given.

467. W(R) THOMAS TRAYE (X) of Bury St Edmunds, parchment maker. 24 September 1632.

Commends soul to God my maker and redeemer.
I give my brother William and his wife Agnes for life all my free and copyhold land and tenements in Bury or elsewhere in Suffolk. They are to keep all buildings in good repair. After the death of the longer liver of William and Agnes Traye, I give my messuage with yard and land in Northgate Street to Agnes their eldest daughter for ever. My messuage in Southgate Street, wherein George Turle now dwells, I give to Elizabeth another daughter of William Traye for ever, and I give her sister Mary for ever the messuage in Southgate Street where I and Thomas Browne glover now live. I give John Warryn, late my servant, 2 dozen of new harrows and 200 of pelts (otherwise called working stuff) and 3 of my working knives. All the rest of my household goods, working stuff, tools, wares, money and immoveables I give to Susan, daughter of my brother William. Exors: brother William Traye and my brother-in-law Richard Wilkenson, to each of whom I give 20s over and above their reasonable charges. Wit. George Turle (X), Francis Wilkenson (X), Oliver Johnson. Pr. at Bury 27 October 1632.

468. W(R) MARGARET ADAMS (X) of Bury St Edmunds, widow. 22 September 1632.

Commits soul to God trusting to Jesus Christ for salvation.
I give Mary Leavold my daughter the forechamber with its present furnishings of which an inventory has been made, my best gown, petticoat and kirtle, a tipped can, 5 silver spoons and 5 sheets (one of which is a casting sheet) which are at pawn. If the sheets are redeemed my daughter Margaret Clarke is to have half the money, and if not she is to have 1 pair of the best of them. My will is that Mary shall lend the casting sheet to her sisters when they are in childbed. I give my daughter Constance Brand a tipped pot and 1 of the best pairs of holland sheets. I give my daughter Margaret Clarke my other gown and kirtle. I give my daughter Jane Lowdall a silver bowl and a pair sheets which I bought of my sister Glover. The rest of my goods are to be divided among my daughters part and part alike, but Mary is to have the better part. Amongst them they are to see that out of my goods my debts and funeral charges are paid and to make up £14 which I bequeath as follows: £5 each to my grandsons

197

Edmund Clarke and Edmund Brand, and £4 to my grandchild Jane Lowdall. Within 2 months of my decease these sums are to be put out until the children are 21. If they die before then their parents are to have their legacies. I give my sister Glover my ring now on my hand and my best pot of gilliflowers. I give my son-in-law Henry Brand my bible which I commonly used, and I give my son-in-law Henry Clarke my other bible which is in the bottom of the great hutch. I give John Lowdall 20s to buy him a ring, and to John Adams my son-in-law household stuff to furnish a room as my exors shall think fit for him. I give Richard Adams my son-in-law 20s. Exors: Mary Leavald and Robert Glover. Craving pardon of all those whom in any way I have offended and freely forgiving all that have offended me, and in the peace of God and a good content I take my leave of this world hoping one day to rise again in the resurrection of the just. Wit. William Grange, Francis Mowle (X) of Hadleigh, John Buckenham (X). Pr. at Bury 21 October 1632.

469. W(R) JOHN RYVETT (X) of Bacton, yeoman. 26 January 1628/29.

Commits soul to God my saviour and redeemer.
I give my eldest son Robert, if he shall at any time return home to demand it, 10s to be paid to him by my son William. I give my wife Mary, if she survives me, all my houses and land in Bacton for life if she remains a widow, but if she remarries I give them immediately to my son William who must pay my legacies to my 2 daughters Helen, wife of Thomas Webber, and Mary. I give my son William all my land in the parish of Cotton on condition he pays my daughter Helen £60 at £15 each half year starting 6 months after my decease, and my daughter Mary £20: £10 when 22 and £10 when 23. These legacies are to be paid in my dwelling house in Bacton. Daughters have power to distrain. I give my son William after the death of myself and my wife my horsemill, my cart and my plough. All the rest of my goods I give to my wife to dispose of at her will and pleasure. Exors: wife Mary and son William. Wit. John Symondes (X), James Jaques (X), John Watcham who wrote will. Pr. at Stowmarket 27 September 1632.

470. W(R) SUSAN DRAPER (X) of Combs, widow. 29 May 1632.

Bequeaths soul to God believing to have pardon of sins and everlasting life through Jesus Christ.
I give my son Robert my long table and form in the hall with the cupboard standing there, a livery bedstead with 2 flockbeds, a red and yellow darnick coverlet, 2 pillows, a flock bolster and 1 pair hempen sheets. I give my daughter Elizabeth Ellet my standing bedstead in the parlour with my middle feather bed, a feather bolster, 2 pillows, a black and white coverlet, 1 pair blankets, my keep in the hall and a great latten candlestick. I give my daughter Susan Draper my standing bedstead in the buttery chamber with my worst featherbed and best bolster, a blue and orange tawny coverlet, 2 pillows, 1 blanket, a long table in the same

chamber, 4 buffet stools, a great chest and a little one in the same room, a stone jar tipped with silver, 1 cobiron and 1 spit. I give my daughter Anne Draper a posted bedstead in the hall chamber with my best featherbed, a red and yellow darnick coverlet, my best blanket, the worst feather bolster, 2 pillows, a great and a little chest in the buttery chamber, a cupboard and a glass keep in the parlour, 2 little square tables, a brazen mortar, a latten candlestick, a cobiron, a spit and a great chair. I give my daughter Susan a bud bullock and a great chair. I give my daughter Elizabeth Ellet a weaned calf. I give my 3 daughters my 3 cows and all my brass, pewter and linen to be equally divided between them. I also give them my 4 acre copyhold close held of the manor of Bavents which I took up at a court held on 7 October 1595 on the surrender of Richard Edgore. I give my grandson Thomas Ellet £5 when 21: 25s to be paid by each of my 4 exors. All the rest of my goods and chattels I give to my son Robert and my 3 daughters and I make my 4 children exors. Wit. Thomas Sothebie, Anne Sothebie, Thomas Martin (X). Pr. at Stowmarket 27 September 1632.

471. W(R) ROBERT NEWMAN (X) senior of Acton, husbandman. 30 July 1632.

Commends soul to God hoping to be made partaker of everlasting life through Jesus Christ.
I give my eldest son Robert 10s to be paid by my exors within 2 years of my decease. I give my youngest son Thomas and my 2 youngest daughters Temperance and Sarah the profits of the house where I now dwell and my close of free land, new broken up and sown with oats, for 4 years and 10 weeks from the date of my will. After this term is up I bequeath the house, yard and 3 rod close of land to my eldest son Robert. I give my eldest daughter Anne, wife of Robert Ingall, £5 within 2 years of my decease. I give Temperance and Sarah £10 each within 2½ years and I also give them all my household stuff except the bed wherein I usually lie which I give to my sons Robert and Thomas. I give my son Thomas all the ungiven residue of my money unspent at the day of my death, on condition he pays my debts and funeral charges. Exors: son Thomas and daughter Sarah. Wit. John Hix (X), Henshawe Ellistone and me Edward Ellistone. Pr. at Sudbury 5 October 1632.

472. W(R) WILLIAM PRIOR (X) of Bradfield St George, yeoman. 2 August 1632.

Commends soul to God trusting to be saved.
I give Martha my dear and loving wife all my money, goods and chattels for life provided she pays my debts and legacies and brings up my 7 children in fear of God and with good meat, drink and clothing during their minority. I give my eldest son William £100: £50 to be paid within 3 years of my decease and £50 after my wife's death. I give my eldest daughter Honor £30 half to be paid within 2 years and half after my wife's

decease. I give my son John £50: half when he is 24 and half after the death of my wife. I give my sons Thomas, Hamlet and Ambrose £40 each to be paid in the same way as John's legacy. I give my youngest daughter Susan £30, half when she is 21 and half after my wife's decease. Benefit of survivorship. If my wife remarries, her husband is to give sufficient security for the payment of my legacies to my brothers William Orbell and Thomas Flack. If my wife finishes the purchase which I have begun to make from John Tastar of Gedding of the house and land now occupied by me, she is to hold them for life towards the maintenance of my children, and after her decease I bequeath them to my son William, who is to pay the legacies left to my 4 sons and 2 daughters. Ex'trix: wife. Wit. Samuel Crossman, William Orbell, Thomas Stearne, Thomas Flacke. Pr. at Bury 22 October 1632.

473. W(R) RICHARD LEWICE (X) of Needham in the parish of Gazely, husbandman. 15 December 1630.

Commends soul to God trusting to be saved.
I give Elizabeth Pond my bed as it stands furnished in the upper chamber, 3 kettles and the lesser brass pot, 4 pewter dishes, the cupboard in the hall and the table and form in the hall. I give my god-daughter Elizabeth Barrett the cupboard and hutch standing under the window in the parlour. All the rest of my goods and chattels I give to Robert Norman, whom I make exor. Wit. Thomas Barcocke, John Prick. Pr at Bury 22 October 1632.

474. W(R) JOHN STOCKEN (X) of Glemsford, weaver. 30 July 1632.

I give my wife Mary for life the messuage in which I dwell with yard and garden, and after her decease to my daughter Mary wife of George Crick. I give my wife all my goods and chattels towards her maintenance, asking her to leave them at her decease to my son John and daughter Mary. Ex'trix: wife. Wit. George Crispe senior, Thomas Crosse, John Gardner (X), Richard Gardner. Pr. at Bury 8 October 1632.

475. W(R) EDWARD FILBRIGG (X) the elder of Bury St Edmunds, blacksmith. 30 October 1632.

Commends soul to God my maker and redeemer.
I give my eldest son Edward the bed and bedstead he lies on, and all my shop stuff, wares, iron, tools, stithes, hammers, bellows and other implements in my shop belonging to my trade. Also all my coals and the grindstone as it now hangs in my yard. I also give him all debts and money due to me at the time of my death from my customers, which are standing or marked up on marks or chalked scores in my shop. I give to my ex'trix the debts and money set down in my debt books and any that I have bonds for, and the debts owing to me from Frances Clarke widow of

Rushbrooke. I give 20s each to all my grandchildren to be paid to them within a month of the decease of my wife Elizabeth. I give my son Thomas, my daughters Margaret and Audry and my son-in-law Robert Darby 10s each within a month of my decease to make them each a ring of gold to wear in remembrance of me. All the rest of my goods and chattels I give to my wife Elizabeth and make her ex'trix. Wit. Stephen Doughty, Oliver Johnson who wrote will. Pr. at Bury 12 November 1632.

476. W(R) JOHN GODDARD (X) of Harleston, husbandman.
2 November 1632.

The unprofitable servant of God. Commends soul to God and body to be buried in Harleston churchyard trusting through Jesus Christ that my soul will be placed in the company of heavenly angels and blessed saints.
I give my son John £60 to be paid by my exors when he is 14 towards his education and upbringing. If John dies before he is 14, my wife Mary is to have £30 of this gift and £20 is to be divided among the children of John Last and Richard Hunt. I give my son John a brass pot and a cupboard when 21. I give George, son of Richard Hunt, and Thomas, son of John Last, 40s each when 21. If the latter dies before he is 21 his mother Ellen is to have his legacy. The residue of my goods and chattels I give to my wife Mary and my father-in-law John Muskett, whom I make exors. Wit. Bryan Parker clerk, Audry Muskett (X). Pr. at Bury 19 November 1632.

477. W(R) JOHN SMYTHE (X) of Stradishall, husbandman. 12 August 1632.

Commends soul to God my saviour and redeemer.
I give my son William 40s within a year of my decease. I give my other son George 40s and his sons George 10s and William 5s to be paid at once. I give my daughter Bridget 20s, my grandchild Benjamin Smythe 10s and my grandson Jonas Smythe 10s. I give my son Benjamin my tenement where he now lives on condition he pays his brother George 10s p.a. for 4 years. I give my sister Alice Ruggells 10s. I give my other son Acquilla 5s. Exor: son Benjamin. Wit. Thomas Raye, Richard Wrighte (X). Pr. at Bury 25 November 1632.

478. W(R) JOHN INGOLL (N) of Barton by Bury, husbandman.
25 October 1632.

He bequeathed all his goods and chattels to be equally divided into 4 parts to be bestowed on his 3 sisters and his brother, but his brother to have the best part and all his apparel. He willed the dividing of his goods to be done by his uncle William Ingoll. Wit. George Crakenthorpe clerk, Ambrose Baker. Let. ad. granted to testator's brother William at Bury 20 November 1632.

479. W(R) WALTER BOOLIN (X) of Wicken [Cambs]. 26 October 1632.

Bequeaths soul to god and body to be buried in Wicken churchyard.
I give my house to my wife Anne for life on condition that if she lives until my son Walter is 24 she pays him £5, but if she dies before then this legacy is void. I give Susan Stookes my sister £4 to be paid 1 and 2 years after my decease. The rest of my goods I give to my wife, whom I make sole ex'trix, to pay my debts and see my body brought honestly to the ground. Wit. John Talbut (X), Jonas Goody (X). Pr. at Bury 20 November 1632.

480. W(R) GILBERT SPALDINGE of Hawstead, yeoman. 8 November 1632.

Commends soul to God hoping to be saved by merits of Jesus Christ.
I will that Gilbert my eldest son shall have all my rights and interest in those messuages and land settled upon me in reversion by my father Gilbert Spaldinge, except for 2 pieces of arable, meadow and pasture amounting to 11 acres and called Isabrookes, the reversion of which I bequeath to my youngest son George. I give my wife Susan all my moveable goods and chattels, corn and cattle, out of which she is to pay my son George £40 when he is 24, and 20s to the poor inhabitants of Hawstead a week after my decease. Ex'trix: wife. Wit. John Steward, John Gilly, John Smith. Pr. at Bury 22 November 1632.

481. W(R) ROGER BARDWELL (X) of Bacton, yeoman. 12 November 1632.

Commends soul to God hoping to be saved through Jesus Christ.
I give Frances my wellbeloved wife for her life my messuage in Bacton wherein I dwell with its free and copyhold land totalling 20 acres, and after her decease to my youngest son Roger. I give my wife for the better maintenance and bringing up of my young children, all my household stuff and ready money, and all my milk neat, cattle and horses; she is to pay my legacies. I give my daughter Mary £20 at Michaelmas after my decease. I give my daughter Frances £20 at the following Michaelmas, I give my daughters Elizabeth, Susan and Anne £20 each when 21. Power to distrain and benefit of survivorship. I give my eldest son Thomas a tenement called Sugg in Bacton where he now dwells and 1 acre belonging to it. I also give him £15: £10 within 1 year and £5 within 2 years of my decease, he behaving himself well towards his mother. I give Thomas another £40 to be paid at £5 p.a. by his brother Roger after my wife's decease. Power to distrain. If Thomas dies before his legacies are paid, they are to be divided among his children. If my wife dies before my son Roger is 21, I appoint Stephen Keable and John Daynes of Bacton as his guardians and ask them to hold his land and pay my legacies. Ex'trix: wife. Wit. Stephen Keble, John Daynes, Robert Spencer.

Memorandum: If my son Thomas by the death of Roger inherits the land left to the latter, he is to pay my daughters £10 each at one a year starting with the eldest. I will that my horse mill remains in my house where it now is to the use of he who inherits this house. Wit. Stephen Keble, John Daynes, Robert Spencer. Pr. at Bury 26 November 1632.

482. W(R) RICHARD ELLIGOOD of Tostock, carpenter. 23 October 1632.

Bequeaths soul to God believing to be saved through Jesus Christ.
I give my son Henry £8 when 21. I give my son Robert £8 when 21 and my land in Bury St Edmunds on the north side with houses standing on it, and a little piece of freehold land next to the Abbey yard with a stable on it. I give my son Thomas a tenement in Bury with a yard on its north side extending as far as within 7 feet of the barn, and part of the yard within the high stone wall so far as where the stable stands. I give my daughters Frances, Elizabeth, Mary and Sarah £8 each when 21 or on their marriage days. The residue of my goods and chattels I give to my wife Mary and make her ex'trix. She is to pay my debts and legacies and maintain my daughter Sarah in good and sufficient sort for 4 years after my decease. I hope she will perform my will according to my trust reposed in her and as she will answer before God. Within a month of my decease she is to enter into a bond of £40 with Robert Bally, yeoman of Norton, to perform my will. Supervisor: Robert Bally. If my wife refuses to enter a bond, Robert Bally is to be my exor and have my goods and chattels to divide among my children. Wit. John Bulbrook, Abraham Hinard (X). Pr. at Bury 26 November 1632.

483. W(R) FRANCIS WRIGHT of Walsham le Willows, shoemaker. 23 October 1632.

Commends soul to God expecting through Jesus Christ to enjoy life everlasting.
I give my wife Alice for life my messuage with yard and garden in Walsham where I now live, and after her decease to my kinsman John Wright, son of my brother Roger, joiner of Wymondham [Norfolk]. I also give John after my wife's decease my cupboard in the room called the parlour. I give Mary, daughter of Roger, £30 when 24 or to her brother John if she dies before that time. All the rest of my goods, plate and money I give to my wife Alice. Exors: my wife and my brother-in-law Thomas Smyth. Wit. George Compton, Robert Gleede, John Page. Pr. at Bury 26 November 1632.

484. W(R) NICHOLAS BELL (N) of Bury St Edmunds, gentleman.
24 February 1631/32.

Being moved by his son Anthony to dispose of his estate, he said I give
my wife Kate [meaning Katherine his wife] all that I have in goods, plate
and money for her to dispose of. Wit. Anthony Bell gentleman, his wife
Martha Bell, the wife of Francis Hicks and Francis Hicks himself. Let.
ad. granted at Bury 30 November 1632 to widow.

485. W(R) THOMAS SKEPPER (X) of Stradishall, carpenter.
13 October 1626.

Commends soul to God.
I give Edward French my brother-in-law and Thomas Pratt my kinsman,
carpenter of Stradishall, all my goods and chattels towards payment of my
debts. They are to have the use of my freehold land and tenements in
Stradishall until all my debts are paid. When this has been done, my land
and tenements are to descend to my son Thomas, who must pay to my
daughters Anne and Martha £20 each when 21. Power to distrain.
Forasmuch as I earnestly desire that all my debts be speedily paid, I
authorise Edward French and Thomas Pratt to sell my tenement in
Stradishall wherein Ambrose Frost now dwells with 3 acres adjoining it,
sometime Combes land, and which I purchased from Francis Periman.
Exors: Edward French, Thomas Pratt. Wit. John Raye of Farley in
Stradishall, John Raye of the parsonage. Pr. 5 November 1632. No place
given.

486. W(R) AUGUSTINE COPPEN (X) of Stanstead, carpenter.
23 November 1632.

Bequeaths soul to God my maker and redeemer.
I give Martha my wife for life all my houses and land in Stanstead and
after her decease I bequeath the houses and land I bought of Thomas
Hynes and half an acre meadow which I bought from Mr Wright to my
son Augustine. I give to my daughters Ann and Mary, equally to be
divided between them, the houses, orchard and meadow which I bought
of Henry Griggs and which are partly occupied by me and partly by
Francis Willson junior and Alice Marris widow. All the residue of my
goods, money and debts I give to my wife whom I make sole ex'trix. Wit.
Thomas Negus, Henry Wallford, William Daye. Pr. at Bury December
1632 [no day].

487. W(R) CHRISTIAN SKINNER (X) wife of George Skinner of
Icklingham. 15 September 1632.

Gives spirit into hands of God and Jesus Christ hoping for a joyful
resurrection.
First as touching my husband with whom I coupled myself in fear of God
refusing all other men and by whom I now have 2 sons and 3 daughters,

and although I have no doubt that God will provide for them, yet as God has blessed me with some worldly substance I give to my husband all my houses and 17 acres land in the field in Icklingham for his life, and after his decease to my 2 sons George and James. I give my 3 daughters Ann, Enneter and Ellen 9 acres land in the Peacke field, but if this land cannot be sold for as much as £30 my 2 sons are to make up my daughters' legacies to £10 each. Wit. Henry Craske, Simon Britall. Pr. 3 December 1632. No place given.

488. W(R) ROSE HYNARD (X) of Bury St Edmunds, widow. 10 April 1632.

Commends soul to God.
I give my daughter Barbara Bland widow and my daughter Rose, wife of John Normanton, my lease of my messuage in Brentgovel Street, formerly in the tenure of my late husband Edmund and now occupied by me, Barbara Bland and William Medleditche. I authorise my 2 daughters, whom I make ex'trices, to sell my messuage and use the money to pay the following legacies: £10 to my grandchild Rose Marshall, £15 to my grandchild Anne Pettyward, £20 to my grandchild Anne, wife of Frederick Godfrye, £15 to my grandchild Bridget Pettyward and 40s to my grandson John Bland; all to be paid within a year of my decease. I give my son-in-law John Normanton 40s to make him a ring. I give my cousin Thomas Cheston of London 40s and Richard Cooper of Bury clothier 40s; both to be paid 1 year after my decease. I will that my daughter Barbara Bland shall dwell in that part of my house where she now inhabits for 30 years if she live so long. I give her a feather bed, a feather bolster and my best covering. I give Anne Pettyward the featherbed that was her mother's, a feather bolster, a covering, 2 pairs sheets and a pillow. I give Bridget Pettyward a flockbed, a flock bolster, 2 pairs sheets and a covering. I give Mary Yonges widow, late wife of Thomas Yonges, my gold hoop ring. My late husband in his will gave legacies of £5 to Rose Marshall (by the name of Rose Bland) and of £10 each to Anne and Bridget Pettyward, and my will is that, if the law of the realm allows this sum of £25 to be recovered by my ex'trices, my legacies to these 3 shall be reduced by the sums left to them by my late husband. If Anne and Frederick Godfrye attempt to sue my ex'trices or refuse to release their interest in my messuage within 10 months of my decease, the legacy of £20 to Anne shall be void. The residue of my unbequeathed goods, plate, money, jewels and household stuff I give to my 2 daughters Barbara Bland and Rose Normanton my ex'trices. I give to my grandchildren John Normanton the younger, Thomas, Rose and Elizabeth Normanton 40s each to be paid by my daughter Rose Normanton when they are 24. I give my grandson Andrew Bland my silver wine cup. I give Edward, George, Edmund, Frances, Anne and Mary Bland my grandchildren 40s to be paid by my daughter Barbara Bland when 24. Wit. John Hyll, George Sparrowe (X). Pr. at Bury 3 December 1632.

489. W(R) ISABEL QUARREY (X) of Bacton, widow. 4 November 1632.

Bequeaths soul to God.

I give William my youngest son 20s to be paid by William Margerie, my brother and exor, 1 week after my decease. I give my youngest daughter Frances my white cow calf immediately after my decease. My will is that the interest of all my money, except £3 owed to me by Thomas Bennett of Bacton which is to be used to pay my debts, shall be used to bind forth my son William as an apprentice as soon as my brother William Margerie can place him with a master. The rest of my money is to be equally divided between my 5 children Thomas, William, Mary, Elizabeth and Frances. I give all my goods and chattels to be parted among my 5 children within a fortnight of my decease with the consent of my exor. I will that my 5 children pay the charges of proving my will and of my burial. I make my brother William Margerie sole exor. Wit. John Talbott junior, John Hogger, Thomas Bennett (X). Pr. at Bury 3 December 1632.

490. W(R) EDMUND DENNYE of Hopton, yeoman. 12 November 1632.

Bequeaths soul to God trusting to be saved.

I give Mary my wife for life my messuages and land in Hopton and Palgrave. She must keep the buildings in repair and commit no waste, and bring up and educate Arthur, son of my brother John Dennye in decent and husbandly manner until he is 24. If both my wife and Arthur Dennye are living at the Michaelmas day after the latter is 24, Arthur is then to inherit my messuage and land in Palgrave now occupied by my kinsman John Denny. After my wife's decease Arthur is also to have my other messuages and land in Palgrave except for the land called North Bradelond, which I lately purchased from Thomas Potter and which I bequeath to Thomas son of my brother John. I give £5 each to all the children of my brother Robert, £20 each to my brothers Thomas, George and Nathaniel, £10 each to the daughters of my brother John, £20 to John Palmer the younger, son of my sister the wife of John Thurston and £10 to Mary daughter of Andrew Cullam; all to be paid within a year of my wife's decease. Immediately after the death of my wife I give to Thomas Shrife of Palgrave, William Prentice the elder of Palgrave, John Denny of Palgrave, my kinsman the son of George Denny of Palgrave, my tenant John Spurgen of Brome and Henry Spurgen of Hopton all my messuages and land in Hopton, They, or any 3 or 2 of them, are to sell the messuages and land within a year of my wife's decease and use the money to pay my legacies given above. Any surplus money is to be equally divided between the towns of Hopton and Palgrave to be used as a stock for ever for the benefit of the poor. I give my brother John 40s p.a. for life to be paid by my wife, and after her decease by Arthur Denny. I give Elizabeth Howes my servant £5 within a year, and to Phoebe Darkin 40s when 21. I give my servant Robert Coocke 10s to be paid within a year by my wife. I give the poor of Hopton 30s and the poor of Palgrave 30s to be paid by my wife, whom I make ex'trix. I give her all my moveable goods and cattle to pay my debts. Wit. William Dennye, Thomas Denny (X), Henry Spurgen who wrote will. Pr. at Bury 10 December 1632.

491. W(R) THOMAS PALSEY alias PAWSEY (X) of Hartest, yeoman. 22 November 1632.

Yields soul into hands of God.
I give my eldest son Thomas my dwelling house or cottage in Hartest now occupied by George Albon and the yard it stands in, except for 3 feet in breadth from one end of the barn adjoining the yard to the other end of the barn. I also give him that part of the orchard adjoining the east end of the yard and from the outmost corner of the barn southward straight down to the pale there, a 3 acre close which is an enclosed part of a field called Hiefield in Hartest and lies next to the highway leading from Boxted to Somerton on the south and to the rest of Hiefield to north, and with its west head abutting on a piece of land called Snowes. I give my daughters Elizabeth and Barbara a 6 acre piece of land and pasture, part of Crosse croft in Hartest and divided from the rest of it by a hedge and fences extending from the highway on the west to the land of Hartest rectory on the east, and lying next to the highway from Boxted to Hartest on the north side and next to the rest of Crosse croft on the south side. I give my daughters Dorothy and Margaret the rest of Crosse croft containing 5 acres and lying next to Burnt house field on the south. I give Dorothy £15 and Margaret £10 when 21. I give my eldest daughter Alice £40 to be paid by my exor. I will that my household stuff be equally divided amongst all my children. The rest of my unbequeathed land and goods I give to my son William, whom I make exor. Wit. William Gault (X), George Albone, Thomas Wright, William Segrave. Pr. at Bury 10 December 1632.

492. W(R) ARNOLD SUTHILL (X) of Barnardiston, husbandman. 11 November 1632.

Commits soul to God my maker and redeemer.
I give my eldest son William £12 and my second son John £10 within 1 year of my decease. I give my third son Arnold £10 when 21, and Robert my fourth and youngest son £10 when 21. I give my eldest daughter Elizabeth and my youngest daughter Helen £10 each when 21. I will that my tenement in Barnardiston wherein I now dwell and its land shall be sold by my wife Elizabeth, my brothers-in-law John and Robert Davage and William Scott yeoman of Barnardiston within a year of my decease to pay my legacies. Any money left over I give to my wife. Legatees have benefit of survivorship. All my moveable goods I give to Elizabeth my wife to pay my debts, prove my will and bring my body to Christian burial and I make her sole ex'trix. Wit. Robert Davage (X), William Scott (X), William King. Pr. at Bury 26 December 1632.

493. W(R) MARGARET PETTYCOTE (X) of Stradishall, widow.
8 March 1631/32.

A note of goods given by her. I give my 3 daughters 20s each. I give the 2 daughters of Anthony Pettycote 15s: 10s to Susan and 5s to Margaret. I give 10s to Thomasine daughter of Ambrose Pettycote and 5s to George son of George Sparrowe. These legacies are to be paid by my son Anthony within half a year of my decease. He is to lay out 10s for my funeral expenses. These sums of money to be paid by Anthony and other debts due to me from him I do forgive him. All the rest of my goods I give to be divided among my 3 daughters. Wit. William Pettycote, Ambrose Pettycote. Let. ad. granted 3 December 1632 to testatrix's daughter Alice, wife of George Sparrow. No place given.

494. W(R) ROBERT STUBBINGE (X) of Wicken [Cambs].
4 September 1632.

Gives soul to God.
I give my wife Anne 2 acres arable land in the fields of Fordham, 1 acre in Barrons field and 1 acre in Kenengell field. I give my daughter Anne 40s when 21. All my other goods and chattels I give to my wife whom I make ex'trix. Wit. Robert Grymner, John Jervis (X) senior. Pr. at Newmarket 3 October 1632.

495. W(R) JOHN MURIELL (X) of Wetheringsett, husbandman.
2 December 1631.

Bequeaths soul to God.
I give all my worldly estate to my wife Thomasine and make her ex'trix. Wit. Robert Sheppard, Samuel Sheppard (X). Pr. at Bury 14 December 1632.

496. W(R) THOMAS WYNTER (N) of Bury St Edmunds. 28 November 1632.

He gave his wife Anna his goods and chattels. Wit. John Hunt, Margaret wife of Richard Strangham. Let. ad. granted 14 December 1632 to widow. No place given.

497. W(R) AMBROSE BRIDON senior of Bury St Edmunds, grocer.
22 January 1630/31.

Bequeaths soul to God being assured to be freed from all my sins through merits of Jesus Christ.
I give to the poor of St James's parish 40s. I give my son Henry £60 within 2 years, and I also forgive him the £40 he owes me by bond. I give my son Jasper all my houses and grounds on the market hill in Cambridge, which I had by gift of my deceased cousin William Bridon of

208

Cambridge, master of arts. I also give Jasper £200 within 2 years. I give my wife Ann for ever my houses and grounds in Bury next to the school hall, which I bought from Thomas Simonds and Thomas West of Bury. I also give my wife my free and copyhold houses and grounds in Fornham St Genevieve, which I bought from Henry Keene gentleman of Brandon Ferry, for her life and after her decease to my son Jasper. I give Edward Page clothier one of my clocks at the discretion of my ex'trix. I give Francis Asty the elder a ring of 10s price. The rest of my goods, bonds, bills, plate and money I give to my wife and make her ex'trix. Wit. Edmund Asty, John Medows. Pr. at Bury 20 December 1632.

498. W(R) LAWRENCE PAGE of Rattlesden. 14 December 1632.

Commends soul to God desiring him to receive me into his heavenly kingdom.
I give old Mr Devereux parson of Rattlesden 10s. I give Mr Chamberlayne of Hunston 10s. I give the poor of Rattlesden 20s and the poor of Hunston 5s. I give my son John all my land both free and copyhold, and he must pay my wife Anne quarterly £18 p.a. Power to distrain. If my wife demands any thirds, this gift shall be void. I give my youngest daughter Elizabeth £200 to be paid the Michaelmas after my decease. I give my daughter Mary Fisher £10 within 2 years, and her son John £10 when 21. The residue of my goods and chattels I give to my son John and make him exor. Wit. Jonathan Jordan, Thomasine Lister. Pr. at Bury 25 December 1632.

499. W(R) PAUL PAGE of Ixworth Thorpe, yeoman. 2 December 1632.

Commends soul to God trusting to have sins pardoned through Jesus Christ and hoping for a joyful resurrection to eternal life.
I give my wife Helen until my son Paul is 21 my tenement and land in Icklingham, now occupied by Henry Craske the younger, except for a piece of arable land lying at New Cross. Paul is to inherit this property after he is 21 or after my wife's remarriage or death whichever happens first. Paul must pay my wife £3 p.a. I give my son Thomas after my wife's decease the tenement in Icklingham that is my wife's jointure, and half an acre of land at Church Lanes end in the occupation of Thomas Talbot and abutting to the west on Church Way. All my goods and chattels are to be sold for the best price within a year of my decease by my wife and supervisors, but my wife is to have for her use £20 of goods at her choice. The money from the sale of my goods I entrust to my supervisors to divide between my 4 youngest children Thomas, Anne, Dorothy and Elizabeth when 21 or married. Until these children are 21 my supervisors are to use their money either to purchase land for them or to put it out. Benefit of survivorship. I give to the poorest people of Icklingham 10s, and to the poor of Thorpe next Ixworth 3s 4d to be paid within a month of my decease by my ex'trix to the churchwardens and overseers of the poor and to be distributed by the minister of each parish. Ex'trix: wife.

Supervisors: my loving cousins William and Edmund Craske of Bardwell. My father in his will left my mother a bequest of 6 combs rye and 6 combs barley to be given to her every year by me. My will is that my wife shall pay these 12 combs of corn to my mother as long as she holds the tenement and land given to my son Paul, who himself must fulfil this legacy after he inherits this property. My debts are to be paid by my ex'trix out of the money raised by the sale of my goods before my 4 youngest children's portions are set out. Wit. William Craske, Henry Craske (X), Thomas Legat, Ralph Whitney. Pr. at Bury 24 December 1632.

500. W(R) ROBERT SYMONDES (X) of Langham, tanner.
14 December 1632.

Bequeaths soul to Jesus Christ through whom I am sure of my salvation.
I bequeath to my wife Margaret for life a pasture close in Langham called the Layd close, which I had by gift of William Munnings of Bury St Edmunds, maltster. She must pay my son George 20s p.a. in my now dwelling house. After her decease I give this close to my son George on condition he pays my daughter Joan £30 within 2 years of my decease. If he refuses to do so, the 20s p.a. left to him and the close are to go to my daughter Joan. I give Joan after my wife's decease a bed in the hall complete as it stands, a cupboard in the hall, a kettle containing 2 pailfuls, a brass pot, and a hutch in the lower chamber with its contents. All the rest of my moveables, bills, bonds and ready money I give to my wife. I give my grandchild Robert Sapster £20 when 27; at age of 24 he is to be paid the interest on this sum. I make my son George sole exor and he must enter into a bond of £40 with William Browne and Thomas Syer the younger of Langham to pay the £20 to Robert Sapster and to prove my will. If he refuses to do this within 14 days of my decease I make my wife ex'trix. Wit. Thomas Syer senior (X), William Browne, Thomas Syer junior. Pr. at Bury 28 December 1632.

501. W(R) JOHN HUNT (X) of Burwell [Cambs]. 19 November 1632.

Bequeaths soul to God.
I will that my house in North Street be sold within 6 months of my decease and the money divided between my sons Jarrett and John. I give my son Jarrett my cow known by the name of Old Wilson. I give my son John my black horse. I give my sons William and Robert £15 each within 12 months of my decease. I give my son Henry £20 within 12 months. I give all the rest of my moveables to my wife Ellen and son Robert, who are my exors. If they do not agree about the performance of my will my son Robert is to pay my wife £15 and she shall have nothing more to do with my goods. I make John Casbon and Stephen Izatson supervisors, asking them to sell my house for my sons Jarrett and John, and I give them 40s for their pains. The legacies given to my sons Henry and William are to be paid by my exors to the supervisors of my will, who are

210

to put the money out until my sons are 21. If my son Henry has a mind to be put forth as an apprentice, my supervisors are to pay his master out of his legacy. I have surrendered to the use of my will my copyhold messuage into the hands of John Casbon and in the presence of Stephen Izatson, tenants of the manor. Wit. John Casburne, Stephen Izatsone, Richard Iveson. Pr. at Burwell 2 January 1632/33.

502. W(R) JOHN HUBBARD the elder of Great Waldingfield, yeoman. 27 June 1632.

Commends soul to God trusting to be saved by merits of Jesus Christ.
I give my daughter Sarah £100 and my daughter Ann £100, both to be paid within a year of my decease. I give my daughter Mary £100 when 21. I give my son William 20s. I give my son Timothy £200 when 21. If any of my children die before their legacies are paid they are to go to their children if they have any, and if not my wife is to have these legacies towards bringing up my children and paying my other legacies. I give the poor of Great Waldingfield £4, 40s to be paid 2 days after my decease and 40s 2 years later. I give my cousins Thomas and William Cason 20s each. I give 20s each to the children of my cousin Ann Cason. I give my sister Joan Lumley 40s, and 20s within 2 years to each of my cousins Judith Sudburie, Lydia Berriffe, Marian Whitehead, Ann Foster and Amy [blank in MS]. All these cousins are the children of my brothers or sisters. I give my wife Joan for life my messuage in Great Waldingfield called Castlins with yard, orchard and moat, and now occupied by Joan Lumley widow, my close called the Netherlay, a piece of arable called the Middlelay and a piece called the Upperley now doled out for my son John and conveyed to him. This land totals 12½ acres and is occupied by Thomas Lumley. I also give Joan my wife a 3 acre piece of the Logge meadow now doled for John and conveyed to him, and occupied by Thomas Lumley, 9½ acres arable in Farm field in my occupation, and a 1½ acre piece of pasture ground called the farm yard lying in the manner of a harp with a barn built on it and occupied by me. I also give my wife as her dower my lease of the manor of Brampton Hall in Great Waldingfield, which I hold from Sir Percivall Hart. My wife is to bring up my children until they receive their legacies. I bequeath to my son John 10s and to my daughter Hannah Browne 10s. I give my daughter Eunice Lovell £5, and my daughter Elizabeth Peachie 10s. I bequeath to my daughter Joan Hamond 10s. I give my loving and faithful friend Mr Richard Peachie £3 and to Mr Edward Elliston 20s within a year of my death. My ex'trix is to pay my legacies, carefully bring up and maintain my son William during her life, discharge my funeral charges and carefully pay my debts. To enable her to do this, I bequeath her all my money, plate, bonds, goods and chattels, and I give her full power to sell within 3 years of my decease my messuage and land as follows: my capital messuage called Belchame with barns, stables, yards, orchards, garden, dove house, drying close, taynter close, a field called Hempland and one adjoining called Great Hempland containing together 11 acres. Also I

211

give her those copyhold crofts called Shadow crofts containing 9 acres, a 9 acre piece of ground called the Newbottom, 2 adjoining arable fields called Great Okefields and containing 14 acres, and that part of the Overlaye not conveyed to my son John and containing 2½ acres, and the 8 acres of Logge meadow not conveyed to John. I give £10 each when 21 to Sarah, Priscilla and Dorothy, daughters of my daughter Eunice Lovell. If my wife marries again, she is to enter into a bond approved of by my supervisors to perform my will. Supervisors: Mr Richard Peachie and Mr Edward Elliston, clerks, desiring them to aid my ex'trix with their best advice according to my trust reposed in them. Wit. Simon Crow, John Pinchbecke, John Westop (X). Pr. at Bury 7 January 1632/33.

503. W(R) HENRY MASON (X) of Exning. 2 November 1631.

Bequeaths soul to God. To be buried in Exning churchyard.
I give my wife Alice for life the bedstead, bed and bedding in the chamber wherein I lie and she is to have this chamber, being in my house next to the street, during her life. I give her 1 comb each of wheat, rye and malt to be given to her yearly by my exor when she demands it. I have sold my son William my freehold house with some land in Exning for £100 on condition he leaves it to his son William. The £100 is to be paid as follows: £20 to my wife Alice within a year of my decease, £20 to my son Henry at 20 nobles a year, on condition he gives William a release of all his interest in this house and land, and £60 to my son Edward in 3 annual instalments starting 3 years after my decease. Power to distrain. I give my daughter Audrey £13 6s 8d within 2 years. I give 20s each to be paid within a month of my decease to my daughters Frances, Anne, Margaret and Gillian, and to Richard Frost and Henry Branch. I give my son William my lease of 5½ acres arable, and all my cattle and goods. I make him sole exor. Wit. Thomas Hogg (X), John Curtis minister. Pr. at Bury 14 January 1632/33.

504. W(R) THOMAS TAWNYE (X) of Rougham, shepherd. 11 February 1631/32.

Bequeaths soul to God trusting that my sins are pardoned by merits of Jesus Christ. To be buried in Rougham churchyard.
I give my son Thomas £20 when 21, and in the meantime he is to have the profit of it, namely 16 pence in every pound. I give my son John £15 when 21 and he is to have the profit at 16 pence in the pound. I give my 2 daughters Frances and Martha £15 each for their education and maintenance, and what can be spared shall paid to them by my faithful exor on the day of their marriage or when 21. I give my wife Susan all the goods, money and household stuff she brought unto me at our late marriage, and I give her £5. Exor: my brother-in-law Thomas Thomson of Barrow to whom I give my unbequeathed goods and chattels to pay my debts.

Children have benefit of survivorship. If Thomas Thomson refuses to take on the executorship, I make my wife ex'trix and give her whatever he should have had. Wit. Zachary Catlin, vicar of Thurston, Thomas Briant. Pr. at Bury to Thomas Thomson 14 January 1632/33.

505. W(R) JOHN COLLINE (X) of Langham, husbandman.
31 December 1632.

Bequeaths soul to Jesus Christ by whose death and passion I am sure of salvation.
I give my sister Margaret, wife of James Wilyams of Elmswell, shead-maker, 6d a week to be paid to her by my exor at her dwelling house. I give for life to my nephew Robert Colline of Elmswell, husbandman, my messuage in Langham wherein William Carpenter dwells with barn, yard, garden, orchard and land adjoining the messuage. After his death I give all this to his son Robert and his heirs. I make my nephew Robert Colline exor and give him all my bonds, bills and money. He is to bury me in a decent and comely manner, and prove my will. Wit. Mary Carpenter (X), Thomas Syer junior. Pr. at Bury 17 January 1632/33.

506. W(R) GILBERT SOMERTON, governor of the hospital of the Holy and Blessed Trinity of the foundation of Sir William Cordell in Long Melford. 3 May 1630.

For good causes I have granted to my trusty and wellbeloved friends and familiar acquaintances John Barker clothier and William Creswell cloth worker, both of Melford, all my goods and chattels which are specified in an attached schedule. I do this in special trust and confidence that they will sell my goods to the best advantage and, after my funeral and other expenses including the ringers have been paid, distribute the money together with any debts due to me among the poorest people living on Melford Green, Westgate Street and High Street in Melford as they shall best see need. No witnesses. Pr. 18 January 1632/33. No place given.
The schedule of Gilbert Somerton's goods. 'A noate made by me Gilbart Somerton Governor the Third daye of Maye 1630 of all the howshold stuff in my chamber that is my owne viz Inprimis an olde fetherbed with bolster & pillowe, a livery Cubbard and a litle Table with a huch in it And one other Table like a stole And one desk, certaine singeng Bookes, fower chestes, a litle box of smale lynen And one greate box with lock and keay to it, Twoe Chaires excepting one other chaire that stand by the bedside that belongeth to the howse, And one olde Table being 2 planck & 2 Tressells under it, And six cushins, certaine glasses & boxes standing on the window, my Raper & dagger, twoe botles hanging by the walesid, And one litle pott covered with silver And a pewter pott standing on the cubard, A paire of Cobirons, fire pane & belowes, Twoe large Trenchers, a portmantle & a hedging hoke, my Sadle & bridle, my

213

Boottes and Shoes that are left after me, Twoe hattes, my Cloke and my horsmans cloke, 1 boke called Bollingers deceade And 2 benches. By me Gilbert Somerton.

What money ther shall arise out of my Stock And my paye lett be to my Supervisors herein named to bestowe on my Buriall. And they to have 5s. each of them John Barker and William Creswell. Gilbart Somerton.'

507. W(R) MARY FITCH late of Gipping. 27 September 1632.

Commends soul to God in perfect hope that he will be pleased to accept me, not for any good or holiness of mine own, but for righteousness of my saviour Jesus Christ.

I give all my goods and chattels to my mother Anne Fitch widow in part of a recompense of the great pains, care and costs which she has taken with me in my long and troublesome sickness. I make my mother ex'trix. Wit. John Tyrell, Jane Tyrell, Alice Miller (X). Pr. at Bury 25 January 1632/33.

508. W(R) JOHN FROST the elder of Norton, yeoman. 17 May 1631.

Commends soul to three persons of Trinity in hope of a joyful resurrection to stand before my glorious bridegroom with the rest of the saints my companions both to be judged and to judge the world so to ascend into the kingdom of glory.

I give to my grandchild Mary Frost the whole sum contained in an obligation made to me by her father and dated 1 November 1626. I give Robert Marlton, my sister's son, my best hood, doublet and one of my coats in full satisfaction of the 20s assured to him by my father to be paid on his marriage day. My ex'trix is to pay my niece Martha Marlton on her marriage the 20s assured to her by my father. I give 5s to the poor of Norton and 5s to the poor of Stratford to be distributed by the overseers of the poor. I give all my grandchildren a small remembrance of 10s apiece, and the like sum to my great grandchildren now living to be paid by my ex'trix as she shall think fitting. My son John has in his hands both by gifts and borrowing many sums without security, which stand in my book, as well as cows, horses and household stuff, and my will is that my ex'trix shall receive from him no more than £40 with my tapestry coverlet and my pewter now in his hands. All the rest I give to John for ever. All the rest of my goods, not in John's hands, I give to Anne my beloved wife. I also give her for life, and after her decease to my son John, my house and land in Stratford. I make my wife sole ex'trix in the hope she will do all things contained in my will without deceit or fraud. I appoint my loving cousin Thomas Frost of Hunston Hall as supervisor to aid my wife, hoping that he will be well pleased to do the same, and I give him 5s for his pains. No witnesses. John Frost wrote his will with his own hand. Pr. at Bury 28 January 1632/33.

509. W(R) ROBERT OFFWOOD (X) of Haughley, grocer.
29 December 1632.

Bequeaths soul to God believing to have remission of sins and everlasting life through Jesus Christ.
I give £40 to William Syer, my sister's son, when 24, and to his sisters Ann and Elizabeth £15 each when 21. Benefit of survivorship. My sister shall have the profit of the above sums until the legacies are due to be paid, and if all 3 of her children die she is to have the money given to them. I give Mary Offwood, my brother's daughter, £5 to be paid within 2 months of my decease. I give the poor of Haughley 10s. Exors: my wellbeloved friends Thomas Syer and Thomas Prior, both of Haughley, and I give them 10s each. They are to pay my debts and legacies, and see my body decently buried. The rest of my moveable goods and debts I give to my sister Elizabeth Syer. Within 2 months of my decease my exors are to become bound for the performance of my will in the sum of £100 to such persons as my supervisor shall appoint. If exors refuse to do this, I appoint Robert Offwood of Parham and Thomas Offwood junior of Gislingham as my exors. Supervisor: Robert Newman of Haughley, whom I entreat to see my will performed. Wit. Robert Fiske, William Thorowgood who wrote will. Pr. 8 January 1632/33 to 2 first named exors and Thomas Offwood. No place given.

510. W(R) ANDREW GILLMAN (X) of Stanton, husbandman.
31 March 1631.

Commends soul to God.
I give my wife Joan all my moveable goods for her life, and then to my daughter Katherine, whom I make sole ex'trix. Wit. John Oger alias Harper (X), Robert Fuller. Pr. at Bury 4 February 1632/33.

511. W(R) KATHERINE KEBLE (X) of Old Newton, widow.
17 November 1632.

Commits soul to God being assured of pardon of sins through Jesus Christ.
In satisfaction of a promise made to my son-in-law John Marshall when he married my daughter Elizabeth, I bequeath them £10 to be paid within a year of my decease. This sum is now in the hands of John Fydler of Newton. I give my son Richard a great brass kettle and a moulding trough. I give my daughter Barbara all my bonds, bills and debts due to me, all my linen and apparel, and a bullock which she already has in part in consideration of some money given by her father. I give my daughter Katherine a cow now in the possession of John Fydler on condition she enters into a bond with Thomas Keble gentleman of Old Newton to pay 6d a week to the inhabitants of Mendlesham, according to an order made by the Justices of the Peace. If my son John will pay this weekly sum or make a composition for it, he is to have the cow left to Katherine. I give

215

Katherine part of the rest of my cattle, and to my son John the residue of my household stuff and the other part of my unbequeathed cattle. Ex'trix: daughter Katherine. Wit. Edmund Heywarde, Elizabeth Wolfe (X). Pr. at Bury 4 February 1632/33.

512. W(R) MIRABEL SYER (X) of Stowmarket, widow. 15 October 1630.

Bequeaths soul to God believing to have salvation through Jesus Christ. To be buried in Stowmarket churchyard.
I give my god-daughter Mirabel Burrowe 10s when 21, and 5s each within a year of my decease to the other 4 of Robert Burrowe's children now at home with him: George, Samuel, Blithe and Margaret. I give Anne and Elizabeth Tuffielde 5s each within a year. I give Richard Burrowe 5s within a year of my death. All the rest of my goods and chattels I give to my nephew Robert Thurwood, who is to pay out of them my debts, legacies and funeral charges, and I make him exor. I give and bequeath more to John and Mary Thurwood £5 each when 21. Wit. Richard Draper and me Philip Barne. Pr. at Bury 4 February 1632/33.

513. W(R) GEORGE AVIS (N) of Fornham All Saints. Beginning of August 1632.

He made his will by word of mouth by me John Frost, parson of Fornham St Genevieve, going to visit him when sick and asking if he had made his will. He answered that he gave his wife all (meaning all his goods and chattels) for I mean to give nothing away from her. Wit. John Frost, Joan wife of Richard Horner. Let. ad. granted to widow Sarah 13 February 1632/33. No place given.

514. W(R) WILLIAM SOAME (X) the elder of Hundon, gentleman. 21 March 1631/32.

Knowing my years past to be many and all men to be mortal I make my will, commending my soul to God.
I give £5 to the poor of Hundon to be paid by my exors as follows: 40s to be distributed to 80 of the poorer sort immediately after my burial, and 20s to 40 of the poor on the 3 Ash Wednesdays after my decease. I give my wife Susan for life my 2 houses in Hundon called Myllions, late occupied by Robert Norman, and the Taynter Yard in which William Wheeler now dwells. I also give her my tenement in Cowlinge called Squiers croft with Penns pightle and now occupied by Henry Lanham. After her decease I give my tenements in Hundon and Cowlinge, except Taynter Yard, to my youngest daughter Susan. I also give her immediately after my death my free and copyhold land and tenement in Hundon called Sealandes, Babers, Little Watles and Bovlies, but my wife shall have the use of this land, until Susan is 16, for her education and

maintenance. If my daughter Susan dies before she is 21, my wife is to have all the property left to her for her life, and then it is to go to 4 of my grandchildren: William, William, John and Fletcher sons of my sons Thomas and William. After the death of my wife I give my tenement Taynter Yard to my daughter Susan, and if she has no heir to my son-in-law Thomas Gent. These gifts to my wife Susan are in consideration of her dower and are made on condition that within 3 months of my decease she shall give a release of all her rights in my property to my sons Thomas and William and my daughter Susan. If she refuses to do this my son William and daughter Susan are to hold land left to her until she agrees to make the above releases. If the moveable goods given below for the payment of my debts and legacies are not sufficient, my tenement in Church Street Hundon, occupied by William Pigg, is to be sold by my exors and supervisor within 6 months of my decease. Any money left over from this sale is to be for the benefit of my daughter Margaret, wife of Richard Scryven gentleman of Stradishall [spelt Stradgewell in MS]. If my tenement in Church Street does not have to be sold, my wife is to have it for life and my daughter Susan after her decease, or my 4 grandsons if she has no heirs. I give my daughters Jane Drewery and Margaret Scryven £5 each, and my sons Thomas and William 20s each all to be paid within a year. I give my grandchildren living at the time of my decease 12 pence each when 16. I give my daughters-in-law Ann and Ann 10s each within a year. I give Anthony Thompson, minister of Hundon, 10s to preach a sermon at my burial. All my other goods, debts, plate and money I give to my wife Susan and my daughter Susan to pay my debts and legacies, and I make them ex'trices. Supervisor: Sir William Soame of Little Thurlow, and I give him for his pains the best living thing I shall have at the time of my death at his choice. Wit. Anthony Thompson, William Taylor, William King. Pr. at Clare 4 October 1632.

515. W(R) JOSEPH SMITH (X) of Soham [Cambs], yeoman.
11 November 1632.

Bequeaths soul to God trusting in the merits of Jesus Christ for redemption. To be buried in sanctuary of parish church of Soham.
I give my eldest son Joseph 10s when 21, and £10 each when 21 to my sons Andrew, Jeremy, John, Mark and Luke. I give my daughter Anne £5 when 21, and my best bed standing in the parlour with all its furniture after her mother's decease. Children have benefit of survivorship. All the rest of my goods and chattels I give to my wife Anne to pay my debts and legacies and towards bringing up my children, and I make her sole ex'trix. Wit. Richard Pechey, Thomas Cheavely senior, James Punge and me Robert Carlton the writer of this will. Pr. at Bury 18 December 1632.

516. W(R) EDMUND HUNT (X) of Bury St Edmunds, yeoman. 13 November 1632.

Bequeaths soul to God my maker and Jesus Christ my redeemer.
I bequeath my house wherein I now dwell with yard, orchard and garden to my wife Abigail for life, and then to be sold within a year of her decease and the money divided among my children. If one of my children refuses to agree to sell my house, the others are to do so and he or she that refuses is to have no share of the money. I make my wife sole ex'trix to take my goods and chattels and pay my debts. Wit. John Hunt, John Peren, Thomas Clough. Pr. at Bury 25 January 1632/33.

517. W(R) JOHN HALL (X) of Bury St Edmunds, husbandman. 21 August 1632.

Bequeaths soul to God trusting in Jesus Christ for salvation.
I give my brother Abraham Hall £5 within 6 months of my decease. I give 30s each to his 2 daughters when 18. Benefit of survivorship. I give my brothers John and Thomas £8 each within 6 months. I give my sister Mary, wife of [blank in MS] Wyette, £5 and my sisters Ann and Alice £5 each, all to be paid within 6 months. My exor is to pay my mother 40s p.a. All the rest of my goods and money I give to my brother William Hall to perform my will and I make him exor. Wit. Alexander Gent, Henry Clarke. Pr. at Hundon 5 December 1632.

518. W(R) ROBERT BRIGHTALL (X) of Bury St Edmunds. 3 January 1632/33.

Commends soul to God hoping to be made partaker of life everlasting through Jesus Christ.
I give my wife Mary for life, as long as she remains unmarried, all my copyhold land and tenements held of the manors of Ashfield Hall and Ixworth Hall, and after her decease to my son Henry. I give my daughters Martha and Mary £10 each to be paid by my wife out of the revenues of my land when they reach 21. Power to distrain and benefit of survivorship. If both daughters die before they are 21, my son Henry is to have their legacies. All the rest of my goods, my debts and legacies being paid, I give to my wife Mary whom I make ex'trix. Wit. John White, John Rose (X) Pr. at Bury 28 January 1632/33.

519. W(R) THOMAS POOLE of Combs, yeoman. 1 March 1631/32.

Commits soul to God believing to have eternal life through Jesus Christ.
I give Elizabeth my beloved wife the use of my free and copyhold lands and buildings, and of all my cows until the Michaelmas after my decease. I give my wife for life my parlour and parlour chamber with free access, the use of the copper and oven in the backhouse for her brewing and baking, of the pump for water, half the fruit every year, and a load of

firewood to be laid in the yard for her use every year by my son Thomas. I give my wife an annuity of £10 to be paid quarterly at my dwelling house. Power to distrain. I give my daughter Elizabeth £40 to be paid over 4 years after the decease of my wife. Power to distrain. I give my son Thomas all my lands and tenements, half of my corn growing at the time of my decease, he paying half the charge of reaping and inning it, and paying half the rent, due at Michaelmas after my death, for the lands which I hire of the parishes of Harleston and Haughley. I give Thomas 2 of my cows to be given to him by my ex'trix at Michaelmas after my decease. I give him all the household stuff that usually stands in the hall, a featherbed and a flockbed with the bedstead in the little chamber and 2 pairs sheets. I give him all the shelves about the house, the little brass pot, 2 beer vessels, the copper, the great brewing tub, the cheese press, cheese vats and the lead in the dairy. I give my daughter Elizabeth my cow called Besse to be given to her at Michaelmas after my death. I also give her a trundle bedstead in the parlour with a flockbed and the furniture belonging to it. The rest of my goods I give to my wife and make her ex'trix. Wit. Thomas Sothebie, John Pinswine. Pr. at Bury 7 January 1632/33.

520. W(R) MARTHA EVERERD (X) of Hawkedon, widow. 30 October 1625.

Bequeaths soul to God my maker and redeemer.
I give my sons Richard and Ambrose 5s each, and my daughters Elizabeth, Martha and Dorothy 5s each, all to be paid within one month of my decease. I give Mary Ruse my grandchild a bed and bedstead as it stands furnished in the little chamber. All the rest of my goods and chattels I give to my daughter Sarah to pay my debts and perform my will, and I make her ex'trix. Wit. Nathaniel Raye, Toby Hamond, Ambrose Chapman clerk. Pr. at Bury 18 February 1632/33.

521. W(R) ELIAS STONHAM (X) of Preston, yeoman. 19 January 1632/33.

Bequeaths soul to God hoping to be saved through Jesus Christ.
I give 5s to the poor of Preston to be distributed by my exor where he shall see most need. I give towards the leading of the parish church of Preston 5s to be paid to the churchwardens within a year of my decease. I bequeath my copyhold tenement in Lawshall called Caldewells, wherein Mother Symon now dwells, with 8 or 9 acres land now occupied by William Crycke, to my wife Anne for life and then to my daughter Anne Kembolde. I give my son Elias a tenement newly erected in Lawshall with 13 acres land called Caldwells and now in the tenurs of William Crycke. I give my wife the best bed I have furnished and which she can choose, the best kettle and posnet, a warming pan, a hutch, a gridiron, a pair tongs, a fire pan and a pair bellows. I give my nephew John Wrighte, my late

servant, 6s 8d. I give my daughter Anne Kembolde 40 marks to be paid by my exor within 2 years. All my goods and chattels I give to my son Elias to perform my will, and I make him exor. Wit. Robert Ryece, Robert Goymer (X), Jeffery Beare (X). Pr. at Bury 14 February 1632/33.

522. W(R) AGNES AVIS (X) of Stowmarket, widow. 3 December 1632.

Commends soul to God hoping through Jesus Christ to be made partaker of life everlasting.

I give my brother Richard Lucas 10s to be paid within 1 week of my decease, and 10s half yearly until he has received £5. If he dies before legacy has been fully paid, my sister Rose, wife of William Lowe, is to have the residue of it or, if she is not living, her children. I give my brother Richard the following goods and household stuff for life, that is my 2 flockbeds whereon I lie, 2 coverlets on the same bed, 2 flock bolsters and a pillow, 2 pairs sheets, a little table, a form, a hutch, 2 kettles and a pewter platter. After Richard's decease my sister Rose or her children are to have these goods. I give 20s each to John and Mary and 10s to Thomas, children of my brother-in-law William Lowe. I give William and Anthony Lowe 5s each 6 months after my decease. I give Anne, daughter of William Lowe, my best bedstead, my greatest table, a hutch and 2 pewter dishes immediately after my decease. I give Thomas Lowe an old flockbed, a bolster and a blanket. I give Robert Cuttinge one old flockbed. I give Thomas Avis my son-in-law 30s within 6 weeks of my death. He stands bound to me in the sum of £6 for payment to me of £3 at a day now past; if he does not pay my exor this £3 within 1 month of my decease this gift to him is void. I give Thomas Avis a cupboard, a kettle, 2 pewter dishes and a skillet which were his father's and my late husband's. I also give him a bolting hutch, a pillow and a leather bottle. All the rest of my goods, after debts and funeral charges and 10s to my exor have been paid, I give to my sister Rose, wife of William Lowe. Exor: my very good friend William Emsden hoping that he will see my body decently buried. Wit John Shene, John Goddard. Pr. at Bury 11 February 1632/33.

523. W(R) CHRISTOPHER RUSHBROOKE (N) of Woolpit, husbandman. 4 or 5 February 1632/33.

He gave his wife Mary for life all his houses and land, goods and chattels, and after her decease to be at her disposing. Wit Elizabeth Rushbrooke, Anne Bowe and Mary Rushbrooke the testator's wife. Let. ad. granted to widow 11 February 1632/33. No place given.

524. W(R) JOAN FORNHAM (N) of Rougham, widow. 17 January 1632/33.

First she gave Anthony Fornham her son a posted bedstead ready furnished, a trundle bedstead with a flockbed, a bolster, a pillow, a blanket and 3 sheets, a framed table, a joined form, a chair, 2 buffet stools, 2 hutches, 2 tubs, 2 barrels, a brass pot, a great kettle and a little one, 4 great pewter platters, a brazen candlestick, a pillowbeere, a diaper table napkin, 2 kerchiefs and all his father's working tools. All the residue of her goods she gave to Dorothy her daughter. She gave her son-in-law Ralph Ingoll 1s to be paid within a month of her decease. Exors: her children Anthony and Dorothy. Wit. John Tilden gentleman, John Elmer, John Baker. Let. ad granted 11 February 1632/33. No place given.

525. W(R) FRANCIS BROWNE (N) of Rattlesden. 16 December 1632.

He gave and bequeathed to Elizabeth his wife all his goods and chattels; she to pay his debts. Wit. Adam Ranson (X), Thomas Scotte. Let. ad. granted to widow 21 January 1632/33. No place given.

526. W(R) THOMAS TALBUT (X) of Barton Mills, shepherd. 26 January 1633 [sic].

Bequeaths soul to God that gave it.
I give my daughters Gatterwode and Anne £7 each when 21 or on marriage day. Benefit of survivorship. I give my son Richard £3 when 21. My ex'trix is to pay my legacies. Ex'trix; wife Philippa. Wit. John Godfrey, Abraham Bilney. Pr. at Bury 26 February 1632/33.

527. W(R) EDWARD SILLETT of Great Horringer, yeoman. 13 December 1632.

Commends soul to God hoping to obtain pardon of sins and everlasting life through Jesus Christ.
I give my son Thomas my copyhold tenement in Great Horningsheath called Sefferies with the edifices and land, a copyhold close called Ashmantuft and all my copyhold land lying in the fields of Great Horningsheagh. He must pay my daughter Bridget, wife of John Sparke, £50 at £10 p.a. starting 3 years after my decease; my daughter Margaret £100 within 7 years and 10s every 6 months for 2 years; and £100 to my daughter Mary at £10 p.a. starting 7 years after my decease, and until then £5 p.a. as interest on the £100. Power to distrain. I give my son John my copyhold close in Great Horringer called Amlis Taylers and Jollifers with east end abutting on Sheep Green, on condition he pays £100 to my daughter Elizabeth when 21; until then the annual profits of this close are to be shared between them. Power to distrain. I give my kinsmen Philip and Sebastian Sillett 20s each to be paid by my sons within a year. I give Paul Adhams 5s to be paid by my 4 daughters within a year. Ex'trices: my

daughters Bridget Sparke and Margaret Sillett. Supervisor: Robert Cotton of Horringer. Wit. Robert Cotton, Richard Baker. Pr. at Bury 12 February 1632/33.

528. W(R) WILLIAM SAMPSON (X) of Newmarket, glover. 6 July 1632.

Gives soul to God. To be buried in churchyard of parish of Newmarket.
On 26 September 1629 I bought from William Bathorne, glover, and Susan Bathorne, widow, both of Bury St Edmunds, a messuage in Mustowe Street near the Eastgate with its shops, cellars and yards, and half a well with free access to draw water. I give my wife Alice for life, and after her death to my daughter Anne, the parlour, parlour chamber and garret over it, being the west end of the messuage, with passage from thence into the yard and to the house of easement and the well. I give my son William the other part of the messuage: the hall, hall chamber, buttery, shop and a chamber beyond that on the east end of the messuage with a gallery, and access to the yard and wood house, house of easement and for drawing water. If my son Nicholas is still living, William is to pay him 20s p.a. starting the year after the decease of Susan Bathorne, to whom an annuity of 40s is paid out of the messuage. During her life William is not to enter upon nor take rent for that part of the messuage bequeathed to him, but my wife Alice is to receive the rent and pay the annuity. She is also to pay 5s p.a. to William towards the repair of his part of the messuage. This messuage is leased for a term of years to William Bathorne; if Susan Bathorne dies before the end of the lease, 30s rent p.a. is to be paid to my wife and 40s to my son William. I give my son Nicholas if he be living and come over into England again 40s, and if he come not again I give it to my exor. I give my son William a bell salt cellar of silver and gilt, my table almost 5 yards long, my posted chair, a long form 2 yards in length and 20s within half a year of my decease. I give my daughter Anne a flockbed, bolster, pillow, pair sheets, a blanket, a covering and a little hutch. All the rest of my moveable goods I give to my wife whom I appoint my true and faithful sole ex'trix. Wit. John Chapman, Thomas Cooke, Robert Stannard. Pr. at Bury 18 February 1632/33.

529. W(R) JOHN TALBOTT (X) of Wicken [Cambs], yeoman. 14 January 1630/31.

Gives soul to God and believes to be saved by Jesus Christ.
I give my only daughter Anne £600 when 21 or within 2 years of her marriage, and £20 p.a. from the age of 14 to age of 21. I also give her my posted bed where now I lie with featherbed, 2 bolsters, 2 pillows, a blanket and a covering, 2 pairs sheets and the bed curtains, and two 2-year old heifers, 1 brown and 1 yellow. I give Mary my wife for life 3 messuages with land in Wicken held of the manor of Wicken, and after her decease to my daughter Anne, but if she dies without heirs I leave

them to my nephew John Russeles. I give him £5 within a year of my decease. I give 20s each within 2 years to Edward and Roger Crow, Alice Flecher, Margaret Pigeon and the wife of John Hargrave; and 20s each within 3 years to Ellen, William and Robert Low of Fordham and to Ellen Low's sister. I give 10s each to Alice and Ann, the 2 daughters of John Clake [sic] of Burwell within a year. I give the parishioners of Wicken 10s, the profit of which is to be distributed amongst the poor on Mid Lent Sunday. The churchwardens and some of the abler sort are to put this 10s in such security of land as my ex'trix shall think fit, so that my gift may continue for ever. I give my daughter-in-law Cecily Goodde of Wicken 40s, and 20s each to Ann and Mary Goodde to be paid within a year. If my daughter Anne dies without heirs before she is 21, my wife is to have her legacy of £600. All my goods and chattels I give for ever to my wife, whom I make sole ex'trix. Wit. John Wilkyns, Thomas Croply, Walter Bullyne (X). I have surrendered all my copyhold land to the use of my will by hands of Thomas Croply and in presence of Walter Bullyne. Pr. at Bury 27 February 1632/33.

530. W(R) WILLIAM HAMBLINGE (X) of Hitcham. 13 November 1632.

Bequeaths soul to God and body to earth in certain hope to rise again to eternal life.
I give my wife Anne the lease of the farm wherein I now dwell together with all my goods, corn and cattle. I give my daughter Martha Wood 10s to be paid within a year, and my daughter Mary £20 to be paid at such time as my wife shall think most fit. I desire that my wife show herself a diligent ex'trix of my will. Wit. William Alcock, Isaac Wood (X), Robert Cross (X). Pr. at Bury 28 February 1632/33.

531. W(R) THOMAS COOKE the elder of Combs, yeoman. 2 November 1631.

Bequeaths soul to God believing to have eternal salvation through Jesus Christ. To be buried in Combs churchyard.
I give the poor people of Combs 10s to be distributed at my burial. I give my wife Mary my copyhold tenement with 3 acres in Combs and called Frendes for her life, and then to my son William. I give my wife for ever all the moveable goods which were hers in her widowhood before our marriage, and my 2 beds in the chamber over the bedchamber. These goods and land are in full satisfaction of her dower. I give my wife £30 to be paid by my exor within 6 months of my decease; also 2 bushels of good clean wheat, a quarter of a waye of good hard cheese, a kettle at her own choice, a bushel of malt, and a clock reel to reel white work. All these are to be delivered to her a week after my decease. I give my son Robert my tenement where I now dwell and all my land, except that given to my wife. He must pay the following legacies: £30 within a year to my daughter Mary, wife of John Sowgate; £20 within 1½ years to my son

Thomas, who must discharge my exor of an obligation for £100 in which he and I are jointly bound to Mr Bullwarde for the payment of certain legacies; 20s p.a. to my daughter Sarah Wellham to be paid quarterly; 40s within a year to my daughter Agnes; 40s each to all the children of Mirabel Poolye, to all those of my daughter Sarah and to my grandchild Mary Sowgate; all to be paid when 21. Legatees have power to distrain. If my wife's legacy of £30 is not paid, she may hold Calves close until the full sum is paid. I give my maid servant Mary Randall 5s to be paid within a month. All the rest of my goods I give to my son Robert whom I nominate exor. Supervisor: Thomas Sothebe clerk and I give him 10s for his pains. Wit. Francis Manninge, Robert Curtis (X) and me Philip Barne. Pr. at Bury 5 March 1632/33.

532. W(R) JOHN JERMYN (X) of Stanstead, yeoman. 23 January 1632/33.

I give my wife Elizabeth all the household stuff she brought when we married, and 5s. I give my eldest son John 5s. I give my sons Giles and Peter my copyhold land and tenement in Stanstead. I give my daughter Rose, wife of Richard Dutton, 5s. I give £10 each when 21 to my son James and daughter Grace. The residue of my goods I give to my sons Giles and Peter and make them exors. Wit. Robert Sparrow, Thomas Wright. Pr. at Bury 25 February 1632/33.

533. W(R) WALTER HOWLETT (X) of Wood Ditton [Cambs], yeoman. 20 February 1632/33.

Gives soul to God hoping to be made partaker of life everlasting through Jesus Christ. To be buried in Wood Ditton churchyard.
I give 50s to the poor people at my burial. I give my grandchild Martin Appleyard all my tenements and lands in the fields of Wood Ditton, except 13½ acres meadow and 30 acres arable which I have surrendered to Thomas Ridgwell and 3¼ acres arable bequeathed in this will. My son-in-law Thomas Appleyard is to occupy these lands until Martin is 24. I give my son-in-law Thomas Ridgwell for life 3¼ acres held copyhold of the manor of Saxton Hall and being in 4 pieces: one in Cawdell field and 3 in Saxton Hall field and all abutting on the Lord's land called Moreleys. After his death I give this land to his daughter Anne. Thomas must give my exor an acquittance of a covenant made between myself and his father William Ridgewell assuring him land worth £20. I give Martin Appleyard all my household stuff when 24; until then his father is to have the use of it, and must not remove anything from the house where the goods now are. I give 40s each when 21 to all the children of Thomas Appleyard begotten of my daughter Alice, his late wife. I give my kinswoman Elizabeth Barram widow for her care of me £10 to be paid over 2 years. I give 20s each within a year to the children of my brother Francis and 10s to my grandchild Ann Ridgwell when 21. I give 6d each to all my godchildren within 3 months of my decease. I give 30s to my son-in-law

Thomas Kilborne and 10s to his son Thomas within a year. I give 2s to each of my household servants dwelling with me at the time of my decease. All the residue of my goods and chattels I give to my son-in-law Thomas Appleyard and make him exor. Wit. Thomas Kilborne, John Martin, William Balls. Pr. at Bury 26 February 1632/33.

534. W(R) CHRISTOPHER EASON alias CUTBERT of Poslingford, tailor. 2 April 1631.

Commends soul to God trusting through Jesus Christ to have sins pardoned and to be raised up again.
My body is to be buried at the discretion of William Lynge of Chipley Abbey in the parish of Chipley and my very loving friend, whom I make my exor. I give my sister Mary Eason alias Cutbert my messuage in Poslingford wherein I now dwell with its yard and garden for her life, and then to my brother Thomas for his life and then to Susan, daughter of Thomas Franncis alias Reeve and his wife Katherine my kinswoman. I give 40s to my brother Thomas and 20s to Henry, son of my brother George within 6 months of my decease and 12 pence within 3 months to my sister Ann Holgate. I give Thomas Franncis alias Reeve a debt of about £5 which he and his wife had of me in commodities at various times. If my sister Mary and my brother Thomas die before Susan Franncis alias Reeve is 21 or married, my exor is to let my messuage until she is of age or married. I give my exor 10s. The residue of my goods I give to my sister Mary. Wit. Thomas Donnett who wrote will and Katherine Franncis alias Reeve (X). Pr. at Bury 12 October 1632.

Note: Chipley Abbey is a farmhouse built on the site of Chipley Priory, an Augustinian house, and lies in the parish of Poslingford.

535. W(R) HENRY CRABBE (X) of Boxford, weaver. 9 September 1631.

Bequeaths soul to God steadfastly believing to be saved through Jesus Christ. To be buried in Boxford churchyard.
I give my wife my messuage wherein I dwell with buildings and yard for her life, and all my goods except the shop and shop stuff, which I give to my youngest son William. I give him my messuage after my wife's death. If William dies without heirs, my messuage is to be sold and the money divided among all the rest of my children. William is to pay all my debts. I give 5s to my daughter Alice Sinderland within a month of my decease; my son George 5s within a year; my son Henry 5s within 2 years and my son Richard 5s within 3 years. Exors: my wife Elizabeth and my son William. Wit. Thomas Hunnable (X), Thomas Burche (X). Pr. 4 June 1632. No place given.

536. W(R) NICHOLAS HARGRAVE (N) of Beyton, husbandman.
12 February 1632/33.

Being asked by the wife of Thomas Gippes what wilt thou do with the
money, wilt thou give it me, he said no. Then she asked him wilt thee
give it thy brother and he said no; and the third time she asked him wilt
thee give it to thy master, meaning Thomas Gippes (he standing by), yes
said Nicholas to bury me. And then taking Thomas Gippes his master
with a great deal of affection by the hand and shook it. Wit. Ann Gippes,
Thomas Gippes. Let. ad. granted 13 February 1632/33 to Thomas Gippes
as principal creditor. No place given.

537. W(R) JOHN PASKE (N) of Boxted, husbandman. 26 June 1633.

He gave his brother Josias and his kinsman Ambrose Evered all his goods
and chattels to be disposed of by them for the education and bringing up
of Sarah, Bridget and John his children, being very young, and he made
them exors. Wit. Samuel Graunger, Richard Evered. Let. ad. granted to
Josias Paske 5 July 1633. No place given.

538. W(R) THOMAS TURTLE (N) of Bury St Edmunds, labourer.
15 June 1633.

I give Susan my loving wife my bed and bedstead wherein I lie. I give my
son John my other featherbed and bedstead standing by the first one, and
1 pair sheets. I give my son Thomas my great cupboard and cupboard
cloth, a pair sheets, a chest on the left hand of the stairs coming up, and a
long joined form. I give my son Henry my long table and the frame, and
my flockbed being under the last mentioned feather bed. I give my son
William a great keeler, a keep and my bible. I give Martha, daughter of
my son Thomas, my glass case. All the residue of my goods I give to my
wife Susan and make her ex'trix. Wit. John Jewell, Susan, wife of John
Harbard, Mary wife of Thomas Thurston. Pr. at Bury 5 July 1633.

539. W(R) MARGERY HOLDEN (X) of Thurston. 3 November 1630.

Commends soul to God hoping to be saved by Jesus Christ. To be buried
near my friends in Tostock churchyard.
I give Elizabeth Sample my daughter my best gown and a little porridge
pot, the least I have. I give Sarah Wade my god-daughter the featherbed
in my chamber where I lie with a little bolster and a blanket belonging to
it. I give my daughter Margery the bedstead in the hall, a little bolster, a
sheet, a blanket and a great kettle. I give Esther Beale a pewter dish that
has my husband's name on it. I give a pewter dish each to Dorothy,
Katherine and Sarah Wade. I give Elizabeth, daughter of Robert Sample,
my best ruff. I give Adam Holden the long table and long form in the
malthouse chamber. I give my son James Holden my pightle called Nut
pightle. I give my daughter Sarah Wade 20s to be paid by my son James 1

year after my decease. I give James the bedstocks in my chamber and the featherbed in the chamber where he lies when he comes to me, and the great chair and a little table in the same chamber, another chair called the hooped chair and an old table in the malt house. I give my daughter Rebecca my best cloak, my best hat and best kirtle. I give my daughter Susan all the rest of my moveable goods and make her ex'trix, trusting she will be careful to execute my will as I repose my trust in her. I desire James my son to be supervisor. Wit. James Holden, Thomas Tyler (X). Pr. at Bury 8 July 1633.

540. W(R) ELIZABETH BARRE (X) of Whepstead, widow. 7 October 1631.

Commends soul to God.
I give John Crowch the elder of Hawstead £10 within 1 year. I give Francis, son of Robert Nun, 20s and his sister Elizabeth 20s. I give Edmund, son of John Crowch, 20s, and Peter Manning the elder 40s within 6 months. The children's legacies are to be paid when they are 20. I give John Fordham my kinsman 3 pewter dishes. All the residue of my goods I give to my kinsman Henry Nun and make him exor. Wit. Robert Steward (X), John Stockin. Pr. at Bury 8 July 1633.

541. W(R) WILLIAM SAWYER (X) of Great Horringer, yeoman. 23 May 1633.

Commends soul to God hoping to obtain everlasting life through Jesus Christ.
I give my 2 brothers Thomas and John my tenement and land in Wattisfield, now occupied by my mother Ellen Sawyer and my brother John, immediately after the former's decease. I give my mother £10 and my 3 brothers Thomas, John and Richard £5 each within a year of my decease. I give Margaret my loving wife my copyhold land in Great Horningsheath for life, and then to my brother-in-law Edmund Godfry of Horningsheath. I make my wife sole ex'trix and bequeath to her all my goods and chattels. Wit. Robert Goodrick minister, Andrew Wrighte. Pr. at Bury 8 July 1633.

542. W(R) RICHARD HAWSELL (N) of Clare, weaver. 31 March 1633.

He appointed Richard Hawsell his son to be his exor. Wit. John Hill, Sarah Lotte. Let. ad. granted to son 16 July 1633. No place given.

543. W(R) ROGER COOKE of Brent Eleigh, yeoman. 10 April 1633.

Commends soul to God trusting through Jesus Christ to be partaker of life everlasting.
I give 13s 4d to the poor of Brent Eleigh to be distributed within a month

of my decease. Although I gave my eldest son Roger a sufficient portion on his marriage, in order that he may permit my other children peacably to enjoy the land left to them, I give him 3 pieces land in Great Waldingfield: 3 acre Randes meadow, Petcroste piece of 4 acres and a 3 rod piece lying by the last and the river. I give Roger a rent charge of 8d p.a. on the house of Edward Wasse in Great Waldingfield. I give my second son Richard my messuage in Great Waldingfield now occupied by my brother Richard, and a 3 acre parcel of land on the backside of the messuage. I also give him my close called Bonnetts and Chapmans lying in Great Waldingfield and Chilton, which I had by the will of Richard Firmyn gentleman. He must pay my daughter Edith £100 in the porch of Great Waldingfield church in 2 portions 1 and 2 years after my decease. In case of default Edith is to have this close. I give my third son Samuel my messuage and little stable in Lavenham, which I lately purchased of Robert Jarrold. I give my fourth son John my messuage in Great Waldingfield now occupied by Anthony Denmer. I give my fifth son Henry my tenement called White House in Great Waldingfield and occupied by Richard Abbott, and 3 rods copyhold land adjoining it and held of the manor of Cautwells. I give my sixth son Thomas my messuage called Aylottes alias Berdes in Great Waldingfield and 2 adjoining closes of 3 acres now occupied by Edward Smye, and a 1 acre piece land occupied by Henry Sugar. I give my son Roger my 2 pieces of moor ground in Great Waldingfield and called Badley Moor, which I bought from Robert Colman gentleman. He must pay my son John £22 within 1 year or forfeit Badley Moor to John. I give my son Richard a 1 acre meadow in Great Waldingfield called Cobbes meadow bought from Robert Colman. I give my son Richard my 6 acre close in Great Waldingfield called Cicelye Croft held copyhold of Morres manor. He must pay my son John £40 within a month of his reaching 24 or forfeit this close to John. I give my son Richard my 5 acre copyhold close in Acton called Griffines. He must pay my son Henry £40 within a month of him being 24 or forfeit close to him. Judith my wellbeloved wife is to take her thirds of my land for her maintenance. I give her £5 p.a. to be paid by my exor so long as she remains a widow. I give her my best posted bed in the parlour chamber with all its furniture, the table at its foot and a press in the same room. I give my daughter a dozen of flax napkins. All my other goods and chattels I bequeath to my son Richard whom I make exor. I give my grandchild Elizabeth, daughter of son Roger, 20s when 21 or married, and to her brother Roger 20s when 21. Wit. Samuel Colman, Thomas Colman, Edward Simson (X). Pr. at Bury 8 July 1633.

544. W(R) JOHN BROWNE (X) of Bradfield Combust, yeoman.
28 June 1633.

Commends soul to God hoping to be saved through Jesus Christ.
I will that my brothers-in-law Anthony and John Browne of Cockfield shall have the rent of my messuage and land in Cockfield for 5 years after my decease using it to pay £40 as follows: £30 to be equally divided

between my daughters Jane and Dorothy when 21, and £10 to my daughter Sarah at the end of the 5 years. Benefit of survivorship. I give Jane and Dorothy my 2 posted bedsteads and featherbeds, one standing at Sutton Hall and the other at Roger Steed's, the bedding at Richard Johnson's, and a copper at Roger Steed's at Shimpling. I give the rest of my goods to my son John to pay my debts and funeral charges, and make him exor. Wit. Philip Stearne, John Smith. Pr. at Bury 8 July 1633.

545. W(R) CHARLES GARDNER of Cavendish, tailor. 28 March 1633.

Bequeaths soul to God trusting to be saved through Jesus Christ. To be buried in Cavendish church.
I give my eldest daughter Margaret £20 and my youngest daughter Mary £20 both when 21. Benefit of survivorship. If both die my wife Frances is to have this £40, and she is to have the use of it towards bringing up my daughters until they are of age. I give all my goods, debts and money to my wife. Exors: John Isack, Thomas Revell. Wit. Susan Hart (X), Margaret Crispe (X) widow, John Grigges. Pr. at Bury 22 July 1633.

546. W(R) GEORGE WHITER of Risby, yeoman. 29 August 1630.

Commends soul to God trusting through Jesus Christ to be partaker of everlasting kingdom prepared for the elect.
I give my wellbeloved wife Margaret all my land and tenements in Stradishall, Risby and Horningsheath until my sons Richard and John are 21. She must pay my daughters Margaret and Ellen £100 each when 21. I give my eldest son George immediately after my decease my land and tenements in Wickhambrook. After my wife's death I give my son Richard all my land in Stradishall, and my son John my land in Risby and Horningsheath. All children have benefit of survivorship. I make my wife ex'trix to pay my debts and legacies, and see my children honestly and well brought up. I give her all my money, debts, goods, corn and cattle. Wit. Anthony Duisburgh, John Whithand. Pr. at Bury 29 July 1633.

547. W(R) HENRY AUBREE (X) of Mildenhall, singleman. 16 July 1633.

Commends soul to God nothing doubting that he will receive my soul into his kingdom in company of his blessed saints and angels.
I give my brother William my 5 acres copyhold land in Dullingham [Cambs] called Hall pasture on condition that within a year of my decease he pays my brother Thomas £16 10s 0d and my sister Jane the same sum. All my goods and chattels I give to William and make him exor. I have surrendered my copyhold land to the use of my will into hands of David Ramewe and Walter Collyn copyhold tenants of the manor. Wit. John Blower, Roger Ridley, David Ramew, Walter Collin. Pr. at Bury 5 August 1633.

548. W(R) JOHN MARGARAME (X) of Great Finborough,
husbandman. 7 July 1633.

Bequeaths soul to God hoping to have eternal salvation through Jesus
Christ. To be buried in Great Finborough churchyard.
I give my son John 20s to be paid within a year of my decease by my wife
Elizabeth, and if my wife marries again my ex'trix is to pay John another
£4. I give my son Richard 20s and £4 on same terms. All my goods and
chattels I give to Elizabeth my loving wife and make her ex'trix to
perform my will as my trust is in her. Wit. Mathew Butcher, John Burche
(X). Pr. at Bury 12 August 1633.

549. W(R) JAMES WETHERBY of Haughley, wheelwright.
10 February 1632/33.

Commits soul to God.
I give my son James after my wife's decease all my copyhold land and
cottages in Haughley and Haughley New Street, which I and my wife
Elizabeth had from my father James as appears in the court rolls. He
must pay my daughter Elizabeth £10 within 3 years's of my wife's death.
Power to distrain. I also give James after wife's decease my bed and
bedstead as it stands in my parlour. I give my son Thomas my posted
bedstead and bedding in the parlour chamber after my wife's decease. I
give my daughter Elizabeth £20 when 21, and a cupboard in the hall after
my wife's decease. My exors are to enter a bond of £40 within a month of
my death to pay Elizabeth £20, and the bond is to be given to my
brothers-in-law William Raffe and Thomas May. I give 40s to be equally
divided among all the children of Edmund Acten and his wife Diana, my
sister, which are living 10 years after my decease; if all are dead, legacy to
be paid to their mother. All the rest of my goods and debts I give to
Elizabeth my wife and Edward Fyske my father-in-law, whom I make
exors. If they refuse to enter into a bond to pay Elizabeth £20, then
William Raffe and Thomas May are to be exors. Wit. Mary Wenshard
(X), and me William Payne. Pr. at Bury 12 August 1633.

550. W(R) SUSAN TAWNEY (X) of Rougham, widow. 30 May 1633.

Commits soul to God believing to be saved by Christ. To be buried in
Rougham churchyard.
I give Bridget Wretham my gown, a red petticoat and a ruff. I give Mary
Wretham a hutch, an old gown and a box. I give Roger and John
Wretham my brass pot. I give Elizabeth, wife of Ralph Inghold, my great
chest and a cloak. I give Edward Rose my brother a flockbed and a
coverlet. I give all the rest of my goods to Matthew and Francis Tawney.
I make Mr Wells minister of Rougham my exor. I give Mabel Humphrey
and her brother 5s each. Supervisors: Thomas Bryant, Thomas Borley.
Wit. Thomas Bryant (X), James Margerye. Pr. at Bury 19 August 1633.

551. W(R) ROBERT CRASKE of Icklingham, husbandman. 22 January 1632/33.

Commends soul to God trusting through Jesus Christ to be associated in heaven with elect and chosen people.
I give 10s to the poor of the parish of St James and 5s to the poor of All Saints in Icklingham and 5s to the poor of Worlington to be distributed by overseers of the poor within a month of my death. I give my brother Andrew my free and copyhold houses and land in Icklingham with all the growing corn and all the compasse on condition he gives my brother Henry a release of his interest in the latter's land in Icklingham late Andrew Garrod's. Henry is to pay £10 and Andrew £20 to my brother John within 13 weeks of my decease. Andrew must also pay £20 each to my brother John's children Alice, Robert and John when 21, and £10 to my brother's daughter Elizabeth when 21. If Andrew refuses to fulfil these conditions, property left to him is to go to Henry on the same terms. I give my sister Helen Folkes my houses and land in Worlington and Freckenham, which I lately bought of Rachel Adames, in consideration of the money I owe her. If Helen dies before she receives land, I give it to her son John. I give Elizabeth, daughter of my brother John, £10 when 21. Exors: brothers Henry and Andrew. Wit. Henry Craske, William Ladinan. Pr. at Bury 24 August 1633.

552. W(R) ANNE RAYNER (X) of Great Waldingfield, singlewoman. 1 May 1633.

Bequeaths soul to God looking for everlasting life through Jesus Christ.
I give my tenement with 2½ acres copyhold land in Great Waldingfield, held of the manor of Acton Hall and part of lands called Gyllbriantes to my father John and mother-in-law Elizabeth and after their deaths to John's heirs. I give the poor of Great Waldingfield 5s. The residue of my goods I give to my exor, my father. Wit. Richard Peachie, John Sudbury (X). Pr. at Bury 29 July 1633.

553. W(R) WILLIAM HALL (X) of Drinkstone, tailor. 23 April 1633.

Gives soul to God trusting to be saved by Jesus Christ.
I give my wife Anne for life my tenement where I now dwell with orchard and garden, and then to my son Andrew who must pay my legacies to the rest of my children: £3 to William, £4 to Margaret, £3 to John, £3 to Robert and £4 to Dorothy at one a year starting 1 year after my wife's decease. If Andrew dies before my wife, William is to have my tenement and pay my legacies. Legatees have benefit of survivorship and power to distrain. Wife sole ex'trix and to have all my moveable goods for life, and after her death they are to be equally divided among my children. Wit. Stephen Goddard, Peter Goddard (X), John Goddard (X). Pr. at Bury 17 September 1633.

554. W(R) ALICE GLEEDE, wife of Robert Gleede the younger of Walsham le Willows, yeoman. 15 August 1633.

I make my will with the consent and good liking of my husband. I commend my soul to God.
I give my wellbeloved husband all my goods and chattels, and all the legacies bequeathed to me by the will of my father Thomas Parker. Exor: my husband. Wit. Thomas Rampley, John Rampley, Edmund Baxter. Pr. at Bury 16 September 1633.

555. W(R) MARGARET HAYWARD (X) of Lawshall. 6 September 1633.

Remembrance of certain goods given by Margaret Hayward being very sick and weak. I have a bond from my brother Nicholas for £10, whereof my memory is that he shall have £5 on condition he enters into a bond to pay my cousin Susan Hayward 40s when 21 and pays me or my exors the remainder of the bond. I give Nicholas a chest. I give my brother Andrew a table in his possession. I give my sister Pettett my best waistcoat, my red petticoat and a warming pan. I give Susan Hayward my bed with all that belongs to it, my little bible and my little hutch. I give Robert Hammont, my sister's son, a pair of my best flaxen sheets and all the rest of my best linen. Exors: brother-in-law Robert Hammont and his wife Bridget. I give them all the rest of my goods and apparel, and a bond for £10 due to me from John Hammont of Melford Park. Wit. William Wright, Robert Nun. Pr. at Bury 28 October 1633.

556. W(R) SAMUEL HARGRAVE (X) of Soham [Cambs], husbandman. 30 September 1633.

Bequeaths soul to God and body to be buried in Soham churchyard.
I bequeath my son William £5 when 21. All the rest of my goods and chattels I give to Elizabeth my wife whom I make ex'trix. Wit. Roger Voyce, William Grandsborough and me Robert Carlton the writer. Pr. at Bury 26 October 1633.

557. W(R) ELIZABETH HOWE (N) of Little Whelnetham, spinster. 22 October 1633.

She gave her sister Dorothy, wife of Henry Peach, £6 in the hands of John Adams of Great Whelnetham, her best gown, her best waistcoat, best ruff and best cloak. She gave her god-daughter Elizabeth Peach 20s. She gave her brother John Howe £20 and a chest. She gave Elizabeth Howe her god-daughter 20s. She gave Ann, daughter of her brother Henry How, 40s and to his wife her best petticoat, a ruff, an apron and other small things. Wit. Anne Howe (X) wife of John Howe of Great Whelnetham, Elizabeth Howe (X) of Great Whelnetham. Let. ad. granted 28 October 1633. No place given.

558. W(R) GEORGE STOWERS (N) of Stoke by Nayland, wheel-wright. 12 September 1633.

Being in extremes of sickness and asked by the undersigned to whom he would give his goods, he answered I will give my son George all my working tools and as for the rest I give them to my wife for we laboured together hard for them. Wit. John Hankyns clerk, David Baker (X). Pr. at Bury 3 October 1633.

559. W(R) MARGARET GARDINER (X) of Aldham, widow. 11 October 1622.

Bequeaths soul to God.
I give William Symons of Aldham, husbandman, and his wife Rose my copyhold land called 2 acre piece, being part of Shelles, and now occupied by him; it lies enclosed between land of Thomas Rand called the Tazell field on the west and the rest of Shelles held by William Symons on the east with the north end abutting on the Lord's wood called Churchfield wood, and with south end on the land of Nicholas Timperley esquire. All my goods and chattels I give to William Symons whom I make exor asking him to pay William Buers of Hintlesham the £5 I owe him. Wit. Francis Harison, William Sexton (X), Francis Clifford (X). Pr. at Sudbury 3 October 1633.

560. W(R) JAMES ROGERS of Pakenham, yeoman. 16 August 1633.

Bequeaths soul to God assuredly hoping for salvation through Jesus Christ.
I give my brethren John, Mathew, Robert and Richard all the money due to me by bond or bill to be equally divided among them as soon as it can be gathered in by my exor. There is due to me from John Coldham of Pakenham 22s which I lent him and due to me about a year past; only 20s shall be demanded of him and I forgive him the rest. I am also owed 20s by my brother Mathew; 40s by Thomas Parker cooper of Ixworth, which he is bound to pay me about Christmas next; and £11 in the hands of my wellbeloved master and friend Sir William Spring. I give my brother Robert all my linen, stockings, hose, shoes, boots and all my other wearing things except my doublets, jerkins, hose and coats which I wish to be sold and the money divided equally among my brothers John, Robert and Mathew. If any of my fellow servants want any of my clothes they may have them at a price appointed by my master Sir William Spring. Exor: brother John, whom I charge in the name of God as he will answer for it to perform my will. If any doubt arises among my brethren about my will, my master shall settle it. I give George Waters my fellow servant my best girdle. Wit. John Alger, Philip Blye (X). Pr. at Bury 16 October 1633.

561. W(R) JOSIAS TRAY (N) of Troston, husbandman. 1 October 1633.

He gave all his goods to Alice his wife. Wit. James Hodson, Ann Stutter (X) wife of John Stutter. Let. ad. granted to widow 14 October 1633. No place given.

562. W(R) JOHN GRIGGS (N) of Hawstead, husbandman. 1 June 1633.

He willed all he had, meaning his goods and chattels, to his wife Frances. Wit. Robert Ray clerk, testator's wife. Let. ad. granted to widow 15 October 1633. No place given.

563. W(R) MARY FOLKES (X) of Mildenhall, widow. 23 July 1633.

Bequeaths soul to God trusting that it will live for ever with the Lord.
I give my son Martin £20 to be paid half a year after my decease, and £20 to his daughter Mary when 21. I also give her my great chest, 1 pair sheets, 1 pair holland pillowbeeres, a long board cloth and a short one, a dozen napkins and all the things that were her father's that be at my cabert [sic – chamber?], and a taffeta petticoat that was her mother's. I give £5 each when 21 to John, Anne and Grace, children of my son Martin. Benefit of survivorship. I give Martin and Mary Folkes 40s each, and 20s each when 21 to John and Ann children of John Folkes. I give my daughter Mary Jackson £10. I give Grace Jackson my bedstead and featherbed, a feather bolster, 2 blankets and a coverlet with the curtains and valances belonging to the bed, and 2 pillows. I give Mary Jackson, my god-daughter £6 and 40s each when 21 to Thomas, Edward and Elizabeth Jackson. I give Henry Place 20s. I give Mr Blower 20s to make a sermon at my burial. I give 5s each to Margaret and Lydia Horringall. I give the poor of this town 20s, and the church 10s to be used at the discretion of the churchwardens. I give Edith Fifild my flockbed and 2s. I will that my exor spend £5 on Mary Folkes my god-daughter towards her bringing up in some good place. All the rest of my goods I give to Edward Jackson, whom I make exor. Wit. Christopher Wharton, Abigail Ofild (X). Pr. at Bury 22 October 1633.

564. W(R) ROBERT PASLEY (X) of Hundon, gentleman. 8 December 1630.

Commends soul to God hoping to be saved by Jesus Christ.
I give the poor people of Hundon 40s to be distributed at my funeral. I give my wife Elizabeth half of all my houses and land in Hundon, Barnardiston and Stradishall in lieu of dower as long as she continues a widow, but if she marries again she is to have but a third part for life. I give her all the furniture, household stuff, bedding and bedsteads in the parlour of the house where I now dwell together with the parlour for her

own use, and right of access for herself, children, friends and servants by the usual way through the hall of the house during her widowhood. I also give her 2 pairs sheets, 1 pair pillows and 2 pairs pillowbeeres more than is on the bed in the parlour. I give her £20 to be paid within a month of my decease. I give her half a dozen silver spoons of the best sort I have, a silver bowl, a kettle, a brass pot, a posnet, half a dozen pewter platters – 3 of the greater and 3 of the lesser sort –, the third part of all my brewing and dairy vesels, 2 hogsheads and half my double silver salt. I give the other half of my houses and lands to my exors for 1 year after my decease; they must pay my son Richard £20 during this year. After this year I give these houses and land to my son Richard; if my wife remarries he is to have two-thirds of my property. After my wife's decease I give the rest of my houses and land to Richard. I give Frances, daughter of my son Richard, £20 to be paid when 21 or married; until then my wife is to have this money and give Frances the interest. I give John, son of my son-in-law James Beckham £20 to be put out with security by his father until he is 21. I give Lawrence Pasley my kinsman £3 within 6 months; my godson James, son of Anthony Thompson of Hundon, 50s within a month; 50s each within a year to Richard Peapes gentleman of Stoke by Clare and to Henry Catts gentleman of Clare, and I do entreat them to be supervisors of my will. My exors are to pay them any charges they incur. Any legatees who will not abide by decisions of supervisors will lose their legacies. Unbequeathed residue of my goods and chattels I bequeath to my daughters Sarah and Elizabeth and make them ex'trices. Wit. Anthony Thompson clerk and vicar of Hundon, John Parker, Richard Thompson. Pr. at Bury 21 October 1633.

565. W(R) ROBERT LANMAN alias JANNINGS (X) of Cockfield, yeoman. 7 May 1632.

Commits soul to God trusting through Jesus Christ to have free pardon of sins. To be buried in Cockfield churchyard.
I give the poor of Cockfield 20s to be distributed half a year after my decease. I give my wellbeloved wife Elizabeth for life my copyhold messuage wherein I dwell with 4 pieces of land totalling 8 acres; also a messuage called Moults with 4 acres land; and 10 acres arable and meadow in Colts Tye which I bought from John Fuller. After her decease or if she remarries I give the above messuages and land to Anthony, younger son of the late Anthony Wappole of Thorpe Morieux. If my wife neglects to keep the buildings in repair, or fells, stubs up or lops any trees or quickset fences on my land except what is necessary for repairs my gifts to her are void. I give my wife an annuity of £6 13s 4d to be paid half yearly. I give Anthony Wappole a messuage and 8 acres in Cockfield which I purchased of William Grigges, on condition he delivers every year to my wife's house 2 loads of wood with 40 faggots to the load, and keeps up the fences on the land left to her. If he fails, my wife is to have the last-named house and land for life. My wife is to have the grazing of these 8 acres until Michaelmas after my decease without any payment. It

is my will that John Mosse shall dwell in the house where he now lives in Cockfield for 1 year after my decease without paying any rent. I give Rose Mosse after my wife's decease a boarded bedstead and 2 flockbeds lying on it in the old chamber over the dairy. I give John, Alice, Bridget and Elizabeth, children of John Mosse 20s each when 21. I give Robert Jannings, son of my brother George, £5 4 years after my decease, and William, son of my brother William Jannings, £5 5 years after. Elizabeth my wife is to have for life a bedstead with a featherbed and all its bedding as it now stands in the parlour chamber, a cupboard, a table, a form and a bench in the parlour of my dwelling house in Cockfield. Also a brass standing under the stairs, a cheese press, a brass pot, 1 pair malt querns, a hooped beetle and 8 wedges, a cart, a plough and a pair harrows. She must keep all these goods in repair and leave them when she dies or remarries to Anthony Wappole. The residue of my goods and chattels I give to my wife and make her ex'trix. Wit. Ralph Blythe senior (X), John Berd (X) and me Peter Marshall, writer of will. Pr. at Bury 4 November 1633.

566. W(R) JOHN FROST of Langham. 4 October 1633.

Commends soul to God.

I give the poor people of Langham 10s, of Hartest 10s, of Ixworth 10s, of Badwell Ash 5s, of Stowlangtoft 5s, of Hunston 5s, of Bardwell 5s and of Hepworth 5s to be paid to churchwardens and overseers and distributed within 3 months of my decease. I give my daughter Abigail for life two-thirds of all my lands and tenements in Norton near Woolpit, and after her decease to my son James, and if he has no heirs to my son John Frost clerk. The other third I bequeath to my son James with remainder to John. If all this property comes to John, within a year he is to pay £120 to be equally divided among the daughters of my son Thomas and my daughter Prudence. I give my daughter Prudence 40s to buy a ring of gold, and 20s to her daughter Mary Rushbrooke for the same purpose. I give 5s apiece to all the rest of my grandchildren when 15. I give my daughter Abigail a bedstead with a featherbed and all necessary bedding. All the rest of my goods and chattels I give to my wife Prudence and son James, who must pay Abigail £5 p.a. until she receives her land in Norton, which will be after the decease of Audrey Clarke widow of Norton. Exors: my wife and my son James. Wit. Thomas Frost, Richard Frost, Thomas Sparrow. Pr. at Bury 28 October 1633.

567. W(R) THOMAS OXE (N) of Bury St Edmunds, maltster. About 21 November 1632.

His debts being paid and his bargains fulfilled, and his funeral charges and all other expenses being deducted, he gave one half of all his goods and chattels to John Oxe, his brother's son, and the other half to Mary Hinton. Exor: Roger Hawsted the elder. Wit. William Muninges, John May the elder. Let. ad. granted at Bury 8 November 1633.

568. W(R) EDWARD RAYMENT (N) of Stoke by Clare, husbandman. 17 April 1633.

He gave his 2 brothers, William and John, and William Baram one colt; 20s to William Rayment's daughter and 20s each to the 3 children of John Rayment. He gave 10s to his godson Thomas Cole, and to the ringers that should ring at his burial 10s. Exor: William Baram. His wearing apparel he gave to his brother John, and any overplus to be divided between his brothers John and William. Legacies to be paid within a year of his decease, and until then money to remain in some honest man's hands. Wit. Henry French (X), Thomas Baram (X). Let. ad. granted 6 August 1633. No place given.

569. W(R) THOMAS CHURCH (X) of Newmarket, cooper. 27 March 1633.

Bequeaths soul to God.
I give 12 pence each to my eldest son Thomas, my son John and my youngest son William, and to my daughters Elizabeth, wife of Newell Hichell, and Margaret Mony. All the rest of my goods I bequeath to my wife Margaret to pay my debts, funeral charges and expenses. Ex'trix wife, who must pay my debts and legacies within 3 months of my decease. Wit. Henry Blackwin, John Harcocke, John Barrett. Pr. at Newmarket 5 October 1633.

570. W(R) ROBERT WRIGHT of Stowmarket, joiner. 2 September 1633.

Bequeaths soul to God believing to have salvation through Jesus Christ. To be buried in Stowmarket churchyard.
I give my wellbeloved wife Rose for life my tenement and land, and all my moveable goods out of which she is to pay my debts. If she dies before all my debts are paid, my exors are to pay them, and they are to sell as many of my goods as necessary to pay my debts. I give my son Robert my tenement where I now dwell with its land after my wife's decease, and he must then pay £3 each to his brethren and sisters. If he refuses to pay legacies, exors are to hold land and tenement until they are paid. Exors are to put my children out when they are old enough, and to divide any surplus of my goods among them. Exors: George Anger, Walter Durrante, both of Stowmarket. Wit. Thomas Bloome (X), and me Philip Barne. Pr. at Stowmarket 4 October 1633.

571. W(R) EDWARD THORNE (X) of Mildenhall, gentleman. 13 July 1633.

Commends soul to God trusting to be made an heir to everlasting life through Jesus Christ.
I make my loving wife Anne sole ex'trix, and give her all my goods and chattels within doors and without for ever. She is to pay and receive my debts, and see my body brought decently to the earth. Wit. John Blower, Agnes Brooke (X). Pr. at Bury 4 November 1633.

572. W(R) WILLIAM GLEED (X) of Wattisfield, yeoman. 14 June 1633.

Commends soul to God hoping to be made partaker of eternal life through Jesus Christ.
I give my son Robert for ever all my messuages and land in Wattisfield, Rickinghall and Walsham, except for a pasture called Bowdes wood which I bought from Nicholas Locke of Wattisfield. Robert is to hold this close for life, but must not fell or stub any timber trees growing on it, and after his decease I leave it to my grandson William. I give Robert all my lease lands and tenements. I give my grandson John £100 when 21. I give my grandsons Jonathan and Theophilus £200 each when 21. Jonathan's legacy is to be paid by my son Robert out of my land in Wattisfield called Fyshepond. £100 of Theophilus's legacy is to be paid out of land in Wattisfield called Bigge Close and the other £100 out of the same close when he is 24. Power to distrain and benefit of survivorship. I give my daughter Anne Crowche £80 in 2 halves 1 and 3 years after my decease. I give grandson William Crowche £20 when 21, and my grandchild Joan, daughter of Edward Crowche, £10 within a year. I give Rose Bybye £5 within a year, and my grandchildren Elizabeth and Judith Crowche £10 each when 21. I give the poor of Wattisfield £5 to be paid at £1 p.a. on Candlemas day and to be distributed at the discretion of my exor. The residue of my goods and chattels I give to my son Robert and make him exor. Wit. Thomas Rust, T. Bedwell. Pr. at Bury 11 November 1633.

573. W(R) HENRY WIARD of Great Horringer. 14 February 1628/29.

Bequeaths soul to God my creator, redeemer and sanctifier.
I give the poor of Great Horningsheath 20s within 6 months of my decease. I give my daughter Mary, wife of Richard Deareson, the best cupboard in the parlour, which I myself do much use, and £20 to be paid to her within 6 months. I bequeath to her son Thomas my biggest brass pot, which was bought of Henry Welham, and £15 when 21. I bequeath to John, another son of Richard Deareson, the best bed in the parlour chamber and £12 when 21, and to Henry Deareson my grandson £12 when 21. My exor is to allow the above children towards their education the interest on their legacies at 12d in the pound i.e. 15s to Thomas and 12s each to John and Henry. Benefit of survivorship. I give Elizabeth,

daughter of my son James, £5 and a copper which hangs in the kitchen chimney or 26s 8d in money. I give Jane Ingoll and Grace Fisson, my godchildren 5s each. Exor: son James, to whom I give my 2 pieces of land lying in Stubbinges and containing 6½ acres to pay my legacies. Legatees have power to distrain. Wit. Frederick Godfre, William Sawyerd (X). Pr. at Bury 18 November 1633.

574. R(W) LEWES NYNDGE (X) of Herringswell, yeoman. 27 October 1633.

Bequeaths soul to God hoping through merits of Jesus Christ to be saved. To be buried in Herringswell churchyard.
I give my wife Christian for life my copyhold tenement with 3½ acres land, and after her decease to my eldest son Thomas, who must pay £3 apiece to my other 3 sons; Lewes, Robert and John at one p.a. I also give these 3 sons £10 each and my 2 daughters Anne and Philippa £10 each to be paid by my ex'trix when 18. Benefit of survivorship, but excluding Thomas. I make my wife ex'trix and give her my goods and chattels towards bringing up my children and paying my legacies and debts. I charge her to all monies due to me to the best profit of her children. I have surrendered to the use of my will my copyhold tenement into hands of Thomas Cabeck clerk and John Nindge, both copyholders of this manor. Wit. Thomas Cabeck clerk, John Flower (X). Pr. at Bury 20 November 1633.

575. R(W) EDWARD MEAPOWLE (X) of Nowton, shepherd. 31 December 1627.

Bequeaths soul to God trusting to have remission of sins through Jesus Christ.
I give Anne my beloved wife for her life 2 pieces of arable land, one enclosed and the other lying in the open fields of Nowton, containing 3 acres and which I bought from Richard Sterne. After my wife's death my son Anthony is to receive rents and profits of this land and use them for the maintenance of my daughter Bridget. If he defaults, Bridget is to have this land for life. I give my daughter Elizabeth £10 to be paid when she is 21 by Anthony, but if he refuses to pay this legacy I give the above 2 pieces of land to Elizabeth after the decease of Bridget. I give my daughter Abigail £10 to be paid by my ex'trix within 1 year of my decease, and my daughter Rose £10 within 2 years. The rest of my moveables I give to Anne my wife and make her ex'trix, nothing doubting that she will be careful to the utmost of her power to see my will performed. Wit. Anthony Adames, Joseph Adames, Roger Lowdall. Pr. at Bury 18 November 1633.

576. R(W) CHRISTOPHER OLLIVER (X) of Burwell [Cambs], labourer. 9 October 1633.

Gives soul to God steadfastly believing to be saved through Jesus Christ.
I give Agnes my wife my copyhold house for life, and after her decease to my son Christopher and to his wife Agnes and then to my grandson John. Immediately after my decease my son and his wife are to have the bakehouse and the house adjoining it next to the orchard, the fruit from the trees of which is to be divided between my wife and son. I give my son Christopher 2 pairs sheets, the bed on his own bedstead, the copper in the kitchen, a brass kettle, a skillet, all the tools belonging to the trade of making gingerbread and the hampers, a great chair, a buffet stool and the old hutch in the cellar. He must pay his mother 43s 4d immediately after my death. He and my wife are each to repair the buildings they occupy. All the rest of my goods I give to my wife, whom I make ex'trix. She must see me decently buried and pay my debts and legacies. Wit. John Wylkins, John Casburne, Thomas Stewaurd. Testator surrendered his copyhold house to the use of his will into the hands of John Casburne and in presence of Simon Clymmance. Pr. at Bury 20 November 1633.

577. W(R) ROBERT HARDY (X) of Icklingham, shepherd. 7 November 1633.

Commends soul to God hoping to be made partaker of everlasting life through Jesus Christ.
I bequeath to my wife Agnes for life all my freehold land and houses in Barningham and all my copyhold houses and land in Coney Weston, and after her decease to my daughter Agnes. My wife is to pay my daughter £4 p.a. from the age of 14; if she does not, daughter is to inherit land at once. If any 2 men chosen by my daughter agree that the houses have fallen into decay or that any waste has been allowed to the land, then repairs must be made within 6 months or my daughter is immediately to have my houses and land. I give my wife all my sheep and moveable goods to pay my debts, and I make her ex'trix. I give 40s each to my sister Elizabeth and to Thomas and Mary, children of Edmund Hardie, all to be paid within a year. Children's legacies to be paid to Roger Daye of Barningham, who is to put money out to best use until legatees are 21. I give Edmund Halle of Icklingham 20s within a year. I give 6s 8d to the poor of Icklingham St James and 3s 4d to the poor of Icklingham All Saints to be distributed within a month. Wit. John Pecke, William Ladiman. Pr. at Bury 25 November 1633.

578. R(W) EDWARD COSEN of Stanningfield, yeoman. 20 June 1633.

Commends soul to God trusting to be saved by Jesus Christ.
I bequeath my 4 acre close in Stanningfield called Nactons with a tenement lately built on it and now occupied by Richard Hayward bricklayer to my wife Frances for life towards bringing up my children. If

it shall be thought best by my exor and supervisor, with consent of my wife, to sell the above close for the benefit of my wife and her 2 youngest children, they may do so. From the age of 14 my 2 youngest children, Frances and William, are to be paid 20s p.a. by my wife in the porch of Stanningfield church. Benefit of survivorship. If Nactons is not sold, William is to inherit it and must pay Frances £20 within 3 years of my wife's decease. In case of default Frances is to have the close. I will that the cottage standing in the close belonging to the messuage wherein I dwell, and in which John Howlt lately dwelt, remains with the messuage for ever. I give my son Robert my silver bowl and silver salt gilt. I give 2 silver spoons each to 3 youngest children of my deceased daughter Ager. My exor and supervisor are to pay their charges and have 20s each from profits of my messuage. I give Dorothy Applewhite, my wife's sister, my trunk covered with black leather. I give 2s each to George Dawling, John Parkyn and Edward Cosen, and another 4s to be divided amongst the other poor of Stanningfield by the overseers. The residue of my goods and chattels I give to my wife. I make my tenant Richard Hayward exor, and entreat George Stebbinge to be supervisor. Wit. Richard Coppinge, John Nun, John Smith, William Frost (X). Pr. at Bury 2 December 1633.

579. W(R) RICHARD LARGIANT (N) of Fordham [Cambs], shepherd.
27 November 1633.

First he gave his wife Margaret all the household stuff she brought unto him, and a cow with prick horns and one of his pigs. The rest of his goods he gave to be equally divided between his 2 daughters. Exor. Thomas Sargiant. Wit. Thomas Hynson, Thomas Sargiant. Pr. at Bury 2 December 1633.

580. R(W) THOMAS SHEPPARD (X) of Mendlesham. 8 April 1633.

Commends soul to God hoping assuredly through Jesus Christ to live for ever amongst the elect.
First I make my wellbeloved friend and kinsman John Sheppard of Mendlesham exor of my will, hoping that as I have found him faithful unto me here in my life he will truly perform my will. First of all I will that the debts which I owe be paid immediately after my decease, and that my exor shall on the day of my burial distribute to every poor man, woman and child there assembled 4d each. He is also to cause them to be put first into the church and chancel, and is to give them the money as they come out again. I give 10s to the preacher appointed by my exor to preach at my burial, provided that if Mr Jefferie of Kenton be pleased to preach he shall be chosen. I give my exor all my copyhold and freehold lands and tenements, except my tenement in Mendlesham Street and 3½ acres called Lady Meadow lately bought from John Seaman of Mendle-

sham. If I bequeath £50 more than the value of my personal estate, the property left to my exor is to be charged with this sum. I give £12 within 3 months of my decease to my sister's daughter Faith Blower, wife of [blank in MS] and £60 to be equally divided among her 4 children when 21. Benefit of survivorship. I give Thomas Beales, my sister's son, £40 within 3 months and £15 each to his 6 eldest children when 21. Benefit of survivorship. As many of my poor kindred to whom I have given legacies are under 21 and have nothing with which to maintain themselves until that age, my exor is to pay them interest of 12 pence in the pound on their legacies. I give £20 to be paid 6 weeks after my decease to Thomas Sheppard my godson and brother of my exor. I give 40s each to the rest of my exor's brothers when 21. I give Elizabeth Sheppard, my exor's sister £10 when 19. Benefit of survivorship. I give Matthias Welaye £15 and Mistress Robinson of Kenton 4s within 2 months. I give my god-daughter the widow Manister of Thwaite 40s within 6 weeks, and to Thomas Neattes the elder £3 and to his son John £3, both within 6 months. I give my godson Henry Wattes £3 when 21. I give 20s to the wife of John Fletcher of Mellis. I give my servant Anne Partlett £65 to be used by my exor and supervisors to buy her a house and land. I also give her a load of wood yearly and the use of my parlour chamber to live in and keep her things until a house is bought for her. She is to choose 2 of the apple trees in my orchard and have the fruit from them at the next fruit time after my decease. I give the wife of Matthias Wealye £3 within 2 months, and £4 to my godson Matthias Wealye when 24. I give 12d apiece to my exor's household servants. I give £6 each to John Vice the elder and his son-in-law Henry Burrowes and 20s to Thomas Thurlowe of Thorndon, all within 2 months. I give 20s to be divided among the children of John Phenex. I give Robert, son of John Berrie of Mendlesham, 20s and the widow Berrie, mother of Robert, 20s, both within a month. I give Mary, wife of Thomas Brooke of Gosbeck, 40s. I give Francis Barnes, knacker, £5, and John Phenex of Mendlesham £5, both within 3 months. I give my former servant Sarah Gyner £5 to be paid by my exor when it shall be most useful for her; provided that if her husband will not allow her to use this legacy for herself it shall be void. I give Lady Meadow to my exor to sell and use the money as follows: to add £5 each to the legacies already left to 4 children of Faith Blower, the 3 children of Tufts and the 7 of Thomas Beales; to pay another 20s each to Mary Wealye and her son Matthias; 20s to Anne wife of Thomas Goodwyn esquire of Little Stonham; and 40s to the child of Sarah Gymer of Eye. Any disputes between exor and legatees are to be settled by supervisors. I give all my goods and chattels to my exor towards payment of debts, legacies and other charges. Supervisors: my worshipful and worthy friends Thomas Goodwyn esquire and William Blomefeild the elder gentleman, both of Little Stonham, and Thomas Brooke gentleman of Gosbeck. I give Thomas Goodwyn for his pains and many courtesies received from him £30, and I give Mr William Blomefield and Master Thomas Brooke £3 each for their pains. Wit. Elizabeth Phenex (X), Margaret Blackes (X). Pr. at Bury 3 December 1633.

581. R(W) THOMAS FRENCHE (N) of Clare, weaver. May 1633.

He bequeathed to the 5 children of John Prentice of Clare 40s apiece. All the rest of his goods to be divided among his brothers and sisters. Exor: John French. Wit. John Thorpe (X), William Gridley (X), Rose Prentice (X). Pr. at Bury 3 December 1633.

582. R(W) JOHN GAMAGE of Newmarket. 6 February 1632/33.

Bequeaths soul to God and body to be buried in churchyard of Newmarket St Mary.

I give my wife Mary the mansion house where I now dwell with adjoining pasture close, barn, stables and malt houses, and 6½ acres arable for life, and after her death to my brother Thomas together with the wainscot, doors and glass as now fixed in the house. I have assured to Mary, widow of Richard Hamerton of Newmarket, 20½ acres freehold arable in fields of Wood Ditton and Saxon [Saxon Street] in Cambridgeshire to secure payment of legacies to 2 of her children. I give these 20½ acres to my wife on condition she pays Mary Hamerton £4 16s 0d p.a. at the feast of All Saints commonly called Hollantide until her daughter Mary is 21 or marries, when my wife is to pay her £30. From then my wife is to pay Mary Hamerton the elder £3 p.a. until her son Richard is 21 or marries, when my wife is to pay him £50. I give the poorer sort of people of Newmarket 20s to be distributed by overseers on the day of my burial. The rest of my goods I give to my wife Mary and make her sole ex'trix. No witnesses. Pr. at Newmarket 16 December 1633.

583. R(W) OLIVER JARVIS of Wicken [Cambs], yeoman. 6 November 1633.

Commends soul to God hoping to be saved through Jesus Christ. To be buried in Wicken churchyard.

I will that my house in Candishe [Cavendish in Suffolk?] called Heyden with its land be sold by my exor to pay my debts and bring up my children. I give my daughter Mary the bedstead and bedding in the parlour whereon I now lie and a wainscot chest standing by the bed, a table with a frame in the hall, a form, a cupboard in the hall, a chair and 40s to be paid when she is 21. The rest of my goods and chattels are to be sold and the money used by my exor for bringing up and education of my children until my sons are 24 and daughters 21 when remainder of goods is to be divided among them: John, Elias, Anne and Martha, except that whichever of my 2 sons shall inherit, according to the custom of the manor, my house in Polstead shall not have a share of my goods. Exor: my brother John Jarvis of Worlington, husbandman. Wit. Nicholas Cowper, John Jarvis senior (X). Pr. at Bury 18 December 1633.

584. R(W) JOHN UNDERWOOD (X) of Brettenham, yeoman.
31 December 1633.

Bequeaths soul to God and my body to be buried in the churchyard trusting through Jesus Christ to have a joyful resurrection.
I give my present loving wife Susan my messuage where I now dwell in Brettenham called Kinges with outbuildings and land for life, and after her decease to my son John, to whom she must pay £6 p.a. I give John 2 cows, 1 white and the other black brinded, a grey mare, and the best bed where I now lie in the parlour with all that belongs to it. I give all the rest of my moveable goods to my wife and make her ex'trix. Wit. Simon Chapman, Walter Branston. Pr. at Bury 17 February 1633/34.

585. R(W) MARGARET PATRICK (X) of Great Whelnetham,
spinster. 21 November 1633.

Commends soul to God hoping to be saved by Jesus Christ.
I give my brother John 20s, his son John 40s and his daughter Margaret £5 all to be paid within a year of my decease within porch of Great Whelnetham church. Benefit of survivorship. I give John Patrick the younger my cupboard in the chamber and the long table there and a long hutch. I give Margaret Patrick my best gown, my red linsey woolsey petticoat, my short table, 5 buffet stools, my new chest, my box and my cupboard in the hall, and 6 pieces pewter. The residue of my goods I give to my sister Anne Steward and make her ex'trix. Wit. Robert Pilboroughe, John Smyth. Pr. at Bury 17 February 1633/34.

586. R(W) SUSAN PAYNTER (X) of Stowmarket, widow. 25 May
1629.

Bequeaths soul to God believing to have salvation through Jesus Christ. To be buried in Stowmarket churchyard.
I give my son William my trundle bedstead with a flockbed and flock bolster lying on it, a chest standing in the chamber, a pillow and 2 cushions. I give my grandchild Susan Paynter 2 pewter chargers and my grandchild Elizabeth Paynter 2 pewter platters. I give my daughter Elizabeth a cupboard in the parlour, 2 chairs, a little buffet stool, a pillow, a spit, 2 kettles, a brass pot, a warming pan, 2 chargers, a bason, 2 fruit dishes, a salt, a great candlestick, a pair sheets and a pillowbeere. I give my daughter Bridget Leaman my table in the hall, a pair sheets, a pillow, a pillowbeere, the form in the hall and the great brass pot. I give my grandson Thomas Leaman my posted bedstead in the chamber with flockbed and bolster and a side table in the parlour. I give my grandchild Francis Leaman my table in the parlour and 6 buffet stools belonging to it. I give my grandchild Susan Leaman my casting sheet, a casting kercher, a pillow, a pillowbeere, a pair sheets and a stamell petticoat. I give my grandchild Henry Leaman my cauldron, the great spit and the dripping pan. I give my daughter Elizabeth Paynter my best gown and

best cloak and a petticoat. All these legacies are to be delivered by my exor within a month of my decease. Anything left over I give to my son-in-law Francis Leaman and make him exor. Wit. John Hubbard and me Philip Barne. Pr. at Bury 17 February 1633/34.

587. R(W) EDWARD DEBNAM of Sapiston, linen weaver. 29 January 1633/34.

I give my soul to my maker that gave it me.

I give my wellbeloved wife Mary for life my freehold tenement with all its land and my copyhold land in Sapiston, and after her decease to my eldest son Thomas, who must pay following legacies: £10 each to my sons Edmund, Edward, Roger and John at one p.a. starting 2 years after my wife's death; and £5 to Frances, daughter of my daughter Anne Winter 6 years after. If Thomas fails to pay legacies, my other sons are to share my house and land. I give all my moveable goods to my wife towards bringing up my children and paying my debts. I give my daughter Anne Winter 5s to be paid by my ex'trix within 3 months. I make my wife sole ex'trix. I entreat my loving friend Robert Cersye the elder to be overseer of my will. Wit. Robert Watson, Thomas Atare. Pr. at Bury 17 February 1633/34.

588. R(W) SUSAN RUSSELL (X) of Bury St Edmunds, widow. 30 December 1633.

Commends soul to God nothing doubting to have remission of sins through Jesus Christ and trusting in resurrection to eternal salvation.

I give my son Thomas within 1 year 2 pairs looms and 5s. I give my son Edward 2 pairs looms, my posted bedstead with bed fully furnished in the parlour and a hanging jack in the hall when 21 or married. I give my son John 1 pair looms, 4 silver spoons, 1 silver cup and 2 pairs hempen sheets when 21. I give my daughter Mary immediately after my decease my canopy bed fully furnished in my chamber, 5 pan tongs and cobirons in the parlour, 6 napkins and a board cloth. I give my daughter Susan immediately my other bed in the same chamber fully furnished, my fire pan, cobirons and tongs in the same room, 6 napkins and a board cloth. I give my daughter Elizabeth when 21 a trundle bed with a feather bed on it, 2 pairs sheets, a hutch in my parlour, a square table and the stools belonging to it, 6 napkins and a board cloth. I give my daughter Anne when 21 the bed I lie on in my chamber with a feather bolster, 2 feather pillows and a featherbed, 2 pairs sheets and a little livery board in the little chamber. I give my daughter Joanna when 21 a posted bedstead in the chamber where I lie with 2 of the best feather pillows in my house, a flockbed, 2 pairs sheets, my table and form in the hall, a great skillet and 4 pewter dishes. I give my daughter Martha when 18, 2 pairs sheets, 4 pewter dishes, my cupboard in the parlour with all the pewter and candlesticks on it and a little kettle. Benefit of survivorship except for son Thomas. I give my daughter Susan 20s to be paid within a month. All the rest of my goods and money, after my debts, expenses and legacies have been paid, I give to my daughters Mary and Susan towards their own maintenance and the bringing up of my young children in godly education and maintaining them in a decent manner. Ex'trices; daughters Mary and Susan. Wit. Thomas Johnson (X), Richard Allinson, Robert Walker. Pr. at Bury 6 March 1633/34.

589. W(R) JOHN TYPTOTT of Rickinghall Superior, yeoman. 3 February 1632/33.

Commits soul to God trusting through Jesus Christ in resurrection to eternal life.
I give my wife Prudence her dwelling in the parlour and parlour chamber and 4 cart loads wood a year. I give her £20 p.a. to be paid out of my lands by my son John at Michaelmas and Lady Day. I also give her my cupboard and table in the parlour, my bed complete as it stands in the parlour chamber and the third part of my brass, pewter and linen. I give my son Edmund £120 when 21 to be paid by son John. I give my daughter Prudence £100 when 21 or earlier if she marries with consent of her mother and my exors. I give the child my wife now goes with £100 when 21. Benefit of survivorship except for son John. My exors are to sell my close in Botesdale called Mickell close and use money to pay my debts; anything left over to be divided among all my children except John. I give John all my free and copyhold land and tenements. Legatees have power to distrain. I give John all the household goods given to me by my grandfather John Typtott of Rickinghall Superior. My unbequeathed brass, pewter and linen are to be divided between my children. Exors: father-in-law John Garnon and brothers-in-law William Brock and William Mannynges.
Postcript: I will that my wife has the education and bringing up of my children and is allowed so much a year out of my lands as my exors think fit; remainder of rents and profits to be kept for legacies to be paid by son John. I give Anne Pettoe, my sister's daughter £10 when 21. Wit. Jonathan Burn minister, John Garnon junior, William Greenewood. Pr. at Bury 14 March 1633/34.

590. R(W) ANNE HOYE (X) of Elmswell, spinster. 23 May 1633.

Bequeaths soul to God.
I give John, son of my brother Christopher Hoye, 16s within 2 months of my death. All the rest of my goods and chattels I give to my sister Joan, wife of John Allen of Bildeston, whom I make my sole heir and ex'trix. Wit. Joan Gale (X), Anne Ellitt (X), William Bramfeld. Pr. at Bury 17 March 1633/34.

591. R(W) SAMUEL NORMAN (X) the elder of Heigham Green in Gazeley. 3 February 1634 [sic].

Bequeaths soul to my heavenly father believing to be saved through Jesus Christ. To be buried in Gazeley churchyard.
I give my son John all my houses and land in Gazeley and Heigham. I give my son-in-law Walter Pricke 5s because I have given him a greater portion before. I give my son-in-law Nicholas Livermare 12 pence because I gave him £5 the day after his marriage day. I stand bound to pay him a portion of £10 which my exor shall pay. I give my son Samuel 20 nobles within a year, and my daughter Susan £15 within 2 months of my decease. I also give her the bed she lies in, 2 pairs sheets which she is to choose out of all my sheets, the best pillow and pillowbeere which I have, a yard kerchief, one of the little kettles, a skillet, a wheel and a reel, a skep of bees at her own choice, and one of my wicker chairs which she is to choose. She is to live in my house for a year after my decease with free access as she had in my life time. I give my son John all the rest of my moveable goods and make him exor. Wit. John Francige, Andrew Barnard. Pr. at Bury 17 March 1633/34.

592. R(W) THOMAS KEABLE (X) of Cotton, blacksmith. 22 October 1629.

Commends soul to God and Jesus Christ.
I give my messuage and free and copyhold land in Cotton to my son Thomas for life and then to his son Thomas. My freehold land is to be charged with payment of £20 to my son-in-law Richard Maninge in 2 portions, 2 and 6 years after my decease, and of £5 each to my grandsons John and Thomas Seamon 4 years after my death. My daughter Agnes Sparkinge is to be paid an annuity of 26s 8d out of my freehold land. When my grandson Thomas inherits my freehold land he is to pay £10 each to my grandchildren Jonas and Bridget Keble 1 and 2 years after, and another £10 to Jonas after 3 years. I give my grandson Edward Coates £5 when 21 and £5 when 22, and £10 to grandchild Mary Coates in same way. All legatees have power to distrain. I give Richard Manynge my son-in-law 40s within 6 months, and to my daughter-in-law Frances, wife of Thomas, £5 to be paid after her husband's death by my grandson Thomas, who is also to give her a cartload of wood p.a. Power to distrain. I give my son Thomas all my moveable goods and appoint Richard Manynge exor. Wit. Francis Ellis, John Keable, Thomas Ellis. Pr. at Bury 17 December 1633.

593. R(W) CHARLES DRURYE esquire of Rougham. 2 December 1633.

Bequeaths soul to heavenly father and body to earth hoping for a joyful resurrection.
I have already made a jointure to my dearly beloved wife Sarah by an indenture dated 1 October 1632, and I now further give her these lands

247

and tenements and also my manor of Rougham Lawnes and Netherplace, and all my other land and tenements in Rougham, Thurston, Barton, Pakenham, Hesset, Bradfield, Drinkstone, Rushbrook and Beyton for 21 years if any children of ours live so long. She is to pay my debts and raise a portion for my daughter Dorothy. I give my son Seckford all the above property with remainder to my brother Roger. If the latter inherits, he is within 2 years to pay my daughter Dorothy £2000 and £500 each to my sisters Cicely Douglas and Anne Drurye. Power to distrain. If Roger has no heirs and my land comes to my daughter Dorothy, she is to pay £2000 each to my 2 sisters if they be living. Power to distrain. I give my 2 sisters £100 each within 2 years of my decease, and £100 to my brother Roger one month after his apprenticeship has ended. I give £15 to the poor people of Bury, Rougham and Ixworth (£5 to each town) and another £5 to the poor of some of the other places near Rougham. I give my wife Sarah the advowson and next presentation to the rectory of Rougham. The rest of my goods and chattels I give to my wife and make her sole ex'trix. Wit. Henry White, Charles Willoughby, Arthur Payne, Anthony Adams. This will was proved in PCC.

594. R(W) JOHN HALL (X) the elder of Cowlinge, yeoman. 16 January 1633/34.

Commends soul to God and body to be buried in Cowlinge churchyard.
I give my eldest son John the house wherein I dwell in Cowlinge with 3 closes, after the decease of my loving wife Margaret. I give my other 3 sons Samuel, Thomas and Robert all my land in Cowlinge called Shorlies after wife's decease. If these sons die without heirs John is to have their portions. I give my daughter Margaret when 21 a cottage in Stradishall and £40 at same age, but if she is unmarried not until she marries. I give my daughter Lydia £60 when 21 or if she is not married on marriage day or within 6 months of demanding it. Benefit of survivorship. If both daughters die, my sons are to share their legacies. I give my wife for life my house where I dwell, its 3 closes and my land called Shorlies, and my cottage in Stradishall until daughter Margaret is 21. I give my wife all my goods and chattels to pay my debts and legacies, and bring up my children, and I make her sole ex'trix. Wit. Thomas Finch (X), Edward Barker. Pr. at Bury 17 March 1633/34.

595. R(W) LUCY PEAKE (X) of Fordham [Cambs], widow. 31 May 1631.

Bequeaths soul to God.
I give my daughter-in-law Audrey Peake widow 2 of my best kirtles. I give her daughters Marian and Winifred 30s each within 6 weeks of my decease. Benefit of survivorship. I give my other daughter-in-law Anne, now wife of Thomas Kinsley, a kirtle and to her daughter Anne Peake 30s. I give John Crispe, son of my brother Luke, 30s and a new suit of

apparel, both within 6 weeks. I give my above 3 grand-daughters all my small wearing linen to be equally divided between them. The rest of my unbequeathed goods I give to my son Thomas and make him exor. Wit. William Hill, William Frost. Pr. at Bury 24 February 1633/34.

596. R(W) JAMES FULLER (X) of Mildenhall. 20 January 1633/34.

Bequeaths soul to God.
I give my sons William and John the messuage I now dwell in with a little tenement in the same yard to let out for 4 years to pay my debts and legacies. When this is done William is to have the messuage and east half of yard and John the little house and west side of yard. I give William my half acre freehold arable at the yard's end to sell towards paying my debts and legacies. I give my daughter Margaret 10s and the table that stands under the window next to the yard, one of the best forms next to the cupboard, a feather pillow and one of the little hutches. I give my daughter Agnes, wife of Henry Younges, 30s within 2 years and my grandchild Agnes Younges one ewe hogg or sheep. I give Emma my youngest daughter 30s within 3 years, a wheel and reel, a flock bed, 1 sheet and a pillow. I give my grandson John Graye one ewe hogg or sheep. I give my son John 20s 4 years after my decease. All my other goods, my milk cow and the rest of my sheep I give to my son William and make him exor. Wit. Philip Kendall (X), Robert Wixe (X), Adam Wormall. Pr. at Bury 24 February 1633/34.

597. R(W) ELIZABETH WEETING (X) of Redgrave, widow.
5 November 1633.

Bequeaths soul to God trusting to Jesus Christ for pardon of sins. To be buried in Redgrave churchyard.
I give my 2 sisters Susan Clarke widow and Frances, wife of John Hart the elder of Redgrave, my tenement and ground in Redgrave now occupied by John Hart the younger for their lives and then to John Hart the younger, who must pay following legacies: to my brother-in-law John Hart 40s; to Anne, wife of Samuel Lawes and my sister's daughter, 20s; and to Rebecca, wife of Richard Grome, 40s within a year of inheriting; to Joseph, son of John Hart the elder, £4 and to his sister Anne £4 both within 2 years; to Elizabeth, daughter of my sister Ethelred and her sister Mary, £3 each within 3 years; to Anne, daughter of Thomas Dale, 20s and to Elizabeth Dale 10s within 4 years; and to Mary, wife of Richard Goulde, 20s within 5 years. All these legacies to be paid in Redgrave church porch. I give 20s each to Richard and Rebecca Grome to be paid by John Hart when they are 21. Legatees have power to distrain. The residue of my goods I give to my sister Frances Hart to distribute among my kinsfolk at her discretion, and I make her sole ex'trix. Wit. John Hart (X) the elder, John Denton. Pr. at Bury 27 January 1633/34.

598. R(W) FRANCES BALLARD (X) of Bury St Edmunds, widow.
12 October 1632.

Commends soul to God my maker and redeemer.
I give my son John a flockbed, a flock bolster, a flock pillow, a trundle bed, a blanket and 3 sheets immediately after my decease. I give my son Henry 12s he owes me, 1 pair cobirons and the coffer which was his own. I give my son John £10 to remain in hands of my exors, who are to pay him the interest when he needs it and the capital sum when he marries. I give my son Henry £10 within 3 months of my decease. I give my daughter Katherine £10 in same way as to John. Benefit of survivorship. All my other household stuff and money I give to my daughter Katherine, who is to pay John 20s 3 months after my decease. Exors: Mr Francis Astye gentleman and his 2 sons Edward and Francis. I give them their reasonable charges out of my estate, and desire them for God's love to be careful of my children and perform my will as my trust is in them. Wit. Oliver Johnson, his wife Susan Johnson (X). Pr. at Bury 21 February 1633/34.

599. R(W) WILLIAM CAUSTON (X) of Lavenham, woolcomber.
20 January 1633/34.

Bequeaths soul to God believing to be saved through Jesus Christ.
I give Jane my wellbeloved wife for life my messuage with outbuildings, yard and orchard in Aprentice Street [now Prentice Street] in borough of Lavenham, and after her decease to my daughter Jane. If she dies without heirs my property is to go to Isaac, Thomas, John and Ann, the children of Isaac Canston clothier of Lavenham and my brother-in-law. They are to pay £5 to my brother Thomas Cawston of Chelsworth. The residue of my goods I give to my wife and make her ex'trix. Wit. Thomas Paine (X) junior and me Peter Marshall. Pr. at Bury 17 March 1633/34.

600. R(W) KATHERINE TILLETT (X) of Rickinghall Inferior, singlewoman. 10 February 1633/34.

Commends soul to God hoping to have remission of sins through Jesus Christ. To be buried in Rickinghall the Nether.
I will my debts paid before all other things. I give my sister Alice all my clothes and household stuff, 2 kettles, a brass pot, a cupboard, a bedstead and a flock bed, 3 coffers and a skillet pan with other lumber. I also give her £10. I give her son William £5 or, if he be dead and she has no other children, to William son of my brother Thomas. I give 10s apiece to 6 of the youngest children of Robert Morse late of Hinderclay; 6s 8d each to the children of Roger Scarfe of Hinderclay and 20s to the children of John Strangman. I give Robert, son of John Jeffery, 6s 8d. I give my brother Thomas 40s and his daughter Elizabeth 20s. I give the wife of Amos Reeve 5s and his son Amos 5s. I give John and William Hamon my cousins 20s between them. All these legacies to be paid within a year of

my death. Exors: John Parker, brother Thomas and Humphrey Padnall and I give them 20s for their expenses. The rest of my goods I give to my exors. If sister Alice departs this life before it shall please God to call me, £10 left to her is to be equally parted between Thomas, Elizabeth and William Tillet and Mary wife of Amos Reeve. Wit. John Gagge (X), John Litton. Lawrence Baxter. Pr. at Bury 24 March 1633/34.

601. R(W) ANTHONY COOKE (X) of Cavendish, husbandman.
10 November 1630.

Humbly yields soul to God.
I give Bridget my wife all the household goods which were hers before we married and £10: half within 6 months and the rest within a year of my decease. She is to have her diet and board with my exor at his charge for 6 months after my death. I give her a load of wood yearly or 12s at her choice. I give my son John £20: £10 when 23 and £10 when 25. I give my daughter Joan £12 when 26. I give £3 each to my grandsons Anthony and Edward Matroe when 21, and until then my exor is to allow them 3s p.a. each. Exor: son Anthony. Wit. Richard Gardner, Thomas Wright. Pr. at Bury 24 March 1633/34.

602. R(W) JOHN BOLDERO of Bury St Edmunds, gentleman.
8 February 1631/32.

Commends soul to God in trust of salvation through Jesus Christ.
I give my grandchild Elizabeth Boldero £20 within a year of my decease. I give my son Edward £40 within 2 years. I give my wife Mary all my plate, jewels and household stuff, and the debts due to me by bills and bonds or otherwise, desiring her to give so much money to my sons George and Henry as she shall think meet. I make her sole ex'trix. Wit. Edward Elsinge, Oliver Johnson, who wrote will. Pr. at Bury 25 February 1633/34.

603. R(W) THOMAS RAINEBERD (X) of Stowupland, freemason.
8 June 1633.

Commends soul to 3 persons of Trinity.
I will that my debts and charges of burial and proving my will be paid out of my goods. The remainder my wife Joan shall have for life, but if she is in want it shall be lawful for her to sell part or all my goods for her maintenance. Any goods left at her death are to be divided by the then churchwardens between my children, and my son Thomas shall have the better part. If my wife remarries, within 1 month she is to pay Thomas 40s and the rest of my children 20s each, and my former gifts to them will then be void. I nominate my wife Joan ex'trix. Wit. John Goddard (X) senior, Thomas Foorde (X), John Goddard. Pr. at Stowmarket 4 October 1633.

604. R(W) THOMAS SPENCER (X) the elder of Dalham. 8 September 1631.

Bequeaths soul to God and body to be buried in Dalham churchyard trusting to be saved through Jesus Christ.
I give my eldest son Thomas all my free and copyhold land and houses in Dalham on condition he pays my debts. I give my son Robert £5 within a year and to his daughter Unica and son Robert 20s each when 21. I give Robert, son of Thomas Spencer the younger, a table and a cupboard in the hall, a bed and bedding and a square table in the parlour, a walnut tree chest in the parlour chamber and the best brass pot after his father's decease, but if he dies first his mother Katherine is to have these goods. I give Thomas Shilling my godson 10s when 21. I give Katherine, wife of Thomas Spencer, for life 3 acres freehold land, 1 acre of which is called the Long acre at the elder bush, an acre in Stowden field, half an acre and half a rod lying in the short went and 1½ rods in the meadow. All the rest of my goods I give to my son Thomas whom I make exor. Wit. Reuben Bridge, Hammond Uttinge.
Memorandum: This will was read to the testator on 1 January 1633/34 and he acknowledged it to be his will. Wit. William Copin, John Ramberlowe, Robert Mosse (X). Pr. at Bury 3 February 1633/34.

605. R(W) MARY PYNDAR (N) of Kentford, widow. 12 September 1633.

She disposed of her goods, lying sick in Kentford. She gave to Alice Wills her grandchild £5 and to 5 other grandchildren by her daughter Mary £5 apiece to be paid to them either at their days of marriage or when 21. She gave her grandson William Alcocke the cup of plate in the cloak bag, and she gave Sarah Thurston her best petticoat. The rest of her goods she gave to her son Alcocke, whom she made exor, to pay her debts, legacies and funeral expenses. Wit. Thomas Barcocke, Edmund Remching, Sarah Thurston. Pr. at Bury 14 January 1633/34.

606. R(W) GEORGE RUFFLE (X) of St Bartholomew next Sudbury, yeoman. 30 May 1633.

Commends soul to God hoping to enjoy everlasting life in kingdom of heaven.
I give Katherine my wellbeloved wife £20. I give £20 each when 21 to all my children: William, Anne, George, Thomas, Elizabeth and John. Within 1 week of my decease all my goods and chattels are to be viewed and prized by John Bragg yeoman of Borley [Essex] and Thomas Poollye yeoman of Sudbury and so many other persons as they shall think necessary. They shall set down in writing the particulars and value of my goods. My wife is to have the use of my goods and of my children's legacies until they are 21 towards their education and upbringing. She is not to waste or embezzle any of my goods, the value of which is to be

divided between my children when 21. Benefit of survivorship. Ex'trix: wife. If my wife refuses to prove my will, or remarries without consent of John Bragg and Thomas Poollye, or wastes my goods, then I make the aforesaid men my exors to see my children educated according to their capacities and employ their portions to their benefit. Wit. Thomas Howe (X), Robert Kingsburie (X) and me William Pricke. Pr. at Bury 27 January 1633/34.

607. R(W) JOHN ABRY (X) of Lakenheath, husbandman.
21 December 1632.

Bequeaths soul to God.
I give Mary my now wife a tenement with 14 acres arable land, late Thomas Geeson's, in Eriswell for her life and after her decease to my son John. I give him a bed with bedstead as it now stands and a cupboard at Eriswell after my wife's death. I give my son Thomas a tenement with 3 rods arable and 1 rod copyhold land in Eriswell after my wife's decease. I give my daughter Mary £14 to be paid as follows: £9 by John and £5 by Thomas 2 years after my wife's death. Power to distrain. If either of my sons die single men, the other is to pay Mary 40s more. The residue of my goods and chattels I give to my wife whom I make ex'trix. Testator surrendered 1 rod copyhold to the use of his will by hand of Miles Marrum. Wit. Francis Hunt (X), Thomas Flatman. Pr. at Bury 21 September 1633.

608. R(W) ELIZABETH DOWNAM (X) of Assington, widow.
3 December 1633.

I desire the Lord to receive my soul.
I give my son John my house and yard in Bures hamlet now occupied by James Potter tailor in part and the other part is standing empty. John is to have the remainder of £10, given him by the will of my late husband, within 1 year of my decease. I give him 12 pence when he shall demand it on condition he takes charge for 1 whole year of bed, board and schooling of my daughter Elizabeth. My son Joseph is to have £10 given by his father and £10 more within a year. The legacy given to my son James by his father, to be paid 3 years after my death, is to be employed for his use until he is 21. The 50s due to William Dickson, cooper of Bures, shall be paid to him at the time agreed on for his apprenticeship. My son Samuel is to have the house bequeathed to him by his father at age of 21 and meanwhile the profits from it are to be used for his education by William Bowes tailor of Bures, to whom £5 is to be paid for the same purpose before 20 May next. My daughter Bridget is to have £10 bequeathed to her by her father when 21, and she shall have her grandmother's gift made up in household stuff to the value of £10 immediately after my decease. My daughter Elizabeth's gift from her father is to be paid when she is 21 and in the meantime employed for her benefit, and I give John Grimes £4 towards bringing her up. I give my

sons James and Samuel 12 pence apiece. If my estate falls short of what is bequeathed, my debts are to be paid first and the legacies equally lessened. Children have benefit of survivorship. I give Thomas Downam my son-in-law 5s and Jane my daughter-in-law 7s, and my daughter-in-law Joan a red petticoat. I give 20 groats to be given to 20 poor people of this parish at the discretion of the minister. Exors: son Joseph and John Thorpe of Assington. Wit. Thomas Rowlington, Robert Rose (X), Thomas Carter. Pr. at Bury 4 February 1633/34.

Note: The will of the husband of this testator is number 335.

609. R(W) ANNE PAGE (X) of Icklingham, widow. 20 February 1632/33.

Bequeaths soul to God my maker and Jesus Christ my redeemer.
I give William Ladie my grandchild my warming pan. I give the poorest people in Icklingham 10s to be paid to them within 1 week of my decease. I give my daughters Dorothy, Margaret and Sarah all my linen and woollen except 1 pair good sheets and 1 pillowbeere which Thomas my son is to have. I give my daughter Margaret the bed standing in the hall, all that belongs to it and all those things she had before. I give my grandchildren William and Francis Ladie and Anne and Thomas Skinner 5s each within a year. The rest of my goods I give to my son Thomas and make him exor. Wit. Henry Craske, Francis Craske. Pr. at Bury 20 January 1633/34.

610. R(W) HUGH DRAKE (X) of Ampton, husbandman. 23 February 1632/33.

Bequeaths soul to God. To be buried in Ampton churchyard.
I appoint my son John to be sole exor and give him my houses and land in Ampton; he is to pay my debts. I will that he pays my son William £8 in 2 portions within 1 and 2 years of my decease. My moveable goods are to be equally divided between my 2 sons. Wit. Robert Stafford, Thomas Davy (X), Susan Bland (X). Pr. at Bury 3 March 1633/34.

611. R(W) MARTHA ARNOLD (X) of Bury St Edmunds. 18 July 1633.

Commends soul to God nothing doubting through Jesus Christ to be received into his blessed kingdom to eternal salvation.
Within a year of my decease my exors are to sell the house wherein I now dwell and the 2 let to James Cobb and Thomas Turle, all in Bury, and use the money to pay my legacies. I give £20 each to my sons Edmund and John Pond, and to my son-in-law John Harrison and his wife and my daughter Anne; all 3 legacies to be paid within 3 months of sale of houses. Wives and children of legatees to have benefit of survivorship. John Waller, cordwainer of Bury, is to hold £10 of the sale money for the use of my grand-daughter Anne, daughter of Thomas Webb and my

daughter Barbara, during the lifetime of her mother. Within a month of Barbara's death £10 to be paid to Anne. If any of the above dislike their legacies and trouble my exors, gifts to them shall be void. I give Edmund, son of my son Edmund Pond, £5 when 21 and until then money is to be put out at yearly rate of 18 pence in the pound. I give my grandson John Pond, son of my son John, £5 on same terms. Brothers and sisters of Edmund and John have benefit of survivorship. I give my servant Elizabeth Arnold £5, 1 pair sheets and a hutch within 1 month of sale of my houses. I give Martha, daughter of my son Edmund, all the household stuff in the hall where I now lie within a month of my decease. I give Anne Webb all the household stuff in hall chamber of the house where I live within a month. I give George Cooke gentleman a gold ring which I now wear. All the rest of my goods and chattels are to be equally divided between my 4 children: Edmund and John Pond, Barbara Webb and Anne Harryson. Exors: my reverend friend Mr John Jewell master of arts and John Waller, and I give them 40s each. Wit. Thomas Gibbon, Valentine Elsden, Robert Walker. Testator surrendered her copyhold premises to the use of her will and into the hands of Robert Browne gentleman and Thomas Gibbon, customary tenants of the manor. Pr. at Bury 14 January 1633/34.

612. R(W) BRIDGET BARWICK of Hitcham, singlewoman.
1 December 1633.

I give my soul to Almighty God.
I give my brother Mr William Barwick all my freehold lands and his son Hugh my copyhold lands held of manor of Hitcham and Kettlebaston. I give Mr Hurd Smith, curate of Hitcham, 20s and entreat him to preach at my burial. I give the poor people of Hitcham 40s to be distributed on day of my burial, and £4 to other poor people fearing God wheresoever they dwell. The above £7 is in hands of William Chaplin, who is to distribute gifts to poor at his own discretion and give my exors an account. I give my brother James the £10 he owes me upon a bill made to my mother Joan Barwick. I give my brother Richard £7 10s 0d and other reckonings mentioned in a bill made to my mother, and forgive him all other demands. I give him my brass pot, my old trunk with its contents, and a little chair with a back which are all in his own house. I give Mr Benjamin Barwick my brother my silver and gilt cup and the 40s he owes me upon his bill, my feather bed, feather bolster and pillow and a coverlet, which are all in his own house. I give my sister Mary, wife of Hugh Backe, an annuity of £3 to be paid to her for her own use and not into hands of her husband, and to be paid out of my lands given to William Barwick and called Stonn fields; to be paid in south porch of Hitcham church at Michaelmas and Lady Day. If William defaults in paying annuity, my friend William Chaplin is to hold Stonn fields during Mary's life and pay her annuity and 10s rent to William. I give Mary my best holland sheet and 3 other sheets when 2 pairs of next best have been taken out for my kinswoman Elizabeth Barwicke. I give Mary 6 diaper napkins and all

things formerly lent her and now in her hands. I give Elizabeth Barwick, daughter of my deceased brother John, £10 when 21 or married to be paid by my brother William out of freehold meadow given to him and lying between Hitcham church and Bildeston. If legacy not paid, Elizabeth is to have this land for life and Hugh Barwick is to fence this piece of meadow and the fence is to be set out by William Chaplin and Robert Gardner the elder. I give Elizabeth when 21 the £5 due to me by a bill made to my mother by my brother Mr Benjamin Barwick, but if she dies my brother William is to have £5. I also give Elizabeth a box at Brownesmith's, a silver spoon, 2 pairs of my best sheets, a trundle bedstead which is at my brother Richard's, my feather bed at William Chaplin's with 2 feather pillows, an old feather bolster, a birded coverlet, 2 pairs blankets whereof one is worth little, a flockbed with a flock bolster and a long buffet stool at Edward Brownesmithe's, my best cloak, my least joined chest and a high buffet stool at my brother Richard's. I give towards the placing of John Randole's lame boy £3. I give Katherine, wife of William Chaplin, my riding suit, my best petticoat, my posted bedstead, my old livery cupboard in her use, my trundle bedstead and my great joined chest at Edward Brounesmithe's, my bason, a low cushion stool and 2 high buffet stools. I give Christian, wife of John Randole and my kinswoman, my second hat, my second cloth waistcoat and my blue stuff petticoat, my best pair shoes and my best upper bodice. I give my sister Mary my best hat, my third petticoat, my best gown, my best cloth waistcoat and my needlework waistcoat. I give Agnes, wife of my brother Richard, my best holland apron. I give my sister Mary and my cousin Elizabeth all the rest of my linen and pewter to be divided between them. I give my sister-in-law Agnes my second petticoat. I give my godson Richard Barwick a silver spoon. All the rest of my unbequeathed goods I give to my brother Mr William Barwick towards payment of my legacies and decent burial of my body, and I make him exor. Wit. William Chaplin, John Chaplin, Ralph Bennitt (X). Pr. at Bury 20 January 1633/34.

613. R(W) WILLIAM BARKER (X) of Brandon Ferry. 10 January 1631/32.

Aged above 80 years yet of whole and perfect remembrance. Commits soul to God trusting to be saved by merits of Jesus Christ.
I give Audrey my now wife the tenement where I dwell for life and after her decease to my nieces Joan, daughter of John Barker of Thetford, and Margaret, daughter of Robert Hubberd deceased. My moveable goods and chattels I give to my wife in regard of her former care of me and that which I yet expect, and I make her ex'trix. Wit. John Rous clerk, John Tilbrooke, Robert Mashe (X). Pr. at Bury 28 January 1633/34.

614. R(W) THOMAS DOCKINE (X) of Mildenhall. 30 December 1633.

Bequeaths soul to God and body to earth trusting that it will be raised again at last day.

I give my wife Katherine for life my house and land, and after her decease my house to my son John, who must pay my daughter Anne £10 within a year and my son Thomas £8 within 2 years. Power to distrain. I give my son Richard 1 acre copyhold and son Thomas half an acre freehold land. Benefit of survivorship. If John dies before my wife, Thomas is to have my house and pay John's children £10 in equal portions when 21. All the rest of my goods I give to my wife and make her ex'trix. Wit. Edward Jackson, Martin Folkes. Pr. at Bury 13 January 1633/34.

615. R(W) MARGARET PATTLE (N) of Thwaite, widow. 8 August 1633.

She willed that her debts should be paid and what remained after burial and probate charges she gave as follows: half to her kinsman Anthony Knappe and other half to children of Walter Reade late deceased, and 10s out of this half to Ann, daughter of William Allen. Wit. Richard Cobbold, John Vise (X). Let. ad. granted to Anthony Knappe 17 September 1633 in St Wolstan's chapel in St Mary's church in Bury.

616. R(W) JOHN FRYER of Finningham, gentleman. 24 September 1631.

Commends soul to God hoping to be made partaker of life eternal through Jesus Christ.

I give my loving wife Anne an annuity of £35, to be paid out of my freehold lands by my son John in my dwelling house in Finningham at Lady Day and Michaelmas, on condition that within 14 days of my decease she gives John a release of all her rights of dower. Wife has power to distrain. I give my son John all my messuages and free and copyhold land and lease land. I give my wife a third part of my household stuff and utensils, and the rest to John; to be divided between them by good discretion of Richard Pretyman gentleman, Thomas Sherief and Thomas Bedwall within a month of my decease. I give my wife 6 of my best milk cows and my roan saddle mare. If my wife refuses to release her dower rights in my land, the gift to her of household goods is void. I give Millicent Browne £10 within a year. My son John is to pay my sister Thomasine an annuity of 40s. I give my sister Esther Norman 40s and my god-daughter Sarah Norman 20s within a year. I give the poor people of Finningham the yearly interest of £5 to be paid to the churchwardens, who are to distribute it in Easter week. I give 20s to poor of Finningham,

Wickham Skeith and Cotton, and 13s 4d to poor of Bacton, Westhorpe and Gislingham. The rest of my goods and chattels, cattle and corn I bequeath to my son John and make him exor. Supervisors: my loving friends Richard Pretyman gentleman and Thomas Shereiff the elder. Wit. Richard Pretyman, Thomas Bedwall. Pr. at Bury 14 January 1633/34.

617. R(W) GEORGE MILLER (X) of Semer, yeoman. 21 March 1633/34.

Bequeaths soul to God looking for salvation through Jesus Christ.
I give my eldest son John my house and land in Whatfield and Semer, now occupied by Hugh Wright, on condition he makes following payments: £5 p.a. to my wife Alice at Michaelmas and Lady Day, and legacies to my other children: £12 to daughter Elizabeth, wife of Thomas Cosen of Whatfield, within 20 days of Michaelmas 1636; £12 to my daughter Martha 2 years later; £12 to son Thomas 2 years after that and £12 to daughter Mary 20 days after Michaelmas 1642. Also £12 to daughter Sarah in 1644; £12 to son Edward in 1646; £12 to daughter Anne in 1648 (to be paid by my wife); £12 to son Richard in 1650; 20 marks to youngest daughter Susan in 1652. Wife and childen have power to distrain. If my wife desires to dwell in the house and land left to my son John, she is to enter them as a tenant at Michaelmas next, paying £7 p.a. to John as long as she remains a widow. She must not fell any trees and must keep buildings in repair with thatching and daubing. I give my wife any 2 of my cows and 4 of my ewes which she pleases to choose at Michaelmas next, all the household stuff she brought to me, the cupboard and table that stand in the hall, a pair cobirons in the parlour, my warming pan, a dozen of my best trenchers, the bedstead in the parlour chamber, a pair of the best sheets and 1 odd sheet. I give Anne, my daughter by my first wife, the bed I lie on in the chamber and all that belongs to it and a chest that stands between the 2 beds in the chamber. I give my daughter Sarah the other bed in the chamber where I lie, 3 table napkins and 2 buffet stools. I give my daughter Mary 2 forms in the parlour and 3 table napkins. All the rest of my goods and chattels I give to my son George provided he pays my debts and funeral charges, and pays my daughter Anne 40s at Michaelmas next and £10 when 21. George must pay my son Daniel £12 when 24. Exor: son George. Wit. John Brunning, Richard Chapline, John Harvie (X). Pr. at Bury 27 March 1634.

618. R(W) THOMAS HILL (N) the elder of Bury St Edmunds, innholder. 26 March 1634.

His debts being paid, he gave the overplus of his goods to his loving wife Eleanor. Wit. his son John Hill, daughter-in-law Susan Hill, Mary Hill. Pr. at Bury 31 March 1634.

619. R(W) MARTHA LILLY of Wetherden, widow of Thomas Lilly of Wetherden. 4 September 1632.

Commends soul to God hoping to be made partaker of everlasting life through Jesus Christ.
A marriage is intended before Michaelmas next between me and William Kendall, cordwainer of Bury St Edmunds, and immediately after it he is to receive £25 now in the hands of my good friend Mr Kilborne clerk of Wetherden, and is bound to use it to pay such persons as I shall appoint in this my will. He also has in his hands certain household goods listed in an inventory and part of my household stuff not inventoried and remaining in my house called Thinges in Wetherden, where I now dwell; all of which, by an agreement made between us, I shall have the power to dispose of by will after our marriage. Within 3 months of my decease William Kendall shall pay £20 of the £25 to my exors in the porch of Wetherden church towards payment of my legacies; the other £5 I give to him. I give John, son of William Kendall, a cupboard, a great chest, 4 boxes with locks and keys and a needlework cushion named in the inventory. I give [blank in MS] Turner, son-in-law of William Kendall, 2 tables, 4 framed or joined stools and the rest of the household stuff in the inventory. All these goods are to be given to the legatees within 1 month of my decease in William Kendall's house in Guildhall Street in Bury. I give Roger, son of my sister Frances Brookes, 40s and to her daughter Martha Sayer £3 13s 4d, being the remainder of £6 13s 4d promised to her on her marriage. I give John Harbor, my sister Pepper's son, 40s and John, son of my brother Jeremy Westlye, 40s. I give Elizabeth Wright, daughter of Frances Brookes, 30s, and to another of her daughters, Susan Keteringham the £3 her husband William owes me. I give Susan 20s, her daughter Margaret 30s, her daughter Elizabeth 20s and her son John 20s. All these sums are to be paid in Wetherden church porch within 4 months of my decease. Benefit of survivorship. I give Martha Sayer my best open seamed sheets, my black wrought pillowbeeres and my blue wrought table cloth. I give Elizabeth Wright 1 pair sheets of taring cloth and a pillowbeere. I give Susan Keteringham 1 pair good sheets and a pillowbeere, to her daughter Margaret a brass pot and to her daughter Elizabeth 2 pewter platters and 4 pewter porringers. All these goods are in my house called Thinges in Wetherden and are not mentioned in the inventory. I give Alice, wife of Joseph Petto of Mendlesham and daughter of widow Brookes, all the rest of my goods in my house in Wetherden on condition she pays 10s towards payment of my legacies. I give my godson Humphrey Markes the younger of Wetherden 10s, and to all the rest of my godchildren in Wetherden 2s 6d each within 3 months. I give the poor people of Wetherden 13s 4d and 10s to the poor of the parish where I die, within 3 months of my death. Exors: my loving kinsman William Sayre of Colchester [Essex] and Joseph Petto and I give them £3 for their pains. Wit. William Kilborne clerk, William Stokes, Edmund Basse, Andrew Kilborne, Humphrey Markes (X). Pr. at Bury 2 April 1634.

620. R(W) EDMUND HAWARD (X) of Cockfield, yeoman. 17 March 1633/34.

Bequeaths soul to God trusting through Jesus Christ for free pardon of sins. To be buried in Cockfield churchyard.
I give Alice my loving wife all my moveable goods so long as she keeps herself unmarried. After her decease my son John is to have half my goods as inventoried after my death, my debts being paid first. The other half I give to my wife to dispose of to my son and 3 daughters as she thinks good. If my wife remarries she is to have half my goods and the rest are to be divided between son John and daughters Anne, Alice and Mary. Benefit of survivorship. Supervisor: brother-in-law John Rabe. Ex'trix: wife. Wit. John Scott (X), Thomas Milles. Pr. at Bury 8 April 1634.

621. R(W) JOHN FLAWNER (X) of Mildenhall, blacksmith. 4 March 1633/34.

Commits soul to God hoping to attain kingdom of heaven through merits of Jesus Christ.
I give my wife Anne my messuage in Mildenhall where I now dwell for ever. She is to pay my debts and bring up my children. I also give her all my implements and household goods, not doubting that she will see my debts honestly paid and continue a careful and loving mother to my poor children after my death. I make her sole ex'trix. Wit. John Hargrave, William Dalleson. Pr. at Bury 8 April 1634.

622. R(W) GEORGE TAYLER of Lidgate, gentleman. 20 May 1633.

Commends soul to God trusting through Jesus Christ to enjoy everlasting life in kingdom of heaven.
I give the poor people of Lidgate 20s to be distributed at my burial. I give my wife Katherine for life all my copyhold land and tenements in Lidgate. After her decease I give to my daughter-in-law Blanche, now the wife of Thomas Loveringe gentleman and formerly wife of my deceased son George, for 4 years all the following copyhold land: a close of meadow called Mullinge; a piece of copyhold called Mullyes lying between highway leading from Lidgate to Bury on the south east and a field called Mully went on north west and abutting to west on a close of Lidgate parsonage and my copyhold ground called Reeves; my copyhold land called Reeves abutting to west on parsonage ground sometime called Marrall; 2 pieces of land lying together in East Good Deane went between William Almer's land on north and his and George Hall's on south and abutting on my land to west and on a way from Lidgate to Cowlinge on east; 2 pieces lying together in Small Meadow field between my free land to north and John Dereslye's land to south and abutting on Portway to east; 2 pieces lying together between Green Portway to south and George Hall's land to north and abutting on John Almer's land to

east and those of divers men to west; 2 more pieces in Small Meadow field between John Dereslye's land to east and Thomas Wakefeild's to west and abutting on a hedge called Trundle hedge to south; 2 pieces called Short Lands in Small Meadow field and lying next to John Almer's land to south and abutting on John Cater's meadow to east and George Hall's land to west; 2 pieces of land lying lengthwise by the highway from Lidgate to Cowlinge and abutting on John Deresley's land to south and the Lord's land to north; 2 pieces of land and meadow lying together in More field between John Almer's land to north and Lidgate parsonage land to south and abutting on Lord's meadow to east and John Warren's and my free land to west; 2 pieces land lying together in Huntsawe between my free land and that of divers men to north and my lands and those of John Warren to south and abutting on the Lord's meadow to east; 2 pieces called Short Lands lying together in Croplyes meadow field between Jeffry Hall's land to north and mine that I exchanged with Thomas Hall to south; 1 piece meadow in Croplye meadow between highway from Lidgate to Newmarket on west and Lord's meadow to east and abutting on John Warren's meadow to south and my land to north; 2 pieces lying in or near North field with way from Ousden to Newmarket passing through them and lying between Mathew Roger's land to north and Ousden parsonage land to south and abutting on land of Ousden manor to east and highway to west; 2 pieces lying together in Cropley meadow field between George Hall's land to south and Almer's to north and abutting on Jeffrey Hall's land to east and on Lord's meadow called Cropley meadow to west. Blanche and Thomas Loveringe must within 20 days of my will being proved make, at their house in Cambridge, an acquittance to my wife of all demands on her or me by them or by the administrators of late John Hilles, doctor of divinity of Fulbourn [Cambs], and enter a bond of £200 to ensure my wife has no demands made on her. After 4 years I give all my copyhold land to my grandson John Tayler, son of my late son George, who must pay £50 in Lidgate church porch to 4 of my grandchildren: £10 to Anne Dereslye, £10 to George Dereslye, £10 to Katherine Tayler, £10 to George Tayler and another £10 to Katherine. Payments to be made 1 p.a. starting 1 year after John inherits land. If he defaults in payments, my copyhold land is to be divided into 5 parts and given to above 4 grandchildren. I give all my goods and chattels to my wife and make her ex'trix. Wit. Adam Webb, Thomas Wakefield. Pr. at Bury 14 April 1634.

623. R(W) ROBERT HOGG (X) of Wortham, yeoman. 19 January 1633/34.

Commits soul to God.
I give Margaret my wife £3 to be paid when she releases her right to dower in 1 acre 3 rods freehold land in Oxcroft field to John Jeashoppe and his wife Frances. I give my wife my bed whereon I lie, all my linen except that given to Sarah Jeasoppe, 2 coffers in chamber where I lie, a little cupboard, a little box, 2 pillows at her choice, the hangings about

the chamber, all the candlesticks in the house except the pewter one and half the pewter. John Jeasoppe is to divide the pewter and my wife is to choose her part. I also give her all the dishes, spoons, cups and trenchers, and all the brass in the house except a great kettle and a brass pot given to John Jeasoppe, all the tubs except the great one, the table in the hall, 3 joined stools and the form, 4 chairs, a stool, 2 pails, 2 flitches bacon, a hook and hatchet, the brazen warming pan, an old hutch in the lower chamber, a little roasting iron, tongs, fire pan, cobirons, 2 hales, the bellows and all my clothes except my best doublet and jerkin and best stockings, and all the pans in the house except the cream pot and 3 little pans that hang together, a little churn at her choice, 4 shelves, 2 little beer vessels, the beer stools, 3 cheese vats, a keeler at her choice, 4 bowls of the middle sort, the store butter and pot, 12 cheeses at her choice, 4 bushels mislyn, 1 of barley and all the hemp, the bunching block, beetles and tow comb, a pashel, a little spit, 3 minging bowls, 2 pokes and the feathers in them, an old hutch, the maund peel, the coal staff, the cradle and a child's chair, all the fowls, 1 sheep and lamb, a bunch of woollen yarn, half the wood in the yard, and a skep of bees. I give the other skep to my grandson John Jessoppe, and I will that my cushions be equally divided between my wife and John Jessoppe. I give my wife a chafing dish, a skimmer, a wash basket and all her wearing apparel, the great wash bowl and a mortar and pestle. I give my daughter Frances 2 acres copyhold held of Wortham Abbottes manor and called Pearles Coate and another 2 acres in the same close and held copyhold of Wortham Hall manor, 1 acre 3 rods in Foxcroft field, and a close called Gyles Albons if my wife is not expecting a man child, but if she is he is to have this close. If my wife bears a woman child, Frances is to pay her £5 within a month of child's birth and £10 a year later. Wife has power to distrain. If my wife has no child, my exor is to pay her £10 within a year of my decease. I give my wife 2 loads of wood from Giles Albon close within a year of my death. I give my grandchild Sarah Jeashoppe my best cupboard in the hall, her sister Elizabeth my great copper kettle and their brother John my great brass pot. I give Robert Neale the flockbed he lies on with a bolster. All the rest of my goods, corn and cattle I give to John Jessoppe to pay my debts and the legacies given by my father in his will, and I make him exor. Wit. Thomas Leaverington rector of Wortham, Mark Corbold, John Rookes. Pr. at Bury 9 April 1634.

624. R(W) ADAM HALL (X) of Hargrave, yeoman. 22 February 1633/34.

Commends soul to God hoping to be saved by merits of Jesus Christ. I will my body be laid in a coffin and decently buried in Hargarve churchyard.
I give my wife Mary all my copyhold land in Chevington for life and then to my nephew John Hall, son of my brother John, yeoman of Lidgate. I also give him all my copyhold land and tenements in Hargrave, but my

wife is to hold them for 1 year after my decease. My nephew John is to pay his sister Elizabeth £5 within 2 years of my decease. I give the poor of Hargrave 20s and the poor of Chevington 20s to be paid to the overseers of the poor within a month, and distributed on Sabbath following. The rest of my goods I give to my wife and make her ex'trix. Wit. Thomas Pratt, John Waade. Pr. at Bury 14 April 1634.

625. R(W) THOMAS COOKE of Hitcham, yeoman. 10 April 1634.

Commends soul to God hoping through Jesus Christ to be a partaker of eternal happiness in Kingdom of heaven. My body to be interred next to my ancestors in Hitcham churchyard.

I will that my brother Isaac has all my free and copyhold land and tenements until my son James is 21. My mind is that my exor shall bring up my 3 children Robert, James and Anne to learning; Robert and Anne for 3 years and James for five or longer if my exor think fit. When my sons are 16 they are to be bound apprentices to some good trade in a corporate or other town, except that if Robert be apt for learning he shall have a better education if my exor sees good cause. Anne is to be put into good service when 16. The Michaelmas after James is 21, I give all my free and copyhold land and tenements to 4 of my 5 children: Thomas my eldest son, Robert, James and Anne. My brother Isaac is to be guardian of my son John's land until he is 14 and afterwards if John thinks fit, for I trust he will be careful for his education and estate. I give John £10 at Michaelmas after James is 24 and Thomas £10 the Michaelmas after James is 23. This £20 is to be raised out of my stock after my debts are paid, but if there is not enough money my daughter Anne is to pay these legacies out of the land left to her, and if she refuses bequest to her is void. I give my brother Isaac my lease land called Ely fields and all my outdoor goods, stock, crops on the ground, goods, debts and credits, except for my late wife's apparel. These goods are to be appraised and sold towards paying my debts and legacies and bringing up my children. Any surplus is to be disposed of among my children, but if there is not enough to pay my debts my children are to make it up. Until Thomas is 21 he is to allow my exor to take profits of the land left to him called Thorne crofts, and if he refuses legacy to him is void. My daughter Anne is to have all the linen and woollen that was her mother's wearing apparel, and it is to be laid up in a chest for her. Exor: my brother Isaac Cooke. Supervisors: my loving brother Mr George French and my loving cousin Thomas Maye of Wetherden. If Isaac refuses to be exor or dies before my son James is 21, Thomas Maye is to be exor. I give the poor of Hitcham 20s to be distributed by my exor. My supervisors are to help about the selling of my stock and goods, and my exor is to give them a note of my debts and a copy of the inventory of my goods, and they are to advise my exor in the education of my children. Wit. Thomas Corbould, George Frenche, Gregory Cooke. Pr. at Bury 1 April 1634.

626. R(W) THOMAS WROE (X) of Thornham Parva, linen weaver.
9 April 1632.

Commends soul to Jesus Christ through whom I hope for eternal life.
I give Margery my beloved wife the east end of the house where I now
dwell called the parlour and parlour chamber, and all my land for life or
until she remarries. After her decease or marriage I give my daughter
Dorcas the east end of my house, the piece of yard adjoining it and 1 acre
land next to it. She must allow owners of other part of house free access
through the yard to the ditch to draw water. The rest of my house and
land I give to my son Henry and his wife Emma. I also give them 1 pair
looms complete as it now stands with 10 pairs slayes, and I charge them
carefully to bring up and educate their son Thomas. If Dorcas wishes to
sell her share she is to offer Henry first refusal for £18. I give my wife all
the rest of my goods and chattels and make her ex'trix. Wit. Robert
Revet, Samuel Colbye, Henry Dune. Pr. at Stowmarket 16 April 1634.

627. R(W) GILBERT SEAMAN of Mendlesham, singleman. 27 March
1634.

Bequeaths soul to God.
I give my brother William, during the life of my mother Elizabeth, all my
lands and tenements: 8 acres copyhold land called Coymans which I had
by gift from my father, and the land I purchased from John Man the
younger. He must pay my mother £10 p.a. in my house in Mendlesham at
Michaelmas and Lady Day. Power to distrain. After my mother's death,
William is to sell land I bought from John Man within a year and give the
money to my 2 sisters: Elizabeth wife of John Packard and her children
Elizabeth and Anne, and Anne Seaman. If land is sold for more than
£100, extra is to go to Elizabeth and her children. If Anne dies without
children before her legacy is paid, £30 of it is to go to children of my
brother William and £20 to Elizabeth's children. If William dies before
our mother, my brother-in-law John Packard is to sell land and pay
legacies. My exor is to give two pence each to the poor people who come
to my burial. I give Mr Wragg and Mr Penn 20s each. I give to Mr Jacob,
Mr Springe, Mr Symondes, Mr Burroughe, Mr Whitbye, Mr Andrews,
Mr Carr, Mr Jefferie, Mr Neech, Mr Devorickes, Mr Young, Mr
Stansbye, Mr Greenehill, Mr Burroughes and Mr Candler, all preachers
of God's word, 10s each when they come to preach at Mendlesham
according to their courses next after my decease. I give 10s each to Mr
Mosse, Thomas and Grace Docker, William Lockwood, Henry Burton,
Thomas Lord the younger and Katherine Sheringe. I give 5s each to
Anne, wife of John Goddard, Elizabeth Hall and Alice Knightes. I give
Bartholomew Knightes 2s 6d. All these gifts to be paid 6 months after my
decease. The rest of my goods I give to my brother William and make
him exor. Wit. Christopher Wragge clerk, Barnabas Gibson, Mathias
Wealy (X). Pr. at Stowmarket 16 April 1634.

628. R(W) ROBERT CLIFFORDE (X) senior of Aldham, yeoman.
30 July 1633.

Commends soul to God in full assurance of salvation by Jesus Christ.
I give my loving wife Elizabeth my mansion house wherein I now dwell with outbuildings and garden and called Bertles tenement, the field before the door called the home field and the adjoining meadow until Michaelmas 12 months after my decease. I also give her for life the copyhold land belonging to Bertles tenement: a close called Tanwell and Tanwell Bottom, a laye field called Goslie i.e. Great and Little Goslies and Goslie Groune, a close called Little Collilands, 2 adjoining pieces called Dead Grounes and a close called Great Hollidaies with an adjoining orchard. She must not take more than 6 cartloads of wood p.a., and must not claim any thirds in my freehold land. I give my son James, and then my grandson James, my messuage the brick house called Parkers tenement with outbuildings and garden, a 6 acre close called Parkers, a close called Frogging field and about an acre of land next to it which I lately bought out of Hovells tenement, a little close called Collyns Hatches and all other land belonging to Parkers tenement. After my wife's decease I give my son Richard Great Hollidaies close with its orchard, and he must pay my son Robert £100 within a year of my decease or I give this close to Robert after my wife's death. I give my wife for ever a 1 acre piece meadow in the common meadow in Whatfield. She is to pay my debts out of land left to her for life. If she dies within 2 years of my decease, her exors are to hold land left to her for 3 years to pay my debts. I give my son Richard a long joined table in the parlour, a great square table there, 6 three-cornered joined stools and a great joined chair, 1 pair cobirons, a firepan and tongs, a great cupboard in the hall, a salting trough, 1 pair malt querns, a brass as it hangs, a great chest and 1 other chest. All the residue of my goods and chattels I give to my wife and make her ex'trix. Wit. John Pagett, Richard Wyeles, William Glead. Pr. at Bury 21 April 1634.

629. R(W) THOMAS INNOLD of Haughley, yeoman. 26 March 1634.

Commends soul to God and Jesus Christ assuredly trusting to be saved through latter.
I bequeath to poor people of Haughley 20s to be distributed on day of my burial at discretion of Mr Cropley our minister and Goodman Thurgood of Haughley. I give 20s to the poor of Hessett to be distributed on the same day by my brother Dedman and William Adkyn of Hessett. I give my wife Mary for life my copyhold messuage wherein I dwell with 18 acres land belonging to it in Haughley, and after her decease to Francis Innold my eldest brother's son on condition he pays £20 within 2 years to be equally divided among the 4 children of my brother John: Thomas, Francis, Mathew and Elizabeth. Benefit of survivorship and power to distrain. I give these 4 children another £20 to be paid within a year of my decease by my exor. I give my brother John £10 within 3 months. I give

Susan, daughter of Mathew Innold, £10 within 1 year and my brother Thomas £20 within 6 months. I give Thomas Dedman, my sister's son, £10 within 1 year. I give my kindred at Bury 20s to be equally divided between them within 6 months. I give my nephew John, son of my brother John, £40 within 8 months. I give my wife Mary my 3 cows, all my hay and wood, all my moveables and household stuff. I give my exors all my bonds and debts and all money owing me to prove and perform my will. Exors: nephews Francis, son of my brother Mathew, and John, son of my brother John. Wit. Thomas Burrowe (X), Thomas Walker, John Burrowe (X). Pr. at Stowmarket 16 April 1634.

630. R(W) ROBERT GILBERT (X) of Burwell [Cambs]. 20 March 1633/34.

Bequeaths soul to God hoping to be saved by merits of Jesus Christ. To be buried in churchyard of St Mary in Burwell.
I give my son Theodore all sums of money due to me by bond and £10 at Christmas next. I give him the lease I now have of Mr Tyndall, my little brown nag, 13 acres of copyhold held of manor of Ramsies of which 3 acres were purchased of Richard Canforth and 10 of Thomas Oliver. I give my daughter Agnes Fuller £20 within a year of my decease, the posted bed in the parlour with all things belonging except the feather bed and instead of it the one on the soller, and 1 cow. I give my godchild and her son Thomas Fuller £6, and £5 each to all her other children. Benefit of survivorship. I give my daughter Elizabeth Fuller £20 within a year, the posted bed in the chamber with its bedding and my other cow. I give my godchild Robert Fuller, son of Elizabeth, £6 and £5 apiece to rest of her children. Benefit of survivorship. Exors to pay these children's legacies to Thomas and William Fuller to be put out for benefit of their children. I give my apprentice William Sowth 10s within a year. I give the poor of Burwell 20s to be paid among them on my burial day. All the rest of my goods I give to my son Robert and make him exor. I give more to my son Theodore £10 now in the hands of William Fuller and not mentioned in a bond. Wit. Robert Carsbury, Daniel Lyvermore. Pr. at Newmarket 10 April 1634.

631. R(W) FRANCIS FULLER (X) of Bury St Edmunds, yeoman. 16 December 1633.

Commends soul to God trusting to have remission of sins through Jesus Christ and to reign in his heavenly kingdom with his holy angels and elect children for ever.
I give my brother Robert Fuller of Mildenhall for life a 4 acre piece of copyhold arable in Stockfield in Mildenhall, and after his decease to his sons Richard and Robert, and if they have no heirs to their brother John and to Francis my eldest brother's youngest son. I give John Fuller £10 to be paid by his father within a year of decease of my wife Frances, or by his brothers if their father has died. I give the above Francis Fuller £5 to

be paid by Robert and Richard Fuller 1 year after my wife's death. My wife is to have an annuity of 20s out of land left to my brother Robert. Power to distrain. Within half a year of my decease my wife is to pay £80 to my brother Robert, which he is to distribute as follows: £8 each to Richard and Robert sons of my eldest brother; £4 each to 2 children of his daughter Anne Powle, wife of [blank in MS] Powle; £8 each to his daughters Frances and Margaret; and £8 to his youngest son Francis. My brother Robert is also to pay out of the £80 £8 each to his youngest son John and to his daughters Mary, Anne and Anne [sic]. All these legatees have benefit of survivorship. Interest on legacies is to be paid to my wife during her life. My son-in-law Daniel Chapman is to pay out of the money he owes me the following legacies: £5 to Thomas son of George Wood within a year; £5 each to his sisters Frances and Emma within 2 years and 3 years; £5 to George son of George Wood within 4 years; £13 6s 8d each to Daniel and Roger sons of Daniel Chapman within 6 and 7 years. If any of these children die before receiving their legacies, Daniel Chapman the elder is to keep them. He must pay the interest on all these legacies to my wife during her life, and if he refuses to pay legacies my exor is to call in at once the money he owes me. I give Anne Tailer, my sister's daughter, £5 to be paid by my brother Robert at 10s p.a. I give her husband my old russet suit and my riding coat. I give Richard Fuller my russet coat and Robert Fuller my best cloak. I give Frances, my brother Richard's eldest daughter, my best hat. I give Thomas Wood my black stuff suit, and Frances Wood my best worsted stockings within a month and, after the decease of my wife, my biggest silver bowl and 2 silver spoons, and to Emma Wood a silver beer bowl and 4 silver spoons. I give my brother Robert all my unbequeathed wearing apparel with the stockings he wears, all my boots and shoes, my bible, a holland shirt, 2 of my best caps and 1 of my best waistcoats. All the rest of my goods, after my debts and funeral expenses have been paid, I give to my loving wife Frances and make her ex'trix. If she dies within 6 months of my decease, it shall be lawful for my brother Robert to take £80 worth of goods. Testator surrendered to use of his will his copyhold land held of the manor of Mildenhall to Thomas Childerston and John Drifte, customary tenants. Wit. Peter Bales (X), Robert Walker. Pr. at Bury 23 April 1634.

632. R(W) JOHN TILBROOKE of Brandon Ferry, parish clerk. 3 November 1633.

Commends soul to God and Jesus Christ my saviour. To be buried in Brandon churchyard.
I will that my debts be paid. Margaret my wife is to have all such moveable goods which she had before we married to give at her own will. She is also to have all those children's goods which were Payne's, and are either in Edward Howtchin's hands or mine, according to her father's will. I give her my house and ground where I now live for life. She must keep buildings and fences in repair, and not allow the fruit trees to decay but do her best to preserve them. If she remarries or when she dies my house and land are to be sold by the then minister and churchwardens,

and the money divided into 8 parts among my kindred as follows: 2 parts each to John Lillege and Nicholas Stallom or his children, and one part each to Nicholas and Abraham Tilbrooke, to Frances Parson and Philippa Duffild or their children. Benefit of survivorship. The minister and churchwardens to keep 40s for their pains. All the rest of my goods and chattels I give to my wife and make her ex'trix. Within 1 year of my decease she is to pay 20s each to John Lillege, Nicholas and Abraham Tilbrooke, Frances Parson, Philippa Duffeild and Abigail Payne, and 10s each to Susan, daughter of Nicholas Stallom, and William Whydbe. Susan Stallom's father is to employ her money for her use. Wit. Richard Holmes, John Ransom (X). Pr. at Bury 28 April 1634.

633. R(W) ROBERT BARON (X) of Burwell [Cambs], waterman. 13 January 1633/34.

Gives soul to God and hopes to be saved by Jesus Christ.
I give Margaret my beloved wife my house where I now dwell for life, and then to be equally divided among my 5 daughters or their heirs. I also give my wife my house and croft and 1 acre in the open field of Burwell after my mother's decease, and then to my daughters. I give my daughters Margaret, Ann, Alice, Mary and Martha £10 each when 21. All the rest of my goods I give to my wife and make her ex'trix. Wit. John Wickyns, Edward Wilson, Thomas Goodchilde (X). Pr. at Bury 28 April 1634.

634. R(W) MARTHA LOCKWOOD (X), wife of William Lockwood of Combs. 12 January 1630/31.

Commends soul to God my merciful saviour and redeemer.
I give my husband William the £300 that he stands bound in, in a bond of £600 to Edward Dandye gentleman and Mr Thomas Sowtherbie, that I might make my will. In consideration of this £300 he is to pay the following annuities: £5 to my mother Joan Bowle widow and, after her decease, 40s p.a. to my brother David and 40s p.a. to my sister Anne Bowle. He is also to pay £60 to my brothers Fernando and Robert within 4 and 6 years of my decease; and £20 each to my sisters Thomasine and Alice 5 years after my death. If my sister Anne marries without the consent of my husband, she shall not have her annuity. I make my husband exor. Wit. Robert Small, William Keble. Pr. at Stowmarket 16 April 1634.

635. R(W) MICHAEL CARR (X) of Monk Soham, yeoman. 24 June 1626.

Commends soul to God and saviour Jesus Christ.
Anne my wife is to have for ever all my goods and chattels, plate and jewells, and ready money. I make her ex'trix. This was sealed and signed in the mansion house of William Parslye. Wit. me Francis Godfrey, William Parslye (X). Pr. at Stowmarket 16 April 1634.

636. R(W) JOHN PATTELL of Cotton, husbandman. 3 March 1632/33.

Commends soul to God my father looking to life and salvation from him by merits of my saviour Jesus Christ.
I give my son Thomas my bible. I give Joan my wellbeloved wife all my goods towards her maintenance, bringing up my children, and paying my debts, and I make her exrx. Wit. Henry Skynner, Francis Skynner (X). Pr. at Stowmarket 16 April 1634.

637. R(W) DOROTHY TILLETT (X) of Brandon Ferry, widow.
2 October 1632.

Bequeaths soul to God and body to be buried in Brandon churchyard.
I give John Franncis my eldest son a brass pot, a pair of my best sheets, my best pillow and pillowbeere, and my framed table paying half the price of it to my daughter Audrey Fuller, also a trundle bedstead and a bed blanket. I give my daughter Audrey Fuller my bed wherein I lie with all that belongs to it, my hemp, my best bullock and all my linen except 2 pairs sheets given to John Franncis and Robert Tillett. I give my son Robert Tillet my other bullock, and all my other moveable goods I give to him and Robert Fuller whom I make exors. Supervisor: my son John Franncis. Wit. John Tilbrooke, John Drake (X). Pr. at Bury 21 April 1634.

638. R(W) ROBERT ROSE (X) of Hopton, miller. 10 March 1633/34.

I bequeath my soul to God trusting to be saved.
I give my daughter Frances my messuage in New Buckenham [Norfolk] with orchard and land, and she is to pay my daughter Mary, wife of John Chase, £12 and my daughter Anne £10. Both legacies to be paid alternately at £4 p.a. over 6 years. I give my daughter Anne within 10 days of my decease a bed, the trundle bed and a bolster set together, a leather pillow, 2 brass kettles one of lesser and other of next size, a brass pot, half my linen and half my pewter. I give John Chase my son-in-law all my apparel within 10 days. All the rest of my goods I give to my daughter Frances and make her ex'trix. I make Henry Spurgen of Hopton supervisor and I give him 20s for his pains. Wit. John Spurgen, Thomas Man alias Muskett (X). Pr. at Bury 28 April 1634.

639. R(W) WILLIAM COOPER alias ROBINSON (X) of Mildenhall, yeoman. 14 February 1633/34.

Commits soul to God trusting through Jesus Christ to obtain kingdom of heaven. To be buried in Mildenhall churchyard.
I give my son James for life my messuage in High Town, Mildenhall at a place called the Pynnefold Slowghe and now occupied by Katherine Revell widow, and which I bought from the heirs of Emma Long, widow. After James's decease, I give this messuage to his son William. I give my

son Robert 20s. I give my kinswoman Anne Hasted 10s. The residue of my goods and chattels, after my debts, legacies and expenses have been paid, I give to my son James and make him exor. Wit. James Knight senior, William Dalleson. Pr. at Bury 28 April 1634.

640. R(W) AGNES BRADNAM (X) of Icklingham, widow. 20 June 1632.

Bequeaths soul to our blessed Saviour hoping to be saved.
I give my grandchild Thomas, son of widow Woods, my bed and bedstead as it now stands in full satisfaction of 20s that I am to pay him when 21. I give my daughter Frances, wife of William Bull, my red petticoat. I give Peter Woods a bedstead which is now in his father's possession and a chest in my chamber to be given to him when 18, and meanwhile to be in custody of William Smyth. I give my son Thomas Woods a kneading trough. I give my grandson Thomas Woods my gown to make him a coat, and a pewter dish. I give James, son of James Bradnam of Icklingham, a candlestick. I make William Smyth of Icklingham my exor and will him to sell what remains of my goods and divide the money between my grandson Thomas Woods, Peter Woods, James Bradnam and Anne, daughter of Thomas Woods. Wit. Samuel Gary clerk, John Ward (X) and others. Pr. at Bury 28 April 1634.

641. R(W) ELIZABETH PARKER (X) of Culford, widow. 1 April 1628.

Bequeaths soul to God hoping for salvation. To be buried in Culford churchyard.
I give my son William Bowles a 2-hand cutting saw and my greatest chest. I give my grandson William Bowles a great charger, being the greatest of all my pewter dishes. I give Frances, wife of my son William, a pewter dish and a pair sheets. I give my daughter Elizabeth, wife of Joseph Johnson, a flockbed, a blanket, a bolster, 2 pillows, a pair sheets, a kettle bound about with an iron band, my greatest skillet, a hutch, a pair pillowbeeres, a little pewter pot, a brass candlestick and a pewter dish. I give my grandchild Susan Johnson, daughter of Elizabeth, a little coffer and a tow comb. I give my grandchild Mary Johnson a little painted box and her sister Elizabeth another such painted box. I give my grandchild Katherine Johnson a little hutch and my grandson Stephen Johnson the greatest save one of my pewter dishes. The rest of my goods I bequeath to my daughter-in-law Anne Parker, whom I make ex'trix. Wit. John Guibon, James Warwell. Pr. at Bury 21 April 1634.

642. R(W) DOROTHY SHARPE (X), widow. 20 April 1634. No place.

I give my son John 2 pairs sheets, 6 silver spoons, 2 kettles and a featherbed. I give my son James the best coverlet, 1 pair sheets, a flock of bed of linsey wolsey bed [sic] and a pillow. I give my son Henry all the goods that I have as they stand in my house. Wit. Simon Barker (X), his wife Susan Barker (X), Katherine Hayward (X) widow, Ann Wayt (X). Let. ad. granted at Bury 6 May 1634 to son Henry.

643. R(W) RICHARD KING (X) of Brockley. 26 February 1633/34.

Bequeaths soul to God hoping to be saved by Jesus Christ.
I give my eldest son Richard my houses and land in Chedburgh, and my brass pot which is to be given to him in porch of Brockley church when 20. I also give him my bed and bedstead in the parlour, but my wife Dorothy shall have them for life if she gives my exors security to preserve them and not sell them. I give my son Michael my grounds called Millers meadows alias Millers croft in Somerton; my exors are to receive rent of this land to bring up Michael until he is 21 when they are to give him an account. I also give him my biggest brass kettle to be given to him in church porch when 21. I give my daughter Mary 20 marks when 18, my long table, 6 joined stools and a square table, all in my parlour. I give my wife Dorothy 40s and the press in the hall with all that is in it 2 days after she has surrendered her rights in my free land in Pakenham. I give the bed and bedstead in the chamber over the parlour to my brother-in-law John Nunne of Stanningfield. If one son dies, other to pay daughter Mary £20 when 21; power to distrain. If Mary dies her portion is to be divided between my wife and son Michael. The rest of my household stuff to be divided into 4 equal parts: 2 to be given to Richard and one each to Michael and Mary when 21. I give 10s each to Ralph Apslee yeoman and Edmund Copping carpenter, both of Brockley, and make them exors, desiring them to be provident and careful as much as they can for good of my children. Wit. John Brooks, Elizabeth Lewes (X), John Brinknell. Exors renounced exor'ship and let. ad. granted to widow at Bury 5 May 1634.

644. R(W) JOHN COCKE (X) of Hopton, yeoman. 29 March 1634.

Commends soul to God.
I give Helen my wife for life 3 pieces land in Hopton in Fen field: 1 acre in Smithfield furlong between land of John Murriell on south and of Knettishall rectory to north; a 1½ rod piece in Gayrode furlong between lands of John Tostock on both sides; and a third piece of half an acre in Huntstond furlong between land of John Spurgen on west and of John Tostock on east. I give my wife my tenement in Hopton where John Grigges now dwells and all the rest of my land for 12 years from Michaelmas after my decease. She is to bring up my daughter virtuously and make no waste on my houses and land. When 12 years are up, I give

land and tenement to my daughter Beatrice [Bettrise], but if she dies without heirs, to Humphrey, son of my brother Humphrey Cock of Coney Weston. I give my wife all my goods except my brazen mortar and my best brass pot, which I give to my daughter. Wife sole ex'trix. Wit. John Muryell, Humphrey Cock (X), Thomas Goddard. Pr. at Bury 12 May 1634.

645. R(W) MARIAN CLARKE (X) of Mildenhall, widow. 12 April 1634.

Commits soul to God and Jesus Christ hoping to have eternal life through latter. To be buried in Mildenhall church or churchyard.
I give my son Robert all my cows, calves and mares. He must pay my daughter Elizabeth £20 at Michaelmas after my decease and another £20 at following Lady Day. I give Robert £5 on condition he puts out 40s to best use immediately after my death and pays this sum with interest to Robert and Marian Adhams, children of my daughter Mabel, when 21. I give my daughter Elizabeth my best gown, best hat, and best neckerchief. All the rest of my clothes and wearing linen I give to be equally divided between my daughters Elizabeth and Mabel. I give my son Robert a pair querns and my biggest pair andirons. All the rest of my household stuff I give to my children Robert, Simon and Elizabeth to be equally divided, and the rest of my goods I give to Robert and make him exor. Wit. Theodore Adhams (X), Thomas Potter, Lancelot Gerold. Pr. at Bury 21 May 1634.

646. R(W) JOHN CLARKE (N) of Exning, singleman. Thursday sevenight after Easter last past i.e. 17 April 1634.

In presence of William Clarke his brother and other witnesses he said to his brother, brother William I give thee all that I have willing thee to pay my debts and bring up my 2 children until they shall be placed in service. These being 2 of his sister's children which he had maintained and brought up until his death. A little before his death John Clarke said that his brother William should have all that he had in the presence of divers persons, whom he desired to bear witness of his words. Wit. Thomas Lynwood, Bridget Lynwood, John Howlett, Bridget Howlett. Pr. at Bury 16 May 1634.

647. R(W) WILLIAM GATTEWARD of Nayland, scrivener. 6 February 1633/34.

Commends soul to God trusting to have pardon of sins through Jesus Christ.
Richard Barnard, tailor of Nayland deceased, did in his will give me all the profits of the lands and tenements which he held and which were to come to him after the death of his mother until his son Richard reached age of 21, and also entrusted me with education of his son until 21. He

asked that if I died before Richard was 21, I should make provision for his education. My will is that my loving and faithful friend William Blyth, grocer of Nayland, should have charge of his education, and I bequeath to him until Richard is 21 the rents and profits of above land. William Blyth shall bring up Richard at school until he is fit to be an apprentice and then bring him up to his own trade or another chosen by Richard or himself. When Richard is 21, William Blyth is to give an account of rents and profits of his lands. My wife Alice is to receive the rents for first half year after my decease, and I give her £4 p.a. for life out of Richard Barnard's lands. I give my wife all my goods and chattels, bills and bonds and money, and all my linen, woollen, brass and pewter except what is hereafter bequeathed. I give John the boy in my education and commonly called John Heard £5 within 1 year of my death and all my wearing apparel. I desire William Blyth to bind out John to some good trade that he shall like. I make my wife sole ex'trix and desire William Blyth to help her. Wit. James Blythe, George Frost, Thomas Russells. Pr. at Bury 19 May 1634.

Note: Richard Barnard's will is number 166.

648. R(W) THOMAS BURD (X) of Wickhambrook, husbandman. 17 May 1633.

Commends soul to God and Jesus Christ. To be buried in Wickhambrook churchyard.
I give my nephew Henry Burd £5, and my nieces Mary Harvy and Margaret Burd 20s each within 3 months of my decease. I bequeath my nephew Thomas Burd all my tools and implements in my shop, all my timber, my grindstone and my apparel. I give my nephews Thomas and Robert Burd all my household stuff, money and debts, provided that Katherine my wife shall have use of my household goods during her widowhood; she must not purloin or embezzle them. My exors are to pay my wife annually the interest on my ready money which comes to their hands and that owed to me on bond at 18 pence in the pound. My wife is to lose use of my goods if she purloins any of them. Exors: Thomas and Robert Burd. Wit. John Shere, Anthony Graunger (X). Pr. at Bury 12 May 1634.

649. R(W) ELIZABETH BARTON (X) of Alpheton, widow. 2 April 1634.

Bequeaths soul to God believing in its resurrection.
I give my kinsman Thomas Bigges my best bed ready furnished, my cupboard, my table, 2 buffet stools, my wicker chair, 2 cushions and my brass pot. I give his wife Katherine 1 sheet and a pillowbeere. I give Elizabeth Tillet my kinswoman a bedstead in my chamber below ready furnished, a chair, 2 cushions and my best kettle save one. I give my kinswoman Mary Tillet my posted bed in the chamber ready furnished,

my hutch in the chamber, my best kettle, one box and 2 cushions. I give John Foskue the elder my best tub and my cloak, and to his son John my godchild 10s and a platter. I give my godchild Francis Laurence 5s. I give Mary Barton a hutch in my chamber, my red coat and a green apron. I give my god-daughter Mary Wheler a fine sheet and a pillowbeere. I give Goodwife Wheler her mother 2 pails and 2 bowls. I give her daughter Ann a platter. I give my god-daughter Mary Lister a pillowbeere and godchild Elizabeth Baulden a pillowbeere and my biggest platter. I give Elizabeth Folker my best petticoat and best ruff. I give god-daughter Mary Paske my joined chest in my chamber, and godchild Ann Roote my black russet coat. I give Emma Fordum a sheet and a smock. I give my son-in-law John Barton a pair querns and my great tub in the cellar. Cash legacies to be paid within a month of my decease. My exor is to sell my 3 cows to pay legacies and expenses of my funeral and probate. The rest of my goods, except my powdering trough, I give to be equally divided between Thomas Bigges and Elizabeth and Mary Tillet. I give Andrew Hayward clerk my powdering trough and make him exor. Wit. Nicholas Hayward (X), Faith Lister. Pr. at Bury 26 May 1634.

650. R(W) THOMAS DEANE of hamlet of Bures in Essex, husbandman. 16 July 1633.

Bequeaths soul to God hoping to be saved by Jesus Christ.
I give the poor of the hamlet of Bures 10s. I give my mother £6 to be paid at 10s a quarter, but if she dies before it is all paid my sister Elizabeth is to have the remainder. I give my mother my best hat, my shirt and petticoat. I give my brother James all my stock at Wormingford [Essex] and all my sheep, except 1 sheep and lamb that are John Deane's, which I give to young John Maynard, and 1 ewe that is in my master's ground and which I give to John Parmiter together with a bond of £3 which he has in his hands and of which 20s is paid. I give my sister Agnes £4 she owes me and 20s to be paid by my brother James and 20s more. I give my sister Elizabeth £3, as much of the bedding at Wormingford as is mine, my hutch and my old coat. I give my brother John £4, my brother Robert 40s and to Mr Sparsmok 20s. I give Tamazen [sic] 5s and my best jerkin, and to Goodwife Myller my best shirt. I give Rolfe my best shoes and John Polle my best breeches. Any residue I give to my master Mr Thomas Walgrave to use at his discretion. I give John Parminter half of my wool. I make my master and my brother James my exors. Wit. Jeffrey Hist, John [surname illegible]. Pr. at Bury 2 June 1634.

651. R(W) THOMAS HOULDEN (X) of Drinkstone, labourer. 24 September 1630.

Bequeaths soul to God.
I give my wife Anne all my moveable goods. The tenement I bought from Henry Mickelfeild is to be sold to pay my debts and legacies. I acknowledge myself to be indebted to my daughter Margaret for £5; £4 is

to be paid her when tenement has been sold. I give my daughter Alice 40s from sale of tenement. I make my wife Anne ex'trix. She is to dispose of any sum left from sale of tenement as she thinks good. Wit. John Maninge, Peter Baker (X). Pr. at Bury 9 June 1634.

652. R(W) RICHARD WARD (X) of Mildenhall, husbandman. 1 May 1634.

Commends soul to God.
I give my wife Martha for life my messuage now in the use of Richard Pollington and after her decease to John, son of Nicholas Shellie of Isleham [Cambs], but if my wife is with child at time of my decease, I give messuage to that child. In this case the child must pay £8 to Marian, sister of John Shellie, within a year of inheriting messuage. If John Shellie inherits it, he is to pay his sister £8. I give Marian Shellie my tenement in the market place now occupied by widow Shephard after her decease, and in meantime Marian is to have the rent of tenement. I give my wife for ever 1 acre copyhold at Swadge cross. If my wife is with child, it is to inherit the tenement in the market place. I give all my goods to the use and discretion of my wife, whom I make ex'trix. Wit. James Sharpe (X), Edmund Hornigolde (X). I give Mary, daughter of Robert Daines deceased, £4 within half a year of my decease. I give the children of James Turner deceased 10s apiece within a year. I give Alice Banyard my god-daughter 10s within a year. Wit. same as above. Pr. at Bury 9 June 1634.

653. R(W) JOHN CROWNE of Rickinghall Inferior, yeoman. 7 January 1633/34.

Commends soul to God trusting to be saved by Jesus Christ.
I give my sister Anna all my lands and tenements in Thelnetham, Hopton, Weston Market, Barningham and Hepworth, and she must pay following legacies: annuity of £10 to my uncle Thomas Crowne and his wife Anne to be paid half yearly in porch of Thelnetham church; £60 each to Frances and Anne daughters of Thomas Crowne within 4 years of my decease; £10 to Helen, one of daughters of Thomas Seman of Well [sic] my deceased uncle, within 3 years; £8 to churchwardens and overseers of Thelnetham to be paid in 20s instalments at Christmas and Easter; £100 to John, son of my late uncle Thomas Offwood of Gislingham, within 3 years; £30 each within 5 years to Elizabeth, Anne and Frances Offwood, daughters of Thomas; £10 to Susan, a daughter of my uncle Thomas Seaman, within 3 years; £40 to Bridget, daughter of my uncle Edmund Seaman, within 1 year; £40 to John, son of my uncle Roger Seaman, within 9 years; £10 within 2 years to my godson John, son of my tenant John Payne; £10 when 21 to my kinsman and godson John, son of Richard Browne of Stanton. All legacies to be paid in porch of Thelnetham church. Legatees have power to distrain. My sister Anna is to pay £5 to churchwardens and overseers of Weston Market: 20s within

14 days of my decease, and then 20s p.a. She is also to pay £6 to churchwardens and overseers of Nether Rickinghall: 20s at Christmas and 20s at Easter for 3 years. I give all the rest of my goods and chattels to my sister Anna and make her ex'trix. Wit. Philip Jacob, Nicholas Dex (X). Pr. at Bury 14 April 1634.

654. R(W) RALPH COOKE of Great Saxham, yeoman. 16 May 1634.

Bequeaths soul to God. To be buried in church or churchyard of Great Saxham.

I give Jane my wife the chest of linen as it stands in the hall chamber. I give my daughters Rebecca, Margaret and Honoria all the rest of my goods to be equally divided between them after my debts and funeral expenses have been paid and when they are 21. If my wife is with child and has a son, he is to pay his sisters £60 each 4 years after he is 21 as follows: to Rebecca when 22, Margaret when 23, and Honoria when 24. This son is to have all my land in Barrow, Great Saxham and Hargrave, but if he does not pay his sisters' portions they are to have the land. If my wife bears a daughter, my land is to be equally divided among all 4 daughters. I give the child my wife is with 10s to be paid when he is 31. I make Stephen Cooke of Bury, my wife's sister's husband, my exor and I give him all the rents and profits of my land until the child my wife is carrying is 21, but if it dies, only until my youngest daughter is 21. He is to use money for godly and virtuous education of my children. Wit. John Cooke, Roger Cooke (X), Alice Covill (X). Pr. at Bury 25 June 1634.

655. R(W) GEORGE SINDERLAND (X) of Nayland, clothier. 28 November 1633.

Commits soul to God hoping to have everlasting life through Jesus Christ. I give my wife Alice the house where I now dwell in Nayland with outbuildings and gardens, and a messuage in Boxford in Callis Street and now occupied by [blank in MS] Wheeler, broad weaver. I also give her 2½ acres meadow ground in Lewhis meadow in Nayland. After my wife's decease I give land and messuage to Samuel Styleman and his wife and my daughter Alice for their lives. I also bequeath to them for life 2 other tenements in which George Frost and Andrew Fytt now dwell. After their death, I bequeath the house where I now live to their son John, but if he sells his reversion to this property this gift shall be void and I give house to his brother Samuel. After decease of my daughter and son-in-law I give the messuage in Callis Street, Boxford to their son Samuel and 2 acres meadow in Lewhis meadow. I give his brother Henry, after their parents' decease, the tenement in Nayland occupied by George Frost and to his brother James the one occupied by Andrew Fytt and half an acre meadow in Lewhis meadow. I give my brother Edward an annuity of 20s to be paid quarterly by my wife and after her death by Samuel and Alice Stileman. I give my daughter Alice £10 within a year. All the rest of my moveable goods I give to my wife Alice and make her ex'trix. Wit. Thomas Russells, William Gatteward. Pr. at Sudbury 13 April 1634.

656. R(W) WILLIAM KNOPP (X) of Great Waldingfield, yeoman. 21 April 1634.

Bequeaths soul to God trusting only in merits of Jesus Christ for eternal salvation.
I give my son William £20 within a year of my decease, my son John £20 within 18 months, my daughter Dorcas £20 within 2 years and my daughter Rachel £20 within 2½ years. Benefit of survivorship. I make my wellbeloved wife Rachel ex'trix. Supervisor: my brother John Knopp yeoman of Middleton [Essex] and my brother-in-law Henry Taner, yeoman of Great Cornard and I give them 5s each. Wit. Rachel Campine and me William Maperant [spelt Marchant in register]. Pr. at Bury 7 July 1634.

657. R(W) THOMAS ALLEN (X) of Glemsford, clothier. 1 June 1634.

Commits soul to God.
I give my 2 sons Thomas and John a messuage and toft, with adjoining garden, called Bumpsteds, and an half acre adjoining pasture in Egremon Street in Glemsford, and now occupied by me, but I give my wife Katherine for life a nether room in the messuage called the parlour. She is to have room at the fire in the messuage for her comfort and to do what is needful, and she is to have the fourth part of fruit on the trees belonging to the messuage. Thomas and John are to occupy the messuage together and pay my wife an annuity of £4 according to an indenture made between me and Henry Kerington and Richard Gardner, both clothiers of Glemsford, on 28 September 1626. Thomas and John must also pay £25 10s 0d to William Biggs, clothier of Glemsford, and £30 12s 0d to John Gilman, tailor of City of London. Both payments are to be made on Thursday next 3 months after decease of my wife according to an indenture dated 29 September 1626 and made between me and the same 2 men as the first one. I give my daughter Katherine, wife of William Bredges, 50s; to daughters Alice and Anne £8 each; to daughter Mary, wife of Samuel Minckes, 50s; all to be paid within 6 months of my decease. I give my son William £6 to be paid by son John within 6 months. After my wife has taken all such household stuff as she brought me, the rest is to be equally divided among 4 of my children: Thomas, John, Alice and Anne. Exors: sons Thomas and John. Wit. John Gardner, Richard Gardner. Pr. at Bury 2 July 1634.

658. R(W) JOHN LARGANT of Barningham, yeoman. 8 January 1633/34.

Bequeaths soul to God.
I give Talmisen my daughter £10. I give my daughter Joan and her husband £10 and my daughter Newelle and her husband £10; all to be paid within a year of my death. I give Talmisen that part of my house in which I do now keep at the time of making my will with a little house

adjoining on east side. She is to have free access through yard and to well to draw water. I will that she has a convenient place in the yard next her house to lay her firing. I give John Boone and his wife Sarah the unbequeathed part of my house and yard and the reversion to that part given to Talmisen. I give latter £3 within 2 years; daughter Joan and her husband £3 within 3 years and daughter Newelle and her husband £3 within 4 years of my decease. Joan's and Newelle's children have benefit of survivorship. I give £5 within 5 years to Thomas, son of my son John, and to his daughter Susan £5 within 6 years. Benefit of survivorship. I give 30s each to John, Robert, Edmund and Elizabeth, children of my son John, to be paid when they are of age to give a lawful discharge to my exor. I give my daughter Talmisen the bedstead on which I lie at the making of this will, and the use of a brass pan for life with remainder to my daughter Susan and her children. I give all the rest of my goods to be equally divided among my children. I make John Boone, my son-in-law, my sole exor. My will is that my daughter Talmisen shall keep the house given her in repair with claying and thatching. Wit. William Cussen (X) of Lackford, Benjamin Cope, John Bowen. Pr. at Bury 14 June 1634.

659. R(W) WILLIAM PASKE (X) of Wickhambrook, yeoman. 10 June 1634.

Commends soul to God by whom I trust to have forgiveness of sins and everlasting life. To be buried in Wickhambrook churchyard.
I give 10s to son of my brother George, £6 to my Abraham Paske [sic] and to my sister Mary Bowles £4; all within 3 months of my decease. I give Rebecca, wife of Daniel Loftes, £6 within 3 months, the bedstead in the corner with flockbed, bolster and pillow, 2 pairs sheets, 2 blankets, 1 coverlet, the hutch at the bed's foot, the brass pot that we daily use, a pewter dish and a buffet stool. I give Ann Lyllye my servant, within 3 months, £10, the bedstead where the trundlebed standeth under, the flockbed, the bolster, pillow, 2 pairs sheets, 2 blankets, 1 coverlet, the hutch at the bed's end, a little brass pot, a little square box, a pewter dish and a low buffet stool. I give 40s each within 3 months to William, David, George, Abraham, Richard and Edward Smyth. I give my kinsman William Lyllye 20s and a hutch in the chimney within 3 months. I give my sister Rose Lyllye 20s and a pair sheets, and Alice, wife of William Elliott, £3; all within 3 months. I give poor of Wickhambrook 40s to be divided the Sabbath day after my decease by my exor, and Thomas Barton, Robert Mertyne and Thomas Raye. I give Alice, wife of John Goodchild, 10s. All the rest of my goods, corn, bills and debts I bequeath to my servant John Lyllye and make him exor. Wit. Thomas Barton, Thomas Raye. Pr. at Bury 4 July 1634.

660. R(W) JOHN MORLY (X) of Cockfield, yeoman. 21 June 1634.

Bequeaths soul to God trusting through Jesus Christ to have free pardon of sins. To be buried in Cockfield churchyard.
I give my son William my tenement wherein I dwell with all my free and copyhold land on condition he pays my debts and legacies. I give my daughter Susan Wheeler £4 within a year of my decease, or to her son Henry if she has died. I give Susan Wheeler my nephew [sic] a boarded bedstead with a flockbed and all its furniture at once and £3 within 2 years. I give Joanna Wheeler £3 within 3 years and Anne Wheeler £3 within 4 years. I give £3 each when 21 to my daughter's children Mary, Henry and Mathew Wheeler. Benefit of survivorship and power to distrain. Exor: son William. Wit. Thomas Smith (X), Thomas Milles. Pr. at Bury 14 July 1634.

661. R(W) LEONARD NEWTON (X) of Brandon, yeoman. 6 July 1634.

Humbly resigns soul to God being assured to have pardon of sins through Jesus Christ.
I give my wife Elizabeth all my houses, tenements and lands in Brandon for life and then to my nephew Thomas, son of John Racke late of Brandon. I give my wife that annuity of £4 which Thomas Racke pays me for my land at Stanford [Norfolk]. After decease of my wife, I give Elizabeth, daughter of William Racke of Brandon, my best posted bed completely furnished. I give my wife for life my messuage and ground in Barton near Mildenhall [Barton Mills] now occupied by Richard Plowman, and after her decease to John, son of Thomas Grigge of Lakenheath, provided he pays £5 each to his sisters Elizabeth, Grace and Mary when 21. I give Elizabeth and William, children of William Racke deceased of Brandon, the moveable goods I now enjoy and which my wife shall leave behind her when it shall please God to call her. I make Mr John Stalham of Brandon my exor and give him £5 to be paid within a year by John Griggs. Wit. Thomas Lawson. Pr. at Bury 16 July 1634.

662. R(W) WILLIAM GRIGGE of Bury St Edmunds, yeoman. 20 April 1630.

Gives soul to God in sure hope to be saved by Jesus Christ.
I give £10 each within a year of my decease to my 3 daughters Anne Baker, Susan Bond and Elizabeth Lyllie. I give my grandchild Margaret Sellowes £25 within a year, and £20 each when 21 to Anne, Mary, Judith and Sarah Sellowes, 4 other grandchildren. Benefit of survivorship. I give my son John towards payment of my debts and legacies all my messuages and tenements. I give my grand-daughter Margaret Sellowes my trundle bedstead, my worst featherbed, my worst flockbed, my worst feather bolster, my worst flock bolster, my flock coverlet, an old blanket, my new kettle, my iron pot, my warming pan, my mantle tree jack rack, my best

skillet, a little spit, my gridiron and my 2 little iron spit racks. I give my son John my gowns, my best doublet and breeches. I give the poor people of Pentlowe in Essex 30s and to poor of Bury £5 as follows: to the high and east wards 30s, to the north ward 30s, to west and south wards 40s. The residue of my goods and chattels I give to be equally divided between daughters Susan Bond and Elizabeth Lyllye. Exor: my son John. Wit. James Turell. Will signed 22 March 1630/31 after crossing out 7 lines in the original will. Pr. at Bury 17 July 1634.

663. R(W) JEFFREY PECHIE (N) of Bures, yeoman. March 1633/34.

He gave his goods and chattels to pay his debts and anything left over for his wife and children, and his wife to have the better part. He appointed his son Jeffrey sole exor. Wit. Henry Waldegrave esquire, William Waldegrave gentleman, both of Bures. On 10 July 1634 in the house of Mr Henry Tanner clerk, being the parsonage house of Wissington, the 2 above witnesses swore to Mr George Carter Bachelor of Divinity, substitute for the Archdeacon of Sudbury during his Visitation, that the above nuncupative will was that of Jeffrey Pechie. Pr. at Wiston 10 July 1634.

664. R(W) ROBERT BRAND of Boxford, clothier. 6 July 1634.

Bequeaths soul to 3 persons of Trinity.
I give my wife Susanna for life all my tenements and land in Boxford, and then for 1 year after her decease to my 3 younger sons Joseph, James and Benjamin. Afterwards I give the house I now dwell in to my eldest son John with the land belonging to it, except one 12 acre arable field called Leidger land, which I give to my son Joseph. I give my son James a tenement in which John Cole now lives with arable and pasture belonging to it, and he must give Benjamin £10 to be paid within 1 year of my wife's death in the south porch of Boxford church. Power to distrain. I give my son Benjamin a tenement with 2 meadows in Boxford, which I purchased of John Hardie. I make my wife sole ex'trix and give her all my goods and chattels. I give the poor of Boxford 10s. Wit. Christopher Goodday, John Wheler (X). Pr. at Boxford during Visitation of Archdeaconry 11 July 1634.

665. R(W) ROBERT NEELE (X) of Wattisfield, yeoman. 26 June 1634.

Commends soul to God hoping through merits of Jesus Christ to be made partaker of life everlasting.
I give my wife Anna for life my tenement and grounds in West Street in Walsham in the Willows. After her decease it is to be sold by her brother Robert Nunn and the value of it divided among my 5 children: Anna my eldest daughter, Elizabeth my second daughter, Sarah, Mary and Alice my youngest daughter. I give my wife all my goods and chattels, and make her and Robert Nunne of Westhorpe exors. Wit. Stephen Vincent, Samuel Margery. Pr. at Bury 14 July 1634.

666. R(W) WILLIAM DIESDEN (X) of Westley, shepherd. 13 July 1634.

Bequeaths soul to God.
I give my son William £20 to be paid by my exor when he is 21. After my debts and funeral charges are paid, I give my wife Ann and my daughter Elizabeth all my moveable goods in equal portions. I make my wife ex'trix. Wit. Robert Emyns the elder, Robert Emyns. Pr. at Bury 4 August 1634.

667. R(W) JOHN CANHAM (X) the elder of Soham [Cambs], husbandman. 28 June 1632.

Commends soul to God trusting that it will be saved through Jesus Christ.
I give Mary my now wife my tenement in Mare Street, Soham where I now dwell, with yard, garden and orchard, and all my moveable goods within it; she must keep house in repair and not destroy any plantation or fruit ground. She is to have the property for life if she remains a widow, but if she remarries my son John is to have it at once. I give my wife for her widowhood my half acre freehold land in Clipsall field, half an acre freehold in Neddiche field, 1 rod freehold in the Hales and half an acre demesne in Windmill crofts, being a hempland. I give her 4 of my best milk cows, 2 of my mares with cart and cart gears, plough and plough gears. I give my daughters Anne Sergent and Ellen Winter £5 each, and my daughter Mary Elsden 20s. I give my son Thomas £5, my son Richard 10s and £5 each to son Robert and daughter Rose. I give my son Stephen £6. My exor is to pay these bequests at £5 p.a. starting 1 year after he inherits the tenement and land left to my wife. If my exor dies without heirs, any 2 of my sons are to sell my tenement and land and divide the money equally among my surviving children, but Stephen is to have £5 more than the rest of them. I give my son John my tenement in Hall Street immediately after my death. I give him all my goods and chattels on condition he faithfully performs my will and I make him exor. If he refuses to pay my debts and burial charges, I make my sons Thomas and Richard exors and give them all bequests made to John. I appoint my trusted friends William Goldsburrowe and Elias Staples as supervisors and give them 2s each to buy a pair of gloves. I have surrendered my copyhold land to use of my will into hands of William Gouldsburrowe and in presence of William Tompson, tenants of manor. Wit. William Goulsborowgh, William Tompson and me William Howe. Pr. at Bury 5 August 1634.

668. R(W) REUBEN FEVERYEARE (X) of Bacton, yeoman. 25 January 1633/34.

Commits soul to God being assured through Jesus Christ of pardon of sins and to be raised up at last day and made a living member of Jesus Christ.
I give all my land in Kenton held copyhold of manor of Debenham or

Butley to my wife Abre for life, and then to 4 of my children which I had by her: Robert, Thomas, John and Anne. I give my wife all my apparel and make her sole ex'trix. Wit. William Jesopp (X), Robert Jesopp (X), Edmund Peteywarde, Henry Jesopp (X). Pr. at Bury 11 August 1634.

669. R(W) JAMES ALBON (N) of Hartest, yeoman. November 1633.

He gave Alice his wife all his goods and chattels to be at her own disposing. Wit. James Albon, George Albon (X). Pr. at Bury 11 August 1634.

670. R(W) MARGARET VINCENT of Stowmarket, widow. 25 May 1632.

Gives soul to God trusting through Jesus Christ to obtain everlasting life. I give my son Miles my freehold tenement with yard wherein I now dwell on condition that within 14 days of my decease, my will having been made known at his mansion house, he pays my daughter Margaret £18 in porch or steeple of Haughley church. If he fails Margaret is to have the tenement and pay Miles £18 in south porch of Stowmarket church within a month of my decease. I give my son Lawrence my great joined table in his hall at Stonham, to my son Miles the posted bedstead in the hall chamber, the chest at the bedhead, a red covering, a pair woollen blankets, 2 pairs coarse sheets, 2 pillows, 2 kettles (a broad kettle and the other my lesser kettle) and 1 skillet. I give my daughter Margaret Andrews the chest in my hall chamber by the geeame [jamb?] of the chimney and all that is in it. I give her also my linen in the chest that stands at my bedside in my hall, 2 great fustian pillows, a little fustian pillow, 1 bird covering, 1 great kettle in the hall chamber and my least kettle save one. I also give her all my apparel, a joined table and 2 joined forms in the hall, a ceiled posted bedstead and the trundle bedstead that runs under it, my great tub and a keeler. I give my grandchild Margaret Andrews a pillion cloth of fustian Alpes, a brass pot, a brass skillet and my great dripping pan. I give my grandson Thomas Vincent 10s to be paid by son Miles in south porch of Stowmarket church 1 year after my death. I give my grandson Robert Vincent 10s to be paid by daughter Margaret in porch or steeple of Haughley church within a year. I give my son Miles and daughter Margaret all my pewter and all my unbequeathed goods and chattels to be equally parted between them by my exor, and they are to pay costs of my burial and proving my will, and my debts. If they refuse to do this, all gifts to them are void. Exor: Hugh Andrews, my son-in-law. Wit. John Raynold, Nicholas Randale (X). Pr. at Bury 11 August 1634.

671. R(W) GEORGE SPARROW (X) of Bury St Edmunds, baker.
1 April 1634.

Bequeaths soul to God hoping that he will receive it through merits of Jesus Christ.
Because my loving wife Mary has been a means to help increase my poor estate by her labour and industry, and because she has faithfully vowed carefully to educate all mine and her children in the fear of God and to allow them means for their maintenance according to her ability to bring them up, I give her all my houses and land in Bury for ever. I also give her all my goods and chattels for her maintenance and that of my children, trusting that she will be a loving and careful mother providing for them according to her promise made to me and my trust reposed in her. I make her ex'trix. Wit. William Middleditch, Robert Kiddall (X). Pr. at Bury 21 August 1634.

672. R(W) GEORGE PRIGG (X) of Stansfield, tailor. 14 July 1634.

Commits soul to God hoping through merits of Jesus Christ to be partaker of everlasting life.
I give my brother Thomas my best suit of apparel and a skep of bees. I give his daughter Alice a skep of bees. I give my brother William my stuff suit of clothes. I give Anne Ward of Hawkedon, singlewoman, my best bedstead in the house where I dwell with all its bedding. I give my sister Anne my wearing coat and my other suit of clothes. I will that my exor sells my house and orchard in Stansfield where I dwell to pay my debts, and any overplus to be equally divided between all my brothers and sisters, as are all my unbequeathed goods. I appoint my brother Daniel Prigg of London my exor, and Mr Ambrose Chapman of Hawkedon supervisor. Wit. Charles Derisley, Walter Derisley. Pr. at Bury 25 July 1634.

673. R(W) GILBERT SPALDYNG of Hawstead, yeoman. 8 June 1634.

Commits soul to God hoping through Jesus Christ to inherit eternal kingdom prepared for elect people of God.
I give my wellbeloved wife Bridget (over and above the thirds of my freehold lands which law casts on her) all my moveable goods and chattels in the house where I now dwell and which are set down in an inventory signed by me and of which she and my son Robert have copies. I also give her £10 which I have given her with my own hands, and her choice of one of my 5 skeps of bees. I give my daughter Bridget £100 within a year of my decease, and 50s in the meantime for her maintenance, which legacies are in discharge of all legacies I have received for her. I promised my son-in-law John Gillye £50 at my decease in addition to his wife's portion, and I give him £50 to be paid within 6 weeks of my death. I give my son Samuel £100 within 2 years and until then 40s p.a. for his maintenance. Bridget and Samuel have benefit of

survivorship. I give a skep of bees each to John Gillye, my daughter Bridget and my sons Robert and Samuel. I give Robert the messuages and land in Boxted, Shimpling, Hartest and Somerton, which I inherited from my mother Elizabeth Spalding. He must pay £100 to Samuel within a year. Power to distrain. All the residue of my goods I give to Robert and make him exor, but if he dies before my will is performed Samuel is to be exor. Any doubts about my will are to be resolved by my good friends and neighbours George Scarpe and Thomas Paige. Wit. George Scarpe, John Alvis. Pr. at Bury 9 August 1634.

674. R(W) HENRY COWPER the elder of Bradfield St George, yeoman. 18 January 1633/34.

Bequeaths soul to God hoping for its salvation through Jesus Christ.
I give my beloved wife Anne the bedstead, bed and bedding in the hall chamber, 2 pairs sheets and half my pewter. I give my son Henry all my other goods and chattels to pay my debts and I make him exor. I also give him after my wife's decease all my copyhold land and tenement called Smalewood Hall and belonging to the manor of Bradfield St George, and all my copyhold land held of Lovells manor. He must pay £50 apiece to my sons James and Joshua when 21, and until then he is to take care for their education and upbringing. Wit. John Drury, Samuel Wright (X), William Hempton. Pr. at Bury 21 April 1634.

675. R(W) MARY STERNE (X) of Cockfield, widow. 14 July 1634.

Bequeaths soul to God trusting through Jesus Christ to have free pardon of sins.
I give the poor of Cockfield 20s to be distributed on Sabbath day after my burial. I give my daughter Susan Manning £20 and £10 to my son-in-law William Manning, both within a year of my death; the latter sum to be given to their son William when 21. I give my son Charles Sterne the elder and his wife an annuity of 16s p.a., and their son Charles 40s 12 months after my decease. I give John, son of Charles Sterne, 20s within a year, and Francis, David and Philip, sons of Charles Sterne, 20s when 21. Charles Sterne the younger is to have the legacies of any who die. I give £5 to my son-in-law Henry Frost within a year for him to pay to his son and my godson Henry when 21. I give my son-in-law David Sterne £5, a little chest standing by my bedside and a pair sheets to be given to his daughter Susan when 21. I give £5 to my son Thomas for his son Charles when 21. I give my maid Sarah Spilman 20s within 6 months. Exors: sons Thomas and Francis. Wit. John Smyth clerk, Thomas Milles. Pr. at Bury 15 September 1634.

676. R(W) FRANCIS FOLKNER (X) of Icklingham, herdsman.
16 August 1634.

Commends soul to God and Jesus Christ hoping for a joyful resurrection.
I give my wife Margery all my freehold houses and land in Icklingham for
life and then to my son Philip. I give my daughter Priscilla 20s within a
year of wife's decease to be paid by son Philip. I give my wife all my
moveable goods and make her ex'trix. Wit. John Goslinge, William
Ladiman. Pr. at Bury 1 September 1634.

677. W(R) JAMES COPPING of Bury St Edmunds, public notary.
6 February 1633/34.

Commends soul to God. To be buried in St Wolstan's chapel in church of
St Mary in Bury.
I give my wellbeloved wife Mary all my free and copyhold lands,
tenements and messuages in Brockley, Rede and Bury, and the reversion
to the property left to me after my mother's decease, for her life towards
the education and upbringing of my sons William, John and Richard.
After my wife's decease, I bequeath to John and Richard the house
wherein Henry Leay of Rede is my tenant, the copyhold land held of
Brockley Hall and the use of the way I bought from John Sparrow of
Rede to go to and from the aforesaid land. I give my son William my
copyhold land held of the manor of Talmayes and Wilfold and the
freehold long pasture I purchased of [blank in MS] Potter. I give my wife
for ever my tenement and ground in Rede bought for her jointure by my
father of one Wiseman, and my house wherein I now dwell in Bury. She
must pay my daughter Ann £80 within a year of my decease. If my
mother resigns her right of thirds in my house and land in Rede and
allows my wife to have this property for life, she is to have an annuity of
£8 paid quarterly. As I leave my wife but a poor estate, I earnestly
entreat my old friend Mr John Legate to take on him the education of my
son John, his godson, for which I hope God will reward him. I give my
wife's god-daughter Mary Tayler a piece of plate worth £3, and to my
god-daughter Hester, daughter of Reginald Browne, a similar piece. I
give my servant Frances Mickborough 40s. I earnestly entreat my uncle
Pead that he will aid my wife in managing my poor estate and educating
my children, especially William that he may be brought up to learning, if
he be capable, to be a clerk in the profession I was brought up in. I make
my wife sole ex'trix. I had in my hands in trust for the children of John
Copping of Kersey £20. I disbursed 33s 4d long since, so with the interest
at 8 pence in the pound there is but £20 in my hands. I entreat my wife to
use her good conscience in this business. Wit. John Jewell. Pr. at Bury 9
April 1634.

678. W(R) JOHN HAYLOCK (X) of Great Saxham, shepherd. 9 August
1634.

Commends spirit to Lord God who gave it trusting to be saved by merits
of Jesus Christ.
I give my wife Alice all my household stuff now in the dwelling house. I
give my son Thomas 40s, part of which I owe him. I give my daughter
Frances Everard 10s and daughter Alice Browne 30s. Legacies to be paid
in Saxham church porch 1 year after my decease. Residue of my goods I
give to my exors, my wife and my son John. I exhort them to agree
together so that the blessing of God may be with them. No witnesses. Pr.
at Bury 1 September 1634.

679. W(R) MARY GATTYWARD (X) of Bury St Edmunds,
singlewoman. 20 August 1634.

Commits soul to God trusting assuredly to be saved by Jesus Christ.
I give my sister Elizabeth my half of the messuage in Guildhall Street in
which widow Kent now dwells, and of which Elizabeth has other half. I
give my brother William £30 within 3 months. I give £5 each when 21 to
Robert and James, sons of Robert Hayward of Bury clothier. My exor is
to pay these legacies with interest at 5%. I give my brother-in-law
William Ollyet of Bury glazier, £5 within 6 months. I give the poor of St
Mary's parish 20s to be distributed on day of my burial. I give Ann Berry
of Bury widow, 20s within 3 months. I give my sister Elizabeth my best
gown, my best petticoat and my scarf. My legacies are to be paid by my
exor out of £100 owing to me by my cousin Edward Gattyward of Risby,
yeoman. The rest of my money and goods I give to my brother-in-law
William Ward, whom I make exor. Wit. Jude Whyte, Thomas Purdy (X),
William Sarson. Pr. at Bury 1 October 1634.

680. W(R) GEORGE KIRBY of Bury St Edmunds, musician. 10 March
1633/34.

Yields soul to God being fully assured to be an inheritor of kingdom of
heaven through Jesus Christ.
I give Agnes Seaman my servant and kinswoman to my late wife my
messuage in Whiting Street, wherein I dwell and which I purchased from
Mr Lancaster, for ever. I give my brother Walter and my sister Alice
Moore widow £10 each within 6 months. My ex'trix must pay £7 each
when 24 to John and Thomas, sons of Adam Hille tailor of Bury
deceased, in satisfaction of the money I received for their benefit. All my
goods and chattels I bequeath to Agnes Seaman and make her ex'trix. I

give the poor people of south and west wards in Bury £3 to be distributed within a month of my decease. Wit. Thomas Wright, John White. Pr. at Bury 7 October 1634.

681. W(R) RICHARD COPPING of Stanningfield, yeoman. 27 August 1634.

Renders spirit to God in certain hope of resurrection to everlasting happiness in God's kingdom.

I give my wife Margaret for life, if she stays unmarried, my parlour and parlour chamber with vance roof over the latter and the furniture in these rooms, my best buttery with all the shelves, and the use of my copper in the kitchen, of the oven to bake in, my yard to set her wood and hang her linen in, of the garden for pot herbs, of the pond for water and a third part of the fruit in the orchard. She is to have 4 loads of best sort of good wood set in the yard for her every year during her widowhood. If she marries again these gifts become void. In lieu of thirds I bequeath her £10 p.a. to be paid at Michaelmas and Lady Day; also £10 within 8 months and £10 within 18 months of my decease. I give my wife a gilt bowl and a church bible; all my bedding and bedsteads except the 2 bedsteads with valances and curtains in the parlour chamber; all my linen and napery; all my brass and pewter, except my copper in the kitchen; all my brewing and beer vessels, keelers and tubs; and the use of my gilt salt and silver bowl with remainder to my nephew Richard Copping after my wife's decease. I give my brother John my houses and lands in Burgate and Wortham for life and then to his son Richard, except what is given to my wife for her life. After my wife's decease I give my nephew Richard the bedsteads in the parlour chamber with valances and curtains, a tapestry coverlet, 6 cushions and a table carpet of Turkey work, all my joined tables in the parlour, the chairs, joined stools, and a great pair cobirons with firepan and tongs. I also give him a long table with frame and a long form in my hall. I give John, my brother's son, £10 when 24 and to his sister Elizabeth £10 when 20. I give George Rewse, my wife's son, £5 within a year. I give my god-daughter Hester Copping of Bury 20s; 40s each to Joan Bennett and Elizabeth Pallesie; 40s each to my half sisters Frances Neall and Margaret Payne; 40s to the children of my half sister Mary Stead; 20s to my godson Richard Rewse of Market Harling [East Harling] in Norfolk; all within 1 year of my death. I give my godson George Copping of Cretingham 20s when 21, and Dorothy Appelwite of Stanningfield 20s within a year. I give my cousin widow Taylor of Gazeley 20s within 6 months. I give my godson John Steward of Whepstead and my kinswoman Anne Steward of Lawshall 20s each within a year. I give my loving friend Mr Doctor Rames of London 40s to buy him a ring to wear for my sake. I give Martha Lea my wife's grandchild £10 when 21, or if she dies to the 2 daughters of my wife's deceased son Simon Rewse of Newmarket. I give every servant in the house where it shall please God to call me 5s within a month of my decease. I give poor of Stanningfield 20s within a month and poor of Burgate 40s within 5 months. I give my wife one of my trunks at her choice with some of my gally pots and boxes, and a wicker chair. The residue of my goods and chattels I give to my brother John and make him exor. I make my loving nephew Mr Philip Jacob of Nether Rickinghall, minister of God's word, supervisor of my will and I give him 20s. Wit. John Steward, Thomas Steward, John Steward. Pr. at Bury 8 October 1634.

682. W(R) BARBARA LAMBE (X) of Thelnetham, widow. 6 August 1634.

Commits soul to God and Jesus Christ.
The cottage wherein I dwell, late Humphrey Lyttone's of Kenninghall [Norfolk], and adjoining croft are to be sold by my 2 sons Thomas and George within a year of my decease. They are to use money to pay £4 each to my daughters Mary, Barbara, Sarah and Anne in porch of Thelnetham church within 2 years. Any surplus is to be divided between my 2 sons and used to pay my debts. Daughters have benefit of survivorship. They are to receive rent of my cottage and croft until they are sold. All my goods and chattels I give to be equally divided, within a month of my decease, between my 4 daughters in a loving and sisterly manner. If they cannot agree, I will that the minister of the parish and my brother-in-law John Wyx divide my goods. I make my 4 daughters ex'trices. Wit. John Wyxe (X) and me William Payne. Pr. at Bury 30 September 1634.

683. W(R) WILLIAM WHIGHTINGE (X) of Mendlesham, yeoman. 17 June 1633.

Commends soul to God trusting through Jesus Christ to enjoy blessed state of eternal life.
I give my daughter Susan my pasture close called Langlond which I purchased of Robert Loppkins. She must pay my daughter Mary £5 within 2 years in north porch of Mendlesham church. I give my wife Elizabeth my best bedstead, featherbed and bolster in my parlour, all my linen, the best brass pot and my little chest standing by the parlour door. I also give her all my cattle and corn on the ground, and my horse mill. I give my son William my copper hanging in the kitchen. All the rest of my goods and chattels are to be divided between my wife and my children Mary, Susan and John. I make my wife sole ex'trix hoping she will perform my will according to the trust I repose in her. Wit. John Kewe, John Murdocke. Pr. at Stowmarket 2 October 1634.

684. W(R) THOMAS GARRAD (X) senior of Wickhambrook. 17 March 1633/34.

Bequeaths soul to God in assured hope sins will be pardoned through Jesus Christ. To be buried in Wickhambrook churchyard.
I give my wife Ann the pied cow, a brinded bullock, the hay in the hay

288

house, a cheese press, the biggest churn, 2 of the biggest keelers and 2 of the biggest bowls, 2 milk pans, the newest kettle and one of biggest of the others, 2 skillets, 3 cheese vats and 2 cheese breads, a great cup, all my dishes, spoons and trenchers, a skimmer, my least kettle, 3 pewter dishes with crosses on the bottoms, 2 pewter saucers, a pewter salt with a cover and a pewter candlestick, 3 beer vessels, 2 of the best pails, a beer stool, 3 tubs and a swill tub, a bedstead with featherbed, feather bolster and 2 feather pillows, 2 pillowbeeres, a flockbed, 1 pair blankets, a covering lying on the bed in the lower chamber, all my sheets, 1 board cloth and 4 table napkins, a coffer that was her own before, a cupboard, an almery, a great chest, a great chair, 2 small chairs, 3 joined stools, 3 other stools, a little table, a hale, a firepan and a pair tongs, a pair andirons, a pelle, a gridiron and a pair pot hooks, a spit, a pair bellows belonging to the hall, a pestle and mortar, a pint, a hook and a hatchet, all my wood, 1 pair malt querns, a pashell, a tow comb, a woollen wheel, a boulting hutch, 4 cushions in the hall and 1 shott. I give my 4 unbequeathed cows to be sold and the money parted amongst my 6 children: Thomas, John, Robert, Katherine and Mary Garrad and Elizabeth Catlin. I give my best looms with 1 pair warping bars to my son Robert, and another pair of looms now in his possession I give to be sold and the money parted between my sons John and Robert. I give my temple heads to Robert, and other implements belonging to my trade are to be equally parted between John and Robert. I give my daughter Mary a livery bedstead and flockbed now in possession of my son Robert, a feather pillow, a covering, a joined table and a napkin. I give my daughter Katherine a coffer in the lower chamber, my best pewter platter and a napkin. I give my son Thomas my coat, my son John my jerkin, 1 pair breeches, 1 pair netherstocks and my best pair shoes. I give Robert my best doublet, best pair breeches, best pair netherstocks, my new boots and my best hat. All the rest of my apparel I give to my son-in-law Thomas Catlin. I give my wife Ann all my bacon and cheese, my warming pan, my meal pokes and bottles. The rest of my goods to be equally parted among my 6 children. After my wife's decease my house and land are to be sold by my exor or the churchwardens, if he is dead, and the money divided between those of my children then living. If any of my sons want to buy my land they shall have it at £5 less than it is valued. I give Thomas and Ann Garrad my grandchildren 5s apiece. I give Thomas, son of Robert Garrad, 10s and 5s to his brother John. I give 20s to be divided among my grandchildren Thomas, Elizabeth, Ann and Margaret Catlen within a year of the decease of Rachel Colby, widow of Cotton. Exors: my wife and son Robert. Wit. John Goddard, John Brightwaie (X). Pr. at Stowmarket 2 October 1634.

685. W(R) JOHN CHASE (X) of Hopton, weaver. 15 May 1627.

Bequeaths soul to God trusting to be saved.
I give my son Anthony 1 pair looms at Jude Pearse's and another pair at Thelnetham with all implements belonging to them. I give my son Robert

1 pair looms in my shop with the implements belonging, my best doublet, hose and jerkin. All the rest of my goods and chattels I bequeath to my wife Alice and my son Anthony whom I make exors. If either of them marries, they are to pay my son Robert £5 in 2 portions within a year. Wit. William Cocke, Henry Spurgen, writer of will. Pr. at Hopton 13 June 1634.

686. W(R) JAMES LAUND alias PALLANT of Cowlinge, yeoman. 12 May 1634.

Bequeaths soul to God.
I give Mary my wife all my moveable goods and chattels for life. She is to pay all my debts, and receive all those due to me. I give my sons Robert, Thomas and George £5 each to be paid on their marriage days or 1 month after my wife's decease. I give £10 to my daughter Elizabeth, and £5 each to daughters Martha and Alice as above. I give my daughter Herington's 4 children 10s each a month after my wife's death. I give poor of Cowlinge 10s to be paid a month after my decease to churchwardens and given by them where most need is, and I will that Hekes has a part. I give my 6 children a silver spoon each after my wife's death. My wife is to dispose of my goods after her death among my children where she shall see most need. Wife sole ex'trix. Wit. Thomas Land, George Land. Pr. at Cowlinge 18 June 1634.

687. W(R) JOHN GARDENER of Wetheringsett, yeoman. 30 September 1634.

Bequeaths soul to 3 persons of Trinity trusting to have sins pardoned through Jesus Christ.
I give my capital messuage where I now dwell with outbuildings and land, and all my other messuages and land to my ex'trix on condition that within 2 years of my decease she sells them all for best price and uses money to pay my debts, keeping overplus for her benefit and for maintaining and bringing up my children. I also give my ex'trix all my goods and chattels, bonds, bills and money. I make Elizabeth my most dear and loving wife my ex'trix, desiring her in fear of God to be good to my children, and to help them with such portions as she can give them, as my trust is she will. Wit. John Frythe, Anthony Aldrich, William Mylls. Pr. at Bury 27 October 1634.

688. W(R) RICHARD MUNNES (X) of Bures hamlet in Essex, labourer. 2 April 1634.

Bequeaths soul to God hoping for remission of sins through Jesus Christ.
I give my wife Helen £5 10s 0d to be paid within 8 months. I give my wife and son George all my household stuff to be equally divided between them by William Simson gentleman and John Simson clerk. My wife is to live in that part of my house where I now dwell for life. I give my son

Thomas my messuage called Digglons with a croft of land in Bures hamlet on condition he pays my son George £20 within a year of my decease. If he does not, gift to him is void. All the rest of my goods I give to Thomas and make him exor. Supervisor: my good friend John Rayner and I give him 20s for his pains. I give my wife all the wood cut and made ready for the fire. Wit. John Cryspe, Jeffrey Harst. Pr. at Bury 13 October 1634.

689. W(R) JOHN HOE alias HOWE (X) of Bradfield St George, yeoman. 2 May 1634.

Commends soul to God hoping to be saved by merits of Jesus Christ.
I bequeath to my grandchild John Howe my 2 messuages and all my land in Bradfield. I give my grandchild Margaret Howe £100 to be paid 4 days after she is 21 in porch of Bradfield St George parish church. I will that Thomas Hamond my son-in-law has rents of my messuage and land in Hawkedon and Rede, paying out of them £20 p.a. to my wife Dorothy in 2 portions in his house. I give my grandson Anthony Howe £100 to be paid in the church porch when 21. If my wife tries to claim thirds, bequest to her is void. All my moveable goods I give to my grandson John Howe to pay my legacies and I make him exor. If he does not prove my will within 10 days of my decease, my bequest to him is void and goes to grandson Anthony who is then to be exor. Wit. Ralph King, John Smith. Pr. at Bury 3 November 1634.

690. W(R) ELIZABETH GRANGER (X) of Ashfield, widow. 26 July 1634.

Commends soul to God.
I bequeath Margaret Bougen, widow of Hinderclay, £20 for the educating and bringing up of my daughter Margaret. I give £15 each for bringing up and apprenticing to some honest trade of my sons William and Thomas. I give my daughter Elizabeth £10 to be put to best use by my ex'trix and paid to her when 21. I give my son Giles £10, part to bind him apprentice, and rest to be given to him when 24. Benefit of survivorship. I give my daughters Elizabeth and Margaret my wearing linen and apparel, and my elder daughter Elizabeth is to choose first; the meaner part to be given to Margaret. I give Margaret Bougen my house and land in Elmswell wherein Nicholas Ule now lives and abutting on the green to the south, with 2 acres adjoining land, to pay my legacies and burial charges. I make her ex'trix. I appoint my brother Francis Bougen supervisor and bequeath him 10s. Wit. Francis Bowgen, Miles Raphe. Pr. at Ixworth 4 October 1634.

691. W(R) ELIZABETH ALLEN (X) of Glemsford, widow. 27 August 1633.

I give my son Israel 3s 4d within a month of my decease provided he gives my exor a release of all claims for debts and legacies; if he refuses I give the 3s 4d to my daughter Sarah. I give my son John my trundle bedstead, and to my daughter Abigail, wife of John Mayes, a boarded hutch. I give my daughter Anne, wife of Richard Farr, a stool with a back and 1s. All the rest of my goods and chattels I give to my daughter Sarah and make her ex'trix. Wit. Anne Griggs (X), Thomas Gardner, Richard Gardner. Pr. at Glemsford 22 July 1634.

692. W(R) ANNE COOPER (X) of Old Newton, widow. 21 June 1634.

Commits soul to God hoping to be made partaker of eternal life through Jesus Christ.

I give my daughter Anne the bedstead with bed, bolster, blankets and coverlets in the parlour, and a pair sheets. I give my daughter Joan the bed and bedstead, bolster, blankets and coverlets in the parlour chamber, a pair sheets and a bullock. I give these 2 daughters all my linen, except 5 pairs sheets given to my sons John, Thomas, Robert, Edward and James, and my wearing apparel and linen. I give my son John the table and form in the parlour, a joined stool and a pair sheets. I give my son Thomas a bolting trough and a pair sheets. I give my son Robert one of my cows to take at his choice, a new chair and a pair sheets. I give my son Edward a trundle bedstead with the bed on it, the bolster, blankets and coverlets in the parlour chamber, 1 pair sheets, the table and a cupboard in the hall. I give my son James my other cow, a load of wood, 1 pair sheets and 40s. My son John owes me 20s which I give to his son John, my godson. My son Thomas owes me 40s of which I give 20s to his son Thomas and 20s to himself. I give my godson Robert, son of my son Robert, 20s. I give my daughter Joan my biggest brass pot and my son Edward my other brass pot. By the will of my late husband John Cooper I am liable to pay my daughter Anne £20 when 22. Thomas Ecie is indebted to me for this sum by bond, which I give to Anne and this money is to be paid immediately after my decease. I give Anne the little table in the parlour chamber, and James my husband's cloak and doublet. The rest of my goods and chattels are to be equally divided among my children. Exors: sons John, Thomas, Robert and Edward. Wit. Robert Tyrell, James Hogges, John Hogges. Pr. at Newton 2 July 1634.

693. W(R) ROBERT NORMAN (N) of Gazeley, yeoman. 11 September 1634.

He gave Margaret his wife all his goods and chattels to pay his debts, and if his goods came to more than his debts, the remainder to be equally divided between his wife and 6 children: Elizabeth, Mary, William, John, Miles and Susan. He made his wife ex'trix. Wit. John Pricke, Jervis Barrett and others. Pr. at Bury 15 September 1634.

694. W(R) MARGARET MATHEW (X) of Great Ashfield, widow.
21 October 1634.

Commends soul to God trusting to be saved by Jesus Christ. To be buried in churchyard of parish where I now live.
Out of my goods 40s is to be paid to each of my children Thomas, Alice, William and Elizabeth, which money was given them by their father in his will. I will that my son William be paid £8 I borrowed of him at several times. I give my daughter Alice Lock a black bullock which I bought of her husband when a calf, a new feather bed that lies on a bedstead aloft in the chamber together with a feather bolster and pillow and a coverlet, and an old buffet stool. I give her 4 children Elizabeth, Robert, Anne and John 10s each and 10s to the child she is now with. I give my son William £6, half within 1 and the rest within 2 years of my decease. I also give him a feather bed in the low chamber to the east with a livery bedstead, a bolster, a pillow, a coverlet, a blanket and a pair sheets, my great brass pot, the middle kettle, a 3-legged joined chair in the hall, a broad buffet stool and 2 pewter platters standing on the shelf in the hall which his godmother gave him. He is to have benefit of corn in the ground and grass at the green, which I hire of Robert Fowler and is to pay rent. I give my daughter Elizabeth Cosen 20s and to her husband a cloak which I bought of Mr Fyrmage. I give my daughters Alice Locke and Elizabeth Cosen my wearing apparel and all my linen, except the sheets given to William and another pair of the best sheets which my son Thomas is to have according to his father's will. I give my daughter Alice's 2 daughters, Elizabeth and Anne, 2 pewter platters in the buttery. I give Rebecca Martyn my maidservant a comb of barley. All the rest of my goods I give to my son Thomas and make him exor. Wit. Thomas Peake, Katherine Syer (X), Rebecca Martyn (X). Pr. at Bury 31 October 1634.

695. W(R) JOHN BILHAM (X) of Barrow, yeoman. 4 July 1634.

Bequeaths soul to God hoping to be saved by Jesus Christ.
I give my son Robert my house wherein I dwell with all my land, except 4 acres purchased by my father of John Warner. I give him the excepted 4 acres on condition he pays my daughter Anne £7 within 2 years, daughter Elizabeth £7 within 3 years and £7 more each to both daughters within 4 years of my decease. In case of default I give my daughters half each of the 4 acres. Benefit of survivorship. I give my 2 daughters £6 6s 8d each to be paid by my exor within a year. My daughters are to have upper chamber next the street, in which I lie, and the hall chamber so long as they remain unmarried, with liberty to use the chimney and fetch water from the pond. I give my son Robert my best featherbed, bolster, blanket, coverlet, a pair sheets, a pillow and my silver spoon. I give my daughter Elizabeth a bed, a bolster, a pillow, a blanket and a coverlet if there be so many. I give Robert my best brass pot, to Anne my next brass pot and to Elizabeth my best kettle. I give each of my daughters, while single, a comb of apples every year if the orchard produces 3 combs. The

rest of my goods to be divided into 3 equal parts by my neighbour Simon Pitts for my 3 children. I make my friend Simon Pitts of Great Saxham my exor, entreating him to advise my son and daughters for the best. Wit. James Cooke, Abraham Day. Pr. at Bury 27 October 1634.

696. W(R) ELIZABETH CALLOWE (N) of Hepworth, singlewoman. January 1633/34.

Commended her soul to God and body to earth.
She gave Alice Stabbinge, her dame, her hat, petticoat, waistcoat and apron. She gave her master John Stabbinge all her money and debts, saying that he best deserved it. Being desired by one Reeve's wife to forgive her 6s she owed the testatrix she said no, her master should have it. Wit. Lydia, wife of Thomas Reeve, John Stabbinge the younger, John Stabbinge the elder and his wife. Let. ad. granted 26 November 1634. No place given.

697. W(R) THOMAS GRIGGES (X) of Cavendish, yeoman. 25 October 1634.

Commends sinful soul to God.
I give Elizabeth my loving wife my mansion house and all my free and copyhold houses and lands in Cavendish for life. She must pay £40 4 years after my decease to my daughter Anne for her portion in south porch of Cavendish church. The rest of my children, who have not received their portions before my death, have benefit of survivorship. If my wife dies within 4 years, my son William is to pay Anne £40 a year after wife's decease. I give the rest of my children portions as follows: to William £40 within 2 years of my wife's death; to Margaret £40 within 6 years of my decease; to Temperance an annuity of £5 for life; £50 to Hugh within 9 years of my decease; to Humphrey £40, of which £10 owed to me by Robert Sandall of Cavendish is to be paid when he is 24; until then the increase of £10 to be paid to Thomas Sandall of Cavendish to teach Humphrey to comb and learn his trade until hs is 24; my wife or her exor to pay him £30 11 years after my decease. I give my son George £50 to be paid when he is 21, and £40 to my daughter Martha when 24, both to be paid by my wife. I give my grandson Thomas Sandall £5 when 21. I give my son Thomas 40s to be paid by my wife 6 months after my death. If my wife dies before she has paid my legacies, my son William is to pay them by selling all my land and tenements in Cavendish within a year of her decease. Legatees have benefit of survivorship, but, if they are married, their children are to benefit. I make my wife sole ex'trix and give her all my goods and household stuff, milk beasts, horses, carts, implements of husbandry and credits. If the sale of my land raises more money than is needed to pay legacies, surplus is to be divided among those of my children who are then unmarried. I give unto the poor people of Cavendish [no sum given] to be distributed at the discretion of my ex'trix. Wit. Roger Bell, William Linge (X), John Abbott. Pr. at Bury 10 November 1634.

698. W(R) WILLIAM GLADWYN of Nayland, yeoman. 29 September 1634.

I give and bequeath my soul to three persons of Trinity.
I give the Minister of God's word appointed by my exors to preach at my burial 10s. I give my son William £20 within a year after my exors have paid my debts. All the rest of my goods and chattels I give to my wife Ann and son Thomas, whom I appoint exors and charge to pay my debts from the rent of the house in Nayland where Thomas dwells and from the yearly profits of my leases and goods. After debts have been paid my wife is to have rent of my house for life and then to son William. My wife is to have benefit of my lease of Wickerland after my debts are paid, and after her decease my son Thomas is to have residue of lease. Thomas is also to have my lease of Fair field in Nayland after my debts have been paid. I request Mr Thomas Blythe the elder of Nayland to be supervisor of my will and assist my exors, who are to pay him 3s 4d. Wit. Hugh Tayler, John Plampen, Mathew Howe. Pr. at Bury 6 November 1634.

699. W(R) NICHOLAS BURREDGE (X) of Soham [Cambs], labourer. 8 February 1633/34.

Gives soul to God and body to be buried among the faithful.
I give my wife Martha all my goods and chattels and make her sole ex'trix. to pay my debts and perform my will. Wit. John Hynkyn (X), Richard Field, Thomas Lawrence (X). Pr. at Bury 20 November 1634. [Of Barrow in will; there is a hamlet of Barway in Soham parish.]

700. W(R) ROBERT NEALE (N) of Wattisham, yeoman. November and December 1633.

Being in perfect mind and lying sick upon his bed at his house where he dwelt in Wattisham, he was required by some of the company that were about him to make his will. He did answer, speaking to Elizabeth wife of William Neale and daughter of testator's wife, all that I have came by your mother and when I die I will that you and your husband shall have all that I have. Wit. John Harlond of Wattisham and Diana his wife and Mary Hawkins. Let. ad. granted to William Neale 4 August 1634. No place given.

701. W(R) RICHARD MARTIN of Buxhall, yeoman. 3 October 1634.

Bequeaths soul to God and Jesus Christ. To be buried in church or churchyard of Buxhall.
I give Mary my wife for life a messuage called Windishes with its garden, yard and orchard, a 9 acre close called Hamlinges, a 2 acre meadow called the Meadowgate, 4 pieces of land totalling 1½ acres, 1½ acres called Calves pightle, a 5 acre close called Wallell, a 3 rod piece of meadow called Wallell meadow, 3 rods meadow adjoining former piece

and a 1½ acre close called Mearcroft; all lying in Buxhall and Great Finborough. After my wife's decease my son Richard is to have all this land, and my free and copyhold land held of Fenhall and Buxhall when 21. I give him when 21 my tenement Highams with barn, stables, garden and orchard; 2 closes of arable and pasture containing 11 acres and known as Barnardes and an adjoining 1 acre meadow. I give my daughter Mary £100 to be paid by Richard, half when she is 21 and half at 24. I give my daughter Elizabeth £100 to be paid in same way. Power to distrain. I give my wife all my moveable goods in my dwelling house, bake house and dairy house, except 2 silver spoons which I give to my 2 daughters, and my musket and fowling piece which I give to my son. I give my wife 4 cows or heifers as she pleases. I give all my goods in my barns and outhouses to be sold by my exors to pay my debts and maintain my 3 children with meat, drink and lodging. My intention is that learning be bestowed on my son Richard to write and read in a reasonable manner as far as his capability extends, and my wife is to have the bringing up of my children with my exors allowing her sufficient maintenance. If she refuses to do this, my exors are to have the goods formerly given to her to maintain my children. I give the poor in Buxhall 20s within 4 days of my decease. Exors: John Towler and my brother Peter Martyn. Supervisor: my wife Mary. Wit. Richard Wright, Robert Wright. Pr. at Bury 24 November 1634.

702. W(R) HENRY ROYSE of Exning, husbandman. 12 June 1631.

Bequeaths soul to God trusting to be saved. To be buried in Exning churchyard.
I give my wife Lucy my house I dwell in, 4½ acres free land and my lease of 5 acres, all in fields of Exning, for her life and then to my son Henry, except for my lease land which I give to my son Robert, who is to pay Henry 2s. Henry is to pay Robert £10 p.a. after my wife's decease. I give my daughter Grizel £10 2 years, £10 to my daughter Katherine, wife of John Turner, 4 years and £10 to daughter Jane 6 years after my decease. If my wife dies before my legacies are paid, son Henry is to pay them. Legatees have power to distrain. I give my wife all my moveable goods and after her death they are to be equally divided among my 3 daughters, who must pay my eldest son Henry 12 pence. I make my wife sole ex'trix. Wit. John Howlett, Richard Shearman. Pr. at Bury 8 November 1634.

703. W(R) MATHEW LANCASTER of Bury St Edmunds, gentleman. 2 September 1634.

Commends soul to God my maker and Jesus Christ my redeemer.
I give £5 to the poor of St Mary's parish and £3 to those of St James's parish in Bury, and 20s to the poor of Fornham All Saints to be distributed by the churchwardens and overseers within a month of my decease. I give 20s each to John Jewell, clerk and reader, and to Edmund

Callimy, clerk preacher, both of St Mary's parish, within 6 months. I give my brother Thomas Manock my best Turkey grosgrain gown faced with black velvet, and to Dorothy his wife and my sister-in-law two 20s pieces of gold within 2 months. I give Robert and Esther, children of Simon Stepney and Ann his wife deceased, 40s each within 6 months. I give my sister Dorcas Waters £5 within 12 months, and my sisters Frances Spaldinge and Mary Adams 40s each within 6 months. I forgive my brother-in-law Thomas Gille all the money he owes me. I give Alice Hubberd widow, my sister-in-law, £12 to be paid at 40s p.a. I give her son Edmund Ravens 40s and her daughter Elizabeth Ravens £3 within 6 months. I give my tenants Richard Godfrey and Roger Petchell 20s each within 3 months. I give my grandchild Mary Gippes £20 when 18 in addition to £10 I have in my hands bequeathed to her by her grandmother Gippes. She is to have interest on this latter sum at 8% until it is due to be paid to her. I give children of my brother Thomas Lancaster 40s each within 12 months. I give my son John £200 when 24, and daughter Margaret £200 when 21 or on marriage day. If latter dies her portion to be divided between my children and my wife. I forgive Margaret Lancaster, my brother John's widow, all the money she owes me for rent or otherwise. I give my servant Ann Bright 40s within 6 months. I give my wife Margaret my lease of 3 acres meadow lying by Friars Lane in Bury and now occupied by Richard Plumbe, and after her death to my son Thomas. I give Thomas my copyhold shop in Newmarket and to his wife a piece of plate worth £3. I give her daughter Sarah, my grandchild, 50s worth of plate to be delivered to her father within 3 months. I give the feoffees of the town lands of Bury £20 as a stock to be employed for the poor. I give my son Thomas 3 adjoining messuages in Bury now occupied by him, Richard Godfrey and Roger Petchell, on condition that he pays my wife £20 p.a. quarterly. Power to distrain. I give Thomas my land and tenement in Emney [Emneth?] and adjoining towns in Norfolk and Cambridgeshire, which I purchased of my brother John, on condition that, if my son John serves out his time of apprenticeship to a woollen draper and afterwards follows this trade he may hold for 12 years the house and shop in Bury now occupied by Roger Petchell and my shop and house in Newmarket; the 12 years to begin when John is 24. John is to pay rent of £6 p.a. for the house and shop in Bury and 40s p.a. for those in Newmarket. If Thomas will not allow John to occupy the shops, latter is to distrain on my land in Emney. I give my son John when 24 my free and copyhold land and tenements in Fornham All Saints and Hengrave which I bought from my brother Thomas Manock, and my freehold land in Fornham All Saints now occupied by Robert Croply. Until John is 24 my wife is to have rents and profits of this land. I give my wife for life, and then to son John, the following: my free and copyhold land bought from Thomas Pocket gentleman and his mother Susan and lying in the fields of Bury and Westley; the land in the fields of Bury which I bought from Thomas Hunt and his mother Margaret; and Plumbes close with the barn and stable near it, which I lately purchased of William Revell the elder, gentleman. I give my daughter Margaret my free and copyhold land in East Barton [Great Barton] now occupied by Thomas Salisbury when she is 20 or marries; until then my wife is to have rents and profits. If John dies without heirs, the land I bought from Thomas Manock is to go to the rest of my children and my wife. I give my wife all my plate, jewels and household goods, and my lease of the house where I now dwell. I give my grandchild Mary, daughter of my son Thomas, a piece of plate worth 50s. The residue of my goods and chattels I give to my wife and son Thomas and make them exors. Supervisor: Thomas Manock. Wit. John Shewe, John Cranmeere, Thomas Bell. Pr. at Bury 5 November 1634.

704. W(R) JOHN HAMOND (N) of Assington. April 1632.

Bequeathed soul to God and body to earth.
He bequeathed all he had amongst his wife and children, allowing out of his goods sufficient for the bringing up of his children, and committed the education of his son Thomas to his kinsman John Hamond. The rest of his goods were to be divided between his wife and children. Exor: John Hamond. Wit. John Thorpe, James Grimes. Pr. at Sudbury 12 April 1634.

705. W(R) WILLIAM PARKER (X) of Lavenham, singleman. 26 May 1627.

I give my sister Sarah my messuage wherein my mother, Joan Parker, now dwells in the High Street in the borough of Lavenham. Ex'trix: sister Sarah. Wit. Isaac Creme, Richard Ridnall, John Pinchbecke. Pr. at Bury 26 November 1634.

706. W(R) WILLIAM ADAMS (X) of Haverhill, fustian maker. 25 October 1634.

I give Stephen my eldest son my reversion, after death of Margery Rombold widow, to messuages and land in Kedington. He must pay following legacies: £60 to my son Joseph when 21, £60 to my son-in-law William Ravens and his wife and my daughter Martha and £60 to my daughter Mary, wife of Alexander Satterthwaite of Bocking [Essex] 1 year after death of Margery Rombold; and £20 each when 21 or married to my 3 daughters Alice, Elizabeth and Mary. If Stephen fails to pay legacies, other children to have messuages and land for ever. I give my goods and chattels to my wife Mary and make her ex'trix. Wit. Peter Hubberd, John Browne, Thomas Argent. Pr. at Bury 16 December 1634.

707. W(R) ALICE REINOLDS of Cowlinge, widow. 2 October 1634.

Bequeaths soul to God. To be buried in Cowlinge churchyard.
I give my eldest daughter Elizabeth, wife of Thomas Fintche, £20. I give my daughter Frances, wife of William Mallat of Hessett, £10 on condition

she makes no claim to the household stuff I brought from Hessett to Cowlinge. I give my daughter Frances all the household stuff I left behind at Hessett. I give my daughter Margaret £20 6 months after my decease. I give my daughter Anne £28, which I have promised on her marriage to Richard Ginne of Wickhambrook, but if marriage does not take place and she marries another man, I give her £20 and the other £8 I give to daughter Margaret. I give my godson William Mallat and my god-daughter Elizabeth daughter of Thomas Fintch 20s each when 21. I give my brother Samuel Barrett a table chair which is at his house at Saxham. I give my son-in-law Thomas Fintch 20s to see me honestly and Christianly buried, and I make him exor. Wit. Edward Barker, Samuel Barrett. Pr. at Bury 26 November 1634.

708. W(R) GEORGE PARKER (X) of Bacton, weaver. 27 November 1634.

Commends soul to God trusting in a glorious resurrection and to be saved by Jesus Christ.
My mind is that my grandchild Thomas Parker should have all my corn growing, my 2 horses, tumbril, plough, harrows, all my implements of husbandry, my hay, a livery and a trundle bedstead in the parlour chamber and vance roof, a great cauldron, a great trunk, a hutch, all my slayes and other implements belonging to weaving, a great tub and 2 bowls now in the hands of Robert Cressy, and a cheese vat and a little cooler in the hands of John Goddard. Thomas is to pay, before Michaelmas next, £3 out of these goods to my brother Robert, which he is to give to my grandchildren, the sons and daughters of my son Thomas when they are 21 as follows: 20s to Henry and 10s each to Mary, Elizabeth, Frances and Rachel. Benefit of survivorship. I give my grandchild Audrey Parker the rest of my unbequeathed goods, and she is to pay 20s to Henry Sharp of Ixworth due to him for a bedstead in my parlour. If Mary Parker, my daughter-in-law, will not allow Robert Smyth to hold the piece of meadow now in his hands, and for which he pays rent of 40s p.a., she is to repay him 15s I have received. I give my grandson Thomas all my wearing apparel. Exors: my grandchildren Thomas and Audrey; the latter is to pay for my burial. I appoint my loving brother Robert Parker of Wickham [Market] supervisor. Wit. Stephen Keble, John Goddard (X), John Daynes, Robert Spenforth. Pr. at Bury 15 December 1634.

709. W(R) JOHN BARKER (X) of Chevington, yeoman. 30 May 1632.

Bequeaths soul to God.
I give Ellen my good and loving wife all my lands and tenements for life, and after her decease I give my house in Chedburgh with its land, now ocupied by George Sparrow, to my younger son Edward until 1 year from Michaelmas after my wife's decease. When this term is over I give the house and land to my eldest son John and his wife Alice and their heirs. I

give my house and land in Stradishall, now occupied by [blank in MS] Coe, to my son Edward after my wife's decease. I give him £10 to be paid 6 months after my wife's death. Daughters Susan and Ellen have benefit of survivorship. I give these 2 daughters £40 each half a year after my wife's decease. I make my wife sole ex'trix and my loving friend John Sparrow of Downings in Rede overseer of my will, desiring him to aid my wife and children. If within a month of my decease my wife has not entered into surety to John Sparrow to perform my will and pay my legacies, I then make my 2 daughters ex'trices. Wit. Robert Laman. Pr. at Bury 20 November 1634.

710. W(R) ROGER MANNING (X) of Cockfield, yeoman. 27 June 1631.

Bequeaths soul to God. To be buried in Cockfield churchyard.
I give Elizabeth my wellbeloved wife an annuity of £5 to be paid quarterly by my ex'trix. She is to have her dwelling, firing, lodging and being with Dorothy my daughter, and is to be carefully tended and looked unto during her life. I give 30s to be divided among the children of my sister Rose Sylverstone within a year. I give 20s to poor of Cockfield within 3 months. I give all my land and houses to my daughter Dorothy, and all my goods and chattels and I make her ex'trix. She is to pay my debts and bring my body to the ground in a decent and comely manner. Wit. John Fincham (X), and me Thomas Curtis. Pr. at Bury 29 December 1634.

711. W(R) MARIAN LYSTER (X) of Alpheton, widow. 20 March 1628/29.

Bequeaths soul to God firmly believing in resurrection of body.
I give my son John the desk that was his father's. I give my youngest daughter Joanna Cunisby the pair of virginals that were her father's. The residue of my goods and chattels I bequeath to be equally divided among my 4 daughters, Mary Hornsby, Martha Hayward, Faith Lyster and Joanna Cunisby, by the discretion of Richard Floode of Melford and Richard Ridnall of Lavenham, both yeoman, whom I make exors. I give them 5s apiece for their pains. Wit. Thomas Chinery, Martha Raye (X). Pr. 23 November 1634. No place given.

712. W(R) THOMAS RAYNEBERD (N) of Stowupland, husbandman. 1 November 1634.

We Philip Garrard and John Goddard of Stowupland certify that Thomas Rayneberd did order his will to be put in writing in the form here set down. I give Vinca my loving wife all my goods and chattels for life; any left at her death to be divided into 3 equal parts to be given to my sons

300

Thomas and John and daughter Joanna. If my wife marries again I give
£5 each to my 3 children out of my goods. Benefit of survivorship.
Ex'trix: wife. Wit. John Goddard, Philip Garrard. Pr. at Bury 4
December 1634.

713. W(R) AMBROSE HARVY (X) of Honington, yeoman. 12 October
1634.

Bequeaths soul to God and body to be buried in church or churchyard of
Honington.
I make Peter Sponer of Thetford [Norfolk] gentleman and John Goody
the elder of Sapiston, yeoman, exors of my will, and John Mann the elder
of Honington supervisor; my exors are to pay him £5. I give 10s to the
minister my exors shall appoint to preach at my burial and 10s more to
Mr Hodsonne, minister of Honington, to give leave to the preacher. I
give £5 to the poor at my burial. My will is that on the day of my burial
my exors shall expend £10 on a dinner for the entertainment of my
friends. I give my godson Ambrose, son of Roger Wright, £10 and to his
brothers Roger and Thomas £5 each. I give Ann, wife of [blank in MS]
Cockermore of Dickleburgh [Norfolk] £10, and [blank in MS] Bridgham,
daughter of my kinswoman Elizabeth Noble, £5. I give £5 to be divided
among 3 children John Brigham the elder had by his first wife. I give £10
to be divided among Peter, Nicholas, Frances and Susan, children of my
cousin Thomas Becke, late of Timworth. I give 20s to Margery, daughter
of Thomas Noble the elder late of Stanton. I give John Nunn the younger
of Honington £6. I give 40s each to the children of my exor John Goody:
John, Robert, Jane, Mary, Thomas, Michael, Alice, Susan and Elizabeth.
I give 20s each to John, Ann, Frances and James children of Augustine
Noble, butcher of Sapiston. I give 20s to my god-daughter Mary,
daughter of John Martyne the elder late of Sapiston, and 10s each to 2
daughters of Thomas Noble the younger late of Sapiston deceased. I give
20s each to Dorcas, Susan and Rebecca, daughters of John Garvie late of
Bardwell deceased, and 10s each to 4 daughters of Henry Martine of
Ixworth Thorpe. I give 10s to Thomas, son of Thomas Aslie. I give £30 to
be divided among my exor Peter Spooner, and John, Ann, Jane, Mary,
Elizabeth, Martha and Susan, all children of Peter Spooner late of
Thetford deceased. All legacies to be paid within a year of my decease.
All the rest of my goods and chattels I give to my exors for their care and
pains. Wit. Mary Goodday, William Stubbes (X). Pr. at Bury 22
December 1634.

714. W(R) WILLIAM HATFIELD alias MAIOR (X) junior of
Elmswell, husbandman. 13 May 1634.

Commends soul to God.
I give my son William £50 when 21. I give my father William all my goods
and chattels for maintaining my son with meat, drink, lodging, linen,
woollen, hose and shoes until he is 21. I make my father my exor. Wit.
Timothy Aumont, Miles Raphe. Pr. at Bury 25 November 1634.

715. W(R) THOMAS GOSS (X) of Hitcham, yeoman. 13 September 1634.

I yield my soul to God who gave it me.
I give my eldest son William £4 when 21, but, if my wife Judith remarries before then, he is to have £4 within 20 days. I give William a bed, bedstead, bolster, pillow. blanket, pair sheets and my cloak. I give my daughter Judith £4 when 24, and a bed, bolster, pillow, coverlet, blanket and a great cupboard standing in the best room below. I give my daughter Elizabeth £3 and 2 joined stools when 24. I give my daughter Dorothy £2, a bed, bedstead and bedding when 24. My wife is to have the best bed and bedstead in the best room below and I make her ex'trix. Wit. John Sparrow, Richard Stafford. Pr. at Sudbury 27 September 1634.

716. W(R) WILLIAM LEWES (X) of Stoke by Clare, husbandman. 2 June 1634.

Commends soul to God trusting through Jesus Christ to enjoy everlasting life.
I give Ellen my wife my house in Stoke for life, and then to my son William and his wife Lydia, and after their deaths to my grandson William. If he has no heirs, my grandson Joseph is to have my house. I give my son William my baulte colt, my grandson William my black sheep and her lamb, and my grandson Joseph my broad hutch standing in the parlour. I give the rest of my moveable goods to my wife and make her ex'trix. Wit. George Pratt, Simon Hall. Pr. at Stoke by Clare 20 July 1634.

717. W(R) BLOYSE ENGLISH of Bury St Edmunds, joiner. 12 December 1634.

Bequeaths soul to God.
I will that my exors sell so much of my land in Hargrave as shall suffice to pay my debts and other charges, and the admission fines for my mother Elizabeth English widow to my copyhold land. Any money left over to be given to my mother. I give my unsold land in Hargrave, and my land and tenement in Bury to my mother for ever. I also give her all my household stuff. I make my loving friends John Mallowes and Edward Kelam gentleman exors. Wit. Robert Browne, Edward Cock, Thomas Sargant, Oliver Theobald. Pr. at Bury 3 January 1634/35.

718. W(R) HENRY SPARKE (X) of Hawstead, yeoman. 22 July 1633.

Commends soul to God hoping assuredly for salvation through Jesus Christ.
I give my son Robert my messuage called Reades with its land in Hawstead, and another adjoining tenement occupied by John Jaggard and John Innold, except for a tenement with a yard which belongs to

Reades tenement. I give my grandson Henry, son of Robert, 20s and the same sum to all my other grandchildren within 12 months of my decease. I give Frances my wellbeloved wife the tenement and yard excepted from gift to Robert for her life and then to Robert. I give my wife and Robert right of access to the well of my tenement called Gippes to draw water. I give my son John my messuage called Gippes with its land wherein I now dwell from Michaelmas after my decease, until which time Robert is to occupy this tenement. I give my daughter Rose, wife of Robert Steward, an annuity of 40s to be paid quarterly by my 2 sons. I have already surrendered my copyhold land in Hargrave to my sons Robert and John, but have since then taken the rents and profits myself and I intend to do so during my life. Within a month of my decease, my son John must give my exors an acquittance for these rents or forfeit gift formerly made to him. John is to give my wife every year a cart load of wood. I give my wife £10 to be paid by my 2 sons within 3 months. She must give my sons a release of all her rights of dower in my land, except what is left to her, or all gifts to her shall be void. I give my godson Robert Sparke 5s and all my other godchildren 12 pence within 3 months. I give £5 to the township of Hawstead to be used as a stock to set the poor to work and for their relief. All the residue of my goods and chattels I give to Robert and make him exor. Wit. Jasper Sharpe, John Spaldinge. Pr. at Bury 5 January 1634/35. Inventory exhibited totalling £130 13s 6d.

719. W(R) WILLIAM LEVERICKE (X) of Hopton, linen weaver.
7 December 1634.

Bequeaths soul to God.
I give my son John my messuage and land in Ringland in Norfolk when 21; until then Mary my wife is to have the use of them to bring up my 2 sons John and Stephen. If John dies without heirs, Stephen will inherit, and if he too dies my sisters Susan and Elizabeth are to have my messuage and lands. I leave my son Stephen £40 to be paid within a year of my decease by my ex'trix to Anthony Parker of Great Ellingham and Nicholas Larkin of Shipdham, both in Norfolk. They are to pay my wife £2 p.a. for the use of £40 until Stephen is 21. John has benefit of survivorship. If my wife is with child at the day of my death, this child is to have my messuage and land in Ringland if my 2 sons both die before they are 21. If both sons die, £40 left to Stephen is to be divided; £30 to my 2 sisters and £10 to my wife. I give John Hurrold, my brother, a new pair of looms which were made by Luke Cocke and 1 slay, which he now works with, and a shuttle and my buck bleacher. I give all the rest of my goods and chattels to my wife to pay my debts, and I make her ex'trix and will her to give the poor people of Hopton 6s 8d at her discretion. Wit. John Halles, Luke Cocke (X), Richard Barker. Pr. at Bury 12 January 1634/35.

720. W(R) DIANA GOSSE (X) of Brettenham, widow. 22 November 1634.

Bequeaths soul to God in hope through Jesus Christ of glorious resurrection.

I give my son George my tenement where I now dwell with free and copyhold land in Hitcham and Brettenham, and he must pay my debts and legacies. I give my son William £14 and my son Edward £15 in full discharge of legacies in their father's will; both within 6 months. I give my grandchild Diana Gosse £5 within a year, and immediately my black cow, my best feather bed with all things belonging, my cupboard and my brass pot. I give George, son of my son George, 20s within a year, and to his sisters Margaret and Agnes 20s when 21. I give £5 each when 21 to William, Judah, Elizabeth and Dorothy children of my son Thomas. I give £5 each when 21 to my grandchildren Josias, John and Robert Camblim, and 20s each to William, Rose and Elizabeth, children of my son Edward when 21. Those who are already 21 are to be paid within a year of my decease. I give my grandchildren William, Thomas and Elizabeth Janinges 20s each within a year. I give Diana Janinges, wife of John Ofward, 5s within a year. Legatees have benefit of survivorship and power to distrain. I give the residue of my goods to my son George and make him exor. He is to lay out 20s for my burial. Wit. George Buckenham, John Durent. Pr. at Bury 15 January 1634/35.

721. W(R) ANNE BROOKE (N) of Bury St Edmunds, singlewoman.

About a fortnight before her death she willed that when she died her sister Elizabeth Stevenson should have her suit of clothes, which words were spoken in presence of Robert Moore and Goodwife Symonds. Let. ad. granted at Bury 12 January 1634/35.

722. W(R) GILES PITCHES (N) of Kirtling [Cambs], yeoman. 1 December 1634.

Being sick of the sickness whereof he died and desirous to dispose of his estate, he desired those present to take notice what he said: I give to Anne my wife all my goods and chattels and I charge and desire her to pay my debts and bring up my 2 children in the fear of God. Wit. Benjamin French, Henry Stanton. Let. ad. granted to widow 12 January 1634/35. No place given.

723. W(R) MARGARET PLEASANCE, wife of Richard Pleasance, parson of Hargrave. 3 July 1633.

Bequeaths soul to God and Jesus Christ hoping to be saved through latter.

I make my will with the consent of my husband. I give Jonathan Slacke my son one piece black grograin of 12 yards. I give my daughter Frances

Fordam one half dozen of cushions unmade, 2 pair sheets, 1 pair pillowbeeres and a dozen table napkins. I give Sarah, Elizabeth and Mary Fordham, children of Frances, 20s each when 21. I give my daughter Mary Slacke a silver spoon if it be demanded. I give my daughter Sarah Mosse for life my house with orchard, yard, barn and 3 acres copyhold land in the fields of Fornham All Saints. I give my goods to the paying of my legacies to Frances Fordham's children. I give the inheritance of my house, orchard, yard and barn after decease of Sarah Mosse, to her daughters Mary Cokes alias Slacke and Sarah Mosse. I give my 3 acres copyhold to John Mosse after his mother's death. Ex'trix: daughter Sarah Mosse. This will made by my wife I Richard Pleasance do allow. Wit. Arthur Heigham, Thomas Underwode. Pr. at Bury 13 January 1634/35.

724. W(R) WILLIAM MARKES (X) of Combs, shoemaker.
5 December 1634.

Commends soul to God and body to earth in assurance of glorious resurrection through Jesus Christ.
I give the backhouse of the tenement Saygoodes, where I now dwell, with free access to my wife Dorothy so long as she remains a widow. I give the dwelling house, all the rest of the tenement and, after my wife's decease, the backhouse to Edward Estow of Barham my son-in-law and his wife and my daughter Mary and their heirs for ever. They must pay my wife an annuity of £3. Power to distrain. I give my wife all the household stuff that was her own before our marriage, and the use for life of my cupboard in the hall and the bedstead there with feather bed and bedding. I give these after her decease, and the rest of my household stuff immediately after my death, to my daughter Mary Estow. My wife is to pay her own fine and 40s towards that of my son-in-law and daughter. All the rest of my goods I give to my wife and make her ex'trix. Wit. Thomas Sothebie, Richard Gildersleve. Pr. at Bury 8 January 1634/35.

725. W(R) PHILIP SMITH (X) of Kedington, husbandman. 2 December 1633.

Bequeaths soul to God hoping to have life everlasting through Jesus Christ. To be buried in some convenient place in Kedington churchyard.
I give Thomasine my daughter £20 to be paid to her by my exor, my trusty and wellbeloved Edmund Betts, who shall keep the money until she is 20. I desire him to see my daughter brought up to learning in the fear of God, and to see that she has all things necessary. I give all the rest of my goods to my wife Thomasine for her maintenance, and to bring up my daughter in good education in the nurture and fear of the Lord. I appoint my wife to join with Edmund Betts as exors. If it please God to take away my daughter before she is 20, my exor is to pay £5 to Philip, son of Jeremy Shelly, when 21 and the other £15 I leave to his disposing. Wit. Thomas Reeve, Clement Howton. Pr. at Clare 11 April 1634.

726. W(R) ROBERT ROBINSON alias SANDER (X) of Wangford, shepherd. 2 October 1634.

Commends soul to God trusting to merits of Jesus Christ for redemption and salvation.
I will that my daughters Elizabeth, wife of Richard Futter, and Dorothy shall enjoy for 6 years after my decease my messuage in Brandon, wherein Jeffrey Capp and Richard Futter now inhabit, and my arable land in the fields of Brandon. They must pay 40s p.a. to my son Robert, who is to have the messuage and land for ever after the 6 years have expired. During the 6 years my 2 daughters are to give my wife Millicent every year 2 bushels good, sweet and well-dressed rye and 2 of the like barley at the messuage next to Brandon churchyard belonging to me and my wife. Power to distrain. I give my wife 3 of my cows: one speckle faced, another brinded and the third a little black one; a great black steer and a little one; 5 ewes and lambs in Wangford flock which are already earmarked for her; 2 hoggs, 2 pigs and a skep of bees. I also give her all the household stuff she had when we married. I give all my other household goods to be equally divided between my 3 children. I give my son Robert 30 ewes and hoggs in Wangford flock, which are already earmarked with his earmark. I make my 2 daughters ex'trices and give them the unbequeathed residue of my goods. Wit. Robert Wright, Henry Munninges, John Marshall. Pr. at Bury 12 October 1634.

727. W(R) WILLIAM RUMBALL (N) of Wangford, husbandman. 1 January 1634/35.

In the presence of Samuel Coxe, rector of Wangford, and Marian Statham he made his wife Susan sole ex'trix of all his goods and chattels on condition that within the space of a year next after his departure she paid 30s to his 3 children: 10s each to Mary, Margaret and Thomas his son. Wit. Samuel Coxe, Marian Statham. Pr. at Bury 2 February 1634/35.

728. W(R) SIMON LARGEANT (X) of Mildenhall, shepherd. 5 November 1634.

Commends soul to God assuredly hoping for salvation by Jesus Christ. To be buried in Mildenhall churchyard until the resurrection of the dead.
I give the copyhold cottage in which I dwell, and held of King's manor, to my wife Elizabeth for life and then to my son Miles, who must pay my daughter Anne £3 in south porch of Mildenhall church within 2 years of my wife's decease, £3 to my son John after 4 years and £3 to son Robert within 6 years in the same place. If Miles refuses to pay legacies, Anne is to have my cottage and pay the legacies; and if she refuses, John, and if he refuses, Robert. My wife is to keep the cottage in good repair. I give my eldest son William 2s within a month of my death. All my goods and chattels I give to my wife towards paying my debts, and I make her ex'trix.

Memorandum: I have surrendered my cottage to use of my will into hands of Thomas Pechey and Robert Thurston, copyhold tenants of the manor. Wit. Robert Thurston (X), Robert Greengrasse (X), Thomas Pechey, William Dalleson. Pr. at Bury 1 December 1634.

729. W(R) WILLIAM MAYER of Denston, yeoman. 23 October 1634.

Humbly bequeaths soul to God hoping for salvation through Jesus Christ. I give Thomas and William, sons of my brother-in-law Thomas Ashfeild, and his daughters Susan and Amy £10 each to be paid by my ex'trix within 18 months of my death. I give my kinswoman Hannah Dearsley £5, and my servant William Rowly £5 within 2 years. I give my servant Elizabeth Browne 40s within a year. All the rest of my goods, cattle and money, after my debts, legacies and funeral expences have been paid, I give to my dear sister Hannah Mayor and make her ex'trix. Wit. Thomas Westrop, Henry Roger. Pr. at Bury 9 February 1634/35. Inventory exhibited with total value of £377 7s 8d.

730. W(R) AUGUSTINE PARKER the elder of Stanton, gentleman. 14 September 1630.

Commends soul to God hoping to obtain everlasting life through Jesus Christ.
I give my wife Elizabeth for life all my messuages and lands in Stanton and Bardwell on condition she brings up my children in the fear of God and learning until 21, and pays my debts and legacies. I give her all my moveable goods. She must keep my house walls and fences in good repair, taking sufficient wood for this. She has power to let my land until Michaelmas 12 months after her decease. I give my son Augustine, after his mother's death, all my land and tenements in Stanton and Bardwell except the tenement with the pasture lying by it called Hallhead land. He must pay any of my debts and legacies left unpaid by his mother, and if he refuses my daughters Katherine and Mary are to hold my land and perform my will. If Augustine dies without heirs, my son John is to have land on same conditions. I give Augustine £10 p.a. for his maintenance to be paid by his mother until he is 30, after which time she is to pay 20 marks p.a. if she is still alive. If he molests my wife in possession of my land, the annuities given to him are void. I give John my tenement and meadow called Hallhead land, now in occupation of [blank in MS], when 21; if he dies without heirs Augustine is to have it. I give my daughters Katherine and Mary £50 each when 21. Benefit of survivorship and if both die, John is to have their legacies. I give my daughters £100 each to be paid by Augustine 1 year after my wife's decease if they are 21, and, if not, when they reach that age. If my daughters marry any man without consent of my ex'trix, my brother John Chapman of Thetford [Norfolk] and my cousin Mr Robert Cotton of Horringer, legacies to them become void. I make my wife sole ex'trix, but if she refuses to act or remarries, then I make my son Augustine exor. Wit. Robert Cotton, Alice Waller (X). Pr. at Bury 16 February 1634/35.

731. W(R) OSMUND MILES (X) of Redgrave, yeoman. 17 December 1634.

Gives soul to God hoping for joyful resurrection through my saviour Jesus Christ.

I give Mary my loving wife for life my messuage in Hockwell in Norfolk with outbuildings and orchard, and now in occupation of Thomas Watson. After her decease, I give it to my brother John Miles for life and then to my godson Osmund, son of Edward Stallon yeoman of Feltwell in Norfolk. I give my brother John a piece of copyhold land in Feltwell for ever, and £20 within a year of my decease. I give 20s each to 6 children of Edward Stallon within 6 months. I give my good friend Thomas Brackells of Wilton in Norfolk 20s, and to Alice and Susan Bishopp my wife's sisters 20s each. I give William Ansell my 'fellow' and good friend 20s. I give my god-daughter Frances, daughter of William Reade my 'fellow', 5s. I give unto all my 'fellows' in Redgrave Hall 12 pence apiece for a pair of gloves, and unto 8 of my 'fellows' which shall carry me to church 2s 6d apiece. All these legacies to be paid by my wife Mary, whom I make ex'trix. I give my brother John all my clothes both linen and woollen, except one shirt. All the rest of my goods I give to my wife. Wit. George Gardner, John Limborn. Pr. at Bury 16 February 1634/35.

732. W(R) AMBROSE BIGGES of Glemsford, gentleman. 24 August 1634.

Humbly yields soul to God trusting to be saved by merits of Jesus Christ.

I give £5 to poor of Glemsford to be distributed on day of my burial or within a month. I give my wife Anne for life my messuage called Balles with buildings and 3 acres land and now occupied by George Grigges and lying at Egremont Street in Glemsford, and my 7 acres copyhold land in Glemsford called Brises and lying next to the wood lately converted to pasture ground and called Brises alias Betney wood. I also give her a 1.5 acre freehold meadow, sometime Crosses, lying at Broad meadow in Glemsford, a 2 acre close of land called Langcrofte and sometime Pettit's, and a messuage called Wards with 18 acres in Little Maplestead and Pebmarsh in Essex and now let to [blank in MS] Smith. I give my wife this land in lieu of dower, and I give her all the goods and chattels, woollen cloths, bonds and bills which in truth were her's at time of our marriage; and also all bills and bonds that I have taken for Suffolk cloth which was my wife's when we married. Also all money and bills which William Grigges, clothier of Stansfield, is engaged to pay me; this money being due to my wife before our marriage. If my wife is with child with a son at time of my decease, I give him, after her death, all my land and tenements in Little and Great Maplestead and Pebmarsh, and I make my wife his guardian. I give my daughter Margery, wife of William Hall, the messuage where I now dwell with its buildings used by me and situated at Tye Green in Glemsford, and all the land in Glemsford which was John Strutt's her deceased grandfather. I give her a 2 acre freehold close in Glemsford next to the wood called the Parsonage wood on west and called the Harpe, a 3 rod piece in Millfield in Glemsford and now enclosed, which I bought of Roger Cricke, and a piece of land with a small pightle adjoining with a pond in it and called Hunden mere or Mill mere. I give my daughters Mary and Anne, in satisfaction of legacies given to them by the will of their deceased uncle John Halle, the messuage at Tye Green now occupied by Robert Warren, and the tenement, yards and orchards at Tye Green now occupied by John Byford, John Locken, Mary Page and Robert Raye, and the adjoining smith's shop. If either of my daughters refuses to accept these premises in discharge of their legacies, being as I remember not more than £92, or if daughter Margery takes liking to them, then upon payment of £92 to be shared by Mary and Anne, Margery shall have these buildings and land. I give my son-in-law William Hall, whom I make sole exor, my woods in Glemsford called Smithes grove and Hillishinch to sell towards paying my debts and legacies. He is also to sell my 2 pieces copyhold land in Cobbes croft and Jacksons croft. If my wife is with a female child, I give her and my daughters Mary and Anne the reversion to all the rest of my land and tenements in Essex and Glemsford not already bequeathed. I give my unbequeathed land in Melford to my daughter Margery to sell to pay my debts. If my wife is not with child, after her decease I bequeath Mary my property in Little Maplestead and Pebmarsh, and Anne the property in Glemsford. I give Anne my messuage called Slaughters with adjoining green and a grove called Oxenholt and my water mill called Glemsford mill, and my land in Glemsford and Melford now in tenure of John Cricke of Glemsford. I give Thomas Gardner my nephew £5 and his brother and my godson John £5; both when 21. I give my wellbeloved friends and cousins John Bigges and Thomas Wright of Hartest 50s each in token of my love to buy a piece of plate. If I have no child by my now wife, I give my grandchildren William and Anne Hall one third of my household stuff and plate; the other 2 parts, set out by indifferent neighbours, I give to my daughters Mary and Anne. All the rest of my goods to be divided among my 3 daughters, provided that if I have any issue by my wife my grandchildren and my daughter Margery shall have no portion of my household stuff. Memorandum made 30 November 1634. Since signing and sealing of this will, I have received from Mr Nore merchant of Ipswich £118 10s 0d for cloths which were my wife's before our marriage. I will that my exor pays this sum to my wife. Robert Howe, clothier of Glemsford, is bound by an obligation dated 24 March 1633/34, to pay £97 4s 0d on 26 March 1635. I give my wife this bond as the money was due to her before we married. I also give her all money due for cloth sold by Robert Howe since my will was made. Wit. Thomas Wright, Richard Gardner. Pr. at Bury 12 January 1634/35.

733. W(R) CHRISTOPHER GOODAY of Chevington, yeoman.
29 January 1634/35.

Bequeaths soul to God hoping for salvation by merits of Jesus Christ.
I give all my copyhold lands and tenements held of manor of Chedburgh
Hall with Arneboroughs and Chevington to my 2 sisters Ellen and Anne
if my wife Christian be not now with child, but if she is, I give this land to
the child. If my sisters have my land, they are to pay following annuities:
to my loving mother Elizabeth Gooday £7 and to my loving wife £7; both
to be paid half yearly at south door of Chevington church. Power to
distrain. I have mortgaged certain freehold land to my kinsman John
Gooday of Chevington to secure payment to him of £106 at a day yet to
come, and I have also secured the payment of £6 interest. If my 2 sisters
and their husbands pay the capital sum when due and the interest on it, I
give them the above freehold land, but if they do not, my ex'trix is to pay
the several sums and I give her the same land for ever. If my sisters and
their husbands do not within 2 months of my decease secure my wife from
any claim against her, I give her the land until the day of redemption of
the mortgage. I give the poor people of Chevington £5 to be paid to
churchwardens and overseers within a year. I give my mother £10 to be
paid by my ex'trix 6 months after my decease. All the residue of my stock
and household stuff I bequeath to my loving wife and make her sole
ex'trix. Wit. Robert Paman, Robert Underwood, John Gooday, Richard
Spenser. Pr. at Bury 27 February 1634/35.

734. W(R) THOMASINE MURRELL (X) of Wetheringsett, widow.
22 October 1634.

Bequeaths soul to God believing that by his free mercy and love unto me
for sake of my sweet saviour Christ Jesus he will pardon my sins and
receive me into everlasting happiness.
I give Julian my daughter, wife of Robert Pinswan, my smallest
featherbed with feather bolster belonging to it and 2 of my best
petticoats. I give Sarah, daughter of Julian, 3s 4d. I give Sarah Pinson my
best hat, I give my son John 10s within half a year. I give my son Joseph,
to whom I have freely been beneficial, 12 pence. I give his daughter
Sarah a coffer. I give Jeremy Tinker, youngest son of my daughter Alice,
20s when 21 or if he dies before then, to John Tinker, Alice's son, to
whom I give when 21 a chest with lock and key, a keep, my best feather
bed, a feather bolster, 2 feather pillows, 2 curtains, 2 coverlets, a blanket,
a wicker chair, a turned chair, 3 pairs sheets and 2 pillowbeeres. I give my
grandson John Tinker a brass pot, a warming pan, 2 kettles, 2 skillets and
7 pieces pewter when 21. I also give him a casting sheet, 6 napkins, 2
pillowbeeres, 3 kerchers and a long table when 21. If he dies before then,
all these gifts are to go to Jeremy Tinker, except the 5 last named and the
turned chair, which I will Anne, daughter of Samuel Sheperd, shall have.
I give him 13s 4d in recompense of his pains as my exor. I give him the

rest of my goods to be sold towards the costs of my burial and proving my will; any overplus to be given to John Tinker when 21. Wit. Samuel Sheppard junior, William Boce. Pr. at Bury 10 March 1634/35.

735. W(R) JOHN WIXE (N) of Bury St Edmunds, linen weaver. 1 February 1634/35.

He made his will in the presence of Anne Cooper widow and Priscilla, wife of John Archer. Being moved to make his will by Anne Cooper, he answered that he would give Mary his wife all he had, meaning all his personal estate of goods, debts and chattels, and did use the same words divers times in his sickness, bidding his wife not to be grieved for she should have all. Wit. Anne Cooper, Priscilla Archer. Let. ad. granted to widow at Bury 9 February 1634/35.

736. W(R) RICHARD GAGES of Drinkstone, yeoman. 13 November 1634.

Commends soul to God trusting through Jesus Christ to inherit eternal life.
I give my well beloved wife Margaret a 9 acre close called Cawdelles in Drinkstone for ever, and all my other freehold land in Drinkstone for life, and after her decease to my son Thomas. I give my wife all my copyhold messuage and land until Thomas is 21, towards her maintenance and that of my 2 children Thomas and Margaret with meat, drink, lodging and virtuous education until they are 21. When Thomas is 21 I give him all my copyhold land and he must pay my wife, if she be living, £6 13s 4d p.a. at Lady Day and Michaelmas in porch of Drinkstone church. Power to distrain. I give my daughter Margaret £100 when 21. If both my children die before 21, I give all my messuage and land to my wife for life and then to my sisters Margaret and Susan and my brother Theodore and their heirs. The residue of my goods I give to my wife, whom I make sole ex'trix. Within 1 month of my decease she is to enter into a bond with my loving uncle Mr George Scarpe for the payment of £100 to my daughter when 21. Wit. Anne Mason (X), Margaret Avis (X), George Scarpe. Pr. at Bury 23 February 1634/35.

737. W(R) ROBERT DAY the elder of Great Ashfield. 24 May 1631.

Commits soul to God trusting to be saved by merits of Jesus Christ. To be buried in parish of Ashfield where I now dwell.
I give my son Robert all my copyhold land held of Ashfield manor, being 26 acres, the homesetting and houses on it and another 2 acres before surrendered to him on his marriage. After his death I give this land to his son Robert the elder. I give Anne my wife £10 p.a. to be paid quarterly out of my lands by Robert. Power to distrain. I give my wife a posted bedstead with a feather bed and the bedding belonging to it as it stands in the little chamber between the 2 doors, the cupboard in the hall, a little

brass pot, a little kettle, a pair bellows, firepan and tongs, a gridiron, a wicker chair, 2 buffet stools and 2 loads of wood every year to be provided by owner of my land. I give all my other moveable goods, and after my wife's decease those left to her, to my son Robert whom I make exor. He is to pay the poor of Ashfield 20s in 3 annual instalments to be disposed of at discretion of the minister of the town and my exor. A legacy of 5 marks a year for 12 years is due to be paid, as appears by several bonds, by my son to Thomas Cartar of Hinderclay; if Robert dies before this £40 is paid, my grandson Robert is to pay remainder, but if he refuses my son's exors shall have power to distrain. As I have given almost all my moveables to my son, he shall presently after my decease give my wife 3 bushels of wheat and 2 of malt, a quarter of his best cheese that he makes and a firkin of butter for her provision between my death and her first annuity payment. I trust my son to perform my will as he will answer at the dreadful day of judgement. Wit. Robert Alderton, George Day (X), Thomas Peake. Pr. at Bury 16 February 1634/35.

738. W(R) RICHARD SPINCKE of Ixworth, carpenter. 20 May 1628.

Bequeaths soul to God trusting to be saved by merits of Jesus Christ.
I give my loving wife Agnes my 2½ acres and 5 rods of copyhold land held of Sir John Corrold of his manor of Ixford, on condition that within 12 months she pays my daughter-in-law Ruth Maior £10. If she refuses or has died, I bequeath above land to my son-in-law Isaac Maior on condition he pays £10 to Ruth, but if he fails or dies, I give the land to Ruth. I give all my goods and chattels to my wife and make her ex'trix. Wit. William Bannok (X), John Cowper. Pr. at Bury 23 February 1634/35.

Note: Sir John Carrell held Ixworth manor c.1618–1630.

739. W(R) STEPHEN KEBLE of Combs, yeoman. 20 January 1634/35.

Commends soul to God and body to earth in confident persuasion of a joyful resurrection to eternal life through merits of Jesus Christ.
I give Stephen my eldest son £20 when 24, and 20 marks each when 24 to my other 6 children: Mary, Elizabeth, Edmund, Martha, Anne and Thomas. If my wife, whom I make ex'trix, marries again, she must enter into a bond of £200 with my supervisor to pay these legacies. If she refuses she must pay all the unpaid portions to my supervisor. I give the poor people of Combs 10s. All the rest of my goods I give to my wife for her own use and towards the education of my children. I make my cousin Thomas Brooke of Combs supervisor, desiring him to assist my wife and for his pains I give him 20s. Wit. Thomas Sothebie, Richard Gildersleeve. Pr. at Bury 3 March 1634/35.

740. W(R) DANIEL GOSNOLD (X) of Boxford, yeoman.
28 November 1634.

Bequeaths soul to God.
I give my daughter Bridget when 21 the house wherein my mother Bantoft lives with its yard and adjoining orchard. I give my loving wife Frances for life the 2 houses where Robert Wysson and Thomas Rafe now live with the croft late in occupation of John Stiggall and the orchard and gardens. After her decease I give them to my son Francis. I give my wife the messuage where I now dwell with yard, garden and backside for life, and then to my son Daniel together with my unbequeathed land. Daniel must pay my eldest son Thomas £30 in 3 annual instalments after my wife's decease, and my son John £20 4 and 5 years after. Power to distrain. I make my wife sole ex'trix. Wit. John Spenser, George Carter (X). Pr. at Bury 23 February 1634/35.

741. W(R) JOHN WHITE (X) of Newton, husbandman. 13 March 1625/26.

Bequeaths soul to God believing to obtain everlasting life through Jesus Christ.
I give Dorothy my wellbeloved wife £20 to be paid over 4 years. Power to distrain. I give my wife her dwelling in my bakehouse with liberty to fetch her water at my usual pond. If she dies before her £20 is fully paid, I give her full power to dispose of residue as she wishes. I give my son John my house and all my copyhold land in Newton on condition he pays my legacies and proves my will. I give my eldest son Thomas £10 to be paid 5 and 7 years after my decease, my son Edward £10 to be paid 6 and 8 years after and my daughter Dorothy £13 6s 8d to be paid 9 years after. Children have power to distrain and benefit of survivorship. I give my wife all my moveable goods except my best posted bedstead and all that belongs to it; I give this to my son Edward. I make my son John exor.
Memorandum that before the sealing of this will I called to mind that I owe £5 to my son Thomas. John is to pay this sum within a year. Thomas has power to distrain. Wit. Samuel Alston, Thomas Frethes (X), Thomas Dearslye. Pr. at Bury 12 January 1634/35.

742. W(R) JOHN RUSSELL of Stowmarket, yeoman. 13 February 1634/35.

Commits soul to God being assured of remission of sins through Jesus Christ.
I give the messuage wherein I dwell with yard and garden, which I purchased of John Garnham, to my beloved wife Joan for life, and after her death to my son Thomas, and if he has no heirs to my grandson John Wright. I give my wife all such goods as were hers before our marriage; these goods being set down in a note dated 12 March 1630/31. I also give

her £20 and all the corn and grain in my house when I die. I give my sons John and Thomas £30 each; my daughter Anne, wife of Robert Wright, £20; my daughter Mary, wife of John Warde, £12; my grandson Samuel Hakinge £5; William Wilton £5; and my daughter Elizabeth Stinson 20s. All these legacies to be paid by my exors within 6 months of my decease, provided the legatees demand them at my dwelling house in Stowmarket and give my exors a receipt. I give my grandchild Mary Hine £5, and £9 each when 21 to my grandchildren Thomas and Elizabeth Stinson. There is due to me by bond from my son-in-law John Ward £12; I give him this bond. I give my son Thomas a cupboard, a featherbed, 1 pair sheets, 1 pair blankets, a coverlet, a kettle of the middle sort, a brass pot, 6 pieces pewter, a short table, a joined form and another form, a chest, a chair, a beer vessell and a bowl; all to be given to him within 3 months of my decease if he has not received these goods in my lifetime. All my other goods I give to my wife towards paying my legacies. Exors: wife and son-in-law Robert Wright, to whom I give 5s for his pains. Wit. John Garneham, Edmund Peteywarde. Pr. at Bury 9 March 1634/35.

743. W(R) RALPH SEAMAN (X) of Bury St Edmunds, smith. 28 February 1634/35.

Commends soul to God hoping through my saviour Jesus Christ to be received into his blessed kingdom and trusting in resurrection to eternal happiness.
At a convenient time after my decease all my moveables shall be sold by my exors and, after my funeral expenses and debts have been paid, the money is to be used as follows: to pay my son Ralph £30 when 24 and my daughter Anne £10 when 21 or when she marries. I bequeath my wife Anne £10 as soon as my goods are sold. Any money remaining to be equally divided between my wife and daughter. If the money from the sale of my goods is not sufficient to pay my debts and legacies, the latter are to be reduced. My exors are to take out of my son's legacy so much as they shall lay out on his binding as an apprentice. Exors: Stephen Rayner, Henry Lawrence. Wit. John Jellowe, John Sudbury, Robert Walker. Pr. at Bury 7 March 1634/35.

744. W(R) NICHOLAS ANDERSON (X) of Kirtling [Cambs], husbandman. 9 February 1634/35.

Commits soul to merciful hands of God.
I give my lease of certain houses and grounds in Moulton to Margaret my wellbeloved wife for life and after her decease to my son Henry. After my debts and funeral expenses have been paid, I will that the rest of my estate be divided into 3 equal parts; 2 to be equally divided between my wife and son, and the third I give to my daughter Elizabeth and her husband. Exors: wife and son. Wit. Thomas Creeke, James Hodge (X). Pr. at Bury 23 March 1634/35.

745. W(R) HENRY WHITINGE (X) of Mendlesham, yeoman. 4 March 1634/35.

Commits soul to God being fully assured of being raised up at last day and made a living member of Jesus Christ.
I give Bridget my beloved wife for her life my messuage where I now dwell with land belonging to it, and after her decease I will that they be sold by my exors within a year and the money used to pay my legacies. If my kinsman Henry Shipp thinks good to give £400 for my land and tenement, he shall have the first offer. I give to William, son of my brother William, £20, and to Thomas, Samuel, Sarah and Margaret, children of my brother-in-law John Calthrop £20 each; all within a year of my wife's decease. I give the children which Thomas Goulston had by my kinswoman, unto 2 of them being twins £10 each and to the other 4 £5 each, all when 21. I give my sister Margaret Turner an annuity of £5 to be paid quarterly out of my goods. I give my wife all my moveable goods, cattle and implements of husbandry. I give the 3 children of John Muning and the children of William Turnor £5 each when 21. I give John Whitinge the elder of Boadesdale [Botesdale] £40 and to his son John £20; and I give John, son of William Whitinge of Mendlesham deceased, £10; all within a year of my wife's death. I give my god-daughter Mary £10 and her sister Alice £5 to be paid to their father Samuel Rout within a year of my decease. I give Frances and Richard, children of Thomas Muninge, £20 to be divided between them when 21. I give my kinswoman Lettice Turnor £20 within a year of wife's decease. Henry Nasie formerly mortgaged to me a tenement and land which fell unto me as certain monies were not paid. I give them back to him on condition he pays my exors within a year of my decease the money due for them. All my unbequeathed goods, bills and ready money I give to my exors to pay my debts and legacies; any surplus to be divided between them. Exors: my kinsman William Turnor and John Muninge of Drinkstone. Wit. Edmund Heywarde, Samuel Rowte, Henry Shipp. Pr. at Bury 23 March 1634/35.

746. W(R) ANN KINGSBERY (N) of Little Cornard, widow. 17 February 1634/35.

She gave Ann Kingsbery her daughter all her linen, the best bed as it stood and £5 to be paid within a year of her decease. She gave her son Edward £5 within 2 years, son George £5 within 3 years, son Barnabas £5 within 4 years, and to 2 of her grandchildren Mary and Joan, daughters of John Kingsbery deceased, 20s each. She gave all the residue of her goods to her eldest son Richard, whom she made exor. Wit. Robert Holborowe (X), John Crispe. Let. ad. granted to exor 24 March 1634/35. No place given.

747. W(R) JANE CLARKE (X) of Bildeston, spinster. 15 December 1634.

Bequeaths soul to God hoping to be made heir of his everlasting kingdom.
I give my father Henry Clarke my meadow ground in Chelsworth. My mind is that he should pay £5 each to my brother Richard and sister Elizabeth within a year of my decease. I give Elizabeth all my apparel, linen and woollen, and all my other goods. I make my father sole exor. Wit. John Bateman (X), Thomas Andrew. Pr. at Bury 24 March 1634/35.

748. W(R) THOMAS LITTON (X) the elder of Thelnetham. 1 March 1634/35.

Bequeaths soul to God my creator and Jesus Christ my redeemer.
I give my eldest son Robert £30 to be paid to him before 1 December 1635. I give my son Thomas £10, daughter Susan £10, daughter Joan £9, son John £14, daughter Thomasine £14, and to Robert Dade minister of Thelnetham £6; all to be paid before 1 December 1635. I give my daughter Mary 1 pair of my best sheets and daughter Thomasine 1 pair sheets. I give 5s to Elizabeth, daughter of my son Thomas, before 1 December 1635. I give all my money, bills and moveable goods to my son Thomas and son-in-law Robert Churchyard and make them exors. Wit. John Locke, John Wixe (X), John Parker. Pr. at Bury 24 March 1634/35.

749. W(R) CHRISTIAN SEAMAN (N) of Wattisfield, singlewoman. No date.

About a quarter of a year next before her decease lying sick of the sickness whereof she died, being desired to make her will to dispose of such small estate as she had, she said Goodwife Nun in whose house she did lie sick should have all that she had. Wit. Anne Bridges, Elizabeth Bert, Stephen Barker. Let. ad. granted 23 March 1634/35. No place given.

750. W(R) MARGARET PORTER (N) of Mildenhall, widow. 2 January 1634/35.

She bequeathed her soul to God and body to earth.
She gave her daughter Margaret all her best linen and the best coverlet lying over her. She gave her son John the black milk cow, and her daughter Marian her best hat. All the rest of her goods, after the charges of her sickness and funeral had been deducted, she gave to be equally divided among her above 3 children and her other daughter Elizabeth. Exor: her brother Thomas Sterne. Wit. Francis Bugge, John Winge. Let. ad. granted to exor at Bury 23 March 1634/35.

751. W(R) ALICE WHIGHTE (X) of Bures St Mary, widow. 5 July 1630.

Bequeaths soul to God trusting to be saved by Jesus Christ.
I give the poor of Bures 20s to be distributed by my exor on day of my burial, and 20s more within 6 months of my decease. I give all my lands and tenement called Bongays and Sorells in Bures ad montem [Mount Bures] and Wakes Colne in Essex to be sold by William Simpson, John Garrad gentleman and John Whight all of Bures St Mary, and the money to be equally divided between children of my daughter Priscilla Whight when 21 or married. I give my sister Ellen Greene one whole year's rent of the land she holds of me by farm. I give my daughter Priscilla my best horse. I give my grandchild Alice Whight my best bed but one with its bedstead and bedding. I give my grandchild Alice Felipe £20 and £10 each to grandchildren John and Elizabeth Felipe when 21 or married. I give my daughter Margery £5 which Jeffrey Pechie the younger owes me. I give my grandchildren Alice and Elizabeth Balle £20 each when 21 or married. I give Richard Carter my servant 16s which Thomas Meller owes me. I give my tenant John Haywarde all the rent now due to me from him, and I give his wife Mary one sheep and one cow to be kept for their son John until he is 12. I give Ellen Greene my sister my black stuff gown, my daughter Priscilla my violet coloured gown, mother Hayward my old gown, Mary wife of John Hayward a new piece of stuff for a petticoat cloth, my daughter Priscilla my stammell petticoat, my grand-child Elizabeth Balle my best hat, my servant Margery Hoye my old saye petticoat and to Christian Nutt my daughter-in-law my second stammell petticoat and my working day waistcoat. I give Margaret Hayward the quarter's rent she owes me. I give £10 to be equally divided among children of John White, and £10 to children of my daughter Margery when 21 or married. The residue of my goods and chattels I give to my daughter Priscilla and make her ex'trix on condition her husband John Whight within 14 days of my decease enters into a bond with William Sympson for the fulfilling of my will. If he refuses, all gifts to Priscilla are void and I make William Sympson exor. Wit. Andrew Smithe, Robert Stebbinge (X), William Simpson. Pr. at Bury 24 March 1634/35.

752. W(R) REGINALD BROCKE (X) of Undley in the parish of Lakenheath, husbandman. 22 January 1634/35.

Bequeaths soul to God believing through merits of Jesus Christ to enjoy a place in his celestial kingdom with the rest of his elect children.
I give Alice my wife my house for life and then, if she be with child, to her and her heirs, but, if she is not now with child, to Reginald son of Thomas Brock. I will my 2 brothers William and Elisas 20 marks each within a year of my decease, and £5 each to William's 3 children when 21. I give the 2 children of Thomas and Alice Reynold £5 each, and as they are young my wife shall give Thomas Brock their father [sic] good

security for the payment of this money. I give Susan Bentlie £5 when 21 or married. I give the 5 children of my sister Catherine Hunt £5 each when 21: Giles, Margaret, Elizabeth, Margery and Anne. Benefit of survivorship for all minor legatees. I give Anne Leighton £8 to be put out to her use. I give Robert, son of Robert Eagle the elder, 40s to be put out to his use. All the rest of my goods I give to Alice my wife, whom I make ex'trix. Wit. Francis Bugg, Thomas Troyse. Pr. at Bury 23 March 1634/35.

753. R(W) WILLIAM MAN of Kersey, joiner. 3 August 1629.

Commends soul to God hoping through Jesus Christ to be made partaker of life everlasting in his kingdom of glory.
I give Elizabeth my wellbeloved wife my messuage where I now dwell with all its free and copyhold land for life, and then to my son James. He must pay my son Robert £30 and my daughters Elizabeth, Alice and Bridget £10 each within 3 years of my wife's decease. Daughters have benefit of survivorship. If Robert dies before his legacy is paid, James is to pay my 3 daughters £5 more each. If James fails to pay legacies, Robert is to have land and pay them and if he fails, daughters are to have land for 21 years. I give James my copyhold tenement in Kersey in which [blank in MS] Stanley now lives. I give Robert my copyhold tenement in Kersey in which William Revell now dwells. I give James all my goods belonging to husbandry: cart, plough, tumbril, harrows, collars and traces. I give Robert all my joiner's tools and my best bible. All the residue of my goods and chattels I give to my wife for life and she is to leave them to my children. If she sells any cattle she is to leave others as good in their place. If she remarries, she is to give my children good security for my goods. Exors: wife and son James. Wit. James Braby. Pr. at Bury 10 March 1634/35.

754. W(R) THOMAS WELLES of Ballingdon [Essex], innholder. 24 November 1634.

Commits soul to God believing to be saved by my saviour Jesus Christ.
I give my brother George 12 pence and my sister Sarah 2s 6d. I appoint that the messuage where I now dwell, called the White Horse, being mortgaged is to be sold for its full worth to redeem the mortgage. Any overplus to be used to pay my debts and legacies. I give my wife Margaret for life a bedstead, a down bed, a blanket, a green rug, a bolster, a feather pillow with a beere and all other things belonging to it as it stands in my parlour chamber, and after her death to her daughter Catherine. I give my wife the bed and bedding wherein I now lie in the parlour for life and then to her daughter Emma. I give my cousin Thomas Welles the coat I did usually wear. All the residue of my goods and debts I bequeath to my wellbeloved wife whom I make ex'trix to take up and pay my debts and see my body decently buried. Wit. William Elliston (X), William Godwell (X) and me Edmund White. Pr. at Bury 3 February 1634/35.

755. W(R) ELIZABETH COOSTEN (X) of Denston, widow.
27 October 1634.

Commends soul to God. To be buried in Denston churchyard.
I give Frances, daughter of my son John, £60, her brother John £40 and her sister Elizabeth £20, all when 21. Benefit of survivorship. I give Frances and Elizabeth all my household stuff to be divided between them when 21. I give John Genne 10s and Christopher Genne 16s. I give William Mayer 5s, William Coppen 2s 6d, Thomas Barnewell 2s and Richard Feilde 2s. I give John Parker the first half year's interest after my decease of the money he owes me. If any of my 3 grandchildren marry without their parents' consent, they shall not have their legacies. All the rest of my goods I give to my son John whom I make exor. Wit. Thomas Raye, Susan Eason (X). Pr. at Bury 1 November 1634.

756. W(R) JOHN REEVE (N) of Mildenhall, shepherd. 20 June 1634.

He gave his eldest son Robert all his best apparel and 12 pence, his second son Frances a coat, a jerkin and a pair breeches, and his third son Thomas 20s. The residue of his goods and chattels he gave to his wife Alice towards bringing up his son John. If John would not be ruled and governed by Alice, he gave him half his goods and chattels for his maintenance and his wife to be freed of him. Wife sole ex'trix. Wit. Richard Bull (X), John Costen, John Reeve (X). Let. ad. granted to widow 1 July 1634. No place given.

757. W(R) SARAH ALLSTONE (X) of Edwardstone, spinster and one of the daughters of Gregory Allstone deceased of Edwardstone. 24 June 1634.

Bequeaths soul to God steadfastly hoping for salvation by Jesus Christ.
I give my brother Robert £8 to be paid by my exor within 6 months of my decease. I give my sister Abigail £4 within a year, and all my linen and apparel and a box. I give Sarah, daughter of William Cooper, £5 when 21 or if she dies to her mother Sarah. The rest of my goods and chattels I give to my wellbeloved brother Samuel whom I make exor. Wit. John Bluette, John White. Pr. at Bury 15 September 1634.

758. R EZECHIEL ADAMS (X) the elder of Sudbury, gentleman.
30 January 1623/24.

Commits soul to God hoping through Jesus Christ to be made partaker of everlasting joys in kingdom of heaven.
I give Elizabeth my wellbeloved wife the messuage wherein I dwell in the parish of St Peter in Sudbury for ever. I give my son Ezechiel 10s and my 3 daughters Dorcas, Alice and Mathusala 10s each within 6 months of my decease. All the rest of my goods I give to my wife towards her maintenance and paying my debts, and I make her ex'trix. Wit. John and Andrew Brownesmyth and me Philip Clarke. Pr. at Sudbury 27 September 1634.

759. R ROGER HARDECK (X) of Polstead, husbandman. 21 August 1632.

Bequeaths soul to God and body to ground.
I give my daughter Anne my oldest brended cow. I give my daughter Alice a black calf with a white face. I give my son Leonard a brended bullock and a black horse colt. I give my son Martin my sorrel mare's colt, 2 sheep and 2 lambs. I give my wife Anne my copyhold land in Polstead for life, and I make her sole ex'trix and give her all my unbequeathed goods to pay my debts and legacies. Wit. John Marten, Robert Shadd. Pr. at Sudbury 12 April 1634.

760. R(W) MARGARET PRICKE (X) of Chevington, singlewoman. 16 March 1634/35.

Commends soul to God hoping steadfastly to be received into celestial joys. Body to be laid in a coffin and buried in Chevington churchyard.
I give my dear and beloved mother Margaret Pricke all my brass, pewter, boxes and apparel, and £10 to be paid to her within 9 months. I give my loving brothers William, Simon, George and Samuel £15 each within 9 months of my decease. Benefit of survivorship. I give George and Simon my colt, and William and Samuel a hogg lamb. I give to William a little table and to Simon a latten candlestick. My mother is to have the use for life of my pot tipped with silver, a drinking glass and 6 cushions, and after her death my exor is to have them. I give my cousins Mary, Alice and George, children of my uncle George Sparrow, 3s each within a month of my decease, and 5s each to all my godchildren within 3 months. I give the poor people of Chevington 40s to be paid to the churchwardens and overseers to add to the stock of the town for the use of the poor. My exor is also to pay 12 pence a house to 12 poor people dwelling in the parish. I make my dear and loving brother John, singleman of Chevington, my exor. Wit. George Sparrow, John Goodday, Joshua Wade. Pr. at Bury 31 March 1635.

761. R(W) WILLIAM AGGAS of Long Melford, yeoman. 11 June 1634.

Bequeaths soul to God and body to Christian burial.
I give my sister Anne, John son of my brother John and my kinsman John Golding £10 each within a year of my decease. I also give John Golding all my apparel. I give the poor people of Melford 10s. All the rest of my goods and chattels I give to my brother Francis to pay my debts, legacies and funeral expenses and I make him my exor. Wit. Ambrose Evered, Richard Gardner. Pr. at Bury 13 April, 1635.

762. R(W) ROBERT TYLER (X) of Long Melford, husbandman.
8 March 1634/35.

Bequeaths soul to God.
I give my wife Anne for life my freehold tenements in Long Melford High Street; one occupied by Edward Baxter and the other by Jeremy Groome, and after her decease to my youngest daughter Anne. I give my wife 2 other tenements in Melford High Street; one occupied by Robert Ambrose and the other by Barnaby Cowle, until my son Robert and daughter Alice are 21, when Robert is to have the second tenement and Alice the first. Children have benefit of survivorship. I give my wife all my goods and chattels to pay my debts and make her sole ex'trix. Wit. Ambrose Davy, John Evered, Oliver Haylocke. Pr. at Bury 13 April 1635.

763. R(W) RICHARD YONGE of Bury St Edmunds, mercer. 6 April 1633.

Bequeaths soul to God trusting through Jesus Christ to have pardon of sins.
Whereas Mary my beloved wife is now with child by me, I give this child £80 when 20. If my wife remarries she is to give good security to her father, William Mayor, and to my good friend John Normanton the elder for payment of this sum. My late father Yonge of Thetford in Norfolk in his will devised to me and [blank in MS] my sister all his moveable goods in his messuage or inn in Thetford called the White Hart after the decease of my mother Mary. I give all my share of these goods to my wife to perform my will, and I make her ex'trix. Supervisors: William Mayor, John Normanton. No witnesses. Pr. at Bull Inn, Bury 9 April 1635. Inventory exhibited 28 July 1635.

764. W(R) ARTHUR CLARKE (X) of Cockfield, tailor. 3 March 1634/35.

Commends soul to protection of God trusting to have pardon of sins through Jesus Christ.
I give my wife Bridget for life my cottage with outhouses and orchard. It is to be sold within 2 years of her decease by the minister and churchwardens of Cockfield, and the money divided between my children Arthur, Frances, Bridget, John, Joseph and Ambrose. Benefit of survivorship. I bequeath my wife all my moveable goods, and make her sole ex'trix. Wit. John Nutking (X), Thomas Milles. Pr. at Bury 1 April 1635.

765. W(R) ELIZABETH HILLES (X) of Sudbury All Saints, widow.
4 February 1634/35.

Bequeaths soul to God hoping to be saved by Jesus Christ. To be buried in churchyard of All Saints, Sudbury.
I give Joan, wife of my son Ralph Raynham, a silver spoon. I give all my

woollen wearing apparel to be equally divided between my daughters Mary, wife of John Johnson, and Joan, wife of Thomas Corder. I give my youngest son Brian Raynham my posted bed which I lie on with all belonging to it if he be yet living to come for it, but if he come not again I will that my son Ralph has it. I bequeath my daughter Alice, wife of Robert Grum, a gold ring if I need it not before my death. I will that my grandson William, son of John Hilles, has my great joined chair. I give my grandson John Johnson a great charger and a trundle bedstead, and my grandson John Hilles a cupboard which is at Lappideyes. I give my eldest son Ralph my husband's gown. I give my kinswoman Katherine Harte a pair of pillowbeeres, and my grandchild Elizabeth Hardye a pair of cobirons. I give my daughter Katherine, wife of John Hilles, a pot tipped with silver. I make my son Ralph Raynam sole exor and will him to use all my unbequeathed goods to see my body decently buried and my debts paid. Wit. Vincent Cocke, William Garard (X) and me Stephen Wilson. Pr. at Bury 13 April 1635.

766. W(R) THOMAS CHEESE of Bury St Edmunds, bellfounder. 26 February 1634/35.

Bequeaths soul to God hoping to have remission of sins by Jesus Christ. I make Mary my wife ex'trix and give her all my goods, debts and household stuff for life. After her decease, I give my son Thomas all the goods and household stuff in the parlour chamber where I now dwell, £14, my greatest kettle and my greatest brass pot. I give my 2 daughters Mary and Elizabeth £10 each after my wife's decease. If my wife marries again, her husband is to be bound in sum of £100 to perform my will to Thomas Andrews, whom I appoint supervisor of my will. Wit. John Jewell, George Baker, Giles Baxter (X). Pr. at Bury 1 April 1635.

767. W(R) THOMAS GRAYE (N) of Fordham [Cambs], singleman. Made between St Peter's Day [1 August] and Michaelmas Day 1634.

To my mother £4, to Susan, wife of Robert Steven, the bed in which I lie and £3 10s 0d. I give Susan and Christian, daughters of Robert Steven, 20s each. I give my aunt Mason, wife of Henry Mason, 20s, and my aunt Porter, wife of Randall Porter, £3 10s 0d. I give the poor of Fordham 20s, and to Margaret, daughter of Philip Graye, 20s. I make Robert Steven my exor. Wit. Charles Eliott, Thomas Cheswright. Pr. at Newmarket 25 March 1635.

768. W(R) MARGARET BARET (N) of Lavenham, singlewoman. Made about 3 days before her death, she dying about 22 March 1634/35.

She did give 20s each to her aunt Collinge, her cousin Dorothy Hordeset, Thomas, John, Henry and Elizabeth Barit. All the rest of her goods she gave to Mary, wife of John Sowter. Wit. Mary, wife of Isaac Cawston, Martha, wife of Henry Cumbe. Let. ad. granted to Mary Sowter 17 April 1635. No place given.

769. W(R) WILLIAM WATERS (X) of Eriswell, yeoman. 26 April 1634.

Commits soul to God.
I give my wife Margaret for life my copyhold messuage and lands in Eriswell belonging to the manor of Priors, and after her decease to my son Thomas according to custom of manor. I give my daughter Elizabeth £15 to be paid by Thomas over 3 years after wife's decease, and to my son John £30 to be paid by Thomas 4, 5 and 6 years after her decease. Power to distrain. I give my wife all my goods and chattels and make her sole ex'trix. I have surrendered my copyhold tenement to the use of my will by the hands of Miles Marham and William Roote, customary tenants of the manor. Wit. Samuel Sutton, Thomas Geeson, Thomas Fuller (X), Miles Marham (X), William Roote (X). Pr. at Bury 20 April 1635.

770. W(R) THOMAS SHELDRAKE (X) of Chilton Street in Clare. 7 March 1634/35.

Bequeaths soul to God hoping through Jesus Christ for pardon of sins and to remain eternally amongst his chosen and elect children.
I give my grandchild James Jarmen all my houses and land, both copy and free, after decease of my wife Grace. She is to have the profit of them as long as she lives, except the house and orchard I purchased from Richard Longe, which my grandson is to have immediately after my decease. I give my grandchild Grace Jarmen £60 within a year of my death. If my wife remarries, James is to have my houses and land at once, and pay her £4 p.a. My debts and legacies being paid, I give all my goods, chattels and debts to my wife, and make her sole ex'trix. Wit. Henry Wright (X), Giles Jarmen (X), Roger Warren. Pr. at Bury 28 April 1635.

771. W(R) JOHN RANEHAM (X) of Brettenham, yeoman. 7 March 1634/35.

Bequeaths soul to 3 persons of Trinity. To be buried in Brettenham churchyard.
I give my loving wife Judith for life my tenement and land in Combs occupied by [blank in MS] Sowgate, and after her decease to my eldest son John. I give my other son Lawrence my tenement in Bildeston now occupied by John Hempsted; he must pay his mother 30s p.a. quarterly. After my wife's decease, I give Lawrence my other tenement in Bildeston, now occupied by [blank in MS] Huggens widow, on condition that he allows my daughter Margaret Osborne widow to have the only habitation of the east end of this tenement, which is next to dwelling house of one Addams. The house is to be divided at the backside of the chimney with the chamber over the east end and the entry now there; Margaret is to have half the yard and the benefit of the well and free access to her end of the tenement. I give my son John 2 silver spoons and my greatest tipped pot, and my son Lawrence 2 silver spoons and my

other tipped pot. I give my other daughter Susan Strutt widow a silver spoon and my tipped can, and my daughter Margaret Osborne one silver spoon. My wife is to have the use of the spoons, pots and can for life. I give my wife for life my best posted bedstead, best trundle bedstead, my best featherbed and best flockbed, half my pewter and brass, all my linen, a framed cupboard, 2 framed chests, a hutch, a turned chair, 3 high joined stools, 2 little joined stools, a framed form, a joined table with a cupboard, another framed table of like length, 1 pair cobirons, a firepan and tongs, a warming pan, a pair bellows and 4 of the best cushions. After my wife's decease I give my best posted bedstead and best featherbed to my daughter Margaret and all the rest of my goods left to my wife are to be equally divided among my 4 children. I give John a posted bedstead, a featherbed, a bolster and 2 blankets. I give my daughter Margaret my worst posted bedstead in the hall chamber, a featherbed, a feather bolster and a bible. I give my grandson Richard Rainham 40s within 2 years of my decease. I give the poor of Brettenham 10s to be paid to the churchwardens within a year. I give my son-in-law Francis Hall 10s within 6 months. I give my daughter Susan 50s within a year, and daughter Margaret £5 within 6 months. I give my grandchildren 6s 8d each when 21. Exor: son Lawrence. Wit. Edward Wengeve. Pr. at Bury 28 April 1635.

772. R(W) JAMES REYNOLDES (X) of Woolpit, yeoman. 19 March 1633/34.

Bequeaths soul to God trusting through Jesus Christ to be partaker of his everlasting kingdom of glory.
I give the poor people of Woolpit 40s and those of Cockfield 20s to be distributed on the day of my burial or within a short time after. I give my daughter-in-law Mary, widow of my late son Thomas, all my houses, tenements and free and copyhold land in Woolpit for life, on condition she keeps houses in repair and remains a widow. After her decease I bequeath this property to my grandson Thomas or, if he has no heirs to grandson James. On 20 September 1611 I conveyed to my deceased son-in-law George Muskett of Coney Weston 14 acres of land and 2 acres meadow in Cockfield on condition that my exors should pay him or his exors £100 in 5 annual instalments starting at the second Michaelmas after my decease; payments to be made in my dwelling house in Woolpit. I bequeath this land to my ex'trix for 7 years to pay my debts and legacies, and she must pay the £100 as set out above. To better enable my ex'trix to pay my debts, being many, and to perform my will I give her all the rest of my houses and lands in Cockfield for 7 years. After this time is up, I bequeath all my houses and land in Cockfield to my grandson Thomas with benefit of survivorship to grandson James. Thomas must pay James £20 p.a. half yearly in my dwelling house in Woolpit. I give my grandchild Susan Reynoldes £10 p.a. to be paid by Thomas starting 1 year after he inherits land. Power to distrain. I give my grandson James £4 p.a. for 7 years after my decease to be paid half yearly by my ex'trix. I give my

grandchild Susan £30 to be paid within 7 years of my decease out of lands given to my ex'trix to perform my will, and my posted bedstead with the bed and bedding belonging to it as it stands in the chamber next to the entry within 3 months of my decease. I give my grandsons William and Edmund Muskett 10s each within a year. I give Katherine, daughter of John Pearson of Rowdham [sic ? Rudham] Norfolk 5s within a year, and to my apprentice Emma Goare 5s when 21. All the rest of my goods and chattels I give to my daughter-in-law Mary for her own use and make her sole ex'trix. Supervisor: John Watson, clerk of Woolpit, my trusty and wellbeloved friend, entreating him to appease any quarrel or strife or debate that may arise over anything in my will, and I give him 20s for his pains. Wit. John Catton (X), Charles Woodward, Robert Jaques.
Codicil made 9 April 1634. Whereas in my will all my goods and chattels not previously disposed of I left to my ex'trix, my mind is now altered and I give my long table in the hall with bench and form there standing with the stained cloth there, my cupboard in the buttery, an ale stool and the shelves there, the salt trough, my malt querns and the tramels in the chimney to my grandson Thomas, but my ex'trix is to have the use of them so long as she continue in my house. Wit. John Catton (X), Charles Woodward.
Codicil made 4 September 1634. My ex'trix is to take only 4 loads of wood a year from my land in Woolpit, but she is to have liberty to top and lop any wood she pleases on my land in Cockfield. Wit. William Woodward, Charles Woodward, Robert Jaques. Pr. at Bury 27 April 1635.

773. R(W) JOHN WESTHROPP of Hundon, yeoman. 28 February 1634/35.

Commends soul to God.
I give my eldest son John my messuage and land in Stansfield, now in tenure of John Sturton, for 5 years and then to my son Ambrose with remainder to my grandchild John, second son of my son John, if Ambrose has no heirs. If my messuage and land come to this grandson he must pay my grandson John, son of my son Joseph, £40 within a year; £20 to Susan, eldest daughter of Joseph, within 2 years; and £40 to Mary, youngest daughter of Joseph, within 3 years. If any of these 3 are under age when their legacies fall due, John is to leave paying them until they are 21. Power to distrain. I give 20s each to my children Ambrose, Joseph, Rose, Susan and Mary to be paid by my exor within a year of my death, and 20s each when 21 to my grandchildren: John, Jean and Mary, children of my son John; John, Susan and Mary, children of my son Joseph; William, Thomas, Samuel, John, Susan and Mary Dersey; and John and Susan Pytches. I give the poor of Hundon £4 to be paid by my exor as follows: 40s on day of my burial, and 20s on each of 2 succeeding Ash Wednesdays. I give 10s to be paid to overseers of town of Kitton

[Kedington] for the use of the poor there within 2 days after my death. I give my exor all my goods and chattels to pay my debts and legacies. I make my eldest son John exor. Wit. Joseph Westhropp, Thomas Westhropp. Pr. at Bury 28 April 1635.

774. R(W) BARNABAS GIBSON of Haughley, gentleman. 1 October 1634.

I do with mine own handwriting make this present writing to be my last will. I yield my soul to God confidently believing that by grace and mercy of Jesus Christ, who died for my sins and rose again for my justification, my sins be in him fully and absolutely forgiven and that I shall be partaker of joys of kingdom of heaven. My body I leave to be buried as near unto my son John his grave as it may be made. At my burial I desire a sermon to be preached by some godly divine for the instruction of such persons as shall be there to learn to live and die well. I give the preacher 10s. I leave to the discretion of my ex'trix the distribution of relief to such poor as be at my burial. I give my eldest son Barnabas my messuage wherein I dwell in Haughley called Young Bells [at Haughley Green] with 107 acres land belonging to it for his life, and then to his son Barnabas and his heirs. My son and grandson must pay my wife Jane £20 p.a. half yearly. During her life my wife is to have her dwelling in the little parlour and closet and the chambers over them in my house. She is to have free access to the yards and gardens, to other rooms to bake, brew and wash and to all the waters for her use. She is to have a fourth part of the pigeons and fruit, and Barnabas is yearly to lay at her door 5 loads of wood. If he fails to give her wood, she may take it herself. If my wife marries again all these gifts to her are void and she is to be paid £10 p.a. She has power to distrain. Her annuity is to be paid in my house called Young Bells. Within 2 months of my decease my wife is to surrender to my son and grandson her 2 closes called Walshes, but if she refuses her legacies and annuity will be void. I am bound to pay John Sharpe of Hessett £45 with interest and Mr Wells £20 with interest, which sums are debts of my son Barnabas which he must pay or find security for so that my ex'trix is not charged with them. If he does not do this, my daughter Ann is to take an 11 acre piece of ground called Oxe hall and lying next to the Green until Barnabas has paid these debts. Within 2 months of my decease Barnabas is to give my ex'trix a release of any demands for the rent of Haughley close or of any annuity made to him upon his marriage. If he refuses, all legacies to him shall be void and my youngest son Samuel and my grandson John shall have the lands and tenements formerly given to Barnabas on the same conditions. Upon the marriage of my son I promised to assure to him in my will my lands and tenements, with reservation of £20 annuity for his mother, on condition he paid £150 to my daughter Ann at a certain time; the writing concerning this is in the keeping of my sister Cropley. If Barnabas my son and his son Barnabas will live in peace, love and friendship with the rest of my children and grandchildren, not vexing or molesting them about any lands left to them,

326

then if Barnabas and his son are loving and kind they shall not pay £150 to Ann but only her board for 4 years after my death. If they behave otherwise, they must pay Ann £150 when 21 in Haughley church porch; power to distrain. My ex'trix shall have 2 months grazing rent free for all my cattle I leave on land belonging to Young Bells to give her time to sell them for the best price. My grandson Barnabas is to pay £200 to his brothers and sisters out of rent of land left to him at a time appointed by his father, but he is not to be compelled to sell any land. If he defaults, his father is to have Wood and Horses closes. But my meaning is that he is not to pay any of the £200 until 2 years after his father's decease. I give my son Barnabas the bedstead in the parlour chamber with the trundle bedstead belonging to it, a flockbed, a coverlet and a pair of blankets to be chosen by my wife Jane. I also give him the desk in the chamber where I lie, the press and short table there, my copper hanged, my cheese press, long table in the parlour, another table in the entry, 4 stools, my best walnut chair, 2 brewing tubs, my stock of hop poles and my 2 fishing nets. I give my grandson Barnabas my biggest desk in the parlour. My wife and my youngest son Samuel are to have the occupying and disposing of my tenement Old Bells with its pasture and rights of commonage on Haughley Green, the land belonging to it in Haughley and Newton and my freehold close called Bardwells in Haughley or Newton; this land totals 60 acres. After paying the entry fine to the lord of the manor, Samuel is to pay Mr John Sharp £30 with the interest due to him from my deceased son John, and then £16 p.a. to my daughter Ann until my grandson John is 12 when he to be paid £16 p.a. until he is 21. When John is 21 he is to have the tenement Old Bells with its 60 acres, but if he dies leaving no heir Samuel is to have it. During John's minority Samuel is not to put into tillage any of Old Bells land, nor to take any timber or firewood from it, and he must keep the houses and fences in repair. If my son and grandson Barnabas make any claim to Old Bells all legacies to them will be void, and Samuel and John shall have the land and goods left to them on same conditions. I give my son Samuel for ever the meadows and grounds I bought from Thomas Goodwyne esquire lying at Stowe town's end [Stowmarket], and also a piece of freehold land in Stowe, which I bought from Thomas Glover, tanner. I give Samuel my biggest silver cup and my viol, my grandson John my lessest silver cup and my daughter Ann my silver cup with a cover. I give my wife Jane all my linen for she has promised me that at a convenient time she will divide it among her children with her own hands. I give my daughter Mary all my goods she has at her house, and my joined chest that stands in the entry with one of my chairs. I give my grandson John Gibson a featherbed with a bedstead, a good pair blankets, a coverlet, my blue rug, a good new feather bolster and a pillow, my longest folding table in the parlour, my lessest walnut tree chair, one of my best cushions, a pair of lessest cobirons and my leastest dansk chest. The residue of my bedding, brass, pewter, joined stuff and household implements in my house where I dwell are to be equally divided between my wife, my son Samuel and my daughter Ann within 10 days of my decease. I give Ann my fat and lean cattle, cows, horses, sheep, hogs, corn, wood, timber sawn and unsawn, and debts. My wife is to sell all these goods and employ the money for benefit of my daughter. If my wife remarries, my son Samuel is to have control of goods and money belonging to Ann until she is of age. I give Samuel my best tumbril with the broad wheels and my old cart with unshod wheels to carry his hay and muck at Stowe meadows. I make my wife sole ex'trix desiring her to be careful in bringing up my daughter Ann in the fear of God, but if she dies or remarries Samuel is to be exor. I beseech God that he will send his blessings to my wife and children that the portions I have left them may prosper with them, and that they may all live in his fear, die in his favour and rest in his joy. I have surrendered my land and tenements held of the manor of Haughley to the use of my will. Wit. Robert Newman (X), William Thorowgood. Pr. at Bury 5 May 1635.

775. R(W) ALICE MASON (X) of Exning, widow. 25 October 1634.

Bequeaths soul to God hoping to be saved by Jesus Christ. To be buried in Exning churchyard.
I give my son William Frost 5s within a month of my decease. I give his wife Elizabeth my best petticoat and my second gown, and 5s within a month. I give 2s each to William, George, Elizabeth, Alice, Susan and Robert, the sons and daughters of William, to be paid within quarter of a year after my decease. I give Alice, daughter of my son Richard Frost, 2s. All the rest of my goods and chattels I give to my son Richard and make him exor. Wit. Charles Eliott, Richard Ballard (X). Pr. at Bury 11 May 1635.

776. R(W) ELIZABETH ORY of Knettishall, singlewoman. 1 April 1635.

Commits soul to God.
I give to Thomas Bartram all my goods and chattels, money and debts, in consideration of the pains he has taken with me and for seeing my body decently to the earth. But I except my stammell petticoat and a ruff band which I give to Susan Cock; and I give the wife of Edward Marten a cloth petticoat, a white apron and 2 bushels corn. I give Mildred Reeve a stuff petticoat and a white apron, and to another maid servant of Edward Marten's a pair of upper bodies. I make Thomas Bartram my exor. Wit. Joseph Tilar, Edward Marten (X). Pr. at Bury 26 May 1635.

777. R(W) GILES FRANCK (X) of Pakenham, yeoman. 7 September 1625.

Commits soul to Jesus Christ trusting to have all my sins pardoned.
I give my son John my messuage with 3 acre adjoining pasture and a 7 acre close, which I hold copyhold of Pakenham Hall manor. I also give him 3 acres copyhold in one piece in Westwalle field in Great Barton held

of Great Barton manor. Within half a year of my decease he is to pay my daughter Jane so much of a bond of £10 as is yet unpaid. I give my son Charles £35 to be paid by my exor within a year of my decease if Charles before that time shall return to this country. He must enter into a bond to pay his son John and his daughter Mary £5 each when 21, and if he refuses my exor is to keep back £10 of his legacy to pay to John and Mary, who have benefit of survivorship. If Charles does not return, my exor is to pay his wife Alice £35 on same conditions. I give my daughters Anne and Mary £5 each within a year of my decease, and I give them my goods and chattels to be divided by my exor at a convenient time. I make my son John exor. Wit. Richard Peacock, John Bettes, Robert Walker.
Codicil: Testator willed his exor should within 2 years of his decease pay £5 each to Thomas and Mary, children of Robert Scott. Wit. same as above. Pr. at Bury 5 May 1635.

778. W(R) ROBERT FULLER alias SNOW (X) of Great Fakenham, labourer. 31 January 1632/33.

Bequeaths soul to God that gave it me.
I give my son William my messuage in Theltam [probably Thelnetham] with 3 acres land. I give my daughter Anne, wife of Edmund Doe, £30 to be paid in 4 annual instalments starting a year after my decease. I give my grandchild Anne Doe £5 within 4 years. I give William all my bills, bonds and ready money, and all the rest of my moveable goods are to be equally divided between him and my daughter Anne. I make William my exor, but, if he refuses to prove my will or pay my legacies, I give Anne my messuage and land and make her husband exor. Wit. John Frost, Thomas Rushbrooke. Pr. at Bury 11 May 1635.

779. R(W) JOAN MINOTT (X) of Lakenheath, widow. 12 November 1634.

Bequeaths soul to God and Jesus Christ. To be buried in Lakenheath churchyard.
I give John Hubberstith the younger, my son-in-law, his bond of 54s, and my son William his bond of 44s. I give John Onsett and his wife Emma all my bonds, debts, goods and chattels, and make him exor, desiring him to see my debts paid and my body decently buried. Wit. Robert Salfar and me Thomas Halman. Pr. at Bury 25 May 1635.

780. R(W) ALICE DEY (X) of Westhorpe, widow. 15 May 1635.

Commends soul to God trusting to be justified and saved by Jesus Christ. My exors are to sell all my goods and chattels within half a year of my decease, and the overplus, left after my debts and expenses of burial and probate have been paid, is to be divided into 7 equal parts. I give 1 part within a year to Nicholas Dey, son of my late husband Thomas in full satisfaction of all his demands on the goods of his father, but if he refuses to be satisfied his share is to go to my children. I give my daughter Mary Roper a seventh part within 6 months, and my daughters Jane and Sarah Roper one part each within a year. I give my 2 younger children Thomas and Frances Roper 3 parts to be equally divided among them when he is 21 and she is 18. Benefit of survivorship. I make my loving kinsman John Hastead, chandler of the City of Norwich, and my daughter Mary exors. Supervisors: Mr Edmund Dandye, Mr Robert Stansbye, Mr Robert Willett, Mr John Bedwall and Lawrence Rainburd. If any question arises about my will it is to be determined according to the literal sense of my will by my supervisors or any 2 of them. Wit. Lawrence Rainberd, John Bedwall. Pr. at Bury 4 June 1635.

781. W(R) JOHN MOORE (X) of Nettlestead, yeoman. 7 July 1629.

Bequeaths soul to 3 persons of Trinity to whom be ascribed all honour, glory, praise, power and dominion.
I give my son Stephen my copyhold land in Rattlesden, a 3 acre piece freehold land in Rattlesden which I lately purchased of Robert Jennings, and a tenement in Poys Street Rattlesden, which I bought of Robert Moore. I give Isaac Moore my freehold tenement and land in Rattlesden now in tenure of Adam Rayson, and 5 acres in Rattlesden now in tenure of my son William and which I purchased from one Chaplen and his son. All my moveable goods and chattels I give to my sons Stephen and Isaac and make them exors. Wit. John Studley, Bartholomew Salter. Pr. at Bury 1 June 1635.

782. W(R) JOHN COSTEN (X) of Denston alias Denerdiston, blacksmith. 24 January 1634/35.

Commits soul to God my maker and Christ my saviour.
I give all my temporal goods to Martha my wife on condition she carefully brings up my children, and pays my debts and funeral expenses. I make her ex'trix and entreat Thomas Usher to be exor with her and helpful to her. As soon as any money becomes due to me by bills or bonds by virtue of the will of Elizabeth Costen my mother, it is to be put out in my children's names to the intent that the portions given to them be not diminished, the annual profits are to be kept by my wife. Wit. John Webb, John Capp (X). Pr. at Bury 1 June 1635.

783. R(W) ROBERT FOORD (X) of Kettlebaston. 16 December 1622.

Commends spirit to God who gave it hoping through Jesus Christ to be received into glory of heaven.
I give all my worldly goods to my loving wife Blanche, whom I make sole ex'trix charging her in the fear of God to see my body Christianly buried and conscientiously to perform my will and pay my debts. I do not doubt that she will have especial godly care as she shall answer before God at the latter day. Wit. John Rayner, clerk, Thomas Foord (X), Margaret Jarvice (X). Pr. at Bury 1 June 1635.

784. R(W) RICHARD LANGTON of Little Waldingfield, gentleman.
9 March 1634/35.

Commends soul to God trusting through Jesus Christ to be made partaker
of life everlasting.
I give my eldest son Jeffrey, after decease of my wife Abigail, my
messuage or dwelling house in Little Waldingfield wherein I now dwell as
it is now fenced and abutting on highway from Little Waldingfield church
to Burndeley, and which I bought from George Richardson and his wife
Frances. I give my son Thomas my tenement in which John Cutchie now
dwells with the orchard belonging to it, now fenced and divided from my
dwelling house and abutting on the same highway. I give my son Richard
the tenement in which John Coller did lately dwell and now occupied by
Margery Leach together with the orchard belonging to it, abutting on the
same road and divided from my tenement in which John Cutchie lives. I
give my daughter Susan £50 when 21; 3 sons have benefit of survivorship.
I give my annuity of £16 out of the manor of Greies or Grayes in Great
and Little Cornard and Newton, which I had from Jeffrey Little, then of
Nayland gentleman and father of my loving wife Abigail, as a portion, to
my 3 sons to sell and equally divide between them a year after my wife's
decease. I give my wife this annuity for life. All my goods and chattels I
give to my loving brother Thomas, whom I make exor. Supervisor: Mr
William Lambert, minister of this parish. Wit. Edward Yeldham (X),
Elizabeth Warren (X), Richard Yeldham, Susan Cant (X) Pr. at Bury 1
April 1635.

785. R(W) WILLIAM HEARNES (N) of Cavenham. 19 May 1635.

On Whitsun Tuesday, being sick of body of the sickness whereof he died,
he said his will was that half an acre of ground that was his in Northfield
should be given to his son Henry, his other son John should have his
other land: a acre called Brome Bushes and 1½ rods lying in the
Howcroftes. He gave his wife Catherine the use of these lands for life,
and all his moveable goods to dispose of at her death as she thought
good. Wit. Edmund Frost (X), John Dowsin (X). Let. ad. granted at
Bury 15 May 1635 to widow. [Dates as in MS].

786. R(W) JOHN FITCH the younger of Rede. 30 May 1635.

Commends soul to God trusting to have sins forgiven by Jesus Christ and
I do look for life everlasting. To be buried in Rede churchyard.
I give my son John £60 when 21, until which time my ex'trix is to use the
interest for his upbringing. I give my daughter Sarah £50 on same terms.
Benefit of survivorship. All the rest of my goods and chattels I give to my
beloved wife Anne, whom I make ex'trix, willing her to be careful in the
education of my children that they may be brought up in the fear of God.
Wit. John Kerington, George Pitches. Pr. at Bury 22 June 1635.

787. R(W) MARGARET MACROE (N) of Risby, singlewoman.
9 April 1635.

Having sent for Edward Gatteward her late master, Frances his wife and Elizabeth, wife of David Church, she said to the first named Master I give all I have to Robert Disse and I pray God that he be not wronged of any of my goods for he shall have all, and I make him exor of my will. Wit. Edward Gatteward, Frances Gatteward, Elizabeth Church. Let. ad. granted 11 May 1635. No place given.

788. R(W) ELIZABETH POWLE (X) of Flempton, widow. 28 April 1628.

Commends soul to God hoping to be saved by merits of Jesus Christ. To be buried in Flempton churchyard.
I give my younger son William £60, and my daughters Elizabeth, Frances and Margaret £20 each, all to be paid by my exor within a year of my decease. I give my 5 children (above 4 and John) all my household stuff to be equally divided among them except a featherbed, a posted bedstead and all the bolsters, pillows and furniture belonging to it, which I give to my daughter Elizabeth. The residue of my goods and chattels I give to my son John and make him exor. Children left cash legacies have benefit of survivorship. Wit. John Shere, John Nockard. Pr. at Bury 11 May 1635.

789. R(W) NICHOLAS HOVELL alias SMYTH (N) of Cotton. 8 June 1635.

The day before his decease, he dying the 9 June 1635, being asked by his sister Anne how he would dispose of his estate, he said he would give all he had to his brother William towards paying his debts. Afterwards being asked what he would give his sister Anne, he said 30 pieces meaning £30. The first legacy was given in the presence of Anne Hovell alias Smyth and the second in the presence of William Hovell the elder and others. Let. ad. granted at the Bull in Bury 30 June 1635 to William Hovell junior.

790. R(W) MARGARET BARQUY (X) of Cavenham, widow. 21 May 1632.

Commits soul to God.
I give my son John my dwelling house in Cavenham and the land next to it, on condition he pays my eldest daughter Margaret 20s (whereof 3s she has already had) within 12 months of my decease, my second daughter Anne 20s within 2 years and my youngest daughter Prudence 20s when 21. I give my daughter Anne my bed and bedding with all that is on it except the wearing apparel on it, my biggest and smallest kettles with all my own pewter, the skillet and the frying pan, my smallest barrel, a chair, the gridirons and the spits. I give my son William 21s a month after he comes to demand it. I give Prudence my best kirtle, and all my other

wearing apparel and linen to my daughter Anne. I give my son John all my other moveables found within the house, and make him exor. If any of my children die before receiving their legacies, John is to have them. Wit. John Belgrave of Cavenham, John Hernes, shepherd of Cavenham. Pr. at Bury 15 June 1635. [Testator's name appears as Anne at foot of will.]

791. R(W) ROBERT NUNNE (X) of Wattisfield, labourer. 2 June 1635.

Commends soul to Christ my saviour.
I bequeath to my wife Helen for life the house where I now dwell and a close of pasture and wood partly in Wattisfield and partly in Thelnetham, which I purchased from Sir Henry Bucknam. I give my wife all my moveable goods. I give my 3 sons Robert, Daniel and Thomas £3 6s 8d each to be paid by my wife when they are 21. Power to distrain. After decease of my wife I give Robert all my houses and land, and he must pay Daniel £8 within 2 years and £8 13s 4d within 4 years, and Thomas £5 within 5 years and £6 13s 4d within 7 years of wife's decease. Power to distrain. I give William Bent of Wattisfield £10 owed to me by John Bridges of Thelnetham and for which I have latter's house in mortgage. I give William Bent this money in satisfaction of £8 I owe him, and he is to pay Abigail Spalle of Wattisfield the 40s I owe her. I make my wife sole ex'trix. Wit. Clement Raie, John Osborn, John Mallowes. Pr. at Bury 8 June 1635.

792. R(W) ANTHONY THEOBALD of the City of Durham, gentleman. 30 January 1634/35.

Bequeaths soul to God trusting to be saved by merits of Jesus Christ. To be buried in parish church of St Nicholas in Durham.
I have surrendered a copyhold orchard I have in Cley [or Aye] Norfolk to the use of my will. By an indenture dated 17 January 1634/35 I have granted in trust for 99 years to Robert Pleasance esquire and my third son Thomas my freehold land in Rushall, Dickleburgh, Brargh [?Brockdish], Langmere, Lincroft and Hulverbush [all in Norfolk] and a parcel of ground in Norfolk called the Clayland. I give the above orchard to my eldest son Henry, and all my other land in Norfolk is to be sold by my lessees. Until the sale is made I bequeath as much of the rents as come to £30 p.a. to my daughter Jane for a term of 10 years to raise a portion for her. The rest of the rents I give to be equally divided between my sons Henry and Thomas and my fourth son William. Benefit of survivorship. If my lessees sell the land, my daughter Jane is to have £300 for her portion less what has already been paid to her, and the remainder is to be divided between my above 3 sons. All my pewter, brass, bedding and household stuff sent from Durham to Norfolk I intended for the use of Jane and I give it to her. All my goods, leases and money at Durham I give to my 3 sons. If my second son Clement when he is 21 gives Mr James Hilton of Durham a release of that part of the house sold by me to him, and which

333

I had purchased in Clement's name, Mr Hilton is to pay £50 as yet unpaid by him to Clement as his portion. Exor William Phillipson gentleman of Stanhope, Co. Durham. Wit. Thomas Foster, John Walton. Pr. at Bury 24 June 1635. This will agrees with that proved in the court of the Bishop of Durham.

793. R(W) GILES KILLINGWORTH of Tostock, esquire. 27 December 1633.

Commends soul to my blessed saviour Jesus Christ by whom I hope for remission of my sins in this world and for eternal life in world to come.
I and my beloved wife Elizabeth have acknowledged a fine sur cognisance de droit come ceo to Giles Allington esquire, Fitznunne Lambe gentleman, John Jones and Hugh Jones, citizens and merchants of London, of the church, rectory and parsonage of Fulbourn [Cambs], Monks Barn in Fulbourn and all the glebe, tithes and land thereunto belonging, to the use of myself during life. After my decease 3 parts of this property are for the use of my wife during her life, and the fourth part to the use of the above 4 men during my wife's lifetime. After her decease the whole property is to be to their use upon trust and confidence that they will sell it and use the money as I shall appoint in my will or, if I make no appointment, to be divided between my son James and daughters Milcha and Elizabeth as expressed in an indenture made between me and my wife and above 4 men on 1 March 1627. If my son James makes no claim to the rectory and parsonage and agrees to the sale, he is to have one third of the money 6 months after the sale. The other 2 parts are to be divided between my younger sons John and Samuel and my daughter Milcha. Benefit of survivorship. If all my children die, my wife's heirs are to have the money. Sale of property is to be made within a year of my wife's decease, and the rents and profits before the sale are to be used as set down in my will. The costs of sale and £3 apiece for the above 4 men are to be paid out of them. I give my son James my gold seal of arms, all my armour and all my books. I give my beloved wife all my goods and chattels, cattle and debts and make her sole ex'trix, nothing doubting but certainly knowing she will be careful in the education of my children, paying my debts and performing my will. Wit. Robert Risby, Lawrence Lomax, John Selby. Pr. at Bury 4 July 1635.

794. W(R) THOMAS ABBOTT of Hawkedon, gentleman. 14 March 1633/34.

By an indenture, dated 10 December 1616, between myself and my brother Ambrose I assured to him my messuage and land in Suffolk for 31 years after my decease to the intent my exors should have the rents and profits to perform my will and pay my debts and legacies. My exors are first to pay my debts and then following legacies: £250 to my eldest son Thomas, £150 to son Edward, £100 to son Robert, £80 to son

William, £50 to son Richard, £80 to son Mathias, £30 to son Bernard, £20 to daughter Frances, £40 to daughter Theodora, £100 to Thomasine, daughter of my deceased eldest son George and £50 to her brother George. Legacies to be paid as money can be raised from profits of my land and tenements. Grandchildren are not to have any part of their legacies until they are 21. Exors: sons William and Mathias. I doubt not they will honestly and carefully perform my will. Wit. Richard Cante, Thomas Hamond, Thomas Wright. Pr. at Bury 2 July 1635.

795. R(W) JOHN TOMPSON of Norton, yeoman. 10 April 1635.

Surrenders soul to God in certain hope of resurrection. To be buried in Norton churchyard.
I give my father John £8 to be paid within a month. I give my brother Thomas £25 within a year and my sister Thomasine £15 within 2 years. I give my father £25 to be paid at £5 p.a. starting 3 years after my decease. All payments to be made in Elmswell church porch. I give my wife Agnes all my goods and chattels and make her and Robert Boalley exors. Wit. William Parker, William Clerke (X), Thomas Hovell alias Smyth. Pr. at Bury 8 June 1635.

796. R(W) ALICE EDMUNDES (X) of Hunston, singlewoman. 14 June 1635.

I give my mother Mary Edmundes 40s, a coat, a tartan waistcoat and 1 pair sheets. I give my sister Elizabeth Spurdance £3, a bed and bedstead as it stands fully furnished at Mayhes at South Lopham [Norfolk], a red cloak, a pillowbeere, a towel and a great kettle. I give my sister Mary a silk coif, a silk forehead cloth and 3 holland coifs, and to her 2 children she had by her first husband to the girl 20s and to the youth 30s. I give my sister Margaret 20s. All the rest of my money, household stuff and clothes, except the cost of my funeral, I give to my mother and sisters to be equally divided among them. Exor: my brother-in-law Robert Spurance. Wit. Richard Chamblayne, Thomas Frost, Robert Draper (X). Pr. at Bury 27 June 1635 to exor, Robert Spurance of Thetford.

797. R(W) MARY BUCKE (X) of Newmarket, widow. 23 September 1634.

Bequeaths soul to God and Jesus Christ.
I give to the poor in the town 40s. I give all the rest of my moveable goods to my son James Ayers and my daughter Anne Farmer equally. To secure a quiet distribution of my goods between them they are each, immediately after my funeral, to choose 2 appraisers to price my goods. I do also charge upon my motherly loving blessing that as they have lived lovingly towards one another during my life so they would continue this their love after my decease in a peacable and equal distribution of my goods between them. I make my son James exor. Wit. John Chapman, Joan Wickes (X), Sarah Lewes. Pr. at Newmarket 1 July 1635.

798. R(W) WINIFRED WATTSONN (X) of Soham [Cambs], widow.
21 May 1635.

Bequeaths soul to God and body to be buried in Soham churchyard.
I give my freehold lake with the tenement thereupon to my daughters
Alice and Mary, and also all my moveable goods. I give my sons Philip
and Richard my copyhold lake with a barn built thereupon. Ex'trices:
daughters. Wit. James Punge, Richard Dowe and me Robert Carlton. Pr.
at Bury 13 July 1635 to Alice Wattsonn.

799. R(W) REGINALD PARFREY (N) of Hepworth, husbandman.
About 2 July 1635.

He gave his wife Ann all his moveable goods, and his sister Mary
Wenlocke divers debts due to him by name: from Thomas Nun 40s, from
Robert Reeve 30s, from Stephen Peck 20s and from John Ketle 20s. He
gave his wife his house and all his ground in Hepworth until Hallowmas
next come 12 month. After which time his wife to hold her thirds for life,
and his brother William to have the rest for ever. He willed his brother to
pay 40s to one Bardwell his sister's son, 40s to Bardwell's child and £3 to
the daughter of his sister Mary Wenlocke. Wit. Archinold Burlingham
(X), Anne Reeve (X). Let. ad. granted 13 July 1635 to widow in William
Colman's house in Bury.

800. R(W) THOMAS DUCKLING (X) of Hopton, husbandman.
30 June 1635.

Bequeaths soul to God.
I give my son William £4 immediately after my decease and £4 more on
the next 2 St John the Baptist Days and 40s on the third one, on receipt
of sums of money owing from William Bigges of Hopton. William must
discharge me and my heirs of any obligations by bonds or bills into which
I entered with him, or my gifts to him will be void. William must give
security to pay my wife Margaret so many shillings p.a. as he has received
in pounds. If William Bigges defaults in payment of sums due to me, the
sale to him of my houses and land will be void and they shall remain to
my wife and my son John. I give John £6 on the St John Baptist Day after
my decease. All the rest of my goods and chattels I give to my wife,
whom I make ex'trix. Wit. Thomas Goddard, Samuel Leeder (X), John
Gilbert. Pr. at Bury 14 July 1635.

801. R(W) BENNET WITTE (X) of Mendlesham, husbandman.
12 March 1634/35.

Bequeaths soul to 3 persons of Trinity with whom I hope to have
everlasting happiness.
I give my house where I now dwell with all the buildings, yards and
orchards to Margaret my wife for life towards bringing up of my young

children, and after her decease to my son Samuel, who must pay my legacies. I give my son Francis £6 within a year of my wife's decease, and £3 each to my daughters Alice, Mary and Ann at one p.a. Power to distrain. I give all my household goods to my wife. Exors: Mr John Sheppard of Mendlesham and William Seman. Wit. Robert Rednall, Richard Rednall, Robert Dennye, Robert Upston (X). Pr. at Bury 22 July 1635.

802. R(W) LUKE HUNT (N) of Bury St Edmunds. 8 December 1632.

He gave his daughter Abigail his bed and bedstead whereon he lay with all the furniture belonging. He gave his daughter Sarah a great cupboard standing in the same room, and his son Hamlet 12 pence. He appointed his wife Thomasine to be ex'trix and gave her all the residue of his moveables and household stuff towards the payment of his debts and funeral charges. Wit. John Jewell, George Baker, Anne Hornigolde widow. Let. ad. granted to widow 27 June 1635. No place given.

803. R(W) ROBERT SCOTT (N) of Boxted, husbandman. February 1634/35.

About 3 days before his decease Robert Scott, who departed this life about 3 or 4 days before Shrove Sunday last past, declared his will. He gave his son-in-law Ambrose Warren his wearing apparel and 12 pence. He willed his exors should bestow 20s in apparel for his daughter, the wife of the said Warren. He gave Richard, son of Ambrose Warren, the bed in which he did lie with its furniture. The rest of his goods he gave to be equally divided among the rest of Mary Warren's children, and willed that the goods should be kept by his exors until they were 21. Exors: Henry Symondes and Henry Ellis of Glemsford. Wit. George Scott (X), Isaac Snape (X). Let. ad. granted 13 July 1635 in William Colman's house in Bury.

804. R(W) GEORGE MORTON (N) of Wood Ditton [Cambs], singleman. 8 July 1635.

He gave his mother Margaret Morton widow £4. The residue of his goods and chattels he bequeathed to his brother William, whom he made exor. Wit. Elizabeth Clarke (X). Let. ad. granted in St Mary's at Bury 28 July 1635 to William Morton.

805. R(W) JOHN CROWCH (X) of Hopton, cordwainer. 20 May 1635.

Bequeaths soul to God.
I give my son John £15: £5 to be bestowed in putting him forth an apprentice and £10 to be paid to him when 21. For 3 years after my decease the interest on the £10 is to be paid to John Allen of Debenham towards the maintenance of my daughter Ruth, and thereafter it is to be

to the benefit of my son John. I give my daughter Ruth £10 when 21; for 3 years the interest is to be paid as above and then for her benefit. Children have benefit of survivorship. All the rest of my goods and chattels are to be divided between my 3 daughters Alice, Elizabeth and Sarah, who are to pay my debts and see my body brought decently to the ground. I give to 10 widows or others of the poorer people of Hopton 5s. Exors: John Muriell and John Gilbert both of Hopton. Supervisor: Thomas Goddard. Wit. Thomas Goddard, Frances Wrigleton (X), Frances Gilbert. Pr. at Bury 14 July 1635.

806. R(W) MARY PLEASEANCE (X) of Wicken [Cambs], widow. 1 April 1634.

Bequeaths soul to God hoping through Jesus Christ to enjoy fruition of his glorious presence in heaven.
I give my son William my 3 cows with the stuff that is in the barn, be it hay or fodder, my long table and the cupboard, a form, a great chest, a great bed which I lie on with the bedding, a trundle bed, a coffer, 2 of my best fine sheets, a pillowbeere and a smock. I give my daughter Bridget Stevens my best kirtle, best waistcoat, 2 green aprons, my wearing linen, 2 tearing sheets and a great chair. I give my son Charles a pot shelf and 12 pence. I give Anne, my son John's wife, my next to best kirtle and my best hat, and to John 12 pence. I give his daughter Mary a weaned calf or 12s at the choice of her father to be given her a year after my decease. All the rest of my goods I give to my son William, whom I make exor on condition he delivers my gifts, pays my debts if any shall happen to be and brings my body decently to the ground. Wit. Robert Everit (X), Zachary Bentham, Mary Everit (X). Pr. 14 July 1635. No place given.

807. R(W) JOHN PAYTON of Thurston, singleman. 1 June 1635.

Bequeaths soul to God through whom I hope to be saved. To be buried in Thurston churchyard.
I give my brother-in-law George Sargant and his wife Elizabeth a bill of £12 if I do not spend it in my lifetime, and if George has nothing to do with it during my life. I give my brother Thomas 10s to be paid by my brother-in-law within 6 months of my decease. I give my kinsman Thomas, son of Thomas Payton, my shortest trunk. I give George and Elizabeth Sargant a featherbed, a bolster, and a green rug and after their decease to my godson John Sargant. I give my kinsman Robert Sargant my longest sword, and my kinsman Thomas Sargant my shortest sword. I give Edmund Caley my grey cloak and John Stevens my tamy cloak, both to be delivered within a month of my decease. I give my godsons Thomas Seadon 5s, John, son of Christopher Coke, 5s when 21, and John, son of Lawrence Rowleson, 5s when 21. I give Charles Bund my best black hat and a pair russet boots within a month. The rest of my moveable goods and apparel I give to George Sargant, whom I make exor. Wit. Edmund Caley, John Muskett. Pr. at Bury 25 July 1635.

808. R(W) ANNE GLEED (X) of Hopton, spinster. 6 June 1635.

Bequeaths soul to God.
I give my third part of a tenement and lands in Thelnetham to John Gilbert of Hopton; these were given to me by the will of my uncle Robert Gilbert of Hopton. I give Bridget Sewell one pillow, and Temperance Catton a green say apron. I make Thomas Goddard of Hopton clerk and Richard Gilbert yeoman of Hopton my exors, and give them all the residue of my goods to pay my debts and legacies. Any overplus I give to Lydia Reve my sister. Wit. Thomas Gayton, Henry Spurgen. Pr. at Bury 27 July 1635.

809. R(W) RICHARD KEY of Eriswell, yeoman. 19 November 1633.

Bequeaths soul to God. To be buried in Eriswell churchyard.
My land and living that I have in Eriswell are to be divided between my 2 daughters Agnes and Dorothy as specified in an indenture dated 9 December 1625. When my daughters are of age and inherit land, each is to pay my wife Alice £150. She is to have the profit or yearly rent of my living until my daughters are 21 to bring them up with such maintenance as shall be fit for them. Daughters have benefit of survivorship. My wife is to have all my goods and pay my debts. £100 of the £300 to be paid to her is for paying my debts, and another £100 she is to pay to my son John when 21. I make my wife sole ex'trix. Wit. Samuel Sutton, Christopher Rushbrooke, Anthony Oliver (X). Pr. at Bury 27 July 1635.

810. R(W) AGNES MORRIS (X) of Lavenham, widow. 2 May 1634.

Bequeaths soul to God.
I give 2s each to my son Edward, my daughter Mary, wife of William Bumsted, my sons William and Stephen and my daughter Anne within a year of my decease. I give Anne and Mary, daughters of my son Edward, and William, son of William Bumsted, 5s each within 2 years. I give my daughter Susan my messuage with yard and garden in Water Street in the borough of Lavenham. The residue of my goods, my debts, legacies and funeral charges being paid, I give to Susan and make her sole ex'trix. Wit. Thomas Poole, Edmund Ryse (X) and me Peter Marshall, who wrote will. Pr. 7 August 1635. No place given.

811. R(W) WILLIAM PLAMPIN of Stoke by Nayland, tailor. 18 April 1635.

Commits soul to God hoping to have everlasting life through Jesus Christ. To be buried in Stoke by Nayland churchyard.
I give my wife Elizabeth for life the tenement in Stoke by Nayland wherein I now dwell with yard and garden, and then to my son Henry. My wife must remain a widow and keep premises in repair. I give my son William £5 within 4 years of my wife's decease, my daughters Margaret

and Elizabeth 20s each within 3 months and my daughter Mary £6 within 6 years. I give all my moveable goods to my wife, and make my son Henry exor, hoping he will carefully fulfill the same. Wit. John Hull, Abraham Bradley, Thomas Russell. Pr. at Stoke by Nayland 2 July 1635.

812. R(W) THOMAS GOLDSON of Gislingham, yeoman. 9 July 1635.

Commits soul to God being assured of forgiveness of sins and to be raised up at last day to be made a living member of Jesus Christ.

I give the messuage wherein I dwell with all its free and copyhold land, being in 3 parcels containing 7 acres, to my son Edward. I give my 10 acre close called Slade meadow, held copyhold of Goldingham manor to my son Thomas. I give 2 acres freehold land, next to Slade meadow in Gislingham to south and to land of William Brett to north, to my daughter Mary. I give to be sold by my exors before my daughter Sarah is 21 an 8 acre parcel of land called Feningham field and lying in Gislingham between highway to east and land of George Foster to west, the procession way on south and Allwood Street on north side. Money from sale is to be used to bring up and to raise portions for my daughters Ann, Sarah and Elizabeth; to be paid within a month of Sarah being 21. All 4 daughters have benefit of survivorship. I give all my moveable goods and cattle to be sold by my exors within a month of my decease; money to be used as above and to pay my debts. Exors: my brother Edward Goulston of Woodbridge and my brother-in-law William Turnor of Bury, whom I make guardians of my children in their minority to let their land and receive the rents. I entreat them to see my children carefully brought up in the fear of God. If my exors do not sell Feningham field, it is to be given to my 3 daughters Ann, Sarah and Elizabeth. Supervisors: Mr Simonde minister of Gislingham, William Freman, William Bedwall. Wit. William Freman, William Bedall, John Levell, Edmund Heywarde. Pr. at Bury 28 July 1635.

813. R(W) ANABELLE MANINGE (X) of Denham, widow. 6 July 1632.

Bequeaths soul to my saviour and redeemer.

I give my son Thomas Smithe 20s, my niece and his daughter Anabelle 1 pair of my best sheets, and my niece Jane, also daughter of Thomas, 20s. I give the poor people of Balsham [Cambs] 20s. All the rest of my goods and chattels I give to my son William Smithe, whom I make sole exor. Wit. Thomas Steward, Bartholomew Maire. Pr. at Bury 13 July 1635.

814. W(R) JOHN WHITTLE (X) of Lavenham. 3 June 1635.

Bequeaths soul to God in sure hope of resurrection to eternal life.

I give my brother George, yeoman of Acton, my messuage in Bolton Street in Lavenham now occupied by me and Susan Ellet, on condition he pays my creditors. Any overplus of the value of the messuage above my debts is to be estimated by the discretion of indifferent men and given to my son Henry and daughter Susan. I give my daughter Alice Ginne 40s within 2 years of my decease. I give my daughters Christian Miller and Alice Ginne all my moveable goods, except my corn and cattle, to be divided between them by my brothers George and Thomas. I choose my brother George as sole exor. Wit. Richard Street and me Thomas Tayler. Pr. at Bury 29 June 1635.

815. W(R) MARGARET PORTER (X) of Stoke by Clare, widow.
4 July 1635.

Commends soul to God trusting through Jesus Christ to enjoy everlasting life.
I give my son Robert 20s within a year of my decease, and my daughter Margaret my stamill petticoat and 20s each to her and my daughter Rose Barick at same time. I give my daughter Ann Baker my cloth gown with my murry petticoat and 20s at the same time. I give my daughter Elizabeth £10 within 18 months and the trundle bed that is over the parlour with all its furniture, a great white chest in the same chamber and all my wearing linen, and the suit of linen and woollen for a young child in the same chest. I also give her a square table with 2 joined stools in the same chamber, my riding suit and the kneading trough that was her grandmother's. I give my son George a posted bedstead as it now stands in the parlour with all its furniture, a table, certain joined stools and a great chest in the parlour. I give my grandchild Dorothy Sparke £8 within 6 years of my decease, but if she dies it to be equally divided between my grandsons Robert and Matthew. I give a sheep to each of the following grandchildren: Robert Porter, Robert and Matthew Sparke, and Elizabeth and Anne Baker. I give my daughter Elizabeth my black say gown. I will that my son George abides with my sons John and Walter until he is 24 and they are to provide him with meat, drink and apparel if he remains so long unmarried, but if he marries before he is 24 he to provide for himself. I will that the legacy my husband gave in his will to John be paid to him before my goods are parted between my 2 exors. I bequeath to my sons John and Walter the unexpired term of years of the house and land bequeathed to me in my husband's will. I give my grandsons Thomas Baker and William Sparke 6s 8d each. My unbequeathed moveable goods I give to my sons John and Walter and make them exors. Wit. George Pratt, John Rote (X). Pr. at Bury 1 September 1635.

816. W(R) HENRY COE of Bury St Edmunds, yeoman. 12 April 1632.

Commends soul to God assuredly persuading myself to have remission of sins through Jesus Christ and expecting to ascend at last day into kingdom of heaven to dwell for evermore with God and his saints and angels.
I give Margaret my wellbeloved wife for life all my messuages and lands in Bury, Great Ashfield, Badwell Ash and Rickinghall now occupied by my son Henry, Oliver Johnson, Thomas Page of Ashfield, William Allen,

George Gallant, Toby Earle and myself, all of Bury, and John Calham of Over Rickinghall. After my wife's decease I dispose of my property as follows: the messuage in Guildhall Street in Bury occupied by my son Henry and Oliver Johnson, and all my messuages and land in Ashfield and Badwell I give to Henry for life, and then the property in Ashfiel i and Badwell to my grandson Thomas, son of Thomas Rands late deceased and of my daughter Margaret now wife of Jeffrey Mosse of Norfolk. Benefit of survivorship to his sisters Margaret, Thomasine and Mary. The messuage in Bury I leave to Henry's wife Judith after his decease and then to Thomas Rands as above. Henry must not cut down more than 4 cart loads of wood p.a. or fell any timber except to repair houses and fences. If he commits any waste, Thomas Rands is to enter into the land affected immediately. I give my wife power to take the long chamber over Richard Nunn's workshop, now used as part of the messuage in which my son Henry and Oliver Johnson dwell, back into the messuage where I and Richard Nunne live as it formerly belonged and was purchased. Also the little stable now occupied with the messuage where I dwell is to remain with it. After my wife's decease I give my grandchild Margaret Rands my messuage in Guildhall Street in which George Gallant dwells and which I purchased from Edward Woode and his wife Barbara; my grandchild Thomasine Rands my messuage in Guildhall Street now occupied by William Allen and one other messuage in Whiting Street now occupied by Toby Earle; and my grandchild Mary Rands my messuage and grounds in Over Rickinghall, which I purchased from Thomas Beck. If my son Henry leases for more than 1 year any of the property left to him for life, then my grandson Thomas may enter into possession of it at once. Grand-daughters have benefit of survivorship. I give Henry my long table in the hall. I give 40s to the poor people of the parish of St Mary in Bury. I give my sisters Prudence Clarke and Elizabeth Baldwyn 20s each within 3 months. The rest of my goods and ready money I give to my wife to perform my will and I make her sole ex'trix, willing her to pay Henry 50s p.a. Wit. John Jewell, Alexander Gent, Benjamin Midleditch. Pr. at Bury 26 August 1635.

817. W(R) ROBERT BETTES (N) of Hitcham. 31 May 1635.

His intent was that his eldest children should have 6s 8d apiece, and his youngest children 20s. The rest of his goods and chattels he gave to Saranna his wife. Wit. Thomas Grate, Rose James. Let. ad. granted at Bury 17 August 1635 to widow.

818. W(R) ELIZABETH HAYWARD (X) of Elmsett, widow. 13 July 1635.

Commends soul to God believing to be saved by Jesus Christ.
I give to 20 several families of the poorer sort in the parish of Elmsett 12 pence apiece, a brown loaf of wheat bread as it comes from the mill, a piece of beef and a pitcher of beer to be distributed on the day of my

burial. I give 12d apiece to 4 honest poor men that shall carry me to burial, that is to William Layt, John Largent, Samuel Lewes and Henry Ranson. I give my son-in-law John Hayward my freehold tenement wherein Richard Barnard lately dwelt with all its land, with remainder if he has no heirs to my godson John, son of my kinsman Philip Curtise of Hitcham. I give £7 to John, son of my brother Thomas Gardiner, when 25 and during preceding 2 years my exors are to pay him 10 groats p.a. for his apparelling. If John dies before he is 26, I give his legacy to Thomas Curtise, my sister's son. I give John Gardiner when 26 a low bedstead that stands in the hall chamber, a flockbed, a bolster, a mat, 2 blankets, a pair strong sheets, a pillow and a pillowbeere, a little coffer, a joined stool, a little kettle, a posnet, a little brass pot, pot hooks and 2 pewter dishes. Remainder to Thomas Curtise. I give him 20s within a year, and to John, Philip and Martha, children of my cousin Philip Curtise of Hitcham, 20s each when 21. I give Mary, wife of William Lives of Hoo, 20s within a year and 20s to her daughter Anne when 21. I give 6s 8d each within 3 months to John, Philip and Nathaniel, 3 sons of my deceased sister Smith of Bramford. I give my sons-in-law William and Robert Hayward of Bramford 20s each within a year, and 20s when 21 to John son of Robert. I give to Mr Carter my minister and to Mr Ashley 10s each, desiring one of them to preach at my burial. I give Philip, son of my brother Philip Gardiner, my cauldron, a silver spoon and a gold ring all of which were my father's. I give John, son of my brother Thomas, my linsey-woolsey coverlet which lies on the bed of my son-in-law John Hayward. I give John, son of Philip Curtise, a pair of sheets, a fustian pillow and an holland pillowbeere. I give my godson Thomas, son of widow Pindesynr of Hadleigh, a pewter dish wrought about that stands on my cupboard's head. I give John Hayward my featherbed on which I usually lie. All the rest of my small goods and moveables I give to my 3 sons-in-law John, William and Robert to be equally divided among them, and I make John sole exor. Supervisor: Philip Curtise of Hitcham, to whom I give 20s. Wit. George Carter, Thomas Downes (X). Pr. at Bury 27 July 1635.

819. W(R) ADAM JESOPE (X) of Occold, yeoman. 27 April 1635.

Commits soul to mercies of God purchased by Jesus Christ in assured hope of resurrection and everlasting life.

I bequeath my son William my leases and lease lands which I hold of the lord of the manor of Thorndon, my horse mill and brewing copper as they now stand in my houses in Occold, on condition he peaceably permits my son Elize to dwell in the messuage now occupied by him and myself and the land belonging to it until Michaelmas one whole year after my decease. If I die between Michaelmas and Lady Day Elize is to pay rent of £50 to William in 2 equal portions for a year's rent, but if I die between Lady Day and Michaelmas he is to pay £25 rent for that period and £50 for the year beginning at Michaelmas after my decease. If William prevents Elize from occupying my house and land, I give them to latter. I give William 2 pieces copyhold in Occold held of manor of Occold Hall and which I purchased from Thomas Warne, on condition he allows Thomas Quyntyne and Abigail his wife and my daughter peaceably to dwell in a dwelling house with shop called Wentes in which Thomas now lives, to use the yards and to take water from the ditch or pond there during Abigail's life. Thomas must pay William 10s rent p.a. in my mansion house where I now live in Occold. If William molests or evicts Thomas and Abigail, they are to have for ever my 2 pieces copyhold in Occold. I give my daughter Susan, wife of Simon Harvye, my silver cup. I bequeath my wife Jane for life the use of all my bedding, household stuff and linen, and after her decease to my son Elize except the linen which I give to my wife absolutely. I give Elize all the residue of my goods and make him exor. Wit. Patience Jesope (X), Thomas Cullum. Pr. at Bury 28 July 1635.

820. W(R) THOMAS BARNARD (X) of Badwell Ash, yeoman. 2 February 1633/34.

Commends soul to God.
I give Margery my wellbeloved wife all my lands and tenements for life and then to my daughter Elizabeth, wife of Edmund Clarke and their children. All my goods and chattels I give to my wife for life and then to be divided among my daughter's children. I make my wife sole ex'trix. Wit. William Buttolphe, Richard Andrew, George Harvye. Pr. at Bury 22 July 1635.

821. W(R) THOMAS FLETCHER (X) the elder of Hargrave, singleman. 13 January 1633/34.

Commends soul to God hoping to be received into celestial joys through Jesus Christ. I will my body be laid in a coffin and decently buried in Hargrave churchyard near unto my ancestors.
I give 10s within 3 years to the 4 children of Elizabeth Amys deceased, late wife of George Amys of Hargrave. The residue of my goods and chattels I give to my nephew Richard Waytes the elder, husbandman of Hargrave, towards paying my debts and legacies, and I make him exor. Wit. Samuel Waad, Abraham Sargent. Pr. at Bury 15 June 1635.

822. W(R) HENRY HOWLET (X) of Botesdale, yeoman. 6 July 1635.

Bequeaths soul into hands of God and bosom of Jesus Christ my sweet lord and saviour hoping through his merits to enjoy rewards of righteous with him in his heavenly kingdom. My body to be buried in churchyard of Upper Rickinghall hoping it will arise at last day to possess a crown of glory.
I give Dorothy my loving wife all my household stuff, money, cattle and stock, on condition she pays my brother Thomas £5 on St John Baptist

344

Day after my decease, and pays my landlord Thomas Jessupp the rent due to him. I make my wife sole ex'trix. Wit. Thomas Jessupp, Robert Leich (X) and me Thomas Maier, who wrote will. Pr. at Bury 21 July 1635.

823. W(R) THOMAS AUDWARKE (X) of Stowmarket, clothworker. 4 July 1632.

Bequeaths soul to God believing to have eternal salvation through Jesus Christ. To be buried in Stowmarket churchyard.
I give Sarah my wellbeloved wife all my moveable goods, except my shop stuff, for life and then to my son John, to whom I give my shop stuff immediately after my decease. I give my son James 10s to be paid by John a month after my death. I make Mr John Allebaster of Hadleigh my exor. Wit. William Prigge (X) and me Philip Barne. Let. ad. granted to widow 15 June 1635. No place given.

824. W(R) EDWARD TOMPSON (X) of Bury St Edmunds, clog maker. 21 February 1631/32.

Commits soul to God nothing doubting to have remission of sins through Jesus Christ, and after the end of this vain and transitory life to be received into his holy kingdom to live with his holy angels and elect children in perpetual happiness for ever.
I give my son Thomas 2s to be paid within a month of my decease. All the rest of my moveable goods, my debts and expenses paid, I give to Mary my loving wife towards her maintenance and the bringing up of my children, and I make her ex'trix. Wit. John Bridon, Robert Walker. Pr. at Bury 7 July 1635.

825. W(R) ALICE TILLOTT of Bury St Edmunds, widow. 5 July 1633.

Being willing to provide for the execution of the nuncupative will of my late husband Reginald Tillott, I do make my own will. First I bequeath my soul to God trusting to have remission of sins through Jesus Christ.
I make my son Thomas exor, desiring him in the fear of God to have a care that his brothers and sister that are as yet unsatisfied of their legacies given them in their father's will may be duly paid out of the moneys and debt due from my loving brother Mr Thomas Coell of Depden being £525. If there be not so much of the debt as the unpaid legacies of my children amount to, then I will their legacies shall be made up out of my goods if no other debts come to supply the want. What remains of my goods and household stuff, after my husband's legacies and such small ones as I give by my will are paid, I give to be equally divided among all my children except my daughter Greene to whom I have given some part of my goods. I give her 2 children 10s each to buy a spoon. I will that my

son William shall have 40s more than his share of my goods to buy him a cloak. My exor is to distribute 40s among the poor of St Mary's parish in Bury either at my burial or within some convenient time after. And that it may appear my care hath been duly to execute my late husband's will for the good of my children I have caused to be set down on the backside of my will what I have paid of my husband's debts and legacies, desiring them to rest contented without murmuring for my expenses through my weakness thinking it was better for them to have a sickly mother rather than none at all.

My children's legacies come to £900.

My husband's inventory come to £1012 10s 0d.

I paid due by my husband at time of his death

To Mr Thomas Pope due by bond £110

To John Simonds due by bond £110

To John Adcock for Mr John Eldred £50

To Samuel Stanton £8

Funeral charges £4

Probate of his will £1 4s 0d

To George Baxter £6

Total of above £289 4s 0d

And I have satisfied my children of their legacies

To my son Thomas his legacy of £200 as by his acquittance

To my son Leonard £10

To my son Robert £20

To my son William £8

To my daughter Susan £100

And so I have paid of debts and legacies £657 and then there remains but £243 yet there is behind unsatisfied to my children of their legacies jointly considered £532.

Codicil. The portions of those of my children who are under age at the time of my death are to be put forth by my exor for some moderate gain for the benefit of those that are or shall be apprenticed. I give my son Thomas my diaper suite of linen and my biggest silver cup for his pains in executing his father's will and mine. Wit. John Jewell, William Man. This will has no probate.

Note: Alice Tillott's husband was Reginald Tillott of Troston, gentleman, who made his nuncupative will about 1 June 1619 and it was proved on 19 July 1619. He bequeathed £200 each to his 2 eldest sons Thomas and Leonard, £100 each to his other sons Robert, William and John, and £100 to his daughters Susan and Dorothy. All legacies to be paid when children 21 by his wife and ex'trix.

826. W(R) JOHN HOWE of Great Whelnetham, yeoman. 29 December 1631.

Commends soul to God trusting through Jesus Christ to inherit kingdom of heaven.

I give my son John the messuage wherein I now dwell in Whelnetham

346

with the land belonging to it, on condition he pays my wife Alice an annuity of £12 at Lady Day and Michaelmas. My wife is quietly to possess the parlour and parlour chamber in my house for life, and John is to allow her 3 loads of wood p.a. for her burning. Power to distrain. I give my wife for life, as long as she remains unmarried, my messuage and land in Bradfield St Clare now occupied by Thomas Worton. She is not to take any wood except for fencing, stiles and gates. After her decease or marriage I give this messuage and land to my son George, and I also give him my messuage in Little Whelnetham occupied by Thomas Wiett and its land now occupied by me. I give John my lease of the lands I hired from Mr Gippes, and my daughter Elizabeth my messuage and land in Rougham now occupied by Roger Tillott. If my wife attempts to claim any thirds from my lands and tenements all legacies to her will be void. I give her all the household stuff and furniture now in the parlour and parlour chamber of the house where I now dwell, except a table chair there which I give to George. I give my wife for life the feather bed and bolster in the low chamber, and then to George. All the rest of my corn, cattle and personal estate I give to John, who is to pay George £10 within 3 years. I give the poor people of Whelnetham 20s to be paid within a month of my decease, and to the preacher that shall preach at my funeral 10s. Exors: wife and son John. Wit. George Scarpe, Henry Peach. Pr. at Bury 20 July 1635.

827. W(R) JOHN HOVELL alias SMYTH of Great Ashfield, single-man. 23 May 1635.

Commends soul to God in full assurance of eternal life through Jesus Christ.
I give my brethren William and Nicholas my tenement and lands in Cotton, which my father William lately purchased for me from John Holmes, on condition they pay my father an annuity of £16 on Lady Day and Michaelmas at his dwelling house, and after his decease an annuity of 32s to my sister Elizabeth, wife of Nathaniel Lister. They must also pay my sister's children £20 to be divided between them a year after her decease, £5 to my sister Martha Frost one year and £20 to my other sister Anne 18 months after my father's decease. My brothers must give my father an assurance not to meddle with the money owed me by Owen Tasburge and John Holmes of Cotton for my father lent me those sums to pay the admission fines to my land in Cotton. I give my mother £10 to be paid by my exors within 18 months of my father's decease. Legatees have power to distrain. My goods and chattels I give to my 2 brethren whom I make exors. And also I give Elizabeth Lister, my sister's daughter now living with my father £5 over and above her share of £20 above to be paid within 18 months of my father's death. Wit. Thomas Goch (X), Robert Syer (X). Pr. at Bury 31 July 1635 to William Hovell alias Smyth. The other exor had died [see his will, No. 789].

828. W(R) RICHARD BROOKE of Mellis, weaver. 8 April 1629.

Bequeaths soul to God trusting through Jesus Christ to have eternal bliss. I give my wife Martha my tenement wherein I now live with its freehold land for life, and after her decease it is to be sold by my exor and the money equally divided among my children. I give my wife all my moveable goods, money and bills except 2 pairs of looms with their slayes and warpings. Within 3 months of my decease my wife must enter into security to my other exor to pay so much money as my inventory shall come to, to be equally divided among my children; if she refuses the goods are to be sold at once and money divided among children. My copyhold land, held of the manor of Pountney, is to be sold by my exors and the money divided among my children within a year of my decease. I give my son Daniel my looms, slayes and warpings. Children have benefit of survivorship. Exors: wife and John Nightingale of Mellis. Wit. John Nightingale, Mary Nightingale and others. Pr. at Bury 23 July 1635 to John Nightingale.

829. W(R) ROBERT GLOVER of Bury St Edmunds, vintner. 24 June 1634.

I Robert Glover and Constance Glover my wife who have lived together man and wife for 52 years, praised be almighty God for it, being both of us in good health and prosperity do lovingly and jointly make this our last will and testament truly to be performed by the survivor of us. We bequeath our souls to God hoping for salvation through Jesus Christ.
Concerning the temporal estate we have truly gotten and gathered together with which it has pleased God to bless us in our pilgrimage, we dispose of it as follows. I give my wife my house and garden in Crown Street for life, and after her decease to my son Francis on condition he pays the following sums in the 3 years after his mother's decease: to Mary our daughter and her husband Thomas Scofeild £6 or, if they are both dead, to their daughter Constance; £6 to our daughter Judith and her husband William Kyng or, if they are dead, to their daughter Judith; and in the third year £8 to our daughter Constance or to her husband if she be married, but if she dies before the time appointed £8 to be paid to whom she shall bequeath it. Power to distrain on goods and chattels in house in Crown Street. As for our moveables, there is an inventory written in a roll of parchment of all the things we do bequeath to everyone what they shall have so that there may be no discontent among them, but to be thankful to God for their portions so left by us to them. All my moveables I give to my wife to pay my debts if any be, and all debts owing to me I bequeath to her whom I make ex'trix. Craving pardon of God for all my sins and pardon of all those I have offended and freely forgiving all those that have offended me, I take my leave of the world in the peace of God and good conscience hoping to rise again through merits of Jesus Christ. I have set my hand and seal this 12 day of July being now finished. Wit. William Kinge, Francis Glover, Mary Slofile. Pr. at Bury 11 August 1635 to widow.

830. W(R) JAMES TYRRILL (X) of Soham [Cambs], husbandman. 28 July 1635.

Wills soul to God who gave it me and to be buried in Soham churchyard.
I bequeath my now wife Sarah 4 milk bullocks and 2 white backed burlynns, 5 combs corn viz 6 bushels each of wheat and peas, and a comb each of lentils and barley, and all the moveable goods within the house. I also give her for life, and after her decease to be equally divided among my 4 daughters, my summer lowe to provide winter meat to maintain the 6 cattle and also one of my hogs. I give my daughters Margaret and Sarah £5 each when 21 and a weanling calf; the red howd to Margaret and the yellow red to Sarah. I give my daughter Ellen £5 when 21 and daughter Elizabeth £6 13s 8d. All the rest of my goods, moveable and unmoveable, I give to my son Lowe to pay my debts and legacies and I make him exor. Wit. John Finch (X) and me Robert Carlton. Pr. at Bury 31 August 1635.

831. W(R) RICHARD SHARPE (X) of Hessett, yeoman. 24 April 1634.

Commends soul to God trusting to be saved through Jesus Christ.
I give the poor people of Hessett 20s to be distributed by my exors within 6 days of my decease. I give my daughter Alice Martyn all my houses and lands in Hessett for life. If she fails to keep buildings in repair, my grandson Sylvester Martyn is to enter them until she does so. I bequeath my houses and land to him after Alice's death. I also give him £200 and my grandson James Martyn £100, both to be paid when 21 by my exors. I give my servant Mary Boulye 40s within a month of my decease. All my moveable goods I give to my daughter Alice, provided so much of them as will pay my legacies remain in my exors hands. Exors: my brother John Sharpe and grandson Sylvester Martyn. Wit. Roger Chennery (X) and me Thomas Walker who wrote will. Pr. at Bury 28 September 1635 to John Sharpe.

832. W(R) THOMAS STANTON (X) of Horringer, mercer. 13 April 1633.

Commends soul to God hoping through Jesus Christ to be made partaker of life everlasting.
I give all my messuages and lands in Horningsheath [Horringer], after deccase of my beloved wife Elizabeth, to Thomas, one of my sons, until my eldest son Robert pays him all the sums he justly owes him at time of my death and discharges him from all bonds for his (Robert's) debts. When Robert has done this he is to have my messuages and lands. If he dies without heirs, property to be divided into 4 parts: one to my son George clerk, one to son Thomas, one to my daughter Mary Garrard widow and the fourth to my daughter Elizabeth, wife of Robert Cotton gentleman. I bequeath my wife all my goods, cattle, plate and money. Exors: son George and son-in-law Robert Cotton. Wit. John Woodward, William Covell, Edward Goldsmyth (X), John Sidey.

349

Memorandum that Thomas Stanton at the time of sealing his will was of perfect memory and the same being verbatim read to him did assent and set his name thereunto, but could not see to write his name perfectly his eyesight being so much decayed. Pr. at Horringer 7 September 1635.

833. W(R) CALEB MORRIS of Nayland, tailor. 20 March 1628/29.

Gives soul to God hoping for everlasting life through Jesus Christ.
I give my wife Margaret my 2 little tenements with yards and gardens in Nayland, which I and my late father purchased of Moses Beekes and Abraham Raund and which are now occupied by William Burlingham, Robert Fox and widow Warren. My wife is to keep the tenements in good repair until my son Joshua is 21 when I give them to him. I give my brother Philip 20s, and my wife all my moveables towards bringing up my son. I make her sole ex'trix. Wit. George Sunderland (X), William Gatteward. Pr. at Sudbury 26 September 1635.

834. W(R) ROBERT MAYOR (X) of Lakenheath, husbandman.
12 August 1635.

Bequeaths soul to God believing through Jesus Christ to enjoy a place in his celestial kingdom there to praise him for ever together with the rest of the elect children.
I give my wife Dorcas for ever the tenement which at this time I have bargained for with Edmund Morley husbandman of Lakenheath, on condition she gives him good security for payment of £13 which will be the remainder due to him after she has paid him £6 18s 0d. My will is that Edmund Morley shall surrender the house to my wife on condition that out of it shall be paid a year after her death £12 to my children: £6 to Robert and £3 each to my son Francis and daughter Elizabeth. If my children are not paid they are to sell the house and divide the money. Benefit of survivorship. If the purchase of the house is not completed, Dorcas is to give Francis Bugg security for the payment of my children's portions when they are 21 or marry. My will is that my wife shall keep my son Robert in a decent and orderly manner so that he shall not be chargeable in any way to the inhabitants of Lakenheath. Wife sole ex'trix. Wit. Francis Bugg, Edmund Morlye. Pr. at Bury 28 September 1635.

835. W(R) JOHN FLATT (N) of Walsham le Willows, linen weaver.
3 August 1635.

Being sick of the sickness whereof he died upon the 3rd day of August 1635 and departing this life upon the Saturday following, he did declare his last will and testament. He willed to his son John and the child wherewith his wife was then big £10 apiece when 21, and in the meantime to be employed to their benefit. He did desire his kinsman John Flatt who was then present to see that this money was so employed. Benefit of survivorship. The residue of his goods and chattels he gave to his wife Mary for her maintenance and the education of his children. Wit. John Flatt (X), Thomas Page. Let. ad. granted 7 September 1635 to widow. No place given.

836. W(R) EDWARD YESTAS (X) of Wickham Skeith, husbandman. 20 June 1635.

Commends soul to God who gave it me.
I give Margaret my now wife for life the use of a low room in the house wherein I dwell called the bedchamber, being at the south end of the house, and the necessary use, at times convenient to my cousin Robert Durrant of Wickham Skeith and his sister Mary, of the chimney standing in the hall to make a fire for her and of room in the yard to lay her wood and to wash and hang her linen and to fetch water from the ditch or pond. After my wife's decease I bequeath the bedchamber to Robert and Mary Durrant, whom I make my exors and to whom I give immediately after my decease the residue of my messuage with the use of the chimney in the hall with my wife, and all the buildings and land belonging to the messuage. I also give them all my moveable goods and debts, except my wife's wearing apparel and the goods which were her's before I married her, which I bequeath to her. Robert and Mary must pay my legacies: an annuity of 10s to my wife; 20s p.a. for 5 years to Nicholas Durrant, now servant to Goodman Mann of Hepworth; 20s p.a. for 5 years to my brother's son Edmund Yestas of Soule [?Southwold] if he then be living; and £6 to my cousin Mary Durrant to be paid 6 years after my decease by Robert Durrant. All payments to be made in south porch of Wickham Skeith church. I have made a letter of attorney to my landlord Moses Buxton to recover certain monies due to me by specialty from John Durrant of Yaxley tailor, which money I intend should be equally parted between Moses's children. If my letter of attorney is not of sufficient force after my decease, my exors are to give him another. I give my wife's son John Winter 40s 7 years after my decease. If there is any difference between my wife and my exors, I ask that Mr Harvye and Mr Bedwell of Wickham Skeith should reconcile them; and if either party will not agree to their decision, they must be bound in sum of £10 to these 2 men and Mr Goddarde of the Street in Wickham Skeith to abide by their arbitration. If my wife refuses to do this, she will forfeit her annuity. I give my wife £5 which Stephen Waters of Wickham Skeith stands bound to pay me. This debt is secured by 2 bonds of 40s and one of 40s from John West of Wyverstone. Wit. Anthony Blomfeild, John Goddard. Pr. at Stowmarket 1 October 1635.

837. W(R) ANNE WRIGHT (N) of Clare, wife of Ambrose Wright. June 1635.

About 3 weeks before her decease, she dying about the beginning of July 1635, she gave all that was given to her by the will of John Scott of Bury St Edmunds to her child Anne. Wit. Francis Crosse (X), John Cadge. Let. ad. granted at Clare 25 September 1635 to Margaret, wife of John Cadge.

838. W(R) MARTHA GRIGGS (X) of Boxted, widow. 8 May 1635.

My late husband John Griggs by his will gave me divers household goods and things then in his great chest together with the chest. I now dispose of these things and the residue of my goods. I give my son John 12 pence, and my son Henry a silver spoon and a pair flaxen sheets. I give Henry his son and my godson 20s. I give my daughter Mary a red and blue coverlet, a silver spoon, 2 pairs flaxen sheets, my worst bearing cloth, my casting kerchief, a square board cloth wrought with Coventry thread, a little kettle, the chair which I usually sit in and one other chair. To her daughter Martha and my god-daughter I give 20s, a pair pillow beeres wrought with knot stitch and half a dozen of my newest napkins. I give my son Stephen a silver spoon, a pair flaxen sheets and half a dozen napkins, and my daughter Bridget my yellow coverlet and my bearing sheet. I give my daughter Elizabeth, wife of Henry Sparke, my red and green coverlet and my best bearing cloth; to her daughter Elizabeth my stone jug tipped with silver, a casting sheet for a bed and half a dozen of my newest sort of napkins; and to her daughter Martha a silver spoon and a cupboard cloth wrought with Coventry thread. I give my grandchild and godson Henry Sparke my new chest, a flaxen table cloth and 20s when 21, and his brother John a new flaxen table cloth and a new posnet. I give my godson John Stephens, son of my daughter Martha, 20s when 18. The greater part of the above goods, plate and linen lay in the great chest at the time of my husband's death and still do. I will my son-in-law Henry Sparke bestows £5 of mine in his hands on my funeral, and if the charge amounts to more it is to be defrayed out of my other goods. The residue of my money and goods and the things in the great chest and the chest itself are to be divided between my daughters Bridget and Elizabeth, but my wearing linen, woollen apparel and yard kerchiefs are to be divided among all 3 of my daughters. I bequeath Henry, Stephen and Mary £20 which Edward Fincham woolman owes me. The residue of my goods, cattle and sown corn I give to my son-in-law Henry and daughter Bridget and make them exors. Wit. William Hibble, Philip Hamond, Thomas Wright. Pr. at Bury 12 October 1635.

352

839. W(R) GILES PETTITT (X) of Fordham [Cambs], yeoman. 8 May 1633.

Commends soul to God hoping through Jesus Christ to be made partaker of life everlasting.
I give my son Giles 20s within a year of my decease. I give my son William the messuage with orchard and garden, which I lately purchased of Michael Dalton esquire, on condition he pays the £60 to him hereinafter given in trust. I give my son Robert the pasture closes I bought with above house, my close of pasture purchased of one Reeve of Cavendish, my house and meadow in Carter Street in Fordham lately purchased of Thomas Graye and a close bought of the widow Harvey. All the above lie in Fordham and are given to Robert in full discharge of a legacy of £20 given to him by his aunt Fytch and of another legacy of £20 left to him by his brother Simon. I give £60 to remain in my exor's hands, out of which he is to pay 30s quarterly to my daughter Rose Bruers so long as her husband Cornelius shall keep from her or so long as he lives, if he comes again. If she outlives her husband or if he remains from her for 7 years after my decease, my exor is to pay her the £60 within 6 months, but if she has died the benefit of the money is to be used to bring up her daughter Susan until she is 21 when £60 is to be paid to her. I give my son Robert the posted bed with its furniture whereon I now lie, 2 pairs of my best sheets, my best brass pot except one, my stone jug tipped with silver, my late wife's gold ring, and my silver spoon marked with the late Lord North's cognisance. I give my daughter Rose my framed table in the hall, a great chest which I bought of Robert Slyr, a silver spoon and the form with 2 buffet stools belonging to the table. I give the poor people of Burwell 20s and those of Fordham 20s to be paid to the overseers and distributed within a month of my decease. I give my daughter Rose her dwelling in the parlour over the cellar and the chamber over it in the house where I now dwell with access to the fire kept in the hall chimney during the time her husband shall live from her or when she is a widow. I give my grandchild Susan Bruers £10 when 18. If the £60 is not paid as set out above, beneficaries have power to distrain on land left to William. The residue of my goods and chattels I bequeath to my son William whom I make sole exor. I make my trusty friend William Balls gentleman supervisor and I give him £4 for his pains to be paid within a year of my decease. Wit. John Gamage, Henry Raynes, William Balls. Pr. at Newmarket 2 October 1635.

840. W(R) MARY ANGAUR (X) of Little Cornard. 7 August 1635.

I give my daughters part and part alike all my lands in Little Cornard and Bures St Mary. I make my daughter Elizabeth ex'trix and give her all my goods and corn to pay my debts. Wit. Thomas Bradys (X), Robert Butt. Pr. at Bury 20 October 1635.

841. W(R) MARTIN MOUNDEFORD of Wyverstone. 31 August 1635.

I bequeath my soul into the hands of the most blessed Trinity, and to our blessed lady and all the saints of heaven desiring them all to pray for me.
I give all my goods to my wellbeloved wife Eunica to pay my debts and see my body decently buried. Exors: John Ramply yeoman of Walsham le Willows and George Wright yeoman of Bouton alias Bacton in Norfolk. I make my dearly loved uncle Thomas Goodrich of Ashfield supervisor. Wit. William Osbern, Thomas Syer. Pr. at Bury 7 October 1635 to John Ramplye.

842. W(R) JOHN BRAND (X) the elder of Soham [Cambs], yeoman. 4 June 1635.

Wills soul to God hoping to have sins forgiven through merits of Jesus Christ. To be buried in Soham churchyard.
I give my daughter Alice Johnson 20s within a year of my decease, and my son-in-law Thomas Johnson my biggest widgill. I give 6s 8d each when 21 to my grandchildren Alice, Andrew, Thomas and Elizabeth Johnson, and Roger and Mary Fletcher. All the rest of my goods I give to Marion my now wife to pay my debts and legacies and I make her sole ex'trix. Wit. Richard Dowe, Edward Elsden (X) and me Robert Carlton. Pr. at Newmarket 2 October 1635.

843. W(R) FRANCES STEWARD (X) of Barton Mills [Little Barton]. 9 October 1632.

Renders soul to God that gave it hoping to be saved by merits of Jesus Christ.
I give my son William 20s to buy him a ring. I give my daughter Joanna one of my rings and my daughter Cattlin my other ring. I give my son Thomas's daughter Wright a pair of sheets and 2 pillowbeeres, and to Agnes my son William's daughter £4 to buy her a piece of plate. I give Lucy and Frances, daughters of my daughter Tallakarme £300, which my son William owes me and of which I have received part, to be divided between them. I give Frances Hayward, daughter of my daughter Cattlin, £20. I give my maid Dorothy Smith 20s, and Barbara Frende 20s. I give Thomas, son of Thomas Walker of Herringswell, 5s. I give to all the servants of my son Thomas, except the man that is new come to him, 5s each. I give all the rest of my goods to Thomas and make him exor. Wit. Abraham Bylney, Dorothy Smithe (X), Joan Fearns (X). Pr. at Bury 26 October 1635 to Thomas Steward.

844. W(R) PHILIP BANCKES (X) of Lawshall, yeoman. 10 October 1635.

Gives soul to God trusting through Jesus Christ to be made partaker of life everlasting.
I give Anne my wife for life and then to my son Philip my copyhold

messuage and tenement wherein I now dwell with all its land in Lawshall held of the manor of Hyningfields, and a 3-acre piece of copyhold held of Lawshall Hall manor. If she is alive when Philip attains age of 21, she is to pay him £4 p.a. for his maintenance; to be paid half yearly in south porch of Lawshall church. Philip is to pay my daughter Anne £30 at £10 p.a. starting 2 years after my wife's decease. If he fails to pay, Anne is to have my freehold land for ever. I give Anne £30 to be paid by my ex'trix when she is 21. The residue of my goods I give to my wife whom I make ex'trix. Wit. William Wright, Francis Sparke, Thomas Potter (X), John Smithe. Pr. at Bury 26 October 1635.

845. W(R) WILLIAM GREENEHALL of Lavenham. 2 January 1629/30.

Commends soul to God beseeching him for Christ's sake to receive it into his heavenly kingdom.
The 2 tenements wherein I dwell with yards, orchards, gardens, backsides and mine interest to the pond adjoining the backsides, I give to Alice my loving and beloved wife for life and after her decease to my youngest daughter Alice, wife of John Cocksedge of Rattlesden, and her heirs. I give my daughter Anne, wife of Mr Edmund Nevill of Much Tey [Great Tey in Essex], 10s to buy a gilt silver spoon if she think so good. I give my daughter Cocksedge 10s to be bestowed in like manner if that seem best unto her. My will is that their husbands, and they likewise, rest thankfully satisfied with their large portions already received by the one husband and partly by the other and partly secured to be paid unto him shortly. I give the poor inhabitants of Lavenham £3 and I would that those living in the Church End should especially be considered. The rest of my goods, debts and money, my debts, probate and funeral expenses being discharged, I give to my wife, although being less than I had purposed to give her for her maintenance through my desire to preserve my daughters in their marriages. I make my wife sole ex'trix. Wit. Isaac Creme, Joshua Blower, Peter Blower. Pr. at Bury 14 October 1635. Ex'trix took oath before Ambrose Copinger, rector of Lavenham.
On back of will: 'Good Mr Coleman I have sent you our good old master, Mr Greenehall, his last will and testament which his desire was might bee proved at Burie by you, the Charges of all which I will suddenlie come over and see discharged, and rest Your truly loveinge friend Francis Copinger. Mistress Greenehall will come over at some Convenyent tyme to take her oath, what will be fitting to your occasions I desire to hear.' Directed to 'his loving friend William Coleman at the Registers Office at Bury St Edmund.'

846. W(R) ROBERT HEDGE of Hopton, yeoman. 28 September 1635.

Bequeaths soul to God my creator, sanctifier and redeemer.
I give my wife Anne for life my tenement in Hopton wherein Luke Cocke now dwells with its land. She is to keep buildings and fences in repair.

355

After her decease it is to be sold within a year for the best price by my sons and daughter: Robert, William, Thomas, Nicholas, James and Anne or any 2 of them, and the money equally divided among them. I give £20 each as follows: to Robert and Thomas within a year and to Anne within 2 years of my decease; to Nicholas when his apprenticeship with Leonard Knocke expires and to James 1 year later. All payments to be made in porch of Hopton church and children have benefit of survivorship. I give all my children except William a bed, a bedstead, a pair sheets, a pillow and a pillowbeere when 21. The rest of my moveable goods I give to my wife and son Robert whom I make exors. Wit. Thomas Goddard, John Tostocke, Richard Gilbert (X), and Henry Spurgen who wrote will. Pr. at Bury 14 October 1635. Inventory exhibited by Robert Hedge 9 November 1635.

847. W(R) LORE HARBERT (X) of Clare, widow. 11 February 1634/35.

Gives soul to God and Jesus Christ hoping to remain eternally among latter's chosen and elect children.
I give my god-daughter Margaret, wife of [blank in MS] Cansby of Cambridge locksmith, Samuel, son of Roger Warren of Clare and his brother George 20s each within 9 months of my decease. I make my kinsman Edmund Chapman, clothworker of Clare, sole exor. My debts, legacies and charges being paid, the residue of my goods, bills and money are to be divided between his daughters Grace and Elizabeth. Wit. William Boarom (X), William Quarrey (X), John Howe. Pr. at Bury 10 November 1635.

848. W(R) THOMAS CATER the elder of Lidgate, singleman. 29 August 1635.

Commits soul to God trusting through Jesus Christ to have everlasting life.
I give all my customary land to my nephew Thomas Cater. I give my kinsman Joseph Westhropp £10, being part of the debt he owes me. I give his wife and my niece Katherine my 2 pairs sheets, my warming pan and a kettle. I give 20s to Mary, daughter of my late nephew William Cater, when 21. All the rest of my goods and chattels I give to my nephew Thomas Cater and make him exor. Wit. Thomas Wakefield, John Halles (X). Pr. at Bury 16 November 1635.

849. W(R) RICHARD WILKINSON (X) of Fornham St Martin, yeoman. 19 October 1635.

Commends soul to God hoping through Jesus Christ to be partaker of everlasting life.
I give the poor people of Fornham St Martin a yearly rent of 10s issuing from the messuage where I now dwell to be paid to the churchwardens

and overseers annually on Candlemas Day and distributed by them on Shrove Sunday following. I give Elizabeth my wife all my messuages and free and copyhold land in Fornham, Bury St Edmunds and Horningsheath [Horringer] for ever, provided that if she be with child at the time of my decease she is to have the property for life only. I give my brother Thomas 20s to buy a ring, and his son £4. I give my brother Peter £5 and my brother Francis £30. All to be paid within half a year of my death. I give my father-in-law Richard Theobald and his wife £10 each within a year, and to my wife's brother Robert £5 when 28. I give Richard Holmes my godson £5 to be put out and employed to his use until he is 24, with remainder to his sister Elizabeth. I give my wife's sister Susan, wife of Richard Holmes, £3 within 2 months. I give my loving friend John Spalding gentleman 20s to buy a ring. I give Oliver Theobald the elder gentleman £10 within a year. The rest of my goods and money I give to my wife and make her sole ex'trix. Wit. Robert Beian, Bartholomew Degon (X), John Suttell (X), William Voyce. Pr. at Bury 4 November 1635. Inventory exhibited 12 January 1635/36.

850. W(R) AMBROSE DAVY (N) of Barnardiston, labourer. About 25 August 1635.

He said that his will was that Sarah his wife should have his house in Barnardiston for life, and after her death it should be sold and the money distributed among his children part and part alike. Wit. Francis Arnold, Elizabeth Davy (X), wife of Richard. Let. ad. granted to widow at Clare 25 October 1635.

851. W(R) ROBERT NUNNE (X) of Hopton, miller. 14 October 1635.

Bequeaths soul to God.
I give my daughter Mary £30 to be put out for her within a month of my decease into hands of Stephen Whight my kinsman on security for yearly payment of 45s to my wife Elizabeth towards the education and bringing up of Mary until she is 21 when she is to be paid the £30. I give my daughter Elizabeth £30 on same terms, but security is to be given by my kinsmen Stephen Whight and Henry Spurgen, and payment made at rate of 18d in the pound. I give my wife all my moveable goods. She is to pay each of my daughters 45s apiece p.a. from age of 18 to 21 in Hopton church porch. I make my wife sole ex'trix. Wit. Richard Gilbert senior, John Gilbert and Henry Spurgen who wrote will. Pr. at Bury 29 October 1635.

852. W(R) HELEN HOLYDAYE (X) of Lavenham, widow. 20 November 1632.

Bequeaths soul to God and body to ground.
I give William, son of William Wyles clothier of Lavenham, £15 when 21, and his sisters Alice and Mary £10 each when 20 or on marriage day.

Benefit of survivorship. The residue of my goods and chattels I give to William Wyles and make him exor. Wit. Thomas Poolle, John Goode and me Peter Marshall, who wrote will. Pr. at Bury 29 October 1635.

853. W(R) THOMAS HARVYE (X) of Wicken [Cambs]. 20 May 1635.

Bequeaths soul to God hoping through Jesus Christ to be an inheritor of that heavenly kingdom he hath purchased for me.
I give my son John my 3 mares, cart, plough and all the gears to them belonging. I give my daughter Mary a milk cow, a black bullock of my own breed and a yearling colt. I give my daughter Petronella 2 bullocks or burlings and my other horse colt. I give my grandson John Elis a garle yearling calf and his father is to put it to best use until John is 21. I give my daughter Mary Elis half an acre peas at Upware fore and an acre barley at High Fen banks end. I give Petronella my acre of wheat. I give the rest of my goods and chattels to my son John, whom I make exor. Wit. Alice Goodye (X) and me Zachary Benthame. Pr. at Bury 10 November 1635.

854. W(R) RICHARD EVERED (X) of Long Melford, clothier. 8 September 1635.

I give my soul to God who first gave it unto me.
I give my son Richard £45 when 21, and in the meantime the profits are to be paid half yearly to my wife Mercy towards his bringing up. I give my daughter Margaret £30 when 17, until when profits to be used in same way. Benefit of survivorship, but if both children die their legacies are to be divided among my sisters. I give my wife £20 due to me from Thomas Cadiold, my father-in-law, and all my goods. I make my brother-in-law Francis Hall of Melford sole exor and give him 10s. Wit. Theo Peachie, John Deeks. Pr. at Bury 20 October 1635.

855. W(R) WILLIAM TEBBOLD of Glemsford, tailor. 8 June 1635.

Bequeaths soul to God and body to Christian burial.
I give my wife Sarah for life my copyhold messuage with yard, garden and orchard. After her decease they are to be sold by the minister and churchwardens of Glemsford for the greatest price offered and they are to pay the money as follows: 20s to Agnes, daughter of my son William, and 10s each to his daughters Mary and Dorothy, and 20s each to my grandchildren Rose and John, son and daughter of John Lister. The rest of the money is to be equally divided among my 3 daughters Sarah, Mary and Elizabeth, wife of John Arrowsmith. I make my wife sole ex'trix and give her the rest of my goods and chattels. Wit. Isaac Deikes (X), Ambrose Bridges, Richard Gardner. Pr. at Bury 10 November 1635.

856. W(R) JOHN GARNHAM of Stowmarket, yeoman. 14 June 1632.

Commits soul to God being assured of resurrection and of being made a living member of Jesus Christ.
I give my wife Rose for life, in satisfaction of her thirds, 4 tenements with yards in Stowmarket wherein John Garnham, Richard Buxton, Miles Baye, John Tricker and Joseph Umfrye now dwell. She and her servants are to have free access to fetch water and she is to have half the fruit from the orchard belonging to the messuage where I now dwell. I give the messuage where I now live and which I late purchased of Mr Samuel Davye and the reversion to tenement left to my wife to my son Nicholas, in consideration of the money promised to him on marriage and on condition he pays his own debts for which I stand bound with him. He must pay my wife an annuity of 40s half yearly and she has power to distrain. I promised my son-in-law William Emsden a portion of £100 with my daughter Rose, of which £20 has been paid and the rest is promised at a certain time after my decease. If they will accept it in discharge of the remainder, I give them 2 pieces of land called Aldams Mare containing 8 acres and which I purchased of Robert Aggas, for their lives and then to their children William, Rose and John, on condition they give my ex'trix an acquittance within 10 weeks of my decease. If they refuse, my son Nicholas is to have Aldams Mare and pay £80 to William and Rose Emsden. I give Nicholas the bedstead standing in the great parlour chamber, the cupboard in the hall and the lead in the kitchen. I give my daughter Rose a table in the hall, a back chair and a cistern now in the occupation of her husband. All the rest of my goods and chattels I give to my wife to dispose of at her pleasure, and to pay my debts. I make my wife sole ex'trix giving her power to hold my land and tenements until the Michaelmas after my decease, when legatees are to enter them. I nominate my kinsman Nicholas Garnham of Newton supervisor and give him 5s for his pains. Wit. Nicholas Garnham, Edmund Heywarde. Pr. at Bury November 1635. No day given.

857. W(R) WILLIAM COOKE of Great Livermere, gentleman. 22 September 1635.

Commends soul to God in full assurance of receiving eternal life and salvation through Jesus Christ unto which most blessed state I humbly beseech my most merciful father in Christ to direct and lead me by his most holy spirit. I will my body to be buried in church of Little Livermere by my late wife Martha in sure and certain hope of resurrection.
I give my son Holefernes immediately after my decease all my flock of sheep going at Ringmere called Ringmere flock, my corn growing at Ringmere and 10 combs rye to seed the land if it be not sown before my death. I give my son Stephen £200 to be paid by my exor within 6 weeks of my decease and another £200 6 weeks later. I give my grandchildren Margaret and Martha, daughters of my deceased son John, £200 each when 21, until when my exor is to pay them each £5 p.a. Benefit of

survivorship. I give my grandson William, one of the children of my late son Robert, £200 when 21 and £5 p.a. until then. I give his sister Martha £100 in same way. Benefit of survivorship. I give my daughter Margaret Sparrowe £20 within 6 weeks. I appoint my son Richard sole exor. Wit. William Chapman, John Cooke, Henry Whitehead. Pr. at Bury 2 November 1635.

858. W(R) HENRY BALLES (X) of Hopton, husbandman. 8 February 1633/34.

Bequeaths soul to God.
I give my wife Susan for life my messuage in Hopton wherein I dwell with its land, and then to my daughter Thomasine and her husband Anthony Pearse. I give my wife all my goods and chattels, and make her sole ex'trix. Wit. Thomas Goddard, Thomas Gayton and me Henry Spurgen, who wrote will. Pr. at Bury 30 November 1635.

859. W(R) ELIZABETH FREND (X) of Great Saxham, widow. 22 November 1632.

Bequeaths soul to God humbly thanking him that he hath given me such a long time in the land of the living and I desire him to receive my soul into his glory through merits of Jesus Christ.
So much as is due for my hoard, the charges of my burial and proving my will are to be satisfied out of money due to me. Of the residue I give half to my son-in-law Simon Pitts and his wife Elizabeth, and the other half to my son-in-law Charles Shawe and his wife Katherine, on condition that Charles pays to my exor the money due to me on reasonable demand. I give Anne Parman, servant to my daughter Pitts, 5s, my red coat, 2 aprons, a garter and a neckercher. I give Isaac Milles a pair of gloves and Elizabeth Milles a little box. The residue of my apparel and linen I give equally to my 2 daughters. I make my son-in-law Simon Pitts exor, entreating him to use his best endeavour to see my will performed. More I give Joan Maninge 10s. Wit. Edward Bridgman, Thomas Maninge (X), George Sparrow. Pr. at Bury 23 November 1635.

860. W(R) JOHN DRAKE (X) of Brandon Ferry, yeoman. 2 October 1635.

Commends soul to God being assured to be made partaker of life everlasting, and body to be decently buried in expectation of resurrection at day of Judgement to glory.
I give Margaret my wife my house which I purchased of George Cappe for life and all my other land until my son William is 21. She is to keep houses in good repair as they be at my death and my land in good tillage, and I make her ex'trix giving her all my moveables provided she remains unmarried. If she remarries my son John is to have my house and pay my son Thomas £10 within a year. I give my son Robert the copyhold land in

Brandon I bought from George Cappe. I give Thomas £10 to be paid by ex'trix within half a year of my departure, but if she remarries, within a month she is to pay £10 each to sons Robert, William and Thomas. Benefit of survivorship. I give my eldest son John £5 more to be paid a quarter of a year after my decease. After my wife's death the goods of which she shall then be possessed are to be divided among my children. Wit. William Southoùse, John Baker (X), William Archer (X), Margaret James (X). Pr. at Bury 30 November 1635.

861. W(R) JOHN BISHOPPE (X) of Thornham Magna, yeoman. 4 November 1635.

Commits soul to God relying wholly on his mercy in Christ for my salvation.
I give my son John my messuage and land in Great Thornham on condition he pays following sums: to my wife Mary £10 p.a. in satisfaction of her dower at Lady Day and Michaelmas; £55 to my son Thomas within 6 months of my decease; £100 to my son Robert, half within 6 months and half within a year; £55 to my daughter Rachel, wife of Jeffrey Barker, within 6 months; 5s each when 21 to my grandchildren John and Mary Barker; 10s to my grandson Moses Buxton and 7s 6d each when 21 to my grandchildren Gregory, Elizabeth and Mary Buxton. My wife is to have the best bed and bedstead to dispose of at her discretion, and I give her all my hemp. Legacies to be paid in porch of Great Thornham church. I give my son John all my goods and chattels and make him exor. Wit. John Posford (X), Thomas Bishoppe. Pr. at Bury 3 December 1635.

862. W(R) ABRAHAM GLEED (X) of Rickinghall Inferior, weaver. 14 May 1633.

Commends soul to God and body to earth in certain hope of resurrection to eternal life.
I give my son Nathaniel all my lands and tenements in Rickinghall and he is to pay my legacies. I give my son Thomas an annuity of 32s to be paid at 4 usual terms in Rickinghall church porch. Power to distrain. I give Nathaniel all my goods and chattels towards paying my debts and bringing my body decently to earth. I have mortgaged a messuage and croft to Thomas Beart and [blank in MS] as feoffees in trust for my grandchild Mary Gleed for payment of a certain sum of money to her. I bequeath this messuage and croft to Nathaniel who must pay £20 to Mary at time and place set down in the deed. If he fails, this messuage called Pickerell Stuffe is to be to the use of Mary and her heirs. I make Nathaniel exor. Wit. James Culham, William Greenwood. Pr. at Bury 4 December 1635.

863. W(R) GRACE CHEAPE (X) of Bury St Edmunds, widow. 16 October 1635.

Commends soul to God and body to earth nothing doubting a joyful resurrection to eternal life.
I give my grandchild Christopher Rose £8 when 24 and in meantime my exor is to put money out to best use, but if he dies money is to be divided among my brothers' and sisters' children. I also give him a posted bedstead with a tester, a flockbed, flock bolster, 2 pillows, a pair sheets, a blanket, a coverlet and a pair pillowbeeres with mat and cord, a brass pot with a pot lid and pot hooks, 2 kettles, a trunk, a little wooden chair, a little coffer and 3 great pewter platters. Until he is 24 these goods are to remain in custody of his master. I give my brother John Snell of Cockfield 6s 8d within a month of my decease. I will that after my funeral expenses, legacies and charges of probate have been paid, all my unbequeathed goods except my apparel shall be sold and the money, together with £6 that Nathaniel Rutter owes me, disbursed for binding out Christopher Rose as an apprentice. I give my sister Martine my stammell petticoat, 1 of my hats, a red waistcoat and a russett coat. I give my brother William's wife my gown, my murry coat, a hat, my cloak, 2 waistcoats and a green apron; and to her daughter my blue purwcas coat, a stuff kirtle and a green apron. All my wearing linen I give to be equally parted between my sister Martine and brother William's wife with benefit of survivorship. Exor: Edward Martine, to whom I give 5s for his pains and care to be taken in proving my will. Wit. Nathaniel Rutter (X), Robert Walker. Pr. at Bury 15 December 1635.

864. W(R) HUMPHREY HOWLETT the elder of Tuddenham, gentleman. 17 March 1634/35.

Commends soul to God.
I give my son John my messuage in Hunston, wherein Robert Walford gentleman now dwells, with all its land on condition he pays my debts and brings my body decently to the earth. I give £20 apiece when 21 to my grandchildren Elizabeth, Robert, Francis and Thomas Harte. I give Mr Chamberlayne minister of Hunston 20s. I give my daughter Dorothy Harte and my daughters-in-law Elizabeth and Anne Howlett 20s each to buy a ring of gold engraved with this inscription: Memento mori. I make my son John sole exor and give him all my goods and chattels to defray my funeral charges, debts and performance of my will. Wit. Henry Smyth (X), George Hawys. Pr. at Bury 21 December 1635.

865. W(R) MARGARET CASBURNE (X) of Burwell [Cambs], widow. 1 November 1635.

Bequeaths soul to God trusting by merits of Jesus Christ to be partaker of everlasting life and by no other merits.
I give my daughter Alice £10 when 21. I give Henry Danster the cupboard

and a bedstead with all its furniture in the parlour, 6 pairs of my best sheets, 3 pillowbeeres, half a dozen napkins, 6 pewter platters and all my childbed linen. I give my son Robert £10 when 21 and 2 pairs sheets. I will that he is put out apprentice with his part of the overplus of my goods at the discretion of my exor and supervisor. I give my son John £8 when 21 and 2 pairs sheets, and my son William £5 when 21 and 2 pairs sheets. I give my son Thomas £8 within a year of my decease, 3 pairs sheets, 2 pillowbeeres, the cupboard in the hall, the bedstead in the chamber with all its furniture that he lieth in, my copper and all my brewing vessels. When my debts and legacies have been paid, my exor and supervisor are to divide the overplus of my goods between my daughter Alice and sons William and Robert. Benefit of survivorship. I make my brother John Casburne exor and my brother Robert Casburne supervisor. I give to the poor of the parish 20s to be dealt out at my burial. I give my sister Porter a suit of apparel. I give following sums to my godchildren: 20s to John Waker, 2s to William Ward, 2s to John Norman and 2s 6d to Mary Garner. I give 20s each to Robert and John Casburne, 5s to my godson Robert Porter and 2s to Margaret Chenares. I give my daughter Alice the table in the parlour and the stools belonging to it, the pot shelf in the parlour and the form. Wit. Robert Casburne, Thomas Cooper. Pr. at Bury 21 December 1635.

866. W(R) ALICE WEETING (X) of Redgrave, widow. 19 October 1635.

Commends soul to God hoping for free pardon of sins and resurrection to eternal life.
I give my son John my best livery bed complete as it now stands in the hall chamber, a table and the short form by it in the parlour, the cupboard in the kitchen chamber, my best kettle and my least brass pot. I give my daughter Alice my best gown and petticoat and my best waistcoat, and to my daughter Mary 2 red and 1 green petticoats. I give my son Robert my copper in the kitchen chimney. The rest of my unbequeathed brass and pewter and my linen I will should be divided equally amongst all my children. I give my daughter Elizabeth £15: £10 for her bringing up and £5 to be given to her when 20, and son John £10, half for his bringing up and half when 21. I give my son Jonathan £8, of which £4 is for binding him apprentice and £4 for him when 21. I give my son Stephen £8 in same way, but £3 to be used for his binding out. I give John £6 a month after my decease, my son Nicholas £5 when 21 and daughters Alice and Mary £5 each when 24. Benefit of survivorship. I make my son Robert sole exor, but if he refuses to act John is to be exor. Wit. Henry Mihill, Robert Debenhall, Nicholas Bond (X). Pr. at Bury 14 December 1635.

867. W(R) ELIZABETH MAYER (X) of Long Melford, widow.
22 September 1635.

Commends soul to God and body to be buried in Melford church or churchyard.
I appoint my son Peter my exor. I bequeath my son John a pot with a silver top and cover. I give Elizabeth How my grandchild a great chest, with all that is in it, standing by my bed wherein I now lie. I give my son Peter and my daughters Mary, Susan, Elizabeth and Margaret all the rest of my household stuff to be prized, sold and equally divided between them by sufficient men, whom my exor shall appoint. My debts and burial charges to be paid out of my goods. Wit. John Butcher, John Byggs. Pr. at Bury 28 December 1635.

868. W(R) JOHN BRINKLY (X) of Redgrave, husbandman.
21 December 1635.

Commends soul to God trusting in Jesus Christ for forgiveness of sins and a glorious resurrection.
I give my wife Martha my tenement in which I dwell with its land for life, and then to my son John, who must pay my daughter Thomasine £15 at £4 p.a. starting a year after my decease. I also give her the little tenement that John Braen has with its hempland. I give my wife all my goods and chattels to pay my debts and bring my body to the earth. Wit. Henry Mihill, Nicholas Bond (X), Mathias Bond. Pr. at Bury 4 January 1635/36.

869. W(R) THOMAS SPENCELY (N) the younger of Bury St Edmunds. 24 August 1635.

The day before his decease he was asked how he would dispose of his estate and replied that his will was his wife should have £150 and his son Thomas £100. And being further asked what he would do with the rest of his estate being £50, he replied that his brother Martin should have £20 and then being interrupted by Mr Turner his wife's father, who seemed unwilling thereat, he desisted and did express his mind no futher touching the same. Wit. Martin Spencely, father of Thomas and Mr Turner. Let. ad. granted at William Colman's house in Bury 12 January 1635/36 to Martin Spencely.

870. W(R) CHRISTOPHER DALLESON (N) of Mildenhall, singleman.
10 May 1635.

He desired his body might be decently brought to the ground and willed 3s should be given to be rang for at his burial. He gave his sister Anne Dalleson, singlewoman, 5s, and William, son of his brother William, his best suit of apparel. To Agnes Docking, who attended him in his sickness, he gave an old other pairs of hose [sic] and a jerkin. The residue of his goods he gave to his brother William and his children. Wit. Mary Howse (X), Agnes Docking (X). Let. ad. granted 18 June 1636 to William Dalleson. No place given.

871. R JOHN HILL of Bury St Edmunds, gentleman. 8 July 1635.

Bequeaths soul to God and Jesus Christ.
I give my loving wife Anne all my houses and lands for 1 year after my decease. She is to pay my daughter Elizabeth, wife of Robert Clarke, £5 and my daughters Mary and Sarah £5 each. I give my wife my messuage in Hatter Street now occupied by Richard Nunne[?] pewterer, for life and then to Mary. I give my wife my orchard in Westgate Street, abutting on Mayewater Lane towards west, for life and then to Sarah. I give my wife my lease grounds in St Mary's parish, now occupied by John Petchie, Richard Gotobed, William B[rest illegible], Stephen Burrowe, James Jar[rest illegible], Stephen Dowtie[?] and William Mayer, for 30 years after my decease. If she dies before lease ends, I give the land to Mary and Sarah, who must pay £10 each to my daughters Elizabeth Clarke and Lea, wife of William Hall. I give power to my wife, my son-in-law John Woodward and my daughter Mary or any 2 of them to sell my capital messuage in the Cook Row [now Abbeygate] and Hatter Street and a tenement in Hatter Street now occupied by Thomas Warren and one Sympson, tailor; 2 chambers are occupied by me. The tenement in Hatter Street is in the tenure of John Hack joiner. They are to use the money as follows: to pay £100 each to my daughters Elizabeth, Mary and Sarah and £80 to my daughter Rachel, wife of Robert Chapman clerk; £50 each to my daughters Lea and Anne, wife of John Woodward. Any surplus is to be divided among Elizabeth, Sarah and Mary. My wife is to release her rights of dower in these messuages or pay Sarah and Mary £5 p.a. I give my grandson John Wilson £10 when 21. I give the feoffees of the town lands of Bury 4 tenements, each with a garden, in Westgate Street near the Horse Market to the intent they should place in them such aged, poor and impotent persons of St Mary's parish as they shall think fit. The poor people are to pay 2s p.a. for each tenement and the feoffees are to use this 8s to repair the tenements. None of the tenants dwelling in these tenements at the time of my death shall be put out or displaced except for some misdemeanour. If my capital messuage and tenement cannot be sold within 3 years, my wife is to let them and divide rents between Elizabeth, Mary, Rachel and Sarah, who are to pay her £5 16s 8d. I give my wife £50 of household goods to be chosen by herself, but appraised by 2 indifferent appraisers. I give Elizabeth a featherbed and bolster, a pair blankets, 2 pillows and pillowbeeres, 2 pairs sheets and a coverlet to be delivered to her at my wife's discretion. The rest of my household stuff I give to my daughters Mary and Sarah, but if I am in debt at time of my decease these goods and my plate are to be sold to pay debts. If there is any surplus I give £5 to my grandson Robert Chapman. I will that no mourning apparel be made at my death, but only a gown for my wife if

she pleases. I give my son-in-law Robert Chapman my Tremelius bible, and all my divinity books to my son-in-law John Woodward with my gold ring with my seal of arms, and to my son-in-law Robert Clarke my wearing apparel. I give to the preacher that preaches at my funeral 10s. All the rest of my goods and chattels, money and plate I give to my wife and make her ex'trix. Wit. to will and codicil John Jewell, Elizabeth Hart (X), Mary Symondes (X) widow.

Codicil dated 27 August 1635. The £5 and £10 left to my daughter Elizabeth are to be paid to her and not to her husband, and £100 to come to her after the sale of my capital messuage and tenement is to be put out at the best profit for her benefit by my wife, John Woodward and my daughter Mary. If she survives her husband the £100 is to be paid to her, but if she dies first the money is to be used as above for the benefit of her children until they are 21 when it is to be divided among them. My son-in-law is to have no benefit of the legacies to my daughter Elizabeth, and if he demands any of these sums in a court of justice or equity, the sums left to Elizabeth are to be disposed of at their pleasure by my wife, John Woodward and Mary. Pr. at Bury 1 December 1635.

Note: The register copy of this will is in very poor condition and the original will is missing. The section concerned with John Hill's bequest to the town land feoffees was abstracted from Woodward's Register (H1/6/1).

872. W(R) ROGER TYLER of Soham [Cambs], gentleman.
3 December 1635.

Commends soul to tuition of God that gave it me trusting to be saved by Jesus Christ.

I give the poor people of Soham 40s to be distributed a week after my burial at discretion of William Thompson and William Elsen. I bequeath for life to my wife Anne, whom I make ex'trix, 2 acres copyhold in Cobbes close and 1½ acres lying in Long Meere late one Goodwyn's. I give her an acre of land in Stutfolde leas late Goodwyn's and one string lying in a holt called Kings Wayte, and after her decease to my son Roger with all my freehold land and tenements. All the right and title in the will of my late father John I give to Roger, together with all my copyhold pastures, lakes and meadows. My wife is to hold them until Roger is 21 or marries, and she is to put out £20 p.a. to his use from his 14th year until he is 21 to raise him a stock of money. I give Roger half my household stuff. If he dies before he is 21, my wife is to pay 20 nobles p.a. to Owen Stocking's and Israel Hewit's children, and after her decease I give all my land and tenements to be equally divided between them. They shall pay my sister Moreden's children 40s apiece. I give William Gallant a suit of apparel, a hat and a pair of stockings. I give Robert Higney a doublet and a pair breeches, and Thomas Willson a doublet and a pair breeches. I give John Fynch my grey coat and Robert Prime my grey friese coat. I give my aunt Godlington half the forecrop of my holt called Deare Bolt. I give Jane Goldington 20s within half a year of my decease. I make my wife sole ex'trix to perform my will as my trust is in her. Supervisors: my good friends Thomas Pottes esquire and William Bridge gentleman of Cambridge, who are to assist in all controversies and difficult matters wherein they are requested to assist. For their good will I give them 20 marks in token of my love. I have surrendered to the use of my will the copyhold lands I hold of the manors of Soham, of Nether Hall Tyndalls and of Nether Hall Wigall into the hands of Richard Peachye and in presence of Thomas Cheavely the elder, both tenants of all 3 manors. Wit. Richard Pechey, Thomas Cheavely senior, William Tompson and me Edward Whin. Pr. at Bury 31 December 1635.

873. W(R) JAMES WYMARKE of Cheveley [Cambs], yeoman.
7 December 1635.

Bequeaths soul to God hoping through merits of Jesus Christ to be made partaker of life everlasting. Body to be buried in North aisle of Cheveley church.
I give the poor people of Cheveley 6s 8d to be distributed by the overseers at my burial. I give my daughters Alice and Anne £100 each when 24. Benefit of survivorship includes son James. I give my exor my house in Cheveley with barns and stables wherein Henry Sparrowe now inhabits, and all the arable land, meadow and pasture now occupied by him, and 1 acre in Saxton field in Wood Ditton, which was purchased with the above house. My exor is to sell the land and house to pay my debts and legacies, and he is to have the disposing of all my other land and tenements in Cheveley until James is 24, to bring up my children in a good and decent manner. He is to keep buildings in good repair. If James has no heir, property is to go to my daughters. I give my kinsman Ralph Wymarke of Chedburgh my house and lands there which are in his occupation, provided he pays the debt in which he and I stand bound to Richard Chapman of Livermere within 6 months of my death and delivers the bonds when discharged to my exor. If he refuses, I bequeath the house and land to my exor to sell to pay the debt. I give my kinsman Ambrose Wymarke my land in Dalham fields on condition he pays my kinsman William Wymarke of Kirtling 20s within 6 months. I give John Patriche his dwelling for life in the house wherein he now lives, on condition he pays my exor 10s every half year and does not take in or entertain any inmate. After his death I will my servant William Otely has his dwelling there for his life, paying my exor 20s every half year and keeping the house in repair. Neither of them is to cut or lop any trees on the ground except for fencing and that in an husbandly manner, and they are to preserve the fruit trees from any hurt. I give my kinswoman Sarah, wife of Nicholas Santy, 40s and my kinsman John Tayler of Ashley 20s. I give my servants Jeffrey Gen, Robert Chenery and Alice Elsinge 5s each. Any surplus, after my debts, legacies, exor's expenses and cost of bringing up my children are paid, is to be equally divided among my children but no more than £40 p.a. My exor is to have liberty to reap any crop of corn growing on my arable land at time my son James attains age

of 24. I make my brother-in-law Lawrence Keate exor, entreating him to take the care and charge upon him and I give him £10 for his pains. My exor is to have the use and benefit of the lands and tenement which I purchased from my kinsman Bragge and his wife, of which I have no assurance yet. Wit. Nicholas Stanley, William Overley (X). Pr. at Cambridge 2 January 1635/36.

874. W(R) ANTHONY GREENE (X) of Great Wratting, yeoman. 14 November 1635.

Commends soul to God my maker, Jesus Christ my redeemer and Holy Ghost my comforter, and my body to earth from whence it came, to be buried as a Christian ought to be.
I give my son Thomas a tenement called Evered with all its land in Hundon, lately purchased of Thomas Smyth gentleman, after the death of Mary my wife on condition he allows my son Samuel to take up, at the next court after death of Thomas Smyth, a piece of copyhold land called Miheles Close. If Thomas refuses, Samuel is to have my tenement and land and to pay Thomas 20s. I give my son John a tenement called the Yeld Hall with an adjoining orchard in Wratting, my son William a tenement called Sorrilles with an adjoining yard in Wratting and my son Samuel a copyhold close in Wratting called Miheles, all after the death of Mr Thomas Smyth late of Hundon. I give my daughter Mary £10 a year after and my daughter Elizabeth £10 2 years after and my daughter Sarah £3 3 years after my decease. I give my daughter Anne £10 when 21. All the rest of my goods I give to my wife Mary to perform my will and make her sole ex'trix. Wit. Thomas Onyon, Francis Stoke (X). Pr. at Bury 15 December 1635.

875. W(R) JOHN WRIGHTE (X) of Sudbury, wheelwright. 23 June 1635.

Commends soul to God hoping to be saved at day of general resurrection not by my own merits but by those of Jesus Christ.
I give my sister Joan Jenninges of Ballingdon [Essex] widow, all my messuages in Ballingdon now in tenure of Edward White, Francis Hayward, William Chaplyn, George Wells, William Codwell and the widow Uncle, for life. After her decease I give the messuage occupied by first 3 men above to John Wrighte, brick striker of Cockfield, eldest son of my brother Edward. He must pay £10 each to his brothers Edward and John and sisters Joan and Mary within 4 years of inheriting. Benefit of survivorship. If he refuses, I give the messuage to his brothers and sisters to sell and divide the money between them. I give William Wrighte, miller of Colchester and son of my brother Edward, my messuages and yards occupied by George Wells, William Codwell and widow Uncle after the decease of my sister, and he must pay £20 within 4 years to Arthur, son of my eldest brother Richard. If he refuses, I give the messuages to Arthur. I give my godson John Baker of Ballingdon 10s within 4 years of

my decease. I give William Nicholl gentleman, now mayor of the town of Sudbury, £4 and make him supervisor of my will desiring him to aid my ex'trix with his best skill, advice and knowledge according to my trust and confidence in him reposed. I give the poor people of the parish of St Peter in Sudbury 10s and those of the hamlet of Ballingdon 20s to be paid within 3 months. The residue of my household stuff, timber, working tools, bonds, bills and debts owing to me I give to my sister Joan Jennings and make her sole ex'trix. Wit. Robert Jon, Robert Salmon. Pr. at Bury 12 January 1635/36.

876. W(R) JOHN GILBERT of Hopton, grocer. 20 October 1635.

I give my soul to God and body to be buried according to laws of the realm.
I give my son John, after the decease of my wife Frances, my tenement in Hopton wherein I now dwell with my tenement on the north side of it, sometime Fuller's, and another tenement on the south side of it against the town well. After my wife's decease I give my son Robert my 8 acre close in Weston [Market] which I purchased of Arthur Bristo; my daughter Anne my close in the Mill field in a furlong called Clapscrosse, and commonly called Pond Close and lying between Henry Spurgen's land to east and highway from Hopton to Thelnetham to north; and my daughter Frances my messuage in Hopton now newly built with an adjoining hempland and a pightle of 1 acre lying in Clapscrosse furlong between land of Henry Spurgen to east and his land and that of Hopton Rectory to west and abutting on the highway from Hopton to Thelnetham to north. I give the child or children that my wife is now withall the rest of my lands, which I purchased of Arthur Bristo, immediately after the decease of Mary Pearetre late wife of Joseph Gaze. Anne and Frances have benefit of survivorship. I make my wife sole ex'trix, and she is to bring up my children, pay my debts, prove my will and see my body reverently brought to the ground. Wit. Thomas Asty (X), John Tostocke and Henry Spurgen, who wrote will. Pr. at Bury 9 January 1635/36. Ex'trix took oath before Thomas Goddard, rector of Hopton, on 18 December 1635.

877. W(R) THOMASINE [Tamesinge] RUSTE (X) of Stoke by Nayland, widow. 12 December 1635.

Commends soul to God believing to have free pardon of sins through Jesus Christ.
I give my son Robert a 6 acre close called Messengers in Weston Market for life and then to his son John for ever. I give my daughter Bridget £50. I give my daughter's sons Thomas and John and her daughters Mary and Bridget Buninge £10 each to be paid to their father Thomas Buninge within a year of my decease. He is to be bound in sum of £200 to my son Robert to pay his children their legacies and profits made from them when they are 21. Benefit of survivorship. I give £10 each to my

grandchildren John, Mary and Sarah Newgos. Money to be paid to their father Robert Newgos as above, but he is to be bound in £100. Benefit of survivorship. I give my grandchild Mary Rust a pair of sheets and a silver spoon, and my grand-daughter Sarah Rust 1 pair sheets. I give my daughter Elizabeth's daughters a pair of sheets apiece. I give my 2 daughters Bridget and Elizabeth all such implements of household as are now in my chamber at my tenant Thomas Payne's house in Weston Market, and all my household stuff, brass and pewter which were removed from my house to my son Robert's at my breaking up housekeeping. I give my grandchildren Jemina and Susan Rust £3 each when 12. I give my grandchild Bridget Bunninge my feather bed which I now lie upon, the feather bolster and the blanket now lying on my bed. My daughter Bridget is safely to keep these things until my grandchild is 16. If any of the money owing to me becomes desperate debts and is not paid to my exor, my legacies are to be lessened in equal portions. The residue of my goods I give to my exor, my son Robert. Wit. Samuel Birde (X), Thomas Sydley junior. Pr. at Bury 18 January 1635/36.

878. R(W) SIMON WELLES (N) of Brockley, doctor of divinity and parson. 13 May 1635.

He willed to Augustine Mayhewe, his son-in-law, all his goods and chattels, ready money and debts, except those in hands of his son Francis, to pay his debts. Wit. Edward Johnson, curate of Shimpling, John Brincknell. Let. ad. granted in John Jewell's house in Bury 16 October 1635 to Augustine Mayhewe.

879. W(R) JOHN ROLFE (X) of Mildenhall, husbandman. 9 November 1635.

Humbly commits soul to God hoping through Jesus Christ to inherit eternal life.
I give my wife Frances for life my copyhold messuage wherein I dwell in West Row in Mildenhall and then to my 3 youngest daughters Jane, Frances and Mary. I stand indebted to my son-in-law John Sheene for the sum of £10 in full recompence of my daughter Amy and his wife's marriage portion. To secure payment to him within a year of my decease, I have made a conditional surrender to him of 1 acre copyhold arable lying on the backside of my messuage. After my wife has paid £10 she is to have this acre for life, and after her decease it is to be divided among my above 3 daughters. I have lately made a conditional surrender of my 3 half acres of copyhold land, lying in Mildenhall field near Twamell Hedge, to the use of Elizabeth Childerstone to secure payment to her of £11 at a certain day yet to come. When my ex'trix has paid £11, she is to sell this land towards paying my debts, but if she can pay them without selling the land I give it to her for ever. I give my daughter Amy 3s 4d within 2 months of my decease. All my moveable goods I give to my wife, whom I make sole ex'trix.

370

Memorandum: I have surrendered my messuage and land to the use of my will by hands of William Ellys and John Clyfte, copyhold tenants of the manor. Wit. William Ellis, John Clifte, James Knight, William Dalleson. Pr. at Bury 1 February 1635/36.

880. W(R) BARTHOLOMEW PARKYN (X) of [Market] Weston.
1 November 1622.

Bequeaths soul to God hoping to be saved by Jesus Christ.
I give all my moveable goods to my wife Christian. I give 10s each to Anne and Alice, the 2 daughters of William Ducklen to be paid by my wife within 2 years of my decease. For a whole year after my decease my wife is to have the use of my hempland and the stover house to store such things as be necessary. I give my wife an annuity of 2s 6d a quarter to be paid by my son-in-law William Ducklen. I give his 2 daughters Anne and Alice 5s each to be paid by him when they are 21. I give my sister Marian Greene 20s to be paid within 3 years of my decease by my son-in-law. I give Anne and Alice Ducklen all my lands and tenement in Weston to be equally divided between them after the decease of William Ducklen and his wife Anne. I make Christian my wellbeloved wife my sole ex'trix.
Wit. Robert Ingham (X), Thomas Jermy. Pr. at Bury 8 February 1635/36.

881. W(R) JOHN HEYLOCKE (N) of Little Saxham, singleman.
About the latter end of January last past.

Speaking to Thomas Jenkin, his father-in-law, he said I give unto you all my goods and chattels on condition you pay my debts and bring my body decently to the ground. Wit. John Wymark the elder and John Wymark the younger of Saxham, and Thomas Jenkin. Let. ad. granted in John Jewell's house in Bury 8 February 1635/36 to Thomas Jenkin.

882. W(R) HENRY COBBOLD (X) of Layham, yeoman. 4 January 1635/36.

Commits soul to God believing to have pardon of sins through Jesus Christ.
I bequeath my grandchild Henry Cobbold my tenement or cottage in Layham with outbuildings and land, which I purchased of William Weaver and is now occupied by me and Henry Cobbold, and he must pay my wife Faith £10 p.a. I give my grandchild John Cobbold my 4 acre piece of land in Layham called Heyfield, which I bought from Francis Martin and is now occupied by Henry Cobbold. My wife is to have the profit of my 5 cows until Michaelmas after the date of my will when they are to be divided among my 5 children equally. I give my son Leonard the bedstead, feather bed and all that belongs to it after my decease. I give my wife all my household goods, bills, bonds and other moveables for life and then to be equally divided among my 5 children. I give the poor of

Layham 20s, of Shelley 20s and of Raydon 20s to be divided among them by the discretion of my exor within a month of my decease. I give my son Martin 20s above the rest of my children and make him exor. Wit. Robert Goodwin, Thomas Adames, Thomas Byles (X). Pr. at Bury 26 February 1635/36.

883. R(W) AGNES HOCKNELL (N) of Ixworth, widow. 14 February 1635/36.

Committed soul to God and body to earth.
She gave all her moveable goods and chattels to be equally parted between Anne and Rebecca Sawyer to see her decently buried. Wit. John Bullmer, Edmund Cage (X). Let. ad. granted to Anne Sawyer 22 February 1635/36. No place given.

884. R(W) MARGERY BARRETT (X) of Gazeley, spinster. 10 July 1635.

Commends soul to God trusting that my sins will be forgiven by Jesus Christ who will receive my sinful soul.
I give my brother Nicholas Barrett £20 to be paid at 40s p.a. starting 2 years after my decease. I give the houses and lands in my possession and my goods to my loving cousin Anne Tayler, whom I make sole ex'trix. Wit. Thomas Barcocke, Bartholomew Baker (X). Pr. at Gazeley 15 February 1635/36.

885. R(W) JOHN NORFOLKE the elder of Soham [Cambs], yeoman. 3 February 1635/36.

Recommends soul to God trusting to be saved through Jesus Christ.
Having a feeling of the distressed state of the poor, I give the poorer sort of people in Soham 20s to be distributed the Sabbath day after my decease by the overseers of the poor. I give my son John my tenement in Mare Street in Soham in the occupation of George Musicke, my 1 acre close of pasture on the south side of Soham and abutting on the highway leading to Wicken, 1 acre freehold land in Downe field next to 2 acres copyhold of John Norfolke the younger held of Netherhall Tindalls now Mr Payne's, 1 acre copyhold of Soham manor in Greneditch furlong on north side of Soham and abutting on Metleham way and by land of Thomas Hobie on the south, 1 acre demesne land in Noddich field next land of Frances Grayve widow and held by William Voyce's lease, half an acre demesne in Bancrofte contained in a lease late Edward Cropley's at Elme, which is a hempland in my use, 2 other half acres hempland in Bancrofte in Mr Hamond's lease, one in my use and the other in that of John Nethercoate the younger by my grant. I give my son Luke 1 acre freehold in Downe field next to that left to John, 1 acre copyhold of Soham manor in Greneditch furlong abutting on Metleham way and land of John Norfolke to south. I have purchased of William Bernes esquire 1 acre hempland next to my other one on south side of the town in Mill

croft and now occupied by John Norfolke. After my decease it is to descend to Luke by the grant of William Norfolke gentleman deceased, and assurance of its purchase is to be made to Luke, failing which my ex'trix is to pay him £22 being the price contracted for the hempland. My sons are to enter upon my land immediately after my decease with full advantage of crops of corn and hemp sown by me. I give my wife Alice 6 of the best milk cows amd 1 mare at her choice. The rest of my cows and horses and husbandry tools I give to be equally parted between my 2 sons by my supervisors; John is to have first choice. My sons are to give my wife each year 2 combs good wheat, 2 combs good rye and 1 comb barley at my now dwelling house, and to plough and sow for her the croft of hempland belonging to the house and to bring home out of the commons of Soham such carriages by cart as Alice has to be carried for her own use each year. If sons refuse, I give my wife the 2 freehold acres in Down field and 2 copyhold acres in Greneditch furlong for life. I give my wife all my implements of household, brass, pewter, iron, linen and woollen for life, and after her decease to be separated in 2 parts by my supervisors for my sons with John having first choice. I give all my grandchildren 10s apiece. I give my kinswoman Anne Tabram 20s when 21. All my unbequeathed goods and chattels I give to my wife and make her sole ex'trix. Supervisors: my loving kinsman John Norfolke, and my sons-in-law Francis Eaton, Robert Pechey and John Nethercoate, and I give each of them 6s 8d within a year of my decease. My grandchildren are to have their legacies when 21. Wit. John Norfolke, Robert Petchie and me William Howe.
Memorandum that John Norfolke has surrendered his copyhold land held of the manor of Soham and Fordham to the use of his will into hands of John Norfolke in presence of Robert Pechey. Pr. at Bury 28 February 1635/36.

886. R(W) SIMON STEGLE (N) of Norton, husbandman. 20 January 1635/36.

He gave his son Christopher and daughter Mary the money due on the 6 bonds he formerly gave into hands of Henry Bright gentleman to be equally divided between them after the decease of his wife Mary; to remain meanwhile in hands of Mr Bright. He gave interest on these bonds to his wife for life. The rest of his goods he gave to his wife towards providing a portion for his son Thomas before she proceeded to the solemnization of any second marriage. He nominated his wife ex'trix. Wit. wife and Mr Henry Bright. Let. ad. granted to widow in house of register, William Colman, in Bury 7 March 1635/36.

887. R(W) WILLIAM BROOKE (N) of Pakenham. 13 December 1635.

Sending for one William Mordyboite his neighbour, the testator in the presence also of Elizabeth Osbourne widow, speaking to his daughter Margaret said I give thee all my goods, rights, credits and chattels. Being desired by William Mordyboite to give her something in token thereof, he took a sheet in his hand and gave it to his daughter uttering the words: I do freely give to thee this sheet and with it all such moveable goods as I have at home and abroad, except one little boarded bedstead, a flockbed, flock bolster, 1 pair sheets, a coverlet, a blanket with bed and bedding which he gave to his son William. He further gave him 40s to be paid to him by Margaret the third year after his decease. His intent was his daughter should give William a sufficient security for payment of 40s,and if she refused William to be an equal partner with her in all things that were her father's. Wit. William Mordeboite, Elizabeth Osbourne. Let. ad. granted at Bury to daughter 7 March 1635/36.

888. R(W) THOMAS TAYLER (X) of Thelnetham, yeoman.
13 February 1635/36.

Commends soul to God and Jesus Christ.
I give my wife Alice my tenement wherein I now dwell with buildings and land in Thelnetham and Wattisfield to sell for best price within a year of my decease and to use the money to pay my debts. I give her all my goods and chattels, bills and bonds to pay those of my debts not covered by sale of tenement and land, and my legacies. I give my son Edward £40 and my daughters Margaret and Alice £20 each, all to be paid at Michaelmas 1649. Benefit of survivorship. I make my wife sole ex'trix, but if she fails to prove my will within 6 weeks of my decease, I make my loving neighbour Richard Person of Thelnetham, son of Richard Person deceased, my exor and he in that case to have my lands and goods. Wit. Robert Dade, Valentine Barlyman (X), John Locke. Pr. at Bury 4 March 1635/36 to widow.

889. R(W) MARY CULLEN (X) of Denston, widow. 20 April 1634.

Commits soul to God in name of Jesus Christ.
I give my son Henry and my daughter Mary, wife of Edward Aves, 12 pence apiece. All the rest of my goods and chattels I give to my daughters Ann and Elizabeth equally to be divided between them and I make them ex'trices, willing them to pay my debts and legacies and such funeral expenses as they shall think fitting to bestow upon me. Wit. John Webb, Martha Webb (X). Pr. at Bury 21 March 1635/36.

890. R(W) JAMES WACE of Chevington, yeoman. 24 January 1635/36.

Bequeaths soul to God assuredly hoping for salvation through Jesus Christ.
I give the copyhold messuage wherein I now dwell with its land to my loving wife Anne for ever. I give Mary, daughter of my sister Alice Sowter, 40s to be paid by my ex'trix when she is 18. I give James Palfrey, one of my sister Alice's sons, and William, one of the sons of my brother William, 40s each when 21. I give Richard, son of Moses Lucas of

Ixworth 20s when 21. My ex'trix is to pay all my debts out of my land. The residue of my goods and cattle I give to my wife and make her sole ex'trix. I have surrendered some of my copyhold land to Sarah Howlett widow for payment of a certain sum of money at a day yet to come; my wife is to pay this money and I give the land to her. Wit. Robert Paman, John Goodday. Pr. at Bury 21 March 1635/36.

891. R(W) THOMAS DRAPER (X) of Gislingham, basket maker. 24 August 1627.

Commends soul to God trusting to inherit eternal life through Jesus Christ.
I give my son Edward my house and ground wherein I now dwell and containing 1 rod in Gislingham, on condition he pays my daughter Mary £4 at £1 p.a. starting 1 year after my decease. I give my 2 sons Thomas and Thomas [sic], my daughter Margaret Barram and her son John 2s 6d each to be paid by my exors within 3 months of my decease. The rest of my goods I give to be equally divided between Edward and Mary and make them exors. Wit. William Brett, William Freman. Pr. at Stowmarket 16 April 1631.

892. R(W) THOMAS BROWNE (X) of Soham [Cambs], shepherd. 22 April 1632.

Bequeaths soul to tuition of God hoping it will be saved by Jesus Christ.
I give all my goods and chattels to my now wife Joan to pay my debts and carefully and motherly educate and bring up my children, and I make her ex'trix. Wit. William Longe (X), Richard Denys (X) and me William Howe. Pr. at Soham 31 May 1632.

893. R(W) JOHN CROSSE of Lavenham, clothier. 5 September 1631.

Bequeaths soul to God trusting to be made partaker of life everlasting through Jesus Christ.
I give poor of Lavenham 40s to be distributed among them on day of my burial. I give my wife Margaret for life my messuage with barn, stables, yard and orchard in Water Street in borough of Lavenham provided she keeps the messuage and the cocks, cisterns and lead pipes belonging to it in good repair. After her decease I give the messuage to my son Ambrose. I give my wife all my linen, woollen and household stuff, except the brewing copper and the long and livery tables, the press and the cupboard in the hall, which are to remain with the house for Ambrose. I give my son John £40 to be paid 2 years after my wife's decease in 2 instalments. I give Elizabeth, wife of William Miller, 40s. I release my son John from all bonds and bills due unto me from the beginning of the world until the date of my will. I give my daughter Margaret, wife of John Lea, £10 to be paid within 3 years of my wife's decease, and my daughter Anne, wife of William Wright, £10 within 4

years. I give Thomasine Rye, another of my daughters, £10 within 5 years. I give my 2 sisters Katherine Wyatt widow and Abigail Symondes widow 20s each. The residue of my goods and chattels I give to my son Ambrose and make him exor. Wit. Edmund Nevell, John Lambey, John Comsbye. Pr. at Bury 10 October 1635.

894. R(W) SAMUEL REVETT of Mendlesham, yeoman. 8 January 1634/35.

Commends soul to God trusting to obtain forgiveness of sins and life everlasting through Jesus Christ.
I give my wife Susan for life all my lands and tenements in Mendlesham, except those hereinafter excepted, on condition she keeps herself a widow and brings up my children. After her decease or marriage they are to go to my son Samuel. I give my wife all my lease lands in Mendlesham until Samuel is 26 when he is to have them for the remainder of the lease. I give my wife all my moveables, except those otherwise bequeathed, to use during her life or widowhood and then to Samuel. I give Samuel my bedstead and long table in the shop chamber, my round spruce hutch in the little chamber, my best cupboard in the hall, my counter table, my 2 anvils and all my other tools belonging to my trade. He is to have the use of my shop and new millhouse to enable him to follow his trade. When he reaches 26 he is to have the shop chamber. He is to pay £15 each to my sons John, Thomas, William and James when 24. If they die without heirs, their portions die with them, but if they have had children they are to have these legacies. I give my 6 children, Susan and Anne and my above 4 sons, £15 each to be paid by Samuel as follows: £5 each within 2 years of my wife's marrying and £10 each within 7 years of her decease at one p.a. starting with the eldest within a year of my wife's death. If my wife does not remarry, legacies of £15 each to be paid, starting at Michaelmas after her decease, in south porch of Mendlesham church. I give my son Timothy £12 to be paid by Samuel at Michaelmas 3 years after my wife's decease. If my wife be now with child, Samuel is to give it £10 when the rest of my legacies have been paid. If any of my children die their legacies become void. Exors· William Scaman of Mendlesham and my son Samuel. Wit. Peter Ducke, John Goddard, Barnabas Barker. Pr. at Bury 23 March 1635/36.

APPENDIX

A note on books mentioned in wills.

Will 258. The Works of Mr Eastye. No author of this name has been traced, but Thomas East or Este [c.1540–c.1608] a music publisher and printer, included the Psalter among his many publications. His son, Michael [c.1580–c.1680] was a composer, principally of madrigals. While master of the choristers at Lichfield Cathedral he composed anthems.

Dr Whitaker against Stapleton. William Whitaker [1548–95], Master of St John's College, Cambridge and Regius Professor of Divinity. He held Calvinist views and devoted much energy to refuting Roman Catholic divines, especially Cardinal Bellarmine and Dr Stapleton. In 1594 he published a defence of the authority of the church by the authority of scripture, which was an answer to one of Stapleton's writings. This work was in Latin and entitled 'Defensionem ecclesiasticae authoritatis, duplicatio, pro authoritate S.Scripturae'. Not surprisingly the man in whose will it is mentioned was a clergyman.

Thomas Stapleton [1535–98] emigrated early in the reign of Elizabeth I and held chairs at Douai and Louvain. He was a learned and skilled controversialist.

Will 355. Foxe's Book of Martyrs. This is the popular title of John Foxe's 'Actes and monuments of these latter and perillous dayes, touching matters of the church'. First published in 1563, it went through many editions and was long second in popularity to the bible.

Will 379. Plain Man's Pathway to Heaven, David's Blessed Man and Mr Henry Smith's sermons. The first has proved impossible to trace. David's Blessed Man may be the Psalms, or some of them, as Psalm 1 begins 'Blessed is the Man'. Henry Smith [c.1550–91] was the best known preacher of his day and was called 'silver-tongued Smith'. He was Lecturer of St Clement Dane's in London, where he enjoyed the patronage of Lord Burleigh. After his death many of his sermons were printed both singly and in collections.

Will 506. Bollinger's Decade. Neither the author nor the work have been traced.

Will 871. Tremelius Bible. John Tremelius [1510–80], a converted Italian Jew, translated the Old and New Testaments into Latin from Hebrew and Syriac respectively; they were printed between 1569 and 1579. This was long the standard Protestant Latin translation of the Bible.

Sources: A. W. Pollard & G. R. Redgrave, *Short Title Catalogue of Books Printed in England, Scotland and Ireland 1475–1640*, 2nd edn, 1976; the *Oxford Dictionary of the Christian Church* and the *Dictionary of National Biography*.

INDEX OF TESTATORS

Aliases have been indexed under both names. Variant spellings which do not appear consecutively have been brought together. There are cross-references from the variants to the preferred spelling.

Counter, William of Exning 133
Cowper,
Henry the elder of Bradfield St George 674
John of Old Newton 330
Crabbe, Henry of Boxford 535
Cradock, Richard of Barrow 258
Crane, Thomas of Barnardiston 284
Craske, Robert of Icklingham 551
Cricke, Alice of Milden 150
Cropley, Elizabeth of Bury St Edmunds 185
Crosse, John of Lavenham 893
Crowch, John of Hopton 805
Crowne, John of Rickinghall Inferior 653
Cullen, Mary of Denston 889
Cunolde, Margery of Old Newton 291
Cutbert alias Eason, Christopher of Poslingford 534

Dale, Robert of Botesdale 12
Dalleson, Christopher of Mildenhall 870
Darbey, Edward of Bury St Edmunds 296
Darbye, Agnes of Burwell 426
Davey, John of Hundon 15
Davy, Ambrose of Barnardiston 850
Day, Robert the elder of Gt Ashfield 737
Daye, John of Badwell Ash 75
Daynes,
Mary of Mildenhall 64
Thomas of Bacton 340
Deane, Thomas of Bures 650
Dearman, Reuben of Lidgate 293
Debnam, Edward of Sapiston 587
Dennant, Frances of Stowmarket 42
Dennye, Edmund of Hopton 490
Dey, Alice of Westhorpe 780
Diesden, William of Westley 666
Dix, Richard of Burwell 177
Dobbes, Thomas of Soham 34
Dobbs, John of Aspal 85
Dockine, Thomas of Mildenhall 614
Doe, Stephen of Hopton 86
Dove, Thomas of Chippenham 427
Dowe, Richard of Soham 451
Downham,
Elizabeth of Assington 608
Thomas the elder of Assington 335
Downsdale, Ralph of Nayland 215
Dowsing, Rose of Hardwick 14
Drake,
Hugh of Ampton 610
John of Brandon 860
Draper,
Susan of Combs 470
Thomas of Gislingham 891
Drurye, Charles of Rougham 593
Duckling, Thomas of Hopton 800

Eason alias Cutbert, Christopher of Poslingford 534
Edgley, John of Stanstead 422
Edmond, Robert of Cheveley 288
Edmundes, Alice of Hunston 796
Edwards, Frances of Bury 366
Eggett, Thomas of Soham 61
Eldred,
Joan of Gt Saxham 350

Thomas of Santon Downham 463
Eley, William of Lawshall 77
Elligood,
Richard of Hitcham 184
Richard of Tostock 482
Ellis, Vinca of Cotton 346
Elye, Daniel of Stanstead 189
Emyns, William of Westley 287
English,
Bloyse of Bury St Edmunds 717
William of Bury St Edmunds 233
Englishe, Joan of Bury St Edmunds 381
Erie, Jeffery of Cavendish 17
Evered,
Martha of Hawkedon 520
Richard of Long Melford 854
Everitt, Stephen the elder of Wicken 142

Farrowe alias Francis, Francis of Botesdale 392
Feveryeare, Reuben of Bacton 668
Filbrigg, Edward the elder of Bury St Edmunds 475
Fison, William of Kennett 462
Fitch,
John the younger of Rede 786
Mary of Gipping 507
Flatt, John of Walsham le Willows 835
Flawner, John of Mildenhall 621
Fletcher, Thomas the elder of Hargrave 821
Flower,
Barbara of Mildenhall 222
Robert of Mildenhall 47
Folkes, Mary of Mildenhall 563
Folkner, Francis of Icklingham 676
Fookes, Philip of Lakenheath 246
Foord, Robert of Kettlebaston 783
Ford alias Word, John of Nowton 72
Fordham, Adam of Hargrave 5
Foredom, Edward of Rougham 190
Fornham, Joan of Rougham 524
Francis, Nicholas of Bury St Edmunds 322
Francis alias Farrowe, Francis of Botesdale 392
Franck, Giles of Pakenham 777
Franke, Edmund of Mildenhall 191
French, John of Stradishall 302
Frenche, Thomas of Clare 581.
Frend,
Elizabeth of Gt Saxham 859
Richard of Sudbury 218
William of Gt Saxham 234
Frost,
Edmund of Cockfield 237
John the elder of Norton 508
John of Langham 566
John of Whepstead 294
Robert of Gt Barton 115
William of Mildenhall 171
Fryer, John of Finningham 616
Fuller,
Francis of Bury St Edmunds 631
James of Mildenhall 596
John of Hepworth 203
Richard of Mildenhall 199
Stephen of Bardwell 162
Fuller alias Snow, Robert of Gt Fakenham 778

382

Peach, William 30
Peachie (Pechie)
　Jeffrey of Bures 663
　William of Mildenhall 240
Peake,
　Lucy of Fordham 595
　Richard of Fordham 455
Pechie see Peachie
Pecok, Richard of Pakenham 410
Peirson (Pirson)
　Elizabeth of Lt Saxham 236
　Richard the elder of Thelnetham 156
　William of Wangford 374
Pepper, Elizabeth of Lavenham 201
Perkyn, Thomas of Bury St Edmunds 146
Pettitt, Giles of Fordham 839
Pettycote, Margaret of Stradishall 493
Pirson see Peirson
Pitches, Giles of Kirtling 722
Plampin, William of Stoke by Nayland 811
Playfere, John of Depden 398
Pleasance,
　George of Barrow 415
　Margaret of Hargrave 723
Pleaseance, Mary of Wicken 806
Plummer, Thomas of Dalham 79
Poole, Thomas of Combs 519
Porter,
　Margaret of Mildenhall 750
　Margaret of Stoke by Clare 815
Powle, Elizabeth of Flempton 788
Prentice, John of Wissington 2
Pretty, Thomas of Eye 147
Prick, Ambrose of Lavenham 292
Pricke,
　Dorothy of Barrow 76
　Margaret of Chevington 760
Prigg, George of Stansfield 672
Prigge, Adam of Stradishall 298
Prior, William of Bradfield St George 472
Pyndar, Mary of Kentford 605

Quarrey, Isabel of Bacton 489

Raffe, Elizabeth of Hitcham 371
Raineberd see Raynberd
Raneham, John of Brettenham 771
Raye,
　Frances of Barrow 111
　Richard of Stradishall 387
Rayment,
　Edward of Stoke by Clare 568
　John of Clare 137
Raynberd (Raineberd, Rayneberd)
　Lawrence the elder of Walsham the Willows 368
　Thomas of Stowupland 603
　Thomas of Stowupland 712
Rayner, Anne of Gt Waldingfield 552
Reade,
　John of Soham 276
　Walter of Stoke Ash 396
Reede, John of Stowmarket 112
Reeve,
　Edward of Hundon 241
　Francis of Hepworth 314
　John of Mildenhall 756
　Reginald of Hepworth 25

Reinolds see Reynoldes
Revell,
　John of Cavendish 124
　Mirabel of Chevington 261
Revett, Samuel of Mendlesham 894
Reynoldes (Reinolds)
　Alice of Cowlinge 707
　James of Woolpit 772
Ridnall, Robert the elder of Mendlesham 328
Roberts, Alice of Downham 11
Robinson alias Cooper, William of Mildenhall 639
Robinson alias Sander, Robert of Wangford 726
Robson, John of Soham 333
Rogers, James of Pakenham 560
Rolfe,
　Agnes of Mildenhall 26
　John of Mildenhall 879
Rose, Robert of Hopton 638
Rosier, Walter of Wetherden 318
Rowninge, William of Chippenham 83
Royse, Henry of Exning 702
Ruffle, George of Sudbury 606
Rumball, William of Wangford 727
Rumbelowe,
　Edmund of Dalham 46
　Robert of Dalham 247
Rushbrooke,
　Christopher of Woolpit 523
　William of Thurston 91
Russell,
　John of Stowmarket 742
　Susan of Bury St Edmunds 588
Ruste, Thomasine of Stoke by Nayland 877
Rymill, Robert of Glemsford 82
Ryvett, John of Bacton 469

Saer, Susan of Groton 257
Sampson, William of Newmarket 528
Sancty, Robert the elder of Wickhambrook 356
Sander alias Robinson, Robert of Wangford 726
Sargant, Robert 96
Sargent, John of Stradishall 238
Sawyer, William of Gt Horringer 541
Scarffe, Augustine of Stanton 140
Scott,
　George of Wissington 444
　John of Hawkedon 260
　Robert of Boxted 803
Scroope, Henry of Mildenhall 361
Seaman,
　Christian of Wattisfield 749
　Gilbert of Mendlesham 627
　Ralph of Bury St Edmunds 743
Seriant, Phyllis of Stradishall 271
Seyrd alias Sherd, Bridget of Gt Livermere 37
Sharpe,
　Dorothy 642
　Richard of Hessett 831
　Roger of Bury St Edmunds 217
Shawe, George of Stanstead 196
Sheene, Thomas of Chippenham 363
Sheep, Ann of Burwell 274
Sheldrake, Thomas of Clare 770
Shepheard, William of Wetheringsett 22
Sheppard,
　Edmund of Redgrave 221

INDEX OF PERSONS

Variant spellings which do not appear consecutively, or have more than a few entries, have been brought together. There are cross-references from the variants to the preferred spellings. Aliases are cross-referenced. The following abbreviations have been used: (e) executor or supervisor; (l) legatee; (p) official of probate court; (w) witness. References following these letters are, for example, to legatees when (l) is used. References are not in strict numerical order, as the abbreviations are treated as sub-headings. Two or more members of a family often bore the same Christian name, so in many instances a number refers to more than one individual

Abbott (Abbut),
　Abigail (l) 351
　Abraham (l)(e) 351
　Ambrose 794
　Bernard (l) 794
　Edward (l) 794
　Frances (l) 794
　Francis (l) 351
　George 267, (l) 794
　Isaac (w) 310
　John (w) 697
　Mathew (l) 216
　Mathias (l)(e) 794
　Richard 543, (l) 794
　Robert (l) 794
　Susan (l) 351
　Theodora (l) 794
　Thomasine (l) 794
　Thomas (l) 794
　William (l)(e) 794
Abbut see Abbott
Abry,
　John (l) 607
　Mary (l) 607, (l)(e) 607
　Thomas (l) 607
Acten,
　Diana 549
　Edmund 549
Acton,
　Amy (l) 86
　Anne 86
　Edmund 86
　Mary 86
Adame, Theodore (w) 110
Adames,
　Anthony (w) 575
　Henry (w) 185
　James 110
　Joseph (w) 575
　Katherine (l)(e) 110
　Rachel 551

　Robert (l) 110
　Rose (l) 110
　Stephen (l) 110
　Thomas (w) 882
Adams (Addams, Adhams), 771
　Alice (l) 706, 758
　Anne (l) 208
　Anthony (w) 593
　Dorcas (l) 758
　Elizabeth (l) 706, (l)(e) 758
　Ezechiel (l) 758
　Frances (l) 208
　John (l) 208, 468, (w) 273
　Joseph (l) 706
　Mabel (l) 645
　Marian (l) 645
　Martha (l)(e) 208
　Mary (l) 703, 706, (l)(e) 706
　Mathusala (l) 758
　Paul (l) 527
　Rachel (l) 208
　Richard (l) 468
　Robert (l)(w) 208, (l) 645
　Stephen (l) 706
　Theodore (w) 645
Adbury 10
Adcock, John 825
Adiold, Nicholas (e) 231
Adkyn, William 629
Adson, Alice (l)(e) 87
Adwell, Mary (l) 421
Ager 578
Aggas,
　Anne (l) 761
　Francis (l)(e) 761
　John (l) 761
　Robert 856
　Roger (w) 165
Agnis alias Smith,
　Dorothy (l) 70

388

Elizabeth (l) 70
Henry (l) 70
John (l) 70
Aierese, Ann (l) 308
Albon,
  Alice (l)(e) 669
  George (w) 669
  Giles 623
  James (w) 669
Albone, George (w) 491
Alcocke (e) 605
  William (l) 605, (w) 530
Alders,
  Isaac (l) 120
  Samuel (l) 120
  William (l) 120
  Winifred (l)(e) 120
Alderton,
  Elizabeth (l) 264
  Henry (l) 264
  John (l)(e) 264
  Robert (l) 264, (w) 737
  Rose (l) 264
  Thomas (l) 264
Aldham,
  Christian (l) 179
  Henry 179
  Jane (l)(w) 179
  Joan (l) 179
  Margaret (l) 179
  Mary (l) 179
  Thomas (l) 179, (w) 270
  William (l) 179
Aldrich, Anthony (w) 433, 687
Aleward, Elizabeth (l) 118, 119
Alger, John (w) 560
Alington, Giles 793
Allablaster, Thomas (e) 442
Alldehowse, William (w) 397
Allebaster, John [Mr] (e) 823
Allen,
  Alice (l) 657
  Anne (l) 615, 657
  Bartholomew (w) 419
  Israel (l) 691
  Joan (l)(e) 590
  John 590, 805, (l) 691, (l)(e) 657, (w) 290
  Judith (l) 115
  Katherine (l) 657
  Nicholas (w) 83
  Samuel (l)(e) 115
  Sarah (l)(e) 691
  Thomas (l)(e) 657
  William 615, 816, (l) 657
Allington, Giles [Sir] 131
Allinson, Richard (w) 588
Allstone see Alston
Almer,
  John 622
  William 622
Alston (Allstone, Alstone)
  Abigail (l) 757
  Abraham (w) 461
  Gregory 757
  Richard (w) 7
  Robert (l) 757

Samuel (w) 741, (l)(e) 757
Alston alias Wells, Millicent 878
Alstone see Alston
Alvis, John (w) 673
Ambrose, Robert 762
Ammys, John (l)(e) 125
Amys,
  Elizabeth 821
  George 821
  Mary (l) 125
Anderson,
  Henry (l) 744
  Margaret (l)(e) 744
Andrew,
  Richard (w) 820
  Thomas (w) 747
Andrewe, Edmund (l) 423
Andrewes,
  Edward, (l)(e) 19
  Margery (l) 19
Andrews,
  Elizabeth 117
  Hugh (e) 670
  Margaret (l) 670
  Mr (l) 627
  Thomas (e) 766
Angaur, Elizabeth (l)(e) 840
Anger, George (e) 570
Anis, widow 174
Ankerson, George (w) 144
Ansell, William (l) 731
Appelwite see Applewhite
Appleton,
  Alice (l) 77
  Catherine (l) 459
  Giles (l) 77
  Hannah (l) 459
  Margaret (l) 459
  Mary (l) 459
  Priscilla (l) 459
  Rachel (l)(e) 459
  William (l) 459
Applewhite, Dorothy (l) 578, (l) 681
Appleyard,
  Alice 533
  Martin (l) 533
  Thomas (l)(e) 533
Apslee, Ralph (e) 643
Apten, Henry 10
Archer,
  John 735
  Priscilla (w) 735
  William (w) 860
Argent,
  Ambrose (l) 100
  Anne (l) 100
  Margaret (l)(e) 100
  Mary (l) 100
  Matthew (l) 100
  Richard (l) 100
  Thomas (w) 706
  William (l) 100
Arnold,
  Elizabeth (l) 611
  Francis (w) 850
  Wheatly (w) 459

Banyard, Alice (l) 652
Banyer,
  Andrew (w) 38
  Robert 34, (w) 61
Baram,
  Thomas (w) 568
  William (l)(e) 568
Barber,
  Anne (l) 353
  Robert 360
Barcocke, Thomas (w) 473, 605, 884
Bardwell 799
  Anne (l) 481
  Elizabeth (l) 481
  Frances (l)(e) 481
  Mary (l) 481
  Roger (l) 481
  Susan (l) 481
  Thomas (l) 481
Bareham, William (w) 355
Barick,
  Margaret (l) 815
  Rose (l) 815
Barit see Barret
Barker,
  Alice (l) 709
  Anne (l) 230, (l)(e) 94
  Audrey (l)(e) 613
  Barnabas (w) 894
  Christopher (l) 230
  Edward (l) 709, (w) 594, 707
  Elizabeth (l) 230
  Ellen (l)(e) 709
  Francis (l)(e) 439
  Jeffrey 861
  Joan (l) 613
  John 230, 613, (l) 709, 861, (l)(e) 506
  Joseph (l) 94
  Katherine (l) 439
  Margaret (l) 94, 230, 449
  Mary (l) 861
  Mr Serjeant (e) 85
  Philip (w) 375
  Rachel (l) 861
  Richard (w) 25, 159, 193, 719
  Roger (w) 252
  Sarah (l) 94
  Simon (w) 642
  Stephen (w) 749
  Susan (l) 94, 709, (w) 642
Barly, Thomas (w) 416
Barlyman,
  Anne (l)(e) 282
  Robert (l) 282
  Thomas 282
  Valentine (w) 889
Barnard,
  Anabel (l) 155
  Andrew (w) 591
  Edward (e) 155, (w) 414
  Elizabeth 182
  Jane (w) 126
  Margery (l)(e) 820
  Richard 647, 818, (l) 182
Barne, Philip (w) 42, 339, 408, 512, 531, 570, 586,
  823

Barnes (Bernes)
  Audrey (w) 347
  Francis (l) 580
  William 885
Barnewell, Thomas (l) 755
Baron,
  Alice (l) 633
  Ann (l) 633
  Grace (l)(e) 223
  John (l) 223, (w) 20, 274
  Margaret (l) 633, (l)(e) 633
  Martha (l) 633
  Mary (l) 23, 633
  Robert (e) 23, (w) 223, 274
Barone, John (w) 23
Barquy,
  Anne (l) 790
  John (l)(e) 790
  Margaret (l) 790
  Prudence (l) 790
  William (l) 790
Barram,
  Elizabeth (l) 533
  John (l) 891
  Margaret (l) 891
Barret (Barit)
  Anne (l) 262
  Elizabeth (l) 453, 768
  George 379
  Henry 379, (l) 768
  Jervis (l)(e) 262
  John (l) 262, 768, (l)(e) 453
  Margery (l) 379
  Mary (l) 379
  Roger (l) 379
  Thomas (l) 768, (l)(e) 379
  William (l) 453
Barrett,
  Elizabeth (l) 473
  Jervis 693
  John 131, (w) 79, 137, 569
  Nicholas (l) 884
  Samuel (l) 707, (w) 707
Barrow, Thomas 131
Barrowe,
  Mistress 131
  [Mrs] 20
Bartlett,
  Anne (l) 252
  Edmund (l)(e) 252
  James (l) 252
  John (l) 252
  Katherine (l)(e) 252
  Margaret (l) 252
  Robert (l) 252
  William (l) 252, (w) 243
Barton (Berton)
  Elizabeth (l)(e) 341
  John 385, (l) 341, 649, (w) 418
  Mary (l) 649
  Robert (l) 341
  Thomas (l) 341, (w) 30, 130, 163, 659
Bartram, Thomas (l)(e) 776
Bartropp,
  Mary (l) 346
  Thomas (l)(e) 346

391

Vinca (l) 346
Barwick,
  Benjamin [Mr] (l) 612
  Hugh (l) 612
  James (l) 612
  Joan 612
  Richard (l) 612
  William [Mr] (l)(e) 612
Barwicke,
  Agnes (l) 612
  Elizabeth (l) 612
  John 612
  Mary (l) 612
Base, William 126
Basse,
  Edmund (e) 126, (w) 619
Bateman, John (w) 747
Batement, Anne (w) 206
Bathorne,
  Henry (w) 48
  Susan 528
  William 528
Baulden, Elizabeth (l) 649
Bawley, John (w) 332
Bawlye,
  Margaret (l) 367
  Robert 367
Baxter,
  Anne (l) 410
  Edmund (l) 60, (w) 554
  Edward 762, (e) 60
  George 825, (w) 160
  Giles (w) 766
  Isaac (l) 60
  James (l) 60
  Lawrence (w) 600
  Margaret (l) 60
  Marian (l) 256
  Nicholas (l) 60
  Peter 234, (l)(e) 256
  Richard (l) 60
  Susan (l)(e) 60
Baye, Miles 856
Baylye, John (w) 370
Beale,
  Anthony (l) 296
  Goodwife (l) 183
  Theodore (w) 412
Beales,
  Robert 11, (l)(e) 308
  Thomas (l) 580
Beame, wife (l) 179
Beamonds,
  John 332
  Susan (l) 332
Beamont (Bemond)
  Michael 213
  Stephen (w) 311
Beane,
  Elizabeth (l) 139
  Margaret (l)(e) 139
  William (e) 139, (w) 322
Beare, Jeffery (w) 521
Beart, Thomas 862
Beast, Margaret (l) 28

Beaton,
  Anne (l)(e) 53
  Richard (w) 53
Beck, Thomas 816
Becke,
  Frances (l) 713
  Nicholas (l) 713
  Peter (l) 713
  Susan (l) 713
  Thomas 713
Beckham,
  James 564
  John (l) 564
Beddall alias Ostiler, James 24
Bedell, William (w) 365
Bedford,
  Alice (l) 294
  Christopher 294
Bedingfeild, Francis (e) 252
Bedwall,
  John [Mr] (e)(w) 780
  Thomas (w) 616
  William (e)(w) 812
Bedwell,
  Mr 836
  T. (w) 572
  William 342
Beekes, Moses 833
Beere, Mistress (l) 179
Beerewaye, Alice (l) 35
Beetes,
  John (l) 316
  Katherine (l) 316
  Robert 316
  Seereine (l) 316
Beian, Robert (w) 849
Bele, Esther (l) 539
Belgrave, John (w) 790
Bell,
  Alice (w) 183
  Anne (l) 382
  Anthony (w) 484
  Joan (l) 382
  Katherine (l)(e) 484
  Martha (w) 484
  Mary (l) 382
  Reginald (w) 17
  Robert (l) 382
  Roger (w) 167, 697, 379
  Thomas (l) 382, (w) 703
  Zachary (l) 382
Bellman,
  Martin (l) 315
  Mary (l) 315
Bellowbie, William 114
Bemond see Beamont
Beniefeild, Thomas 131
Bennet,
  Andrew (l) 316
  Anne (l) 316
  Christian (l) 316
  Denis (l) 316
  Humphrey (i) 316
  John (l) 316
  Joseph (l) 316

Mary (l) 316
Robert 113
Susan (l) 316
Bennet alias Sweatman, Rebecca (l)(e) 53
Bennett,
  Anne (l)(e) 442
  Joan (l) 681
  Mary (l) 442
  Thomas (l) 442, (w) 489
Bennitt, Ralph (w) 612
Bens, Francis 11
Benson, Rose (l) 316
Bensted,
  Frances (l)(e) 416
  Peter (l) 426
  Robert (l) 416, (w) 416
  William (l) 416
  Zachary (l) 416
Bent, William 791
Bentham, Zachary (w) 142, 344, 806, 853
Bentley (Bentlie, Bently, Bentlye)
  Elizabeth (l)(e) 113
  John (w) 363
  Mr 38
  Rachel (l) 268
  Richard 34
  Robert 34
  Stephen (l)(e) 113
  Susan (l) 752
Benton, Mr 385
Berd see Bird
Bernes see Barnes
Berrie see Berry
Berriffe, Lydia (l) 502
Berry (Berrie)
  Ann (l) 679
  John 580
  Robert (l) 580
  Widow (l) 580
Bert, Elizabeth (w) 749
Berton see Barton
Betes see Betts
Betteney, Jeremy 465
Bettes see Betts
Bettony, Jeremy (w) 465
Betts (Betes, Bettes)
  Edmund (e) 725, (w) 300
  John (l) 427, (w) 777
  Saranna (l)(e) 817
  Stephen 384
Beutton, Anne (l) 328
Bevill, Elizabeth (l)(e) 6
Biat, Daniel (w) 458
Bickner 70
Bigg,
  Henry (l) 204
  John (l) 204
  Katherine (l)(e) 204
  Mary (l) 204
  Robert (l) 204
  Thomas (l) 204
Bigges (Byggs, Biggs)
  Ambrose (w) 82
  Anne (l) 649, 732
  John (l) 732, 800, (w) 867
  Katherine (l) 649

Margaret (e) 800
Mary (l) 40, 732
Thomas 40, 381, (l) 649, (w) 139, 233
William 657, 800
Biggs see Bigges
Bilham,
  Anne (l) 695
  Elizabeth (l) 695
  Robert (l) 695
  Thomas 6
Bilney, Abraham (w) 526
Bird (Berd, Birde, Burd, Burde, Byrd, Byrde)
  Agnes 294
  Anne (l)(e) 432
  Henry (l) 648
  Jane (l) 295
  John (l) 295, (w) 341, 565
  Katherine (l) 648
  Margaret (l) 315, 648
  Phoebe (l) 432
  Robert 145, (l)(e) 648, (w) 390
  Samuel (w) 877
  Susan (l) 315
  Thomas 294, (l)(e) 432, 648
Birde see Bird
Bishopp,
  Alice (l) 731
  Susan (l) 731
Bishoppe,
  John (l)(e) 861
  Mary (l) 861
  Robert (l) 861
  Thomas 135, (l)(w) 861
Blackaby (l) 380
Blackborne, George 91
Blackes, Margaret (w) 580
Blackwin, Henry (w) 569
Bland,
  Andrew (l) 488
  Anne (l) 409, 488
  Barbara (l)(e) 488
  Edmund (l) 488
  Edward (l) 488
  Frances (l) 488
  George (l) 488
  John (l) 488, (w) 270
  Mary (l) 409, 488
  Robert (l) 409
  Robert [Mr] 115
  Stephen (l) 409
  Susan (l)(e) 409, (w) 610
Blewet (Bluett, Bluette)
  Elizabeth (l) 257
  John 257, (w) 214, 757
  Mary (l) 257
  Nathaniel (l) 257
  Sarah (l) 257
Blogget, Elizabeth (w) 53
Bloggette,
  Anne (l)(e) 408
  John (l) 408
  Thomas (l) 408
Blome see Bloome
Blomefeild (Blomfeild, Blumfeilde)
  Anthony (w) 836
  Katharine (l) 85

393

William 112, (w) 85, 347
William the elder (e) 580
Bloome (Blome)
    Thomas 112, (w) 570
Blowe,
    Alice (l)(e) 138
    Barnaby (l) 138
    Elizabeth (l) 138
    Frances (l) 138
Blowein, Richard 113
Blowen, Richard (w) 113
Blower,
    Faith 580
    John (w) 382, 547, 571
    Joshua (w) 395, 845
    Mr (l) 563
    Peter (w) 845
Bluett see Blewet
Bluette see Blewet
Blumfeilde see Blomefeild
Blye, Philip (w) 560
Blyth, William (l)(e) 647
Blythe,
    James (w) 647
    Ralph senior (w) 565
    Thomas the elder (e) 215
    Thomas [Mr] (e) 698
Boalley, Robert (e) 795
Boarom, William (w) 847
Bobie, Christopher senior (w) 301
Bobye,
    Anne (l) 97, 301
    Christopher 97, (l)(e) 301
    Dorothy (w) 149
    Nicholas (l) 301
    Robert (l) 301
Boce, William (w) 734
Boldero,
    Edward (l) 602
    Elizabeth (l) 602
    George (l) 602
    Henry (l) 602
    Mary (l)(e) 602
Bond,
    John (w) 147
    Nicholas (w) 866
    Susan (l) 662
Bone,
    Mathias (w) 868
    Nicholas (w) 868
Bonner, Anne (l) 435
Boolin,
    Anne (l)(e) 479
    Walter (l) 479
Boone,
    John (l)(e) 658
    Sarah (l) 658
Booth,
    Abigail (l) 249
    Elizabeth (l) 249
    Henry (l) 249
    John (l) 249
    Mary (l) 249
    Nathan (l) 249
    Richard (l) 249
    Robert (l) 249

Thomas (l)(e) 249
Boothe, Robert (w) 249
Borbart, Robert (w) 428
Borley, Thomas (w) 39, 550
Borough see also Burrowe
    John (l) 43
    Rebecca (l) 43
    Rose (l) 43
    Thomas (l)(e) 43
Borrows, Stephen 6 399
Botthamley, John (w) 121
Bougen,
    Francis (e) 690
    Margaret (l)(e) 690
Bouging,
    Frances (l) 74
    Francis (l) 74
    Giles (l) 74
    Lydia (l) 74
    Thomas (l) 74
Bouginge,
    Elizabeth (l) 59
    Frances 59
    Francis (l) 59
    Giles 59
    Margaret (l) 59
    Thomas 59
Boulye, Mary (l) 831
Bovell alias Lanur, Thomas 128
Bowe, Anne (w) 523
Bowen, John (w) 658
Bowes, William (l) 6080
Bowgen, Francis (w) 690
Bowier, Henry 112
Bowle,
    Alice (l) 634
    Anne (l) 634
    David (l) 634
    Fernando (l) 634
    Joan (l) 634
    John 171
    Robert (l) 634
    Thomasine (l) 634
Bowler, Alice (l) 160
Bowles,
    Frances (l) 641
    Mary (l) 659
    William (l) 641
Bowman,
    Elizabeth (l) 180
    John (l) 180
Bowser, Henry (w) 422
Boxe,
    Anne 66
    Simon (e) 45
Boyton,
    Edward 29
    George (l) 29
    John (l) 29
    Susan (l)(e) 29
Braby, James (w) 753
Brackells, Thomas (l) 731
Bradley,
    Abraham (w) 811
    Anthony (l) 426
Bradnam, James (l) 640

394

Bradnham,
  Dorothy (l) 279
  Mary (l)(e) 279
Bradys, Thomas (w) 840
Braen, John (l) 868
Bragg, John (e) 606
Bragge 873
Brame,
  George (w) 433
  Philippa (l) 183
Bramfeld, William (w) 590
Brampton,
  Frances 147
  John 147
Branch, Henry (l) 503
Brand,
  Benjamin (l) 664
  Constance (l) 468
  Edmund (l) 468
  Henry (l) 468
  James (l) 664
  John (l) 664, (w) 451
  Joseph (l) 664
  Marion (l)(e) 842
  Mistress 316
  Richard (w) 333
  Susanna (l)(e) 664
  William 266
Branston, Walter (w) 584
Bray,
  Ann (l) 93
  Nicholas 93
Bredges see Bridges
Brett,
  Grace (l) 173
  Robert (l) 89, (w) 318, 342
  Sarah (l) 268
  Thomas (e) 78
  William 812, (w) 140, 891
Brettam, Elizabeth (l) 436
Bretten,
  Elizabeth (l) 327
  Thomas (l) 327
Bretton 218
Brewerton,
  Alice (l) 121
  Anne (l) 121
  Clement (l) 121
  Elizabeth (l) 121
  John (l)(e) 121
  Thomas (l) 121
  Ursula (l) 121
Brewett, Thomas (w) 246
Brewster,
  Ambrose (l) 35
  John (l) 35
  Martha (l) 35
  Thomas (l) 35
  William 35, (l) 35
Briant see Bryant
Bridge,
  Elizabeth (l) 355, (l)(e) 131
  Giles 455, (w) 73
  John (l) 131, (w) 441
  Margaret (l) 355
  Ralph (l)(e) 355

Reginald (l) 355
Reuben (w) 288, 604
Robert (l) 131
Thomas (w) 125, 355
William (e) 872, (l) 131
Bridges (Bredges),
  Ambrose (w) 855
  Anne (l) 5, (w) 749
  John 791
  Katherine (l) 657
  William (l) 657
Bridgham see Brigham
Bridon,
  Ann (l)(e) 497
  Henry (l) 497
  Jasper (l) 497
  John (w) 824
  William 497
Brigham (Bridgham) (l) 713
  John 713
Bright,
  Ann (l) 703
  Henry [Mr] (w) 886
Brightall,
  Henry (l) 518
  Martha (l) 518
  Mary (l)(e) 518
  Robert (w) 394
Brightwaie, John (w) 684
Brightwell, William (w) 233, 436
Brincknell, John (w) 878
Brinkly,
  John (l) 868
  Martha (l)(e) 868
  Thomasine (l) 868
Brinknell, John (w) 643
Bristo, Arthur 876
Britall, Simon (w) 487
Brock,
  Reginald (l) 752
  Thomas 752
  William (e) 589
Brocke,
  Alice (l)(e) 752
  Elisas (l) 752
  William (l) 752
Brome (Broome),
  Alexander (w) 401
  George (w) 22
  John (w) 339
Brond, John (w) 7
Bronwyne, William (w) 115
Brooke,
  Agnes (w) 571
  Alice (l) 95
  Anne (l) 395
  Daniel (l) 828
  George (l) 55
  Grace (l) 115
  John (l)(e) 55
  Lea (l) 395
  Margaret (l)(e) 887
  Martha (l)(e) 828
  Mary (l) 580, (l)(e) 55
  Rebecca (l) 95
  Robert (e) 95, (w) 429

395

Thomas (e) 580, 739, (l) 95
William (l) 887, (l)(e) 55
Brooks (Brookes),
  Frances 619
  John (w) 643
  Roger (l) 619
  Widow 619
Browne (Brown),
  Alice (l) 452, 678
  Anne (l)(e) 311
  Anthony 544
  Arkknoll (w) 218
  Caleb 381, (w) 139
  Dorothy (l) 544
  Elizabeth (l) 257, 729, (l)(e) 525
  Francis 257
  George 358, (l) 452
  Hannah (l) 502
  Henry 358
  Hester (l) 677
  Isaac 268, (l) 311
  Jane (l) 411, 544
  Joan (l)(e) 362, 892
  John 544, (l) 51, 311, 653, (l)(e) 544, (w) 706
  Katherine (l) 452
  Mary (l) 311, 452, (w) 381
  Millicent (l) 616
  Nicholas the elder 51
  Nicholas (w) 51
  Reginald 677
  Richard 653, (l) 77, 452
  Richard the elder (w) 55
  Robert 131, 611, (l) 311, 452, (w) 223, 717
  Roger (w) 412
  Sarah (l) 544
  Simon 411
  Stephen 97
  Susan (l)(e) 176
  Thomas 263, 467, (l) 452, (w) 84, 104
  William 148, 268, (l) 452, (w) 132, 178, 450, 500
Brownesmithe, Edward (l) 612
Brownesmyth,
  Andrew (w) 758
  John (w) 758
Browning, Thomas 88
Bruers,
  Cornelius 839
  Rose (l) 839
  Susan (l) 839
Brundishe, James 384
Brunning, John (w) 219, 617
Bryan, Thomas (l)(e) 80
Bryant,
  Agatha (l) 113
  John 217, (w) 334, 373
  Mary (l) 146
  Matthew (l) 114
  Thomas (e)(w) 550, (w) 272
  William 113
Bryce, Edmund (w) 409
Bryde,
  John 157
  Mary (l)(e) 157
Bubbe, Nicholas (w) 384
Bucher, Richard (w) 238

Buckenham (Bucknam),
  George (w) 720
  Henry 296
  Henry [Sir] 791
  John (w) 468
Buckle,
  Anne (l)(e) 105
  Richard (l) 440
  Robert (w) 58
Bucknam see Buckenham
Budley,
  Elizabeth (l)(e) 212
  John (l) 212
Buers, William 559
Bugg, Francis (w) 319, 752, 834
Bugge,
  Francis (w) 750
  John (w) 38
  Robert (w) 340
  Thomas (e)(w) 275
Bulbrock, Stephen (w) 193
Bulbrook, John (w) 482
Bulbrooke,
  James (l) 315
  John (w) 89
Bull,
  Frances (l) 640
  Henry (w) 144
  Richard (w) 341, 756
  William 640
Buller,
  Anne (l) 117
  Robert 117
Bullocke,
  Dorothy (l) 207
  Elizabeth (l) 207
  Jeffery (l) 207
  Ralph (l)(e) 207
  Robert (l) 207
  Thomas (l)(e) 207
Bullwarde, Mr 531
Bullyne, Walter (w) 529
Bulman, Richard (w) 253
Bulmer, John (w) 883
Bulwer, Robert (w) 272
Bumpsted, Francis 237
Bumsted,
  Edward 810
  Elizabeth (l)(e) 458
  John (l) 458
  Mary (l) 810
  Robert (l) 458
  Thomas (l) 458
  William (l) 810
Bun, Robert (w) 387
Bund, Charles (l) 807
Buninge,
  Bridget (l) 877
  John (l) 877
  Mary (l) 877
  Thomas (l) 877
Buntinge,
  Anne (l) 418
  John 418
  Richard (l) 418

396

397

Campine, Rachel (w) 656
Campion,
  Edmund (l) 99
  Elizabeth (l) 99
  Joan (l) 99
  John (l) 99
  Nicholas (l) 99
  Richard (l)(e) 99
Camplin, John (l) 456
Camplyn alias Campill see Camphill alias Camplyn
Candler, Mr (l) 627
Canford,
  Alice (l) 253
  Benjamin (l) 253
  Richard (l) 253
  Robert (l) 253
Canforth,
  Isabel (l)(e) 426
  Richard 630, (l)(e) 426
Canham,
  John (l)(e) 667
  Mary (l) 667
  Richard (l) 667
  Robert (l) 667
  Rose (l) 667
  Samuel (w) 368
  Stephen (l) 667
  Thomas (l) 667
Cannam, William (w) 265
Cannt see Cant
Cansby, Margaret (l) 847
Canston,
  Anne (l) 599
  Isaac (l) 599
  John (l) 599
  Thomas (l) 599
Cant (Cannt, Cante),
  Katherine (l) 164
  Richard (w) 794
  Susan (w) 784
Cante see Cant
Capp,
  Anne (l) 376
  John (l) 376, (w) 782
  Thomas (l) 376
Cappe, William (w) 373
Carleton see Carlton
Carliells, Randolph (w) 346
Carlton (Carleton)
  Edniah (l) 38
  Edward (l) 38
  Elizabeth (l) 38, (l)(e) 38
  Erasmus (l) 38
  Henry (l) 38
  John (l) 38
  Philip (l) 38
  Richard (l) 38
  Robert 798, (l) 38 (w) 61, 333, 455, 515, 556,
    830, 842
  Thomas (l) 38
  William (e) 9, (l) 38
Carpenter,
  John 11
  Mary (l) 11, (w) 505
  William 505

Carr,
  Anne (l)(e) 635
  Mr (l) 627
Carrell, John [Sir] 738
Carsbury, Robert (w) 630
Cartar see Carter
Carter (Cartar)
  Alice (l) 149
  Andrew (l) 149
  Anne (l) 149
  Edward (l) 307
  George [Mr] 663
  George (w) 54, 312, 338, 460, 740, 818
  Gregory (w) 173
  John 189, (l)(e) 149, (w) 422
  Margaret (w) 460
  Marian (l)(e) 307
  Mr (l) 818
  Nathaniel (l) 149
  Richard (l) 751
  Robert 93
  Thomas 737, (l) 149, (l)(e) 74, (w) 59, 608
Cartner, Elizabeth (l) 400
Cartwrite, Edmund 263
Casbon see Casburne
Casborne see Casburne
Casburne (Casbon, Casborne, Caseburne),
  Alice (l) 153, 865
  John 153, (e) 865, (l) 865, (w) 418, 576
  Margaret (l)(e) 153
  Robert 23, (e) 865, (l) 153, (l)(w) 865 (w) 404,
    406
  Thomas 153, (l) 153, 865
  William (l) 153, 865
Caseburne see Casburne
Casen, Mabel (l) 135
Cason,
  Anne 502, (w) 200
  Thomas (l) 502
  William (l) 502
Cassam, William (w) 142
Castleton, William 45
Catchpoole, Gabriel (l)(e) 205
Cater,
  Alice (l) 141
  Elizabeth (l) 141
  John 622, (l)(e) 141, (w) 37
  Katherine (l) 141
  Margaret (l) 158
  Mary (l) 158, 848
  Peter (w) 8
  Ralph (l)(e) 158
  Thomas (l) 141 (l)(e) 848
  William 848
Catherall (l) 350
Catlen see Catlin
Catlin (Catlen),
  Anne (l) 684
  Elizabeth (l) 684
  Margaret (l) 684
  Thomas (l) 684
  Zachary (w) 504
Catton,
  John (w) 772
  Temperance (l) 808

Vincent (w) 765
William (w) 685
Cockermore, Ann (l) 713
Cocksadge, Martin (e) 80
Cocksedge (Coxsage)
  Alice (l) 845
  Anne (l) 268
  John 268, 845
  Luke 194
Codd,
  Frances 112
  Miles 112
Codde, Frances (w) 145
Codwell, William 875
Coe 709
  Henry (l) 816, (w) 81
  Judith (l) 816
  Margaret (l)(e) 816
Coell see Cole
Coggshall, John (w) 15
Coke see Cooke
Cokes alias Slacke, Mary (l) 723
Cokey, Nicholas (l) 56
Colbey, Samuel (w) 24
Colby, Rachel 684
Colbye, Samuel (w) 626
Coldham, John (l) 560
Coldom, Grace (l)(e) 448
Cole (Coell) 101
  Anne (l)(e) 466
  Elizabeth (l)(e) 393
  John 664, (l)(e) 393
  Robert 466
  Thomas 398, 825, (l) 568, (w) 101, 349
Coleman see Coleman
Colle, Robert (w) 297
Coller, John 784
Collin (Colline, Collyn), (l) 768
  Edward (l) 379
  John 343
  Robert (l)(e) 505
  Susan (l) 433
  Walter (w) 547
Colline see Collin
Collinge see Collin
Collyn see Collin
Collyns, wife (l) 379
Colman (Coleman),
  Henry (w) 225, 420
  Mary (l) 113
  Robert 543, (w) 401
  Samuel (w) 543
  Thomas 113, (w) 405, 543
  William 845, 869, (p) 886, (w) 401
Colt (Coult),
  Elizabeth (l) 201
  Henry [Sir] 17
  John (l) 201
Combes,
  Edward (l) 465
  John (e)(w) 465, (l) 465
  Margaret (l)(e) 465
Compton, George (w) 483
Comsbye, John (w) 893
Coo, John (w) 56
Coocke see Cooke

Cooke (Coocke), 183
  Abigail (l) 286
  Agnes (l) 531
  Alexander (l) 401
  Anne (l) 129, 625
  Anthony 294, (e) 601, (w) 17
  Bridget (l) 601
  Christian (l)(e) 401
  Edith (l) 543
  Edmund (l) 129
  Edward (l) 401
  Elizabeth (l) 129, 375, 543, (l)(e) 129
  Ellis (l) 401
  George (l) 401, 611
  Gregory (w) 625
  Henry 225, (l) 543
  Holefernes (l) 857
  Honoria (l) 654
  Isaac (l)(e) 625
  James (l) 286, 625, (w) 695
  Jane (l) 654
  Joan (l) 601
  John 45, 857, (l) 129, 375, 543, 601, 625, (w) 129, 158, 175, 654
  Judith (l) 543
  Katherine (l)(e) 286
  Margaret (l) 654, 857
  Martha (l) 857
  Mary (l) 375, 531
  Nathaniel (w) 375
  Rebecca (l) 654
  Richard 45, 543, (e) 857, (l)(e) 543
  Robert 857, (l) 129, 286, 375, 490, 625, (l)(e) 531
  Roger (l) 543, (w) 654
  Rose (l) 375
  Samuel (l) 543
  Stephen (e) 654, (l) 857
  Thomas 5, 294, 528, (l) 129, 375, 531, 543, 625
  Timothy (l) 286
  wife (l) 367
  William 367, (l) 531, 857, (l)(e) 375
Cooper see also Cowper,
  Alice (l) 160
  Anne (l) 692, (w) 735
  Barsheborne 342
  Edward (l)(e) 692
  George (l) 160
  Henry (l) 418
  James (l) 692
  Joan (l) 692
  John 692, (l)(e) 692
  Mistress (l) 372
  Richard 365, (l) 160, 488, (w) 160, 394
  Robert 296, (l)(e) 692
  Sarah (l) 757
  Thomas (l)(e) 692, (w) 865
  wife (l) 365
  William 418, 757
Cooper alias Robinson,
  James (l)(e) 639
  Robert (l) 639
  William (l) 639
Coosten,
  Elizabeth (l) 755
  Frances (l) 755

401

402

John 650
Robert (l) 650
William (w) 252
Deareslie *see* Derisly
Deareslye *see* Derisly
Deareson,
  John (l) 573
  Mary (l) 573
  Richard 573
  Thomas (l) 573
Dearman,
  Henry (l) 293
  Prudence (l) 293
  Reuben 293
  Robert (l) 293
  Thomasine (l) 293
  William (l)(e) 293
Dearsley *see* Derisley
Dearslye *see* Derisley
Death, George 5, 413
Debenhall, Robert (w) 866
Debnam,
  Edmund (l) 587
  Edward (l) 587
  John (l) 587
  Mary (l)(e) 587
  Roger (l) 587
  Thomas (l) 587
Dedman 629
  Thomas (l) 629
Dednam, William 445
Deekes, John (e)(w) 299
Deeks (Deikes),
  Isaac (w) 855
  John (w) 854
Degon, Bartholomew (w) 849
Deikes *see* Deeks
Delamare, Thomas 363
Denmer, Anthony 543
Dennant, Walter (l)(e) 42
Dennell, Thomas (w) 355
Dennye,
  Arthur (l) 490
  George (l) 490
  John 490
  Mary (l)(e) 490
  Nathaniel (l) 490
  Robert 490, (w) 801
  Thomas (l) 490, (w) 490
  William (w) 490
Denton, John (w) 597
Denys, Richard (w) 892
Dereslye *see* Derisley
Derisley (Deareslie, Deareslye, Dearsley,
    Dearslye, Dersly),
  Anne (l) 622
  Charles (w) 672
  Francis (w) 343
  George (l) 622
  Hannah (l) 729
  Jeffrey (w) 393
  John (w) 337, 622
  Thomas (w) 228, 349, 741
  Walter (w) 343, 672
Dersey,
  John (l) 773

Mary (l) 773
Samuel (l) 773
Susan (l) 773
Thomas (l) 773
William (l) 773
Dersly *see* Derisley
Devereux (Deverex, Deverux),
  John (w) 264
  Mr (l) 498
  Peter (e) 9, 416
Deverex *see* Devereux
Deverux *see* Devereux
Devonshire, Earl of 241
Devorickes, Mr (l) 627
Dex, Nicholas (w) 653
Dey (Deye) *see also* Day
  John (l)(w) 282
  Nicholas (l) 780
  Robert 282
  Thomas 780
Deye *see* Dey
Dickson, William 608
Diesden,
  Ann (l)(e) 666
  Elizabeth (l) 666
  William (l) 666
Dillamore,
  Rose 323
  Thomas 323
Disborough, George (w) 78
Disborowe, Anthony (w) 258, 362
Disse, Robert (l) 787
Dister, Elizabeth (l)(w) 40
Dix (Dixe),
  Elizabeth (l) 177
  Oliver (l) 177
  Rachel (l) 177
  Richard (l) 177, (w) 20
  Susan (l) 177
  Thomas (l) 177
  William (l)(e) 177
Dixe *see* Dix
Dobbes *see* Dobbs
Dobbs (Dobbes)
  Agnes (l) 34
  Alice (l)(e) 34
  Anne (l) 85
  Frances (l) 85
  John (l)(e) 85
  Margaret (l) 85
  Robert (l) 85
  Thamar (l) 85
  Thomas (l) 34
  William (l) 34
Docker,
  Grace (l) 627
  Thomas (l) 627
Dockine *see* Docking
Docking,
  Agnes (l) 870, (w) 870
  Anne (l) 614
  John (l) 614
  Katherine (l)(e) 614
  Richard (l) 614
  Thomas (l) 614

405

Doe,
  Anne (l) 778
  Edmund 778
  John (l) 280
  Robert (l) 2880
  Stephen (l)(e) 86
  William (l) 68
Donnell, Thomas (w) 70
Donnett, Thomas (w) 534
Doughty (Dowghtie, Dowtie),
  Stephen 871, (l) 435, (w) 475
Douglas, Cicely (l) 593
Dove,
  Anne (l) 427
  Richard (l) 427
Dowe,
  Anne (l) 451, (l)(e) 451
  Richard (l) 34, (w) 798, 842
  Thomas (l) 451
Dowghtie see Doughty
Downam see Downham
Downes, Thomas (w) 818
Downham (Downam),
  Bridget (l) 335, 608
  Elizabeth (e) 335, (l) 335, 608
  James (l) 335, 608
  Jane (l) 608
  Joan (l) 608
  John (l) 335, 608
  Joseph (l) 335, (l)(e) 608
  Samuel (l) 335, 608
  Thomas (l) 335, 608
Downsdale,
  Priscilla (l)(e) 215
  Ralph (l) 215
  Roger (l) 215
  William (l) 215
Dowsen see Dowsing
Dowsin see Dowsing
Dowsing (Dowsen, Dowsin),
  John (l) 90, (l)(e) 14, (w) 785
  Robert (l) 90
  Thomas (l) 90, (l)(e) 14
Dowtie see Doughty
Drake,
  John (l)(e) 610, (w) 637
  Margaret (l)(e) 860
  William (l) 610, 860
Draper,
  Anne (l)(e) 470
  Edward (l)(e) 891
  Mary (l) 891
  Richard (w) 512
  Robert (l)(e) 470, (w) 796
  Susan (l)(e) 470
  Thomas (l) 891
Drewery see Drury
Drifte, John 631
Drinkmylke,
  Gregory (l) 290
  Mary (l) 290
Drurie see Drury
Drury (Drewery, Drurie, Drurye),
  Anne (l) 593
  Dorothy (l) 593
  Jane (l) 514

John (w) 39, 674
Mr 38
Roger (l) 593
Sarah (l)(e) 593
Seckford (l) 593
Drurye see Drury
Ducke, Peter (w) 894
Ducklen,
  Alice (l) 880
  Anne (l) 880
  William 880
Duckling, William (l) 800
Duffild, Phillipa (l) 632
Duisburgh, Anthony (w) 546
Duncon (Dunkon), 183
  John 339, (l) 147
  Judith (l) 147
  Susan (l) 183
Dundon,
  John (l) 147
  Judith (l) 147
Dune, Henry (w) 626
Dunkon see Duncon
Dunnyngham, Richard 349
Durent, John (w) 720
Durrant,
  John 836
  Mary (l)(e) 836
  Nicholas (l) 836
  Robert (l)(e) 836
Durrante, Walter (e) 570
Dutton,
  Richard 532
  Rose (l) 532, (w) 197
Dyke, Mathias (w) 351

Eagle,
  John (l) 45, (w) 30
  Robert the elder 752
  Robert (l) 45, 752
Ealsinge see Elsinge
Earle, Toby 816
Eason, Susan (w) 755
Eason alias Cutbert,
  George 534
  Henry (l) 534
  Mary (l) 534
  Thomas (l) 534
Eastgates, Edmund 35
Easton, Thomas (w) 252
Eaton 327
  Francis (e) 885
  William 128
Ecie, Thomas 692
Edes, Organ (w) 334
Edgar,
  Ezechiel 324
  Susan (l) 324
Edgore, Richard 470
Edmond, Anne (l) 288
Edmundes,
  Margaret (l) 796
  Mary (l) 796
Edwardes, Francis (l) 216
Edwards,
  Audry (l) 366

Elizabeth (l)(e) 366
Nicholas (l)(e) 366
Thomas (l) 366
Thomas senior (w) 70
William (w) 70
Eggett (Egott),
Bridget (l) 104
Elizabeth (l)(e) 61
John (l) 61
Robert (l) 61
Thomas (l) 61
Egott see Eggett
Elcocke,
John (l) 179
Richard (w) 259
Eldred,
Elizabeth (l)(e) 463
John (e) 350, (l) 350, (w) 234
John [Mr] 825
Thomas (l) 463
William (l) 350, 463
Eley (Elye),
Francis (l) 189
John (l) 77
Robert (l)(e) 77
Thomas (w) 94, 330
Eliott see Elliott
Elis see Ellis
Elles see Ellis
Ellet see Elliott
Elligood,
Elizabeth (l) 482
Frances (l) 482
Henry (l) 482
Jane (l)(e) 184
Mary (l) 482, (l)(e) 482
Robert (l) 482
Sarah (l) 482
Thomas (l) 482
Elliott (Eliott, Ellet, Ellitt),
Alice (l) 659
Anne (w) 590
Charles (w) 767, 775
Elizabeth (l)(e) 470
Susan 814
Thomas (l) 470
William 659
Ellis (Elis, Elles),
Francis (w) 592
Henry (e) 803
John (l) 853
Mary (l) 853
Nicholas 346
Thomas (l) 346, (w) 592
Thomazine (l) 81
William 346, (w) 879
Elliston,
Edward [Mr] (l)(e) 502
William (w) 754
Ellistone,
Edward (l) 471
Henshawe (w) 471
Ellitt see Elliott
Elmer, John (w) 524
Elsden,
Edward (w) 842

Francis 207
Mary (l) 667
Valentine (w) 611
Elsen, William 872
Elsinge (Ealsinge)
Alice (l) 873
Edward (w) 602
John 199
Elson, Anne (w) 197
Elye see Eley
Emduce (l) 205
Emsden, William (e) 522
Emyns,
Elizabeth (l) 287
Mary (l) 287
Robert the elder (w) 666
Robert (w) 287, 666
Roger (w) 236
Susan (l)(e) 287
English (Englishe, Inglishe),
Elizabeth (l) 233, 381, 717
Joan (l)(e) 233
Mary (l) 118, 381
Robert 119
Susan (l) 118, 119
Erie,
George (l) 17
Jeffery (l)(e) 17
Joan (l) 17
Margaret (l) 17
Estow,
Edward (l) 724
Mary (l) 724
Ethelred,
Elizabeth (l) 597
Mary (l) 597
Evans, Richard 73
Everard (Evered),
Ambrose (l) 520, 537, (w) 761
Dorothy (l) 520
Elizabeth (l) 520
Frances (l) 678
John [Mr] 66, (w) 762
Martha (l) 520
Mary (l) 66
Mercy (l) 853
Richard (l) 520, 854, (w) 141, 537
Robert (w) 323
Sarah (l)(e) 520
Thomas 267, (w) 141
Evered see Everard
Everit see Everitt
Everitt,
Anne (l) 142
Joan (l) 142
Margaret (l) 142
Mary (l) 142, (w) 806
Robert (l)(e) 142, (w) 806
Ezard, Mirable (l) 109

Fann,
Elizabeth (l) 248
Henry 248
Farmer, Anne (l) 797
Farr,
Anne (l) 691

407

408

Sarah (l) 723
Thomas (l) 5, (w) 118
Fordum see Fordham
Foredom see Fordham
Forman, Richard (l) 410
Fornham,
  Anthony (l)(e) 524
  Dorothy (l)(e) 524
Foskue,
  John the elder (l) 649
  John (l) 649
Foster,
  Ann (l) 502
  George 812
  Thomas (w) 792
  widow 218
Fothergell, Richard (w) 187
Fothergill,
  Elizabeth (l) 461
  John (e) 461, (w) 420
Fowle,
  John (l) 150
  Michael (l) 150
Fowler,
  James 101
  Robert 694
Fox,
  Robert 833
  Thomas (w) 436
Foxton, Robert (w) 259
Francige, John (w) 591
Francis,
  John 363, (w) 37
  John the elder (w) 427
  John the younger 427
  Katherine (l)(e) 322
  Mary (l) 427
  Robert (l) 427
Francis alias Farrowe, Edmund (l)(e) 392
Franck see Franke
Francke see Franke
Franke (Franck, Francke), 350
  Alice (l) 777
  Anne (l) 777
  Charles (l) 777
  Edmund (l) 191
  Isaac (w) 62
  Jane (l) 777
  John 60, (l) 191, 777, (l)(e) 777
  Judy (l) 191
  Margaret (l)(e) 191
  Mary (l) 777
  Samuel (w) 60
  Thomas (l) 191
Franncis, John (l)(e) 637
Franncis alias Reeve,
  Katherine (w) 534
  Susan (l) 534
  Thomas (l) 534
Frary, James (w) 354
Freanch see French
Freiston, Thomas (w) 153, 406
Freman,
  William (e)(w) 812, (w) 90, 891
French (Freanch, Frenche), 84
  Barbara (l) 302

Benjamin (w) 722
Edward (e) 485
George 302, (w) 184
George [Mr] (e)(w) 625
Henry (w) 568
Joan (l) 207
John (e) 581, (w) 298
Margaret (l)(e) 302
Susan (w) 335
William 207, (l) 422
Frenche see French
Frend (Frende),
  Barbara (l) 843
  Elizabeth (l) 234
  George (l) 218
  John (l) 218
  Joseph (l) 218
  Mary (l) 218
  Roger 218, (l) 218
  Rose (l) 218
  Thomas (l) 218
Frende see Frend
Freston (Fryston),
  Thomas 223, (l)(e) 274
Frethes, Thomas (w) 741
Frost,
  Abigail (l) 566
  Abraham (l) 115
  Agnes (l) 189, 196
  Alice (l) 171, 775
  Ambrose 485
  Anne (l) 66, 196, 455, (l)(e) 237, 508
  Bridget (l) 115, 196
  Edmund (w) 785
  Elizabeth (l) 66, 115, 196, 775
  Frances (l) 294
  Gabriel (l) 237
  George 655, (l) 455, 775, (w) 336, 647
  Henry (l) 455, 675, (w) 34
  James 219, (l)(e) 566
  John 174, 294, (l) 66, 68, 171, 508, 566,
    (l)(e) 66, (w) 148, 466, 778
  Judith (l) 219
  Lettice (l) 196
  Lydia (l) 115
  Margaret (l) 115, 455
  Marian (l) 455, (l)(e) 294
  Martha (l) 827
  Mary (l) 115, 196, 508
  Prudence (l)(e) 566
  Richard 242, 267, (l) 503, (l)(e) 775, (w) 566
  Robert (l) 294, 455, 775, (w) 198, 466
  Roger 294
  Rose (l) 66
  Sarah (l) 115
  Simon (l)(e) 171
  Susan (l) 171, 775
  Thomas (e) 508, (l) 66, 171, 237, (w) 566, 796
  Vincent 115
  William (l) 171, 775, (w) 114, 578, 595
Fryer,
  Anne (l) 616
  Edward (w) 346
  John (l)(e) 616
  Thomasine (l) 616
Fryston see Freston

Frythe, John (w) 687
Fulcher, John 147
Fuller,
    Agnes (l) 630, (l)(e) 199
    Alice (l) 162
    Anne (l) 162, 199, 631, (l)(e) 162
    Arthur 335
    Audrey (l) 647
    Charles (l) 162
    Elizabeth (l) 630
    Frances (l) 199, 631, (l)(e) 631
    Francis (l) 199, 631
    Giles (w) 159
    James (l) 162, (w) 309
    John 565, (l) 154, 162, 596, 631
    Margaret (l) 199, 596
    Mary (l) 631
    Richard 199, (l) 199, 631
    Robert (l) 199, 630, 631, (l)(e) 637, (w) 72, 140,
        186, 239, 309, 510
    Stephen (l) 162
    Thomas (l) 154, 630, (w) 133, 274, 769
    William 114, 630, (l) 206, (l)(e) 596
Fuller alias Snow, William (l)(e) 778
Futter,
    Elizabeth (l)(e) 726
    Richard 726
Fydler, John 511
Fyler, Nicholas (l) 31
Fynch see Finch
Fyrmage,
    John (w) 180
    Mr 694
Fyrman (Firmyn),
    Richard 543
    Thomas (l) 148
Fysher, Edward (w) 425
Fyske,
    Edward (l)(e) 549
    Jeremy (e) 388
Fyson see Fison
Fytch 839
Fytt,
    Andrew 655
    James (l) 187
    Thomas 187

Gage, William 263
Gages,
    Anne (l)(e) 193
    Humphrey (l) 193
    Margaret (l) 193, 736, (l)(e) 736
    Richard (l) 193
    Susan (l) 193, 736
    Theodore (l) 193, 736
    Thomas (e) 193, (l) 736
Gagge, John (w) 600
Gainford (Gaynford),
    Anne (l) 403
    Gabriel 403, (l) 403
    John (l) 403
    John the elder (e) 403
    Peter 403
    Rose 403
    Thomas (l) 403

William (l) 403
Gale,
    Joan (w) 590
    Robert 225
Gallant,
    George 816
    William (l) 872
Gamage,
    John (w) 839
    Mary (l)(e) 582
    Thomas (l) 581
Game,
    Alice (l) 188
    Frances (l) 186
    Joan (l) 188
    Robert (l) 186
    Susan (l)(e) 186
Garard see Garrard
Gardener see Gardiner
Gardiner (Gardener, Gardner),
    Elizabeth (l)(e) 687
    Frances (l) 545
    George (w) 731
    Henry (w) 388
    John (l) 732, 818, (w) 474, 657
    Margaret (l) 545
    Mary (l) 545
    Philip (l) 818
    Richard 5, 265, 657, (l) 474, (w) 82, 87, 267,
        601, 657, 691, 732, 761, 855
    Robert the elder 612
    Thomas 818, (l) 732, (w) 82, 691
Gardner see Gardiner
Garland, Thomas 342
Garneham see Garnham
Garner,
    Barnaby (w) 20, 426
    Mary (l) 865
Garnham (Garneham, Garnon),
    John 742, 856, (e) 589, (w) 742
    John junior (w) 589
    Nicholas (e)(l) 856
    Rose (l)(e) 856
Garnon see Garnham
Garrad see Garrard
Garrade see Garrard
Garrard (Garard, Garrad, Garrade, Garrod),
    Andrew 551
    Ann (l)(e) 684
    John 751, (l) 684, (w) 118
    Katherine (l) 684
    Mary (l) 684, 832
    Philip 291, (w) 712
    Robert (l)(e) 684
    Thomas (l) 684
    William (w) 765
Garret, John (l) 425
Garrett, John (w) 12
Garrod see Garrard
Garvie,
    Dorcas (l) 713
    John 713
    Rebecca 713
    Susan (l) 713
Gary, Samuel (w) 640
Gaskines, John 125

410

411

412

Goslinge (Goslen, Goslin, Goslyn, Gostlin, Gostlyn),
  Anne (l) 67
  Elizabeth (l) 67
  George (l) 67
  James (l) 67
  Katherine (w) 67
  John (w) 364, 403, 676
  Priscilla (l) 67
  Robert (l) 67
  Thomas (l)(e) 67
  Thomas [Mr] 228
  William(l) 67
Goslyn see Goslinge
Gosnold,
  Bridget (l) 740
  Daniel (l) 740
  Frances (l)(e) 740
  Francis (l) 740
  John (l) 740
  Thomas (l) 740
Goss see Gosse
Gosse (Goss),
  Agnes (l) 720
  Diana (l) 720
  Dorothy (l) 715, 720
  Edward (l) 720
  Elizabeth (l) 715, 720
  George (l)(e) 720
  Judah (l) 720
  Judith (l)(e) 715
  Margaret (l) 720
  Rose (l) 720
  William (l) 715, 720
Gostlin see Goslinge
Gostlyn see Goslinge
Gotheram, John (w) 433
Gotobed, Richard 871
Goulde,
  Mary (l) 597
  Richard 597
Goulding,
  Joan (l) 167
  John 167, (l)(e) 167
  Mark (l) 167
  Richard (l) 167
  Robert (l) 167
  Roger (l) 167
  Thomas (l) 167
  William (l) 167
Goulston,
  Edward (e) 812
  Mary (l) 257, (w) 257
  Robert 257
  Thomas 745
Goymer,
  Robert (w) 521
  Stephen (w) 219
Grandsborough, William (w) 556
Grange, William (w) 468
Granger (Graunger),
  Anthony (w) 648
  Elizabeth (l) 59, 74, 690
  Giles (l) 690
  John (l)(e) 59, 74
  Margaret (l) 690

  Samuel (w) 537
  Thomas (l) 690
  William (l) 690
Grate, Thomas (w) 817
Graunger see Granger
Grave (Grayve),
  Frances 885
  Robert (l) 327, (l)(e) 327
  Susan (l) 327
  William 327
Gravett, John 85
Graye,
  Edward (w) 161
  John (l) 161, 596
  Luke (l) 161
  Magdalene (l)(e) 161
  Margaret (l) 767
  Philip 767
  Robert (l) 161
  Seth (l) 161
  Thomas 839, (l) 161
  William (l) 161
Grayve see Grave
Greene,
  Abraham (w) 310
  Anne (l) 874
  Charles (w) 217
  Dorothy 825
  Elizabeth (l) 874
  Ellen (l) 751
  John 306, (l) 874, (w) 95, 186
  Marian (l) 880
  Mary (l) 874, (l)(e) 874
  Rose (l) 67
  Samuel (l) 874
  Sarah (l) 874
  Thomas (l) 874
  William (l) 874, (w) 214
Greenegras see Greenegrasse
Greenegrasse (Grennegras, Greenegresse, Greengrasse),
  Bridget (l) 109
  Edmund (l) 423
  Elizabeth (l) 109
  Francis 109
  John (l) 109
  Margaret (l) 109
  Robert (w) 163, 728
  Roger (l)(e) 109
  Susan (l)(e) 423
  Thomas (l) 109
Greenegresse see Greenegrasse
Greenehall, Alice (l)(e) 845
Greenehill, Mr (l) 627
Greeneward,
  Elizabeth 12
  William (e) 12
Greenewood see Greenwood
Greengrasse see Greenegrasse
Greenwood (Greenewood),
  William 589, (w) 235, 392, 862
Greeton,
  Avis 405
  Randall 405
Grengres see Greenegrasse
Gridley, William (w) 581

413

414

Robert (l) 553, 594
Samuel (l) 594
Simon (w) 716
Thomas 622, (l) 517, 594
Thomasine (l) 164
William 193, 871, (e) 732, (l) 553, 732, (w) 358
Halle *see* Hall
Halles *see* Halls
Halls (Halles),
  Adam 5
  Giles (l) 343
  Jeffrey 115
  John (l) 343, (w) 719, 848
  Mary (l)(e) 343
  Nicholas (l) 343
  Richard (w) 141
  Stephen (e) 343
Hallydaye,
  Elizabeth (l) 395
  Helen (l) 395
  John (l) 395
  Margaret (l) 395
Halman, Thomas (w) 211, 246, 779
Halstead, Roger the elder (l) 296
Hamand *see* Hammond
Hamant *see* Hammond
Hamblinge,
  Anne (l)(e) 530
  Mary (l) 530
Hamblyn, John (l) 232
Hamerton,
  Mary 581
  Richard 581
Hammerton,
  Anne (l) 372
  Joan (l) 372
  Mary (l) 372
Hammond (Hamand, Hamant, Hammont,
  Hamon, Hamond),
  Abraham (l)(e) 266
  Ambrose (l) 57, (l)(e) 266
  Anne 111, (l) 57, 358, (l)(e) 57
  Bridget (l)(e) 555
  Elizabeth (l) 271, (l)(e) 358
  Francis (w) 19
  George (l) 57
  Joan (l) 502
  John 385, 555, (e) 118, 704, (l) 600, (l)(e) 266,
    (w) 120, 196
  Joseph (w) 77
  Lydia (l) 57
  Margaret (l) 127
  Mary (l) 385
  Mr 885
  Philip (l) 358, (w) 266, 838
  Rebecca (l) 57
  Robert 127(l) 358, 555, (w) 266
  Susan (l) 266
  Thomas 271, (l) 111, 358, 689, 704, (w) 72, 520
  Toby (w) 520
  William (l) 600
Hammont *see* Hammond
Hamon *see* Hammond
Hamond *see* Hammond
Hanham,
  Christopher (w) 316

Em (w) 316
Hankyns, John (w) 558
Harbard,
  John 538
  Susan (w) 538
Harbor,
  John (l) 619
  widow 218
Harcocke, John (w) 569
Hardeck,
  Alice (l) 759
  Anne (l) 759, (l)(e) 759
  Leonard (l) 759
  Martin (l) 759
Harded,
  Abigail (l) 170
  Dorothy (l) 170
  John (l)(e) 170
  Katherine (l) 170
Hardey, John (w) 297
Hardie,
  John 664
  Richard 448
Hardy (Hardey, Hardie, Hardye),
  Agnes (l)(e) 577
  Bridget (l)(e) 48
  Edmund 577
  Elizabeth (l) 577, 765
  John 664, (w) 297
  Mary (l) 577
  Richard 448
  Thomas (l) 48, 577
Hardye, Elizabeth (l) 765
Hargrave,
  Elizabeth (l)(e) 556
  John 529, (w) 64, 621
  wife (l) 529
  William (l) 556
Harison *see* Harrison
Harlond,
  Diana (w) 700
  John (w) 700
Harne, Mary (l) 179
Harper,
  Christopher (w) 292
  Francis 179
  Joseph (w) 99
  Nan 179
Harper alias Oger, John (w) 510
Harris, Elizabeth (l) 37
Harrison (Harison, Harryson),
  Anne (l) 611
  Edward 75
  Francis (w) 559
  John 461, (l) 611
  John [Mr] (l) 420
  Thomas 144
Harryson *see* Harrison
Harssante, Francis (w) 328
Harst, Jeffrey (w) 688
Hart (Harte),
  Anne (l) 597
  Dorothy (l) 864
  Elizabeth (l) 864, (w) 871
  Frances (l)(e) 597
  Francis (l) 864

Hugh (w) 117
John 165, (w) 103
John the elder (w) 597
John the younger (l) 597
Joseph (l) 597
Katherine (l) 765
Percival [Sir] 502
Richard 337
Robert (l) 864
Susan (w) 545
Thomas (l) 864, (w) 259, 317
Harte *see* Hart
Harvey (Harvie, Harvy, Harvye),
  Bridget (l) 321, (l)(e) 446
  Elizabeth (l) 392
  George (w) 122, 820
  Grace (l) 321
  John 15, (l) 179, 392, (l)(e) 321, 853, (w) 12, 34,
    354, 617
  Mary (l) 446, 648, 853
  Mr 836
  Petronella (l) 853
  Simon 819
  Susan (l) 819
  Thomas (l) 321
  Widow 839
Harvie *see* Harvey
Harvy *see* Harvey
Harvye *see* Harvey
Hasell, Jeremy (l) 216
Hasellwood,
  Agnes (l) 27
  Edward (l)(e) 27
  Elizabeth (l) 27
  Joan (l) 27
  John (l) 27
  William (l) 27
Hasfeilde,
  Martha (l) 295
  Richard 295
Hastead, John (e) 780
Hasted,
  Andrew (l) 448
  Anne (l) 639
  John (l) 175
Hatchet,
  John (l) 126
  Thomas 126
Hatfeild alias Maior,
  Anne (l) 58
  Elizabeth (l) 58
  Joan (l) 58
  John (l) 58
  Robert (l) 58
  Thomas (l)(e) 58
  William (e) 714, (l) 58, 714
Hatton, James (w) 18
Haward,
  Alice (l) 620, (l)(e) 620
  Andrew (l) 111
  Anne (l) 620
  John (l) 620
  Mary (l) 620
Hawes (Hawis, Hawys),
  Frances (l)(e) 173
  Francis (w) 25, 55, 136

George (w) 864
Gregory (w) 434
Jane (w) 239
John (w) 192, 434
Thomas 9
William 9
Hawis *see* Hawes
Hawkes,
  John 282
  Mary (l) 282
Hawkins, Mary (w) 700
Hawsell, Richard (e) 542
Hawsted,
  Roger (e) 386
  Roger the elder (e) 567
Hawys *see* Hawes
Haxall,
  John (w) 284
  Miles (w) 19
Haxoll, Susan (l)(e) 331
Hayes,
  Thomas (l)(e) 125
  William (l) 125
Haylock (Haylocke),
  Alice (l)(e) 678
  Bridget 42
  Edmund (w) 344
  John (l)(e) 678
  Oliver (w) 762
  Thomas (l) 678
  William 42, (w) 191
Haylocke *see* Haylock
Hayward (Haiward, Haywarde, Heyward,
  Heywarde),
  Andrew (l) 555, (l)(e) 649, (w) 415
  Anne (l) 445, (w) 251
  Cattlin (l) 843
  Deborah (l) 23
  Edmund (w) 94, 291, 330, 511, 745, 812, 856
  Frances (l) 843
  Francis 875
  George (l) 405
  Hannah (l) 445
  James (l) 679, (w) 116
  John 9, 445, (l) 23, 50, 405, 445, 751, (l)(e) 818
  Katherine (w) 642
  Margaret (l) 23, 751
  Martha (l) 711, (l)(e) 405
  Mary (l) 23, 751
  Mother (l) 751
  Nicholas (l) 555, (w) 649
  Richard (e) 578, (l) 23
  Robert (l) 405, 679, 818
  Rose 23
  Stephen (l) 23
  Susan (l) 555
  Thomas (l) 23
  Thomazine (l) 50
  William (l) 23, 818, (w) 112
Haywarde *see* Hayward
Heard (Herd), John 91, (l) 647
Hearne, Katherine (l) 83
Hearnes,
  Catherine (l)(e) 785
  Henry (l) 785
  John (l) 785

416

Heath,
Joan (l) 134
Roger 134
Hebble, Edmund (w) 247
Hedge,
Anne (l) 89, 846, (l)(e) 846
James (l) 846
John (l) 218
Nicholas (l) 846
Robert (l)(e) 846
Thomas (l) 846
William (l) 846
Heigham 209
Arthur [Mr] (l) 258
Arthur (w) 415, 723
Francis (w) 76, 415
Henry (l) 185
Hekes 686
Helder, Richard (l)(e) 116
Heley, Mr 385
Hempsted,
Abigail (l) 231
Anne (l) 231
Constance (l) 231
Elizabeth (l) 231
John 771
Reuben (l) 231
Susan (l)(e) 231
Hempton, William (w) 674
Hengames,
Anthony 135, (l) 135
Margaret (l)(e) 135
Thomas (l) 135
Herd see Heard
Hering, Simon 20
Herington 686
Hernes, John (w) 790
Heromer, Robert (w) 369
Hershame, John (l) 433
Hewit, Israel 872
Heynor, Philip (w) 128
Heyward see Hayward
Heywarde see Hayward
Hibbe, Priscilla (l) 102
Hibble,
Edmund (l) 247
William (w) 838
Hichell,
Elizabeth (l) 569
Newell 569
Hicks,
Francis (w) 484
wife (w) 484
Higney, Robert (l) 872
Hill (Hille, Hyll),
Adam 680
Anne (l)(e) 871
Eleanor (l) 618
Elen (l) 423
Elizabeth (l) 423
Emma (l) 333
Gilbert 202
John 384, (l) 680, (w) 146, 488, 542, 618
Lea (l) 871
Mary (l) 871, (w) 618
Sarah (l) 871

Stephen 333
Susan (w) 618
Thomas (l) 680
William (w) 327, 455, 595
Hille see Hill
Hilles see Hills
Hills (Hilles),
Ellen (l) 78
John 622, (l) 765
Katherine (l) 765
Martin (w) 363
Robert 78
William (l) 765
Hilton, James [Mr] 792
Hinard see Hynard
Hindes (Hyndes),
Anne 281
Francis (l) 281
Jane (l) 78
John 281
Richard 78
Thomas (l) 281
Hindle,
Alice (l) 114, (l)(e) 114
Faith (l) 114
James (l) 114
John (l) 114
Peter (l) 114
Thomas (l) 114
Hine, Mary (l) 742
Hinsebye,
Barbara (l)(e) 8
Esther (l) 8
James (l) 8
Mary (l) 8
Hinson (Hinsone, Hynson),
Anne (l) 455
Elizabeth (l) 455
John (e) 38, (l)(e) 455
Margaret (l) 455
Marian (l) 455
Mary (l) 455
Richard (l) 455
Rose (l) 455
Thomas 104, (l) 455, (w) 131, 161, 579
William (l) 455
Hinsone see Hinson
Hinton, Mary (l) 567
Hist, Jeffery (w) 650
Hitchcocke, Edward (w) 359
Hix, John (w) 471
Hixe, William (l) 157
Hobbard see Hubbard
Hobie, Thomas 885
Hockett, George 114
Hodge, James (l) 744
Hodgkine, John (w) 275
Hodgkin (l) 83
Hodgkyn, John 402
Hodson, James (w) 109, 423, 561
Hodsonne, Mr (l) 713
Hoe alias Howe, Dorothy (l) 689
Hogg,
Elizabeth (l) 623
Margaret (l) 623
Thomas (w) 503

418

419

Jaques,
Jarmen,
James (w) 469
Robert [gent] (w) 88
Robert (w) 772
Jarmen,
Giles (w) 770
Grace (l) 770
James (l) 770
Jarrold, Robert 543
Jarves see Jarvis
Jarvice see Jarvis
Jarvis (Jarves, Jarvice, Jervis),
Alice (l) 402
Anne (l) 402, 583
Christian (l) 402
Elias 402, (l) 583
Elizabeth (l) 402
John (e) 583, (l) 402, 583, (w) 402
John senior (w) 494, 583
Margaret (w) 783
Martha (l) 583
Mary (l) 402, 583, (l)(e) 402
Jaslyn,
Anne (l) 297
Philip (l) 297
Rose (l) 297
Jasper,
Anne (l) 392
Henry (l) 392, (l)(e) 392
Ruth (l) 392
William (w) 221
Jeames see James
Jeashoppe see Jesopp
Jeffe,
John 455
Robert 455
Jefferie see Jeffery
Jeffery (Jefferie),
John 600
Mr 580, (l) 627
Robert (l) 600
Jelley (Jellye),
Mary (l)(e) 378
Robert (w) 143
William (l)(e) 378
Jellowe, John (w) 743
Jellye see Jelley
Jelson,
Henry 300
Mary (l) 300
Jenepie, Robert (l) 55
Jeninges see Jennings
Jenkin, Thomas (l)(e)(w) 881
Jenninges see Jennings
Jennings (Jeninges, Jenninges),
Francis the elder (l) 334
Francis the younger (l) 334
James (w) 233
Joan (l)(e) 875
Robert 781
Samuel (l)(e) 334
Susanna (l) 334
Thomas (w) 92, 152, 187
Jenor, Robert (w) 444
Jermy, Thomas (w) 880

Jermyn,
Elizabeth (l) 532
Giles (l)(e) 532
Grace (l) 532
James (l) 532
John (l) 532
Peter (l)(e) 532
Robert [Sir] 194
Thomas 398
Jerrold, Simon (w) 110
Jervis see Jarvis
Jesop see Jesopp
Jesope see Jesopp
Jesopp (Jeashoppe, Jesop, Jesope, Jessope,
   Jessopp, Jessoppe, Jessupp),
Anne (l) 452
Constance (l)(e) 24
Elize (l)(e) 819
Frances (l) 623
Henry (w) 668
Jane (l) 819
John 135, (e) 623, (l) 452, 623, (l)(e) 452
Mary (l) 452
Patience (w) 819
Robert (w) 668
Sarah (l) 623
Thomas (w) 822
William (l) 819, (w) 397, 668
Jessope see Jesopp
Jessopp see Jesopp
Jessoppe see Jesopp
Jessupp see Jesopp
Jewell,
Anne (w) 160
John (e) 611, (l) 703, (p) 538, 677, 766, 802,
   816, 825, 871, 881, (w) 81, 160, 202, 315, 367,
   421
Jiggins,
Edith (l) 167
John 167
John (Jon),
Mary (l) 233
Robert (w) 875
William 233
Johnson (Johnsonne), 181
Alice (l) 842
Andrew (l) 842
Dorothy (l) 232
Edward 232, (w) 878
Elizabeth (l) 641, 842, (l)(e) 342
Grace (l) 360
Henry (l) 360, (w) 30, 240
John 765, (l) 765
Joseph 641
Katherine (l) 641
Mary (l) 233, 360, 368, 641, 765
Oliver 816, (w) 29, 322, 467, 475, 598, 602
Peter (w) 181
Reginald 368
Richard 544, (l)(e) 449
Robert (l) 342
Simon (l) 360
Stephen (l) 641
Susan (l) 641, (w) 598
Thomas (l) 842, (w) 588

420

421

Judith (l) 829
Mary (l) 643
Michael (l) 643, (l)(e) 220, 370
Ralph (w) 689
Richard (l) 220, 643
Robert (w) 170
Rose (l) 189
Sarah 101, (l) 175
Stephen 257
Thomas 161
William (l)(w) 829, (w) 19, 241, 284, 492, 514
Kinge *see* King
Kingesburye *see* Kingsbery
Kingsberie *see* Kingsbery,
Kingsbery (Kingesburye, Kingsberie, Kingsburie),
Alice (l) 226
Anne (l) 746
Barnabas (l) 746
Edward (l) 746
George (l) 746
Joan (l) 226, 746
John 155, 746, (l) 226
Mary (l) 155, 746
Richard (l)(e) 746
Robert (l)(e)(w) 226, (w) 606
William (l) 226
Kingsburie *see* Kingsbery
Kinsley,
Anne (l) 595
Thomas 595
Kirby, Walter (l) 680
Kirbye,
Amy 10
George 10
Kirke, Edward 440
Kittleburrough *see* Kettleborough
Knapp (Knappe),
Anthony (l)(e) 615
Beatrice (l) 296
John 296, (w) 60
Knappe *see* Knapp
Knight,
James 382, (l)(e) 382, (w) 879
James senior (w) 639
Joan (l) 382
Robert (w) 319
Knightes,
Allce (l) 627
Bartholomew (l) 627
Knock (Knocke),
Diana (l) 38
Francis (l)(w) 109
Henry (w) 447
Leonard 846
Mihill 93
William 38
Knocke *see* Knock
Knopp,
Dorcas (l) 656
John (e) 656, (l) 656
Rachel (l)(e) 656
William (l) 656
Kyng *see* King

Ladie,
Francis (l) 609

William (l) 609
Ladiman *see* Ladyman
Ladinan, William (w) 551
Ladyman (Ladiman),
Alice (l) 205
Anne (l) 205
Benjamin (l) 205
Elizabeth (l) 205
Ezekiel (l) 205
Frances (l) 205
Joseph (l) 205
Nathan (l) 205
Susan (l) 205
William (w) 577, 676
Lagger, Philip (w) 300
Laman, Robert (w) 709
Lambe,
Anne (l) 682
Barbara (l) 682
Fitznunne 793
George (l) 682
Mary (l) 682
Sarah (l) 682
Thomas (l) 682
Lambert,
Richard 178
William [Mr] (e) 784
Lambey, John (w) 893
Lancaster,
John (l) 703
Margaret (l) 703, (l)(e) 703
Mary (l) 703
Mr 680
Sarah (l) 703
Thomas 703, (l)(e) 703
Land,
George (w) 686
Thomas (w) 686
Widow (l) 174
Landemer, Mary (l) 183
Lane, Theophilus (w) 4
Langham,
Henry (l) 104
Thomas 51
Langton,
Abigail (l) 784
Jeffrey (l) 784
Richaid (l) 784
Susan (l) 784
Thomas (l) 784, (l)(e) 784, (w) 118, 119
Lanham, Henry 514
Lanman alias Jannings, Elizabeth (l)(e) 565
Lanur alias Bovell, Thomas 128
Largant *see* Largent
Largeant *see* Largent
Largent (Largant, Largeant, Largiant),
Agnes (l) 130
Alice (l) 428, (l)(w) 11
Anne (l) 428, 728
Edmund (l) 658
Edward (l) 246
Elizabeth (l) 658, (l)(e) 728
Frances (l) 428
George (w) 41
John 246, 658, (l) 130, 658, 728, 818, (w) 117
Margaret (l) 579, (l)(e) 428

422

Mary (l) 428
Miles (l) 728
Philip (l) 246
Richard (l) 428
Robert (l) 658, 728, (l)(e) 428
Simon (l)(e) 130
Susan (l) 658
Talmisen (l) 658
Thomas (l) 658
William (l) 130, 728
Largiant see Largent
Larke, John (w) 316
Larkin, Nicholas 719
Last,
  Ellen (l) 476
  Francis 294
  John 476
  Thomas (l) 476
Laund alias Pallant,
  Alice (l) 686
  Elizabeth (l) 686
  George (l) 686
  Martha (l) 686
  Mary (l)(e) 686
  Robert (l) 686
  Thomas (l) 686
Launder, James (l) 308
Laurence see Lawrence
Lawes,
  Anne (l) 597
  Samuel 597
Lawrence (Laurence),
  Barbara (l) 146
  Francis (l) 649
  Henry (e) 743
  Thomas (w) 699
Lawson, Thomas (w) 661
Lay, Valentine 218
Laye, William (w) 359
Layman, John (w) 256, 279
Layt, William (l) 818
Lea see Lee
Leach, Margery 784
Leaman (Lemon),
  Bridget (l) 586
  Francis (l) 395, (l)(e) 586
  Henry (l) 586
  John (l) 395, (w) 400
  Susan (l) 586
  Thomas (l) 586, (l)(e) 395
Leaverington, Thomas (w) 623
Leavold, Mary (l)(e) 468
Leay see Lee
Lee (Lea, Leay),
  Henry 677
  John 893
  Margaret (l) 893
  Martha (l) 681
  Thomas (l) 456, (w) 331
Leeder, Samuel (w) 800
Legat, Thomas (w) 499
Legate, John [Mr] 677
Le Gris, John [Mr] 321
Leich, Robert (w) 822
Leichfeild,
  Edward(l) 6

Francis (l) 6
Henry (l) 6
Leigh see also Lee
  Mr 7
  Thomas (e) 154
  William (w) 213
Leighton, Anne (l) 752
Lelam,
  Bennett (l) 439
  Edward (l)(w) 439
  Margaret (l) 439
  Thomas (l) 439
Lemon see Leaman
Leonard, James (e) 11
Levell, John (w) 812
Levericke,
  Elizabeth (l) 719
  John (l) 719
  Mary (l)(e) 719
  Stephen (l) 719
  Susan (l) 719
Leverington, Thomas (w) 51, 623
Levett, Thomas (w) 204
Levick, Elizabeth (l) 35
Lewes (Lewis),
  Elizabeth (w) 643
  Ellen (l)(e) 716
  John (w) 211
  Joseph (l) 716
  Lydia (l) 716
  Samuel (l) 818
  Sarah (w) 797
  William (l) 716
Lewis see Lewes
Leywarde, Edmund (w) 251
Lillege, John (l) 632
Lillie see Lilly
Lilly (Lillie, Lyllie, Lyllye), (l)(e) 659
  Anne (l) 659
  Barnaby (l)(e) 438
  Elizabeth (l) 662
  John (l) 175
  Rose (l) 659
  Margaret (l) 175
  Stephen (l) 44
  Thomas 175, 294, (w) 14
  William (l) 659
Limborn, John (w) 731
Linge (Lynge),
  John 337
  Judith (l) 281
  Susan (l) 309
  Thomas (l)(e) 309
  William (e) 534, (w) 697
Linwoode (Lynwood),
  Bridget (w) 646
  Robert (l) 348
  Thomas (w) 646
Lister (Lyster),
  Elizabeth (l) 827
  Faith (l) 711, (w) 649
  John (l) 711
  Mary (l) 649
  Nathaniel 827
  Rose (l) 855
  Thomasine (w) 498

Little, Jeffrey 784
Litton (Lyttone),
  Elizabeth (l) 748
  Humphrey 682
  Joan (l) 748
  John (l) 748, (w) 600
  Mary (l) 748
  Robert (l) 748
  Susan (l) 748
  Thomasine (l) 748
  Thomas (l)(e) 748
Livermare see Livermore
Livermore (Livermare, Lyvermer, Lyvermore),
  Daniel (w) 223, 630
  Nicholas (l) 591
  Peter (l) 393
Lives,
  Anne (l) 818
  Mary (l) 818
  William 818
Lock (Locke),
  Alice (l) 694
  Anne (l) 694
  Elizabeth (l) 694, (l)(e) 122
  John 394, (l) 694, (w) 748, 889
  Margaret (l) 328
  Nicholas 572
  Robert (l) 148, 694
  Susan 394
Locke see Lock
Locken, John 732
Lockwood, William (l) 627, (l)(e) 634
Loft, Richard (w) 263
Loftes,
  Daniel 659
  Rebecca (l) 659
Loker,
  Ann (l) 227
  Bridget (l) 227
  Elizabeth (l)(e) 227
  Henry (l)(e) 227
  John (l) 227
Lomax, Lawrence (w) 793
Long see Longe
Longe (Long),
  Emma 639
  Francis (w) 295
  James (w) 107
  John 333, (l) 277
  Richard 770, (w) 31
  William (w) 892
Loppkins, Robert 683
Lord,
  Jeffery (w) 263
  John 218
  Thomas the younger (l) 627
Lorkin, John (w) 87
Lorkyn,
  John (l) 216
  John the younger (l) 216
Lotte, Sarah (w) 542
Lovell,
  Dorothy (l) 502
  Eunice (l) 502
  Priscilla (l) 502
  Sarah (l) 502

Lovenes, Benjamin (l) 464
Lovenis, Isabel (l) 67
Loveringe,
  Blanche (l) 622
  Thomas 622
Loves,
  Joan (l) 441
  Margaret 441
  Matthew (l) 441
  Sarah (l) 441
  William (l) 441
Lovette, Edward 11
Low see Lowe
Lowdall,
  Jane (l) 468
  John (l) 468
  Roger (w) 575
Lowe (Low),
  Anne (l) 522
  Anthony (l) 522
  Benjamin (l) 263
  Ellen (l) 529, (l)(e) 263
  John (l) 522
  Mary (l) 522
  Robert (l) 529
  Rose (l) 522
  Thomas (l) 263, 522
  William (l) 263, 522, 529
Lowes, John (w) 377
Lucas,
  Moses 890
  Richard (l) 522, 890
  Samuel 384
Lumley,
  Joan (l) 502
  Thomas 502
Lummis,
  Agnes (l) 457
  Nathaniel (l) 457
Lumpkyn, Charles (w) 361
Lurkyn, John (w) 68
Lurkyne, John 148
Lusher,
  Francis (w) 130, 341
  James 391
  Joan (w) 206
Lyllie see Lilly
Lyllye see Lilly
Lynge see Lingo
Lynwood see Linwood
Lyster see Lister
Lyttone see Litton
Lyvermer see Livermore
Lyvermore see Livermore

Madwell, Elizabeth (w) 152
Maier see Maior
Maies see Mayes
Maior (Maier, Maire) see also Mayer
  Bartholomew (w) 813
  Isaac (l) 738
  Ruth (l) 738
  Thomas (w) 822
Maior alias Hatfield see Hatfield alias Maior
Maire see Maior
Makeinges, William (w) 305

425

Milles *see* Mills
Mills (Milles, Mylles, Mylls),
  Agnes (l) 188
  Anthony 188
  Elizabeth (l) 84, 188
  Frances (l)(e) 84
  Francis (l) 234
  George 100
  Isaac (l) 84
  John 12, (l) 188, (l)(e) 188
  Richard (l) 188, (w) 299
  Rose (w) 374
  Simon (l) 84
  Thomas (w) 84, 170, 188, 620, 660, 675, 764
  William (l) 188, (w) 687
Minckes,
  Mary (l) 657
  Samuel 657
Minott, William (l) 779
Mony, Margaret (l) 569
Moodye, Edmund (w) 121
Moorden *see* Moreden
Moore (More), (l) 205
  Alice (l) 680
  Ambrose (l) 379
  John (l) 379
  Isaac (l)(e) 781
  Katherine (w) 62
  Margery (l) 379
  Michael (l) 379
  Robert (l) 781, (w) 721
  Stephen (l)(e) 781
Mordyboite, William (w) 887
More *see* Moore
Moreden (Moorden), 872
  Oliver 113
Morgane, Humphrey (e) 305
Morley (Morly),
  Edmund (l)(e) 211, (w) 246, 834
  Henry (e) 13
  John (l) 13, 211
  Mary (l) 13
  Thomas (l)(e) 211
  William (l)(e) 660
Morly *see* Morley
Morrice *see* Morris
Morris (Morrice), 437
  Alice (l) 6
  Anne (l) 810
  Caleb (w) 155
  Edward (l) 810
  Joshua (l) 833
  Margaret (l)(e) 833
  Mary (l) 810
  Philip (l) 833
  Stephen (l) 810
  Susan (l)(e) 810
  William (l) 810
Morse,
  Philip (w) 386
  Robert 600
Mortlock,
  Elizabeth (l) 169
  James (l) 169
Morton,
  Margaret (l) 804

William (l)(e) 804
Mosse,
  Alice (l) 565
  Bridget (l) 565
  Elizabeth (l) 565
  Jeffrey 816
  John (l) 565
  Margaret 816
  Mr (l) 627
  Robert (w) 604
  Rose (l) 565
  Sarah (l) 723, (l)(e) 723
Motham,
  Isaac (w) 193
  Mr 193
Motte, Thomas (w) 7
Moulton,
  Edward (w) 452
  Elizabeth (l) 51
  John (l) 51
  Mawnlinge (l)(e) 51
  Sibilla (l) 51
Moundeford, Eunica (l) 841
Mounsey, John (l) 372
Mountecute,
  John 228
  John the younger (l) 228
  Mary (l)(e) 228
Mowle, Francis (w) 468
Mullyner, Francis (l)(e) 69
Muning *see* Munninge
Muninge *see* Munninge
Muninges *see* Munnings
Munnes,
  George (l) 688
  Helen (l) 688
  Thomas (l)(e) 688
Munninge (Muning, Muninge),
  Abigail (l) 305
  Ellen (l) 305
  Francis (l) 745
  Humphrey (l) 305
  John (e) 745, (w) 193
  Katherine (l) 305
  Leonard (l) 305
  Richard (l) 305, 745
  Theophilus (l) 305
  Thomas 745, (w) 463
  William (l) 305
Munninges *see* Munnings
Munnings (Muninges, Munninges),
  Henry (w) 726
  William 500, (w) 567
Munns,
  Agnes (l)(e) 429
  Elizabeth (l) 429
  John (l) 429
Murden, Roger [Mr] (e)(w) 38
Murdocke, John (w) 683
Muriell *see* Murrell
Murrell (Muriell, Muryell),
  John (e) 805, (l) 734, (l)(e) 448, (w) 86, 446, 644
  Joseph (l) 734
  Richard (w) 357
  Robert (e) 209
  Sarah (l) 734

Thomasine (l)(e) 495
Murriell *see* Murrell
Muryell *see* Murrell
Musant, William 207
Musicke, George 885
Musket *see* Muskett
Muskett,
Audry (w) 476
Edmund (l) 772
George 772
John (l) 251, (l)(e) 476, (w) 389, 807
Mary (l) 251
Robert (l)(e) 251
Thomas (l) 308
William (l) 251, 772
Muskett alias Man, Thomas (w) 638
Musscit *see* Muskett
Mutton,
Christopher 179, (w) 179
John 179, (l) 179
Mistress (l) 179
Myller *see* Miller
Mylles *see* Milles
Mylls *see* Milles
Myne, Nicholas (w) 13
Mynett, Nicholas (w) 222
Mynnes,
John (w) 249
Judith (w) 249

Nasie, Henry 745
Nasy, goodwife (l) 183
Neale (Neall, Neele),
Alice (l) 665
Anna (l)(e) 665
Edward (w) 411
Elizabeth (l) 665, 700
Frances (l) 681
George 17
James (w) 434
Juda (l) 17
Mary (l) 665
Robert (l) 623
Sarah (l) 665
Ursula (l) 17
widow 330
William (l)(e) 700, (w) 29
Neall *see* Neale
Neattes,
John (l) 580
Thomas the elder (l) 580
Neave, Richard (l) 41
Nebbett, Edward 215
Neech, Mr (l) 627
Neele *see* Neale
Negus,
Frances (l) 267
Henry (l) 267
John (l)(e) 267
Mary (l) 267
Richard 267
Sarah 267
Thomas (l) 267, (w) 486
Nelson, John 113
Nethercoate *see* Nethercote

Nethercote (Nethercoate),
Anne (l) 104
Edward (l) 104
John (e) 104
John the younger (e) 885
Margaret (l) 104
Richard (l) 104
Thomas (l)(e) 104
Nevell (Nevill),
Amy (l) 225
Anne (l) 845
Edmund (l) 845, (w) 893
John 225
Newgos,
John (l) 877
Mary (l) 877
Robert 877
Sarah (l) 877
Newham,
Bridget (l) 436
John (w) 439
Thomas 436
Newman,
Anne (l) 135
Frances (l) 135
Joan (l) 135
John (w) 444
Robert (e) 264, 509, (l) 471, (w) 774
Sarah (l)(e) 471
Temperance (l) 471
Thomas (l)(e) 471
Walter 135
Newton,
Elizabeth (l) 661
John 430
Katherine 430
Nicholas, Mary (l) 183
Nicholl, William (e) 875
Nicholson, Thomas 215
Nickolson Mr (l) 56
Nightingale,
John (e)(w) 828
Mary (w) 828
Nobbett, Thomas 384
Noble,
Ann (l) 713
Augustine 713
Elizabeth 713
Frances (l) 713
James (l) 713
John (l) 713
Margery (l) 713, (l)(e) 136
Thomas 713, (l) 136
William (w) 158
Nockard, John (w) 788
Nodson, Elizabeth (w) 280
Noothe,
Anne (l) 414
Bridget (l) 414
Hugh (l)(e) 414
Margaret (l) 414
Mary (l) 414
Robert (l) 414
Thomas (l) 414
William (l) 414

428

429

John (w) 94, 291, 791
Margaret (l) 771
Thomas (w) 432
Osbourne *see* Osborne
Ose, John (l) 386
Ostiler alias Beddall, James 24
Otely, William (l) 873
Overley, William (w) 873
Owers, Charles (e)(w) 57
Owles,
  Francis (l) 174
  Thomas (l) 174
Oxe, John (l) 567

Packard,
  Anne (l) 627
  Elizabeth (l) 627
  John 627
Padnall, Humphrey (e) 600
Page,
  Anne (l) 498, 499
  Dorothy (l) 499, 609
  Edward 193, (l) 497
  Elizabeth (l) 498, 499
  Helen (l)(e) 499
  John (l) 179, (l)(e) 498, (w) 307, 368, 463, 483
  Katherine (l) 268
  Margaret (l) 609
  Mary 732
  Paul (l) 499
  Robert 148, 161, (w) 132
  Sarah (l) 609
  Thomas 673, 816, (l) 179, 268, 499, 609, (w) 835
Pagett, John (w) 628
Paige *see* Page
Paine *see* Payne
Palfrey, James (l) 890
Pallant alias Laund *see* Laund alias Pallant
Pallesie, Elizabeth (l) 681
Palmer,
  Emma (l) 85
  John (l) 490
  Richard (w) 46
Palsey alias Pawsey,
  Alice (l) 491
  Barbara (l) 491
  Dorothy (l) 491
  Elizabeth (l) 491
  Margaret (l) 491
  Thomas (l) 491
  William (l)(e) 491
Palsie, William (l)(e) 189
Paman,
  Clement (w) 198
  Henry (w) 293
  Robert (w) 16, 127, 285, 398, 733, 890
Pament, Henry 294
Pamplyn, Goodman 223
Pamplyne, Thomas 253
Pangham, Charles (w) 179
Parfrey,
  Ann (l)(e) 799
  William (l) 799
Parish, Nicholas 112
Parke,
  Anne (l) 219

Robert 219
William (l) 219
Parker,
  Alice (l) 434, (l)(e) 383
  Anne (l) 383, (l)(e) 641
  Anthony 719
  Audrey (l)(e) 708
  Augustine 434, (l) 730, (w) 55
  Bryan (w) 476
  Elizabeth (l) 708, (l)(e) 730
  Frances (l) 708
  Henry 91, (l) 708
  Joan 705
  John (e) 600, (l) 730, 755, (w) 564, 748
  Katherine (l) 730
  Mary 708, (l) 708, 730
  Rachel (l) 708
  Richard (l)(e) 434, (w) 208
  Robert (e) 708, (w) 192
  Sarah (l)(e) 705
  Thomas 554, 560, (l) 383, (l)(e) 708
  William (l) 383, (w) 795
Parkin, John (w) 36
Parkyn,
  Christian (l)(e) 880
  Ezechiell (w) 153
  John 153
  John (l) 578
Parkyns, William (w) 453
Parman, Anne (l) 859
Parmiter, John (l) 650, (w) 227
Parre,
  Francis (l)(e) 180
  Henry (l) 180
  John (l) 180
  Robert (l) 180
Parslye, William (w) 635
Parson,
  Frances (l) 632
  John (w) 349
  Peter (w) 411
  William 349, (w) 180
Partaredge *see* Partridge
Partlett, Anne (l) 580
Partridge (Pataredge, Pattrage),
  Alice (l) 299
  Elizabeth (l)(e) 299
  John (l) 299
  Mary (w) 308
  Thomas (l) 299, (w) 331
Paske,
  Abraham (l) 659
  Bridget 537
  George 659
  John 537
  Josias (l)(e) 537
  Mary (l) 649
  Nathaniel 298
  Sarah 537
Pasley,
  Elizabeth (l) 564, (l)(e) 564
  Frances (l) 564
  Lawrence (l) 564
  Richard (l) 564
  Sarah (l)(e) 564
Patriche, John (l) 873

Patrick (Pattrick),
  John (l) 585
  Margaret (l) 585
  Stephen (w) 311
Patrick John the younger (l) 585
Pattell see Pattle
Pattle (Pattell),
  Adam 134
  Alice (l)(e) 134
  Joan (l)(e) 636
  Margaret (l)(e) 337
  Martha (l) 28
  Thomas (e) 28 (l) 636
  William (l) 337
Pattrage see Partridge
Pattrick see Patrick
Pawsey alias Palsey see Palsey alias Pawsey
Pay, John (w) 30
Payne (Paine), 632
  Abigail (l) 99, 632
  Alice (l) 185
  Arthur (w) 593
  Benjamin 20, (l) 253
  Christian (l) 323
  Edward (w) 288, 320
  Elizabeth (l) 185, 253
  Henry 323, (e) 372, (l)(e) 40
  John 99, 253, (l) 99, 653, (w) 156
  Margaret (l) 491, 681
  Mr 885
  Prudence (l) 21
  Richard (w) 213, 409
  Robert (w) 114
  Stephen (l)(e) 253, (w) 426
  Thomas 877, (l) 185
  Thomas junior (w) 599
  Walter (e) 157
  William (l) 185, (w) 156, 549, 682
Paynter,
  Elizabeth (l) 586
  Susan (l) 586
  William (l) 586
Payton, Thomas (l) 807
Peach,
  Agnes (l) 30, (l)(e) 30
  Dorothy (l) 557
  Elizabeth (l) 557
  Henry 557, (w) 826
  John (l) 30
  Mary (l) 30
  Robert 30
  Thomas (l) 30
  William (l) 30
Peachey see Peachie
Peachie (Peachey, Pechey, Pechie),
  Agnes (l) 240
  Elizabeth (l) 240, 502
  Henry 199
  Jeffrey 751, (e) 663
  John 319, 871, (w) 455
  Katherine (l) 333
  Mary (l) 333
  Mathew 104
  Nicholas (l)(e) 240
  Richard 319, (w) 377, 515, 552, 872
  Richard [Mr] (l) 120, (l)(e) 502

Robert (e)(w) 885, (l)(e) 333, (w) 382
Theo (w) 854
Thomas 199, (w) 341, 728
William (l) 240
Peacock (Peacocke, Pecok),
  John (l) 410
  Richard (w) 777
  Robert (l) 410
  Thomas (l) 410, (w) 106
Peacocke see Peacock
Pead 677
  Richard (p) 88
Peake,
  Anne (l) 455, 595
  Audrey (l) 595
  Ellen (l) 455
  John 455, (l) 455
  Margaret (l) 455
  Margery (l) 455
  Marian (l) 455, 595, (l)(e) 455
  Richard (l) 109
  Robert 455
  Thomas (l) 455, (l)(e) 595, (w) 194, 347, 694, 737
  William 455
  Winifred (l) 595
Peapes, Richard (l)(e) 564
Pearelye, John (w) 215
Pearetre, Mary 876
Pearse (Peirse),
  Anthony (l) 858
  Francis (l)(e) 447
  Thomasine (l) 858
Pearson (Peirson, Person, Pirson),
  Abraham (l) 236
  Anne (l) 156
  Avis (l)(e) 156
  Gualcher (w) 388
  John 772
  Lionel (w) 388
  Lucy (l) 374
  Katherine (l) 772
  Mary (l) 156
  Richard 888, (l)(e) 156
  Robert (w) 95
  Rose (l) 156
  William 156
Pechey see Peachie
Pechie see Peachie
Peck (Pecke),
  John 186, (w) 577
  Mary (l) 186
  Stephen 799
  Susan (l) 186
  William (l) 186
Pecke see Peck
Pecok see Peacock
Peirse see Pearse
Peirson see Pearson
Penall, Isaac 3
Penn, Mr (l) 627
Penny,
  Barbara 248
  Francis 248
  Margery (l) 248
Pennynge, Robert (w) 138

431

Pennynnge, William (w) 138
Pepper 619
  Margaret (l) 250
Percifall,
  Elizabeth 371
  Thomas 371
Peren, John (w) 516
Periman, Francis 485
Perkyn,
  Lettice (l)(e) 146
  Mary (l) 146
  Rebecca (l) 146
Person see Pearson
Petchell, Roger (l) 703
Petchey (Petchie),
  Dorothy (w) 62
  Edmund (w) 44
  Henry (w) 276
  John 871
  Robert (w) 276
Petchie see Petchey
Peteywarde see Pettyward
Pett, Samuel (w) 242
Pettet see Pettit
Pettit (Pettet, Pettitt), (l) 555
  Ambrose (l) 46
  Bridget (l) 46
  Esther (l) 46, 247
  Giles (l) 839
  John (l) 46, 247
  Mary (l) 46, (w) 45
  Robert (l) 839
  William (l)(e) 839
Pettitt see Pettit
Pettiward see Pettyward
Pettiwate see Pettyward
Petto (Pettoe)
  Alice (l) 619
  Anne (l) 589
  Joseph (e) 619
Pettoe see Petto
Pettycote,
  Ambrose (w) 493
  Anthony (l) 493
  Margaret (l) 493
  Susan (l) 493
  Thomasine (l) 493
  William (w) 493
Pettyward (Peteywarde, Pettiward, Pettiwate),
  Anne (l) 488
  Anthony (w) 271
  Bridget (l) 488
  Edmund (l) 742, (w) 668
  Henry (w) 32
Phenex,
  Elizabeth (w) 580
  John (l) 580
Phenexe, John (w) 328
Phillippes see Phillipps
Phillipps (Phillippes), see also Felipe
  George 85
  Mary (w) 457
  Oliver (w) 464
  Roger (w) 457
Phillipson, William (e) 792
Pigeon, Margaret (l) 529

Pigg, William 514, (w) 15, 98
Pilboroughe, Robert (w) 585
Pilborowe, Michael (w) 232
Pilgrime 100
Pinchbecke, John (w) 502, 705
Pinswan (Pinswayne, Pinswine),
  John (w) 519
  Julian (l) 734
  Robert 734
  Sarah (l) 734
  Thomas (l) 818
  Widow 818
Pinswayne see Pinswan
Pinswine see Pinswan
Piper, John the elder (e)(w) 213
Pirson see Pearson
  William 156
Pistor, Alexander (w) 208
Pitches (Pytches),
  Anne (l)(e) 722
  George (w) 786
  John (l) 773
  Susan (l) 733
  William (w) 443
Pittes see Pitts
Pitts (Pittes, Pyttes),
  Avis (l) 234
  Elizabeth (l) 234, 859
  Richard (e) 134
  Simon (e) 695, 407, (e)(w) 84, (l)(e) 234, 859,
    (l)(w) 56, (w) 108, 329
  William (l) 234
Place, Henry (l) 563
Plampen see Plampyn
Plampin see Plampyn
  Elizabeth (l) 811
  Henry (l)(e) 811
  Margaret (l) 811
  Mary (l) 811
  William (l) 811
Plampyn,
  Anne (l) 232
  Dorcas (l) 232
  Dorothy (l) 232
  Elizabeth (l) 232, 811
  Frances (l) 232
  Henry (l)(e) 811
  John (l) 232, (l)(e) 232, (w) 698
  Margaret (l) 811
  Mary (l) 232, 811
  Robert (l) 232
  William (l) 811
Playfere,
  Abigail (l) 398
  Anthony (l) 398
  Dorcas (l) 398
  Dorothy (l) 398
  Margaret (l)(e) 398
  Sarah (l) 398
  Susan (l) 398
  Thomas (l) 398
Pleasance (Pleasannce, Pleasaunce, Pleaseance),
  Alice (l)(e) 415
  Anne (l) 806
  Charles (l) 806
  George (w) 424

432

John (l) 415, 806, (w) 224
Judith (l) 415
Mary (l) 806
Richard 723
Robert 792
Thomas (w) 370
William (l) 415, (l)(e) 806
Pleasannce see Pleasance
Pleasaunce see Pleasance
Pleaseance see Pleasance
Pledger, Robert (w) 241
Plowman, Richard 661
Plumbe,
  Henry (w) 48
  Margaret (l) 403
  Richard 703
Plummer,
  Edward 79
  Elizabeth (l) 79
  Joan (l)(e) 79
  Margaret (l) 79
  Robert 79
  Susan (l) 79
  Thomas 79, (l) 79
Pocket,
  Susan 703
  Thomas 703
Polle, John (l) 650
Pollington, Richard 652
Pollye see Pooley
Pond,
  Edmund (l) 611
  Edward (e) 453
  Elizabeth (l) 473
  John (l) 611
  Margaret (l) 453
  Martha (l) 611
Ponder (l), 42
Poole (Poolle),
  Elizabeth (l)(e) 519
  Thomas (l) 519, (w) 810, 852
Pooley (Pollye, Poollye, Poolye),
  Anne 102
  Dorothy (l) 56
  John 102
  Mirabel 531
  Thomas (e) 606, (w) 852
Poollye see Pooley
Poolye see Pooley
Pope, Thomas [Mr] 825
Porter, (l) 865
  Elizabeth (l) 411, 750, 815
  Francis (l) 83
  George (l) 815
  John (l) 750, (l)(e) 815
  Margaret (l) 750
  Marian (l) 750
  Randall 767
  Robert (l) 815, 865
  Thomas 411
  Walter (l)(e) 815
  wife (l) 767
Portte,
  Judith (l) 90
  Rachel (l) 90

Posford,
  Joan 229
  John 229, (w) 861
Potter 677
  Henry (l)(e) 174
  James 608
  John (w) 230
  Oliver (e) 377
  Thomas 490, (w) 645, 844
Pottes, Thomas (e) 872
Poulter see Powlter
Powle 631
  Anne 631
  Elizabeth (l) 788
  Frances (l) 631, 788
  Francis (l) 631
  John (l)(e) 788
  Margaret (l) 631, 788
  William (l) 788
Powlter (Poulter),
  John 27, 113
Powlyn, John (l) 307
Poyner, John (l) 179
Pratt,
  George 97, (w) 716, 815
  John 46, (e)(w) 201
  Richard 145
  Thomas (e) 485, (w) 298, 624
Prentice,
  John 581, (l) 2
  Mary (l) 2, (l)(e) 2
  Peter (l) 2
  Philip (l) 2
  Rose (w) 581
  Sarah (l) 2
  Thomas (l) 2
  William 490, (l) 2
Preston, Thomas (w) 90
Pretty,
  Dorothy (l) 147
  Edmund (l) 147
  Elizabeth (l) 147
  George (l)(e) 147
  Jane (l) 147
  John (l) 147
Pretyman, Richard (e)(w) 616
Prewer,
  Anne (l) 70
  Anne the younger (l) 70
Prick see Pricke
Pricke (Prick),
  Ambrose (l) 292
  Anne (l)(e) 292
  Charles (e) 76
  Christopher (w) 127
  George (l) 760
  John (e) 760, (w) 473, 693
  Margaret (l) 760
  Richard (w) 415
  Robert (e) 76
  Samuel (l) 760
  Simon (l) 760
  Thomas (w) 105, 378
  Walter (l) 591
  William (l) 760, (w) 606

433

434

Rayneberd *see* Raynberd
Rayner (Reyner),
 Elizabeth (l) 552
 John (e) 688, (l)(e) 552, (w) 783
 Mr (l) 179
 Robert (w) 179
 Stephen (e) 743
Raynes, Henry (w) 839
Raynham (Rainham, Raneham),
 Brian (l) 765
 Joan (l) 765
 John (l) 771
 Judith (l) 771
 Lawrence (l)(e) 771
 Ralph (l)(e) 765
 Richard (l) 771
Rayniad, Thomas (w) 399
Raynold *see* Reynold
Rayson, Adam 781
Read *see* Reade
Reade (Read, Rede, Reede),
 Anne (l) 112
 Edward (l) 112, 276
 Elizabeth (l) 276, 427
 Ellen 396
 Frances (l) 731
 Jane (l)(e) 112
 John (l) 112, 276
 Margaret (l)(e) 276
 Mary (l) 112, 396
 Prudence (l) 112
 Robert (l) 276
 Thomas (l) 112, 276, 448
 Walter 615
 William 731, (l) 112
Redder, Robert 11
Rede *see* Reade
Redewlon, John 181
Redgyn, Miles 174
Rednall,
 Richard (w) 801
 Robert (w) 801
Reede *see* Reade
 Anne (l) 112
 Edward (l) 112
 Jane (l)(e) 112
 John (l) 112
 Mary (l) 112
 Prudence (l) 112
 Thomas (l) 112
 William (l) 112
Reeve (Reve), 839
 Alice (l)(e) 756
 Amos (l) 600
 Anne (w) 799
 Avis (l) 241
 Elizabeth (l) 241
 Francis (l) 756, (l)(e) 25
 Henry (w) 230
 John (l) 241, 756, (w) 756
 Lydia (w) 696, 808
 Margaret (l) 25, (l)(e) 241, 314
 Mary (l) 241, 600
 Mildred (l) 776
 Parnall (l) 25
 Richard (w) 256

Robert 799, (l) 756
 Thomas 696, (l) 756, (w) 725
 William 455
Reeve alias Franncis *see* Franncis alias Reeve
Reighnoldes *see* Reynolds
Reinolds *see* Reynolds
Remching, Edmund (w) 605
Reve *see* Reeve
Revell (Revill), (l) 311
 Edmund (l) 120
 Katherine 639
 Martha (l)(e) 261
 Prentise (l) 124
 Thomas (l)(e) 124, (w) 379, 545
 William 753
 William the elder 703
Revet *see* Revett
Revett (Revet),
 Anne (l) 894
 James (l) 894
 John (l) 894
 Samuel (l)(e) 894
 Susan (l) 894
 Thomas (l) 894
 Timothy (l) 894
 William (l) 894
Revill, Edmund (l) 120
Rewse,
 George (l) 681
 Henry (w) 254
 Richard (l) 681
 Simon (l) 681, (w) 254
Reyner *see* Rayner
Reynold (Raynold),
 Alice 752
 John (w) 43, 670
 Thomas 752
Reynoldes *see* Reynolds
Reynolds (Reighnoldes, Reinolds, Reynoldes),
 Anne (l) 707
 Francis (l) 77
 James (l) 772
 Margaret (l) 707
 Mark (w) 100
 Mary (l)(e) 772
 Susan (l) 268, 772
 Thomas (l) 772
Richardson,
 Frances 784
 George 784
 Joan (w) 449
 Philip (w) 179
Rickard, Richard (l) 382
Rideldale, wife (l) 56
Ridgwell,
 Ann (l) 533
 Thomas (l) 533
 William 533
Ridley, Roger (w) 547
Ridnall (Rednall, Rydnall),
 Anne (l) 328
 Elizabeth (l) 328
 John 194, (l) 328
 Richard (e) 711, (l) 328, (w) 705, 801
 Robert (l)(e) 328, (w) 134, 801
 William (l) 328

435

Risby, Robert (w) 793
Rise,
  Reginald 368
  William 368
Rivers, Lord 362
Roberts,
  John (l) 11
  Thomas (l) 11
Robertsonne, Thomas (w) 206
Robinson,
  Mistress (l) 580
  Richard (w) 2, 155
Robinson alias Cooper see Cooper alias Robinson
Robinson alias Sander,
  Dorothy (l)(e) 726
  Millicent (l) 726
  Robert (l) 726
Robson, Emma (l) 333
Rockett, Thomas (w) 304
Rodwell, Richard (w) 465
Roger,
  Henry (w) 729
  Mathew 622
Rogers,
  Arthur (w) 102
  John (l) 426, (l)(e) 560, (w) 438
  Mathew (l) 560
  Mr (l) 335
  Richard (l) 560, (w) 174
  Robert (l) 560
  Thomas (w) 448
  William (w) 20, 223, 448
Rolfe, (l) 650
  Agnes (l) 26
  Andrew 110, (w) 26
  Elizabeth (l) 26
  Frances (l)(e) 879
  Jane (l) 26, 879
  Mary (l) 879
  Richard (l)(e) 26
  Simon 26
Rombold, Margery 706
Roockeard, Robert [Sir] 266
Rookes, John (w) 623
Roote,
  Ann (l) 649
  Frances (w) 190
  Susan (l) 372
  William 402, (w) 769
Roper,
  Frances (l) 780
  Jane (l) 780
  John (w) 290
  Mary (l)(e) 780
  Sarah (l) 780
  Thomas (l) 780
Ropp, Robert (w) 429
Rose,
  Alice (l) 132
  Anne (l) 638
  Christopher (l) 863
  Edmund (w) 395
  Edward (l) 550
  Ezechias 68
  Ezekias (l)(e) 132
  Frances (l)(e) 638

John (w) 518
Mary (l) 132
Robert (w) 608
Thomas 409, (w) 63
Thomasine (l) 409
Rosier,
  Alice (l) 318, (l)(e) 318
  Anne (l) 318
  Mary (l) 318
  Thomas (l) 318
  William (l) 318
Rosse, Anne (w) 249
Rosyar, George (w) 126
Rote, John (w) 815
Rouland, Thomas (w) 32
Rous (Rowse), John (w) 454, 613
Rout (Rowte),
  Alice (l) 745
  Mary (l) 745
  Samuel 745, (w) 745
Rowe,
  Christopher 404
  Jonas (w) 442
Rowleson,
  John (l) 807
  Lawrence 807
Rowlington, Thomas (w) 608
Rowly, William (l) 729
Rowneing see Rowninge
Rowninge (Rowneing),
  James (l) 83
  John (l) 83, 284
  Phyllis (l)(e) 83
  William (l)(e) 83
Rowte see Rout
Royse,
  Grizel (l) 702
  Henry 702
  Lucy (l)(e) 702
  Robert (l) 702
Rudland, William (w) 225
Ruffle,
  Anne (l) 606
  Elizabeth (l) 606
  George (l) 606
  John (l) 606
  Katherine (l)(e) 606
  Thomas (l) 606
  William (l) 606
Ruggells, Alice (l) 477
Rumball,
  Margaret (l) 727
  Mary (l) 727
  Susan (l)(e) 727
  Thomas (l) 727
Rumbelowe,
  Anne (l) 46, 247
  John (l)(e) 46, 247
  Martin (l) 46
  Robert (l)(e) 46
  Thomas 46, 247
Ruse, Mary (l) 520
Rush (Rushe),
  Edward (l) 90
  Jasper (l) 90
  John (w) 371

437

Sawyer (Sawer),
  Anne (l) 272, (l)(e) 883
  Ellen (l) 541
  Henry (l) 272
  John (l) 541
  Margaret (l)(e) 541
  Rebecca (l) 883
  Richard (l) 541
  Thomas (l) 541
Sawyerd, William (w) 573
Sayer, Martha (l) 619
Sayre, William (e) 619
Scarfe (Scarffe),
  Augustine (l) 140
  Elizabeth (l)(e) 140
  George (l) 140
  Roger 600
Scarffe see Scarfe
Scarpe (Skarpe),
  Anthony (w) 10
  George (w) 324, 673, 736, 826
  George [Mr] 10
Scofeild,
  Constance (l) 829
  Mary (l) 829
  Thomas (l) 829
Scofen,
  Austen 257
  Elizabeth (w) 257
Scotchmer,
  Alice 145
  Thomas (w) 145
  William 145
Scott (Scotte), 9
  Abigail (l) 367
  Austin (w) 427
  Christopher (w) 444
  Edward (l) 260
  George (w) 803
  John 837, (l)(e) 444, (w) 385, 620
  Martha (l) 260
  Mary (l)(e) 260, (w) 777
  Richard 367
  Thomas (l) 777, (w) 152, 525
  William (l) 260, (w) 492
Scotte see Scott
Scroope,
  Anne (l)(e) 361
  John (l) 361
Scrutton, William (l) 112
Scryven,
  Margaret (l) 514
  Richard 514
Seadon, Thomas 807
Seaman (Seamon, Seman),
  Agnes (l)(e) 680
  Anne (l) 627, 743
  Barber 104
  Bridget (l) 653
  Edmund 653
  Elizabeth (l) 627
  Helen (l) 653
  John 580, (l) 592, 653
  Ralph (l) 743
  Roger 653
  Susan (l) 653

  Thomas 653, (l) 592
  Widow (l) 183
  William (e) 801, 894, (l)(e) 627
Seamon see Seaman
Seargeant see Sargant
Seawell, Agnes (l) 395
Seffray, Thomas (w) 442
Segrave, William (w) 491
Selby, John (w) 793
Seley, James (w) 440
Selfe, William (w) 18
Seller,
  John [Mr] 436
  Mary (l) 436
Sellowes,
  Anne (l) 662
  Judith (l) 662
  Margaret (l) 662
  Mary (l) 662
  Sarah (l) 662
Seman see Seaman
Sergent see Sargant
Seriant, (l) 56
  Anne (l)(e) 271
  John (l) 271
Sewell,
  Bridget (l) 808
  Henry (w) 423
  William 215
Sexton, William (w) 559
Shadd, Robert (w) 759
Sharp see Sharpe
Sharpe (Sharp),
  Alice 323
  Anne (l) 217
  Grace (l)(e) 217
  Henry 708, (l) 217, (l)(e) 642
  James (w) 652
  Jasper (l) 217, (w) 718
  John 323, 774, (e) 831, (l) 217, 642
  Margaret (l) 217
  Phoebe (l) 217
  Richard (w) 332
  Robert (l) 217
  Roger (l) 217
  Thomas 9
  William 267
Shary, Rebecca (w) 435
Shaw see Shawe
Shawe (Shaw),
  Anne (l) 196, 234
  Charles (l) 234
  Edward (l) 234
  Francis (l) 234
  George (e) 196, (l) 196
  Grace (l) 196
  John (e) 196, (l) 196
  Katherine (l) 234
  Roger (l) 196
  Simon (l) 234
  Susan (l) 196, 234
  Thomas (l) 196
Sheader,
  Jane (w) 201
  Walter (w) 201
Shearman see Sherman

438

Sheene (Shene),
  Amy (l) 879
  Anne (l) 363
  Elizabeth (l) 363
  John (l) 363, 879, (w) 147, 522
  Margaret (l) 363
  Thomas (l)(e) 363
  William (l)(w) 363
Sheep,
  Anne (l) 274
  Elizabeth (l) 274
  Henry (l) 274
  John (l) 274
  Thomas (l) 274
Sheldrake, Grace (l)(e) 770
Shelley see Shellie
Shellie (Shelley, Shelly),
  James (w) 316
  Jeremy 725
  Joanna (l) 110
  John (l) 64, 652
  Katherine (l) 110
  Marian (l) 64, 652
  Nicholas 110, 652
  Philip (l) 725
  Rose 110
Shelly see Shellie
Shene see Sheene
Sheperd see Sheppard
Shephard see Sheppard
Shepheard see Sheppard
Sheppard (Sheperd, Shephard, Shepheard),
  Ambrose (l) 183
  Anne (l) 734
  Benjamin (l) 22
  Edmund (l) 183, 221
  Elizabeth (l) 183, 221, 580
  Francis (l) 183
  John (l) 22, (l)(e) 183, 221, 580
  John [Mr] (e) 801
  Joshua (l) 22
  Richard (l)(e) 221
  Robert (w) 495
  Samuel (e) 734 (w) 495
  Samuel junior (w) 734
  Sarah (l) 22, (l)(e) 22
  Thomas (l) 183, 221, 580, (w) 183
  William (l) 22, 183, 221
Shere, John (w) 648, 788
Sherief, Thomas the elder (e) 616
Sheringe, Katherine (l) 627
Sherman (Shearman),
  Anne (l) 372
  Richard (w) 181, 348, 702
Shewe, John (w) 703
Shilling, Thomas (l) 604
Shipp, Henry (w) 745
Shippe, Timothy (l) 282
Shornebise, Robert (w) 221
Shreve, Thomas (e) 193
Shrife, Thomas 490
Sibbs,
  John (w) 272
  Thomas (w) 272
Sidey, John (w) 832

Sillett,
  Elizabeth (l) 527
  John (l) 527, (w) 244
  Margaret (l)(e) 527
  Mary (l) 527
  Philip (l) 527
  Richard 10
  Sebastian (l) 527
  Thomas (l) 527
  William (w) 162
Silvester (Sylvester),
  James 294
  Martha (l) 9
  Robert (w) 91
  William 9
Simionde, Mr (e) 812
Simonds see Symondes
Simpson (Simson, Sympson), 871
  Alice 337
  Edward (w) 543
  John 688
  William 688, (e)(w) 751
Simson see Simpson
Sinderland,
  Alice (l) 535, (l)(e) 655
  Edward (l) 655
Sippes, Thomas (w) 66
Skarpe see Scarpe
Skepper,
  Anne (l) 485
  Constance (l) 272
  George (l)(e) 272
  John (l) 272
  Martha (l) 485
  Peter (l)(e) 272
  Thomas (l) 485
Skevington,
  Edward (e) 152
  Susan (l) 152
Skinner (Skynner),
  Anne (l) 461, 487, 609
  Ellen (l) 487
  Enneter (l) 487
  Francis (l) 268, (w) 636
  George (l) 487
  Henry (w) 212, 636
  James (l) 268, 487
  Martha (l) 268
  Mary 268
  Robert (w) 212
  Thomas (l) 609
  William (l) 461
Skynner see Skinner
Slacke,
  Jonathan (l) 723
  Mary (l) 723
Slacke alias Cokes, Mary (l) 723
Slofile, Mary (w) 829
Slyr, Robert 839
Small, Robert (w) 634
Smeare, William 342
Smeth see Smith
Smethe see Smith
Smith (Smeth, Smethe, Smithe), 91, 732
  Abigail (l) 347

439

Alice (l) 33, 230
Anabelle (l) 813
Andrew (l) 3, 515, (w) 751
Anne (l) 3, 33, (l)(e) 33, 312, 515
Avis (l) 33
Bartholomew 33, (l)(e) 33
Bridget (l) 123
Charles 335, (w) 2
Christopher (l) 33
Deborah (l) 347
Dorothy (l)(w) 843
Edmund 347
Elizabeth (l) 3, 313, 347
Francis (w) 21
Hannah (l) 347
Henry (l) 230
Hurd [Mr] (l) 612
Jane (l) 813
Jeremy (l) 525
John (e) 77, (l) 3, 33, 347, 515, 818, (w) 21, 480, 544, 578, 689, 844
Joseph (l) 515, (w) 360
Lucy (l)(e) 404
Luke (l) 515
Lydia (l) 347
Mark (l) 515
Martha (l) 347
Mary (l) 33, 347
Matthew (l)(e) 460
Nathaniel (l) 818
Olive (l) 347
Philip (l) 818
Rachel (l) 347
Robert (l) 33, 70, 219, 347, 460
Rose (l) 96
Simon (l) 347
Thomas 347, (l) 3, 813, (w) 333, 660
Thomasine (l)(e) 725
William (l) 219, 347, (l)(e) 404, 813, (w) 24, 424
Smith alias Agnis *see* Agnis alias Smith
Smithe *see* Smith
Smye, Edward 384, 543
Smyth (Smythe), 10
Abraham (l) 659
Acquilla (l) 477
Agnes 17
Alice (l) 103, 364, (l)(e) 364
Anne (w) 105
Bartholomew (w) 169
Benjamin (l) 477, (l)(e) 477
Bridget (l) 477
Clement (l) 102
David (l) 659
Edward 202, (l) 659, (l)(e) 385
Elizabeth (l) 102, 364
Fabian (l)(e) 364
Francis 878
George (l) 477, 659
Henry (l) 102, 200, (w) 864
Joan (l) 102
John 103, 114, (e) 243, (l) 103, 364, 385, (w) 165, 205, 237, 585, 675
Jonas (l) 477
Lancelot (l) 385
Margery (l) 102
Mary (l) 102, (l)(e) 413

Peter (w) 376
Rebecca (l) 392
Reginald (l) 243
Richard (l) 659
Robert 708, (l) 385
Rose (l) 200
Samuel 97
Sarah (l) 420
Soffiny (l) 364
Thomas 385, 874, (e) 102, 483, (l) 102, 420, (w) 413
William 385, (e) 640, (l) 200, 393, 477, 659, (w) 315
Smyth alias Hovell *see* Hovell alias Smyth
Smyth alias Hovill, John 126
Smythe *see* Smyth
Snape, Isaac (w) 803
Snell,
John (l) 863
John the younger 445
Mary (l) 445
Snelling, John (w) 89
Snow alias Fuller, William (l)(e) 778
Soame,
Ann (l) 514
Fletcher (l) 514
John (l) 514
Susan (l)(e) 514
Thomas (l) 514
William (l) 514
William [Sir] (e) 514
Soles,
Bridget (l) 196
Edward (l) 196
Frances 196
Susan (l) 196
Somer,
John (l)(e) 39
Margaret (l) 39
Sorrell, William 407
Sothebe *see* Sothebie
Sothebie (Sothebe, Sothebye, Sowtherbie),
Anne (w) 470
Thomas (e) 531, (w) 28, 470, 519, 724, 739
Thomas [Mr] 634
Sothebye *see* Sothebie
Sowgate 771
Helen (l) 97
John 531, (l) 97, (w) 69
John junior 145
Mary (l) 531
William (l) 97
Sowter,
Alice 890
Edmund (l)(e) 365
Francis (l) 391
John 768, (l)(e) 379
Mary (l) 379, 768, 890
Sowth,
Agnes (l) 253
Benjamin (l) 253
John (l) 253
Mary (l) 253
William (l) 253, 630
Sowtherbie *see* Sothebie
Spaldin *see* Spalding

440

442

444

Thomas (l) 98
Tilar *see* Tyler
Tilbrooke,
  Abraham (l) 632
  John (w) 613, 637
  Margaret (l)(e) 632
  Nicholas (l) 632
Tilden, John (w) 524
Tiler *see* Tyler
Tillet *see* Tillett
Tillett (Tillet, Tillott, Tyllet),
  Alice (l) 600
  Anne (l) 437
  Cicely (l) 139
  Edmund 139, (l) 437
  Elizabeth (l) 600, 649
  John 825, (l)(e) 437, (w) 231
  Leonard 193
  Margaret (w) 437
  Mary (l) 649
  Reginald 825
  Robert (l) 825, (l)(e) 637
  Roger 826
  Thomas (l)(e) 600, 825
  William (l) 600, 825
Tillott *see* Tillett
Timperley, Nicholas 559
Tinker,
  Alice 734
  Jeremy (l) 734
  John (l) 734
Tirrill *see* Tyrrill
Titterell, William (l) 315
Tolwardes, Thomas (w) 83
Tolwardye,
  Agnes (l) 425
  Ambrose (e) 425
  Frances (l)(e) 425
  John (l) 425
  Judith (l) 425
Tompson *see also* Thompson
  Agnes (l)(e) 795
  Grace (l) 13
  John 228, (l) 795
  John the younger (l) 228
  Margaret (l) 366
  Mary (l)(e) 824
  Mathew (l) 315
  Thomas (l) 795, 824
  Thomasine (l) 795
  William (w) 667
Topley, John (w) 332
Torell (Torrell),
  Ellen (l) 441
  James (l)(e) 441
  Love (l) 441
  Margaret (l) 441
  Sarah (l) 441
Torladie, Thomas 181
Torrell *see* Torell
Tostock, John 644
Tostocke, John (w) 846, 876
Tovell, George senior 85
Towler,
  Holyfernus (w) 277
  John (e) 701

Townsend, Elizabeth 109
Trapet, Margaret (l) 309
Trapper, widow 11
Tray, Alice (l)(e) 561
Traye,
  Agnes (l) 467
  Elizabeth (l) 467
  Mary (l) 467
  Susan (l) 467
  William (l)(e) 467
Treake, William (l) 175
Tricker, John 856
Troyse,
  Thomas (w) 752
  William (w) 289
Tuffeild (Tuffielde),
  Anne (l) 512
  Edmund 60, (l) 80
  Elizabeth (l) 512
  Margaret (l) 80
  Susan (l) 80
Tuffielde *see* Tuffeild
Tufts 580
Tunrer (l) 619
Turell *see* Turrill
Turells, Godfrey (w) 435
Turle,
  George (w) 467
  Thomas 611
  Widow 367
Turner (Turnor),
  Alice (l) 64, 380
  Anne (l) 101
  Barnabas 253
  Bartholomew 380
  Daniel (l) 101
  George (l) 380
  James 64, 652
  Jane (l) 702
  John 363, 702
  Katherine (l) 702
  Lettice (l) 745
  Lydia (l) 367
  Margaret (l) 745, (l)(e) 290
  Mark (w) 26
  Martin (l) 380
  Mary (l) 64, 101
  Mr (w) 869
  Ralph 355
  Richard 367
  Samuel (l) 101, 380
  Simon (l) 380
  Susan (l) 101
  wife (w) 380
  William (e) 745, 812, (w) 366
Turnor *see* Turner
Turrill (Turrell),
  James (l) 662
  Marion (l) 122
  Mary (l) 122
Turtle,
  Henry (l) 538
  John (l) 538
  Martha (l) 538
  Susan (l)(e) 538
  Thomas (l) 538

446

447

448

Whight *see also* White
  Alice (l) 751
  John 751
  Priscilla (l) 751
  Stephen 851
Whightinge,
  Elizabeth (l)(e) 683
  John (l) 683
  Mary (l) 683
  Susan (l) 683
  William (l) 683
Whin, Edward (w) 872
Whitacre, (l) 115
Whitbye,
  Mr (l) 627
  William (l)(e) 174
White (Whyte) *see also* Whight
  Arnold (w) 228
  Bridget (l) 56
  Dorothy (l) 741
  Edmund (w) 754
  Edward 875, (l) 741
  Elizabeth (l) 113
  Henry [Mr] (l) 296
  Henry (w) 593
  John 56, (l)(e) 741, (w) 332, 463, 518, 680, 757
  Jude (w) 679
  Thomas (l) 741
Whitehead (Whithead),
  Henry (e) 57
  Marian (l) 502
  Margaret (l)(e) 300
  Robert (l) 300
  Thomas (l) 300
Whiter,
  Ellen (l) 546
  George (l) 440, 546, (l)(e) 440
  Helen (l) 440
  John (l) 440, 546
  Margaret (l)(e) 440, 546
  Richard (l) 440, 546
Whithand,
  John (l) 127, 440, (w) 25, 546
  Mary (l) 127
  Susan (l) 127
Whithead *see* Whitehead
Whiting (Whitinge),
  Anne (l) 101
  Bridget (l) 745
  John (e) 101
  John the elder (l) 745
  William (l) 745
Whitinge *see* Whiting
Whitney,
  Ralph (w) 202, 499
  Ran (w) 306
  Reginald (w) 162
  Thomas (w) 306
Whittle,
  George (l)(e) 814
  Henry (l) 814
  Susan (l) 814
  Thomas 814
Whydbe, William (l) 632
Whyte *see* White

Wiard,
  Elizabeth (l) 573
  James (l)(e) 573
Wickes,
  Joan (w) 797
  Mary (l) 80
Wickyns, John (w) 633
Wiett *see* Wyatt
Wiffin (Whiffine, Wyffen),
  Dorothy (l) 168
  Mary (l) 168, 247
  Richard (e) 420, (l)(e) 168
  William (e) 420, (l)(e) 168
Wildes (l) 179
  Edward (l) 179
  Elizabeth (l) 179
  Nan (l) 179
  Thomas (l) 179
Wilken *see* Wilkin
Wilkenson *see* Wilkinson
Wilkin (Wilken, Wilkyn),
  Elizabeth (l) 333
  John (l) 333
  Thomas 104, 333, (e)(w) 275
Wilkinson (Wilkenson),
  Elizabeth (l)(e) 849
  Francis (l) 849, (w) 467
  Peter (l) 849
  Richard (w) 81
  Thomas 333, (l) 849
Wilkyn *see* Wilkin
Wilkyns (Wylkins),
  John (w) 253, 274, 369, 404, 406, 529, 576
  Thomas (w) 276
Willasonne, Joseph (w) 214
Willett,
  John 92
  Robert [Mr] (w) 780
Williames (Wilyams),
  James 505
  John (w) 432
  Margaret (l) 505
  Thomas (w) 221
Williamson, Thomas (w) 173
Williment, William junior (e) 136
Willis (Wyllis),
  Anne (l) 103
  Samuel, 103, 296
  Thomas 103
  Thomas [Mr] (l) 395
Willmott, [Mr] (l) 124
Willon (Wyllon),
  Avis (l) 12
  Robert 12
Willoughby, Charles (w) 593
Wills,
  Alice (l) 605
  Mary 605
Willson *see* Wilson
Wilson (Willson),
  Edward (w) 633
  Francis junior 486
  John (l) 871
  Stephen (w) 765
  Thomas (l) 872

INDEX OF PLACES

Numbers immediately following place names refer to wills of testators who lived there. References to land given only when not in testator's parish.

Acton 471
  fields etc (named) in 543
  persons of 814
Aldham 54, 559, 628
  fields etc (named) in 559, 628
  persons of 559
Alpheton 649, 711
Ampton 409, 610
  churchyard, burial in 409, 610
Ashfield 690
  manor of 518, 737
  persons of 841
Ashfield, Gt 194, 264, 347, 430, 694, 737, 827
  burial in parish of 347, 737
  churchyard, burial in 430, 694, 737
  fields etc (named) in 264
  land in 115, 816
  minister of 347
  poor of 347
Ashfield Hall, manor of 518
Ashley [Cambs] 250
  flock of sheep at 46
  land in 288
  persons of 873
Aspall 85
  fields etc (named) in 85
Assington 335, 411, 608, 704
  churchyard, burial in 411
  land in 225
  persons of 214, 608
  poor of 225, 335, 608
  vicarage house in 335
Attleborough [Norf], persons of 11

Bacton 269, 317, 340, 389, 465, 469, 481, 489, 668, 708
  Breisworth New Hall manor in 465
  fields etc (named) in 465, 481
  persons of 340, 481, 489, 4889
  poor of 317, 616
Bacton [Norf], persons of 841
Badwell Ash 75, 820
  land in 115, 202, 816
  persons of 75
  poor of 68, 566
Ballingdon [Essex] 114, 754
  houses in 114
  inn (named) in 754

persons of 875
poor of 461, 875
Balsham [Cambs], poor of 813
Bardwell 162, 244
  Bardwell Hall manor in 162, 202
  churchyard, burial in 244
  fields etc (named) in 244
  land in 179, 730
  persons of 259, 423, 499, 713
  poor of 566
  Wykes manor in 162
Barham, persons of 724
Barking,
  Barking manor in 384
  land in 384
Barnardiston 195, 284, 383, 492, 850
  churchyard, burial in 383
  land in 564
  overseers of 195
  persons of 284, 492
Barnby, poor of 179
Barnham 117
Barningham 36, 149, 282, 658
  churchyard, burial in 149
  fields etc (named) in 36
  fold courses in 36
  land in 242, 577, 653
  persons of 282, 577
  sheep walks in 36
Barrow 76, 111, 258, 286, 337, 415, 424, 695
  Barrow Hall in 258
  churchyard, burial in 337, 415, 424
  fields etc (named) in 6
  land in 654
  persons of 258, 504
  poor of 111, 258
Barton 80
  fields etc (named) in 80
  persons of 296
  poor of 80
Barton, Gt 60, 115, 478
  churchyard, burial in 60
  fields etc (named) in 60, 777
  land in 593, 703, 777
  manor of 272, 777
  poor of 60
Barton Mills 526, 843
  land in 661
Beccles, poor of 179

Bedfield,
  land in 148
  persons of 148
Belchamp Otton [Essex], manor of 420
Beyton 172, 304, 536
  fields etc (named) in 304
  land in 593
  property in 89
Bildeston 419, 747
  land in 305, 612, 771
  land near 612
  minister of 305
  persons of 590
Blo' Norton [Norf], land in 448
Bocking [Essex], persons of 461, 706
Borley [Essex], persons of 606
Botesdale 12, 392, 822
  fields etc (named) in 589
  land in 12
  persons of 745
Boxford 349, 535, 664, 740
  Callis St in 655
  churchyard, burial in 535
  fields etc (named) in 664
  house in 535, 655
  land in 155, 225
  persons of 56, 213
  watermill in 56
Boxted 358, 412, 537, 803, 838
  land in 673
  road to 491
Bradfield, land in 593, 689
Bradfield Combust 390, 544
  land in 208
Bradfield St Clare,
  land in 194, 826
  persons of 229
Bradfield St George 229, 472, 674, 689
  fields etc (named) in 194, 674
  Lovells manor in 674
  manor of 229, 674
  persons of 229
Bradley, Gt, land in 46
Bradley, Lt 320
Braintree [Essex],
  land in 367
  persons of 367
Braiseworth 52, 401
Bramford, persons of 818
Brandon 35, 92, 152, 169, 187, 376, 613, 632, 637,
  661, 860
  burial in church of 169
  churchyard,
    burial in 92, 169, 632, 637
    house next to 726
  house in 726
  persons of 497, 661
  poor of 35, 92
Brandon Ferry see Brandon
Brargh (unidentified) [Norf], land in 792
Braxted, Much [Essex], persons of 137
Brent Eleigh see Eleigh, Brent
Brettenham 305, 584, 720, 771
  churchyard, burial in 584, 771
  fields etc (named) in 9, 584
  house (named) in 9

land in 107
  persons of 229
  poor of 9, 771
Bricett, persons of 449
Brinckley [Cambs], persons of 113
Brockford 24
Brockley 65, 466, 643, 878
  fields etc (named) in 115
  house in 466
  land in 65, 677
  persons of 345, 643
Brockley Hall manor 677
Brome,
  persons of 490
  poor of 357
Bulmer [Essex], land in 420
Bures 225, 663
  churchyard, burial in 375
  curate of 225
  hamlet of 335
  land in 375
  persons of 335, 608, 663
  poor of 225, 751
Bures [Essex] 650, 688
  fields etc (named) in 688
  poor of 650
Bures hamlet 608
  house in 335, 608
Bures, Mount [Essex],
  fields etc (named) in 751
  persons of 228
Bures St Mary 227, 375, 751
  churchyard, burial in 225, 227
  fields etc (named) in 225
  land in 840
  persons of 751
Burgate, land in 681
Burwell [Cambs] 20, 23, 131, 153, 177, 223, 253,
  274, 369, 404, 406, 417, 418, 426, 501, 576,
  630, 633, 865
  churchyard, burial in 223, 630
  fields etc (named) in 153, 223, 253
  High Town End in 20
  manor of Dullingham in 404
  manor of Ramsies in 20, 253, 404, 630
  North St in 501
  Parsonage Lane in 20
  persons of 529
  poor of 20, 426, 630, 839, 865
  repair of parish church of 20
  windmill in, 253
Bury St Edmunds 10, 29, 32, 48, 49, 62, 81, 103,
  139, 144, 146, 160, 185, 212, 216, 217, 233,
  255, 280, 296, 322, 366, 367, 381, 386, 394,
  399, 421, 436, 439, 467, 468, 475, 484, 488,
  496, 497, 516, 517, 518, 538, 567, 588, 598,
  602, 611, 618, 631, 662, 671, 677, 679, 680,
  703, 717, 721, 735, 743, 763, 766, 802, 816,
  824, 825, 829, 863, 869, 871
  Abbey yard in 482
  alderman of 296
  Brackland in 144
  Brentgovel St in 488
  burgesses of 296
  Churchgate St in 367
  Cook Row in 871

454

Crown St in 829
Eastgate in 528
Eastgate St in 212
fields etc (named) in 703
Friars Lane in 703
Garland St in 103
Guildhall St in 619, 679, 816
Hatter St in 871
Horse Market in 871
hospital of St Petronilla in 10
house in 217, 233, 296, 373, 394, 439, 516, 528,
    611, 816, 829, 871
land in 482, 849
market cross in 103
Mayewater Lane in 871
Mustow St in 91, 528
Northgate St in 103, 296, 367, 467
persons of 76, 78, 81, 103, 178, 216, 231, 254,
    274, 296, 385, 394, 403, 421, 435, 438, 488,
    497, 500, 528, 611, 619, 629, 654, 681, 703,
    812, 816
poor of 139, 367, 593, 662, 703
Raingate St in 32
Risbygate St in 144
road to 622
St Andrews St in 81
St James's parish in,
    poor of 185, 217, 296, 439, 497, 703
    preacher of 296
St Mary's churchyard, burial in 48
St Mary's parish in 48, 871
    poor of 394, 439, 703, 816, 825, 871
    preacher of 703
St Wolstan's chapel in St Mary's church in 677
school hall in 497
shop in 703
south ward in 10
    poor of 680
Southgate St in 10, 467
town lands, feoffees of 871
Vinefield in 10
wards in 662
west ward in, poor of 680
Westgate St in 139, 871
Whiting St in 29, 81, 816
Buxhall 701
    Buxhall manor in 328
    churchyard, burial in 701
    Cockereels manor in 328
    fields etc (named) in 184, 328, 701
    poor of 70

Cambridge,
    furniture at 125
    house in 622
    King's College in 56
    market hill in 497
    persons of 248, 497, 622, 847, 872
    University of 272
Cambridgeshire,
    Ashley 46, 250, 288
    Balsham 813
    Brinckley 113
    Burwell 20, 23, 131, 153, 177, 223, 253, 274,
        369, 404, 406, 417, 418, 426, 501, 529, 576,
        630, 633, 839, 865

Cheveley 288, 873
Chippenham 83, 154, 166, 363, 402, 427
Ditton, Wood 273, 533, 582, 804, 27
Dullingham 547
Ely, Isle of 441
Fordham 38, 131, 161, 327, 455, 494, 579, 595,
    767, 839, 885
Fulbourn 622, 793
Hingestone 220
Isleham 78, 652
Kennett 462
Kirtling 282, 323, 380, 428, 722, 744
Littleport 441
Reach 38
Shudy Camps 326
Soham 34, 38, 61, 78, 275, 276, 333, 377, 402,
    441, 451, 515, 556, 667, 699, 798, 830, 842,
    872, 885, 892
Wicken 142, 344, 372, 402, 479, 494, 529, 583,
    806, 853, 885
Candishe (unidentified) 583
Catlidge see Kirtling
Cavendish 17, 124, 167, 351, 379, 545, 601, 697
    burial in church of 545
    churchwardens of 351
    churchyard, burial in 545
    fields etc (named) in 351
    house in 207, 583
    minister of 351
    persons of 216, 697, 839
    poor of 351, 379
    preacher of 124
Cavenham 8, 785, 790
    churchyard, burial in 8
    fields etc (named) in 785
    persons of 407, 790
Chedburgh 220
    Chedburgh Hall with Arneboroughs manor in
        733
    fields etc (named) in 220
    land in 643, 709, 873
    persons of 873
Chelmsford [Essex], land in 146
Chelsworth 249, 310
    land in 747
    persons of 599
Cheveley [Cambs] 288, 873
    church, burial in 873
    churchyard, burial in 288
    poor of 873
Chevington 16, 127, 261, 285, 370, 709, 733, 760,
    890
    church 16
    churchyard, burial in 370, 760
    fields etc (named) in 285, 294
    land in 391
    manor of 391
    manor of Chedberg with Armborowes in 391
    persons of 127, 261, 285, 733, 760
    poor of 16, 127, 624, 733, 760
Chilton, fields etc (named) in 543
Chipley (unidentified), land in 175
Chippenham [Cambs] 83, 154, 166, 363, 427
    Badlingham in 83
    churchyard, burial in 83, 166, 363, 427
    fields etc (named) in 363

456

457

houses (named) in 514
land in 15
minister of 514
persons of 98, 564, 874
poor of 514, 564, 773
windmill in 241
Hunston 796
land in 68, 864
minister of 864
persons of 68, 498, 508
poor of 68, 498, 566
Hunston Hall 508

Icklingham 180, 403, 487, 551, 577, 609, 640, 676
All Saints parish in 551, 577
fields etc (named) in 403, 487, 499
persons of 403, 577, 640
poor of 403, 499, 551, 577, 609
St James's churchyard, burial in 180
St James's parish in 551, 577
Ingham, persons of 403
Ipswich,
house in 296
persons of 74, 296, 439, 458, 732
Isleham [Cambs],
Beckhold manor in 78
house in 78
persons of 78, 652
Ixworth 202, 738, 883
house in 87
land in 306
manor of 518, 738
persons of 560, 708, 890
poor of 45, 68, 566, 593
priory of 148, 179
Ixworth Hall, manor of 518
Ixworth Thorpe 306, 391, 499
crops in 391
fields etc (named) in 306
persons of 713
poor of 499

Kedington 300, 725
churchyard, burial in 300, 725
land in 706
poor of 300, 773
Kennett [Cambs] 462
Kenninghall [Norf], persons of 282, 682
Kentford 605
Kenton,
Debenham or Butley manor in 668
land in 668
persons of 580
Kersey 442, 753
churchyard, burial in 442
Kesgrave, house in 388
Kettlebaston 783
manor of 612
tenement in 292
Ketton hamlet [Essex] 70
poor of 70
Kirtling [Cambs] 323, 380, 428, 722, 744
fields etc (named) in 323, 428
persons of 282, 873
Knettishall 448, 776
poor of 448

Lackford 174
bridge in 403
persons of 174
poor of 174
Lakenheath 211, 246, 289, 290, 607, 752, 779, 834
churchyard, burial in 779
persons of 661, 834
Undley in 752
Langham 68, 132, 148, 178, 450, 500, 505, 566
fields etc (named) in 148, 178, 500
manor of Ixworth Priory in 148
persons of 68, 75, 132, 178, 450, 500
poor of 68, 178, 566
tenement (named) in 68
Langmere [Norf], land in 792
Larling [Norf], persons of 11
Lavenham 200, 201, 292, 599, 705, 768, 810, 814,
845, 852, 893
Bolton St in 814
Church End in 845
Church St in 292
churchyard, burial in 292
High St in 705
house in 543, 599, 845
persons of 9, 56, 599, 711, 852
poor of 845, 893
Prentice St in 599
tenement in 42
Water St in 810, 893
Lawshall 21, 77, 555, 844
fields etc (named) in 77, 521
land in 65, 844
manor of 844
Laxfield, persons of 388
Layham 882
fields etc (named) in 882
poor of 882
Lidgate 102, 141, 205, 293, 622, 848
churchyard, burial in 141
fields etc (named) in 622
persons of 624
poor of 141, 622
Lincroft (unidentified) [Norf], land in 792
Lindsey 214
persons of 214
Little Bradley see Bradley, Lt
Little Cornard see Cornard, Lt
Little Livermere see Livermere, Lt
Little Saxham see Saxham, Lt
Little Stonham see Stonham, Lt
Little Thurlow see Thurlow, Lt
Little Waldingfield see Waldingfield, Lt
Little Whelnetham see Whelnetham, Lt
Littleport [Cambs], persons of 441
Livermere, persons of 873
Livermere, Gt 37, 158, 857
burial at 158
furniture at 391
persons of 45
Livermere, Lt 129
church, burial in 857
fields etc (named) in 129
London,
citizen of 56, 85, 420
Foster Lane in, persons of 367
persons of 109, 218, 258, 367, 657, 672, 681, 793

459

Long Melford *see* Melford
Lopham, South [Norf], furniture at 796

Maplestead,
  Gt [Essex], land in 732
  Lt [Essex], fields etc (named) in 732
Market Weston see Weston Market
Melford, Long 19, 266, 299, 331, 506, 761, 762,
    854, 867
  churchyard, burial in 867
  fields etc (named) in 266, 299
  Green in 506
  Hall Street in 19
  High St in 506, 762
  Holy Trinity hospital in 506
  houses in 19, 762
  land in 732
  persons of 266, 299, 458, 506, 555, 711
  poor of 506, 761
  Westgate St in 506
Mellis 828
  churchyard, burial in 90
  persons of 580
  Pountney manor in 828
Mendlesham 134, 183, 328, 580, 627, 683, 745,
    801, 894
  fields etc (named) in 580, 627, 683
  payment to inhabitants of 511
  persons of 339, 580, 619, 745, 801, 894
  poor of 580
Middleton [Essex],
  land in 461
  persons of 656
Milden 150
  persons of 56
Mildenhall 13, 26, 44, 47, 64, 106, 110, 128, 130,
    163, 171, 191, 199, 222, 240, 319, 341, 352,
    353, 360, 361, 382, 547, 563, 571, 596, 614,
    621, 639, 645, 652, 728, 750, 756, 870, 879
  Beck Row in 199
  church,
    burial in 110, 645
    repair of 106, 128, 199, 319, 382
  churchyard, burial in 191, 639, 728
  fields etc (named) in 26, 64, 128, 171, 199, 319,
    352, 360, 631, 639, 652, 879
  High Town in 639
  house in 341, 596, 621
  King's manor in 728
  land in 391, 614, 631
  manor of 631
  market place in 64, 652
  persons of 631
  poor of 199, 319
  West Row in 879
Monk Soham *see* Soham, Monk
Monks Eleigh *see* Eleigh, Monks
Moulton, land in 744
Mount Bures *see* Bures, Mount

Naughton, land in 80
Nayland *see also* Stoke by Nayland 182, 215, 647,
    655, 698, 833
  churchwardens of 215
  Court St in 215
  fields etc (named) in 155, 215, 655, 698

house (named) in 215
land in 655
overseers of 215
persons of 182, 215, 228, 647, 698, 784
Needham Market,
  Church Lane in 384
  land in 384
Nettlestead 781
New Buckenham [Norf], house in 638
Newmarket 113, 528, 569, 582, 797, 582
  churchyard, burial in 113, 528
  house in 582
  inns (named) in 113
  persons of 38, 113, 273, 582, 681
  poor of 113, 582, 797
  road to 622
  St Mary's churchyard, burial in 582
  shop in 131, 703
Newton 297, 741
  fields etc (named) in 774
  land in 774
  manor of Grayes in 784
  persons of 4, 119, 296, 856
Newton, Old 94, 291, 330, 511, 692
  manor of Dagworth Hall in 94
  persons of 511
Norfolk,
  Attleborough 11
  Bacton 841
  Blo' Norton 448
  Brargh (unidentified) 792
  Cley 792
  Dickleburgh 713, 792
  Diss 113
  Ellingham, Gt 719
  Feltwell 731
  Forncett 385
  Foulden 24
  Harling, East 681
  Hevingham 124
  Hockham 11
  Hockwell 731
  Hulverbush (unidentified) 792
  Kenninghall 282, 682
  Langmere 792
  Lincroft (unidentified) 792
  New Buckenham 638
    persons of 816
  Postwick 219
  Ringland 719
  Ropham (unidentified) 174
  Rudham 772
  Rushall 792
  Shipdham 719
  Stanford 661
  Stoke 174
  Thetford 613, 713, 730, 763
  Weeting 463
  Wicklewood 456
  Wilton, 731
  Wormegay 179
  Wramplingham 385
  Wymondham 483
North Cove *see* Cove, North
Norton 123, 263, 508, 795, 886
  bridge in 263

churchyard, burial in 263, 795
land in 566
manor of Norton Hall in 88
persons of 367, 482, 566
poor of 123, 508
Norwich, persons of 780
Nottinghamshire, persons of 258
Nowton 72, 575
land in 405, 575
fields etc (named) in 10

Oakley 357
poor of 357
Occold 397, 819
Benningham in 397
house (named) in 819
persons of 178
Occold Hall, manor of 819
Old Newton *see* Newton, Old
Ousden,
land in 453
manor of 46, 622
road to 622

Pakenham 410, 560, 777, 887
churchyard, burial in 410
Hall manor in 777
land in 45, 593, 643
persons of 36, 45, 109, 178, 560
poor of 45, 410
Palgrave,
fields etc (named) in 490
persons of 490
poor of 490
Parham, persons of 509
Pebmarsh [Essex], fields etc (named) in 732
Pentlow [Essex] 662
persons of 107, 420
Polstead 155, 316, 364, 759
churchyard, burial in 316
fields etc (named) in 155
house in 583
land in 759
persons of 297
poor of 316
Poslingford 343, 534
Chipley Abbey in 534
house in 534
land in 175
Postwick [Norf], farm (named) in 219
Preston 395, 521
church, repair of 395, 521
minister of 395
persons of 395
poor of 395, 521

Rattlesden 209, 416, 498, 525
fields etc (named) in 9
house (named) in 9
land in 367, 781
parson of 498
persons of 9, 845
poor of 9, 498
Poys St in 781
Raydon,
persons of 297

poor of 882
Reach [Cambs], persons of 38
Rede 443, 786
churchyard, burial in 786
fields etc (named) in 443
land in 470, 677, 689
persons of 370, 766, 709
Redgrave 221, 235, 597, 731, 866, 868
churchyard, burial in 597
fen 221
fields etc (named) in 221, 235
persons of 258, 597
Redgrave Hall 731
Redlingfield 243, 252
persons of 252
Rickinghall, land in 572, 816, 862
Rickinghall Inferior 600, 653, 862
burial in 600
churchwardens of 653
fields etc (named) in 165
persons of 681
Rickinghall Superior 589
churchyard, burial in 822
land in 816
persons of 589, 816
Ringland [Norf], land in 719
Ringmere, flock of sheep at 857
Risby 362, 440, 546, 787
churchyard, burial in 440
persons of 679
Ropham (unidentified) [Norf], persons of 174
Rougham 39, 190, 231, 437, 504, 524, 550, 593
Barton Hall manor in 272
churchyard, burial in 504, 550
fields etc (named) in 210, 272
land in 826
minister of 550
Netherplace manor in 593
persons of 202, 437
poor of 593
rectory of 593
Rougham Lawnes manor in 593
Rowdham [Norf], persons of 772
Rudham [Norf] *see* Rowdham
Rushall [Norf], land in 792
Rushbrooke 385
land in 593
persons of 194, 421, 475
poor of 385

St Ives [Hunts], persons of 248
Sandon [Essex], persons of 357
Santon Downham see Downham
Sapiston 270, 587
land in 179
manor of Sapiston Grange in 179
persons of 179, 713
poor of 179
rectory in 179
Saxham, house in 707
Saxham, Gt 108, 198, 234, 350, 407, 654, 678, 859
churchyard, burial in 654
persons of 463, 464, 695
poor of 198
Saxham, Lt 6, 236, 431, 881
Saxtead 452

Thaxted [Essex], land in 94
Thelnetham 156, 682, 748, 888
  cottage in 682
  fields etc (named) in 156
  land in 653, 778, 791, 808
  looms at 685
  manor of 156
  minister of 748
  persons of 888
Thetford [Norf],
  persons of 613, 713, 730, 763
  White Hart Inn at 763
Thorndon 50, 135, 388
  manor of 819
  persons of 580
Thornham Magna 861
Thornham Parva 626
Thorpe Morieux 107
  land in 127
  persons of 565
Thurlow, persons of 113
Thurlow, Gt 393
  churchyard, burial in 393
Thurlow, Lt, persons of 514
Thurston 88, 91, 210, 272, 281, 303, 539, 807
  church, repair of 91
  churchyard, burial in 91, 123, 210, 807
  fields etc (named) in 91, 210, 272
  house (named) in 272
  land in 263, 593
  manor of Netherhall in 272
  persons of 80, 123, 281
  poor of 123
Thwaite 18, 615
  persons of 580
Timworth, persons of 713
Tostock 59, 67, 74, 89, 482, 667, 793
  churchyard, burial in 539
  land in 89
  poor of 89
Trimley St Martin, land in 388
Trimley St Mary, land in 388
Troston 45, 109, 423, 561
  persons of 825
  poor of 109
  sheepwalk in 104
Tuddenham 143, 378, 457, 864
  churchyard, burial in 143, 378
  land in 46, 407

Wakes Colne, see Colne, Wakes
Waldingfield, Gt 120, 502, 552, 656
  Acton Hall manor in 552
  Badley Moor in 543
  Brampton Hall manor in 502
  Cautwells manor in 543
  fields etc (named) in 502, 543
  house (named) in 502, 543
  Morres manor in 543
  persons of 543
  poor of 120, 552
Waldingfield, Lt 118, 119, 784
  persons of 118
Walsham le Willows 307, 368, 434, 483, 554, 835
  fields etc (named) in 307, 368
  land in 306, 483, 572, 665

persons of 465, 841
poor of 68, 368
West St in 665
Wangford 374, 726, 727
  persons of 179
  rector of 727
Washbrook, persons of 54
Wattisfield 572, 665, 749, 791
  fields etc (named) in 572
  land in 541, 888
  persons of 156, 791
  poor of 572
Wattisham 700
Weeting [Norf], land in 463
West Stow see Stow, West
Westhorpe 780
  land in 465
  poor of 616
  rector of 259
Westley 287, 438, 666
  land in 703
  persons of 287, 395, 644
Weston, Coney
  land in 577, 772
  poor of 448
Weston Market 95, 880
  churchwardens of 653
  land in 282, 653, 876, 877
Wetherden 126, 318, 619
  fields etc (named) in 619
  land in 317, 437
  persons of 126, 619, 625
  poor of 126, 619
  Pulham Hall manor in 318
  way leading to 58
  Wetherden Hall manor in 318
Wetheringsett 22, 433, 495, 687, 734
  houses in 687
Whatfield 151, 312, 338, 405
  Barrardes manor in 338
  churchyard, burial in 338
  land in 617, 628
  poor of 151
Whelnetham,
  house at 205
  poor of 826
Whelnetham, Gt 585, 826
  land in 10
  persons of 557
  poor of 826
Whelnetham, Lt 208, 557
  land in 10, 826
Whepstead 294, 336, 540
  churchyard, burial in 115
  Dunston St in 115
  fields etc (named) in 115, 294
  land in 370
  persons of 115, 681
  poor of 115, 294
Wicken [Cambs] 142, 344, 372, 402, 479, 494, 529,
    583, 806, 853
  churchyard, burial in 344, 402, 479, 583
  fields etc (named) in 142
  land in 402
  manor of 402, 529
  persons of 402, 529

463

poor of 372, 402, 529
road leading to 885
Wicken manor in 529
Wickham, persons of 708
Wickham Skeith 192, 836
churchyard, burial in 192
persons of 192, 836
poor of 616
the Street in 836
Wickhambrook 356, 648, 659, 684
churchyard, burial in 648, 659, 684
land in 546
persons of 707
poor of 659
Wicklewood [Norf] 456
fields etc (named) in 456
Wilton [Norf], persons of 731
Wimbish [Essex], land in 94
Wissington 2, 321, 444, 459
churchyard, burial in 2, 321
fields etc (named) in 2
house in 335
parsonage house of 663
poor of 2, 321
Wood Ditton [Cambs] *see* Ditton, Wood
Woodbridge, persons of 812
Woolpit 523, 772
clerk of 772
fields etc (named) in 328
land in 9, 367
persons of 9
poor of 772
smith's shop in 9

Worlingham, poor of 179
Gt, land in 179
Lt, land in 179
Worlington 40
churchyard, burial in 40
land in 81, 551
persons of 583
poor of 40, 551
Wormegay [Norf],
land in 179
poor of 179
Wormingford [Essex], stock at 650
Wortham 51, 623
churchyard, burial in 51
fields etc (named) in 623
land in 681
persons of 51
Wortham Abbottes manor in 623
Wortham Hall manor 623
Wramplingham [Norf],
land in 385
persons of 385
poor of 385
Wratting, Gt 874
fields etc (named) in 874
Wymondham [Norf], persons of 483
Wyverstone 53, 841
churchyard, burial in 317
land in 367, 465
persons of 836

Yaxley, persons of 836

INDEX OF OCCUPATIONS
AND STATUS OF TESTATORS

INDEX OF SUBJECTS

467

debtors, named 97, 115, 358, 418, 489, 799, 800, 836
debts,
    chalked up in shop 475
    owed by testator, list of 337
dinner for friends after funeral 56, 713
dish, marked with initials 392
ditch, water from 819, 836
Dominican Friary, former 461
doors, as a fixture 582
dove house 502
drying close 502

easement, house of 528
education,
    of children 9, 730
    of daughter 608
    by godfather 677
    in reading and writing 74, 182, 701
    at school 437
    of son 107
executor's accounts 825

feathers, poke of 623
firehouse 209
firewood for wife 36, 58, 112, 170, 193, 252, 264, 306, 565, 589, 601, 681, 718, 737, 774
fish ponds 142
flaxen yarn 183
flowers, pot of 468
fold course 36
foodstuffs, perishable 306
fowling piece 701
fruit 519, 657, 774
fruit trees 632, 873
funeral,
    bearers at 818
    bell ringers at 455, 568
    cost of 825
funeral sermon 74, 179, 225, 372, 395, 420, 435, 514, 563, 580, 612, 698, 713, 774, 818, 826, 871
furnishings 19, 33, 35, 44, 67, 85, 90, 115, 125, 139, 141, 150, 158, 167, 187, 192, 193, 195, 200, 205, 248, 269, 349, 356, 357, 379, 385, 411, 425, 440, 450, 453, 470, 506, 522, 524, 539, 586, 588, 604, 612, 617, 619, 623, 628, 641, 649, 659, 662, 670, 681, 684, 692, 694, 734, 771, 774, 815, 818, 838, 863, 866, 894
furniture, measurements of 528

gally pots 681
garden, pot herbs in 681
gilt,
    goblet 56
    salt 205, 681
    spoon 268
glass 56
    drinking 760
    with silver foot 56
gloves, bequest of 667, 731, 859
gold pieces 703
goods at sea 74
gown,
    money owed for 274
    sale of 64
grindstone 411, 475, 648
grograin, length of 723

hall house 356
hampers 576
harrows 306, 565, 708, 753
hemp 333, 392, 623, 637
hemp crop 885
hens 272
hop plants 112
hop poles 112, 774
horses,
    colour of 163, 194, 324, 501, 584, 616, 630, 716, 759
    names of 9, 226
horse mill 35, 113, 115, 127, 186, 330, 347, 439, 481, 683, 819
house,
    division of 771
    measurements of 190
    name of 38, 224, 248, 502
    newly built 245, 248, 521, 578, 876
    price of 186, 201, 335, 580
    repairs to 144, 252, 341, 407
husband, choice of 487

inn, name of 113, 754
interest, rate of 228, 504, 611, 677, 703, 733

jewel 182

kettle, capacity of 500
kiln house 439

Latin, learning of 9
lawsuit 9, 175
lease 56, 530
legacy, dispute over 346
linen,
    made by testator 183
    washing of 836
looms 147, 235, 299, 588, 626, 684, 685, 719, 828
    maker of 719

malt house 81, 125, 453, 539, 582
malt mill 56
marriage,
    length of 829
    objection to 371
    planned 619
    proposed 707
mill 424, 449
millhouse 56, 81, 894
money, due to wife before marriage 732
mortgage 30, 46, 55, 81, 112, 144, 323, 342, 358, 384, 418, 733, 745, 791
musket 91, 701

nets, fishing 774
New Testament 262

orchard, fruit in 323, 576, 681, 856

pawned goods 468
pictures 258, 372, 465
pig, colour of 104
pigeons 774
pillion 141
pillow, leather 638

469

GLOSSARY

ale/beer stools	stand for cask of ale/beer
almery (aumbry)	large cupboard with doors used for food, linen or clothes
andirons	horizontal iron bars supported on 3 short feet with upright in front; used to support logs in fireplace
backhouse	outhouse or lean-to used for variety of domestic purposes
bald (colour)	piebald
band	neckband
barley screen	implement for separating corn from dust
baulte (colour)	streaked or marked with white i.e. piebald or skewbald
baymaker	maker of bayes, a cloth made with worsted warp and woollen weft
bearing cloth or sheet	christening robe
bed	mattress
bedline	cord laced through holes bored horizontally in bed frame, making a network on which to lay a rush mat and mattress
bedsteadle	bedstead
bedstocks	bed frame supporting mattress
beetle (hooped)	implement with heavy head used to drive stakes into ground, ram stones, etc
bird/birded coverlet	perhaps coverlet embroidered with birds
birding piece	gun for shooting birds
black howed	black hued (colour)
blage (colour)	perhaps black
board cloth	table cloth
book debts	debts recorded in a book
boules	perhaps feet (on bottom of a hutch)
boulting/bolting hutch	chest for storing sifted flour
bowe	curved line dividing an enclosure
brend wood	obscure, perhaps streaked or burnt wood; if latter, then charcoal
brinded/brended	tawny brown colour
brindle	tawny brown colour
broad weaver	weaver of broad cloth
bud	bull, bullock or heifer between 1 and 2 years old
buffet stool	high or low stool, usually for use at a long table; also foot stool
burlynn/burling	yearling bullock or heifer
bushel	vessel for measuring grain, or a quantity of grain
buttery	store room for food, drink and kitchen equipment
cabert	obscure
canvas	unbleached linen cloth usually made of hemp
casting sheet	obscure, perhaps connected with childbirth
casting kercher	obscure
caverings	chaff or husks of corn used to fill mattress
ceiled bedstead	panelled
ceiled chamber	panelled
chair house	obscure
chicksell	perhaps a chisel or jigsaw
clock reel	reel to measure length of skeins
cobirons	irons supporting spit in front of fire
coif	close-fitting cap worn by women and rarely by men
comb	measure, usually of grain, equal to 4 bushels
compasse	manure or night soil
coolers	*see* keelers
copper	large vessel, usually used for brewing

471

copyhold	land held by unfree tenure
counter/counter table	writing table or desk for counting money or side table
Coventry thread	thread made in Coventry, usually blue
croft	small piece enclosed ground, usually attached to a house
crome	wooden-handled rake with 2 long metal teeth
cross cloth	head cloth
danske chest	chest made of spruce imported from Denmark
darnacke/darnick	coarse linen fabric, originally made at Dornick (Tournai) in Belgium, and used for hangings and coverlets
daubing	plastering
daunce chest	*see* danske
deroy	light-weight worsted, usually for men's clothing; as a colour, obscure
dornix	*see* darnacke
dower	dowry
draught hook	iron hook used for pulling heavy objects
entry fine	lump sum paid by copyholder when buying or inheriting copyhold land
fan	flat, fan-shaped basket used in winnowing corn; winnowing fan
farm, holds by	pays rent for
fatt	*see* vat
fellow	servant
feoffee	trustee
field bed	folding bedstead, which could be packed for travelling
firehouse	heated room, probably only one in house
firkin	cask holding 56 lbs butter or 9 gallons liquid
flock	wool refuse used for stuffing mattresses, etc
fold course	area over which flock of sheep can be grazed
forehead cloth	triangular strip of material worn round forehead with point facing backwards
fother ground	obscure
fustian	coarse cloth of cotton or hemp, or of wool mixed with these; originally from Fostat, a suburb of Cairo
fustian Alpes	obscure
gallypots	small, glazed earthenware pots, used by apothecaries for ointments
garled cow	obscure
gears	harness
groat	coin worth four pence
grograin	coarse fabric of silk and mohair
hagg saw	hack saw
hake	hook from which pot or kettle hung over fire
halberd	long-handled axe or military weapon
hale	iron bar from which hooks hung, *see* hake
hall house	hall of house
Hallowmas	All Saints Day
harp	harp-shaped field
harrows	used by parchment maker; obscure
hassocks	clump of turf, tussock of matted vegetation
hearst	wooden framework
hempland	field where hemp grown, usually small in area
hogget sheep	from 6 months old to first shearing
holdfast	perhaps vice or clamp
holland	good quality linen, often imported from Holland
holt	plot where willows grow
home setting	land surrounding house
horse mill	mill driven by horse, harnessed to a beam connected to gearing, walking in a circle
howd	hued, coloured
hutch	chest or cupboard
infield land	land near farmstead, land regularly cropped
jack	mechanical device for turning a spit
joined	furniture made by a joiner with morticed and tenoned frame
jointure	property provided for wife during widowhood

472

keeler/coller	shallow tub in which liquids, particularly milk, set to cool
keep/glass keep	small storage cupboard
kercher	kerchief or cloth used to cover head or neck
kersey	coarse, narrow cloth, woven from long (combed) wool
kettle	open cooking pot with semi-circular handles fixed to both sides
kneading trough	trough in which dough was kneaded
kyne	cows
lake	perhaps peat diggings
latten	an alloy of copper and zinc
lead	vessel made of or lined with lead and used for brewing and other domestic purposes
leas	pasture or meadow
linsey wolsey	coarse, inferior cloth made from mixture of wool and linen
livery cupboard	small, ventillated cupboard
lockeram	coarse, loosely-woven linen
lodge	obscure
mark (money)	thirteen shillings and four pence
mash vat	vat in which malt and boiling water mixed in first stage of brewing
mat	placed over cord/line laced across bedstead
maund	woven rush or wicker basket
meere/mere	boundary
messuage	house
mirrell	perhaps mulberry coloured
moulding board	board on which bread shaped before baking
narrow combs	obscure
neat	cow or ox
netherstocks	stockings
noble	gold coin, originally worth 6s 8d, later 10s
overbody	garment worn over bodice
pashell	pestle, beetle or mallet
peel/pelle	long-handled shovel to remove loaves from oven
petticoat	skirt for women, small coat for men
pied (colour)	piebald
pightle	small field or enclosure
pillion	pad or small saddle attached to rear of proper saddle for a second rider
pillowbeere	pillow case
pint	measure
poke	small bag or sack
porrengers	bowls for porridge or soup, made of earthenware, pewter or silver
posnet	small metal pot with long handle and three feet, used for boiling
post axe	obscure
pottengers	*see* porrengers
powdering trough	tub used for salting or pickling meat
purwcas	obscure
reel	spool of spinning wheel, or frame used to hold bobbins
rent capons	paid for rent
rod of land	quarter of an acre
rofe/ruff	starched linen neckwear, worn by both sexes
running house	obscure
russet	coarse cloth of a reddish brown colour
salting trough	tub for salting meat
saucer	dish used to hold sauce
sheadmaker	perhaps a maker of slayes or reeds
sheep combs	obscure, but perhaps for scraping skins
shift	division of open field for cropping rotation; tripartite in Breckland
shoate/shott	young pig
sholve	shovel
shop	usually a workshop
shred trees	lop off branches

473

skep	straw or wicker beehive
skillet	cooking pot with long handle and 3 feet, to stand over fire
slayes	part of a loom: wooden frame holding reeds through which warp threads pass
solar/soller	upper chamber
spalter	obscure
spong	long, narrow strip of land
spreading sheet	*see* casting sheet
spruce hutch	*see* dansk hutch
stained cloth	cloth painted with coloured designs and used as wall hanging
stammell	fine worsted cloth
still	stand for barrel or tub
stithe	blacksmith's anvil
stock cards	wool or hemp cards fastened to stock or support
stover	winter food for cattle
string of land	basic unit of ploughing, same as selion
stryces	perhaps hemp ropes
stuff	worsted cloth without nap
swathe rake	used between rows of hay or corn to collect loose stalks into the swathes or rows
tamy	cheap worsted cloth, possibly originally made at Tamworth in Staffordshire
taring/tearing	cloth or sheets made from finely dressed hemp
tassell	teazels, used to raise nap on cloth
temple heads	contrivance for keeping cloth stretched to its proper width on loom during weaving
tenement	house/holding of land/house with land
tester	canopy of wood or cloth over a bed
thirds	wife's right to a third of husband's real estate in her widowhood
throwyer	knife used for cleaning laths
thurdale	obscure
tick	hard linen used for cases for pillows and mattresses
tow	coarse part of flax or hemp
town	any settlement, usually means parish
tramell	bolster
transome	mattress or bolster
trencher	wooden plate or dish
trevet	3-footed metal stand for a pot, used over or before fire
truckle/trundle bed	low bed on wheels which could be pushed under a high bed when not in use
trundle	perhaps wheeled frame to move loom around
tumbrel	2-wheeled cart
tunn of silver	drinking vessel
turves	turf or peat for burning
use	interest
vaunce	attic
waistcoat	garment covering upper part of body, worn by both sexes
warping bars	bars round which yarn wound to make the warp to be placed on loom
watchet	pale blue colour
way/weye	measure of cheese, usually 256 lbs or 312 lbs in Suffolk
weanling	weaned
went	sub-division of field
whipple tree	cross bar to which traces fastened
white work	same as cut work, cut and slashed lace
widgell	obscure, but some kind of young horse
wimble	gimlet, auger or brace
winding corpse	to wrap in shroud
wool driver	obscure
wrought	embroidered
yard kerchers	yard square
yealde vat	wort (gile) tub in which malt and hot water ferment